DICTIONARY
OF POPES
AND THE PAPACY

THE ENCYCLOPEDIA OF THEOLOGY AND CHURCH

based on the third edition of the

LEXIKON FÜR THEOLOGIE UND KIRCHE

Michael Buchberger
Series founder

Edited by
Walter Kasper
Konrad Baumgartner
Horst Bürkle
Klaus Ganzer
Karl Kertelge
Wilhelm Korff
Peter Walter

DICTIONARY

OF

POPES

AND THE

PAPACY

Edited by
BRUNO STEIMER AND MICHAEL G. PARKER

Translated by
BRIAN McNEIL AND PETER HEINIGG

A Herder and Herder Book
The Crossroad Publishing Company
New York

The Crossroad Publishing Company
481 Eighth Avenue, New York, NY 10001

Originally published in German under the title
Lexikon der Päpste und des Papsttums
©2000 by Verlag Herder, Freiburg im Breisgau

Printed in the United States of America

Library of Congress Cataloging-in-Publication Data

Lexikon der Papste und des Papsttums. English.
    The dictionary of popes and the papacy / edited by Bruno Steimer ;
translated by Brian McNeil and Peter Heinigg.
        p. cm. — (The encyclopedia of theology and church)
    "A Herder and Herder book."
    Includes bibliographical references (p.   ) and index.
    ISBN 0-8245-1918-3
    1. Papacy—Dictionaries. 2. Popes—Biography—Dictionaries. I.
Steimer, Bruno. II. Title. III. Series.
    BX955.3 .L4913 2001
    262'.13'03—dc21
                                                                2001005154

1 2 3 4 5 6 7 8 9 10 05 04 03 02 01

Contents

PREFACE

THE CONTINUAL REFORM AND RENEWAL of the papacy require a theological and historical understanding of its origins and development. In order to participate and contribute to this process of reform and renewal, Roman Catholics and other Christians require knowledge of the papacy as well as of the popes. This work provides the reader with a reliable source of information about both.

Dictionary of Popes and the Papacy is the first in the series The Encyclopedia of Theology and Church, a theological reference library being planned in cooperation with Verlag Herder in Freiburg, Germany. The intention of the series is to make the wealth of information contained in the new third edition of the *Lexikon für Theologie und Kirche* (*LThK*) available to the English-language public in the form of a series of thematic dictionaries. In addition to translations, there will also be supplements to the English-language edition that give greater attention to the Anglo-American historical and theological context.

As its title suggests, this work is divided into two parts: persons and subjects. The first part includes short biographical articles on the popes and antipopes of historical record, and the second contains articles on the institutional, canonical, and theological aspects of the papacy. In addition, articles of contemporary interest such as the Holy (Jubilee) Year are included. By contrast, entries on historical events involving the papacy, such as the Western Schism, will be treated in a subsequent volume on church history.

An international bibliography as well as a list of general reference works make this volume useful to the scholar and student alike. Maps and drawings complement the text. In short, this compact one-volume reference work offers a unique source of reliable and up-to-date information about the popes and the papacy.

MICHAEL G. PARKER
Academic Editor
The Crossroad Publishing Company

Acknowledgments

I would like to take this opportunity to thank the Verlag Herder and especially the LThK Redaktion (Dr. Bruno Steimer, Johannes Weitzel, Joachim Fähndrich, Matthias Bergedick, Wolfgang Herkel, and Evelyn Nebor) for their hospitality to me during the nearly two years I have spent working in Freiburg, Germany. In particular, I would like to thank Bruno Steimer for introducing me to the *Lexikon für Theologie und Kirche* and for showing me how much work a highly talented, disciplined, and professional editorial team can accomplish.

In addition, I would like to thank the translators, especially Dr. Brian McNeil, who translated the bulk of the entries for this volume. Finally, I would like to acknowledge Dr. Paul Kobelski and Dr. Maurya Horgan of The HK Scriptorium, copyeditors and compositors of this work, for their patience, good humor, and dedication to the tools of the trade.

Michael G. Parker
Freiburg, Germany

Frequently Cited Reference Works

AAS	*Acta Apostolicae Sedis* 1 (Rome, 1909–).
ACO	*Acta Conciliorum Oecumenicorum,* ed. E. Schwartz. 1st series, 4 vols. (Berlin, 1914-84; 2nd series, 1984–).
ActaSS	*Acta Sanctorum,* ed. Bollandists (S. Bolland et al.). Original ed., 70 vols. (Antwerp, 1643-1770; Tongerloo, 1794; Paris, 1875-87; Brussels, 1780-1944; reprint, vols. 1-43, Brussels, 1734-70; vols. 1-60, Paris, 1863-70; reprint of 1st ed., Paris, 1966-71).
AHC	*Annuarium historiae conciliorum* (Paderborn, 1969–).
AHP	*Archivum historiae pontificiae* (Rome, 1963–) (containing *Bibliographia historiae pontificiae*).
AnPont	*Annuario Pontificio* (Rome, 1912–).
ASS	*Acta Sanctae Sedis* 6-41 (Rome, 1870-1908). Vols. 1-5 (to 1869) published as *Acta ex iis decerpta quae apud Sanctam Sedem geruntur in compendium opportune redacta et illustrata.* From 1909: *AAS.*
BBKL	*Biographisch-bibliographisches Kirchenlexikon,* ed. F. W. Bautz (Hamm, 1975–).
Bertolini	O. Bertolini, *Roma di fronte a Bisanzio e ai Longobardi* (Bologna, 1941).
BiblSS	*Bibliotheca Sanctorum,* ed. Istituto Giovanni XXIII, 12 vols., index vol. (Rome, 1961-70; Prima Appendice, 1987).
Borgolte	M. Borgolte, *Petrusnachfolge und Kaiserimitation* (Göttingen, 1989; 2nd ed. 1995).
Caspar	E. Caspar, *Geschichte des Papsttums von den Anfängen bis zur Höhe der Weltherrschaft,* 2 vols. (Tübingen, 1930-33).
CATH	*Catholicisme: Hier—Aujourd'hui—Demain,* ed. G. Jacquemet et al., 15 vols. (Paris, 1948-2000).
CCEO	*Codex Canonum Ecclesiarum Orientalium,* 1990.
CIC	*Codex Iuris Canonici,* 1983.
CIC/1917	*Codex Iuris Canonici,* 1917.
CPL	*Clavis Patrum Latinorum,* ed. E. Dekkers (Steenbrugge, 1951; 2nd ed. 1961; 3rd ed. 1995).
DACL	*Dictionnaire d'archéologie chrétienne et de liturgie,* ed. F. Cabrol and H. Leclercq, 15 vols. (Paris, 1907-51).
DBI	*Dizionario biografico degli Italiani* (Rome, 1960–).
DDC	*Dictionnaire de droit canonique,* ed. R. Naz, 7 vols. (Paris, 1935-65).
DECL	*Dictionary of Early Christian Literature,* ed. S. Döpp and W. Geerlings, trans. M. O'Connell (New York, 2000).
DH	H. Denzinger, *Enchiridion symbolorum, definitionum et declarationum de rebus fidei et morum,* 37th ed. with German trans. by P. Hünermann (Freiburg, 1991).

DHGE	*Dictionnaire d'histoire et de géographie ecclésiastiques,* ed. A. Baudrillart et al. (Paris, 1912–).
DHP	*Dictionnaire historique de la papauté,* ed. P. Levillian (Paris, 1994).
DizEc	*Dizionario ecclesiastico,* ed. A. Mercati and A. Pelzer, 3 vols. (Turin, 1953-58).
DMC	*Dictionarium morale et canonicum,* ed. P. Palazzini et al., 4 vols. (Rome, 1962-68).
DSp	*Dictionnaire de spiritualité, Ascétique et Mystique: Doctrine et historie,* ed. M. Viller, 16 vols., index vol. (Paris, 1932-95).
DTHC	*Dictionnaire de théologie catholique,* ed. A. Vacant and E. Mangenot, continued by E. Amann, 15 vols. (Paris, 1903-50; 3 index vols., 1951-72).
EC	*Enciclopedia Cattolica,* 13 vols. (Rome, 1949-69).
GKG	*Gestalten der Kirchengeschichte,* ed. M. Greschat (Stuttgart et al., 1978–).
HCMA	*Hierarchia Catholica medii (et recentioris) aevi,* founded by K. Eubel: vols. 1-3, ed. L. Schmitz-Kallenberg (Münster, 1898-1910; 2nd ed. 1913-23); vol. 4, ed. C. Gauchat (Münster, 1935); vols. 5-8, ed. V. Ritzler (Padua, 1952-79).
HDRG	*Handwörterbuch zur deutschen Rechtsgeschichte* (Berlin, 1971–).
HKG	*Handbuch der Kirchengeschichte,* ed. H. Jedin, 7 vols. (Freiburg, 1962-79); Eng., *History of the Church* (New York, 1980-81).
HKKR	*Handbuch des katholischen Kirchenrechts,* ed. J. Listl, H. Müller, and H. Schmitz (Regensburg, 1983; 2nd ed. 1999).
LMA	*Lexikon des Mittelalters,* 9 vols. (Munich/Zurich, 1980-98; study ed., Stuttgart, 1999).
LP	*Liber Pontificalis,* ed. L. Duchesne, 2 vols. (Paris, 1886-92; reprint, 1955); vol. 3, ed. C. Vogel (Paris, 1957).
Mansi	J. D. Mansi, *Sacrorum conciliorum nova et amplissima collectio,* 31 vols. (Florence/Venice, 1759-98); reprint and continuation, ed. L. Petit and J. B. Martin, 53 vols. (Paris, 1901-27).
MGH	*Monumenta Germaniae Historica inde ab a.C. 500 usque ad a. 1500,* indexes by O. Holder-Egger and K. Zeumer (Hanover and Berlin, 1826–).
MGH.AA	—*Auctores antiquissimi* (1877-1919).
MGH.Cap	—*Capitularia regum Francorum* (1883-97).
MGH.Conc	—*Concilia* (1893–).
MGH.Const	—*Constitutiones et acta publica imperatorum et regum* (1893–).
MGH.Ep	—*Epistolae* (1887–).
MGH.ES	—*Epistolae selectae* (1916–).
MGH.LL	—*Libelli de lite imperatorum et pontificum saeculis XI et XII conscripti* (1891-97).
MGH.PL	—*Poetae latini medii aevi* (1880–).
MGH.SRG	—*Scriptores rerum Germanicarum in usum scholarum ex Monumentis Germaniae historicis recusi (separatim editi),* Oktav series (1826-1913); *Nova series,* Oktav series (1922–).
MGH.SS	—*Scriptores* (1826-1934).
MKCIC	*Münsterischer Kommentar zum Codex Iuris Canonici unter besonderer Berücksichtigung der Rechtslage in Deutschland, Österreich und der Schweiz,* ed. K. Lüdicke (Essen, 1985–; published in fascicles).
NBD	*Nuntiaturberichte aus Deutschland nebst ergänzenden Aktenstücken,* I., III., und

IV. Abteilung ed. Deutsches Historisches Institut in Rom, II. Abteilung ed. Österreichisches Historisches Institut in Rom. I. Abteilung (1533-59): vols. 1-12 (Gotha/Berlin, 1892-1912; reprint Frankfurt a.M., 1968); vols. 13ff. (Tübingen, 1959–); additional vols. 1-2 (1530-31 and 1532) (Tübingen, 1963-69). II. Abteilung (1560-72): vols. 1-8 (Vienna/Leipzig, 1897-1939; Graz/Cologne, 1952-67). III. Abteilung (1572-85): vols. 1-5 (Berlin, 1892-1909; reprint Turin, 1972); vols. 6ff. (Tübingen, 1982–). IV. Abteilung (17th cent.): 3 unnumbered vols. (Berlin, 1895-1913; reprint Turin, 1973). Further volumes in preparation.

NBD(G)	*Nuntiaturberichte aus Deutschland nebst ergänzenden Aktenstücken,* ed. Görres-Gesellschaft (no continuous numbering of vols.). I. Abteilung: *Die Kölner Nuntiatur,* vols. 1 and 2/1 (1585[84]-90) (Paderborn, 1895-99; reprint 1969); vols. 2/2ff. (1590-1630); (Munich et al., 1969–). II. Abteilung: *Die Nuntiatur am Kaiserhofe,* 3 vols. (1585[84]-92) (Paderborn, 1905-19).
NCE	*New Catholic Encyclopedia,* ed. W. J. MacDonald et al., 15 vols. (New York et al., 1967).
Pastor	L. von Pastor, *Geschichte der Päpste seit dem Ausgang des Mittelalters,* 16 vols. (Freiburg, 1885-1913; reprint 1955-62).
PL	*Patrologia Latina,* ed. J. P. Migne, 217 vols., 4 index vols. (Paris, 1841-64).
PLS	*Patrologia Latina,* suppl. vols. 1-5, ed. A. Hamman (Paris, 1958-70).
PRE	*Paulys Real-Encyklopädia der classischen Altertumswissenschaft,* new revised ed. G. Wissowa and W. Kroll (Stuttgart, 1894-1980).
PuP	*Päpste und Papsttum* (Stuttgart, 1971–).
QFIAB	*Quellen und Forschungen aus italienischen Archiven und Bibliotheken* (Rome, 1897–).
RGG	*Die Religion in Geschichte und Gegenwart* (Tübingen, 1909-13; 2nd ed. 1927-32; 3rd ed. 1956-62; index vol. 1965; 4th ed. 1998–).
Richards	J. Richards, *The Popes and the Papacy in the Early Middle Ages 476-752* (London, 1979).
RPR(J)	*Regesta Pontificum Romanorum ad a. p. Chr. n. MCXCVIII,* ed. P. Jaffé (Leipzig, 1851); 2 vols., ed. S. Löwenfeld et al. (2nd ed.; Leipzig, 1881-88; reprint Graz, 1956).
RPR(P)	*Regesta Pontificum Romanorum inde ab a. 1198 ad a. 1304,* ed. A. Potthast, 2 vols. (Berlin, 1874-75; reprint Graz, 1957).
RPR.GP	*Regesta Pontificum Romanorum: Germania Pontificia,* ed. A. Brackmann (Berlin, 1911–).
RPR.IP	*Regesta Pontificum Romanorum: Italia Pontificia,* vols. 1-8, ed. P. F. Kehr (Berlin, 1906-35); vol. 9, ed. W. Holtzmann (Berlin, 1962); vol. 10, ed. D. Girgensohn (Zurich, 1975).
RQ	*Römische Quartalschrift für christliche Altertumskunde und Kirchengeschichte* (Freiburg, 1887–).
Schmidlin	J. Schmidlin, *Papstgeschichte der neuesten Zeit,* 4 vols. (Munich, 1933-39) (continuation of Pastor).
TRE	*Theologische Realenzyklopädie,* ed. G. Krause and G. Müller (Berlin/New York, 1976–).

VATL   *Vatikanlexikon,* ed. N. Del Re. German revision by E. Bordfeld (Augsburg, 1998) of Italian original, *Mondo Vaticano* (Rome, 1995).

Zimmermann

J   H. Zimmermann, *Das dunkle Jahrhundert* (Graz, 1971).

Pa   H. Zimmermann, *Papstabsetzungen im Mittelalter* (Graz et al., 1968).

Pt   *Das Papsttum im Mittelalter: Eine Papstgeschichte im Spiegel der Historiographie* (Stuttgart, 1981).

Pu   *Papsturkunde: 896-1046,* ed. H. Zimmermann, 3 vols. (Vienna, 1988-89) (continuous pagination).

Reg   *Papstregesten 911-1024,* ed. H. Zimmermann, Regesta Imperii 2,5 (2nd ed.; Vienna, 1998).

Select Bibliography

Full bibliographical details are usually not given
when these works are cited in articles

G. Arnaldi, ed., *Enciclopedia dei papi* (Rome, 2000).

G. Barraclough, *The Medieval Papacy* (London, 1968; reprint 1979).

R. Barth, *Taschenlexikon der Päpste* (Munich, 2000).

P. Brezzi, *Roma e l'impero medioevale (774-1252)* (Bologna, 1947).

G. Buchheit, *Das Papsttum: Von seiner Einsetzung bis zum Pontifikat Pauls VI.* (Neuenburg, 1962).

M. E. Bunson, *The Pope Encyclopedia: An A to Z of the Holy See* (New York, 1995).

G. Castella, *Illustrierte Papstgeschichte,* 3 vols. (Zurich, 1999).

O. Chadwick, *A History of the Popes 1830-1914* (Oxford, 1998).

A. Ciaconius, *Vitae et res gestae Pontificum Romanorum et S.R.E. Cardinalium,* 2 vols. (Rome, 1601-2); continued to Clement VIII by A. Victorelli et al. (2nd ed.; Rome, 1630); continued to Clement IX by A. Oldoini, 4 vols. (3rd ed.; Rome, 1677); continued to Clement XII by M. Guarnacci, 2 vols. (4th ed.; Rome, 1751); vol. 7 (Rome, 1787).

F. J. Coppa, *The Modern Papacy since 1789* (London, 1998).

———, *Encyclopedia of the Vatican and Papacy* (London, 1999).

H. E. J. Cowdrey, *Popes and Church Reform in the 11th Century* (Aldershot, 2000).

G. Denzler, *Das Papsttum: Geschichte und Gegenwart* (Munich, 1997).

E. Duffy, *Saints and Sinners* (New Haven, 1997).

C. Falconi, *Storia dei papi e del papato,* 4 vols. (Rome/Milan, 1967-72).

C. Fichtinger, *Lexikon der Heiligen und Päpste* (Gütersloh, 1980; Frankfurt a.M. /Berlin, 1995).

R. Fischer-Wollpert, *Lexikon der Päpste* (Regensburg, 1985; 2nd ed. 1988).

A. Franzen and R. Bäumer, *Papstgeschichte: Das Petrusamt in seiner Idee und seiner geschichtlichen Verwirklichung in der Kirche* (Freiburg, 1974; 3rd ed. 1982; updated new ed. 1988).

H. Fuhrmann, *Von Petrus zu Johannes Paul II: Das Papsttum: Gestalt und Gestalten* (2nd ed., Munich, 1984).

———, *Die Päpste von Petrus zu Johannes Paul II.* (Munich, 1998).

J. Gelmi, *Die Päpste in Lebensbildern* (Graz, 1983; 2nd ed. 1989).

M. Greschat, *Das Papsttum,* 2 vols. (Stuttgart, 1985; reprint 1993).

M. Greschat and E. Guerriero, *Storia dei papi* (Milan, 1994).

M. Guerra Gomez, *Los nombres del Papa: Estudio filológico-teológico de varios nombres del Papa en los primeros siglos del cristianismo* (Burgos, 1982).

B. Guillemain, *Les papes d'Avignon 1309-76* (Paris, 1998).

J. Haller, *Das Papsttum,* 3 vols. (Stuttgart, 1934-45); 5 vols. (2nd ed.; Stuttgart, 1950-53; reprint, Esslingen, 1962).

Y.-M. Hilaire, *Histoire de la papauté: 2000 ans de mission et de tribulations* (Paris, 1996).

C. Hollis, ed., *The Papacy* (London, 1964).

J. N. D. Kelly, *Oxford Dictionary of Popes* (Oxford, 1986).

H. Kühner, *Lexikon der Päpste: Kirchengeschichte, Weltgeschichte, Zeitgeschichte: Von Petrus bis heute* (Zurich, 1956; updated ed., Wiesbaden, 1991).

P. Levillain, ed., *Dictionnaire historique de la papauté* (Paris, 1994).

A. Lopes, ed., *Die Päpste: Ihr Leben im Laufe der 2000 jährigen Geschichte* (Rome, 1997).

M. Maccarrone, ed., *Romana ecclesia: Cathedra Petri*, 2 vols. (Rome, 1991).

J. Mathieu-Rosay, *La véritable histoire des papes: Du royaume des cieux aux royaumes terrestres* (Paris, 1991).

B. Mondin, *Dizionario enciclopedico dei Papi: Storia e insegnamenti* (Rome, 1995).

C. Morris, *The Papal Monarchy: The Western Church from 1050 to 1250* (Oxford, 1989).

M. Pacaut, *La papauté, des origines au concile de Trente* (Paris, 1976).

I. S. Robinson, *The Papacy 1073-1198: Continuity and Innovation* (Cambridge, 2000).

K. Schatz, *Der päpstliche Primat: Seine Geschichte von den Ursprüngen bis zur Gegenwart* (Würzburg, 1990); Eng., *Papal Primacy: From its Origins to the Present* (Collegeville, 1996).

B. Schimmelpfennig, *Das Papsttum von der Antike bis zur Renaissance* (Darmstadt, 1984; 2nd ed. 1996); Eng., *The Papacy* (New York, 1992).

M. Schellhorn, *Der heilige Petrus und seine Nachfolger: Eine Geschichte der Päpste* (1958), continued to John Paul II by K. Friedrich (Vienna/Munich, 1982).

G. Schwaiger, *Papsttum und Päpste im 20. Jahrhundert von Leo XIII. bis Johannes Paul II.* (Munich, 1999).

F. X. Seppelt, *Geschichte der Päpste von den Anfängen bis zur Mitte des 20. Jahrhunderts*, 5 vols. (vols. 4 and 5 revised by G. Schwaiger) (2nd ed.; Munich, 1954-59).

W. Ullmann, *A Short History of the Papacy in the Middle Ages* (2nd ed.; London, 1974).

M. Walsh, ed., *The Papacy* (London, 1997).

C. Weber, *Genealogien zur Papstgeschichte*, 2 vols. (Stuttgart, 1999).

A. D. Wright, *The Early Modern Papacy from the Council of Trent to the French Revolution, 1564-1789* (London, 2000).

A. Wucher, *Von Petrus zu Paul: Eine Weltgeschichte der Päpste bis Johannes Paul II.* (3rd ed.; Frankfurt a.M., 1991).

G. Zizola, *Les papes du XXe siècle* (Paris, 1996).

LIST OF POPES

Peter	-67?	Leo I	440-461	Gregory II	715-731
Linus	67?-79?	Hilary	461-468	Gregory III	731-741
Anacletus I	79?-91?	Simplicius	468-483	Zachary	741-752
Clement I	91?-101?	Felix II (III)	483-492	Stephen (II)*	752
Evaristus	101?-107?	Gelasius I	492-496	Stephen II	752-757
Alexander I	107?-116?	Anastasius II	496-498	Paul I	757-767
Sixtus I	116?-125?	Symmachus	498-514	Constantine II*	767-768
Telesphorus	125?-138?	Laurence*	498-507	Philip*	768
Hyginus	138?-142?	Hormisdas	514-523	Stephen III	768-772
Pius I	142?-155?	John I	523-526	Hadrian I	772-795
Anicetus	155?-166?	Felix III (IV)	526-530	Leo III	795-816
Soter	166?-174?	Dioscurus	530	Stephen IV	816-817
Eleutherus	174?-189?	Boniface II	530-532	Paschal I	817-824
Victor I	189?-198?	John II	533-535	Eugene II	824-827
Zephyrinus	198?-217?	Agapitus I	535-536	Valentine	827
Calixtus I	217?-222	Silverius	536-537	Gregory IV	827-844
Hippolytus*	217?-235	Vigilius	537-555	John (VIII)*	844
Urban I	222-230	Pelagius I	556-561	Sergius II	844-847
Pontian	230-235	John III	561-574	Leo IV	847-855
Anterus	235-236	Benedict I	575-579	Benedict III	855-858
Fabian	236-250	Pelagius II	579-590	Anastasius III*	855
Cornelius	251-253	Gregory I	590-604	Nicholas I	858-867
Novatian*	251-258?	Sabinian	604-606	Hadrian II	867-872
Lucius I	253-254	Boniface III	607	John VIII	872-882
Stephen I	254-257	Boniface IV	608-615	Marinus I	882-884
Sixtus II	257-258	Adeodatus I	615-618	Hadrian III	884-885
Dionysius	259?-268?	Boniface V	619-625	Stephen V	885-891
Felix I	268?-274?	Honorius I	625-638	Formosus	891-896
Eutychian	274?-282?	Severinus	640	Boniface VI	896
Gaius	282?-295?	John IV	640-642	Stephen VI	896-897
Marcellinus	296?-304	Theodore I	641-649	Romanus	897
Marcellus I	307?-309?	Martin I	649-653 (655)	Theodore II	897
Eusebius	309?-310?	Eugene I	654-657	John IX	898-900
Miltiades	310-314	Vitalian	657-672	Benedict IV	900-903
Silvester I	314-335	Adeodatus II	672-676	Leo V	903
Mark	336	Donus	676-678	Christopher	903-904
Julius I	337-352	Agatho	678-681	Sergius III	904-911
Liberius	352-366	Leo II	682-683	Anastasius III	911-913
Felix (II)*	355-358	Benedict II	684-685	Lando	913-914
Damasus I	366-384	John V	685-686	John X	914-928
Ursinus*	366-367	Conon	686-687	Leo VI	928
Siricius	384-399	Theodore*	687	Stephen VII	929-931
Anastasius I	399-402	Paschal*	687	John XI	931-936
Innocent I	402-417	Sergius I	687-701	Leo VII	936-939
Zosimus	417-418	John VI	701-705	Stephen VIII	939-942
Boniface I	418-422	John VII	705-707	Marinus II	941-946
Celestine I	422-432	Sisinnius	708	Agapitus II	946-955
Sixtus III	432-440	Constantine I	708-715	John XII	955-964

* An asterisk following a name indicates those who should not be regarded as legitimate bishops of Rome.

Leo VIII	963-965	Innocent III*	1179-1180	Innocent VIII	1484-1492
Benedict V	964	Lucius III	1181-1185	Alexander VI	1492-1503
John XIII	965-972	Urban III	1185-1187	Pius III	1503
Benedict VI	973-974	Gregory VIII	1187	Julius II	1503-1513
Boniface VII	974-985	Clement III	1187-1191	Leo X	1513-1521
Benedict VII	974-983	Celestine III	1191-1198	Hadrian VI	1522-1523
John XIV	983-984	Innocent III	1198-1216	Clement VII	1523-1534
John XV	985-996	Honorius III	1216-1227	Paul III	1534-1549
Gregory V	996-999	Gregory IX	1227-1241	Julius III	1550-1555
John XVI*	997-998	Celestine IV	1241	Marcellus II	1555
Silvester II	999-1003	Innocent IV	1243-1254	Paul IV	1555-1559
John XVII	1003	Alexander IV	1254-1261	Pius IV	1559-1565
John XVIII	1003-1009	Urban IV	1261-1264	Pius V	1566-1572
Sergius IV	1009-1012	Clement IV	1265-1268	Gregory XIII	1572-1585
Benedict VIII	1012-1014	Gregory X	1271-1276	Sixtus V	1585-1590
Gregory VI*	1012	Innocent V	1276	Urban VII	1590
John XIX	1024-1032	Hadrian V	1276	Gregory XIV	1590-1591
Benedict IX	1032-1045	John XXI	1276-1277	Innocent IX	1591
Silvester III	1045	Nicholas III	1277-1280	Clement VIII	1592-1605
Gregory VI	1045-1046	Martin IV	1281-1285	Leo XI	1605
Clement II	1046-1047	Honorius IV	1285-1287	Paul V	1605-1621
Damasus II	1048	Nicholas IV	1288-1292	Gregory XV	1621-1623
Leo IX	1049-1054	Celestine V	1294	Urban VIII	1623-1644
Victor II	1055-1057	Boniface VIII	1294-1303	Innocent X	1644-1655
Stephen IX	1057-1058	Benedict XI	1303-1304	Alexander VII	1655-1667
Benedict X	1058-1059	Clement V	1305-1314	Clement IX	1667-1669
Nicholas II	1059-1061	John XXII	1316-1334	Clement X	1670-1676
Alexander II	1061-1073	Nicholas V*	1328-1330	Innocent XI	1676-1689
Honorius II*	1061-1072	Benedict XII	1334-1342	Alexander VIII	1689-1691
Gregory VII	1073-1085	Clement VI	1342-1352	Innocent XII	1691-1700
Clement III*	1084-1100	Innocent VI	1352-1362	Clement XI	1700-1721
Victor III	1086-1087	Urban V	1362-1370	Innocent XIII	1721-1724
Urban II	1088-1099	Gregory XI	1370-1378	Benedict XIII	1724-1730
Paschal II	1099-1118			Clement XII	1730-1740
Theodoricus*	1100-1101	*Western Schism (Rome,*		Benedict XIV	1740-1758
Albert*	1101	*Avignon, Pisa)*		Clement XIII	1758-1769
Silvester IV*	1105-1111	Urban VI [R]	1378-1389	Clement XIV	1769-1774
Gelasius II	1118-1119	Boniface IX [R]	1389-1404	Pius VI	1775-1779
Gregory VIII*	1118-1121	Innocent VII [R]	1404-1406	Pius VII	1800-1823
Calixtus II	1119-1124	Gregory XII [R]	1406-1415	Leo XII	1823-1829
Celestine (II)*	1124	Clement VII [A]	1378-1394	Pius VIII	1829-1830
Honorius II	1124-1130	Benedict XIII [A]	1394-1417	Gregory XVI	1831-1846
Innocent II	1130-1143	Clement VIII*	1423-1429	Pius IX	1846-1878
Anacletus II	1130-1138	Alexander V [P]	1409-1410	Leo XIII	1878-1903
Victor IV*	1138	John XXIII [P]	1410-1415	Pius X	1903-1914
Celestine II	1143-1144			Benedict XV	1914-1922
Lucius II	1144-1145	Martin V	1417-1431	Pius XI	1922-1939
Eugene III	1145-1153	Eugene IV	1431-1447	Pius XII	1939-1958
Anastasius IV	1153-1154	Felix V*	1439-1449	John XXIII	1958-1963
Hadrian IV	1154-1159	Nicholas V	1447-1455	Paul VI	1963-1978
Alexander III	1159-1181	Calixtus III	1455-1458	John Paul I	1978
Victor IV*	1159-1164	Pius II	1458-1464	John Paul II	1978-
Paschal III*	1164-1168	Paul II	1464-1471		
Calixtus III*	1168-1178	Sixtus IV	1471-1484		

THE POPES

Adeodatus I (formerly Deusdedit I) (Oct. 19, 615-Nov. 8, 618). Saint (feast day Nov. 8). A Roman and son of a subdeacon named Stephanus. In contrast to his predecessors, he reverted to the practice of giving preference in appointments to church office to clerics rather than monks. He gave an honorable reception in Rome for the exarch Eleutherius of Ravenna during the latter's campaign of pacification against Naples. The report remains unclear: "Hic constituit secunda missa in clero" (*LP*). He is buried in Rome.

■ **Sources:** *LP* 1:319-20; *RPR*(J) 2nd ed. 1:222; 2:698, 739.
■ **Bibliography:** *LMA* 3:738; *VATL* 4-5; Caspar 2:517-23; Bertolini 300ff.

GEORG JENAL

Adeodatus II (Apr. 11, 672-June 17, 676). A Roman, he was a monk in the Erausmus monastery in Rome. Generally described as kindly; hardly anything else is known about him except for his opposition to Monothelitism and the fact that he fostered various monasteries (Rome, Tours, Canterbury).

■ **Sources:** *LP* 1:346-47; *PL* 87:1141-46.
■ **Bibliography:** *LMA* 1:149; *VATL* 5.

BERNHARD KRIEGBAUM

Adrian → Hadrian

Agapitus I (May 535-Apr. 22, 536). Son of the Roman priest Gordianus and archdeacon to John II; he exerted influence upon the church in Gaul, Illyria, and North Africa. Sent by the king of the Ostrogoths to Constantinople because of the impending threat of Italian reconquest, he solidified the church's ties with Justinian; he recognized Chalcedon, deposed Anthimus, consecrated Menas, and excommunicated the followers of Severian by means of a synod. Having died suddenly, Agapitus was taken back to Rome.

■ **Sources:** *LP* 1:287ff.; *RPR*(J) 2nd ed. 1:113ff.; 2:694; *ACO* 3:4.
■ **Bibliography:** *DHGE* 1:887-90; *VATL* 6-7; Caspar 2:199f., 221-29; *RPR*(J) 2nd ed.; W. Esslin, "Papst Agapet I. und Kaiser Justinian I.," *Historisches Jahrbuch* 77 (1957) 459-66; J. Hofmann, "Der hl. Papst Agapet I. und die Kirche von Byzanz," *Ostkirchliche Studien* 40 (1991) 112-32.

JAKOB SPIEGEL

Agapitus II (May 10, 946-December 955). A Roman, he was dependent on Alberic II; he promoted monastic reform and strengthened papal authority. In 947/948 he approved the establishment of dioceses in Denmark (Schleswig, Ripen, Aarhus) and in the East Elbe region (Brandenburg, Havelberg). In 948 he confirmed the metropolitan rights of Hamburg over northern lands. In 949 he decided the dispute over the archbishopric of Rheims in favor of Artold and against Hugo of Vermandois. In 952 he denied entry to Rome and coronation to Otto I; nevertheless, in 955 he approved the establishment of the archbishopric of Magdeburg and a church organization in the eastern regions of the empire.

■ **Sources:** *LP* 2:245; Zimmermann *Pu* 1.1.191-249; *MGH.Conc* 6:128-202.
■ **Bibliography:** *DHGE* 1:890ff.; W. Kömel, *Rom und der Kirchenstaat im 10. und 11. Jh.* (Berlin, 1935); Zimmermann J.

FRIEDRICH LOTTER

Agatho (June 27, 678-Jan. 10, 681). A saint (feast day Jan. 10), from Sicily. Once Emperor Constantine IV had abandoned Monothelitism, amicable relations were restored between Rome and Constantinople. Agatho was able to strengthen papal authority in England (supporting Wilfrith of York, dispatching the Roman archcantor John), Ravenna (weakening the autonomy of its bishops), and Milan. He arranged for a unanimous profession of faith by the Western church in Christ's two wills and operations, as opposed to the Monothelites (Roman Synod of 679; Synod of Hatfield [England], presided over by Theodore of Canterbury; Roman Synod in March 680). He was represented by an impressive delegation at the general Council of Constantinople (680-681), which laid down the doctrine of the two wills and operations in Christ—in agreement with papal doctrinal writings—and, with the approval of the papal legates, he also condemned Honorius I.

■ **Sources:** *LP* 1:350-58; 3:96; *RPR*(J) 1:238ff.; 2:609, 741; A. Potthast, *Bibliotheca historica medii aevi*, vol. 1, (2nd ed. Berlin, 1896) 26.
■ **Bibliography:** *DHGE* 1:916ff.; *VATL* 8; Caspar 2:588-608, 684ff.; G. Kreuzer, *Die Honoriusfrage im Mittelalter*

1

und in der Neuzeit (Stuttgart, 1975) 76-94; A. Angenendt, *Das Frühmittelalter* (Stuttgart, 1990) 251.

GEORG SCHWAIGER

Albert (antipope). Bishop of Sabina, appointed cardinal archbishop of Silva Candida in 1084 by Clement III. At the end of 1101, after the banishment of his predecessor Theodoric, he was elected pope in the Roman basilica of the Twelve Holy Apostles without the participation of King Henry V. With the help of bribes he was delivered to the party of Paschal III and condemned to imprisonment in the monastery of San Lorenzo in Aversa.
■ **Sources:** *RPR(J)* 1:773.
■ **Bibliography:** C. Servatius, *Paschalis II* (Stuttgart, 1979) 52-53, 71, 339; J. Ziese, *Wilbert von Ravenna* (Stuttgart, 1982) 104.

ODILO ENGELS

Alexander I (107?-116?). A Saint (feast day May 3); according to the oldest list of Roman bishops (Irenaeus of Lyons, *Adversus haereses* 3.3.3), he was the fifth successor of Peter. According to the (unhistorical) reckoning of the third or fourth century, he is supposed to have led the Roman community for about ten years. Nothing certain is known about his origins, life, or activities. Since a monarchical episcopate had not fully developed in Rome before the middle of the second century, we may assume that he exercised a leading role in the directorship of the presbyters (*episcopi*). The tradition of his martyrdom is possibly based on confusion with a Roman martyr of the same name on the Via Nomentana.
■ **Sources:** *LP* 1:XCI-XCII, 127; 3:72, 239; *Quellen zur Geschichte des Papstums und des römischen Katholizismus* (C. Mirbt, founder and original series editor), ed. K. Aland, vol. 1 (6th ed. Tübingen, 1967) 15.
■ **Bibliography:** P. von Winterfeld, *Neues Archiv der Gesellschaft für Ältere Deutsche Geschichtskunde zur Beförderung einer Gesamtausgabe der Quellenschriften deutscher Geschichten des Mittelalters* 26 (1901) 751-54 (translation by Freissing); Caspar 1:8-16; R. M. Hübner, "Die Anfänge von Diakonat, Presbyterat und Episkopat in der frühen Kirche," in A. Rauch and P. Imhoff, eds., *Das Priestertum in Einen Kirche* (Aschaffenburg, 1987) 45-89; J. Hoffmann, "Die amtliche Stellung der in der ältesten römischen Bishofsliste überlieferten Männer in der Kirche von Rom," *Historisches Jahrbuch* 109 (1989) 1-23; N. Brox, *Der Hirt des Hermas* (Göttingen, 1991).

GEORG SCHWAIGER

Alexander II (Sept. 30/Oct. 1, 1061-Apr. 21, 1073). Formerly *Anselm,* he was born ca. 1010-1015 as a son of the Milanese captain Andericus of Baggio and attended the cathedral school in Milan. From 1056 to 1073 he was bishop of Lucca. His election as pope can be traced back to the influence of the reform party in the College of → Cardinals and was met with bitter resistance. As early as October 29, 1061, a coalition of Romans, Lombards, and Germans elevated a rival antipope—Cadalus of Parma (Honorius II). Not until the Synod of Mantua (1064) was Alexander also recognized by the German royal court. His pontificate had far-reaching consequences for the Gregorian Reform: he expanded the legate system, reformed the distribution of the → pallium by demanding that the new archbishop appear in person before the pope and swear a special oath, intensified the struggle against simony and Nicolaitism, supported the Pataria in Milan, reformed the canons at the → Lateran in Rome, defended the principle of canonical election, as opposed to their appointment by the German and French kings, concluded a pact with the Normans in southern Italy and with England, and established the first contacts with Mozarabic Spain. In promoting these reforms, Alexander became one of the most important precursors of Gregory VII and was one of the most significant popes of the eleventh century.
■ **Sources:** *RPR(J)* 2nd ed. 1:566-92; *PL* 146:1279-1430.
■ **Bibliography:** *DBI* 2:176-83; *TRE* 2:235ff.; *LMA* 1:371f.; *VATL* 18-19; W. Goez, "Papa qui et episcopus: Zum Selbstverständnis des Reformpapstums im 11. Jh.," *AHP* 8 (1970) 27-59; T. Schmidt, "Die Kanonikerreform in Rom und Papst Alexander II. (1061-1073)," *Studi Gregoriani per la storia della Libertas Ecclesiae* 9 (1972) 199-221; C. Morton, "Pope Alexander II and the Norman Conquest," *Latomus* 34 (1975) 362-82; T. Schmidt, *Alexander II. (1061-1073) und die römische Reformgruppe seiner Zeit* (Stuttgart, 1977); F.-J. Schmale, "Synoden Papst Alexanders II. (1061-1073)," *AHC* 11 (1979) 307-38; R. Schieffer, *Die Entstehung des päpstlichen Investiturverbots für den deutschen König* (Stuttgart, 1981) 84-110; L. Laudage, *Priesterbild und Reformpapsttum im 11. Jh.* (Cologne-Vienna, 1984) 251-91.

JOHANNES LAUDAGE

Alexander III (Sept. 7, 1159-Aug. 30, 1181). Formerly *Rolando Bandinelli,* born 1100-1105, in Siena. He was a canon in Pisa, Magister in Bologna, and in 1150 he became cardinal deacon of Sts. Cosmas and Damian. In 1151 he was cardinal priest of San Marco, and in 1153 he became papal chancellor of the Roman church. He was a legate and an important advisor of Eugene III and Hadrian IV, who, in opposition to the German emperor Frederick I, defined the Western imperial office as something conferred by the pope, and who lay claim to the *regalia beati Petri* as a free property of the church of Rome. These differences of opinion led to a papal schism in 1159. A two-thirds majority of the cardinals decided in favor of Alexander III; the remainder chose Cardinal Octaviano de Montecello (Victor IV), who was friends with the emperor. Victor seemed to enjoy stronger political support intially. Although Alexander was generally recognized in the west and south of Europe, the imperial councils of Pavia (1160) and Lodi (1161) declared their support for Victor. At the end of 1161 Alexander had to flee to France, where in 1162 negotiations between the German and French over ending the schism took place; but these attempts failed, as did the later efforts of the emperor to profit from the dispute over Thomas Beckett and to draw support from Henry II of England. Alexander's position solidified after 1168. His coalition with the Lombard League and William II of Sicily forced Frederick Hohenstaufen to enter into peace negotiations, which were concluded in Venice in 1177. The question of the *regalia Petri* was not resolved, but Alexander adhered to the papal legal standpoint, so that Urban III, Celestine III, and Innocent II could later invoke him in support of their demands for recuperation. Within the church Alexander achieved prominence above all as a legislator through decretals and as the convoker of the Third Lateran Council (1179). Admittedly, the normative force of his decisions rested largely on their reception by canon lawyers in the twelfth and thirteeth centuries, but from the outset they were laid out in very general terms. Of particular importance was a decree of 1179 that placed the papal election (→ Election, Papal) entirely in the hands of the College of → Cardinals and introduced the principle of the two-thirds majority (*Conciliorum oecumenicorum decreta* 211 c. 1). Alexander was a theological and canonical defender of Roman → primacy; but he is no longer considered to be the author of a *summa* on the *Decretum Gratiani* and the dogmatically significant *Sentences*.

■ **Sources:** *LP* 2:397-446; *PL* 200; *Epp. Pontificium Romanorum ineditae,* ed. S. Loewenfeld (Leipzig, 1885; repr. Graz, 1959) nos. 237-348; *Corpus Iuris Canonici,* ed. E. Friedberg (Leipzig, 1881); *Conciliorum oecumenicorum decreta,* ed. G. Albergigo et al. (4th ed. Bologna, 1991) 202-25.
■ **Bibliography:** *TRE* 2:237-41; H. Reuter, *Geschichte Alexanders III. und der Kirche seiner Zeit,* 3 vols. (2nd ed. Leipzig, 1860-64); W. Holtzmann, "Die Register Papst Alexanders III. in den Händen der Kanonisten," *QFIAB* 30 (1940) 13-87; M. Pacaut, *Alexandre III* (Paris, 1956); M. W. Baldwin, *Alexander III and the Twelfth Century* (Glen Rock, N.J., and New York, 1968); R. Foreville, *Lateran I-IV* (2nd ed. Mainz, 1970); T. A. Reuter, *The Papal Schism, the Empire and the West 1159-69* (Oxford, 1975); J. T. Noonan, "Who was Rolandus?" *Law, Church and Society: Festschrift for S. Kuttner* (Philadelphia, 1977) 21-48; W. Madertoner, *Die zwiespältige Papstwahl des Jahres 1159* (Vienna, 1978); F. Barlow, *Thomas Beckett* (London, 1986); *Miscellanea Rolando Bandinelli papa Alessandro III,* ed. F. Lotta (Siena, 1986); J. Laudage, *Alexander III. und Friedrich Barbarossa* (Cologne, 1990); G. Viti, "La canonizzazione di San Bernardo di Clairvaux tra politica e religiosità," *Vivens homo* 10 (1999) 53-78.

JOHANNES LAUDAGE

Alexander IV (Dec. 12, 1254-May 25, 1261). Formerly *Rainald,* son of Count Philip of Ienne (near Subiaco); in 1219 he became Magister and *domini pape subdiaconus.* In 1227, thanks to his uncle, Gregory IX, he was made cardinal deacon of Sant' Eustachio; from 1217 to 1231 he was a papal chamberlain; before August 11, 1231, cardinal bishop elect of Ostia and Velletri; but he remained a cardinal deacon until early 1235 and was not consecrated a bishop until sometime before May 5, 1235. Having been tried and tested in various diplomatic missions and by now familiar with the Hohenstaufen issues, he was chosen in Naples as a compromise candidate to succeed Innocent IV and was consecrated on December 20, 1254. The refusal to become the guardian of the orphaned Conradin, his excommunication of Manfred (March 25, 1255), and simultaneous recognition of the investiture of King Edmund of England as king of Sicily (April 9, 1255) dashed all the hopes that Alexander (the choice of name was significant) might be able to mediate between the legal position of the curia and the Hohenstaufen interests. The uncertain state of affairs in the south forced Alexander to seek refuge in Viterbo. In spite of the ecclesiastical penalties he imposed on Manfred and his adherents (1259-1260), the

Guelph position worsened. But in the German empire he remained indecisive in his choice of candidates for the throne during the interregnum. For a time he made overtures to Richard Rufus of Cornwall, who became a senator of Rome at the same time as Manfred.

Alexander's handling of the great political issues facing the church in his day was inadequate. Nevertheless his efforts, most of which were unavailing, should be noted: the union of the Latin and Greek churches, the coexistence of Latins and Greeks on Cyprus, a crusade, the defense of Christendom against the danger posed by the Mongols as well as the hierarchy (appointment of a Maronite patriarch in Antioch, elevation of Riga to an archbishopric). Moreover, he strove to remove blatant abuses; he imposed a waiting period of only six months between election and consecration; he enforced the obligation to perform → *ad limina* visits, set out in the constitution *Execrabilis;* he canceled all broadly phrased dispensations and awarded commissions. Through the bull *Licet ecclesia* (April 9, 1256) he joined together numerous eremitical groups into the Augustinian order. In 1255 he had the Servite orders confirmed. Having been the cardinal protector of the Franciscans and Poor Clares for many years (de facto since 1227), Alexander maintained that preference for the mendicant orders after becoming pope. He expanded the scope of the Inquisition, canonized Clare of Assisi, and fought the limitations on pastoral care by the mendicants by nullifying the regulations of his predecessor through the bull *Nec insolitum* (December 22, 1254). He repelled the vehement attacks of their critics and secured the right of the mendicants to teach at the University of Paris (in the bull *Quasi lignum vitae* of April 14, 1255). But he also condemned the impugned *Liber introductorius* of Gerardo de Borgo San Donnino (October 23, 1255) and forbade disputations between lay people and heretics (*Corpus Iuris Canonici* VI° 5.2.2).

■ **Sources:** C. Bourel de la Roncière et al., *Les Registres d'Alexandre IV,* 3 vols. (Paris, 1895-1959); *RPR*(P) 2:1286-1473, 2124-29.

■ **Bibliography:** *DBI* 2:189-93; *LMA* 1:373; F. Tenckhoff, *Papst Alexander IV.* (Paderborn, 1908); G. Barraclough, "The Constitution 'Execrabilis' of Alexander IV," *English Historical Review* 49 (1934) 193-218; E. Dupré Theseider, *Roma dal commune di popolo alla signoria pontificia* (Bologna, 1952) 34-86; S. Sibilia,

Alessandro IV (Anagni, 1961); S. Andreotta, *La famiglia di Alessandro IV e l'abbazia di Subiaco* (Rome, 1962); *Registro degli atti e delle lettere di Gregorio di Monte Longo (1233-69)* (Rome, 1965); T. T. Haluscynski and M. M. Wojnar, *Acta Alexandri P.P. IV* (Rome, 1966); L. Pellegrini, *Alessandro IV e i Francescani* (Rome, 1966); P. Linehan, *The Spanish Church and the Papacy in the Thirteenth Century* (Cambridge, 1971); W. R. Thomson, "The Earliest Cardinal-Protectors of the Franciscan Order," *Studies in Medieval and Renaissance History* 9 (1972) 52ff.; A. Paravicini Bagliani, *Cardinali di curia e "familiae" cardinalizie dal 1227 al 1254* (Padua, 1972) 41-60; G. F. Nüske, "Untersuchungen über das Personal der päpstlichen Kanzlei 1254 bis 1304 [I]," *Archiv für Diplomatik, Schriftgeschichte, Siegel- und Wappenkunde* 20 (1974) 39-240; I. Rodríguez de Lama, *La documentación pontificia de Alejandro IV* (Rome, 1976); H. Hénaff, "Les conservateurs apostoliques et les decrétales d'Alexandre IV," *Revue de droit canonique* 3 (1985) 194-221; F. Liotta, "I papi Anagnani e lo sviluppo del diritto canonico classico," *AHP* 365 (1998) 33-47; M. K. Wernicke, "Die Bulle 'Oblata nobis' Alexanders IV. vom 20. April, 1256," *Analecta Augustiniana* 63 (2000) 51-57.

LUDWIG VONES

Alexander V (June 26, 1409-October 3, 1410). Formerly *Petrus Philargis* (also known as *Philaretus* or *Petrus of Candia*), the first pope of the Pisan obedience (Council of Pisa) in the Western Schism, born in 1340 in Crete, he died in Bologna. A Franciscan from 1357, he studied in Padua, Oxford, and Paris, and taught in Paris and Pavia, where he was considered a first-rate theologian. Promoted by the Viscontis, he was made bishop of Piacenza (1386), Vicenza (1388), and Novara (1389); in 1402 he was consecrated archbishop of Milan and in 1405 he was made a cardinal by Innocent VII. As such he was engaged mostly in diplomatic activity. He had a decisive influence on the Council of Pisa, which elected him pope. Alexander strove successfully for the recognition of the Pisan obedience. In Italian politics he turned to Louis II of Anjou for support, who in exchange supported him in the conquest of the → papal states.

■ **Bibliography:** *DBI* 2:193-96; *Dictionary of the Middle Ages,* ed. J. R. Strayer, vol. 1 (New York, 1982) 147-48; F. Ehrle, *Der Sentenzenkommentar Peters von Candia* (Münster, 1925); A. Tuilier, "L'élection d'Alexandre V, pape grec, sujet vénitien et docteur de l'Université de Paris," *Rivista di Studi Bizantini e Slavi* 3 (1983) 319-41; T. Morrissey, "Peter Candia at Padua and Venice in March 1406," *Reform and Renewal in the Middle Ages* *and Renaissance,* Festschrift for L. Pascoe (Leiden, 2000) 155-73.

JOHANNES GROHE

Alexander VI (Aug. 11, 1492-Aug. 18, 1503). Formerly *Rodrigo de Borja* (Borgia), probably born on January 1, 1431, at Játiva near Valencia. He was created a cardinal in 1456 and a vice-chancellor in 1457 by his uncle, Callistus III. The leading concerns of his pontificate were maintaining church-internal equilibrium and limiting the influence of the great powers over Italy, as well as promoting the interests of his own family. In 1495, together with the Holy League, he forced Charles VIII of France to retreat from Italy, but in 1499 he made overtures to Louis XII. In 1493, following earlier models, he enfeoffed Castille with the newly discovered countries of the Americas; and in 1494 he confirmed the dividing up of Spanish and Portuguese expansionary interests in the Treaty of Tordesillas. Along with his children he engaged in purposeful dynastic politics; with the help of his son the condottiere Cesare Borja he pursued the centralization of the → papal states (Romagna). He favored strict law and order. Girolamo Savonarola came into conflict with him only because of French politics. Alexander's often immoral way of life was attacked by his contemporaries primarily for political reasons.

■ **Bibliography:** *DBI* 2:196-205; *TRE* 2:241-44; *LMA* 1:374; 8:873-74; *VATL* 23-24; A. Baragona, *La polemica storiografica sulle bolle alessandrine relative alle grandi scoperte: Miscellanea di storia delle esplorazioni,* vol. 2 (Genoa, 1977) 29-47; F. A. Young, "Fundamental Changes in the Nature of the Cardinalate in the Fifteenth Century and Their Reflection in the Election of Pope Alexander VI" (Diss., University of Maryland, 1978); M. Brion, *Les Borgia* (Paris, 1979); S. Schüller-Piroli, *Die Borgia-Päpste Kalixt III. und Alexander VI.* (Munich, 1980); C. Shaw, "Alexander VI, Cesare Borgia and the Orsini," *European Studies Review* 11 (1981) 1-23; S. Poeschl, *Alexander Maximus: Das Bildprogramm des Appartamento Borgia im Vatican* (Weimar, 1999).

WINFRIED EBERHARD

Alexander VII (Apr. 7, 1655-May 22, 1667). Formerly *Fabio Chigi,* born February 13, 1599, in Siena, where he studied philosophy, law, and theology. He entered the papal service in 1628, which took him to Ferrara, as vice-legate; to Malta, as inquisitor; and in 1635 to Cologne, where he served as nuncio from 1644-1649, and mediated

the the Peace of Westphalia in Münster. In 1651 he became secretary of state. In person he was a pious, experienced diplomat with literary interests and connections; he was elected as the candidate of the politically independent cardinals. He suffered a severe loss of prestige in the dispute with France—he had to sign the humiliating peace conditions dictated by Pisa on February 12, 1664—which was not offset by the lifting of the Venetian ban on the Jesuits (imposed by Paul V) as the price of papal help against the Turks. As secretary of state, he eliminated the patronage system of Innocent X and shifted the center of gravity to the Congregations. Though he initially rejected it, he returned to → nepotism, even though the *nipoti* had no substantial influence on affairs. The measures taken during his pontificate were: (1) A decree of the Congregation of the Propaganda in favor of the Jesuit mission to China (March 23, 1656); (2) Two constitutions against Jansenism (October 16, 1656, and February 15, 1665); (3) Two condemnations of laxism (September 24, 1656, and March 18, 1666). His promotion of the arts and sciences lives on especially in the Chigi and Valentina libraries that he founded (→ Vatican Library) and in masterpieces by Giovanni Lorenzo Bernini (→ St. Peter's).

■ **Works:** *Philomathi Musae juveniles Cologne 1645, Antwerp 1654, Paris 1656, Amsterdam 1680,* ed. H. Hufgenroth (Cologne, 1999).

■ **Sources:** *Bulletino Romano 16 and 17* (Turin, 1869); J. A. F. Orbann, *Bescheiden in Italië omtrent nederlandsche kunstenaars en geleerden,* vol. 1 (The Hague, 1911); G. Hoogewerff, *Bescheiden, etc.,* vol. 3 (The Hague, 1917); G. Brom, *Archivalia in Italië,* vol. 3 (The Hague, 1914); V. Kybal and G. Incisa della Rochetta, *La Nunciatura di Fabio Chigi (1640-51),* vol. 1/1 and 2 (Rome, 1943, 1946); A. Legrand and L. Ceyssens, *La correspondance antijanséniste de Fabio Chigi* (Brussels and Rome, 1957); V. Borg, *Fabio Chigi, Apostolic Delegate in Malta (1634-39)* (Vatican City, 1967); *Diarium Chigi 1639-51,* ed. K. Repgen (Acta Pacis Westphalicae III C 1/1) (Münster, 1984).

■ **Bibliography:** No modern biography exists. There is a fragmentary contemporary one by S. Pallavicino, *Della vita di Alessandro VII, libri cinque* (Prato, 1839-40); *DTHC* 1:730-47; *DBI* 2:205-15; *VATL* 24ff.; Pastor, vol. 14/1; K. Repgen, *Die römische Kurie und der Westfälische Friede,* vol. 1/1-2 (Tübingen, 1962-65); R. Darricau, "Louis XIV et la papauté de 1661 à 1670," *Revue d'histoire diplomatique* 84 (1970) 165-72; M. Albert, *Nuntius Fabio Chigi und die Anfänge des Jansenismus 1639-51* (Rome, 1988); K. Repgen, "Salvo iure Sanctae

5

Sedis? Die Zessionsbestimmungen des Westfällischen Friedens für Metz, Toul und Verdun als Konkordatsrechts-Problem," *Fides et Ius,* Festschrift for G. May (Regensburg, 1991) 527-58.

KONRAD REPGEN

Alexander VIII (Oct. 6, 1689-Feb. 1, 1691). Formerly *Pietro Ottoboni* (family enobled in 1646), born in Venice on April 22, 1610. He studied law in Padua, entered the curial service in 1630, became a → Rota auditor in 1642; he was created a cardinal in 1652, and from 1654 to 1664 he served as bishop of Brescia. Thereafter he was a Venetian cardinal protector; from 1667 to 1669 he was a datary. Elected as an independent *zelante*, he strove by his extreme accommodationism to achieve a political and ecclesiastical reconciliation with Louis XIV. After this failed, he condemned the legal system of the state church as expressed in the four Gallican Articles, having already issued a dogmatic condemnation of thirty-one Jansenist propositions. The attempt at a political rapprochement with France necessitated a cooling off of relations with the emperor. In 1690 during troop movements in the → papal states as part of Venice's war against the Turks, there was political unrest, despite lowered taxes and eased economic restrictions. Alexander's pontificate was marked by a return of papal nepotism. For the → Vatican Library he purchased large parts of Christina of Sweden's library. His tomb is in St. Peter's. No biography exists.

■ **Works:** *Decisiones sacrae rotae Romanae* (Rome, 1657). *Bulletino Romano* 20 (Turin, 1870).

■ **Bibliography:** *DTHC* 1:747-63; *DBI* 2:215-29; *HCMA,* vols. 4 and 5; Pastor, vol. 14/2; M. Langlois, "Madame de Maintenon et le Saint-Siège," *Revue d'histoire ecclési-astique* 25 (1929) 33-72; L. Ceyssens, "Les jugements portés par les théologiens du Saint-Office sur les 31 propositions rigoristes condamnées en 1690," *Antoni-anum* 56 (1981) 451-67; A. Menniti Ippolito, "L'eresia di Santa Pelagia, Pietro Ottoboni e la politica del S. Uffi-cio," *Rivista di storia e letteratura religiosa* 26 (1992) 298-305.

KONRAD REPGEN

Anacletus I (Anenkletos) (79?-91?). A saint and probably a martyr under Domitian. He is the second successor to Peter according to the oldest list of Roman bishops (Irenaeus of Lyons, *Adversus haereses* 3.3.3) and Eusebius of Caesarea (*Historia ecclesiastica* 3.13) and others. He is the second successor to Peter. The order of succession Linus,

Anacletus, and Clement is the original one, while the order of Linus, Clement, Anacletus (*Catalogus Liberianus*) is not attested before the fourth century. Cletus was evidently used early on as an abbreviation of Anacletus. Both names found their way into the Roman liturgical calendar: Cletus on April 26 and Anacletus on July 13. The name Anenkletos was often borne by slaves at this time, which suggests that Anacletus may have been a manumitted slave of Greek extraction. At the time Rome had not yet developed a monarchical episcopate. But we may be sure that Anacletus had a leading position among the presbyters (*episcopi*) of the Roman community. The calculation that his pontificate lasted twelve years dates to the third or fourth century and is unhistorical.

■ **Bibliography:** *LP* 1, Introductio 122, 125; 3:241, 268; *Quellen zur Geschichte des Papstums und des römischen Katholizismus* (C. Mirbt, founder and original series editor), ed. K. Aland, vol. 1 (6th ed. Tübingen, 1967) 19, 33-34; *VATL* 29.

GEORG SCHWAIGER

Anacletus II (antipope, Feb. 14/23, 1130-Jan. 25, 1138). Formerly *Petrus Pierleoni* (from an originally Jewish-Roman noble family), born ca. 1090. He studied in Paris before entering the monastery in Cluny (prior to 1116); he was created a cardinal deacon (of Sts. Cosmas and Damian) in 1112. In 1120 he became a cardinal priest of Santa Maria in Trastevere and a legate for Callistus II. Highly educated and of unimpeachable character, he represented a Cluniac spirituality that was destined to decline in the face of the rapid rise of the Vita Apostolica movement. In 1130 conflicting views of the role of the papacy and the curia led to a papal schism. The fact that Innocent II won out, despite the electoral majority for Anacletus, is to be attributed primarily to the influence of Bernard of Clairvaux, Norbert of Xante, Lothar III, and the Roman chancellor Haimerich. The area subject to Anacletus was essentially limited to Norman southern Italy, the later → papal states, and Scotland. The key to Innocent II's victory was, among other things, the stress on his rival's Jewish extraction.

■ **Sources:** *RPR*(J) 2nd ed. 8370-8432; *PL* 179:687-731.

■ **Bibliography:** *LMA* 1:568-69; *VATL* 29-30; H. W. Klewitz, "Das Ende des Reformpapstums," *Deutsches Archiv für Geschichte des Mittelalters* 3 (1939) 371-412; P. F. Palumbo, *Lo scisma del 1130* (Rome, 1942); F.-J. Schmale, *Studien zum Schisma des Jahres 1130* (Cologne and Graz, 1961); J. Deér, *Papstum und Normannen* (Cologne and Vienna, 1972); M. Stroll, *The Jewish Pope: Ideology and Politics in the Schism of 1130* (Leiden and New York, 1987); G. Knight, "Politics and Pastoral Care: Papal Schism, in Some Letters of Peter the Venerable," *Revue Bénédictine* 109 (1999) 359-90.

JOHANNES LAUDAGE

Anastasius I (Nov. 27[?], 399-Dec. 19[?], 402). Saint (feast day April 27), a Roman, son of Maximus. He repeatedly took a stand against Origenist errors (although Rome had little precise knowledge of the disputes in the East) and admonished the African bishops to intervene against the Donatists. His friends Jerome and Paulinus of Nola speak of him with high esteem.
■ Sources: *LP* 1:218-19; 3:83; 3; *RPR*(J) 2nd ed. 1:42-43; 2:691-92.
■ Bibliography: *DHGE* 2:147ff.; *VATL* 30-31; Caspar 1:285ff., 291-92, 600 (chronology).

GEORG SCHWAIGER

Anastasius II (Nov. 24, 496-Nov. 17, 498). A Roman, son of the presbyter Peter. His pontificate occurred during the Acacian schism and in the early years of the Ostrogoth domination under Theoderic the Great in Italy. More conciliatory than his predecessors Felix II and Gelasius I, he strove for peace and understanding in the imperial church (he sent a legation to the Byzantine emperor Anastasius I), but forbade the mention of Acacius and his successors in the diptychs of the liturgy. The attempts to settle the schism stirred up opposition from part of the Roman clergy and later brought down on him the (unfounded) reproach of heresy, for example in Dante (*Divine Comedy, Inferno* XI, 8-9). After his death the crisis of the Roman church led to the schism of Symmachus and Laurentius. His supposed letter of congratulation on the baptism of the Frankish king Chlodwig is a seventeeth-century forgery.
■ Sources: *LP* 2:258-59; 3:87; *RPR* (J) 1:95-96; 2:693; E. Schwartz, *Publizistische Sammlung zum Akazianischen Schisma* (Munich, 1934) 226-30.
■ Bibliography: *DHGE* 2:1473ff.; I. Döllinger, *Papstfabeln* (2nd ed. Stuttgart, 1890) 146-53; Caspar 2:82-87; H. Rahner, *Die gefälschten Papstbriefe aus dem Nachlaß von J. Vignier* (Freiburg, 1935); *Das Konzil von Chalkedon: Geschichte und Gegenwart,* ed. A. Grillmeier and H. Bacht, vol. 2 (2nd ed. Vienna, 1979) 66-70; Richards, 67ff.

GEORG SCHWAIGER

Anastasius III (presumably from the beginning of September 913 to the end of October 913). A Roman; precise dates as well as details of his tenure in office are unknown. Anastasius's epitaph says that he ran his pontificate in a pleasant fashion, which implies a contrast between him and the troubled pontificates of his predecessors. Patriarch Nicholas I of Constantinople and the Byzantine emperor Alexander sent letters to him during the "tetragamy" dispute (on the fourth marriage of Emperor Leo VI) that he did not answer.
■ Sources: Epitaphium Anastasii III: *MGH.PL* 4/3, 1026; *RPR*(J) 2nd ed. 1:448; 2:706.
■ Bibliography: P. Fedele, "Ricerche per la storia di Roma e del papato nel secolo X," *Archivio della Società Romana di Storia Patria* 34 (1911) 393-423; Zimmermann J.

SEBASTIAN SCHOLZ

Anastasius III (antipope). Also known as *Anastasius Bibliothecarius,* born before 817 in Rome, died there ca. 879. He was probably educated in a Roman monastery of Greek monks. He was created a cardinal of San Marcello in 847 by Leo IV, but then excommunicated and laicized from 850 to 853 on account of opposition to him. From August to September 855 he was antipope to Benedict III, then pardoned by Benedict and readmitted to the priesthood by Nicholas I. He was abbot of Santa Maria in Trastevere and became increasingly engaged in papal policies concerning the East. He was appointed librarian of the Roman church by Hadrian II and thus occupied himself with the papal correspondence. As a representative of Emperor Louis II he took part in the Eighth Ecumenical Council in Constantinople (he is our source of information about the acts of the council). As an opponent of Photius and a promoter of the Apostles to the Slavs, Cyril and Methodius, he had less influence under John VIII. He did not participate in writing the → *Liber Pontificalis* except for the *vita* of Nicholas I. He was mainly a (reliable?) translator from the Greek (he translated the seventh and eighth sessions of the Conciliar Acts, and the lives of the saints with his own prologues). Together with Johannes Diaconus Hymmonides, he compiled, from Greek sources, the *Chronographia tripartita.* He also wrote his own commentaries on the translations by John Scotus Eriugena of the writings of Dionysius the Areopagite and Maximus Confessor, which he sent to Charles the Bald.

■ **Works:** *Epp. sive Praefationes,* ed. E. Perels and G. Laehr, *MGH.Ep* 7:395-442; Acts of the Council: *PL* 129:9-512; *Chronographia tripartita,* ed. C. de Boor, *Theophanis Chronographia II* (Leipzig, 1885) 31-346; for translations of Lives, see the lists in C. Leonardi, *Hagiographie, cultures et sociétés, IVᵉ-XIIᵉ siècles* (Paris, 1981) 471-90; U. Westerbergh, *Anastasius Bibliothecarius, Sermo Theodori Studitae de Sancto Bartholomeo apostolo* (Stockholm, 1963); P. Devog, *Analecta Bollandiana* 83 (1965) 117-87; P. Chiesa, *Studi Medievali* 28 (1987) 879-903 (St. Amphilochios).

■ **Bibliography:** *DBI* 3:25-37; *LMA* 1:573-74; E. Perels, *Papst Nicolaus I. und Anastasius Bibliothecarius* (Berlin, 1920); P. Devos, "Anastase le Bibliothécaire," *Byzantion* 32 (1962) 97-115; D. Lohrmann, *Das Register Papst Johannes' VIII.* (Tübingen, 1968) 239-57 and passim; idem, "Eine Arbeitshandschrift des Anastasius Bibliothecarius und die Überlieferung der Akten des 8. Ökumenischen Konzils," *QFIAB* 50 (1971) 420-31 (Acts of the Council); A. Lapôtre, *De Anastasio Bibliothecario sedis apostolicae: Études sur la papauté au IXᵉ siècle* (Paris, 1985); C. Leonardi, "Anastasio Bibliotecario e l'ottavo concilio ecumenico," *Studi Medievali* 12 (1987) 60-192 (Acts of the Council); M. W. Herren, *The Sacred Nectar of the Greeks* (London, 1988); G. Arnaldi, *Anastasio Bibliotecario, Carlo il Calvo e la fortuna di Dionigi l'Areopagita nel secolo IX: Giovanni Scoto nel suo tempo* (Spoleto, 1989) 513-36; K. Herbers, *Leo IV. und das Papsttum in der Mitte des 9. Jh.* (Stuttgart, 1996) 214-24; B. Neil, "Anastasius Bibliothecarius' Latin Translation of Two Byzantine Liturgical Commentaries," *Ephemerides liturgicae* 114 (2000) 329-46.

CLAUDIO LEONARDI

Anastasius IV (July 12, 1153-December 3, 1154). Formerly *Conrad of Suburra,* a Roman. In 1128 he was made cardinal archbishop of Sabina; in the schism of 1130 he was the vicar of Innocent II in Rome. He was called to be pope at an advanced age. He joined with Frederick I Barbarossa over the appointing of Wichmann to be archbishop of Magdeburg, to whom he gave, as he did to Archbishop William of York, the → pallium that had been denied them by Eugene III. At that time Sweden began to pay the → Peter's Pence.

■ **Sources:** *LP* 2:388; *RPT*(J) 2nd ed. 2:89-102.

■ **Bibliography:** *DBI* 3:24-25; B. Zenker, "Die Mitglieder des Kardinalskollegium von 1130 bis 1159" (Diss., Würzburg, 1964) 46-48; P. Classen, "Zur Geschichte Papst Anastasius IV.," *QFIAB* 48 (1968) 36-63; A. Poppe, "Die Magdeburger Frage: Versuch einer Neubewertung," *Europa Slavica—Europa Orientalis,* Festschrift for H. Ludat (Berlin, 1980) 297-340.

JOHANNES LAUDAGE

Anicetus (155?-166?). Saint (feast day April 17). According to the oldest list of Roman bishops (Irenaeus of Lyons, *Adversus haereses* 3.3.3), he was the tenth successor of Peter, eleventh in other Roman bishops' lists. According to the → *Liber Pontificalis,* he was a Syrian from Emsa. With his tenure, the monarchical episcopate evidently came to prevail in the Roman community. Under Anicetus, Hegesippus and Polycarp came to Rome; Justin and the heretics Valentinus and Marcion were also active there. The negotiations with Polycarp about the celebration of Easter brought no agreement, but neither was there any break-off. Whether or not Anicetus was martyred is uncertain.

■ **Sources:** *LP* 1:58-59, 134; 3:73, 244; *Quellen zur Geschichte des Papsttums und des römischen Katholizismus* (C. Mirbt, founder and original series editor), ed. K. Aland, vol. 1 (6th ed. Tübingen, 1967).

■ **Bibliography:** J. Hofmann, "Die amtliche Stellung der in der ältesten römischen Bischofsliste überlieferten Männer in der Kirche von Rom," *Historisches Jahrbuch* 109 (1989) 1-23; P. Lampe, *Die stadtrömischen Christen in den ersten beiden Jahrhunderten* (2nd ed. Tübingen, 1989); N. Brox, *Der Hirt des Hermas* (Göttingen, 1991).

GEORG SCHWAIGER

Anterus (Nov. 21, 235-Jan. 3, 236). Saint (feast day Jan. 3). Successor to Pontian, who abdicated on September 28, 235. According to his name and the *Liber Pontificalis,* he was of Greek extraction. His short rule fell during the persecution of Christians under Emperor Maximinus Thrax, but he himself cannot be considered a martyr. Anterus was the first pope who was buried in the papal crypt of the catacomb of Callistus. Large fragments of his epitaph, in Greek letters, were found there in 1854.

■ **Sources:** Eusebius of Caesarea, *Historia ecclesiastica* 6.23.3; 29.1-4; *LP* 1:95f., 147; 3:74, 244; *Quellen zur Geschichte des Papsttums und des römischen Katholizismus* (C. Mirbt, founder and original series editor), ed. K. Aland, vol. 1 (6th ed. Tübingen, 1967) 62.

■ **Bibliography:** *DHGE* 3:520f.; *BiblSS* 2: 51f.; J. Wilpert, *Die Papstgräber und die Cäciliengruft in der Katakombe des heiligen Kalistus* (Freiburg, 1909) 16f. Table II; Casper 1: 43f., 48ff.

GEORG SCHWAIGER

Benedict I (June 2, 575-July 30, 579). A Roman, whose pontificate, about which information is sparse, was hard pressed by the Langobard siege of Rome in 579. Benedict and the Roman senate looked to Byzantium for help, but because of the war with the Persians, its assistance was completely inadequate. Benedict consecrated twenty-one bishops, among them the Roman John as archbishop of Ravenna.

■ **Sources:** *LP* 1:CCLV, CCLXI, 308; *RPR*(J) 1:1371; 2:695-96.

■ **Bibliography:** *DHGE* 8:7ff.; *DBI* 8:234-35; Caspar 2:350-51; S. Gasparri and P. Cammarasano, eds. *Langobardia* (Udine, 1990).

GEORG SCHWAIGER

Benedict II (June 26, 683-May 8, 685). Saint (feast day May 7). After his election (in the beginning of June 683), the consecration was delayed for a year, since confirmation of the election had to be obtained from Byzantium. Under the aegis of the peace between Byzantium (under Emperor Constantine IV) and Rome, future papal elections were to be confirmed once again by the exarch of Ravenna; and the autonomy of Ravenna (after the Monothelitism dispute) was abolished. Benedict worked for the recognition of the Sixth Ecumenical Council (Constantinople 680/681) in the West, especially in the self-confident Visigothic churches. He restored Roman churches and intervened (unsuccessfully) on behalf of Bishop Wilfrid of York.

■ **Sources:** *LP* 1:363ff.; *RPR*(J) 1:241f.; 2:699.

■ **Bibliography:** *DHGE* 8:9-14; *DBI* 8:325-29; Caspar 2:614-17, 674ff., 687; J. M. Lacarra, "La iglesia visigoda en el siglo VII y sus relaciones con Roma," *Settimane di studio del Centro Italiano di Studi sull'Alto Medioevo* 7/1 (1960) 378-84.

GEORG SCHWAIGER

Benedict III (Sept. 29, 855-April 7 [not 17], 858). A Roman, Benedict was elected immediately after the death of Leo IV (July 17, 855), but in order to be consecrated he needed the consent of Emperor Louis II. An influential group, supported by the imperial ambassadors, denied him recognition and elevated Anastasius Bibliothecarius, who had been condemned by Leo IV, as antipope. Anastasius had Benedict imprisoned but ran into open opposition as a result. Benedict, a cultivated man intent on compromise, was consecrated, with the consent of imperial ambassadors, on September 29, 855, in St. Peter's. This confusion provided the starting point for the later legend of Pope → Joan. Benedict treated Anastasius gently, strove for peace between Louis II and his brothers, and

managed to strengthen papal authority vis-à-vis Patriarch Ignatius of Constantinople, Archbishop Hincmar of Rheims, and in England. The *Liber Pontificalis* praises his service to the churches of Rome.

■ **Sources:** *LP* 2:140-50; *RPR*(J) 1:339ff.; 2:703, 744.

■ **Bibliography:** *DHGE* 8:14-27; *DBI* 8:330-37; Zimmermann *Pa*, 82-83; K. Herbers, *Leo IV und das Papsttum in der Mitte des 9. Jh.* (Stuttgart, 1996).

GEORG SCHWAIGER

Benedict IV (May/June 900-July/August 903). A Roman, considered a member of the party of Pope Formosus. In 900 he held a Lateran synod. In February 901 he crowned Louis II as emperor, who subsequently was defeated by his Italian opponent, King Berengar, in 903. At this point the papacy was threatening to flounder amid the wildly partisan struggles of the so-called dark ages (*saeculum obscurum*).

■ **Sources:** *LP* 2:233; *RPR*(J) 1:443-44; 2:705.

■ **Bibliography:** *DHGE* 8:27-31; *DBI* 8:337-42; Zimmermann *J*.

GEORG SCHWAIGER

Benedict V (end of May–end of June 964). The learned Roman scholastic and deacon *Benedictus Grammaticus* was chosen by the Romans after the death of John XII instead of the banished Leo VIII and against the wishes of Emperor Otto I. But he was then handed over to the emperor, who was besieging Rome, and was formally deposed at a Lateran synod by Leo and Otto. He died in Hamburg on July 4, 965, supposedly just before his restitution, which the Romans had asked for. His body was transferred to Rome in 988 on orders from Otto II.

■ **Sources:** Zimmermann *Reg*.

■ **Bibliography:** *DBI* 8:342ff.; *LMA* 1:1858; *VATL* 96; Zimmermann *J*.

HARALD ZIMMERMANN

Benedict VI (Jan. 19, 973–end of June 974). Son of Hildebrand Monachus from the sub-Capitolean region of Rome. He was a (cardinal) deacon of San Teodoro before he was elected, probably as early as September 972. The → enthronement did not take place until the emperor gave his consent. Only a few documents have been preserved from his pontificate. Among others, the confirmation of the diocese of Prague has been lost. He was overthrown by a revolt of the Crescentian clan, and in July 974, despite the intervention of an imperial envoy, he was murdered in the → Castel Sant' Angelo on orders of Boniface VII.

■ **Sources:** **Zimmermann** *Reg;* Zimmermann *Pu* vol. 1.

■ **Bibliography:** *DBI* 8:344ff.; *LMA* 1:1858-59; *VATL* 69; Zimmermann *J.*

HARALD ZIMMERMANN

Benedict VII (October 974-July 7, 983). The nephew of the Roman prince Alberic II and bishop of Sutri was elected in the presence of an envoy of Otto II. Many documents have been preserved from his pontificate, which was oriented to cooperation with the emperor and was shaken by Boniface VII and his followers. Among these documents are the confirmation of the German primate for Mainz in 975. In 981 a Lateran synod that had been arranged with Otto condemned simony. He also made important contacts with Spain.

■ **Sources:** Zimmermann *Reg;* Zimmermann *Pu* vol. 1.

■ **Bibliography:** *DBI* 8:346-50; *LMA* 1:1859; Zimmermann *J.*

HARALD ZIMMERMANN

Benedict VIII (May 17, 1012-April 9, 1024). Formerly *Theophylactus.* As the second son of Gregory of Tusculum, he was elevated to the papacy as a layman; he managed to prevail against Gregory VI and was consecrated on May 21. In contrast to his predecessors he sought out contact with the German court, which led to his coronation of Henry II as emperor on February 14, 1014. At a synod in Ravenna in 1014 both men took action against simony, as well as cooperating in other matters. After the uprising against Byzantium in Apulia, which he supported with Norman mercenaries, collapsed in October 1018, he arranged to meet with the emperor at Easter in Bamberg in 1020. In the same year the Privilegium Ottonianum was renewed. In the summer of 1022 the military campaign in southern Italy pursued its largely fruitless course. On August 1, 1022, both Benedict and Henry continued the councils in Pavia, which promulgated regulations against clerical marriage. Since 1014 there had been connections between Benedict and reform-minded circles around Abbot Odilo of Cluny. In the spring of 1016, with help from Genoa and Pisa, Benedict overcame pirates off Sardinia. He did not become involved in German disputes, except in the Hammerstein marriage affair. His pontificate was characterized by close cooperation with the emperor and an effort to strengthen the papacy.

■ **Sources:** *LP* 2:268; *RPR*(J) 1:506-14; Zimmermann *Reg;* Zimmermann *Pu* 2:464-549.

■ **Bibliography:** *LMA* 1:1859; P. G. Wappler, *Papst Benedikt VIII.* (Leipzig, 1897); K. J. Herrmann, *Das Tuskulanerpapsttum* (Stuttgart, 1973); H. Wolter, *Die Synoden im Reichsgebiet und in Reichsitalien von 916 bis 1054* (Paderborn, 1988).

KLAUS JÜRGEN HERRMANN

Benedict IX (Oct. 21, 1032-May 1, 1045). Formerly *Theophylactus,* the nephew of both his predecessors John XIX and Benedict VIII; a layman. With help from his father, Alberic III of Tusculum, he was elevated to the papacy in his youth (not as a child). He maintained a careful distance from the German royal court. In the dispute of Conrad II with Archbishop Aribert of Milan, he supported the emperor, but not until 1038 after a meeting in Spello. In the conflict between Grado and Aquileia he decided (1044) in favor of Grado, contrary to German interests. Making use of family connections and a supple policy vis-à-vis Byzantium he succeeded in extending the Latin church in southern Italy. Contacts are known to have existed between Benedict and reform circles in Italy and France. Banished from Rome by a revolt of the aristocracy in September 1044, he expelled the antipope Sylvester III. On May 5, 1045, he abdicated in favor of Gregory VI in exchange for money paid to his partisans. On December 24, 1046, he was deposed in Rome by Henry III. After the death of Clement II he took up his pontificate again, but on July 16, 1048, he had to give way to Damasus II. A renewed attempt to seize power in April 1054 likewise came to grief. He supposedly died between September 18, 1055, and January 9, 1056, as a penitent in the monastery of Grottaferrata.

■ **Sources:** *LP* 2:270ff.; *RPR*(J) 1:519-23; 2:709, 748ff.; Zimmermann *Pu* 2:598-623.

■ **Bibliography:** *LMA* 1:1859-60; S. Messina, *Benedetto IX: Studio critico* (Catania, 1922); Zimmermann *Pa,* 120-39; K. J. Herrmann, *Das Tuskulanerpapsttum* (Stuttgart, 1973); F. J. Schmale, "Die 'Absetzung' Gregors VI. in Sutri und die synodale Tradition," *AHC* 11 (1979) 55-103; H. Wolter, *Die Synoden im Reichsgebiet und in Reichsitalien von 916-1054* (Paderborn, 1988).

KLAUS JÜRGEN HERRMANN

Benedict X (Apr. 5, 1058-Apr. 1060). Formerly *John of Velletri,* probably not the same person as Bishop Benedict of Velletri, who is mentioned in

1057 as belonging to a circle of reform-minded cardinals. After the death of Stephen IX, he was elevated to the papacy under the leadership of the Tusculans, but he was not recognized by the reform cardinals, who elected Nicholas II in December 1058 in Siena. Benedict was excommunicated in January 1059 at a synod in Sutri. He was banished from Rome and was forced, with Norman help, to submit in Galleria. He was deprived of spiritual honors by the Lateran synod in April 1060; he died under Gregory VII (after 1073) in a Roman monastery.

■ Bibliography: *LMA* 1:1860; G. Tellenbach, *Die westliche Kirche vom 10. bis zum frühen 12. Jh.* (Göttingen, 1988) 134.

TILMANN SCHMIDT

Benedict XI (Oct. 22, 1303-July 7, 1304). Blessed (1736; feast day July 7), a Dominican (1257). Formerly *Niccolò di Boccassio*, born in Treviso in 1240, died in Perugia. He may have studied in Milan (1262-1268); he taught theology in Venice and Genoa; he became provincial of Lombardy (1286-1289, 1293-1296), and General-master in 1296. From 1297 he obliged the order to follow the papal position; he was a member of an embassy to the kings of France and England. In 1298 he was made cardinal of Santa Sabina, in 1300 cardinal bishop of Ostia. He went on only modestly successful legations (Hungary, Vienna); in 1303 after a brief conclave dominated by the pro-Boniface cardinal Matteo Rosso Orsini and massively influenced by Charles II of Anjou, he was unanimously elected pope and crowned five days later. He did not follow the political line of his predecessor Boniface VIII, but his lack of firmness toward the Colonna family, along with pressure from France, forced him to flee to Perugia (April 1304) and made him revoke most of the measures taken by his predecessors (to the point of issuing a general absolution) or at least soften them (lifting the excommunication of Philip IV of France and his family, promulgation of the bull *Clericis laicos*). He wished to call to account (in the bull *Flagitiosum scelus*) only those directly responsible for the attack on Boniface VIII at Anagni— Guillaume de Nogaret and the Colonnas—but he died before promulgating the aggravated judgment of contumacy against the excommunicated men. He canceled the bull *Super cathedram* of Boniface VIII, which limited the pastoral activity of the mendicant orders. He enlarged the College

of → Cardinals with three Dominican cardinals, since the order was practically his only source of support.

■ Bibliography: *DBI* 8:370-78; *LMA* 1:1860-61; *VATL* 72; H. Finke, *Aus den Tagen Bonifaz VIII.* (Münster, 1902) 275ff.; C. Grand-Jean, *Registres de Benoît XI* (Paris, 1905); A. M. Fereero, *Benedetto XI, papa domenicano* (Rome, 1934); T. Schmidt, *Der Bonifaz-Prozeß* (Cologne/Vienna, 1989) esp. 88ff.

LUDWIG VONES

Benedict XII (Dec. 20, 1334-Apr. 25, 1342, Avignon). Formerly *Jacques Fournier*, born ca. 1285 in Saverdun near Toulouse, studied in Paris (Master of Theology), in 1311 abbot of Fontfroide, in 1317 bishop of Pamiers, in 1326 bishop of Mirepoix; he led inquisitional proceedings against the Cathars. In 1327 he became a cardinal and theological advisor to John XXII—as the veteran theological expert and an eradicator of all forms of heresy, he was to end the dispute about the beatific vision, which had broken out in John's pontificate, with the dogmatic bull *Benedictus Deus* in 1336. After his election, the pope, who was inclined to moral strictness, began a comprehensive reform program, at whose center—along with a curial reform combating corruption, → nepotism, and administrative abuses (attempts at reorganizing curial authorities; creation of better organizational and operational instruments for the system of penances and petitions; controversial limits on benefices, improving the selection of candidates through examinations)—was to be the reform of religious orders. From the outset resistance from the Dominicans blocked any thoroughgoing measures, so that apart from the general regulations against vagabond monks and crossing over from one order to another (1335), only slightly effective constitutions on discipline and organization for the Cistercians (*Fulgens sicut stella*, 1335), Benedictines (*Summi magistri*, 1336), Franciscans (*Redemptor noster*, 1337), and canons regular (*Ad decorem*, 1339) could be issued. Benedict's efforts to reorganize the → papal states were highly promising, while his interventions in political matters were mostly unsuccessful (proceedings against Louis IV the Bavarian; attitude of the German electoral princes, Rhens 1338).

■ Bibliography: *DBI* 8:378-84; *LMA* 1:1861-62; É. Baluze and G. Mollat, *Vitae paparum Avenionensium*, vol. 1 (2nd ed. Paris, 1914) 194-240; J.-M. Vidal, *Benoît*

XII: Lettres communes (Paris, 1903-11); G. Daumet, *Benoît XII: Lettres closes . . . se rapportant à la France* (Paris, 1899-1920). J.-M. Vidal and G. Mollat, *Lettres closes . . . intéressant les pays autres que la France* (Paris, 1913-52); B. Guillemain, *La politique bénéficiale du pape Benoît XII* (Paris, 1952); J. Duvernoy, *Le registre d'Inquisition de Jacques Fournier, évêque de Pamiers, Benoît XII (1318 à 1325)*, 3 vols. (Toulouse, 1965). G. Mollat, *Les papes d'Avignon* (10th ed. Paris, 1965) 72-88; B. Guillemain, *La cour pontificale d'Avignon* (2nd ed. Paris, 1966); B. Schimmelpfennig, "Zisterzienserideal u. Kirchenreform: Benedikt XII. als Reformpapst," *Zisterzienser-Studien* 3 (1976) 11-43; idem, "Benedikt XII. und Ludwig der Bayer," *Archiv für Kulturgeschichte* 59 (1977) 212-22; L. Böhm, *Papst Benedikt XII. als Förderer der Ordenstudien. Festschrift für N. Backmund* (Windberg, 1978) 281-341; G. Melville, "Quellenkundliche Beiträge zum Pontifikat Benedikts XII.," *Historisches Jahrbuch* 102 (1982) 144-82; F. J. Felten, *Benoît XII, Arnaud de Verdale et la réforme des chanoines: Le monde des chanoines* (Toulouse-Fanjeaux, 1989) 309-39; *Aux origines de l'état moderne: Le fonctionnement administratif de la papauté d'Avignon*, Actes de la table ronde (Avignon, 23-24 janvier, 1988) organized by the l'école Française de Rome (Rome, 1990); F. J. Felten, *Le pape Benoît XII (1334-42) et les Frères Prêcheurs: La papauté d'Avignon et le Languedoc (1316-42)* (Toulouse, 1991) 307-42; idem, *Die Ordensreformen Benedikts XII. unter institutionen-geschichtlichem Aspekt: Institutionen und Geschichte*, ed. G. Melville (Cologne, etc., 1992) 369-435.

LUDWIG VONES

Benedict XIII (Sept. 28, 1394-July 26, 1417). Formerly *Pedro de Luna*, born in 1342/43 in Illueca from Aragonese nobility, professor of canon law in Montpellier, he was created a cardinal in 1375. At the outbreak of the Western Schism he was the member of the College of → Cardinals to whom Clement VII largely owed his recognition in France and the Spanish kingdoms. As pope he insisted uncompromisingly on his legitimacy, which, as a highly cultured person with wide literary interests, he justified in several works. As a way of resolving the schism he preferred the conquest of Rome with the violent removal of the opposition pope. In order to force Benedict to abdicate, the French besieged the papal palace in Avignon from 1398 to 1403. Negotiations over his resignation failed in 1408, and Benedict had to flee from Italy to the protection of the king of Aragón. The Councils of Pisa and Constance deposed him on June 5, 1409, and July 26, 1417, respectively, as a schismatic and a heretic. His life ended unnoticed

in Peñiscola, probably on November 29, 1422. Two competing candidates were chosen to succeed him, Gil Sánchez Muñoz (Clement VIII) and Bernard Garnier (Benedict XIV).

■ **Bibliography:** *LMA* 1:1862ff.; S. Puig y Puig, *Episcopologio Barcinonese: Pedro de Luna* (Barcelona, 1920); D. Girgensohn, "Ein Schisma ist nicht zu beenden ohne die Zustimmung der konkurrierenden Päpste," *AHP* 27 (1989) 197-247; M.-H. Jullien de Pommerol and J. Monfrin, *La bibliothèque pontificale à Avignon et à Peñiscola,* 2 vols. (Rome, 1991).

DIETER GIRGENSOHN

Benedict XIII (May 29, 1724-Feb. 21, 1730). Formerly *Pietro Francesco Orsini*, he was born on February 2, 1649, in Gravina di Puglia. He entered the Dominican order in 1667, receiving the religious name *Vincenzo Maria*. He was created a cardinal in 1672, in 1675 he became archbishop of Manfredonia, 1680 bishop of Cesena, 1686 archbishop of Benevento. Politically inexperienced, he was already weakened by old age when he became pope. In 1725 Benedict confirmed the bull *Unigenitus* and issued the bull *Pretiosus* in 1727. Mostly occupied with pastoral activity and canonizations, he largely abandoned other matters to the unscrupulous Cardinal Nicola Coscia.

■ **Works:** *Opere tutte Latine ed Italiane,* 3 vols. (Ravenna, 1728-34).

■ **Bibliography:** *DBI* 8:384-93; *VATL* 73-74; B. Neveu, *L'oracle Romain au risque de l'interprétation. Benoît XIII et l'ordre dogmatique: Papes et papauté au XVIIIᵉ siècle* (Paris, 1999) 121-44.

GEORG SCHWAIGER

Benedict XIV (July 7, 1740-May 3, 1758). Formerly *Prospero Lambertini*, born March 31, 1675, in Bologna. He combined talent, legal training, and an amiable nature with a flair for political reality and the requirements of the time. He entered curial service in 1701; by 1727 he was archbishop of Ancona, created cardinal in 1728, and made archbishop of Bologna in 1731. A competent, beloved pastor, as well as an author of important works, primarily about canon law, he was the surprise choice after a six-month conclave. As pope he was intent on reforms appropriate for the times and on reaching settlements with the European powers (agreement with Naples in 1741, Spain in 1753, Austria for Milan in 1757; recognition of the Prussian royal dignity). His decision in the bull *Ex quo singulari* (1742) requiring all Chinese missionaries to take a solemn oath against the rites proved to be a mistake. Along with administrative reforms in the → papal states and the promotion of the arts and sciences, he busied himself in the domain of canon law, reforms in the liturgy, penitential practice, marital law, orders, curial authorities, as well as the → Index of Forbidden Books. The encyclical *Annus qui* (1749) saw to the further development of church music. His works on beatifications and canonizations (*De servorum Dei beatificatione et beatorum canonisatione*, 4 vols. [Bologna, 1734-38]) and on the diocesan synod (*De synodo dioecesana* [Rome, 1755]) became fundamental texts in legal theory and practice. Benedict was the most important pope of his century and one of the most learned of all the popes.

■ **Bibliography:** *DBI* 8:393-408; *TRE* 5:531ff.; R. Reinhardt, "Zur Reichskirchenpolitik Papst Benedikts XIV.," *RQ* 60 (1965) 259-68; T. Bertone, *Il governo della Chiesa nel pensiero di Benedetto XIV* (Rome, 1977); A. Casieri, *La Perfezione cristiana in Benedetto XIV* (Rome, 1979); J. Hermans, *Benedictus XIV en de liturgie* (Bruges, 1979); M. Cecchelli, ed., *Benedetto XIV (Prospero Lambertini): Convegno internazionale di studi storici*, 2 vols. (Cento, 1982); F. Boes-Pflug, *Dieu dans l'art* (Paris, 1984); J. Gelmi, "Die Minutanten im Staatssekretariat Benedikts XIV.," *Papsttum und Kirchenreform: Festschrift für G. Schwaiger* (Sankt Ottilien, 1990) 537-61; N. Schöch, *Die Frage der Reduktion der Feiertage bei Benedikt XIV.: Eine rechtshistorische Untersuchung* (Rome, 1994); D. Biagi Maino, *Benedetto XIV e le arti del disegno: Convegno internazionale, Bologna, 1994* (Rome, 1998); E. Garms-Cornides, *Storia, politica e apologia in Benedetto XIV: Papes et papauté au XVIIIᵉ siècle* (Paris, 1999) 145-61; D. Ligou, *La réception en France des bulles pontificales condemnant la franc-maçonnerie* (Paris, 1999) 205-17.

GEORG SCHWAIGER

Benedict XV (Sept. 3, 1914-Jan. 22, 1922). Formerly *Giacomo della Chiesa*, born November 21, 1854, in Genoa of old Genoese nobility. He became a close collaborator of the nuncio to Madrid and Cardinal Secretary of State Mariano Rampolla. Because of this collaboration he was more or less put on the shelf by Pius X. In 1907 he became archbishop of Bologna, but not until 1914 was he created a cardinal. After the serious diplomatic mistakes and internal church disturbances under Pius X (integralism, modernism, reform Catholicism), Benedict's pontificate introduced a period of necessary consolidation of the church in the older and newly established nation states; but it was entirely overshadowed by World War I and its consequences. In the war Benedict's efforts aimed at political neutrality, a just peace, and alleviating affliction (relief organizations for prisoners, exiles, and the destitute). In 1914 England and the Netherlands set up diplomatic missions with the Holy See, although Italy (on account of the unresolved Roman Question) and France (since the separation of church and state in 1905) maintained no official contacts with the Vatican. The independence of the Vatican was respected by Italy, and Benedict opened a sort of branch office in Lugano for communicating with the Central Powers. The pope's early efforts for peace can be understood only in the framework of the complicated, often parallel and intersecting attempts at mediation by both governments and individuals. These efforts peaked, outwardly, in the peace note of August 1, 1917, but remained fruitless. Benedict was excluded from the peace negotiations, as the Allies had promised Italy in April 1915 that he would be. Benedict viewed the Treaty of Versailles as a vengeful dictate. He demanded justice even for the defeated and strove for reconciliation and internal peace within Europe, which included the necessary consolidation of the church in the older and newly established nation states. With the support of Cardinal Secretary of State Pietro Gasparri, the resolution of the Roman Question and the reorganization of church–state relations were prepared by concordats. Along with the lessening of tension after the modernism crisis, the most important events within the church were the edition of the *Codex Iuris Canonici* (prepared by Pius X, promulgated in 1917, and in force from 1918) and the encyclical on the missions *Maximum illud* of November 30, 1919, with its future-oriented program for Catholic world missions.

■ **Bibliography:** *DBI* 8:408-17; *TRE* 5:533ff.; Schmidlin, 3:179-339; F. Hayward, *Un pape méconnu, Benoît XV* (Paris, 1955); W. H. Peters, *The Life of Benedict XV* (Milwaukee, 1955); E. Kovács, "Papst Benedikt XV. und die Restaurationsbemühungen des Kaisers und Königs Karl von Österreich," *AHP* 27 (1989) 357-99; N. Thevenin, "La Note de Benoît XV du 1ᵉʳ août 1917 et les réactions des catholiques français," *Revue d'histoire diplomatique* 103 (1989) 285-338; V. Cárcel Ortí, "Benedicto XV y el catolicismo social español," *Analecta Sacra Tarraconensia* 63/64 (1990) 7-152; G. Rumi, ed., *Benedetto XV e la pace — 1916* (Brescia, 1990); idem, *Benedetto XV: Un espistolario inedito* (Rome, 1991); V. Cárcel Ortí, "Benedicto XV y los obispos españoles," *AHP* 29 (1991) 197-254; 30 (1992) 291-338; D. Stevenson, "The Failure of Peace by Negotiation in 1917," *Historical Journal* 34

(1991) 65-88; P. Christophe, "Les 'silences' de Benoît XV durant la grande guerre," *Mélanges de science religieuse* 52 (1995) 25-64; R. Morozzo della Rocca, "Benedetto XV e il nazionalismo," *Cristianesimo nella storia* 17 (1996) 541-66; F. M. Requena, "Benedicto XV, un papa entre dos mundos," *Anuario de historia de la iglesia* 6 (1997) 61-76; J. F. Pollard, *The Unknown Pope: Benedict XV and the Pursuit of Peace* (London, 1999); J. Lenzenwege, "Papstwahlen 1914 und 1922," *In factis mysterium legere: Festschrift für I. Rogger* (Bologna, 1990) 187-94; A. A. Giovagnoli, *Roma e Pechino: La svolta extraeuropea di Benedetto XV* (Rome, 1999).

GEORG SCHWAIGER

Boniface I (Dec. 29, 418-Sept. 4, 422). Saint (feast day Oct. 25). After the death of Zosimus, the majority of the Roman presbyters elected him on December 28, 418, in opposition to Eulalius, who had been elected by the deacons on December 27. The resulting schism was ended in 419 by the emperor Honorius: Eulalius was exiled, and Boniface was recognized as the legitimate pope. He strove to still the theological controversies that had arisen under Zosimus and to restore peace within the church as well as to strengthen papal claims to primacy. In the controversy over the right to appeal synodal decisions to the African church, the Carthaginian synod of May 25, 419, instructed Boniface, who had exercised restraint in this matter, about its decisions and forbade any interference from Rome. For his part, Boniface restored the older metropolitan order in Gaul, which under Zosimus had been changed to favor Arles. With the help of Honorius he opposed the attempt to remove Illyricum from papal jurisdiction.
■ **Sources:** *LP* 1:227ff.; *RPR*(J) 1:51-54; *CPL* 1576-91, 1648-49.
■ **Bibliography:** *Augustinus-Lexikon,* ed. C. Mayer, vol. 1 (Basel, etc., 1986) 655-58 (M. Wojtowytsch); *VATL* 81; Caspar 1:360-68, 373-83; W. Marschall, *Karthago und Rom* (Stuttgart, 1971) 161-203; O. Wermelinger, *Rom und Pelagius* (Stuttgart, 1975) 238-44; M. Wojtowytsch, *Papsttum und Konzile von den Anfängen bis zu Leo I. (440-461)* (Stuttgart, 1981) 254-57, 267-83, 300ff.; P. J. Carefoote, "Pope Boniface I, the Pelagian Controversy and the Growth of Papal Authority," *Augustiniana* 46 (1996) 261-89.

PETER DÜCKERS

Boniface II (Sept. 22, 530-Oct. 17, 532). A Romanized Goth, earlier a Roman archdeacon. The dying Felix III designated Boniface as his successor. The majority of the clerics, however, elected the deacon Dioscurus pope, but the latter's death, on October 14, 530, quickly ended the schism. Boniface forced his opponents to reconcile with him; but he failed in his attempt to stipulate the deacon Vigilius as his successor. Boniface confirmed the decisions of the Second Synod of Orange in 529 and tried to solidify the Roman claim to jurisdiction over Illyricum.
■ **Sources:** *LP* 1:281-84; *RPR*(J) 1:111-12; 2:694, 737.
■ **Bibliography:** *DBI* 12:133-36; *VATL* 82; Caspar 2:193-98, 206-9.

PETER DÜCKERS

Boniface III (Feb. 19-Nov. 12, 607). A Roman, under Gregory I he had been a *defensor* (executive agent), deacon, and papal secretary in Constantinople. He got Emperor Phocas to issue a decree confirming the Roman church as the head of all the churches. He made new regulations for the → election of the pope and bishops: the stipulation of one's successors during one's lifetime was prohibited; the clergy and the sons of the church were to hold a free election, but not until three days after the funeral.
■ **Sources:** *LP* 1:316; *MGH.Ep* 1:39 n. 3 and 287 n. 2.
■ **Bibliography:** *DBI* 12:136-37; Richards, 257-63.

SEBASTIAN SCHOLZ

Boniface IV (Sept. 15, 608-May 8, 615). Saint (feast day May 25), born in the modern province of L'Aquila. Under Gregory I he was a deacon and treasurer. Emperor Phocas entrusted him with the Pantheon in Rome, which he transformed into a church (Santa Maria ad Martyres); he held a synod in 610 to deal with questions of monastic life and the English church. He was called upon by Columban to revoke the condemnation of the Three Chapters by his predecessors.
■ **Sources:** *LP* 1:317; Bede the Venerable, *Historia Ecclesiastica* 2:4; *MGH.Ep* 3:170-77.
■ **Bibliography:** Caspar 2:517-22; Richards, 256-64; F. Michetti, *San Bonifacio e il suo pontificato* (Rome, 1969; Avezzano, 1992).

SEBASTIAN SCHOLZ

Boniface V (Dec. 23, 619-Oct. 25, 625). A Neapolitan, he promoted the English church and strengthened the position of the clergy in Rome. He forbade acolytes to preside over the transferring of relics or baptisms.
■ **Sources:** *LP* 1:321-22; Bede the Venerable, *Historia Ecclesiastica* 2:7, 10-11.
■ **Bibliography:** *DBI* 12:1; Richards, 263-64.

SEBASTIAN SCHOLZ

Boniface VI (Apr. 896). A Roman, deposed as a subdeacon and presbyter, not restored after the second deposition. His election was carried out by the enemies of Formosus in the course of a popular uprising. He died after only a fifteen-day pontificate.

■ Sources: *LP* 2:228; Mansi 18A:224.

■ Bibliography: *DHGE* 9:899-900; *DBI* 12:142-43.

SEBASTIAN SCHOLZ

Boniface VII (end of June 974-end of July 985). The Roman deacon *Franco Ferrucci*, who was raised to the papacy in a revolt of the Crescenti party, in place of the imprisoned Benedict VI, was soon banished from Rome by a representative of the emperor in the summer of 974. He was then declared to be deposed by a synod of Benedict VII. After returning in the summer of 980, he fled in March 981 from Otto II, taking the church treasury with him. With Byzantine help at the end of April 984, he drove out John XIV, who was then murdered in prison, not long before Boniface himself was toppled and murdered. Some of his contemporaries derisively called him "Maliface."

■ Sources: Zimmermann *Reg.*

■ Bibliography: *DBI* 12:143-46; *LMA* 2:414; Zimmermann *J.*

HARALD ZIMMERMANN

Boniface VIII (Dec. 24, 1294-Oct. 11, 1303). Formerly *Benedetto Caetani*, born ca. 1235 in Anagni into a noble family from the Campagna, he laid the foundation for its rise. He was trained in Roman law in Todi and Spoleto, and he continued his legal studies in Bologna. He was made a papal chaplain in 1264, a papal notary in 1276, cardinal deacon of San Nicola in Carcere Tulliano in 1281. In 1291 he became a cardinal priest of San Martino ai Monti, after proving himself on a legation to France (1290-1291). He mediated the peace of Tarascon in the Sicilian question (1291) and was active in Paris in the dispute over the mendicant orders (1290). As someone who had originally voted for Celestine V (who resigned on December 13, 1294), and belonging to neither the Orsini nor the Colonna faction, he was unanimously elected pope in Naples. His coronation took place on January 23, 1295. He immediately revoked all the measures taken by his predecessor, except for appointments to the cardinalate. When Celestine died shortly afterward on May 19, 1295, Boniface was blamed for it. Opposition to him spread quickly and became more intense when the church-political conflicts over Sicily (recognition of Frederick II in 1303, to the disadvantage of Anjou) with the Colonna, who questioned his legitimacy (excommunication of the Colonna cardinals in 1297 and their flight to France) as well as with King Philip the Fair of France, eased. The struggle with the French king, to whom Boniface was originally well disposed, took on central importance. With the bull *Clericis laicos* (1296) he forbade any taxing of the clergy without the approval of the curia; but Philip IV forced him to yield on this (cf. the bulls *Ineffabilis* [1296] and *Etsi de statu* [1297], which allowed the taxation of state property in times of governmental emergency). Tensions were temporarily defused with the canonization of Louis IX in 1297, but they broke out all the more violently when the success of the first → Holy Year (1300) seemed to strengthen papal monarchical claims (alteration of the tiara, statues erected in honor of the pope). The king's display of contempt for the church's jurisdiction in the case of Bishop Bernard Saisset of Pamiers offered the immediate occasion to cancel the royal privileges through the bull *Salvator mundi* (1301); the pope summonded the king before a Roman synod (*Ausculta, fili*, 1301) and Philip retaliated with a propaganda campaign against him voicing the suspicion of his heresy; the king appealed to a council through a French gathering of Estates General, and Boniface responded by threatening to have the king deposed. Boniface provided a theoretical foundation for his hierocratic position with the bull *Unam sanctam* (November 18, 1302, although not published until the summer of 1303). In it he reiterated his view that a worldly ruler is responsible to the pope "ratione peccati," without developing this idea in ways that went beyond the prevailing views of the canonists. He argued that the "plenitudo potestatis" meant the subordination of secular to spiritual power, that the "spiritualis potestas" could set up ("instituere") secular power and could judge it when it sinned. When Boniface moved in support of the German kingdom, and at the (controversial) solemn confirmation of the election of Albrecht I clarified his new viewpoint that the French king was subject to the empire "in temporalibus," and additionally ratified an oath of the ambassadors (*Patris eterni filius*, 1304), hinting at his intention of excommunicating the king and the disobedient bishops, Philip IV reacted sharply. He again accused the pope of heresy and appealed to a general council, to which his advisor Guillaume de Nogaret was to summon the pope. The more intensely worded papal constitutions, the plan to excommunicate the French king while dissolving all oaths of loyalty to him (*Super Petri solio* of September 8, 1303), and the pope's contacts with the radical nobleman Sciarra Colonna moved the ambassador to arrest Boniface on September 1 ("the crime at Anagni") to prevent the publication of the bull. Although he was freed on September 8, Boniface died shortly after his return to Rome. He had been defeated by his exaggeratedly hieratic attitude and his notion of the papal "plenitudo potestatis" in the struggle between church and state. Nevertheless, his measures to reform the relationship between the mendicants and the secular clergy (*Super cathedram*, 1300), the benefice system, the training of parish clergy (*Cum ex eo*), and the administration of the → papal states, as well as his efforts to promote a crusade, found widespread approval. His expansion of Gregory IX's collection of decretals in his *Liber sextus* was destined to become an important addition to canon law.

■ **Bibliography:** *DBI* 12:146-70; *TRE* 7:66ff.; *LMA* 2:414ff.; G. Digard et al., *Les registres de Boniface VIII*, 4 vols. (Paris, 1884-1939); J. Muldoon, "Boniface VIII's Forty Years of Experience in the Law," *Jurist* 11 (1971) 449-77; G.G. Nüske, "Untersuchungen über das Personal der päpstlichen Kanzlei 1254-1305," *Archiv für Diplomatik, Schriftgeschichte und Wappenkunde* 20 (1974) 39-240; 21 (1975) 249-431; R.-H. Bautier, "Le jubilé romain de 1300 et l'alliance franco-pontificale au temps de Philippe le Bel et de Boniface VIII: Le Moyen-âge," *Revue d'histoire et de philologie* 86 (1980) 189-216; T. Schmidt, *Libri rationum camerae Bonifatii pape VIII* (Vatican City, 1984); G. de Andrés, "'Speculum Pontificale' de Juan Ignotus: Poema sobre la vida del papa Bonifacio VIII," *Revista española de teología* 45 (1985) 155-99 (and *Hispania Sacra. Revista de historia ecclesiástica* 44 [1992] 745-87); T. Schmidt, "Papst Bonifatius VIII. und die Idolatrie," *QFIAB* 66 (1986) 75-107; idem, "Ein Studenthaus in Bologna zwischen Bonifatius VIII. und den Colonna," *QFIAB* 66 (1986) 108-41; T. M. Izbicki, "The Problem of Canonical Portion in the Later Middle Ages: The Application of 'Super Cathedram,'" in *Proceedings of the Seventh International Congress of Medieval Canon Law*, ed. P. Linehan (Vatican City, 1988) 459-73; T. Schmidt, *Der Bonifatius-Prozeß* (Cologne/Vienna, 1989); P. Herde, "Ein Plan, Benedict Caetani zum Kardinalbischof zu erheben (1291)," in *Ius*

et historia, Festschrift for R. Weigand (Würzburg, 1989) 181ff.; T. M. Izbicki, "*Clericis Laicos*" and the Canonists: Popes, Teachers, and Canon Law in the Middle Ages (Ithaca/London, 1989) 179-90; A. Sommerlechner, "Die Darstellung des Attentats von Anagni," *Römische historische Mitteilungen* 32/33 (1990/91) 51-102; B. Arnold, "Die Erwerbung des Kastells Sismano durch Kardinal Benedikt Caetani (Bonifatius VIII.) im Jahre 1289," *QFIAB* 71 (1991) 169-94; T. Schmidt, "Papst Bonifatius VIII, als Gesetzgeber," in *Proceedings of the Eighth International Congress of Medieval Canon Law*, ed. S. Chodorow (Vatican City, 1992) 227-45; P. Herde, "Die Wahl Bonifaz' VIII. (24.12.1294)," *Cristianità ed Europa*. Festschrift for L. Prosdocimi, vol. 1, 1 (Rome, 1994) 132-53; *Boniface VIII en procès: Articles d'accusation et dépositions des témoins (1303-11)*, ed. J. Coste (Rome, 1995); R. Bartolomei Ramagnoli, "Le bolle di Celestino V cassate da Bonifacio VIII," *AHP* 37 (1999) 61-83; L. Hödl, "Der Jubiläumsablaß Papst Bonifaz' VIII.1300—der Ernstfall der Buße," *Wissenschaft und Weisheit* 62 (199) 292-308; C. Frugoni, *Due papi per un giubileo: Celestino V, Bonifacio VIII e il primo Anno santo* (Milan, 2000); *Bonifacio VIII e il suo tempo*, ed. M. Righetti Tosti-Croce (Milan, 2000).

LUDWIG VONES

Boniface IX (Nov. 2, 1389-Oct. 1, 1404). Formerly *Pietro Tomacelli*, born ca. 1350 from Neapolitan nobility, created a cardinal in 1381. During his pontificate, which was shaped by the Western Schism, he was more fortunate than his predecessor Urban VI. He asserted the authority of Rome against the pope of Avignon; he shored up the threatened → papal states and put down rebellious Rome once and for all. But the means he unscrupulously made use of proved to be fatal. The courting of Christendom away from his rival, the antipope, led to unworthy concessions. The financial losses (halved income on account of the schism, increasing dependence on Florentine banks [rise of the Medici] were all too inventively compensated for by the sale of indulgences and offices, preferential clauses, etc. The compact clan of noble Neapolitan families, which knew how to make itself indispensable amid such straits, was promoted by unheard-of nepotism and for its part blocked every compromise on the question of unifying the papacy. Boniface never took seriously any of the *viae unionis*. All this made contemporaries view the superficially successful pontificate of this unspiritual pope as a symbol of the church's need for reform.

16

■ **Bibliography:** *DBI* 12:170-87; *LMA* 2:416-17; M. Jansen, *Papst Bonifatius IX. und seine Beziehungen zur deutschen Kirche* (Frankfurt [Main], 1904); J. Favier, *Les finances pontificales à l'époque du grand schisme d'Occident* (Paris, 1966); A. Esch, *Bonifatius IX. und der Kirchenstaat* (Tübingen, 1969).

ARNOLD ESCH

Callistus (Calixtus) **I** (Kallistos) (217?-222). Saint (feast day Oct. 14). Our main source of information about Callistus is his opponent Hippolytus (*Refutatio omnium haeresium* 9.11-12; 10.27). Callistus was born a slave. His banking business failed, which led to a conflict with a synagogue. In the trial that followed under Fuscianus, Callistus was exiled to work in the mines in Sardinia. After he was pardoned by the emperor Commodus, Victor I offered him a monthly pension and sent him to Antium (Anzio) for about ten years. Under Zephyrinus, Callistus was probably the deacon in charge of the community cemetery on the Via Appia ("San Calisto"). As bishop he recognized previously nonbinding unions between women from the senatorial clases and lower-class men as ecclesially valid marriages. He allowed men who had been married more than once to serve in church offices; he allowed consecrated persons to marry and let leniency prevail in receiving heretics back into the church (no connection with the "*Edictum peremptorium*" [Tertullian, *De pudicitia* 1.6]). It is hard to know what to make of the report that he introduced a second baptism. Although he excommunicated Sabellius, Hippolytus accuses him of Patripassianism. According to *Liber Pontificalis* 17, Callistus introduced three Saturdays as days of fasting. He may have died as a martyr (*Depositio martyrum* of 354 locates his grave in Trastevere), but the Passio (*Bibliotheca hagiographica latina antiquae et mediae aetatis* 1523ff.) is legendary; two letters in the decretals of Pseudo-Isidor are inauthentic.

■ **Bibliography:** *VATL* 98-99; *RGG*, 4th ed., 2:13-14; O. Bardenhewer, *Geschichte der altkirchlichen Literatur*, vol. 2 (2nd ed. Freiburg, 1914) 636ff. (letters: Caspar 1:22-28, 37-40); J. Schümmer, *Die altchristliche Fastenpraxis* (Münster, 1933) 153-58; B. Poschmann, *Paenitentia secunda* (Bonn, 1940) 348-67; J. Gaudemet, "La décision de Calixte en matière de mariage," Festschrift for U. E. Paoli (Florence, 1955) 333-44; H. Gülzow, *Christentum und Sklaverei* (Bonn, 1969) 144-72; I. Goldhahn-Müller, *Die Grenze der Gemeinde* (Göttingen, 1989) 369-70; R. E. Heine, "The Christology of Callistus," *Journal of Theological Studies* 49 (1998) 56-91; H. J. Vogt, "Die Trinitätslehre des Papstes Kalixt I.," *Theologische Quartalschrift* 179 (1999) 195-209.

CLEMENS SCHOLTEN

Callistus (Calixtus) **II** (Feb. 2, 1119-Dec. 14, 1124). Formerly *Guido*, son of Count William of Burgundy, made archbishop of Vienne in 1088. He sought to win a primacy for this see vis-à-vis Arles and promoted this view as pope. He served as a papal legate, and in 1112 he led the Synod of Vienne, which protested against the privilege of investiture that Henry V had extorted. He was elected by the cardinals who were present at the death of Gelasius II in Cluny and was crowned on February 9, 1119, in Vienne. Callistus carried on negotiations over investiture in Mouzon with the Salian, but they came to naught over the question of temporalities and led to a renewed sentence of excommunication from the Synod of Rheims (October 1119). He was in Rome in 1120 (enthronement on June 3), defeated the antipope Gregory VIII in 1121, and solidified his feudal sovereignty over the Normans. New negotiations with Henry V led, on September 23, 1122, to the Concordat of Worms. The First Lateran Council "tolerated" the peace agreement and issued important reform decrees. His grave is in the Lateran in Rome.

■ **Sources:** U. Robert, *Bullaire du pape Calixte II*, 2 vols. (Paris, 1891); *LP* 2:322-28; *RPR(J)* 1:780-821.
■ **Bibliography:** *DHGE* 11:424-38; *DBI* 16:761-68; *LMA* 2:1397-98; *VATL* 99-100; U. Robert, *Histoire du pape Calixte II* (Paris, 1891); T. Schieffer, "Nochmals die Verhandlungen von Mouzon," Festschrift for E. E. Stengel (Münster/Cologne, 1952) 324-41; S. A. Chodorow, "Ecclesiastical Policies and the Ending of the Investiture Contest: The Papal Election of 1119 and the Negotiations of Mouzon," *Speculum, Journal of Medieval Studies* 46 (1971) 613-40; M. Minninger, *Von Clermont zum Wormser Konkordat* (Cologne/Vienna, 1978) 176-209; R. Somerville, "The Councils of Pope Calixtus II: Reims 1119," in *Proceedings of the Fifth International Congress of Medieval Canon Law* (Vatican City, 1980) 35-50; M. Stroll, "New Perspectives on the Struggle between Guy of Vienne and Henry V," *AHP* 18 (1980) 97-116; idem, "Calixtus II: A Reinterpretation of His Election and the End of the Investiture Contest," *Studies in Medieval and Renaissance History* 3 (Lubbock, 1980) 1-53; B. Schilling, *Guido von Vienne—Papst Calixt II* (Hannover, 1998).

JOHANNES LAUDAGE

Callistus (Calixtus) **III** (Apr. 8, 1455-Aug. 6, 1458). Formerly *Alonso de Borja*, born on December 31, 1378, at Canals near Játiva (Valencia); studied and taught both civil and canon law at the University of Lleida. In the service of Alfonso V of Aragón-Naples he convinced the antipope Clement VIII to abdicate in 1429 (end of the Great Schism). In gratitude the king gave him the bishopric of Valencia. Because he separated the king from the party of the rump council in Basel, Eugene IV named him a cardinal (1444). In the curia, he was valued for his knowledge of the law, his diplomatic experience, and his simple way of life. After becoming pope, Callistus viewed the struggle against the Turks as his main task, less so the promotion of the Reconquista in Spain. But his enthusiasm met with indifference and rejection among the princes. The rising national states would no longer be persuaded to join in a common action. The pope's resources and armaments alone were too weak. Hence his individual successes against the Turks, such as the relief of Belgrade in 1456 (Johannes Hunyadi) and the victories of 1457 (by Skanderbeg of Albania in Tomorniza, the victory of the papal-Aragonese fleet at Metelino under Cardinal Ludovico Scarampo) could not be exploited. When Callistus could not win over either the empire or the Western European kingdoms for economic or military support, he turned to Skanderbeg and King Alfonso of Aragón-Naples. In the promotion of art and the sciences Callistus lagged far behind his predecessor, Nicholas V, for which he incurred the wrath of humanists. His image is greatly tarnished by → nepotism in grand style, which brought the Borgias to Italy, including his nephew Rodrigo de Borja (Alexander VI). After his death the pent-up hatred exploded in riots against the Borgias and the "Catalans," who enjoyed outrageous preferment in the → papal states. The anticurial tendency swelled in Germany. It found expression in, among other things, the "Complaints of the German Nation" at the Frankfurt Assembly of Princes in 1456.

■ **Bibliography:** *DHGE* 11:438-44; *DBI* 16:769-74; *LMA* 2:1398-99; *HCMA* 2:11-12; F. Martorelli, "Biblioteca di Callisto," *Studi e Testi* 41 (1924) 166-91; J. Rius i Serra, "Catalones y Aragoneses en la Corte de Calixto III," *Analecta Sacra Tarraconensia* 3 (1927) 193-330; P. Paschini, "La flotta di Callisto," *Archivio della Società Romana di Storia Patria* 53-55 (1930-33) 177-254; A. Serra, "Relazioni del Castriota con il Papato nella lotta contro i Turchi," *Analecta Sacra Tarraconensia* 114 (1956) 713-33; J. Rius i Serra, *Regesto ibérico de Calixto*

III, 2 vols. (Barcelona, 1948-58); P. Brezzi, "La politica di Calisto III," *Studi Romani* 7 (1959) 31-51; M. E. Mallett, *The Borgias* (London, 1969); E. Pitz, *Supplikensignatur und Briefexpedition an der römischen Kurie im Pontifikat Papst Calixtus' III.* (Tübingen, 1972); S. Schüller-Piroli, *Die Borgia-Päpste Kalixt III. und Alexander VI.* (Munich, 1980); P. Herde, "Johann III. von Grumbach, 'Bischof von Würzburg (1455-66), und Papst Kalixt II.,'" in *Abhandlungen zur fränkischen und bayerischen Kirchengeschichte zu den christlich-jüdischen Beziehungen,* ed. P. Herde (Würzburg, 1996) 169-92.

GEORG SCHWAIGER

Callistus (Calixtus) **III** (antipope) (shortly after Sept. 20, 1168-Aug. 28, 1178; died 1180 or later). Formerly Abbot *John of Struma* (near Arezzo). Elevated to cardinal bishop of Albano by Victor IV and after the death of Paschal III elected the third antipope in opposition to Alexander III. He received recognition from Frederick I Barbarossa until the Peace of Venice (1177); thereafter he lost almost all his authority. He fled from → Viterbo to the fortress of Monte Albano and abdicated in Tusculum in 1178. Alexander III named him rector of Beneventum, where there are records of his presence until 1180.

■ **Sources:** *RPR*(J) 2:429-30.

■ **Bibliography:** *DBI* 16:768-69; *LMA* 2:1398; J. Laudage, *Alexander III. und Friedrich Barbarossa* (Cologne, 1990).

JOHANNES LAUDAGE

Celestine I (Sept. 10, 422-July 27, 432). A saint (feast day April 6), he reinforced the rejection of Pelagianism, opposed Nestorius (by briefs, by means of a Roman Synod of 430, and by sending legates in 431 opposing him to the Council of Ephesus), strove for church unity after the council, coordinated the missions in Ireland and Britain, supported the rights of local churches in the election of bishops (Ep. 4), but met with resistance from the African church against appeals to Rome.

■ **Sources:** Letters; *PL* 50:417-558; *ACO* I/1, 7, 125-37; I/2, 5-101.

■ **Bibliography:** *DACL* 2:2794-2802; *DHGE* 12:56ff.; *BiblSS* 3:1096-1100; *VATL* 143; O. Wermelinger, *Rom und Pelagius* (Stuttgart, 1975) 244-53; J. Speigl, "Die Päpste in der Reichskirche," *GKG* 11:53-54.

JAKOB SPEIGL

Celestine (II) → Honorius I.

Celestine II (Sept. 26, 1143-Mar. 8, 1144). Formerly *Guido de Castello*, a canon at the regulated cathedral chapter in Città di Castello, to which he bequeathed his private library of fifty-six books. In 1127 at the earliest he became cardinal deacon of Santa Maria in Via Lata; in 1133 he was made a cardinal priest of San Marco. From 1130/31 he belonged to the innermost circle around Innocent II and was repeatedly active as a legate. Frequently called Magister, he was considered learned and pious. Gerhoh of Reichersberg dedicated to him the *Libellus de ordine donorum Sancti Spiritus* and the canon Benedict of St. Peter dedicated his *Liber politicus* to him. His studies with Peter Abelard, whom he had met in Morigny in 1131, and two of whose works he owned, is not securely documented. His brief pontificate occurred in the time of the uprising of the Roman communes, which were striving for autonomy. He lifted the interdict he imposed on Louis VII of France in 1142. Celestine delayed the re-enfeoffment of Roger II with Sicily in accordance with the Treaty of Mignano (1129), but shortly before his death he was forced to enter into negotiations with the king. He died in Rome; his tomb is in the Lateran basilica.

■ **Bibliography:** *DHGE* 12:59-62; *DBI* 23:388-92; *LMA* 3:4; W. Bernhardi, *Konrad III.* (Berlin, 1883); L. Mirot, ed., *La chronique de Morigny* (2nd ed. Paris, 1912); A. Wilmart, "Les livres légués par Célestin II à Città-di-Castell," *Revue bénédictine* 35 (1923) 98-102; W. Maleczek, "Das Kardinalskollegium unter Innozenz II. und Anaklet II.," *AHP* 19 (1981) 58-59.

                                            WOLFGANG PETKE

Celestine III (Apr. 10, 1191-Jan. 8, 1198). Formerly *Giacinto* or *Hyacinthus Borbone*, born ca. 1105/6 into a family of Roman nobility, in 1138 he probably became prior subdeacon. He studied with Peter Abelard in Paris, where he would have also been close to Arnold of Brescia. In 1143-1144 he was cardinal deacon of Santa Maria in Cosmedin. As such he was an outstanding diplomat entrusted with politically important missions. He is said to have accepted his election as pope in his old age only in order to prevent a schism. He worked for the reform of the curial administration (→ *Liber censuum*) and of the College of → Cardinals.

An opponent of the Hohenstaufen policy toward Sicily, Celestine signed the Concordat of Gravina (June 1192) with Tancred of Lecce, whom he enfeoffed with Sicily. After achieving the *Unio regni ad imperium* with the seizure of Palermo by Henry VI in November 1194, the emperor believed he could come to an understanding with the pope by planning a crusade, but Celestine rejected the plan of a hereditary kingdom connected to it and an offer, apparently made to him in the course of dramatic negotiations, to grant the emperor investiture with regard to the empire. Celestine's defensive posture toward Hohenstaufen expansionary efforts formed an essential prerequisite for the later achievements of his successor, Innocent II.

■ **Bibliography:** *DBI* 23:392-98; *LMA* 3:4-7; V. Pfaff, "Papst Coelestin III.," *Zeitschrift der Savigny-Stiftung für Reichsgeschichte, Kanonische Abteilung* 47 (1961) 109-28; G. Baaken, "Die Verhandlungen zwischen Kaiser Heinrich VI. und Papst Coelestin III. in den Jahren 1195-97," *Deutsches Archiv für Erforschung des Mittelalters* 27 (1971) 457-513; V. Pfaff, "Die innere Verwaltung der Kirche unter Papst Coelstin III.," *Archiv für Diplomatik* 18 (1972) 342-98; P. Zerbi, *Papato, Impero e "Respublica Christiana" dal 1187 al 1198* (2nd ed. Milan, 1980); W. Maleczek, *Papst und Kardinalskolleg von 1191-1216* (Vienna, 1984) esp. pp. 68ff.; K. Zeillinger, *Konstantinische Schenkung, Kaisertum und Papsttum in salisch-staufischer Zeit (1053-1265)* (Vienna, 1984) MSS. 78-102 and 173-86; K. Baaken, "Zu Wahl, Weihe and Krönung Coelestins III.," *Deutsches Archiv für Erforschung des Mittelalters* 41 (1985) 203-11; C. Reisinger, *Tankred von Lecce* (Cologne, 1992) 146ff., 246ff.

                                            KURT ZEILINGER

Celestine IV (Oct. 25-Nov. 10, 1241). Formerly *Goffredo Castiglione*; born into the Milanese Castiglione family, he was not related to Urban III. From 1223 to 1226 he was chancellor in the archdiocese of Milan; in 1227 he became cardinal priest of San Marco. From the spring of 1228 till the fall of 1229 he was a legate in Tuscany and Lombardy; in the spring of 1228 he was made cardinal bishop of Sabina. Celestine emerged as pope from the conclave of terror in the Septizonium of Rome (→ Election, Papal) and presumably died before being crowned.

■ **Bibliography:** *DBI* 23:398-402; *LMA* 3:7; K. Wenck, "Das 1. Konklave der Papstgeschichte. Rom, August-Oktober 1241," *QFIAB* 18 (1926) 101-70; A. Paravicini Bagliani, *Cardinali di Curia e familiae cardinalizie dal 1227 al 1254,* vol. 2 (Padua, 1972) 407-16.

                                            ANDREAS KIESEWETTER

Celestine V (July 5-Dec. 13, 1294 [abdicated]). Saint (a Benedictine) before 1230, formerly *Pietro de Morrone*, born 1209/10 in Molise (most likely in Sant' Angelo Limosano) as the son of a peasant. Died May 19, 1296 in Castello di Fumone (Frosinone). He entered Santa Maria di Failfula as a hermit ca. 1231, and from around 1235-1240 he lived in the Morone mountains near Sulmona, where he organized a society of hermits, which Gregory X later integrated into the Benedictine order in 1275. From around 1240-1245, he organized a congregation at Santo Spirito in Maiella on the model of the Cistercians. Without any formal education, he proved to be a good director and brought in many donations. His brotherhood spread from the Abruzzi to Rome and Apulia. Pietro soon acquired the reputation of sanctity and was well known at the curia and in the Angevin royal court in Naples. After a long → *sede vacante*, he came under consideration for the papacy through the influence of Charles II of Anjou and was elected pope "*per inspirationem*" in Perugia. He was consecrated and crowned on August 29 in Aquila. He fell under the influence of Charles II, whom he followed to Naples in October. Celestine was not up to the demands of his office. Evidently under the impression of Joachimite speculations, on September 18 he appointed twelve new cardinals, many of whom were monks, as if he were seeking to inaugurate the monastic age of the Holy Spirit. Chaos and corruption prevailed in the curia. Shortly after his arrival in Naples Celestine was overcome by torments of conscience and considered abdicating, which was possible under canon law. Correctly advised by various cardinals (including Benedict Caetani), he carried out the abdication on December 13, 1294, in the presence of the College of → Cardinals, which, given the exceptional conditions, elected Benedict Caetani (Boniface VIII) the new pope on December 24. Boniface wanted to keep Pietro-Celestine under supervision because of the controversial abdication, but the ex-pope fled in January 1296 while traveling from Naples to Rome, at first going to his cell in Sant' Onofrio at Sulmona, later to Apulia. He wanted to flee like the Umbrian Franciscan Spirituals, to whom he had granted the status of an independent association, to Greece. But he was captured and in June 1295 brought to the pope at → Anagni, where he was kept in the Castle of Fumone under house arrest. At the instigation of his confreres, a number of the Spirituals and the Franciscan opponents of Boniface VIII, he was canonized in → Avignon by Clement V on May 5, 1313 (his name has recently been stricken from the liturgical calendar). The simple hermit, whose character could at times be quite harsh, soon became viewed as an angelic pope of the last days and thus the object of eschatological speculation. Today he is considered a contrast to the rigidly ossified church of the time. In reality he was incapable of carrying out reforms, and his abdication preserved the church from greater harm.

■ **Bibliography:** *DBI* 23:402-15; F. Baethgen, *Der Engelpapst* (Leipzig, 1943); P. Herde, *Coelestin V.* (Stuttgart, 1981); Centro Celestiniano, Sezione storica. l'Aquila, Atti del 1⁰ (–5⁰) Convegno storico internazionale . . . , 5 vols., no date (L'Aquila, 1987-91); J. R. Eastman, "Giles of Rome and Celestine V," *The Catholic Historical Review* 76 (1990) 195-211; P. Palazzini, "San Pietro Celestino e la rinuncia al Papato," *Apollinaris* 67 (1994) 841-46; R. Russo, *La sofferta canonizzazione di Celestino V* (Sulmona, 1995); P. Golinelli, *Il papa contadino: Celestino V e il suo tempo* (Florence, 1996); A. Ripa, *Celestino V e Angelo Clareno: Temi e immagini del medio evo. In Memory of R. Manselli* (Rome, 1996) 93-113; *Celestino V: Dalla rinuncia all cattura*, Atti del Convegno Fiorentino, 1995, ed. B. Valeri (Frosinone, 1997); F. Accrocca, "Querebat semper solitudinem," *AHP* 35 (1997) 257-87; A. Bartolmei Romagnoli, "Le bolle di Celestino V cassate da Bonifacio VIII," *AHP* 37 (1999) 61-83; C. Frugnono, *Due papi per un giubileo: Celestino V e Bonifacio VIII e il primo Anno santo* (Milan, 2000).

PETER HERDE

Christopher (Sept. 903-Jan. 904). A Roman. As a presbyter, he overthrew his predecessor, Leo V, and made himself pope. He was deposed by Sergius II and condemned to imprisonment in a monastery or murdered.

■ **Bibliography:** E. Dümmler, *Auxilius und Vulgarius* (Leipzig, 1866) 60-61, 135; Zimmermann *Pa* 63.

SEBASTIAN SCHOLZ

Clement I (Clement of Rome) (91?-101?). Saint (feast day Nov. 23). The earliest access to the personality of Clement comes from the letter ascribed to him by writers as early as Hegesippus and Irenaeus of Lyons (first letter to the Corinthians, before 100). Here he appears as a peace-loving

Christian speaking with authority in the name of the Roman church. According to Irenaeus, he knew the apostles Peter and Paul, had dealings with them, and followed them as the third bishop of Rome (*Adversus haereses* 3.3.3). Origen sees in him the Clement mentioned in Phil. 4:3 (*Commentarii in Johannem* 6.36), which is just a hypothesis, but it is reported by Jerome and others. The so-called Clementines link him to the imperial house, so that in the more recent literature he is on occasion falsely identified with the consul Titus Flavius Clemens. Not until the end of the fourth century did the legend of his martyrdom emerge along the Black Sea. As a result he is listed in the martyrologies, calendaries, and in the first Roman sacramentaries, as well as in the Constantinople Syntaxarium.

For the fourth century a *Dominicum Clementis* is attested; Jerome characterizes it as a church (*De viris illustribus* 15). An inscription found in the church of San Clemente in Rome and still kept there is dedicated to a martyr, whose missing name was completed as "Clement" by the archaeologist Giovanni Battista da Rossi. At the Roman council of 499 two priests of the *titulus Clementis* took part, which in the council of 595 was called *titulus sancti Clementis*. Under Pope Hormisdas (514-523) the titular priest of San Clement, Mercurius, built an altar in the church; as Pope John II (533-535), he decorated the church with the parclose panels, which have been preserved and which bear his monogram. A sixth-century hagiographer collected cultic and literary elements in an expanded version of the legend, rudimentary forms of which can be found in the → *Liber Pontificalis* and in other Roman legends. In 867 the relics of St. Clement were transported by the Apostles to the Slavs, Cyril and Methodius, from Cherson (the Crimea) to the Roman church, which provided the occasion for the Italic Cyril-and-Methodius legend (*Bibliotheca hagiographica latina* 2073) and for the cycle of frescoes preserved in the lower church of San Clemente and dedicated to Cyril. Cyril, who died shortly thereafter in Rome, was buried in San Clemente. The lower church lasted into the eleventh century and was then replaced by the one that stands over it today. The results of the excavations carried out by a Dominican priest Joseph Mullooly in the nineteenth century must nowadays be viewed as outdated after those of Federico Guidobaldi, who

argues that the story of the titulus may be reconstructed as follows: After the city was burned in 64 C.E. a two-storied place of business was built, on the west side of which stood a service dwelling, likewise two stories, whose basement served as a summer residence and was set up in the third century as a Mithraeum. In the same century a rectangular long room (whose purpose must remain unspecified on account of the barely preserved wall sections and entirely missing floor) was added on. Thus, the question of whether this may have been a *domus ecclesiae* (house church) is unanswerable. The one thing certain is that the hall was set up around the middle of the fourth century for Christian worship and in the fifth century was provided with an apse on the western narrow side.

■ **Bibliography:** *DACL* 3:1872-1902; *CATH* 2:1183ff.; *EC* 3:1809-15; *DHGE* 12:1089-93; *TRE* 8:113-23; *DECL* 133-34; *VATL* 121-22; M. Tadin, *La légende intitulée "Translatio S. Clementis"* (Paris, 1955); P. Meyvaert, *Autour de Léon d'Ostie et de sa "Translatio S. Clementis"* (Paris, 1956); A. von Harnack, *Geschichte der altchristlichen Literatur* (2nd ed. Leipzig, 1958) 1:39-47; 2:25-255; H. Delehaye, *Étude sur le Légendier romain* (Brussels, 1968) 96-116; P. Lampe, *Die stadtrömischen Christen Roms in den ersten beiden Jahrhunderten* (Tübingen, 1987); F. Guidobaldi, *San Clemente: Gli edifici romani, la basilica paleocristiana e le fasi altomedievali* (Rome, 1992); F. Guidobaldi, C. Barsanti, and A. Giulia Guidobaldi, *San Clemente: La scultura del VI secolo* (Rome, 1992); J. Hofmann, *Unser heiliger Vater Klemens. Ein römischer Bischof im Kalender der griechischen Kirche* (Trier, 1992); D. Hofmann, *Die Legende von Sankt Clemens in den skandinavischen Ländern im Mittelalter* (Frankfurt [Main], 1997); H. E. Lona, *Der erste Clemensbrief* (Göttingen, 1998); M. Vielberg, *Klemens in den pseudoklementinischen Rekognitionen* (Berlin, 2000).

VIKTOR SAXER

Clement II (Dec. 24, 1046-Oct. 9, 1047). Formerly *Suidger*; from the Saxon nobility, a cathedral canon of Halberstadt, in 1032 chaplain to Archbishop Hermann of Hamburg-Bremen, 1035 court chaplain, 1040 bishop of Bamberg. After the synods of Sutri and Rome he was nominated by Henry III to be pope; immediately after his enthronement he crowned Henry as emperor (December 25, 1046). As pope he continued to hold his bishopric. In January 1047 he arranged a reform synod with important regulations about simony, and he accompanied the emperor to southern Italy. He died—probably on the trip to Germany—in the monastery of St. Thomas on the Aposella near Pesaro perhaps as a result of poisoning. His significance for the Gregorian Reform is disputed. His vestments were preserved. He is buried in the cathedral of Bamberg, the only papal burial site north of the Alps.

■ **Sources:** *RPR*(J) 1:525-28; E. von Guttenberg, *Die Regesten der Bischöfe und des Domkapitels von Bamberg* (Munich/Vienna, 1963) 99-108.

■ **Bibliography:** *LMA* 2:2138-39; K. Hauck, "Zum Tode Papst Clemens' II.," *Jahrbuch für fränkische Landesforschung* 19 (1959) 265-74; W. Specht, "Der Tod des Papstes Clemens II.," ibid., 261-64; S. Müller-Christensen, *Das Grab des Papstes Clemens II. im Dom zu Bamberg* (Munich, 1960); W. Goez, "Papa qui et episcopus," *AHP* 8 (1970) 27-59; H. Beumann, "Reformpäpste als Reichsbischöfe in der Zeit Heinrichs III.," Festschrift for F. Hausmann (Graz, 1977) 21-37; G. Zimmermann, "Bischof Suidger von Bamberg—Papst Clemens II.," *Sorge um den Menschen*. Festschrift for J. Schneider (Bamberg, 1980) 125-35; H. Wolter; *Die Synoden in Reichsgebiet und in Reichsitalien von 916-1056* (Paderborn, 1988) 379-404; G. Zimmermann, "Bambergs Zeichenhaftigkeit für die Reichskirche des 11. Jh.," *Historischer Verein Bamberg für die Pflege der Geschichte des Ehemaligen Fürstbistums* 133 (1997) 83-92; L. Göller and A. Dechant, *Clemens II., der Papst aus Bamberg* (Bamberg, 1997).

JOHANNES LAUDAGE

Clement III (Dec. 19, 1187 [Pisa]-Mar. 28, 1191). Formerly *Paolo Scolari*, a Roman. Succeeded Gregory VIII; under Alexander III he was a papal subdeacon and archpriest of Santa Maria Maggiore. In 1179 he was made cardinal deacon of Saint Sergius e Baccho, in 1880 cardinal priest of Santa Pudenziana, in 1181/87 cardinal bishop of Preneste. Clement was able to move to Rome, where on March 31, 1188, he reached an agreement with the senate regulating relations between the papacy and the city. Evidently under the impression of the impending Third Crusade, Clement applied a policy of rapprochement vis-à-vis Frederick I Barbarossa. He yielded in the dispute over the Trier bishopric and through the Treaty of Strassburg he got back possession of the occupied → papal states, though on condition that imperial rights would be maintained in exchange for the promise to crown Henry VI emperor. After the death of William II of Sicily (November 18, 1189) and the elevation of Tancred of Lecce as the new king

(January 1189), in view of the surrounding troops threatening the Papal States (*Unio regni ad imperium*) he supported Tancred against the claims of Henry VI, without, however, breaking with the Hohenstaufen king.

■ **Bibliography:** *DBI* 26:188-92; *LMA* 2:2140-41; J. Petersohn, "Der Vertrag des römischen Senats mit Papst Clemens III. (1188) und das Pactum Friedrich Barbarossas mit den Römern," *Mitteilungen des Instituts für Österreichische Geschichtsforschung* 82 (1974) 289-337; P. Zerbi, *Papato, imperio e "Respublica Christiana" dal 1187 al 1198* (2nd ed. Milan, 1980); V. Pfaff, "Papst Clemens III. (1187-91)," *Zeitschrift der Savigny-Stiftung für Rechstgeschichte. Kanonistische Abteilung* 56 (1980) 261-316; J. Petersohn, "Kaiser, Papst und Prefectura Urbis zwischen Alexander III. und Innocent III.," *QFIAB* 60 (1980) 168-81; C. Reisinger, *Tankred von Lecce* (Cologne, 1992) 246ff.

KURT ZEILLINGER

Clement III (antipope). Formerly *Wibert of Ravenna*, born between 1020 and 1030 in Parma of a noble family who were related to the margrave of Canossa. He died on September 8, 1100, in Città Castellana. Clement probably became a cleric under Bishop Cadalus of Parma (Honorius II, antipope). From 1054 he was at the German court; at the request of Empress Agnes, he was made chancellor for Italy (1058-1061). He probably took part in the negotiations with Nicholas II about the papal → election decree of 1059. Up until the death of Honorius II, he was the latter's supporter. In 1072 Clement received from Henry IV the archbishopric of Ravenna, and for that he swore an oath of obedience to Alexander II. Clement's relations with Hildebrand-Gregory VII broke off when he sided with the Lombard bishops' critical view of Rome. He was suspended in 1076 because of his hostility to Gregory VII. At the "fasting synod" of 1078 he was excommunicated and deposed along with Thedald of Milan. At the Synod of Brixen (June 25, 1080) he was nominated to be antipope. On March 21, 1084, he was elected in Rome at the prompting of Henry IV and enthroned by the bishops of Modena and Arezzo, who were not legally entitled to do so. His choice of a name was inspired by the first German reform pope, Clement II, rather than by Clement I. On Easter (March 31) he crowned Henry IV emperor. After temporary flight from the Normans, with the support of the majority of the cardinals and the nobles of the city of Rome, Clement managed to stay in Rome for quite some time. In 1091/92 there was a synod against Nicolaitism and simony. As pope, Clement held on to the bishopric of Ravenna and promoted it as best he could, even making use of forged documents. Clement died while organizing the resistance against Paschal II. Even his opponents acknowledged his personal integrity and reform zeal. In the effort to extend his authority (England, Denmark, Portugal, Hungary, Croatia, Serbia, Calabria; he launched negotiations on union with the Russian church and made attempts to reactivate relations with Byzantium), Clement moved out of the shadow of Henry IV, whom he supported during the emperor's life. Under Clement Ravenna became a journalistic center for imperial anti-Roman propaganda. In all likelihood, however, the so-called imperial version of the papal election decree was not composed there. A polemic that Clement wrote against Gregory VIII has been lost, and its contents can be inferred only from the counter-polemic by Anselm of Lucca (*MGH.LL* 1:519-28).

■ **Sources:** *RPR*(J) 2nd ed. 1:649-55; *MGH.LL* 1:621-26; 2:169-72; F. Liebermann, "Drei Briefe an Lanfranc," *English Historical Review* 16 (1901) 328-33; W. Holtzmann, "Brief an Basileios von Reggio," *Byzantinische Zeitschrift* 28 (1928) 59-60; P. Kehr, "Urkunde für Erzbischof Petrus von Doclea," *Nachrichten der Gesellschaft der Wissenschaften in Göttingen* (1900) 148ff., n. 7; *MGH.Const* 1:541-46, n. 383 (cf. H.-G. Krause, *Das Papstwahldekret von 1059 und seine Rolle im Investiturstreit* (Rome, 1960) 271-75; P. Kehr, "Zur Geschichte Wiberts von Ravenna," *Sitzungsberichte der Preußischen Akademie der Wissenschaften* (Berlin, 1921) 355-68, 973-88.

■ **Bibliography:** *LMA* 2:2139-40; O. Köhncke, *Wibert von Ravenna* (Leipzig, 1888); J. Ziese, *Wibert von Ravenna* (Stuttgart, 1982); I. Heidrich, *Ravenna unter Erzbischof Wibert (1073-1100)* (Tübingen, 1984); K. G. Cushing, "Anselm of Lucca and the Doctrine of Coercion," *Catholic Historical Review* 81 (1995) 353-71.

ELKE GOES

Clement IV (Feb. 5, 1265-Nov. 29, 1268). Formerly *Gui Foucqois*, born ca. 1200 in Saint Gilles; studied law in Paris, legal adviser to Raimund VII of Toulouse, later to Alphonse of Poitiers and King Louis IX of France. Repeatedly entrusted with investigations in Languedoc, he came into contact there with the Inquisition. This led to the *Quaestiones quindecim ad inquisitores*, a manual for inquisitors. He became a cleric in early 1255 after the death of his wife; in 1257 he was conse-

crated bishop of Le Puy, in 1259 he was made archbishop of Narbonne, in 1261 cardinal archbishop of Sabina. Despite the failure of a legation to England in 1264, a year later he was elected pope. His pontificate faced pressure to resolve the problem of succession in the kingdom of Sicily. He enforced harder fief conditions on Charles I of Anjou than Urban IV had done. Although his Sicilian policy was successfully crowned with the enfeoffment of the Angevins (June 28, 1265), he had to accept setbacks, since Charles often did not abide by the agreements and tried to extend his dominions to Rome and Tuscany. Clement's constitution *Licet ecclesiarum* (1265) was important for the internal strengthening of the church: it reserved all vacant lower-level benefices for the pope. He died in → Viterbo, where he had the famous papal palace built for himself.

■ **Bibliography:** *DBI* 26:192-202; *LMA* 2:2141-42; *Les registres de Clément IV (1265-68)*, ed. E. Jordan (Paris, 1945); Y. Dossat, "Gui Foucois, enquêteur-réformateur, archêveque et pape (Clément IV)," *Cahiers de Fanjeaux* 7 (1972); P. Herde, *Karl I. von Anjou* (Stuttgart, 1979); M. Thumser, "Zur Überlieferungsgeschichte der Briefe Papst Clemens' IV.," *Deutsches Archiv für Erforschung des Mittelalters* 51 (1995) 115-68.

ANDREAS KIESEWETTER

Clement V (June 5, 1305-Apr. 20, 1314). Formerly *Bertrand de Got*, probably born ca. 1250 in Vilandraut (Gironde). After studying law in Bologna and Orléans, he acquired various benefices in Gascony. In 1285 he became the procurator for Edward I of England in the Parliament of Paris. Through the influence of his brother Bérard, he became general vicar of the archdiocese of Lyons in 1289, bishop of Comminges in 1295, and was made archbishop of Bordeaux in 1299. During the clashes between Boniface VIII and King Philip IV of France he followed a policy of neutrality. In the conclave of Perugia (1304-1305) he was elected pope by the anti-Boniface party. He was crowned on November 14, 1305. Because of his shattered health his repeatedly voiced intention of bringing the curia back to Rome could not be realized. He often changed his place of residence in France, until opting for → Avignon. His pontificate was marked by the trial of Boniface, the proceedings against the Templars and a → nepotism of hitherto unknown proportions. He was dependent on Philip IV, and the cardinals he created were almost without exception French. For procedural reasons the French did not conclude the trial of Boniface, which opened in 1310. On the matter of the Templars, after initial resistance, Clement had to give the French king a free hand. In the fall of 1307 he belatedly sanctioned the arresting of the Templars, and on April 3, 1312, he dissolved the order at the Council of Vienne. He appointed many of his relatives cardinals or bishops and later made bequests to them from the papal treasury. With regard to Emperor Henry VII, Clement vacillated, after initial support; he was pressured by Philip after the conflict broke out between Henry and Robert of Anjou into taking a harder line. At the same time the authority of the pope completely declined in the papal states and in imperial Italy. He was more successful in his activities in the cultural domain and as a legislator: he founded many universities and issued the decretals of the Clementines at the Council of Lyons. He died, presumably from cancer, at Roquemare (Gard).

■ **Sources:** *Regestum Clementis Papae V . . .* , 11 vols. (Rome, 1885, 1957).

■ **Bibliography:** *DBI* 26:202-15; *LMA* 2:2142-43; *VATL* 125ff.; G. Mollat, *Les papes d'Avignon* (10th ed. Paris, 1964) 27-38; T. Schmidt, *Der Bonifaz-Prozeß* (Cologne/Vienna, 1989); A. Luttrell, "The Hospitalers and the Papacy, 1305-14," *Forschungen zur Reichs-, Papst- und Landesgeschichte.* Festschrift for P. Herde (Stuttgart, 1998) 595-622; J. Seiler, "Die Aufhebung des Tempelordens nach neueren Untersuchungen," *Zeitschrift für Kirchengeschichte* 109 (1998) 19-31; A. Gilmour-Bryson, "L'elezione di Bertrand de Got (Clemente V) e l'incontro a St. Jean d'Angely," *Rivista di storia della Chiesa in Italia* 53 (1999) 407-55.

ANDREAS KIESEWETTER

Clement VI (May 7, 1342-Dec. 6, 1352). Formerly *Pierre Roger*, a Benedictine (1307); born in 1290/91 in the fortress of Maumont (Corrèze) to a poor noble family. Entered the Benedictine monastery of La Chaise-Dieu. After studies in Paris (doctor of theology) he was made prior of Saint-Pantaléon in Savigny (diocese of Lyons) and Saint-Baudil (diocese of Nîmes). In 1326 he became abbot of Fécamp, in 1328 bishop of Arras, in 1329 archbishop of Sens, and in 1330 archbishop of Rouen. At the same time he was a close friend of King Philip VI of France and, thanks to that connection, a member of the Chambre des Enquêtes and president of the Chambre des

Comptes, without ever becoming royal chancellor. As a cardinal priest of Saints Nereo and Achilleo (from 1338 onward) he was elected pope on account of his great talent as a preacher and theologian. His splendid court, worthy of a Renaissance prince, his unrestrained → nepotism, his consolidation of curial fiscalism or benefices (provisions, rights of succession) and his emphatic support of French policy as well as his grossly increasing the French share in the College of → Cardinals brought him into disrepute. Nevertheless, his struggle against King Louis of Bavaria (the absolution trial, the promotion of Charles IV), the Franciscan Spirituals and Cola di Rienzo were of major church-political significance. The acquisition of → Avignon and of the county of Venaissin, the expansion of the papal palace, and the path-breaking way that he structured the Jubilee Year of 1350 all had great importance in church politics.

■ **Sources:** É. Baluze and G. Mollat, *Vitae paparum Avenionensium,* vol. 1 (2nd ed. Paris, 1914) 241-308; E. Déprez, J. Glénisson, and G. Mollat, *Lettres closes, patentes et curiales se rapportant à la France* (Paris, 1901-61 [years as continuous series]); E. Déprez and G. Mollat, *Lettres closes, patentes, et curiales intéressantes les pays autres que la France* (Paris, 1960-61); T. Gasparini Leporache, *Le suppliche di Clemente VI* (Rome, 1948).

■ **Bibliography:** *DBI* 26:215-22; *LMA* 2:2143-44; *VATL* 1217ff.; G. Mollat, *Les papes d'Avignon* (2nd ed. Paris, 1966); J. E. Wrigley, "Clement VI Before his Pontificate," *Catholic Historical Review* 56 (1970) 433-73; idem, "The Conclave and the Electors of 1342," *AHP* 20 (1982) 51-82; D. Wood, *Clement VI: The Pontificate and Ideas of an Avignon Pope* (Cambridge, 1989).

LUDWIG VONES

Clement VII (Sept. 20, 1378-Sept. 16, 1394). Formerly *Robert of Geneva*, born in 1342 at the fortress of Annecy, the son of Amadeus III, count of Geneva and Matthilde of Boulogne. He was related to the royal house of France as well as to almost all European princely houses. He was promoted by his uncle, Cardinal Gui de Boulogne, who was a leading churchman and cardinal ("cardinal of Geneva"). After studying canon law in Paris (while at the same time a canon of Notre Dame), he became a papal notary. In 1361 he was consecrated bishop of Thérouanne, in 1368 bishop of Cambrai, and finally cardinal-priest of the Holy Twelve Apostles (1371) with a great assortment of benefices. Under Gregory XI he was a papal legate for the Romagna and the Marches (1376-1378). He was at once lord of the fortresses of Beauregard, Gaillard (perhaps exchanged for Cruseilles), and Morex. His election in Fondi by the cardinals who had broken with Urban VI triggered the Western Schism. After the failure of his policies in Italy and in the → papal states, where despite the support of France and Louis I of Anjou he could not prevail against Urban VI, he returned to → Avignon (1379) and founded the Avignon "obedience" with its own curia and a complete College of → Cardinals, while building up the financial or benefice-economy. Clement rejected all offers to settle divisions within the church (by the University of Paris or Catherine of Siena, for instance). He was a clever tactician, who knew how to get the western European kingdoms on his side and exploit both traditional rivalries and political alliances in the Hundred Years War. He had very little scope for a continuous papal policy, but his promotion of the University of Avignon and expansion of the city stand out.

■ **Sources:** *Repertorium Germanicum,* ed. Deutsches Historisches Institut in Rom, vol. 1 (Berlin/Tübingen, 1916); *Documents relatifs au Grand Schisme,* 3 vols. (Brussels/Rome, 1924-34); *Acta pseudopontificum Clementis VII . . . ,* ed. A. L. Tautu (Rome, 1966).
■ **Bibliography:** *DBI* 26:222-37; *LMA* 2:2144-45; J. Favier, *Les Finances Pontificales à l'époque du Grand Schisme d'Occident* (Paris, 1966); H. Diener, "Die großen Registerserien im Vatikanischen Archiv (1378-1523)," *QFIAB* 51 (1971) 305-68; idem, "Rubriziellen zu Supplikenregistern Papst Clemens' VII.," ibid., 591-605; R. C. Logoz, *Clément VII (Robert de Genève): Sa chancellerie et le clergé romand au début du Grand Schisme* (Lausanne, 1974); *Génèse et débuts du Grand Schisme d'Occident, 1362-1394* (Paris, 1980); M. Harvey, *Solutions to the Schism* (St. Ottilien, 1983); J. Serra Estelles, *Los registros de súplicas y letras pontificias de Clemente VII de Aviñón (1378-84): Estudio díplomatico* (Rome, 1988); idem, "Un registro especial de súplicas dirigidas a Clement VII . . . ," *AHP* 33 (1995) 7-39.

LUDWIG VONES

Clement VII (Nov. 19, 1523-Sept. 25, 1534). Formerly *Giulio de' Medici.* Born May 26, 1478, in Florence, an illegitimate son of the lord of the city, Giuliano de' Medici. In 1514 through his cousin Leo X he was made archbishop of Florence and a cardinal. As a candidate of the imperial party he was chosen to succeed Hadrian VI. At a time of the gravest crisis for the church, Clement acted for the most part like an Italian Renaissance prince on behalf of the → papal states and the Medici, resorting to a sly, untrustworthy diplomacy in all areas. His attempt to restrain the imperial hegemony in Italy in alliance with the French king, Francis I (who was conspiring with the Turks against Emperor Charles V), and Venice (Holy League of Cognac, 1526) led to the sack of Rome in 1527 and his being taken prisoner. The subsequent rapprochement with Charles V (peace of Barcelona, 1529; the crowning of the emperor in Bologna in 1530) brought no papal help in the turmoil of the German Reformation (Imperial Diet of Augsburg, 1530), since Clement always dodged the demand for a council. The weakness of his character also appeared in the delaying tactics with which he handled the question of King Henry VIII of England's marriage and moved against the Scandinavian kingdoms. During his pontificate a third of western Europe broke away from the church (large parts of Germany, England, Scandinavia, etc.), Hence he has been called "probably the most disastrous of all the popes" (Leopold von Ranke). The expansion of the hierarchy into Latin America and his patronage could not compensate for these losses.

■ **Bibliography:** *DHGE* 12:1175-1224; *HKG* 4:246-50, 693; *DBI* 237-59; *TRE* 8:98-101; *VATL* 129ff.; S. Ehses, "Die Politik des Papstes Clemens VII. bis zur Schlacht von Pavia," *Historisches Jahrbuch* 6 (1885) 557-603; 7 (1886) 553-93; J. Fraikin, *Nonciatures de France: Clément VII,* 2 vols. (Paris, 1906-16); T. Pandolfi, "G. M. Gilberti e l'ultima difesa della libertà d'Italia negli anni 1521-25," *Archivio della Società Romana di Storia Patria* 34 (1911) 131-237; Pastor, vol. 4/1 and 4/2; *HCMA* 3:18-22; E. Rodocanachi, *Les pontificats d'Adrien VI et de Clément VII* (Paris, 1933); S. E. Reiss, *Cardinal Giulio de' Medici as a Patron of Art (1513-23)* (Princeton, 1992).

GEORG SCHWAIGER

Clement VIII (Jan. 30, 1592-Mar. 5, 1605). Formerly *Ippolito Aldobrandini,* born February 24, 1536, in Fano to a respected Florentine family. He studied in Padua, Perugia, and Bologna. Under Pius V and Sixtus V he was an outstanding jurist in the curia. He was created a cardinal in 1585. Clement largely conformed to the ideals of Catholic reform. He had political successes in the reconciliation with France (absolution of Henry IV in 1595), the church union of Brest, mediation between France and Spain (the Peace of Vervins in 1598) and the recovery of Ferrara for the → papal states. But the pope's efforts made no headway against the Turks in Hungary and Counter-Reformation expectations in England and Sweden. In the dispute over grace, Clement failed to reach a decision. He promoted new editions of liturgical books (the *Pontificale Romanum*, the breviary, and the *Missale*), of Sixtus V's Vulgate and the → Index of Forbidden Books. Clement intensified the action of the Inquisition (Giordano Bruno was burned at the stake in 1600). In the tragic murder trial of the Cenci (three executions outside the Castel Sant' Angelo), he did not ease the severity of the laws in force. Even if Clement is not to be counted as one of the great reform popes, he did manage to solidify the reforms introduced by earlier popes and reacquired political independence (especially vis-à-vis Spain). His grave is in Santa Maria Maggiore (Cappella Borghese).

■ **Bibliography:** *DHGE* 12:1249-97; *DBI* 26:259-82; *VATL* 132ff.; Pastor, vol. 11; *HCMA* 4:3-8; K. Jaitner, *Die Hauptinstruktionen Clemens' VIIII. für die Nuntien und Legaten an den europäischen Fürstenhöfen,* 2 vols. (Tübingen, 1984); idem, "Il nepotismo di papa Clemente VIII: Il drama del card. Cincio Aldobrandini," *Archivio storico italiano* 146 (1988) 57-93; S. Andretta, *Das Papstum, die Christenheit und die Staaten Europas 1592-1605: Forschungen zu den Hauptinstruktionen Clemens' VIII.* (Tübingen, 1994); R. Zapperi, *Der Neid und die Macht: Die Farnese und Aldobrandini im barocken Rom* (Munich, 1994); C. Alonso, "Una embajada de Clemente VIII a Persia (1600-09)," *AHP* 34 (1996) 7-125; idem, "Una visita de Clemente VIII al Convento Romano de San Agustín," *Analecta Augustiniana* 60 (1997) 341-65.

GEORG SCHWAIGER

Clement VIII (antipope) (June 10, 1423-July 26, 1429). Formerly *Gil Sánchez Muñoz y Carbón,* born 1369-70 in Teruel (Aragón), died December 28, 1446, in Majorca. He was a *doctor decretorum* and served the curia in → Avignon. An intimate of Benedict XIII (Avignon), he was also provost of Valencia. Shortly before Benedict died (May 23, 1423) or, more likely, sometime before that (November 29, 1422, in Peñiscola), he appointed four new cardinals. Three of them chose Clement on June 10, 1423. He had only a few supporters but was used by King Alfonso V of Aragón-Naples against Pope Martin V. He abdicated on July 26, 1429, in Peñiscola; he was later named bishop of Majorca by Martin V.

■ **Bibliography:** *DHGE* 12:1245-49; *LMA* 2:2145-46; F. Ehrle, *Martin de Alpartils Chronica Actitatorum temporibus domini Benedicti XIII* (Paderborn, 1906); D. Gir-

gensohn, "Ein Schisma ist nicht zu beenden ohne die Zustimmung der konkurrierenden Päpste," *AHP* 27 (1989) 197-247, esp. 236-39.

GEORG SCHWAIGER

Clement IX (June 20, 1667-Dec. 9, 1669). Formerly *Giulio Rospigliosi,* born January 28, 1600, in Pistoia; he studied in Pisa and rose through the curia under Urban VIII. From 1644 to 1653 he was a nuncio in Spain; in 1657 he was made a cardinal; he was secretariat of state of Alexander VII. A friend of literature and a composer of religious melodramas, Clement succeeded in breaking down political tensions; he avoided → nepotism, ordered the church's affairs in Portugal (after its independence was recognized by Spain). He made great efforts on behalf of the Peace of Aachen (1668) between France and Spain. A French-papal expedition to support Venice could not prevent the loss of Crete to the Turks. In the dispute over Jansenism the "Clementine peace" brought only a temporary truce.

■ **Bibliography:** *DHGE* 12:1297-1313; *DBI* 26:282-93; A. Cauchie, "La paix de Clément IX 1668/69," *Revue d'histoire et de littérature religieuse* 3 (1898) 481-501; C. Terlinden, *Clément IX et la guerre de Candie* (Louvain, 1905); idem, "La diplomatie pontificale et la paix d'Aix-la-Chapelle de 1668," *Bulletin d'Institut Historique Belge de Rome* 27 (1952) 249-68; Canevazzi, *Papa Clemente IX poeta* (Modena, 1910); *HCMA* 5:3ff.; D. Romei, *Il papa "comico": Sul melodrammi di Giulio Rospigliosi (Clemente IX): Paragone* 41/n. 482 (Florence, 1990) 43-62; M. Fagiolo and S. Roberto, "Un' opera berniniana per Clemente IX," *Palladio* no. 5 (1990) 63-90: P. Blet, "Louis XIV et les papes aux prises avec le Jansénisme," *AHP* 32 (1994) 65-148; M. L. Roden, "Cardinal Decio Azzolini and the Problem of Papal Nepotism," *AHP* 34 (1996) 127-57.

GEORG SCHWAIGER

Clement X (Apr. 29, 1670-July 22, 1676). Formerly *Emilio Altieri,* born July 12, 1590, in Rome from Roman nobility. After legal studies in Rome he became auditor of the Polish nunciature; from 1627 to 1666 he was bishop of Camerino; from 1644 to 1652 he was nuncio in Naples. In 1669 he was created a cardinal, and he was elected pope after a conclave that lasted more than four months and was shaped by French–Spanish conflicts. Clement handed over business to his adoptive nephew Cardinal Paluzzo Paluzzi degli Albertoni. There was sharp hostility with Louis XIV, who laid claim to the *regalia* (i.e., the right to revenues from vacant sees and abbeys). The pope lent his support to the Polish king Jan Sobieski in the war against the Turks. Clement presided over an unusually large number of canonizations.

■ **Bibliography:** *DHGE* 12:1313-26; *DBI* 26:293-302; *VATL* 136-37; C. Bildt, *Christine de Suède et le conclave de Clément X* (Paris, 1906); M. Dubruell, "La cour de Rome et l'extension de la régale," *Revue d'histoire de l'Église de France* 9 (1923) 163-76; *HCMA* 4:34-35, 131; 5:6-9; S. de Dainville-Barbiche, *Correspondance du nonce en France Fabrizio Spada 1674-1675* (Rome, 1982).

GEORG SCHWAIGER

Clement XI (Nov. 23, 1700-Mar. 19, 1721). Formerly *Gian Francesco Albani*, born on June 22, 1649, in Urbino of Umbrian nobility; from 1677 he served in the curia. He was made a secretary of briefs in 1687 and was created a cardinal in 1690. He had great influence under Alexander VIII and Innocent XII. He opposed nepotism but was not up to handling political difficulties. His pontificate was overshadowed by the War of Spanish Succession. Clement strove for neutrality but inclined toward France and at first recognized the Bourbon Philip V as the Spanish king. The tensions with Emperor Leopold I intensified under Emperor Joseph I in 1708 during the war in Italy, when the → papal states were partially occupied. In 1709 Clement had to make peace and recognize the emperor's brother as Charles II of Spain (the future emperor Charles VI), which led to a break with King Louis XIV and his grandson Philip V of Spain. In the Peace of Utrecht, like that of Rastatt in 1714, as well as in later territorial shifts, the papacy's superior feudal rights over Sicily, Naples (Monarchia Sicula), Sardinia, Parma, Piacenza, etc., were disregarded. The pope's protest against the royal titles that the Elective Prince of Brandenburg, Frederick (1701 King in Prussia), claimed for himself remained ineffectual. From 1715 to 1718 Clement supported the emperor and Venice against the Turks, but intrigues by Cardinal Guido Alberoni prevented their successes from being exploited. At the insistence of Louis XIV, Clement issued the bulls *Vineam Domini* (1705) and *Unigenitus* (1713) against the Jansenists. Clement promoted art and science, and strove to advance the missions and the Eastern Christians. In the controversy over the Chinese rites he decided against the Jesuits.

■ **Bibliography:** *DHGE* 12:1326-61; *DBI* 26:302-20; *HCMA* 5:17, 222-23; *Committenze della famiglia Albani: Note sulla Albani Tortonia* (Rome, 1985); L. Ceyssens,

Autour de l'Unigenitus: Recherches sur la génèse de la constitution (Louvain, 1987); idem, "La bulle 'Vineam Domini' et le jansénisme français," *Antonianum* 64 (1989) 398-430; C. Burns, "Pope Clement XI and the British Isles," *Ecclesiae Memoria*, Festschrift for J. Metzler (Rome, 1991) 41-85; S. Åkerman, *Queen Christina of Sweden and Her Circle* (Leiden, 1991); L. Ceyssens, *Le sort de la bulle Unigenitus* (Louvain, 1992); C. M. S. John, *Papal Art and Cultural Politics: Rome in the Age of Clement XI* (Cambridge, 1993); S. Tabacchi, "Tra riforma e crisi. Il 'buon governo' delle comunità dello Stato e della Chiesa durante il pontificato di Clement XI," in *Papes et Paupauté au XVIIIᵉ siècle* (Paris, 1999), 51-85; J. Sgard, "Le pape dans les 'Nouvelles ecclésiastiques,'" ibid., 195-204.

GEORG SCHWAIGER

Clement XII (July 12, 1730-Feb. 6, 1740). Formerly *Lorenzo Corsini*, born April 7, 1652, in Florence of Florentine nobility. He studied in Florence, Pisa, and Rome. In 1690 he was made titular bishop of Nicomedia, in 1691 nuncio in Vienna (the appointment was not carried out because of tensions with the emperor). Elected after a difficult conclave, Clement was too old for his office, and in addition he went completely blind after 1732. He tried to leave behind the difficult legacy of Benedict XIII (Orsini); he regulated the conclave (the constitution *Apostolatus Officium* of 1732) by limiting the cardinals' rights when there was a vacancy (→ *Sede Vacante*) in the papal see. But he managed neither to slow down the decline of the political power of the papacy (as in the Polish War of Succession) nor to push through his claims on Parma and Piacenza. Only with great effort could he avoid a break with Spain (concordat of 1737). He failed in his attempt to promote re-Catholicization through recognition of the secularization of church property in the electorate of Saxony (the bull of 1732). Clement excommunicated Bishop Theodore van der Croon of Utrecht and in 1738 forbade Catholics from joining the Freemasons (bull *In eminenti*). He had notable achievements in the missions to Lebanon, in art (the façade and Corsini chapel in the Lateran basilica, the Capitoline museum), and in the sciences (Bibliotheca Corsini; astronomy).

■ **Bibliography:** *DHGE* 12:1361-81; *DBI* 26:320-28; *VATL* 139-40; *HCMA* 5:24, 288; 6:3-9; L. P. Raybaud, *Papauté et pouvoir temporel sous les pontificats de Clément XII et Benoît XIV* (Paris, 1963); F. Tagell, *Relació de la mort de Climent XII i de l'elecció de Benet XIV (1740)*, ed. J. Mascaró (Barcelona, 1971); E. Garms-Cornides,

"Päpstliche Friedenspolitik und italienisches Gleichgewicht: Zu einigen Vermittlungsversuchen der Kurie im Polnischen Erbfolgekrieg," *Römische Historische Mitteilungen* 28 (1986) 303-38; D. Ligou, "La réception en France des bulles pontificales condamnant la franc-maçonnerie," in *Papes et papauté au XVIIIe siècle* (Paris, 1999) 205-17.

GEORG SCHWAIGER

Clement XIII (July 6, 1758-Feb. 2, 1769). Formerly *Carlo della Torre Rezzonico*, born March 7, 1693, in Venice. After studies in Bologna, Padua, and Rome he joined the curial service in 1716. In 1737 he was made cardinal deacon of San Nicola in Carcere, in 1743 bishop of Padua. He was elected pope after the French exercised their right to exclude consideration of Cardinal Carlo Alberto Cavalchini Guidobono. His entire pontificate was heavily burdened by the "Jesuit question." Clement and his secretary of state, Cardinal Ludovico Torrigiani, who were both pronounced friends of the Jesuits, could no longer prevent Jesuit expulsion and exile, beginning with Portugal under Prime Minister Martquês de Pombal in 1759, and continuing in the Bourbon states of France (1762-1764), Spain (1767), Naples and Sicily (1767), as well as Parma-Piacenza (1768). His intransigent and undiplomatic clinging to the ecclesiastical penalties of the bull of communion (final version of 1627) worsened the situation and strengthened the joint political action of the powers opposed to Clement. The areas belonging to the Papal States of Avignon, with Venaissin, Bevevento, and Pontecrovo were occupied. In Germany danger threatened from effects of the Seven Years War on denominational politics, and once again from the projects of secularization. Clement sought to oppose the Enlightenment, Gallicanism, and episcopalism; and in 1764 he condemned Febronianism. He consigned to the → Index works by Claude-Adrien Helvétius, Jean le Rond d'Alembert, Denis Diderot's *Encyclopédie*, Jean-Jacques Rousseau's *Émile*, and works by François-Philippe Mésenguy. The encyclical *Christianae reipublicae salus* (1766) rejected all publications that did not agree with Catholic dogma.

Clement promoted the arts and sciences, specifically such figures as Anton Raphael Mengs, Giovanni Battista Piranesi, and Johann Joachim Winckelmann. He covered up the nakedness of statues and paintings (Sistine Chapel).

■ **Bibliography:** *DHGE* 12:1381-1410; *HKG* 5:626-31; *DBI* 26:328-43; *VATL* 140-41; Pastor, vol. 16/1; *HCMA* 6:8, 19-24, 330; E. Noé, "Rezzonicorum cineres," *Rivista dell'Istituto Nazionale d'Archeologia e storia dell'arte* 3 (1980) 173-306; J. T. Lukowski, "The Papacy, Poland, Russia and Religious Reform, 1764-68," *Journal of Ecclesiastical History* 39 (1988) 66-94; P. Zovato, "La soppressione della Compagnia di Gesù," in *Atti del XIII Convegno Fonte Avellana* (Urbino, 1989) 55-81; M. Müller, *Die Opposition von Papst Klemens XIII. und des gallikanischen Episkopats gegen die Unterdrückung der Gesellschaft Jesu in Frankreich 1761-65*, 2 vols. (Marburg, 1996).

GEORG SCHWAIGER

Clement XIV (May 19, 1769-Sept. 22, 1774). Formerly *Giovanni Vinzenzo Antonio Ganganelli*, born October 31, 1705, at Sant' Arcangelo near Rimini, he joined the Minorites in 1723; his religious name was Lorenzo. In 1746 he was made a consultor of the Holy Office and was created a cardinal in 1759. Originally favorable to the Jesuits, he later opposed Clement XIII's policy. Elected after a three-month conclave, which was completely dominated by the Jesuit question, Clement was expected to dissolve the Society of Jesus, although he had not given his binding consent to do so. He tried at first to achieve peace with the Bourbon states by major concessions to the established churches there. Pressure from those countries, especially Spain, increased to the point of threatening schism. The Habsburg empress Maria Theresa finally declared that she would remain neutral to a papal decision. After a long hesitation and preparatory steps, Clement decreed the dissolution of the Jesuit order by means of the brief *Dominus ac Redemptor noster* (July 21, 1773). France and Naples thereupon left the occupied territories of the → papal states. The situation of the church was marked by the Gravamina of Coblenz of 1769 and the Salzburg Congress of the Bavarian bishops (1770-1777). Financial and economic reforms in the papal states were largely unsuccessful. Clement rendered outstanding services to art (Museo Pio-Clementino) and the sciences. Since 1802 his grave has been in the church of the Twelve Holy Apostles.

■ **Bibliography:** *DHGE* 12:1411-23; *DBI* 26:343-62; *VATL* 142-43; *HCMA* 6:22, 25-28; Pastor, vol. 16/2; A. Galassi, "La malattia e morte di Clemente XIV," *Rivista di storia delle Scienze* 41 (1950) 153-65; W. Müller, "Die Aufhebung des Jesuitenordens in Bayern," *Zeitschrift für bayerische Landesgeschichte* 48 (1985) 285-352; G. Paris-

Ciani, *Gianvincenzo e Lorenzo Ganganelli "figli" del convento di Urbino* (Ancona, 1988); C. Schmitt, "La fusione degli Osservanti con i Conventuali di Francia decisa da Clemente XIV a Roma nel 1771," *Studi francescani* 87 (1990) 265-82; K. Frammelsberger, "'Dominus ac Redemptor,'" *Geist und Leben* 63 (1990) 373-88; F. Champarnaud, "Sade et le pape," in *Papes et papauté au XVIIIe siècle* (Paris, 1999) 107-19; S. Pavone, "Il paradosso dei Gesuiti," in ibid., 219-38; P. Retat, "La mort de Clément XIV," in ibid., 261-63.

GEORGE SCHWAIGER

Conon (Oct. 21, 686-Sept. 21, 687). Son of a high-ranking officer in the Thracian military corps. He was educated in Sicily and became a priest in Rome. On the death of John V, he was elected pope as a very elderly man, a compromise candidate: the clergy had wanted the archpriest Peter, and the Roman soldiery had wanted the priest Theodore. The tensions continued to smolder during the pontificate of Conon, whose health was poor, and they erupted anew after his death. A revolt broke out in the Sicilian possessions of the papacy during his reign; Emperor Justinian II continued his policy of détente vis-à-vis Rome. Conon is buried in St Peter's.

■ **Sources:** *LP* 1:368ff.; 3:index; *RPR*(J) 1:243; F. Dölger, ed. *Corpus der griechischen Urkunden des Mittelalters und der neueren Zeit,* Reihe A: *Regesten,* Abteilung I: *Regesten der Kaiserurkunden des oströmischen Reiches* (Munich, 1924) 1:565-1024, nn. 254ff.
■ **Bibliography:** *DBI* 28:21-25; *BBKL* 4:379f.; *VATL* 427; Caspar 2:620-23, 631; Bertolini 396-401.

GEORG SCHWAIGER

Constantine I (Mar. 25, 708-Apr. 9, 715). A Syrian. Emperor Justinian II summoned him to his court in 710 in order to end the controversy about the canons of the Quinisext council (691), but nothing is known in detail about the negotiations, which took place in a friendly atmosphere at Nicomedia. In 712/713, Constantine opposed the renewal of Monothelitism by the emperor Philippicus, and had his name removed from the diptychs. Constantine succeeded in resolving the controversy with archbishop Felix about the autocephaly of Ravenna in favor of Rome.

■ **Sources:** *LP* 1:389-95; *RPR*(J) 1:247ff.; 2:700.
■ **Bibliography:** *LMA* 3:170; *VATL* 429f.; Caspar 2:638-43; J.-M. Sansterre, "Le pape Constantin Ier et la politique religieuse des empereurs Justinien II et Philippikos," *AHP* 22 (1984) 7-29.

SEBASTIAN SCHOLZ

Constantine II (antipope) (July 5, 767-Aug. 6, 768). After the death of Paul I, Duke Toto of Nepi forced through the election of his brother Constantine, a layman, as pope, and had him ordained. To begin with, Constantine reigned unchallenged, but he was arrested by the opposition within the city of Rome, with help from the Langobards, on July 31, 768, and was deposed by a Roman synod on August 6. Stephen III was elected the new pope. Subsequently, Constantine was blinded and deposed yet again at the Roman synod of April 769.

■ **Sources:** *LP* 1:468-76; *RPR*(J) 1:283ff.; *MGH.Conc* 2:1, 74-86; *MGH.Ep* 3:649-53.
■ **Bibliography:** *LMA* 3:170f.; Zimmermann *Pa*, 13-25; T. F. X. Noble, *The Republic of Saint Peter* (Philadelphia, 1984) 112-18; J. S. Gibaut, "The clerical cursus of Constantine of Nepi," *Ecclesia orans* 12 (1995) 195-206.

SEBASTIAN SCHOLZ

Cornelius (Mar. 251-June 253). Saint (feast day Sept. 16), a Roman, son of Castinus. Pope Fabian died on January 20, 250, as a martyr in the persecution under the emperor Decius. After the persecution in Rome had abated, the majority chose the Roman presbyter Cornelius as Fabian's successor (Cyprian, *Ep.* 55). In opposition to the upright Cornelius, who, however, represented the milder trend in penitential practice, the stricter minority of the Roman clergy elevated the gifted Novatian, who in the long → *sede vacante* had exercised great influence, as antibishop. But Cornelius, supported by Cyprian of Carthage and Dionysius of Alexandria, managed to prevail in the church as a whole. In the fall of 251 a synod attended by sixty bishops rejected the charge of the Novatians that Cornelius was a Libellaticus or was in communion with the Libellatici (Eusebius of Caesarea, *Historia ecclesiastica* 6.43). His milder form of penitential discipline, which granted forgiveness to those who had apostatized once they had done penance, was approved by the synod. Novatian and his adherents were excluded. Cornelius sent letters to Alexandria, Antioch (in Syria), and Carthage, mostly dealing with the Roman schism. Only two letters to Cyprian have been preserved (*Epp.* 49 and 50 in the latter's correspondence), in addition to the fragment of a letter to Fabius of Antioch (Eusebius 6.43.11), in which the organization of the Roman clergy is mentioned: 46 presbyters, 7 deacons, 42 acolytes, 52 lectors, exorcists, and porters, along with 1,500 widows and needy, which points to a community of about 30,000 persons. When the emperor Gallus renewed the persecution, Cornelius was exiled to Centumcellae (Civitavecchia), where he soon died *cum gloria* (probably not as a martyr, although Cyprian characterized him as one). Cornelius was buried in the Lucina crypt of the catacombs of Callistus. Up until the Enlightenment, especially in the Rhineland, Cornelius was greatly revered as one of the holy marshals (centers: Saint-Corneille-de-Compiègne, Korneliusmüntser, St. Severin at Cologne).

■ **Sources:** *LP* 1:CCVIII-IX, 4-6, 150ff.; *RPR*(J) 1:17ff.; 2:690; *Quellen zur Geschichte des Papsttums und des römischen Katholizismus* (C. Mirbt, founder and original series editor), ed. K. Aland, vol. 1 (6th ed. Tübingen, 1967) 62-72.

■ **Bibliography:** *DHGE* 13:891-94; *Dizionario patristico e di antichità cristiane*, ed. A. Di Berardino, vol. 1 (Casale Monferrato, 1983) 786; *LMA* 3:242-43; *DECL* 144; *VATL* 150; J. Wilpert, *Die Papstgräber und die Cäciliengruft in der Katakombe des heiligen Kallistus* (Freiburg, 1909) 26-27, 32-33; P. Franchi De'Cavaliero, "La persecuzione di Gallo a Roma," *Studi e Testi* 33 (1929) 181-210; Caspar 1:66-70; L. Reekmans, *La tombe du pape Corneille et sa région cémétériale* (Vatican City, 1964).

GEORG SCHWAIGER

Cyriacus, the name of a pope in the legend of St. Ursula. Around 1164, the monk of Deutz, Theodericus Aedituus, cites a supposed grave inscription of Cyriacus. According to the visions of Elizabeth of Schönau, Cyriacus was a Briton by birth and laid down his office in order to follow St. Ursula to martyrdom. His successor is supposed to have been Anterus (235-236). A recension of the legend dating from the end of the twelfth century claims that Cyriacus's birth name was Donatus, and, in order to link the martyrdom of St. Ursula with the invasion of the Huns, it makes him the predecessor of Hilary.

■ **Bibliography:** I. Döllinger, *Die Papstfabeln des Mittelalters* (2nd ed. Munich, 1890) 53ff.; W. Levison, *Das Werden der Ursulalegende* (Cologne, 1928) 140-57; C. M. Cusack, *Hagiography and History: The Immense Panorama*. Festschrift for E. J. Sharpe (Sydney, 1999) 89-104.

MANFRED GROTEN

Damasus I (Oct. 1, 366-Dec. 11, 384). Born ca. 305, his Spanish extraction (*LP* 39) is doubtful. Epigrams (Ferrua 57 10 11) attest to his Roman family origins (his father, Antonius, was a deacon and possibly bishop, his mother, Laurentia, and his sister, Irene). As a deacon of the exiled bishop Liberius, Damasus joined the party of Felix, who had been installed by the emperor. Although Liberius pardoned everyone, an unreconciled minority chose Ursinus before the majority elected Damasus. After bloody clashes, the last of which occurred in the basilica of Sicinini (Liberius?), where more than a hundred persons were killed, Ursinus had to give way to pressure from the state. For years his party gave Damasus a lot of trouble (among other things, the capital trial by Isaac the Jew). In 378 Emperor Gratian awarded the Roman bishop in principle the highest jurisdiction over the metropolitans in the West. Damasus cleverly tried not to force things and shared influence with Ambrose. He ignored the call of the Spanish enthusiast Priscillian, but he wrote to the Spanish bishops in the style of the later decretals. Even when his policies (in Antioch, for example, he recognized Paulinus and rejected Meletius) caused irritation and his profession of faith was felt to be insufficiently clear, the creeds and anathemas (lastly in *Tomus Damasi* [378]) that he repeatedly formulated with the Roman synods did lead to a de facto rapprochement with the churches of the Eastern empire, which had been deeply split under Valens (died 378), and to theological agreement (the synod of Antioch [379]; the edict *Cunctos Populos* of Theodosius [380]). While Theodosius I let the Eastern church regulate its own affairs (the synod of Miletius in Antioch [379]; the Council of Constantinople [381]), and Ambrose overcame the remnants of Arianism in the West with the Council of Aquileia in 381 so that an ecumenical council in Rome was not necessary. Damasus emphatically recalled the apostolic-Petrine qualification of the Roman church (synod of 383, preserved in the *Decretum Gelasianum*).

Damasus promoted Jerome's biblical studies and encouraged him to revise the Latin translation of the Bible (Vulgate). Under Damasus a lively period of church building commenced in Rome (*inter alia* three titular churches, many memorials to the martyrs and fifty-nine metrical inscriptions by the pope in "Damasian characters" by Furius Dionysius Philoclaus).

■ **Sources:** *CPL* 1632-36.

■ **Bibliography:** *DACL* 4:145-97; *EC* 4:1136-39; *DHGE* 14:48-53; *DECL* 161-62.; *VATL* 168-69; A. Ferrua, *Epigrammata Damasiana* (Rome, 1842); Caspar 1:196-256; C. Pietri, *Roma christiana*, vol. 1 (Rome, 1976) 407-884;

Saecularia Damasiana: Atti del covegno internazionale per il XVI centenario della morte di papa Damaso I 1984, ed. Pontificio Istituto di Archeologia Christiana (Vatican City, 1986); J. Guyon, "Damase et l'illustration des martyrs," *Martyrium in Multidisciplinary Perspective: Essays in Memory of L. Reekmans* (Louvain, 1995) 157-77; W. D. Hauschild, "Basilius von Caesarea und die Beziehungen zwischen Ostkirche und Rom," in *Geist und Kirche.* Festschrift for E. Lessing (Frankfurt [Main], 1995) 230-48; A. T. Hack, "Zur römischen Doppel-apostolizität," *Hagiographica* 4 (1997) 9-33; M. Saghy, "Prayer at the Tomb of the Martyrs? The Damasian Epigrams," in *La preghiera nel tardo antico* (Rome, 1995) 519-37; G. Wesch-Klein, "Damasus I., der Vater der päpstlichen Epigraphik," in *Quellen, Kritik, Interpretation.* Festschrift for H. Mordek (Frankfurt [Main], 1999) 1-30; U. Reutter, "Damasus, Bischof von Rome (366-384)" (Diss., Jena, 1999).

JAKOB SPEIGL

Damasus II (July 17-August 9, 1048). Formerly *Poppo*, from the Bavarian nobility. He was made bishop of Brixen by King Henry III in 1039; he participated in the latter's march on Rome in 1046 and in the synods of Pavia (October 25, 1046), Sutri (December 20, 1046), and Rome (December 23, 1046). After the death of Clement II, at Christmas 1047 in Pöhlde, he was designated as his successor by Emperor Henry (as a Roman patrician) through a Roman envoy. Since in the meantime the deposed Benedict IX had returned to power, in the spring of 1048 Damasus had to turn back and leave Italy, until Margrave Boniface of Tuscany conducted him to Rome at the direction of the emperor. He was enthroned on July 17; he evidently held on to the see of Brixen. He died twenty-three days later in Palestrina, probably from malaria, although some sources claim he was poisoned by Benedict IX. His tomb is in San Lorenzo Outside the Walls.

■ **Sources:** *LP* 2:274, 332f. (*Annales Romani*); *RPR*(J) 1:528-29; E. Steindorff, *Jahrbücher des deutschen Reiches unter Heinrich III.,* 2 vols. (Leipzig, 1874-81).

■ **Bibliography:** *DHGE* 14:53-54; *LMA* 3:470; K. Guggenberger, *Die deutschen Päpste* (Cologne, 1916) 38ff.; G. Frech, "Die deutschen Päpste," in *Die Salier und das Reich,* ed. S. Weinfurter, vol. 2 (Sigmaringen, 1991) 308-9; K. Mittermaier, *Die deutschen Päpste* (Graz, 1991).

GEORG SCHWAIGER

Deusdedit → Adeodatus

Dionysius (July 22, 259 [260?]-Dec. 26, 267/268?). Saint (feast day Dec. 30; not a martyr). Emperor Gallienus returned to the Christians the cult sites that had been expropriated by Emperor Valerianus. Dionysius was able to reorganize the Roman community, which had been hard hit during the persecution, and most likely founded a stable order of presbyters. At the insistence of the presbyters of Alexandria, Dionysius held a synod in Rome, which spoke out against Bishop Dionysius of Alexandria. In a letter to the church there he presented the doctrine of the Trinity, while rejecting subordinationism and Sabellianism, which the Alexandrian was using to justify himself (Eusebius of Caesarea, *Historia ecclesiastica* 7.26.1; Athanasius, *De decretis Nicaeae synodi,* c. 25-26; *De sententia Dionysii,* c. 13ff.). He sent a letter of consolation and money to the church of Caesarea in Cappadocia, which was suffering from the barbarian invasions (Basilius of Caesarea, *Ep. 70 ad Damasum*). The letter of the synod of Antioch, which had condemned Paul of Samosata, arrived after Dionysius's death (Eusebius 7.30.2). Dionysius is one of the most important popes of the third century. He is buried in the cemetery of Callistus. The authenticity of the documents concerning the so-called dispute of the Dionysii is debated.

■ **Sources:** *LP* 1:157; 3:279; *RPR*(J) 1:22-23; 2:690, 732.

■ **Bibliography:** *DHGE* 14:247-48; *Dizionario patristico e di antichità cristiane,* ed. A. Di Berardino, vol. 1 (Casale Monferrato, 1983) 984-85; *DECL* 183; *RGG,* 4th ed. 2:863; *VATL* 176-77; A. Jülicher, "Kritische Bemerkungen zu den Papstverzeichnissen," in C. Mirbt, *Quellen zur Geschichte des Papsttums* (3rd ed. Tübingen, 1911) 482-83; C. H. Turner, "The Papal Chronology of the Third Century," *Journal of Theological Studies* 17 (1916) 348-49; Caspar 1:620; H. Pietras, "La difesa della monarchia divina da parte del papa Dionigi," *AHP* 28 (1990) 335-42; L. Abramowski, "Dionysius of Rome (†268) and Dionysius of Alexandria (†264/265) in the Arian Controversies of the Fourth Century," in L. Abramowski, ed., *Formula and Context: Studies in Early Christian Thought* (London, 1992) n. 11; R. Davis, "Pre-Constantine Chronology: The Roman Bishopric from AD 258 to 314," *Journal of Theological Studies* 48 (1997) 439-70.

GEORG SCHWAIGER

Dioscurus (Sept. 22-Oct. 14, 530). Formerly a Roman deacon; originally from Alexandria. As an opponent of Monophysitism in Egypt, Dioscurus came to Rome, where he soon came to be held in high regard. In the first three decades of the sixth century he often appears as an intellectual leader of papal policy. In the schism between Pope Symmachus and antipope Symmachus Laurentius, he successfully represented Symmachus before Theoderic the Great (506). Dioscurus was a leading participant in the embassy of Pope Hormisdas to Constantinople, which ended the schism of Acacius in 519. On his deathbed Pope Felix III (IV), in violation of the traditional law, designated Boniface II as his successor. The anti-Gothic majority of the presbyters, which was friendly to Byzantium, elected Dioscurus, who was consecrated on September 22, 530, in the Lateran basilica. The schism was quickly ended, since Dioscurus died soon afterward on October 14. Boniface II pronounced an anathema over the dead man and forced the sixty presbyters who had previously been in the opposition to subscribe to it. Agapitus I had this document publicly burned. Dioscurus is sometimes unfairly considered an antipope.

■ Sources: *LP* 1:282-87; 3:91; *RPR*(J) 1:111-14; 2:694; *Collectio Avellana* Corpus scriptorum ecclesiasticorum latinorum 35 (Vienna, 1895) 105-243.
■ Bibliography: *DHGE* 14:507-8; *DBI* 40:220-24; *VATL* 177-78; Caspar 2:797.

GEORG SCHWAIGER

Donus (Nov. 2, 676-Apr. 11, 678). A Roman, son of Mauritius. The latent schism between Rome and Constantinople continued. A letter of mediation from Emperor Constantine asked the pope to send an embassy, but Donus was dead by the time it arrived. Archbishop Reparatus of Ravenna was evidently prepared to recognize Rome's supreme authority. Donus promoted the building and adornment of churches in Rome.

■ Sources: *LP* 1:348-49; *RPR*(J) 1:238.
■ Bibliography: *DHGE* 14:671-72; *VATL* 185; Caspar 2:585-88.

GEORG SCHWAIGER

Donus II. An early pope counted in the usual list *Donus II* (Domnus, Bonus), generally inserted in 974, came about through an error by chroniclers who took Domnus (= dominus) as a personal name.

■ Sources: *LP* 2:XVII, 256; *RPR*(J) 1:479.

GEORG SCHWAIGER

Eleutherus (174?-189?). Saint (feast day May 26); according to the → *Liber Pontificalis* a Greek from Nicopolis, and a deacon of the Roman church

under Anicetus. According to the oldest list of Roman bishops (Irenaeus of Lyons, *Adversus haereses* 3.3.3) he was the twelfth successor of Peter; he succeeded Bishop Soter. The Christian community in Rome, while externally secure, was disturbed by the heresies of Marcion and the Gnostic Valentinus. During the persecution in Lyons the presbyter Irenaeus brought a letter from the community (on Montanism) to Eleutherus. The report in the *Liber Pontificalis* that a British king named Lucius asked to be allowed to become a king is probably based on the legendary confusion with King Abgar IX of Edessa.

■ Sources: *LP* 1:CIIff.
■ Bibliography: *DHGE* 15:147-48; *VATL* 194-95; A. Harnack, "Der Brief des britischen Königs Lucius an den Papst Eleutherus," *Sitzungsberichte der Preußischen Akademie der Wissenschaften* (Berlin, 1904) 909-16; A. Poncelet, "La translation des Ss. Eleuthère, Pontien et Anastase," *Analecta Bollandiana* 29 (1910) 409-27; Caspar 1:620.

GEORG SCHWAIGER

Eugene I (Aug. 10, 654-June 2, 657). Saint (feast day June 2), a Roman. After Martin I was deposed and exiled by Emperor Constans II, under pressure from the imperial exarch, Eugene was appointed his successor, even while Martin was still alive. In the dispute over Monothelitism, he resumed contacts with Constantinople. Patriarch Peter sent him a compromise formula in 655. The vehement resistance by the clergy and people in Rome prevented Eugene from accepting this formula.

■ Sources: *LP* 2:341.
■ Bibliography: *LMA* 4:77-78; *VATL* 202-3; Caspar 2:547-80; Richards, 191-94.

SEBASTIAN SCHOLZ

Eugene II (beginning June 824-August 827). Elected while archpresbyter of Santa Sabina as the candidate of the Roman nobility, with support from Walas of Corbie, after a long dispute. His notice of election to Emperor Louis the Pious involved Eugene with a sworn promise of fidelity. In the fall of 824 Eugene received Emperor Lothar I, who tried, by means of the *Constitutio Romana*, to end the disorders in Rome and to secure the Frankish power. When the iconoclastic controversy broke out once more, Eugene allowed the Franks to take their own position (synod of Paris [825]), but he himself stuck to the line of Hadrian

I. In November 826 he held a reform synod in Rome, which tackled the canon law traditions and the beginnings of Frankish reform. In 826 he confirmed the missionary charge for northern Europe to Ebo and Ansgar.

■ **Sources:** *LP* 2:69-70; *RPR*(J) 1:320ff.

■ **Bibliography:** *LMA* 4:78; B. Simson, *Jahrbücher des fränkischen Rechts unter Ludwig dem Frommen*, vol. 1 (Leipzig, 1874) 214-15; W. Seegrün, *Das Papsttum und Skandinavien bis zur Vollendung der nordischen Kirchenorganisation (1164)* (Neumünster, 1967) 20-23; T. F. X. Noble, *The Republic of St. Peter* (Philadelphia, 1984) 308-22; W. Hartmann, *Die Synoden der Karolingerzeit im Frankreich und in Italien* (Paderborn, 1989) 168-77; J. Fried, "Ludwig der Fromme, das Papsttum und die fränkische Kirche," in *Charlemagne's Heir*, ed. P. Godman and R. Collins (Oxford, 1990) 231-73.

SEBASTIAN SCHOLZ

Eugene III (Feb. 15, 1145-July 8, 1153). Blessed (since 1872; feast day July 8). A Cistercian (1138). Formerly *Bernard*, born in Pisa, died in Tivoli (tomb in St. Peter's, Rome). In 1115 he became a Camaldolese of St. Zeno (Pisa); in 1128 he became prior and in 1135/37 vice-dominus of the archdiocese. He then entered Cluny, and in 1141 he became abbot of Tre Fontane in Rome. Amid the turmoil of the city he was elected pope and was consecrated in Farfa on February 18. In 1145 he stayed mostly in → Viterbo, where on December 1 he proclaimed the Second Crusade. Despite two agreements (1145 and 1149) his relations with the citizens of Rome remained tense. At the beginning of 1147 Eugene went to the French royal court, where he was supported by Bernard of Clairvaux, whose sermons promoting the crusade and his "mirror of the pope" *De consideratione* helped Eugene on the road to success. He held great synods, in Paris (1147), Trier (1148), Rheims, and Cremona; otherwise he concentrated on the restoration of papal rule in Rome and environs, on negotiations with Conrad III and Frederick I about their imperial coronations, on relations with Roger II of Sicily, on preventing a Byzantine invasion, and the primacy of the pope within the church. The influence of the College of Cardinals on his policies was considerable. The later popes Adrian IV, Alexander III, and Victor IV were among his advisers. The Treaty of Constance of March 23, 1153, was one of his greatest successes.

■ **Sources:** *LP* 2:386-87; *RPR*(J) 2:20-89; *RPR.IP* passim; J. B. Watterich, *Pontificum Romanorum qui fuerunt inde*

ab exeunte saeculo IX usque ad finem saeculi XIII vitae ab aequalibus conscriptae etc., vol. 1 (Leipzig, 1862) 283-321; Hohn of Salisbury, *Historia pontificalis*, ed. M. Chibnall (London, 1956); *Bibliotheca rerum Germanicarum*, ed. P. Jaffé, vol. 1 (repr. Aalen, 1964).

■ **Bibliography:** *LMA* 4:78ff.; *VATL* 203-4; H. Gleber, *Papst Eugen III. (1145-53)* (Jena, 1936); M. Maccarrone, *Papato ed impero dalla elezione di Federico I alla morte di Adriano IV* (Rome, 1956); F.-J. Schmalle, "Das Papsttum im Zeitalter Bernhards von Clairvaux und der frühen Staufer," *GKG* 11:176-95; O. Engels, "Zum Konstanzer Vertrag von 1153," in *Deus qui mutat tempora*. Festschrift for A. Becker (Sigmaringen, 1987) 235-58; C. D. G. Spornick, *The Life and Reign of Pope Eugene III* (Ann Arbor, 1988); M. Horn, *Studien zur Geschichte Papst Eugens III. (1145-53)* (Frankfurt [Main], 1992); R. Hiestand, "Von Troyes—oder Trier?—nach Reims: Zur Generalsynode Eugens III. im Frühjahr 1148," in *Papstgeschichte und Landesgeschichte*. Festschrift for H. Jakobs (Cologne, 1995) 329-48.

JOHANNES LAUDAGE

Eugene IV (Mar. 3, 1431-Feb. 23, 1447). Augustinian hermit, formerly *Gabriele Condulmer*, a nephew of Gregory XII, born in Venice in 1383, the scion of a Venetian merchant family, whose upbringing was influenced by the spirit of Augustinianism. Co-founder of the Congregation of San Giorgio in Alga, he went through the curial *cursus honorum*. In 1407 he was made bishop of Siena, in 1408 cardinal priest of San Clemente. Elected pope thanks to a compromise between the Orsini and the Colonna, and crowned on March 3, 1431, Eugene revived the crisis of the papacy as in the pre-1417 period of schism, when he tactlessly opposed the College of → Cardinals and formed a front against conciliar tendencies in the church by dissolving the Council of Basel, which had been called by his predecessor, in December 1431. Faced with massive resistance, he had to revoke his decision on December 15, 1433, and recognize the council. Disputes with conciliarism became the leitmotif of his papacy. When pressure increased from the Basel negotiations, which brought forth insuperable conflicts especially on the question of union with the Greek churches, he shifted the synod to Ferrara, his immediate sphere of influence (1437), and finally to Florence. The break became definitive when the members of the synod, who had stayed behind in Basel, deposed him on June 25, 1439, and elected a new pope, Felix V. But Eugene achieved his most important success with the completion of the Church Union

(July 5, 1439), whose effects were admittedly limited, but which won him prestige in the eyes of secular rulers, who mistrusted the idea of church parliament. While the pope, supported by brilliant canon lawyers and promoted by the granting of privileges and the concluding of a concordat for individual countries, was to prevail against Basel and the conciliar pope, he nevertheless had to make still further concessions to the secular rulers (as early as the Pragmatic Sanction of Bourges, 1438). Recognition by Emperor Frederick III and the electoral princes (1445-1447) finally secured his administration. His Italian policy had little success, since it lacked a consistent approach to the dominant powers there (especially Milan, Anjou, and Aragon), and alternated between the brutal use of force and sheer indecisiveness. Receptive to the promotion of education and humanistic trends, in the end Eugene could not shed his demonstrable mediocrity. Any chance of having a successful, necessarily flexible ecclesiastical policy was blocked by his stubborn clinging to the papal *plenitudo potestatis*, as well as the monastic severity he had practiced since his youth.

■ **Sources:** *Reportorium Germanicum*, ed. Deutsches Historisches Institut in Rom, vol. 1 (Berlin/Tübingen, 1916); G. Feadlto, *Acta Eugenii Papae IV* (Rome, 1990).

■ **Bibliography:** *DHGE* 15:1353-59; *LMA* 4:80ff.; J. Gill, *Eugenius IV, Pope of Christian Union* (London, 1961); W. Brandmüller, "Der Übergang vom Pontifikat Martins V. zu Eugen IV.," *QFIAB* 47 (1967) 596-629; J. W. Stieber, *Pope Eugenius IV, The Council of Basel and the Secular and Ecclesiastical Authorities in the Empire* (Leiden, 1978); B. Schwarz, "Die Abbreviatoren unter Eugen IV.," *QFIAB* 60 (1980) 200-274; R. Reinhardt, "Martin V. und Eugen IV.," *GKG* 12:27-38; J. Helmrath, *Das Basler Konzil (1431-49)* (Cologne/Vienna, 1987); Borgolte 267ff.; H. Müller, *Die Franzosen, Frankreich und das Basler Konzil (1431-49)*, 2 vols. (Paderborn, 1990); E. Meuthen, "Eugen IV: Ferrara-Florenz und der lateinische Westen," *AHC* 22 (1990) 219-33; H. Thurn, "Inhaltsanalyse eines Traktats des Giuliano Ceasarini für Papst Eugen IV. gegen das Konzil von Basel," in *De iure canonico medii aevii*. Festschrift for R. Weigand (Rome, 1996) 559-71.

LUDWIG VONES

Eusebius (Apr. 18-Aug. 17, 308 [309? 310?]). Saint (feast day Aug. 17), venerated as a martyr; according to the *Liber Pontificalis*, a Greek. The dispute, which had already broken out under Marcellus I over the *lapsi* in the persecution of Diocletian,

continued during his pontificate. The scanty tradition permits some relatively certain statements only about the brief duration of Eusebius's tenure in office (*Catalogus Liberianus*). After Damasus I, Eusebius seems to have permitted the readmission of the lapsed Christians after an appropriate period of penance, whereas Heraclius, the head of an opposition group, "forbade" this. Emperor Maxentius had Eusebius and Heraclius deported to Sicily, where Eusebius soon died. He was later interred in the catacomb of Callistus.

■ **Sources:** *LP* 1:CVIIff., 8ff., 74-75, 167; 3:284.

■ **Bibliography:** *DHGE* 15:1433; *HKG* 1:386-87; A. Jülicher, "Kritische Bemerkungen zu den Papstverzeichnissen," in C. Mirbt, *Quellen zur Geschichte des Papsttums* (3rd ed. Tübingen, 1911) 482-83; Caspar 1:99-100, 128-29; A. Ferrua, *Epigrammata Damasiana* (Rome, 1942) 129-36; B. Kriegbaum, "Die Religionspolitik des Kaisers Maxentius," *AHP* 30 (1992) 7-54; L. Reekmans, "Les tombeaux des papes Gaius (283-296) et Eusèbe (309 ou 310) et des martyrs Calocerus et Parthenius dans la catacombe Calliste," in *Memoriam Sanctorum venerantes*. Festschrift for V. Saxer (Rome, 1992) 689-709; R. Davis, "Pre-Constantine Chronology: The Roman Bishopric from AD 258 to 314," *Journal of Theological Studies* 48 (1997) 439-70.

GEORG SCHWAIGER

Eutychianus (Jan. 4, 274 [275?]-Dec. 7, 282 [283?]). Saint (feast day Dec. 7, not a martyr). According to the *Liber Pontificalis,* he was a son of Marinus from Tuscany. The Roman church managed in this period to spread and consolidate itself, as the significant expansions of the burial sites in the catacombs attest. Reports are lacking; the documents ascribed to him are inauthentic. He is the last pope to be buried in the papal vault in the catacomb of Callistus (burial inscription discovered).

■ **Sources:** *LP* 1:CXXXI-CLX, 6-7, 10, 159-60; 3:75, 285.

■ **Bibliography:** *DHGE* 16:91-92; *VATL* 206-7; J. Wilpert, *Die Papstgräber und die Cäciliengruft in der Katakombe des heiligen Kallistus* (Freiburg, 1909) 19-20, 35; A. Jülicher, "Kritische Bemerkungen zu den Papstverzeichnissen," in C. Mirbt, *Quellen zur Geschichte des Papsttums* (3rd ed. Tübingen, 1911) 482-83; Caspar 1:43, 84; R. Davis, "Pre-Constantine Chronology: The Roman Bishopric from AD 258 to 314," *Journal of Theological Studies* 48 (1997) 439-70.

GEORG SCHWAIGER

Evaristus (Euaristos; in the *Catalogus Liberianus,* Aristus) (101?-107?). Saint (feast day Oct. 26). According to the oldest Roman bishops' list (Irenaeus of Lyons, *Adversus haereses* 3.3.3), he was the fourth successor of Peter, who, according to calculations of the third and fourth centuries, is said to have guided the Roman community for about eight to thirteen years as its bishop (after Anacletus I and Clement I and before Alexander I). The name points to Greek extraction. Although the system of a single monarchical episcopate had not yet developed, he certainly enjoyed a leading position under the presbyters (*episcopi*). Nothing further is known about him.

■ **Sources:** *LP* 1:XC-XCI, 126; 3:72, 285.

■ **Bibliography:** Caspar 1:8, 13, 53.

GEORG SCHWAIGER

Fabianus (Jan. 10, 236-Jan. 20, 250). Saint (feast day Jan. 20). A Roman, son of Fabianus. After the unrest and the brief, harsh persecution of Christians by Emperor Maximus Thrax, Fabianus succeeded in solidifying and organizing the expansion of the Roman church in the period of peace before the persecution of Decius. Fabianus divided Rome into seven ecclesiastical administrative districts, which were subject to seven deacons (*MGH. AA* 9/1, 75), and devoted particular care to the cemeteries. The impression made by his personality is attested to by, among others, Cyprian of Carthage (*Ep.* 9.1), Novatian (Cyprian, *Ep.* 30.5), laudatory legends (Macarius Magnes, *Aposcriticus* 3.24), and Eusebius of Caesaria, *Historia ecclesiastica* 6.29). Origen sent Cyprian a letter of self-justification (Jerome, *Ep.* 84.10). Fabianus died as one of the first victims of Decius's persecution; he was buried in the catacomb of Callistus (his sarcophagus was discovered in 1915).

■ **Sources:** *LP* 1:4, 148-49; 3:74, 285; *RPR*(J) 1:15ff.

■ **Bibliography:** *DACL* 5:1058-64; *DHGE* 16:317-18; *BiblSS* 5:426-29; *Dizionario patristico e di antichità cristiane*, ed. A. Di Berardino, vol. 1 (Casale Monferrato, 1983) 1326; *VATL* 210; J. Wilpert, *Die Papstgräber und die Cäciliengruft in der Katakombe des heiligen Kallistus* (Freiburg, 1909) 18-19; F. Grossi-Gondi, *San Fabiano* (Rome, 1916); U. Stutz, "Die römischen Titelkirchen und die Verfassung der stadtrömischen Kirche unter Papst Fabianus," *Zeitschrift der Savigny-Stiftung für Rechtsgeschichte. Kanonistische Abteilung* 9 (1919) 288-312; Caspar 1:621-22; O. Bertolini, "Per la storia delle diaconie romane," *Archivio della Società Romana di Storia Patria* 70 (1947) 1-2.

GEORG SCHWAIGER

Felix I (Jan. 5, 268 [269?]-Dec. 30, 273 [274?]). Saint (feast day May 30). He was not a martyr.

According to the *Liber Pontificalis,* he was a Roman, the son of Constantine; he entered the church community with Bishop Domnus of Antioch (Syria), the successor of the deposed Paul of Samosata. Emperor Aurelian decided that the bishop would occupy the episcopal residence of Antioch, which Paul did not wish to leave, with which "the bishops of Italy and the city of Rome stand in connection" (Eusebius of Caesarea, *Historia ecclesiastica* 7.30). Further reports about Felix are uncertain or forged. He is buried in the catacomb of Callistus.

■ **Sources:** *LP* 1:CXXV, 158; 3:75, 286; *RPR*(J) 1:23; 2:690.

■ **Bibliography:** *DHGE* 16:886-87; *VATL* 213-14; A. Jülicher, "Kritische Bemerkungen zu den Papstverzeichnissen," in C. Mirbt, *Quellen zur Geschichte des Papsttums* (3rd ed. Tübingen, 1911) 482-83; C. H. Turner, "The Papal Chronology of the Third Century," *Journal of Theological Studies* 17 (1916) 349; G. P. Kirsch, "Le memorie dei martiri nelle vie Aurelia e Cornelia," *Studi e Testi* 38 (1924) 63-100; Caspar 1:621-22; R. Davis, "Pre-Constantine Chronology: The Roman Bishopric from AD 258 to 314," *Journal of Theological Studies* 48 (1997) 439-70.

GEORG SCHWAIGER

Felix (II) (antipope) (355-358). After the exile of Liberius, the Roman clergy along with Archdeacon Felix swore not to recognize another bishop so long as Liberius was alive. Nevertheless after a few months Felix allowed himself to be appointed pope by Emperor Constantius II, and he was consecrated in the imperial palace in Rome by three Arian bishops. Felix entered into communion with the Arians, but found support only from the Roman clergy and hardly at all from the people. After the return of Liberius in 358, the emperor wanted both bishops to rule jointly, but after bloody riots Felix was soon driven out. After the failure of a violent attempt to return, Felix could stay only in the region around Rome, but up until his death on November 22, 365 (on his estate near Porto), he never gave up his claims. Liberius strove to be reconciled with Felix's supporters. Since the sixth century, Felix, who violated his oath, has been regarded as the legal pope, and, through a series of confusions, he has been celebrated as a holy martyr (feast day July 29), while Liberius has been represented as a traitor.

■ **Sources:** *LP* 1:CXXIIIff., 211; 3:57ff., 82, 286; *RPR*(J) 1:35-36; Corpus scriptorum ecclesiasticorum latinorum 35 (Vienna, 1995) 1-4.

■ **Bibliography:** *DHGE* 16:887ff.; *LMA* 4:340; *VATL* 214; I. von Döllinger, *Die Papst-Fabeln des Mittleralters* (2nd ed. Stuttgart, 1890) 126-45; L. Saltet, "La formation de la légende des papes Libère et Félix," *Bulletin de littérature ecclésiastique* 20 (1905) 222-36; J. P. Kirsch, "Die Grabstätte des 'Felices duo pontifices et martyres' an der Via Aurelia," *RQ* 28 (1925) 1-20; Caspar 1:621; A. Dilhe, *L'Église et l'Empire au IVᵉ siècle* (Geneva, 1989).

GEORG SCHWAIGER

Felix II (III) (Mar. 13, 483-Mar. 1, 492). Saint (feast day Mar. 1). Son of the presbyter Felix of the Roman nobility; previously married, an ancestor of Gregory the Great; elected thanks to the influence of King Odoacer (see *MGH.AA* 12:445). The West was afflicted by the storms of the barbarian invasions (conquest of Italy by Theoderic the Great; in Africa persecution of Catholics by the Arian Vandals). In the East the popular disturbances over the Council of Chalcedon persisted through the Henotikon of Emperor Zeno of 482. Felix demanded the removal of Patriarch Peter III Mongus of Alexandria, and through the Roman synod of 484 he excommunicated and deposed Patriarch Acacius of Constantinople, the author of the Henotikon (Corpus scriptorum ecclesiasticorum latinorum 35 [Vienna, 1895] 155-61). Acacius then removed the pope's name from the diptychs, resulting in the first schism between Rome and the East (until 519). In 487 a Roman synod issued rules about penances for those who had apostatized in Vandal-controlled areas. Felix appears to have been a powerful personality. He attended to the Catholics who had been persecuted by the Vandals and decisively opposed the pressures from the emperor's tutelage. His secretary archdeacon, later Pope Gelasius, continued to work out the distinction between secular and spiritual authority.

■ **Sources:** *LP* 1:252ff.; 3:87, 286; *RPR*(J) 1:80-83; 2:693, 736; A. Thiel, ed., *Epp. Romanorum Pontificum Genuine*, vol. 1 (Braunsberg, 1867; repr. Hildesheim, 1974) 221-84; E. Schwartz, *Publizistische Sammlung zum Akazianischen Schisma* (Munich, 1934) 202-19.

■ **Bibliography:** *LMA* 4:340; *DHGE* 16:889-95; *VATL* 214-25; Caspar 2:24-44; J.T. Milik, "La famiglia di Felice III papa," *Epigrafica* 28 (1966) 140ff.; W. Ullmann, *Gelasius I* (Stuttgart, 1981); P. Nautin, "La lettre de Félix III à André de Thessalonique et sa doctrine sur l'Église et l'Empire," *Revue d'histoire ecclésiastique* 77 (1982) 5-34; idem, "La lettre 'Diabolicae artis' de Félix III aux moines de Constantinople et de Bithynie," *Revue des Études Augustiniennes* 30 (1984) 263-68.

GEORG SCHWAIGER

Felix III (IV) (July 12, 526-Sept. 22, 530). Saint (first accepted into the Roman Martyrology by Caesar Baronius). A son of Castorinus from Samnium. After the death of John I, amid the dispute between the Byzantine and Gothic parties, Theoderic the Great ordered the election of the Roman deacon Felix. In 519 he had taken part in the papal embassy to Constantinople that succeeded in ending the Acacian schism. He ruled in peace with the Ostrogoths (hence the royal court privilege for the Roman clergy, ca. 527; the framework in the Forum for erecting the Church of Saints Cosmas and Damian), and he supported Caesarius of Arles in the struggle against semi-Pelagianism, sending him a *capitula* on the doctrine of grace (taken from Augustinian texts), which Caesarius accepted at the synod of Orange in 529. We owe the mosaics in Sts. Cosmas and Damian to Felix. On his deathbed he (noncanonically) designated Boniface II as his successor, which led to the intervention of the senate and to the double election (Dioscurus).

■ **Sources:** *LP* 1:270, 279-80; 3:91, 286; *RPR*(J) 1:110-11; 2:694-737.

■ **Bibliography:** *DHGE* 16:895-96; *LMA* 4:340-42; *VATL* 215-16; L. Duchesne, "La succession du pape Félix IV," *Mélanges d'archéologie et d'histoire* 3 (1883) 239-66; Caspar 2:798; Borgolte 74f.

GEORG SCHWAIGER

Felix V (antipope). Born September 4, 1383, in Chambéry; died on January 1, 1451, in Geneva. After a long and successful (especially as a legislator) rule as count and duke of Savoy, Amadeus VIII withdrew in 1434, along with the knights of order of Mauritius, which he had founded, into the princely hermitage of Ripaille on Lake Geneva, but he continued to exercise influence on the government. His election as pope by the Council of Basel on November 5, 1439, against the deposed Eugene IV may well have taken place in contact with the leading council fathers from the territory of Savoy-Lyons, especially Cardinal Louis Aleman. This was preceded by a massive influx of Savoyard clergy into the synod. His pontificate soon proved to be a disappointment to both sides, because Felix, who wished in this way to crown his own career and the glory of his house, hardly shared the radical ideas of the council and was put out of sorts by its hesitant supply of beneficiaries and rights. For his part, he brought the synod neither the financial support nor above all hoped-for political support from the most important political powers, who in the wake of a Western schism were horrified by the prospect of another split in the church. In 1443, when Aragon, Milan, and Scotland also announced their obedience to him, this was obviously reduced to the "replacement papal state" of Savoy, where Felix had been residing since November 1442, mostly in Lausanne, and where in 1444 he also assumed the administration of the diocese of Geneva. In the course of the liquidation of the council, which was mostly carried out by France, on April 7, 1449, Felix too was moved into retirement (under richly privileged conditions). Until his death, Nicholas V let him, among others, preside as a permanent delegate and vicar in the domain that had formerly been under his authority.

■ Bibliography: *DHGE* 16:896; *LMA* 4:341; *VATL* 216-17; E. Mongiano, *La cancelleria di un antipapa. Il bollario di Felice V (Amedeo VIII di Savoia)* (Turin, 1988); H. Müller, *Die Franzosen, Frankreich und das Basler Konzil (1431-49)*, 2 vols. (Paderborn, 1990); F. Cognasso, *Amedeo VIII* (Milan, 1991); B. Andenmatten, ed., "Amédé VIII—Félix V: Premier duc de Savoie et pape," in *Colloque international Ripalle-Lausanne, 1990* (Lausanne, 1992) (esp. J. W. Stieber).

HERIBERT MÜLLER

Formosus (Oct. 3, 891 - Apr. 4, 896). Born ca. 816, Formosus began his ecclesiastical career as bishop of Porto near Rome (874-876), proving himself to be a gifted, ambitious assistant to the popes, above all through several legations: in 866 he was part of the mission to the Bulgarians (his appointment as archbishop of Bulgaria came to grief on the resistance of Nicholas I); he was present on papal commissions in Constantinople; and he held negotiations with different Frankish rulers. John VIII (872-882), with whom Formosus, according to Lapôtre, had perhaps already competed at the time of John's elevation to the papacy, excommunicated Formosus on April 19, 876, supposedly because of a conspiracy against the emperor and the pope. Formosus fled to the kingdom of the West Franks; the ban was renewed at the synods of Ponthion (July 876) and Troyes (August 878) (in 878 he was admitted to lay communion). He was reinstated in Porto by Marianus I in 883-884. On April 10, 891, Formosus himself became pope (as an already consecrated bishop in the form of an "inthronizatio," which, however, is not attested

until later polemics). Formosus came into contact with the most important centers of the *orbis christiana*: with England (in matters concerning the appointment of episcopal seats and the primate of Canterbury), with Catalonia (Gerona) with the East Frankish church (especially on account of the dispute over whether Bremen belonged to the royal province of Cologne or to Hamburg), and also with the Western Frankish kingdom (particularly in the dispute between Odo and Charles the Simple over the succession to the throne). However, Formosus failed finally to ease the tensions with Byzantium. In Italy and Rome his relations with the Spoleto party after the imperial coronation of Wido III and his son Lambert (April 30, 892, with the conclusion of a pact) became increasingly problematic (see the entry in the alliance book of Remiremont). On account of this threat, Formosus turned above all against the East Frankish king Arnulf (imperial coronation February 896). After Formosus's death Stephen VI had his corpse exhumed and at the synod of 896/897 posthumously condemned him, in particular because Formosus had violated the ban on *translatio*. Further, Stephen declared his consecration null and void. Theodore II and John IX (Council of Ravenna in 898) revoked this judgment, but the disputes over the validity of Formosus's ordinations continued into the pontificates of Sergius II and John X. The writings of the apologists for Formosus (Auxilius of Naples, Eugenius Vulgaris, and the anonymous "Invectiva in Romam") have been preserved; they praise the pope's piety and learning over against his opponents.

■ **Sources:** *LP* 2:227; 3:288; *RPR*(J) 1:435-39; 2:705, 746; *MGH.Ep.* 7:366-70; Auxilius of Naples, *PL* 129:1037-1102; E. Dümmler, *Auxilius u. Vulgarius* (Leipzig, 1866); *Invectiva in Romam,* ed. E. Dümmler, Gesta Berengarii (Halle, 1871) 137-54.

■ **Bibliography:** *VATL* 225ff.; G. Domenici, "Il papa Formosus," *La civiltà cattolica* 75 (1924) 1:106-20, 518-36; 2:121-35; D. Pop, *La défense du pape Formosus* (Paris, 1933); I. Dujcev, *Medioevo Bizantino-Slavo,* vol. 1 (Rome, 1965) 149-81, 548-51; G. Arnaldi, "Papa Formosus e gli imperatori della casa di Spoleto," *Annali della Fac. di Lettere. Università di Napoli* 1 (1951) 85-104; H. Zimmermann *Pa,* 49-73; A. Lapôtre, *Études sur la Papauté au IXe siècle.,* ed. A. Vauchez, vol. 1 (Turin, 1978) 1-120; V. Peri, "Le ricerche di P. Arthur Lapôtre sulla politica dei Papi alla fine del IX secolo," *Rivista di storia della Chiesa in Italia* 36 (1982) 125-45; *LMA* 4:655-56 (bibl.) (K. Herbers); Borgolte 125; W. Hartmann, *Die*

Synoden der Karolingerzeit im Frankenreich und in Italien (Paderborn, 1989) 389-96; S. Scholz, *Transmigration und Translation* (Cologne, 1992) 216-42; M. Bacchiega, *Papa Formoso* (2nd ed. Foggia, 1998).

KLAUS HERBERS

Gaius (also known as Caius) (Dec. 17, 282 [283?]- Apr. 22, 295 [296?]). Saint (feast day Apr. 22; not a martyr). According to *Liber Pontificalis*, he came from Dalmatia, but this is uncertain. He reigned during a period of peace for the church, before the persecution of Diocletian. Reliable lists of dates of ordination begin with Gaius. He was buried in the catacomb of Callistus, and the inscription on his tomb survives. The legend of Susanna (ca. sixth century) makes him Susanna's uncle and a relative of the emperor Diocletian, linking Pope Gaius to the founder of the *titulus Gaii*. He also plays a role in the *Passion of Saint Sebastian*.
- **Sources:** *LP* 3:291 (index); *RPR(J)* 1:25.
- **Bibliography:** *DHGE* 11:237f.; G. B. de Rossi, *Roma sotterranea* (Rome, 1877) 3:114-20; J. Wilpert, *Die Papstgräber und die Cäciliengruft in der Katakombe des heiligen Kallistus* (Freiburg, 1909) 23f., 30; A. Jülicher, "Kritische Bemerkungen zu den Papstverzeichnissen," in C. Mirbt, *Quellen zur Geschichte des Papsttum* (3rd ed. Tübingen, 1911) 482f.; C. H. Turner, "The Papal Chronology of the Third Century," *Journal of Theological Studies* 17 (1916) 350f.; J. P. Kirsch, *Die römischen Titelkirchen im Altertum* (Paderborn, 1918) 70-74, 152ff.; Caspar 1:621; L. Reekmans, "Les tombeaux des papes Gaius (283-296) et Eusèbe (309 ou 310) et les martyrs Calocerus et Parthenius dans la catacombe Calliste," in *Memoriam Sanctorum venerantes*, Festschrift for V. Saxer (Rome, 1992) 689-709; R. Davis, "Pre-Constantine Chronology: The Roman Bishopric from AD 258 to 314," *Journal of Theological Studies* 48 (1997) 439-70.

GEORG SCHWAIGER

Gelasius I (Mar. 1, 492-Nov. 19, 496). Saint (feast day Nov. 21). Born in Rome. As archdeacon and secretary, he was already active in church politics as writer and counselor under his predecessors Simplicius and Felix III. After King Theoderic I assumed power in 493, Gelasius had close connections with the east Gothic court. During the Acacian schism, his unyielding stance gave proof of his steadfast resistance to the caesaropapist tendencies of the east Roman emperors: Gelasius insisted that Acacius's name be deleted from the diptychs in Constantinople, with the result that the schism lasted until 519. In support of his position, he developed the doctrine of the "two powers" (*utraque potestas*), first outlined in *Letter 12* to the emperor Anastasius I and fully developed in his fourth treatise, in which he emphasized the equally divine origin of the kingship (*regnum*) and the priesthood (*sacerdotium*) and distinguished their spheres of responsibility. Gelasius acknowledged that the *regnum* is responsible for the secular sphere, but he insisted that it was subordinate, in terms of its responsibility vis-à-vis God, to the *sacerdotium,* to which "divine matters" are entrusted. Gelasius's doctrine of the two powers had a decisive influence, in the form of the theory of the "two swords," on the medieval definition of the relationship between church and state.

Gelasius wrote six theological treatises: one against Pelagianism (*Dicta adversus Pelagianam haeresim*), one against the pagan Lupercalia, and four against Monophysitism. Numerous letters and decretals bear his name (more than one hundred complete or fragmentary texts). The so-called *Decretum Gelasianum de recipiendis et non recipiendis libris* and the sacramentary to which Walafried Strabo gave the name *Sacramentarium Gelasianum* have been shown to be pseudepigraphical.
- **Sources:** *CPL* 1667-75; *PL* 59:9-190; *PLS* 3:739-87; A. Thiel, ed., *Epp. Romanorum Pontificum Genuinae* (Braunsberg, 1867; repr. Hildesheim, 1974) 1:285-613; E. Schwartz, *Publizistische Sammlung zum Akazianischen Schisma* (Munich, 1934: contains *Epp. 3*, 8-10, 12, 27, 45, and *Tractatus* II-IV); H. de Lubac and J. Daniélou, eds. Sources chrétiennes 65 (Paris, 1960).
- **Bibliography:** *DHGE* 20:284-94; *TRE* 12:273-76; *LMA* 4:1197; F. Dvornik, "Pope Gelasius and Emperor Anastasius," *Byzantinische Zeitschrift* 44 (1951) 111-16; W. Ensslin, "Auctoritas und Potestas: Zur Zweigewaltenlehre des Papstes Gelasius I.," *Historisches Jahrbuch* 75 (1955) 661-68; A. W. J. Hollemann, *Pope Gelasius I and the Lupercalia* (Amsterdam, 1974); W. Ullmann, *Gelasius I (492-496)* (London, 1979); G. Mancuso, "'Auctoritas sacrata pontificis' e 'auctoritas principis,'" *Apollinaris* 68 (1995) 193-204; P. G. Caron, "L'interpretazione della Lettera gelasiana nel pensiero e nell'azione dei papi del duecento," in Festschrift for P. Bellini (Catanzaro, 1999) 161-74.

MARIO SPINELLI

Gelasius II (Jan. 24, 1118-Jan. 29, 1119). Formerly *John of Gaeta*. He was an oblate and monk in Montecassino and a pupil of Alberich of Montecassino, where he composed a number of biographies. He may have been the nephew of John III, cardinal bishop of Tusculum. He was appointed subdeacon and *prosignator* of Urban II on August 23, 1088, and cardinal deacon on September 23, 1098. He was papal chancellor no later than July 1, 1089; he introduced the *cursus* and may have been hostile to the monks of Cluny. Santa Maria in Cosmedin, which he restored, is first attested as his titular church in a document dated November 30, 1101. He returned to Montecassino in 1116. On the death of Paschal II, the cardinal bishop Peter of Porto brought him back to Rome. He was elected pope in Santa Maria in Pallaria and ordained bishop on March 3, 1118, in Gaeta. He fled from the Frangipani to France in September 1118. He was unyielding on the investiture question. He died in Cluny and was buried there.

■ **Sources:** *PL* 163:473-514 (biography and letters); *LP* 2:311-21; L. A. Muratori, *Rerum Italicarum scriptores ab anno aerae christianae 500 ad 1500* (Milan, 1723) 3:417f. (biography).

■ **Bibliography:** *LMA* 4:1197f.; *VATL* 248f.; R. Krohn, *Der päpstliche Kanzler Johannes von Gaëta* (dissertation, Marburg, 1918); O. Engels, "Papst Gelasius II. als Hagiograph," *QFIAB* 35 (1955) 1-45; idem, "Die hagiographischen Texte Papst Gelasius' II. in der Überlieferung der Eustachius-, Erasmus- u. Hypolistuslegende," *Historisches Jahrbuch* 76 (1957) 118-33; D. Lohrmann, "Die Jugendwerke des Johannes von Gaëta," *QFIAB* 47 (1967) 355-445; R. Hüls, *Kardinäle, Klerus und Kirchen Roms, 1049-1130* (Tübingen, 1977) 231f.; H. E. J. Cowdrey, *The Age of Abbot Desiderius* (Oxford, 1983); R. Volpini, "Documenta nel 'Sancta sanctorum' del Laterano: I resti dell' 'Archivio' di Gelasio II," *Lateran* 52 (1986) 215-64; F. Dolbeau, "Recherches sur les oeuvres littéraires du pape Gélase II," *Analecta Bollandiana* 107 (1989) 65-127, 347-83; K. Schreiner, "Gregor VIII., nackt auf einem Esel," in *Ecclesia et regnum,* Festschrift for F.-J. Schmale (Bochum, 1989) 155-202; G. Andrisani, "Gelasio II a Capua," *Benedictina* 40 (1993) 35-47.

ODILO ENGELS

Gregory I, the Great (590-Mar. 12, 604). Saint (feast day Sept. 3). Born 540 in Rome.
1. *Historical Personage.* — 2. *Life.* — 3. *Pontificate.* — 4. *Missionary Activity.* — 5. *Theological Work.*

1. *Historical Personage*
"God's consul" came from a very wealthy family, to which two earlier popes, Felix III and Agapitus I, had belonged. He is one of the four great doctors of the Latin church; Pope Boniface VIII

bestowed this title on Ambrose of Milan, Augustine, Jerome, and Gregory in 1295. One might describe him as a Janus-figure who looks backward into the classical period and forward into the early Middle Ages: he is the "last Roman" and the first medieval pope.

The Latin West had looked to Eastern Rome in earlier times, but all that now remained of this cultural and political link was the exarchate of Ravenna. The Frankish kingdom had risen since the reign of Clovis to become the dominant power with which other powers in western Europe had to reckon. The Rome of late antiquity had no political role in the interplay between Byzantium, the Langobards, the Franks, and the Goths. Against the background of the Roman heritage, Gregory fashioned a position for the West that was independent of Byzantium. By retaining those elements of the classical past that were of use to the faithful, while at the same time adapting the positive elements produced up to that time by the Christian Latin culture, Gregory brought about a turning point in the history of Christian culture.

In his old age, Gregory was oppressed by a pessimism that led him often to speak of "the world growing old" (*mundus senescens*). This undercurrent is particularly clear in the "funeral sermon" he preached about Rome in 592, when the city was besieged yet again by the Langobards.

2. *Life*
In his youth, Gregory received a thorough education in grammar, rhetoric, and administrative law. He became prefect of the city, the highest official of the civil government of Rome, in 572/573. This made him very familiar with the problems connected with the city's food supply (*annona*), with public order, the state of the buildings, and the maintenance of the city walls. His organizational talent, which developed to meet these challenges, was a great help throughout his later pontificate. Despite his success as an administrative official, he soon withdrew to the family palace on the Clivus Scauri, where he founded a monastic community dedicated to St. Andrew. The sources do not allow us to determine whether Gregory himself was abbot. He was ordained deacon in 578/579 by Benedict I or Pelagius II and was sent as apocrisiary (nuncio) to the imperial court at Constantinople, where he forged important political ties. He returned to the monastery of St. Andrew in

585/586. The year 590 was one of catastrophes, with the plague and the flooding of the Tiber; on the death of Pope Pelagius II, Gregory was elected bishop of Rome. His reluctance to accept ordination, documented in several of his letters, recalls the customary rhetorical expressions of humility.

3. *Pontificate*

Although he emphatically bewailed his frequent illnesses, Gregory worked energetically. As a pastoral pragmatist, he solved the problem of the Langobards by paying a large sum of gold from the Patrimony of Peter; the east Roman emperor Maurice reproached him vigorously for buying peace from Agilulf in this manner, and withheld his support from Gregory in the controversy of the Three Chapters.

He reorganized the papal curia in the synod of 595 and accepted only clerics and monks as collaborators, entrusting a special role to the *vicedominus,* who was charged with organizing and overseeing the episcopal residence of his patriarchate. Within the sphere of his direct influence, Gregory wished to see only bishops with a high sense of responsibility. He appointed only bishops who matched the profile he had elaborated in his *Pastoral Rule,* even where this meant a departure from the previous praxis of the ancient church. Every attempt at simony was ruthlessly suppressed.

Gregory himself administered the extensive lands which the Roman church owned, drawing on the collaboration of Bishop Januarius, the deacon Peter, and the subdeacon Antemius. Church properties in Lower Italy, Sicily, Sardinia, Gaul, Dalmatia, and northern Africa were reorganized in detail. The tenants were given credits, and their rent was kept within acceptable limits. Gregory gave the rectors of the individual regions (most of whom were subdeacons) lists of the bribes to be paid to the various grades of corrupt officials in the exarchate of Ravenna. The income from the domains of the Patrimony which these measures generated were employed primarily for charitable purposes, such as coping with the problem of refugees in Rome. His intervention in Cagliari demonstrated that he was ready to help the Jews.

His pastoral responsibility led Gregory to preach frequently and gladly. When his voice broke down, a notary read aloud the sermon that the pope had prepared.

Gregory's vigorous opposition to the title *patriarcha oikoumenikos,* which had been assumed by the see of Constantinople, was based on a misunderstanding. His own title, *servus servorum Dei,* which all his successors have adopted, expressed his biblical ideal (Mk 10:44).

4. *Missionary Activity*

Gregory displayed prudent reserve in his dealings with Spain. He maintained contact with Bishop Leander of Seville, who had brought about a profound improvement in relations between the bishops and the kingdom of the western Goths after the conversion of Reccared. Through his contacts with Queen Theodelinde, Gregory paved the way for the conversion of the Langobards to the Catholic Church. His dealings with the Frankish bishops were marked by friendly tact. He succeeded in creating a basis for the Anglo-Saxon mission by suggesting reforms to Queen Brunhilde, but without mentioning the bloody feuds in her family. His letters to high-ranking persons were always accompanied by noble gifts from his treasuries of relics. He gave the monk Augustine, from the monastery of St. Andrew in Rome, precise instructions when he sent him to England: the missionaries were directed to take existing pre-Christian practices as their point of departure, not destroying sanctuaries but transforming them into churches, and recasting local cultic celebrations as feasts of the martyrs, since "One who wishes to climb a peak does so slowly, step by step, not in leaps and bounds" (*Ep.* 56a: *MGH.Ep.* 2:331). The local church administrations in northern Africa resisted Gregory's attempts to exercise influence there; he himself saw this as a recrudescence of Donatism.

5. *Theological Work*

The Bible is the criterion of all Gregory's theology. His exegesis requires the exploration of the open (historical) and the hidden meanings of scripture; the inner meaning of the text is disclosed by allegorical contemplation and moral exposition. This twofold meaning of scripture is the basis of his ample commentary on Job in thirty-five books, which was completed in 595. Since the moral-theological reflections, which reveal his exceptional knowledge of human nature, predominate in this work, it functioned as a handbook of moral theology. Gregory's collection of homilies comprises forty sermons on Gospel passages from 590/591 and twenty-two continuous expositions of the book of Ezekiel from 593. The accounts of miracles, prophecies, and visions in his *Dialogues of the Life and Miracles of the Italian Fathers* in four books (from ca. 594) nourished the medieval delight in the miraculous; book 4.55 provides the basis of the so-called Gregorian Masses. Gregory probably composed several thousand letters; 847 survive and are an important historical source not only for theology but also for the history of taxation and economics.

■ **Works:** *CPL* 375-81.

■ **Sources:** *LP* 1:312ff.; *Vita auctore anonymo Anglo,* ed. F. A. Gasquet (Westminster, 1904); *PL* 74:41-59; H. Grisar, "Die Gregor-Biographie des Paulus Diaconus," *Zeitschrift für Katholische Theologie* 11 (1887) 158-73; B. Colgrave (ed.), *The Earliest Life of Pope Gregory the Great by an Anonymous Monk of Whitby* (Cambridge, 1985).

■ **Bibliography:** T. Klauser et al., eds., *Reallexikon für Antike und Christentum* (Stuttgart, 1983) 12:930-51; *TRE* 14:135-45; *LMA* 4:1063-66; *VATL* 265-68; E. H. Fischer, "Gregor der Große und Byzanz," *Zeitschrift der Savigny-Stiftung für Rechtsgeschichte. Kanonistische Abteilung* 36 (1950) 15-144; C. Dagens, "Grégoire le Grand et la culture de la sapientia huius mundi à la docta ignorantia," *Revue des Etudes Augustiniennes* 14 (1968) 17-26; idem, "La fin des temps et l'Église selon saint Grégoire le Grand," *Rivista di storia e letteratura religiosa* 5 (1969) 384-91; S. Frank, "Actio und Contemplatio bei Gregor dem Großen," *Trierer Theologische Zeitschrift* 78 (1969) 283-95; O. Giordano, *L'Invasione Longobardo e Gregorio Magno* (Bari, 1970); C. Dagens, *Saint Grégoire le Grand* (Paris, 1977); P. Meyvaert, *Gregory, Bede and Others* (London, 1977); V. Recchia, *Gregorio Magno e la società agricola* (Rome, 1978); P. Courcelle, *Ascesi e ruolo dei viri Dei nell'Italia di Gregorio Magno* (Paris, 1981); J. Richards, *Gregor der Große: Sein Leben—seine Zeit* (Graz et al., 1983); R. Godding, *Bibliografia di Gregorio magno (1890-1989)* (Rome, 1990); W. Gessel, "Reform am Haupt: Die Pastoralregel Gregors des Großen und die Besetzung von Bischofsstühlen," in M. Weitlauff and K. Hausberger, eds., *Papsttum und Kirchenreform* (St. Ottilien, 1990) 17-36; M. Fiedrowicz, *Das Kirchenverständnis Gregors des Großen* (RQ Supplement, Freiburg, 1995); S. C. Kessler, *Gregor der Große als Exeget* (Innsbruck, 1995); J. C. Cavadini, ed., *Gregory the Great: A Symposium* (Notre Dame, Ind., 1995); P. Riché, *Gregor der Große* (Munich, 1996); V. Recchia, *Gregorio Magno—papa ed esegeta biblico* (Bari, 1996); M. Doucet, "Modernité de Grégoire le Grand," *Bulletin de littérature ecclésiastique* 97 (1996) 119-35; R. A. Markus, *Gregory the Great and His World* (Cambridge, 1997); M. Simonetti, "Gregorio Magno e la nascita dell'Europa," *Vetera christianorum* 34 (1997) 311-27; R. G. Tweed, "The Psychology of Gregory the Great," *International Journal for the Psychology of Religion* 7 (1997) 101-10; E. Gandolfo, *Gregorio Magno servo dei servi di Dio* (Vatican City, 1998); M. Schambeck, *Contemplatio als Missio: Zu einem Schlüsselphänomen bei Gregor dem Großen* (Würzburg, 1999); S. C. Kessler, "Gregor der Große und seine Theorie der Exegese," in *L'esegesi dei padri latini* (Rome, 2000) 691-700.

WILHELM M. GESSEL

Gregory II (May 19, 715-Feb. 11, 731). Saint (feast day Feb. 13). Born in Rome. After the series of "Greek popes," once again a Roman was bishop of his native city. Gregory had spent all his life in papal service; as a deacon, he had accompanied his predecessor Constantine I to Constantinople in 710/711, in the aftermath of the Synod in Trullo. In 721, he presided over a synod of twenty-two bishops. He devoted much attention to the buildings of the city, the churches, the basilicas, and the liturgy. In his relations with Byzantium, he opposed a "national Italian" revolution, on the one hand, and taxation demands, on the other. Two imperial edicts (726 and 730) about the veneration of images, touching on both doctrine and piety, led to a rupture with Constantinople. Gregory replied to these edicts in two letters which most scholars hold to be basically authentic. He resisted caesaropapism. The Langobard king Liutprand bestowed Sutri on the Prince of the Apostles in 728 and negotiated with the imperial exarch outside the gates of Rome shortly after this.

Gregory found support in his missionary endeavors north of the Alps. In 716, the Bavarian duke Theodo came to Rome "as the first of his tribe" and agreed on a metropolitan structure: a church province with four dioceses and the Roman liturgy was to be directly subordinated to Rome (not every detail in this agreement was realized). The missionary commission entrusted to Boniface on May 15, 719 (see Boniface, *Ep.* 12), explicitly charged him to employ the Roman liturgy for baptism and confirmation. On the recommendation of Charles Martel and the Thuringian nobles, Boniface was ordained bishop for Germany east of the Rhine on November 30, 722, taking the same oath of obedience as the bishops of the Roman metropolitanate. These actions had profound consequences.

Erich Caspar called Gregory the "greatest pope of the eighth century," one who looked to the future by detaching Rome from Byzantium and turning to the north.

■ **Sources:** *LP* 1:396-414; 3:99f.; *RPR*(J) 1:249-57; 2:742; *RPR.GP* IV/4:6-12; P. Conte, *Regesto delle lettere dei papi del secolo VIII* (Milan, 1984) 192-200.

■ **Bibliography:** *DHGE* 21:1420f.; Caspar 2:643-64, 691-701, 726ff.; G. Ferrari, *Early Roman Monasteries* (Vatican City, 1957); W. Kelly, *Pope Gregory II on Divorce and Remarriage* (Rome, 1976); H. Grotz, "Beobachtungen zu den zwei Briefen Papst Gregors II. an Kaiser Leo III.," *AHP* 18 (1980) 9-40 (supplement: *AHP* 24 [1986] 365-73); T. F. X. Noble, *The Republic of Saint Peter* (Philadelphia, 1984) 23-43; C. Vogel, *Medieval Liturgy: An Introduction to the Sources,* ed. W. G. Storey et al. (Washington D.C., 1986); W. Hartmann, *Die Synoden der Karolingerzeit im Frankenreich und in Italien* (Paderborn, 1989) 38ff.

ARNOLD ANGENENDT

Gregory III (Mar. 18, 731-Nov. 28, 741). Saint (feast day Nov. 28). Gregory, who was of Syrian origin, continued the policies of his predecessor, Gregory II. A synod excommunicated iconoclasts, including the emperor Leo III, on November 1, 731. A subsequent synod on April 4, 732, with the participation of the suburbicarian bishops, founded a sanctuary of All Saints in → St. Peter's, furnished with numerous relics and images like that in St. Paul's, where an Office of psalms and a Mass were to be celebrated each day. The emperor responded by imposing confiscatory taxes on the possessions of the Roman church in south Italy and Sicily, and by transferring Illyria from the Roman jurisdiction to the patriarchate of Constantinople.

Gregory appealed twice in vain to Charles Martel for help against the Langobard king Liutprand, who was threatening Rome (739/740). In 735, he bestowed the pallium on Egbert of York. He had already bestowed it on Boniface in 732, and he received him in audience in Rome in 738.

Because of the unstable relations between East and West, Gregory's pontificate has been called one of the most difficult in the entire history of the papacy (Theodor Schieffer).

■ **Sources:** *LP* 1:415-23; 3:100f.; *RPR*(J) 1:257-62; 2:742; *RPR.GP* IV/4:12-18; P. Conte, *Regesto delle lettere dei papi del secolo VIII* (Milan, 1984) 200-207.

■ **Bibliography:** *DHGE* 21:1421f.; *VATL* 269f.; Caspar 2:664-68, 701-7, 728-31; G. Ferrari, *Early Roman Monasteries* (Vatican City, 1957); A. A. Häussling, *Mönchskonvent und Eucharistiefeier* (Münster, 1973) 288-97, 360-64; T. F. X. Noble, *The Republic of Saint*

Peter (Philadelphia, 1984) 38ff.; H. Mordek, "Rom, Byzanz und die Franken im 8. Jahrhundert," in *Person und Gemeinschaft im Mittelalter,* Festschrift for K. Schmid (Sigmaringen, 1988) 123-56; W. Hartmann, *Die Synoden der Karolingerzeit* (Paderborn, 1989) 41ff.

ARNOLD ANGENENDT

Gregory IV (autumn 827-Jan. 25, 844). In keeping with the *Constitutio Romana,* he was ordained only after the emperor had given his consent in 828. During his reign, the city of Rome was consolidated and Ostia was given strong defenses against the Saracens ("Gregoriopolis"). He also encouraged the Frankish mission to Scandinavia. During the conflict between Louis the Pious and his sons, Gregory accompanied Lothar I to France in 833 in an unsuccessful attempt at mediation which led to a fundamental debate about papal, imperial, and episcopal authority.

■ **Sources:** *LP* 2:73-85; *RPR*(J) 1:323-27; 2:702, 743f.; *MGH.Ep* 5:71-84, 228-32.

■ **Bibliography:** *LMA* 4:1667f.; G. Ladner, *Die Papstbildnisse des Altertums und des Mittelalters* (Vatican City, 1941) 1:142ff.; H. Löwe, "Gozbald von Niederaltaich und Papst Gregor IV.," in Festschrift for B. Bischof (Stuttgart, 1971) 164-77; U. Broccoli, "Ostia antica, Santa Aurea, Gregoriopoli," in *Lunario Romano XII: Il Lazio nell'antichità romana,* ed. R. Lefèvre (Rome, 1982) 189-95; T. Schieffer, "Adnotationes zur Germania Pontificia und zur Echtheitskritik überhaupt, 1. Teil," *Archiv für Diplomatik, Schriftgeschichte, Siegel- und Wappenkunde* 32 (1986) 503-45; J. Fried, "Ludwig der Fromme, das Papsttum und die fränkische Kirche," in P. Godman and R. Collins, eds., *Charlemagne's Heir: New Perspectives on the Reign of Louis the Pious* (Oxford, 1990) 264-71; H. Spilling, *Opus Magnentii Hrabani Mauri in honorem sanctae crucis conditum: Hrabans Beziehung zu seinem Werk* (Frankfurt a.M., 1992) 36-39; P. Depreux, "Empereur, Empereur associé et Pape au temps de Louis le Pieux," *Revue belge de philologie et d'histoire* 70 (1992) 893-906; M. Suchan, "Kirchenpolitik des Königs oder Königspolitik der Kirche?" *Zeitschrift für Kirchengeschichte* 111 (2000) 1-27.

PETER JOHANEK

Gregory V (Apr. 996-Feb. 999). Formerly *Bruno,* son of Duke Otto of Carinthia of the Salier family and cousin of Emperor Otto III, whom he crowned in Rome in 996. He had studied at the cathedral school in Worms and had been chaplain to Otto III. He owed his election as pope to nomination by the king. The aristocratic opposition party in Rome, the Crescentii, put the antipope John XII on the papal throne, so that Gregory fled the city in October 996. Although the hoped-for cooperation between the emperor and "the first German Pope" had not functioned particularly well (since Gregory had made Roman interests his own), Otto III expelled the antipope and restored Gregory to his see in February 998. No doubt thanks to the influence of Abbo of Fleury, Gregory upheld the Roman and canonical positions in such questions as the schism between Arnulf and Gerbert of Aurillac in Rheims or the divorce of the French king Robert II. In the presence of the emperor, Roman councils in 998 dealt with a schism in Vich and with the reestablishing of the diocese of Merseburg, which had been dissolved in 981. More than thirty documents issued by Gregory have been preserved.

■ **Sources:** Zimmermann *Reg*; Zimmermann *Pu*, vol. 2.
■ **Bibliography:** *LMA* 4:1668; Zimmermann *Pa*; Zimmermann *J*; T. E. Moehs, *Gregorius V.* (Stuttgart, 1972); K. Mittermaier, *Die deutschen Päpste* (Graz, 1991); K. Görich, *Otto III.* (2nd ed. Sigmaringen, 1995).

HARALD ZIMMERMANN

Gregory VI (antipope). After the death of Sergius IV in May 1012, he was made pope by the Crescentii and shortly afterward was expelled by the Tusculan pope Benedict VIII. Gregory went to the German court in Pöhlde at Christmas 1012, but Henry II refused his petition and he was forced to resign.

■ **Sources:** *RPR*(J) 2:514; Thietmar, *Chronicle* 6:101, ed. R. Holtzmann: *MGH.SRG* N.S. 9:394f.
■ **Bibliography:** *LMA* 4:1668; Zimmermann *Pa* 115ff.; K.-J. Herrmann, *Das Tuskulanerpapsttum (1012-46)* (Stuttgart, 1973) 5, 7, 25ff.

JOHANNES LAUDAGE

Gregory VI (May 1, 1045-Dec. 20, 1046). Formerly *Johannes Gratianus,* born ca. 1047, possibly in Cologne. He was probably not a relative of the Pierleoni family. He was archpriest of San Giovanni a Porta Latina and godfather (and possibly confessor) of the Tusculan pope Benedict IX. After riots in the city of Rome, he paid a sum of money as compensation and succeeded Benedict as pope. His character was irreproachable, and Peter Damian greeted him as one who would assist church reform. To begin with, his reign was unchallenged, and he repulsed Silvester III and Benedict IX. As late as November 1046, Henry III concluded a "brotherhood of prayer" with him in

Piacenza, but the same emperor compelled him to abdicate on December 20, 1046, because of simony at the synod of Sutri. He was exiled with Hildebrand (later Gregory VII) "to the banks of the Rhine" (which may mean Cologne). After the death of Clement II, Wazo of Liège made an unsuccessful attempt to secure Gregory's rehabilitation.

■ **Sources:** *LP* 2:270; *RPR*(J) 2nd ed. 1:524f.
■ **Bibliography:** *LMA* 4:1668f.; H. Kromayer, "Über die Vorgänge in Rom im Jahre 1045 und die Synode von Sutri 1046," *Historische Vierteljahresschrift* 10 (1907) 161-95; G. B. Borino, "L'elezione e la deposizione di Gregorio VI," *Archivio della Società Romana di Storia Patria* 39 (1916) 141-252, 295-410; idem, "Invitus ultra montes cum domno papa Gregorio abii," *Studi gregoriani per la storia di Gregorio VII e della riforma gregoriana della Libertas Ecclesiae* 1 (1947) 3-46; A. Hauck, *Kirchengeschichte Deutschlands* (Berlin, 1958) 3:570f., 583-90; Zimmermann *Pa* 122-31; K.-J. Herrmann, *Das Tuskulanerpapsttum (1012-46)* (Stuttgart, 1973) 154-59; F.-J. Schmale, "Die 'Absetzung' Gregors VI. in Sutri und die synodale Tradition," *AHC* 11 (1979) 55-103; J. Laudage, *Priesterbild und Reformpapsttum im 11. Jahrhundert* (Cologne, 1984) 151-54; H. Wolter, *Die Synoden im Reichsgebiet und in Reichsitalien von 916 bis 1056* (Paderborn, 1988) 373-404; P. Engelbert, "Heinrich III. und die Synoden von Sutri und Rom im Dezember 1046," *RQ* 94 (1999) 228-66.

JOHANNES LAUDAGE

Gregory VII (Apr. 22, 1073-May 25, 1085). Saint (feast day May 25). Formerly *Hildebrand,* born ca. 1015 (according to the medical examination of his bones) in Tuscany (Soana?), probably into a non-aristocratic family. He came to Rome early in life and was a monk in the monastery of St. Mary on the Aventine, which was under Cluniac influence. He studied in the Lateran, where one of his teachers was Archbishop Laurence of Amalfi. As chaplain to Gregory VI, he accompanied him into exile in Germany (Cologne?) in 1047, but returned to Rome with Leo IX at the beginning of 1049. He became superior of St. Paul's Outside the Walls in 1050. He was papal legate in France in 1054 and 1056, and legate to the German court in 1057/58. He appears as datary in documents of Victor II and became archdeacon of the Roman church, probably in 1058. This position gave him considerable influence on the course taken by the reforming papacy under Nicholas II and Alexander II.

On the day of Alexander's funeral, the Romans made Hildebrand his successor, in tumultous circumstances, but the process was recognized by the cardinals. He took the name of the monastic pope Gregory I and received episcopal ordination on June 30. As the surviving register of his *Letters* (with 360 entries) and about sixty other surviving letters show, Gregory understood his election as a special commission from God to enforce papal authority and thus overcome abuses that infringed canon law; he respected secular authority to the extent that rulers were willing to serve the church. This reflects not so much a systematic concept as a basic religious intuition, expressed in the lapidary propositions of the *Dictatus papae* (1075). Obedience to St. Peter and his successors became the decisive criterion which, if the need arose, might shatter the boundaries of the hierarchical ordering of the church and even cause a new appraisal of secular rulers. Gregory was the first medieval pope to seek contact with all the rulers of his age—for the simple reason that he wanted to urge them all to accept his reform program. Here he abrogated all terminological distinctions between the king in Germany and other sovereigns; he laid claim to a feudal lordship vis-à-vis Denmark, Hungary, Dalmatia, the Normans in southern Italy, and even England, which was meant to secure him financial and military backing. His concept of a *militia sancti Petri* makes Gregory an intellectual forerunner of the crusades.

The fateful conflict with King Henry IV about investiture led to a confrontation with King Philip I of France that was initially even harsher. This was generated by Gregory's disappointment over Henry's refusal to collaborate with the German episcopate in the papal reform of the church; indeed, Henry intensified the exercise of his sovereignty over the church in Italy. When Henry and the majority of the German bishops withdrew their recognition of Gregory at Worms on January 24, 1076, Gregory drew the strongest possible inferences from his papalist doctrine and held a synod at Rome in Lent 1076 at which he not merely excommunicated the king but took the wholly unprecedented step of deposing him and releasing all the king's subjects from their oaths of loyalty. The extraordinary impact of this action plunged the Salic kingdom into a profound crisis and forced Henry to hasten in penitent's garb to meet the pope, who was traveling to Germany for the election of a new king. Gregory reluctantly absolved him at the fortress of Canossa on January 28, 1077. On the one hand, the power of the clergy to inflict sanctions had triumphed, but on the other hand, Henry now had the political and tactical advantage of having deprived his opponents in Germany of legitimacy. This meant that the election of the rival king Rudolf in the presence of papal legates on March 15, 1077, was essentially a failure. Gregory drew the consequences of his position and issued a total prohibition of investiture, no later than 1078; he vacillated between claiming the right to adjudicate between the two rivals and hoping for a reconciliation with Henry, until he finally broke with Henry in the Lenten synod of 1080.

Henry reacted in Brixen to the papal recognition of Rudolf as king and to his renewed deposition by appointing Archbishop Wibert of Ravenna as antipope (Clement III) on June 25, 1080. After the military defeat of Rudolf, Henry began the march on Rome in 1081. Gregory was left without reliable allies and could muster only a feeble defense. He refused to yield on this matter, but since he was abandoned even by most of the cardinals, he had to stay in → Castel Sant'Angelo and witness Henry's entry into Rome on March 21, 1084 and his coronation as emperor by the antipope in → St. Peter's ten days later. Gregory was liberated at the end of May by the Norman duke Robert Guiscard and spent the last year of his life as a refugee in Salerno, where he issued one last appeal for help to those who had remained faithful to him. His tomb is in the cathedral in Salerno.

Despite his personal failure, Gregory was one of the most significant popes in history, since he helped the church reform of the eleventh century to succeed and imprinted the idea of hierocratic autonomy on the whole of the West. He achieved this not so much by means of his writings, which found remarkably little echo in the tradition of canon law, as by means of his resolute action, which decisively weakened traditional values such as the sacral kingdom and private sovereignty over churches, paving the way for a new kind of "church freedom" (*libertas ecclesiae*) under papal leadership. He was canonized by Paul V in 1606.

■ **Sources:** *Gregorii VII Vitae*, in J. B. Watterich, *Pontificum Romanorum qui fuerunt inde ab exeunte saeculo IX usque ad finem saeculi XIII vitae ab aequalibus conscrip-*

tae etc. (Leipzig, 1862) 1:293-546; *RPR*(J) 2nd ed. 1:594-649; 2:712f., 751; E. Caspar, ed., *Das Register Gregors VII.* (*MGH.ES* 2 [Berlin, 1920-23; repr. Munich, 1978]); L. Santifaller, *Quellen und Forschungen zum Urkunden- und Kanzleiwesen Papst Gregors VII.*, vol. 1 (Rome, 1957); H. E. J. Cowdrey, ed., *The Epistolae Vagantes of Pope Gregory VII* (Oxford, 1972).

■ **Bibliography:** *DHGE* 21:1424-33; *TRE* 14:145-52; *LMA* 4:1669ff.; G. Meyer von Knonau, *Jahrbücher des Deutschen Reiches unter Heinrich IV. und Heinrich V.*, 4 vols. (Berlin, 1890-1903); E. Caspar, "Gregor VII. in seinen Briefen," *Historische Zeitschrift* 130 (1924) 1-30; C. Schneider, *Prophetisches Sacerdotium und heilsgeschichtliches Regnum im Dialog 1073-77* (Munich, 1972); J. Gilchrist, "The Reception of Pope Gregory VII into the Canon Law (1073-1141)," *Zeitschrift der Savigny-Stiftung für Rechtsgeschichte. Kanonistische Abteilung* 59 (1973) 35-82; 66 (1980) 192-229; W. Goez, "Zur Persönlichkeit Gregors VII.," *RQ* 73 (1978) 193-216; R. Schieffer, "Gregor VII., ein Versuch über die historische Größe," *Historisches Jahrbuch* 97/98 (1978) 87-107; I. S. Robinson, "'Periculosus Homo': Pope Gregory VII and Episcopal Authority," *Viator* 9 (1978) 103-31; R. Schieffer, *Die Entstehung des päpstlichen Investiturverbots für den deutschen König* (Stuttgart, 1981); G. Fornasari, "Del nuovo su Gregorio VII?" *Studi medievali* 24 (1983) 315-53; J. Vogel, *Gregor VII. und Heinrich IV. nach Canossa* (Berlin, 1983); I. S. Robinson, "Pope Gregory VII," *Journal of Ecclesiastical History* 36 (1985) 439-83; G. Fornaciari et al., "Il regime di vita e il quadro fisico-clinico di Gregorio VII," *Rassegna storica salernitana*, N.S. 2, no. 2 (1985) 31-90; D. Jasper, *Das Papstwahldekret von 1059* (Sigmaringen, 1986) 34-46; H. Fichtenau, "Cluny und der Mönch Hildebrand (Gregor VII.)," in idem, *Beiträge zur Mediävistik* (Stuttgart, 1986) 3:122-46; G. Tellenbach, "Die westliche Kirche vom 10. bis zum frühen 12. Jahrhundert," in *Die Kirche in ihrer Geschichte*, ed. B. Möller (Göttingen, 1988) II/1, 152-200; H.-W. Goetz, "Tradition und Geschichte im Denken Gregors VII.," in *Historiographia Mediaevalis*, Festschrift for F.-J. Schmale (Darmstadt, 1989) 138-48; H. Thomas, "Gregors VII. imperiale Politik und der Ausbruch seines Streites mit Heinrich IV.," in Festschrift for E. Hlawitschka (Kallmünz, 1993) 251-65; J. Englberger, *Gregor VII. und die Investiturfrage* (Cologne, 1996); H. E. J. Cowdrey, *Pope Gregory VII* (Oxford, 1998); U. R. Blumenthal, "Zu den Datierungen Hildebrands," in *Forschungen zur Reichs-, Papst- und Landesgeschichte*, Festschrift for P. Herde (Stuttgart, 1998) 145-54; T. Struve, "Heinrich IV. in der historiographischen Tradition des 19. und 20. Jahrhunderts," *Historisches Jahrbuch* 119 (1999) 52-64; U. R. Blumenthal, *Gregor VII. Papst zwischen Canossa und Kirchenreform* (Darmstadt, 2001).

RUDOLF SCHIEFFER

Gregory VIII (Oct. 21-Dec. 17, 1187). Augustinian canon, formerly *Albertus de Morra,* born at the beginning of the twelfth century in Benevento. After a period as Master in Bologna, he was created a cardinal in 1155/56 and was entrusted with numerous legations. He became chancellor of the Roman church in 1178. His pontificate was marked by endeavors to reach an accommodation with Frederick I Barbarossa and to start a new crusade, as well as by an extension of papal legislation. Scholars no longer accept his authorship of a *Forma dictandi.*

■ **Bibliography:** *VATL* 276; P. Kehr, "Papst Gregor VIII. als Ordensgründer," *Studi e Testi* 38 (1924) 248-75; W. Holtzmann, "Die Dekretalen Gregors VIII.," *Mitteilungen des Instituts für Österreichische Geschichtsforschung* 58 (1950) 113-23; A. Dalzell, "The Forma Dictandi Attributed to Albert of Morra and Related Texts," *Mediaeval Studies* 39 (1977) 440-65; P. Nadig, "Gregorio VIII e i suoi 57 giorni di pontificato," *Studi beneventani* 1 (1989) 85-158.

ULRICH SCHMIDT

Gregory VIII (antipope). (Mar. 3, 1118-Apr., 1121). Formerly *Maurice Bourdin (Mauritius Burdinus),* born in Burgundy or Limoges, died after 1137. Archbishop Bernard of Toledo brought this Cluniac monk to Spain and ordained him bishop of Coimbra on March 18, 1099. He was elected archbishop of Braga at the beginning of 1109 and received the pallium in the summer of that year. Traveling to the holy land as a pilgrim between 1104 and 1108, he brought back the alleged head of the apostle James the Less. He became involved in legal conflicts with Toledo over suffragan sees and was deposed as archbishop by the Council of Palencia on October 25, 1113. Despite papal decisions in his favor (November 3 and December 4, 1114), his position in Spain had become untenable, and the pope reduced his archiepiscopal jurisdiction. He came to Rome, where he took the emperor's side: he crowned Henry V in a solemn ceremony in St. Peter's on March 25, 1117. Henry made him pope as rival to Gelasius II, who excommunicated him and deposed him on April 7, 1118. After the emperor failed to support him, Gregory was captured by Cardinal John of Crema in Sutri in April, 1121, and was paraded in disgrace through the streets of Rome as *burdinus* ("burden") on an ass. He was imprisoned in the abbey of La Cava, then in San Germano near Montecassino, and finally in Castel Fumone near Alatri.

He is last mentioned as a prisoner in La Cava in August 1137.

■ **Bibliography:** *DHGE* 21:1433-36; *LMA* 4:1671; *VATL* 276; C. Erdmann, "Mauritius Burdinus," *QFIAB* 19 (1927) 205-61; P. David, "L'énigme de Maurice Bourdin," in idem, *Études historiques sur la Galice et le Portugal* (Lisbon/Paris, 1947) 441-501; L. Vones, *Die 'Historia Compostellana' und die Kirchenpolitik des nordwestspanischen Raumes 1070-1130* (Cologne, 1980); K. Schreiner, "Gregor VIII., nackt auf einem Esel," in *Ecclesia et Regnum,* Festschrift for F.-J. Schmale (Bochum, 1989) 155-202.

LUDWIG VONES

Gregory IX (Mar. 19, 1227-Aug. 22, 1241). Formerly *Hugo(lin), count of Segni,* born in Anagni shortly before 1170. He was a relative of Innocent III and Alexander IV. He was ordained to the priesthood in Anagni. He studied in Paris, perhaps also in Bologna. Innocent III made him a chaplain at the curia in 1198 and created him cardinal deacon of Sant' Eustachio at the end of the same year. He carried out important legations in southern Italy and Sicily in 1199 and 1202. In 1206, he became cardinal bishop of Ostia and thereby dean of the College of → Cardinals. He was papal legate in Germany between 1207 and 1209 during the conflict about the throne. He was the most important counselor of Honorius III and was frequently sent as legate to central and northern Italy on questions concerning the crusade, heresies, and the Lombard cities. By the authority of his office, he anointed Frederick II during the imperial coronation in 1220.

His pontificate was overshadowed by political conflicts with Frederick, whom he excommunicated twice (in 1227, when the crusade was broken off, and in 1239, in response to the emperor's antipapal politics, his oppression of the Sicilian church, and his opposition to the war against the Albigensians, etc.); he planned shortly before his death to depose the emperor. The Peace of San Germano or Ceprano in 1230 achieved only a brief accommodation, without removing the deeper causes of the conflict (viz., the church states and northern Italy, Sicilian church politics, the relationship between secular and spiritual authority). These conflicts were accompanied by a propaganda war of apocalyptic dimensions.

Within the church, Gregory was particularly attentive to the new orders (Camaldulensians, Cistercians, Dominicans, Florentines; orders of knights), above all to the Franciscans. He was the first cardinal protector of the Franciscans and helped draw up their first rule (1223) and the adaptation of this rule to the Third Order; he was also responsible for the rule of the Poor Clares (1218/19).

Under the name "Liber Extra," the collection of decretals (1234) which he charged Raymund of Peñafort to draw up as a parallel to the *Liber Augustalis* of Frederick II was one of the elements of the *Corpus Iuris Canonici* (in force until 1917). The chapter "De haereticis" (X5, 7) regulates the procedures of criminal law involved in the persecution of heretics, which Gregory—imitating procedures set up by Frederick II—entrusted to special commissioners, viz. the Dominicans, in the form of the Inquisition (1231).

■ **Sources:** Biographies: L. A. Muratori, *Rerum Italicarum scriptores ab anno aerae christianae 500 ad 1500* (Milan, 1724) 3:570-87; P. Fabre and L. Duchesne, *Le Liber censuum de l'Eglise romaine* (Paris, 1910) 2:18-36; *RPR*(P) 1:680ff.; 2:2099ff.; *MGH.Ep Saeculi XIII* 1:261-739; G. Levi, *Registri del Card. Ugolino d'Ostia* (Rome, 1890); L. Auvray, ed., *Registres de Grégoire IX,* 4 vols. (Paris, 1896-1955); H. Golubovich, "Disputatio Latinorum et Graecorum seu Relatio Apocrisiariorum Gregorii IX. de gestis Nicaeae in Bithynia et Nyphaeae in Lydia (1234)," *Archivum Franciscanum historicum* 12 (1919) 418-70; A. L. Tàutu, ed., *Acta Honorii III et Gregorii IX e registris vaticanis aliisque fontibus* (Vatican City, 1950).

■ **Bibliography:** *DHGE* 21:1437f.; *LMA* 4:1671f.; *TRE* 14:152-55; E. Brem, *Papst Gregor IX. bis zum Beginn seines Pontifikats* (Heidelberg, 1911); S. Sibilia, *Gregorio IX* (Milan, 1961); S. Kuttner, "Raymond of Peñafort as Editor: The 'decretales' and 'constitutiones' of Gregory IX," *Bulletin of Medieval Canon Law* 12 (1982) 65-80; W. Maleczek, *Papst und Kardinalskolleg von 1191-1216* (Vienna, 1984) 126-33; J. P. Lomax, "Ingratus or Indignus: Canonist Argument in the Conflict between Pope Gregory IX and Emperor Frederick II," (dissertation, Kansas, 1987); E. Pásztor, "Saint Francis, Cardinal Hugolino, and the 'Franciscan Question,'" *Analecta Tertii Ordinis Regularis Sancti Francisci de Paenitentia* 19 (1986/87) 461-97; A. Marini, "La 'forma vitae' di San Francesco per San Damiano tra Chiara d'Assisi, Agnese di Boemia ed interventi papali," *Hagiographica* 4 (1997) 179-95; F. Liotti, "I papi Anagnini e lo sviluppo del diritto canonico classico," *AHP* 36 (1998) 33-47; P. Segl, "'Quoniam abundavit iniquitas': Zur Beauftragung der Dominikaner mit dem 'negotium inquisitionis' durch Papst Gregor IX.," *Rottenburger Jahrbuch für Kirchengeschichte* 17 (1998) 53-65.

THEO KÖLZER

Gregory X (Sept. 1, 1271-Jan. 10, 1276). Blessed (feast day Jan. 9). Formerly *Tedaldo Visconti,* born ca. 1210 in Piacenza, died at Arezzo. He studied in Paris and was a canon in Lyons (St. Jean). He became archdeacon of Liège in 1259 and took part in English legations. While on a pilgrimage to the holy land, he was elected pope *in absentia* in → Viterbo. He was a compromise candidate, ending a → *sede vacante* that had lasted nearly three years (since November 29, 1268). He was not yet a priest; he was ordained on March 19, 1272, and crowned on March 27 in Rome. In order to avoid similar situations in the future, he introduced regulations governing the conclave and the papal → election, in the constitution *Ubi periculum* (November 1, 1274). His principal concern was the desire to liberate the holy land by means of a new crusade, which was to be prepared at the Second Council of Lyons. No solutions were found to the confusions of Italian politics, where Charles of Anjou fought against the Ghibellines; nor to relations with Byzantium, where the emperor Michael VIII Palaeologos feared that the imperial plans of Charles of Anjou would mean the conquest of his kingdom and the restoration of the Latin empire; nor to the conflict about the Roman empire, after the election of Rudolf of Habsburg on October 1, 1273. Negotiations about union with the Greek church, in order to ensure that the crusade could go ahead, led to a transitory agreement which could not be put into practice (July 6, 1274). After Alfons X of Castille renounced the Roman kingship and Rudolf promised to come to Rome and to promote the crusade (October 1275), it was possible to make progress toward an agreement with Rudolf; only Gregory's death prevented him from crowning Rudolf as emperor. The sessions of the council also showed that the pope wanted to begin a profound work of reform, in order to put a stop to ecclesiastical abuses.

■ **Bibliography:** *DHGE* 21:1348f.; *LMA* 4:1672f.; L. Gatto, *Il pontificato di Gregorio X* (Rome, 1959); B. Roberg, *Die Union zwischen der griechischen und der lateinischen Kirche auf dem II. Konzil von Lyon (1274)* (Bonn, 1964); idem, "Der konziliare Wortlaut des Konklave-Dekrets Ubi Periculum von 1274," *AHC* 2 (1970) 231-62; idem, "Die Tataren auf dem 2. Konzil von Lyon," *AHC* 5 (1973) 241-302; idem, "Subsidium Terrae Sanctae: Kreuzzug, Konzil und Steuern," *AHC* 15 (1985) 96-158; H. Schmidinger, "Zur Vita Gregorii X.," in *Aus Kirche und Reich,* Festschrift for F. Kempf (Sig-

maringen, 1983) 397-403; B. Roberg, *Das Zweite Konzil von Lyon (1274)* (Paderborn, 1990); idem, "Che cosa è guelfo o ghibellino . . . ? Gregor X. und der mißlungene Friede in Florenz 1273," *AHC* 27/28 (1995-96) 303-23; idem, "Die 'lectura' des Franciscus de Albano aus dem Jahr 1276 über die 'constitutiones novissimae' Papst Gregors X.," *AHC* 31 (1999) 297-366.

LUDWIG VONES

Gregory XI (Dec. 30, 1370-Mar. 27, 1378). Ordained priest Jan. 4 and crowned Jan. 5, 1371. Formerly *Pierre Roger (de Beaufort),* son of Guillaume Roger and Marie de Chambons, born ca. 1330 in Rosiers d'Egletons (Départment of Corrèze). He was a nephew of Clement VI and became cardinal deacon of Santa Maria Nuova in 1348, holding many benefices. He studied in Perugia and was an important canon lawyer.

As pope, he fought against heresy and condemned eighteen propositions of John Wyclif. His policies in the church states were intended to promote the return of the curia to Rome, as Catherine of Siena and others urged. His pontificate ended the period of exile in Avignon in 1376; he himself entered the city of Rome on January 17, 1377. Gregory made peace between Emperor Charles IV and King Louis of Hungary, but his attempts at mediation in the Hundred Years War were unsuccessful. He created twenty-one cardinals, but was not able to achieve church reform or resolve the problems within the curia; this is why his death led to the outbreak of the Western Schism. He is buried in Santa Maria Nuova in Rome.

■ **Sources:** *LMA* 4:1674; additional material: Grégoire XI, *Lettres communes,* 2 vols. (Paris, 1992); P. N. Zutshi, "The Registers of Common Letters of Pope Urban V and Pope Gregory XI," *Journal of Ecclesiastical History* 51 (2000) 497-508.

■ **Bibliography:** *DHGE* 21:1439f.; *LMA* 4:1673f.; *VATL* 279ff.; G. Mollat, *Les Papes d'Avignon* (10th ed. Paris, 1965); Guillemain; M. Dykmans, "La bulle de Grégoire XI à la veille du Grand Schisme," *Mélanges de l'Ecole Française de Rome: Moyen-âge, Temps modernes* 89 (1977) 485-95; *Genèse et débuts du Grand Schisme d'Occident 1362-94* (Paris, 1980); R. G. Davies, "The Anglo-Papal Concordat of Bruges 1375," *AHP* 19 (1981) 97-146; P. R. Thibault, "Pope Gregory XI and the Crusade," *Canadian Journal of History* 20 (1985) 313-35; idem, *Pope Gregory XI: The Failure of Tradition* (New York/London, 1986); M. Hayez, *Les réserves spéciales de bénéfices sous Urbain V et Grégoire XI* (Paris, 1990) 237-49; idem, "D'Urbain V à Grégoire XI: Un dangereux retour au passé?" in *L'écrit dans la société médiévale* (Paris, 1991) 151-64; A. M. Hayez and M. Hayez, "Les débuts du pontificat de Grégoire XI," in *Les Prélats, l'Eglise et la Société* (Bordeaux, 1994) 173-83; A. M. Hayez, "Un aperçu de la politique bénéficiale de Grégoire XI," in *Forschungen zur Reichs-, Papst- und Landesgeschichte,* Festschrift for P. Herde (Stuttgart, 1998) 685-98; G. Battelli, "Gli alloggi assegnati in Roma a Raimondo di Turenne per il ritorno di Gregorio XI (1377)," in *Roma, magistra mundi,* Festschrift for L. E. Boyle (Louvain-la-Neuve, 1998) 1:25-40.

LUDWIG VONES

Gregory XII (Nov. 30, 1406-July 4, 1415). Formerly *Angelo Correr,* pope of the Roman obedience in the Western Schism; born ca. 1335, died Oct. 18, 1417, at Recanati. His contemporaries looked on Gregory as a zealous promoter of church union, a man of irreproachable character and a good theologian. After endeavors to achieve union broke down, the disappointed cardinals of both obediences summoned the Council of Pisa. When this council deposed Gregory in 1409, he lost most of his followers, and he declared his resignation after the Council of Constance deposed the Pisan pope John XXIII.

■ **Bibliography:** *LMA* 4:1674f.; *VATL* 281f.; A. Lando, *Il papa deposto (Pisa 1409)* (Turin, 1985); W. Brandmüller, *Das Konzil von Konstanz 1414-18* (Paderborn, 1991); I. D. Girgensohn, "Reste von Rubrizellen aus einem verlorenen Register Gregors XII.," in *Forschungen zur Reichs-, Papst- und Landesgeschichte,* Festschrift for P. Herde (Stuttgart, 1998) 723-43.

JOHANNES GROHE

Gregory XIII (May 13, 1572-Apr. 10, 1585). Formerly *Ugo Boncompagni,* born Jan. 1, 1502, at Bologna, the son of a merchant. He studied in Bologna and taught law there from 1531 to 1539. He entered the service of the curia at Rome in 1539. The curia sent him to the Council of Trent in 1546 and from 1561 to 1563, where he was largely responsible for the formulation of the reform decrees; in the intervening period, he carried out diplomatic tasks in France (1556) and Brussels (1557). He was made bishop of Viesti in 1558. He was created cardinal in 1565 and sent as legate to Spain, where he won the confidence of King Philip II. Gregory's election as pope, in an unusually brief conclave, was due above all to the influence of Philip and of Cardinal Antoine Perrenot de Granvella.

Although Gregory had grown up in the atmos-phere of the Renaissance, his life as pope remained modest. As a trained lawyer with administrative experience, he expedited the most important business in person. His rule was mild, but he was a decisive promoter of the Catholic reform and the Counter-Reformation, employing harsh and sometimes dubious methods. He supported Henry III of France against the Huguenots and held a public celebration in Rome of the St. Bartholomew's Day Massacre, although he had not been involved in its preparation. He supported the revolt of the Irish and the buildup of Spanish arms against Elizabeth I of England; similarly, he supported the Spanish Counter-Reformation in the Netherlands. While the Catholic Church in Poland was able to regain strength and renew itself decisively, the re-Catholicization of Sweden failed. The nuncio Antonio Possevino did not succeed in forging either a union or a closer relationship to the Russia of Ivan IV, and the endeavors to create a grand alliance against the Turks were unsuccessful. Gregory devoted particular attention to German matters, setting up a "German" congregation of cardinals in 1573 and establishing new permanent nunciatures in Cologne, Graz, and Lucerne. His most important church-political intervention here was the retention of the imperial Electorate of Cologne for the Catholic Church after Archbishop Gebhard II Truchsess von Waldburg became a Protestant in 1583; this ensured both that the imperial church in Lower Germany remained Catholic (despite the grave risks to which it was exposed), and that the imperial throne would continue to be occupied by Catholics.

As a friend of the sciences, church education, and the Jesuit order, Gregory played a decisive role in the foundation of seminaries in all the Catholic countries. In Rome, he founded the English, Hungarian, Greek, Armenian, and Maronite colleges, ensured the survival of the German college by means of a rich endowment, and refounded the Roman College. He promoted the missions, especially in India and Japan. He drew up the official edition of the *Corpus Iuris Canonici,* as desired by the Council of Trent, and carried out the reform of the Julian calendar (so that the day following October 4, 1582, was October 15). He began the reform of the liturgical chants and reorganized the Congregation of the Index. In 1580, Gregory repeated the condemnation of Michael Baius, who submitted.

Gregory was one of the great reforming popes of the post-Tridentine period, who established the Catholic reform on the basis of the council and sought to regain lost territory. The immense expenditure on education, colleges, and diplomatic tasks and the extension of Rome and splendid buildings caused very serious financial problems, which led to unrest. Rome and the → papal states suffered greatly, especially in the final years of his reign, from a plague of bandits, who were often supported by the aristocracy. The aged pope, who was all too inclined toward caution, could not restore order, and this became the most urgent task for his successor, Sixtus V.

■ **Bibliography:** *VATL* 282ff.; *RGG* 4th ed. 3:1261; Pastor, IX; J. Krüger, "Das ursprüngliche Grabmal Gregors XIII. in St. Peter zu Rom," *Korrespondenzblatt des Collegium Germanicum* 95 (1986) 41-59; G. Schwaiger, "Die Päpste der Katholischen Reform und Gegenreformation," *GKG* 12:79-102; F. M. De' Reguardati, "Il fenomeno del banditismo sotto Gregorio XIII e Sisto V," *Rivista araldica* 85 (1987) 198-207; S. Vareschi, *La legazione del card. Ludovico Madruzzo alla dieta imperiale di Augusta 1582: Chiesa, Papato e Impero nella seconda metà del sec. XVI* (Trent, 1990); V. Peri, "Roma e l'idea del patriarcato di Mosca all'epoca di Gregorio XIII," in *IV Centenario dell'istituzione del Patriarcato in Russia* (Trent, 1991) 177-205; A. Fernández Collado, *Gregorio XIII y Felipe II en la nunciatura de Felipe Sega (1577-87)* (Toledo, 1991); E. Olivares, "La bula 'Ascendente Domino,' 1584, y los teológicos posttridentinos," *Archivo teológico Granadino* 62 (1999) 5-75; M. Freiberg, "Going Gregorian, 1582-1752: A Summary View," *Catholic Historical Review* 86 (2000) 1-19; J. P. Donelly, "Antonio Possevino, S.J. as Papal Mediator between Emperor Rudolf II and King Stephan Báthory," *Archivium historicum Societatis Jesu* 69 (2000) 3-56.

GEORG SCHWAIGER

Gregory XIV (Dec. 4, 1590-Oct. 16, 1591). Formerly *Niccolò Sfondrati,* born Feb. 11, 1535, at Somma Lombardo (Varese). He became bishop of Cremona in 1560 and was created cardinal in 1583. He was a friend of Charles Borromeo and Philip Neri. Since his health was always poor and he lacked political experience, he entrusted business to his cardinal nephew Paolo Camillo Sfondrati, who was unsuited to this task and pursued an unsuccessful anti-French policy under Spanish influence, supporting the Holy League in France with money and troops and renewing the sentence of excommunication against King Henry IV.

■ **Bibliography:** *VATL* 284f.; M. Facini, *Il pontificato di*

Gregorio XIV (Rome, 1911); *HCMA* 3:53f., 181; Pastor 10:531-73; L. Castano, *N. Sfondrati vescovo di Cremona al Concilio di Trento 1561-63* (Turin, 1939); idem, *Gregorio XIV* (Turin, 1957).

GEORG SCHWAIGER

Gregory XV (Feb. 9, 1621-July 8, 1623). Formerly *Alessandro Ludovisi,* born Jan. 9, 1554, in Bologna, the son of Count Pompeio Ludovisi. He studied with the Jesuits in Rome and at Bologna. He became archbishop of Bologna in 1612 and was created cardinal in 1616. He was already elderly and in poor health when he became pope, and he left business to his highly gifted cardinal nephew Ludovico Ludovisi. Reform within the church and an active Counter-Reformation program were pursued with vigor: hence the centralization of world missions through the foundation of the Sacra Congregatio de Propaganda Fide (1622), and the re-Catholicization of Bohemia after the victory at White Mountain (1620). Gregory gave diplomatic and financial support to Emperor Ferdinand II and to Maximilian I of Bavaria, who headed the League and who gave Gregory the Palatine Library (→ Vatican Library). Gregory mediated in the conflict of Veltlin; he maintained a strictly neutral line between France and Spain, with the result that he was able to achieve a maximum of success in ecclesiastical matters and in the Counter-Reformation; these possibilities vanished under his successor, Urban VIII. Gregory issued two bulls concerning the papal → election, and canonized Ignatius of Loyola, Francis Xavier, Philip Neri, and Teresa of Avila.

■ **Bibliography:** *VATL* 285f.; Pastor 13/1; G. Gabriele, "Il conclave di Gregorio XV," *Archivio della Società Romana di Storia Patria* 50 (1927) 5-32; *HCMA* 4:15ff., 118; D. Albrecht, *Die deutsche Politik Papst Gregors XV.* (Munich, 1956); G. Schwaiger, "Die Päpste im Zeitalter des Dreißigjährigen Krieges," *GKG* 12:103-27; K. Repgen, ed., *Krieg und Politik 1618-48* (Munich, 1988); S. Samerski, "Akten aus dem Staatssekretariat Pauls V. und Gregors XV.," *AHP* 33 (1995) 303-14; K. Jaitner, *Die Hauptinstruktionen Gregors XV. für die Nuntien und Gesandten an den europäischen Fürstenhöfen 1621-23,* 2 vols. (2nd ed. Tübingen, 1997).

GEORG SCHWAIGER

Gregory XVI (Feb. 2, 1831-June 1, 1846). Camaldulese monk (1783). Formerly *Bartolomeo Alberto Cappellari,* born Sept. 18, 1765, at Belluno as the son of an aristocratic lawyer. He entered the monastery at San Michele di Murano near Venice in 1783 and received the religious name of *Mauro*. He was ordained priest in 1787, and taught in his order. In 1795, he moved to Rome; he became abbot of San Gregorio al Celio in 1803 and general of his order in 1823. He was created cardinal in 1826 and appointed prefect of the Congregation of Propaganda. The conservative → *zelanti* were an important factor in his election after a difficult conclave that lasted fifty days; Prince Metternich also played a significant role in his election, although Gregory was no friend of Austria. He was ordained bishop and crowned on February 6, 1831.

Gregory had a pleasant personality, and he was pious and unassuming; in political matters, he was inexperienced and unworldly. Despite urgent recommendations by the great powers (in the memorandum of May 31, 1831), Gregory did not carry out the necessary reforms of the → papal states, which were heavily in debt and badly administered. His policies were supported by the harshly reactionary Cardinal Secretaries of State Tommaso Bernetti and (after 1836) Luigi Lambruschini. Gregory refused to welcome the Risorgimento, especially the radical "Young Italy" group headed by Giuseppe Mazzini, but he likewise rejected the more moderate demands of the Neo-Guelphs (Vincenzo Gioberti, Gino Capponi, et al.). Gregory was faced by almost continuous revolts in the papal states and could maintain papal sovereignty only with the help of troops from Austria and France. He traveled through his domains in 1841, but this did little to quell the popular dissatisfaction, which was intensified by the activities of secret societies.

During the most difficult tribulations of the papacy, under Pius VI, Mauro Cappellari had published the book *Il trionfo della Santa Sede e della Chiesa contro gli assalti dei Novatori* ("The triumph of the Holy See and the church against the assaults of the innovators" [Venice, 1799; reprinted many times]). Here he defended the monarchy, sovereignty, and → infallibility of the pope in the church and sharply attacked the Febronians and all "innovators," especially Pietro Tamburini, who was the driving force of the synod of Pistoia. This clearly delineated consciousness of the papal "plenitude of power" and medieval ideals dominated the whole of church politics. Thus, Gregory's encyclical *Mirari vos*

(August 5, 1832) condemned the errors and contemporary demands of liberalism (indifferentism, freedom of conscience and of the press, the separation of church and state) and Hugo-Félicité-Robert de La Mennais, who had been celebrated up to that date as a hero. In 1834, he condemned La Mennais' reply, *Paroles d'un croyant.* In the same year, he issued the first of many condemnations of the fideism of Louis-Eugène-Marie Bautain; in 1835, he condemned Georg Hermes. In his opposition to every form of national church, Gregory fought against echoes of Febronianism in Germany, pressed the prince bishop of Breslau, Leopold Count Sedlnitzky von Choltitz, to resign, and extirpated Gallican tendencies in France. He insisted on basic Catholic principles in various controversies about mixed marriages, especially in the "confusions of Cologne" (1837-1841). As a defender of "legitimate" rulers and a foe of all revolts, he disapproved strongly of the Polish rebellion against Russian rule in 1830/31; at the same time, he protested against the harsh persecutions of Catholics in Russia and boldly made this case in person, when Emperor Nicholas I visited Rome in 1845.

Gregory displayed a breadth of vision in the question of world missions and in the creation of new hierarchical structures: he set up ca. 70 new dioceses and apostolic vicariates and appointed nearly two hundred missionary bishops and also promoted the training of local priests. He showed caution when regimes changed, especially in Latin America. The bull *Sollicitudo ecclesiarum* (August 7, 1831) overlooked Spanish and Portuguese protests and established the basis for the definitive resolution of controversies about the appointment of bishops in Latin America and India. Gregory condemned slavery and the slave trade in the brief *In supremo* (December 3, 1839). He set up four new dioceses in Canada and ten in the United States; in England, he supported the endeavors of Nicholas Wiseman, who acted as his representative.

Gregory was a friend of the religious orders. During his pontificate, the scholastic "Roman theology" began to assume its predominant position. He promoted science and culture in many ways: excavations were carried out in the Roman Forum and in the catacombs; he founded the Etruscan and Egyptian museums in the Vatican (→ Vatican Museum) and the Christian museum in the Lateran; he supported scholars such as Angelo Mai and Giuseppe Mezzofanti and artists such as Johann Friedrich Overbeck and Bertel Thorvaldsen; he rebuilt St. Paul's Outside the Walls. In its positive and negative aspects, his pontificate formed both the precondition and the basis for the reign of Pius IX.

■ **Sources:** Mauro Cappellari, *Il trionfo* (see above); A. M. Bernasconi, *Acta Gregorii Papae XVI,* 4 vols. (Rome, 1901-4; incomplete repr. Graz, 1971); *Gregorio XVI, Miscellanea commemorativa,* 2 vols. (Rome, 1948); A. Mercati, *Raccolta di concordati* (Rome, 1954) 1:724-50; *HCMA* 7:19, 24-35.

■ **Bibliography:** *DHGE* 21:1445-52; *HKG* 6/1:311-476; *VATL* 286ff.; *RGG* 4th ed. 3:1261f.; D. DeMarco, *Il tramonto dello Stato pontificio: Il papato di Gregorio XVI* (Naples, 1948; repr. 1992); Schmidlin 1:511-687; R. Lill, "Das Zeitalter der Restauration," *GKG* 12:171-83; A. J. Reinerman, "An Unnatural 'Natural Alliance': Metternich, Palmerston, and the Reform of the Papal States, 1831-1832," *International Historical Review* 10 (1988) 541-58; idem, *Austria and the Papacy in the Age of Metternich,* II: *Revolution and Reaction, 1830-38* (Washington, 1989); G. Maggioni, "Tre lettere inedite di Gregorio XVI," *Archivio Storico di Belluno* 61 (1990) 27-32; idem, "I viaggi di Gregorio XVI," ibid., 193-202; A. Dierkens, ed., *Le libéralisme religieux* (Brussels, 1992); J. S. Panzer, "The Popes and Slavery," *Homiletic and Pastoral Review* 97 (1996) 22-29; A. Marani, "Tra sinodi e conferenze episcopali: La definizione del ruolo degli incontri collettivi dei vescovi fra Gregorio XVI e Pio IX," *Cristianesimo nella storia* 17 (1996) 47-93; M. Martinelli, "La restaurazione della cristianità durante il pontificato di Gregorio XVI," in Festschrift for P. Bellini (Catanzaro, 1999) 457-84; L. Courtois, "La liberté comme mal," in *L'Église et le monde moderne au XIXᵉ siècle: Imaginaires du mal* (Paris, 2000) 221-36.

GEORG SCHWAIGER

Hadrian I (Feb. 9, 772 [date of ordination]-Dec. 25, 795). He was a member of the Roman aristocracy and had been Stephen III's deacon and confidant. He abandoned Stephen's friendly policy toward the Langobards and sent political opponents to be judged in Constantinople (an action that amounted to recognition of the emperor's sovereignty). At the same time, he renewed the Frankish alliance and appealed to the Frankish king for help against the Langobard king Desiderius. Charlemagne abandoned his alliance with the Langobards, conquered Pavia in 774, and deposed the royal house. When he came to Rome at Easter, he was received by Hadrian as *patricius*. Charlemagne swore oaths in → St. Peter's that guaranteed papal safety, celebrated the Easter feast in the Lateran basilica, and renewed Pippin's donation (→ Papal States) on the following Wednesday, bestowing extensive domains on the pope; when Charlemagne visited Rome in 781, he made this donation a reality, though in reduced form. On this latter occasion, Hadrian baptized Charlemagne's son Carloman, with Pippin as godfather; he anointed Carloman and his brother Louis as kings, the former for Lombardy and the latter for Aquitaine. The *compaternitas* ("common fatherhood") was a continuation of the "spiritual alliance" which allowed the pope to appear as "father of the family of peoples."

Hadrian aimed at a position equal to that of the emperor; he stopped the practice of dating the year according to the reign of the emperor in Constantinople, minted coins with his own image, and extended the Lateran opposite the Palatine. The *Constitutum Constantini* probably reflects this situation.

Hadrian entrusted the "Dionysio-Hadrian" collection of canon laws and the Gregorian sacramentary (*Sacramentarium Gregorianum Hadrianum*) to Charlemagne, as instruments for the reform of the Frankish church. During the iconoclastic controversy, Hadrian sent legates to the Seventh Ecumenical Council at Nicaea and welcomed its conclusions in favor of images; these were, however, rejected by Charlemagne and his court theologians, who expressed their dissent in the *Libri Carolini*. The "special council" held by Charlemagne in Frankfurt in 794, attended by papal legates, condemned adoptianism, but held firm to its rejection of Nicaea II, although without giving formal approval to the *Libri Carolini*. Hadrian, who had wanted to be a "pope-emperor" (in the phrase of Josef Déer), was unable to bend Charlemagne to his will, and indeed was rather the king's "provincial Frankish bishop" (Peter Classen).

■ **Sources:** *LP* 1:486-523; 3:105ff.; *RPR*(J) 1:289-306; 2:701; *MGH.Ep* 5:3-57; Codex Carolinus (*MGH.Ep* 3:469-657); P. Conte, *Regesto delle lettere dei papi del secolo VIII* (Milan, 1984) 231-45.

■ **Bibliography:** *DBI* 1:312-23; *DHGE* 1:614-19; 22:1484f.; *TRE* 14:306ff.; *LMA* 4:1821f.; *RGG* 4th ed. 3:1369f.; H. J. Sieben, *Die Konzilsidee der Alten Kirche* (Paderborn, 1979) 324-43; A. Angenendt, "Das geistliche Bündnis der Päpste mit den Karolingern," *Historisches Jahrbuch* 100 (1980) 1-94; H. Fuhrmann, "Das Papsttum und das kirchliche Leben im Frankenreich," *Settimane di Studio del Centro Italiano di Studi sull'Alto Medioevo* 27 (1981) 419-56; T. F. X. Noble, *The Republic of St. Peter* (Philadelphia, 1984) 127ff.; P. Classen, *Karl der Große, das Papsttum und Byzanz* (Sigmaringen, 1985); M. Maccarrone, "Il Papa Adriano I e il Concilio di Nicea del 787," *AHC* 20 (1988) 53-134; W. Hartmann, *Die Synoden der Karolingerzeit* (Paderborn, 1989) 105-15; O. Engels, "Zum Rombesuch Karls des Großen im Jahr 774," *Jahrbuch für fränkische Landesforschung* 52 (1992) 15-24; A. Alexakis, "The Source of the Greek Patristic Quotations in the 'Hadrianum,'" *AHC* 26 (1994) 14-30; R. Berndt, *Das Frankfurter Konzil von 794*, 2 vols. (Mainz, 1997); L. Spera, "Cantieri edilizi a Roma in età carolingia: Gli interventi di Papa Adriano I nei santuari delle catacombe," *Rivista di archeologia cristiana* 73 (1997) 185-254; E. Lamberz, "Studien zur Überlieferung der Akten des VII. ökumenischen Konzils," *Deutsches Archiv für die Erforschung des Mittelalters* 53 (1997) 1-43; B. Neil, "The Western Reaction to the Council of Nicaea II," *Journal of Theological Studies* 51 (2000) 533-52.

ARNOLD ANGENENDT

Hadrian II (Dec. 14, 867-Nov./Dec. 872). Born in Rome, son of Talarus. He came from the same family as Popes Stephan IV and Sergius II and was married. He was ordained subdeacon and priest under Gregory IV. He had already been suggested as a candidate in the papal elections of 855 and 858; he was seventy-five when elected in 867. Immediately after his episcopal ordination, Hadrian persuaded Emperor Louis II to pardon the exiled bishops Gauderich of Velletri and Stephen of Nepi, as well as John the deacon, and he maintained his good relations with the emperor in the following years. In the course of the controversy about Lothar II's marriage, he departed from the strict line of Nicholas I by offering a new synodal decision; but the matter was resolved by Lothar's death. Hadrian could do nothing to prevent the occupation of Lorraine by Charles the Bald after Lothar's death, or the subsequent partition of this territory between Charles and Louis the German. In the conflict about the rebellious prince Carloman and Bishop Hincmar of Laon, who had appealed to the pope, Hadrian was obliged to yield to King Charles and to Archbishop Hincmar of Rheims and to acknowledge the sentence of deposition which the synod of Douzy had passed on Hincmar of Laon in 871. Hadrian did indeed insist on his right to review this sentence, but at the same time he offered

Charles the prospect of succeeding Louis II as emperor. In the East, he failed to win the Bulgarian church to the Roman observance, since he delayed too long over the appointment of an archbishop for Bulgaria. He received Cyril and Methodius in Rome in 868 and gave his approbation to the Slavonic liturgy. He ordained Methodius archbishop of Pannonia in 868. In June 869, the condemnation of Patriarch Photius was renewed at a Roman synod, in the presence of a delegation from Byzantium; this condemnation was repeated at the Fourth Council of Constantinople (869-870) in the presence of papal legates, and Patriarch Ignatius was restored to office.

Hadrian's letter to the synod of Douzy, confirming the translation of Bishop Actard from Nantes to Tours, is the earliest papal letter to contain an indubitable literal quotation from Ps.-Isidore.

■ **Sources:** *LP* 2:173-90; 3:125f.; *MGH.Ep* 6:691-765; Mansi 16.

■ **Bibliography:** *DBI* 1:323-29; *LMA* 4:1822f.; *VATL* 292f.; H. Grotz, *Erbe wider Willen* (Cologne, 1970); F. Dvornik, "Photius, Nicholas I and Hadrian II," *Byzantinoslavica* 34 (1973) 33-50; H. Fuhrmann, *Einfluß und Verbreitung der pseudoisidorischen Fälschungen* (Stuttgart, 1973) 2:273-80; S. Scholz, *Transmigration und Translation* (Cologne, 1992) 130-47; S. Vacca, *Prima sedes a nemine iudicatur* (Rome, 1993) 121-25.

SEBASTIAN SCHOLZ

Hadrian III (May 17, 884-Sept. 17, 885). Saint (feast day July 8). Born in Rome or Teano, the son of Benedict. He was continuously required to address revolts in the city of Rome. The few documents he issued, sent to persons in central and northern Italy and southern France, do not allow the reconstruction of a clear picture of the personality of this pope. At the end of August 885, he accepted the invitation of Charles III to come to the Frankish kingdom, in order to depose a number of bishops and to help Charles's illegitimate son Bernard succeed to the throne. It has been shown that he did not take the → *Liber diurnus* (or *diuturnus*) with him on this occasion. He died en route, near the abbey of Nonantola, where he was buried. The local liturgical cult of Hadrian III (sometimes confused with Hadrian I) was confirmed by Leo XIII in 1891.

■ **Sources:** *LP* 2:191, 225; 3:127; *RPR*(J) 1:426f.; 2:705; *Bibliotheca hagiographica latina antiquae et mediae* *aetatis,* ed. Bollandists, 2 vols. (Subsidia hagiographica 6; Brussels, 1898-1901) 3738; *Vita Adriani,* ed. A. Gaudenzi, *Bollettino dell'Istituto Storico Italiano* 36 (1916).

■ **Bibliography:** *DBI* 1:329f.; G. Quatrini, *Del pontificato e del culto di s. Adriano* (Modena, 1892), III; P. Brezzi, *Roma e l'impero medievale* (Bologna, 1947) 84; E. Hlawitschka, *Lotharingien und das Reich an der Schwelle der deutschen Geschichte* (Stuttgart, 1968) 28; Zimmermann *Pa* 52.

KLAUS HERBERS

Hadrian IV (Dec. 4, 1154-Sept. 1, 1159). Formerly *Nicholas Breakspear,* born 1120 or 1130 at Abbot's Langley in England; died at Anagni and buried in St. Peter's in Rome. He was a canon regular, prior, and from 1135 abbot of St. Ruf near Avignon. His influence played a decisive role in the unification of the kingdom of Aragon and Catalonia to form one realm. He became cardinal bishop of Ostia in 1149 and was legate in Scandinavia in 1152-1153, where he established the Norwegian ecclesiastical province and paved the way for the establishment of the province of Uppsala, which took place in 1164.

As pope, he defended the independence of the sovereign papal rights and the curial understanding of the Western empire. The renewal of the Treaty of Constance in 1153 made it possible for Frederick I to be crowned emperor in 1155, despite resistance on the part of the Roman citizenry and a number of points of conflict with the Staufer court. Another consequence was the execution of Arnold of Brescia. Nevertheless, the planned military action against the Normans was canceled at short notice. The end of this political union was sealed by the Treaty of Benevento in July 1156, in which Hadrian recognized the Norman kingdom, set up the feudal structures pertaining to this kingdom, and entered a formal alliance with William I of Sicily, who had been victorious against Byzantium. This decision, which was supported by only some of the cardinals, led to a grave conflict with the emperor. Other points of conflict were the controversy about the nature of the imperial dignity initiated in the assembly of the royal court at Besançon in 1157, and the capture of Eskil of Lund. These disputes were only partly resolved in June 1158. Shortly after this, the emperor disregarded the sovereign papal rights and applied the legal regulations of Roncaglia about sovereign rights to those papal possessions in Rome and other parts of Italy that were guaran-

teed by the *Constitutum Constantini.* Hadrian protested via diplomatic channels and entered an alliance in July or August 1159 with the cities of northern Italy which were hostile to the emperor, threatening Frederick with excommunication. He died before he could carry out this threat. Scholars disagree about whether he urged King Henry II of England to conquer Ireland, but it is certain that Hadrian's church politics formed one of the main causes of the papal schism of 1159.

■ **Sources:** *LP* 2:388-97; *RPR*(J) 2:102-45, 720f., 760f.

■ **Bibliography:** *LMA* 4:1823; *VATL* 294f.; *RGG* 4th ed. 3:1370; E. M. Almedingen, *The English Pope (Adrian IV)* (London, 1925); M. Maccarrone, *Papato e impero dalla elezione di Federico I alla morte di Adriano IV (1153-1159)* (Rome, 1959); W. Heinemeyer, "'Beneficium—non feudum sed bonum factum': Der Streit auf dem Reichstag zu Besançon 1157," *Archiv für Diplomatik* 15 (1969) 155-236; J. Déer, *Papsttum und Normannen* (Cologne/Vienna, 1972) 247ff.; H. Enzensberger, "Der 'böse' und der 'gute' Wilhelm," *Deutsches Archiv für Erforschung des Mittelalters* 36 (1980) 385-432; J. L. Heady, *Adrian the Fourth: The Pontifical Pragmatist* (Ann Arbor, 1986); J. Laudage, *Alexander III. und Friedrich Barbarossa* (Cologne, 1990); O. Engels, "Friedrich Barbarossa und Dänemark," in *Friedrich Barbarossa,* ed. A. Haverkamp (Sigmaringen, 1992) 353-85; U. Vones-Liebenstein, *Saint-Ruf und Spanien* (Turnhout, 1995) 225-64; O. Engels, *Die Staufer* (7th ed. Stuttgart et al., 1998) 59-82.

JOHANNES LAUDAGE

Hadrian V (July 7-Aug. 18, 1276). Formerly *Ottobuono Fieschi,* born ca. 1220 to a noble family of Genoa, the counts of Lavagna; died in → Viterbo, where his tomb in the Cosmatesque style is in the church of San Francesco. He was a nephew of Innocent IV. He studied in Paris and held benefices in England and Italy. His uncle made him a papal chaplain and created him cardinal in 1251. From this date on, he exercised decisive influence on papal politics. He was a specialist in English affairs and supported the policy of Urban IV and Clement IV, who appealed to Charles I of Anjou. He was the most successful legate to England in medieval times (1265-1268), achieving peace between King Henry III and the baronial opposition. He upheld the Angevin position and supported the return of the Guelphs to Genoa. He was elected pope in Rome on July 11, 1276, under a rigorous application of the regulations governing the conclave issued by Gregory X (*Ubi periculum;* papal → election), but fell seriously ill and was neither ordained bishop nor crowned. Hadrian abolished the conclave regulations by declaration; this abolition was documented in writing by John XXI, but the conclave was reintroduced by Celestine V.

■ **Sources:** *LP* 2:457; *RPR*(P) 2:1709f.

■ **Bibliography:** *DBI* 1:335ff.; R. Graham, "Letters of Cardinal Ottoboni," *English Historical Review* 15 (1900) 87ff.; N. Schöpp, *Papst Hadrian V.* (Heidelberg, 1916); Sir M. Powicke, *The Thirteenth Century 1216-1307* (Oxford History of England; 2nd ed. London, 1962) 207ff.; G. Ladner, *Die Papstbildnisse des Altertums und des Mittelalters* (Vatican City, 1970) 2:185ff.; 3 (1984) 56; P. Herde, "Die Entwicklung der Papstwahl im 13. Jahrhundert," *Österreichisches Archiv für Kirchenrecht* 32 (1981) 23ff.; idem, "Adriano," in *Storia della Chiesa,* ed. D. Quaglioni (Milan, 1994) 11:29f.

PETER HERDE

Hadrian VI (Jan. 9, 1522-Sept. 14, 1523). Formerly *Adrian Florensz Boeyens,* born Mar. 2, 1459, in Utrecht, the son of a carpenter; his tomb is in Santa Maria dell'Anima. He was a pupil of the Brethren of the Common Life and studied at the University of Louvain, where he taught theology from 1491 to 1507. He was influenced by late scholasticism, and his principal interests lay in the fields of canon law and casuistic moral theology. Emperor Maximilian I appointed him tutor of his grandson, later Emperor Charles V, in 1507. Boeyens ensured that Charles retained the full right of inheritance in the Spanish monarchy. From 1516 onward, he and Cardinal Francisco Jiménez Cisneros governed Spain; after the cardinal's death, Boeyens ruled alone. He became bishop of Tortosa in 1516, and inquisitor and cardinal in 1517. While Charles V was absent for the imperial election, Boeyens was once again regent in Spain and played a part in subduing the revolt in Castille (1520-1522). In the conclave that followed the death of Leo X, which was lacerated by political rivalries, he was elected pope *in absentia,* thanks to his position in Spain, to his close links to Emperor Charles V, and to his exemplary life.

The pious and severely ascetic Hadrian encountered hostility and rejection on the part of the worldly curia and the Roman populace as soon as he entered Rome on Aug. 29, 1522, taking the sea route to emphasize his political neutrality. He saw his principal task as the checking of the Reformation which Martin Luther had unleashed and the achieving of a common front of the Christian powers against the Turks (Belgrade had fallen in 1521, and Rhodes in 1522). He earned resentment by his policy of thrift (in contrast to his predecessor, who had piled up debts) and by his serious intention to carry out reform; he was also disliked as a foreigner. Hadrian was isolated, supported only by a few Spanish and Dutch associates such as Cardinal Willem van Enkevoirt.

He sent Francesco Chiericati as → nuncio to the imperial parliament at Nuremberg in 1523. In the instructions he gave Chiericati, Hadrian spoke of the abuses in the curia and expressed his will to bring about reforms. He was unsuccessful in his attempt to have the Edict of Worms applied to Luther. He was similarly unsuccessful in his mediation between Charles V and King Francis I of France; when France applied sanctions to him, Hadrian saw no other course than to enter an alliance against France with Charles V, England, and Venice. Other areas of concern in Hadrian's pontificate were Switzerland, Poland, Hungary, and the Scandinavian kingdoms.

■ **Bibliography:** *DHGE* 22:1487ff.; 24:379f. (s.v. Hezius [Thierry] secrétaire d'Adrien VI); *TRE* 14:309f.; *RGG* 4th ed. 3:1370f.; Pastor 4:2; A. Mercati, *Diari di concistori del pontificato di Adriano VI* (Rome, 1951); *Ephemerides theologicae Lovanienses* 35 (1959) 513-629; J. Posner, *Der deutsche Papst Adrian VI.* (Recklinghausen, 1962); R. E. McNally, "Pope Adrian VI and Church Reform," *AHP* 7 (1969) 253-85; P. Berglar, "Die kirchliche und politische Bedeutung des Pontifikats Hadrians VI.," *Archiv für Kulturgeschichte* 54 (1972) 97-112; K. H. Ducke, *Handeln zum Heil: Eine Untersuchung zur Morallehre Hadrians VI.* (Leipzig, 1976); J. Bijloos, *Adrianus VI: De Nederlandse Paus* (Haarlem, 1980); K. Mittermaier, *Die deutschen Päpste* (Graz, 1991); R. B. Hein, *"Gewissen" bei Adrian von Utrecht (Hadrian VI), Erasmus von Rotterdam und Thomas More* (Münster, 2000); P. Nissen, *Adrianus VI: Een biografie* (Amsterdam, 2000).

GEORG SCHWAIGER

Hilary (Nov. 19, 461-Feb. 29, 468). Saint (feast day Feb. 28), born in Sardinia. He became archdeacon in Rome and was papal legate at the "Robbers' synod" in Ephesus in 449, where he energetically took the side of Patriarch Flavian and was obliged to flee. Hilary had a strong and vigorous character and followed the example of Leo I in his prudent and measured exercise of Roman preeminence. He frequently intervened to resolve conflicts about jurisdiction in the Gallican church, protecting the metropolitan rights of Leontius of

Arles (*MGH.Ep* 3, n. 16) and of Ingenuus of Embrun. He disciplined Archbishop Hermes of Narbonne at the Roman synod in 462 and sent a letter on December 3, 462, to the bishops of southern Gaul, exhorting them to hold annual provincial synods, reminding them of their obligation to reside in their dioceses, and discussing church property. In a similar way, the Roman synod of November 19, 465 (the first synod whose exact minutes have been preserved), regulated controversial questions in the Spanish church, including a prohibition on bishops designating their own successors. Hilary opposed Philotheus's heretical ideas about the Holy Spirit and fought against the Arians, who were protected by Ricimer, the de facto ruler of Italy. He made use of the period of peace that followed the sack of Rome by the Vandals in 455 to make rich donations to Roman churches and monasteries. He built three splendid chapels alongside the baptistery of the Lateran and a monastery beside San Lorenzo fuori le Mura; he is buried in the crypt of the latter church.

■ **Sources:** A. Thiel, ed. *Epp. Romanorum pontificum* (Braunsberg, 1868) 1:126-74; *PL* 58:11-31; *PLS* 3:379ff., 441ff.; *LP* 1:242-48; *RPR*(J) 1:75ff., 2:692, 736.

■ **Bibliography:** *DTHC* 6:2385-88; *LMA* 5:8; *VATL* 304f.; Caspar, vols. 1, 2; G. Langgärtner, *Die Gallienpolitik der Päpste im 5. und 6. Jahrhundert* (Bonn, 1964).

GEORG SCHWAIGER

Hippolytus (antipope?). Saint (feast day Aug. 13), also known as Hippolytus of Rome. Since Johann Ignaz Döllinger's influential 1853 monograph, *Hippolytus und Kallistus,* the basic biographical facts of Hippolytus's life have been widely accepted. Döllinger's account relies largely on the anonymous *Refutatio* and diverse traditions of the fourth and fifth centuries. Accordingly, the Roman presbyter Hippolytus is thought to have come into conflict with Zephyrinus, bishop of Rome, as well as with his successor, Callistus, over dogmatic and ethical questions. Hippolytus accused them (among other things) of modalism and founded a schismatic church—hence he is counted as the first antipope. The schism continued during the reigns of Urban I and Pontian. Emperor Maximinus Thrax banned and deported Hippolytus and Pontian around 235 to Sardinia, where the two were finally reconciled and died. Under bishop Fabian (236/237) Hippolytus was buried in Rome on the Via Tiburtina in a catacomb later named after him and was subsequently venerated as a martyr. In 1551 a torso was found there of a seated figure in a chair, which, because of the inscription engraved on the armrests, was taken to be a statue of Hippolytus.

Criticism of the above historical reconstruction, while never completely absent, has mounted in recent years. The extensive writings attributed to Hippolytus (all in Greek), in fact originate from different authors of the same name; for critics the biographical facts point only to a controversy with Callistus. Other data (the first antipope, the deportation, and martyrdom) are untrustworthy. The controversy continues unabated. But for the history of the papacy, Hippolytus is of only minor importance.

■ **Bibliography:** *DECL* 287-89; A. Brent, *Hippolytus and the Roman Church in the Third Century* (Leiden, 1995).

BRUNO STEIMER MICHAEL G. PARKER

Honorius I (Oct. 27 or Nov. 7[?)] 625-Oct. 12, 638). He belonged to a wealthy family in Campagna which had a house in Rome, and his father, Petronius, held the title of consul. Honorius's *Vita,* consciously composed in imitation of the biography of Gregory I, lavishes special praise on Honorius's building activity, which he financed from his private wealth; by the time of his death, he had considerably enriched the church. He worked together with the Langobard king Arioald to achieve a resolution (at least for a time) to the schism of the Three Chapters in the area around Venice and in Istria. He continued Gregory's policy with regard to the christianization of England, but he was unable to persuade the Irish church to accept the Roman date for Easter. The privilege of exemption that he granted to Bobbio established an important precedent. Shortly before his death, acting on defective information, he reproached the Spanish bishops for proceeding with excessive mildness against unbelievers (637/638); Braulio of Saragossa repudiated this accusation in a masterly letter with an ironic undertone.

Honorius's affirmations about the question of the energies in Christ were to have fatal effects (the "Honorius question"). Patriarch Sergius I of Constantinople had achieved an agreement with the Monophysite Theodosians in Alexandria in 633 on the basis of the doctrine of one single energy in Christ. When Sophronius of Jerusalem expressed his reservations about this, it was agreed that the question of the energies would be excluded from the proclamation of the faith in the future. In the course of this discussion, however, Sergius wrote to Honorius, who had no taste for theological discussion and replied in two letters with propositions outlining the doctrine of one will in Christ (Monothelitism). Only after Honorius's death, under the influence of Maximus the Confessor, was the doctrine of the two wills and the two energies in Christ elaborated. The Sixth Ecumenical Council, held at Constantinople in 680-681, declared this doctrine—which in the meantime had established itself in the West—to be a dogma, condemning those who asserted that there was only one will and one energy in Christ. These included Honorius. Pope Leo II accepted completely the anathema pronounced by Constantinople III, and this sentence was repeated by the Seventh (787) and Eighth (869-870) Ecumenical Councils. The case of Honorius was soon forgotten in the West, and after the close of the ninth century, no one recalled that the condemned heretic Honorius had been a pope; by the mid-twelfth century, his name had disappeared completely from the Western sources. Throughout the Middle Ages, however, the Greeks recalled that the Sixth Ecumenical Council had anathematized a Pope Honorius.

The case of Pope Honorius interested scholars in the West from the fifteenth century onward. Nicholas of Cusa, who was convinced of the inerrancy of the papal see, was untroubled by the condemnation of Honorius; nor did the Cardinals Johannes de Torquemada and Gasparo Contarino doubt that the Sixth Ecumenical Council had indeed reckoned Honorius among the heretics. The Dutchman Albert Pigge, an extreme defender of papal → infallibility, was the first to assert that Honorius could not possibly have been condemned. Accordingly, he maintained that the Greeks had added the pope's name to the acts of the Sixth Ecumenical Council. This so-called forgery hypothesis was further elaborated by Caesar Baronius and others and found adherents even in the twentieth century.

Opponents of Pigge's hypothesis from the mid-sixteenth century onward (e.g., Melchior Cano) affirmed that a pope as private person could be a heretic; but the papalist tendency which has dominated since the seventeenth century prevented this view from prevailing. In the modern period, scarcely any scholars other than Protestants and adherents of Gallican ideas have looked on Pope Honorius as heretical. Vatican I changed little here: in order to tone down the categorization of Honorius as a heretic at the Sixth Ecumenical Council, the proponents of infallibility judged the anathema to be a disciplinary measure rather than a judgment about the pope's faith.

It is, of course, unhistorical to study the case of Honorius only from the perspective of the discussion about infallibility. There is no doubt that the Sixth Ecumenical Council condemned him as a heretic because it genuinely held him to be a heretic. The specific context of the anathema does not allow us to water down the meaning of the verdict pronounced against him.

■ **Sources:** *ACO* Series II 2/2:548; 4:559; 8:620; 22:625; 19; *LP* 1:323-27; F. Wilkelmann, "Die Quellen zur Erforschung des mononergetisch-monotheletischen Streites," *Clio* 69 (1987) 525f. ("Quellen" 44 and 47).

■ **Bibliography:** *DHGE* 24:1049f.; *LMA* 5:119f.; *TRE* 15:566f.; G. Kreuzer, *Die Honoriusfrage im Mittelalter und in der Neuzeit* (Stuttgart, 1975); P. Conte, "Nota su una recente appendice sulla questione di Onorio," *Rivista di storia della Chiesa in Italia* 37 (1983) 173-82; F. Carcione, "Enérgheia, Thélema e Theokínetos nella lettera di Sergio, patriarca di Costantinopoli, a Papa Onorio Primo," *Orientalia christiana periodica* 51 (1985) 263-76; E. Zocca, "Onorio I e la tradizione occidentale," *Augustinianum* 27 (1987) 571-615; A. Thanner, *Papst Honorius I.* (St. Ottilien, 1989); E. Zocca, "Una possibile derivazione Gregoriana per il 'monotelismo' di Onorio I," *Augustinianum* 33 (1993) 519-75.

GEORG KREUZER

Honorius II (Dec. 16/21, 1124-Feb. 13, 1130). Formerly *Lambert Scannabecchi*. He was born in modest circumstances in the region of Bologna (Fiagnano near Imola) and became a canon regular at Santa Maria in Rhino (Bologna), where he also served as archdeacon. He was created cardinal priest of Santa Prassede and became cardinal bishop of Ostia in 1117. He accompanied Gelasius II to France and was counselor to Calixtus II. He led the papal legation for the negotiation of the Concordat of Worms.

After Cardinal Theobald of Sant' Anastasia had been elected and had taken possession of the papal office as Celestine (II) in 1124, Haimerich, the cardinal chancellor, and the Frangipani acted quickly to exclude him from the succession before he could be ordained bishop and enthroned. Theobald resigned, and Scannabecchi was canonically elected pope.

The results of his policies were mixed. He was successful in France and England, and had a good relationship with Lothar III; he excommunicated Conrad of Staufen in 1128, but the measures he took against Roger II of Sicily were a failure, and he was obliged to bestow the lordship of Apulia on Roger in the Peace of Benevento (August 22, 1128). Disputes within the church led him to depose the abbots Oderisius of Montecassino and Pontius of Cluny in 1126. He recognized the order of Premonstratensians in the same year. He displayed profound skepticism vis-à-vis questionable claims to legal rights (e.g., in the case of Santiago de Compostela).

■ Sources: *LP* 2:237, 379; 3:136ff., 170f.; *RPR*(J) 2nd ed. 1:823-39; *PL* 166:1217-1320; J. B. Watterich, *Pontificum Romanorum qui fuerunt inde ab exeunte saeculo IX usque ad finem saeculi XIII vitae ab aequalibus conscriptae, etc.* (Leipzig, 1862), vol. 2 (1099-1198), 157-73; *Lothar III.* (Regesta Imperii 4,1; Cologne, 1994).

■ Bibliography: *LMA* 5:129; *VATL* 306f.; F.-J. Schmale, *Studien zum Schisma des Jahres 1130* (Cologne, 1961); G. Tellenbach, "Der Sturz des Abtes Pontius von Cluny," *QFIAB* 42/43 (1963) 13-55; H. Hoffmann, "Petrus Diaconus, die Herren von Tusculum und der Sturz Oderisius' II. von Montecassino," *Deutsches Archiv für Erforschung des Mittelalters* 27 (1971) 1-109; J. Déer, *Papsttum und Normannen* (Vienna, 1972); R. Somerville, "Pope Honorius II, Conrad of Hohenstaufen, and Lothar III," *AHP* 10 (1972) 341-46; R. Hüls, *Kardinäle, Klerus und Kirchen Roms 1049-1130* (Tübingen, 1977) 106f., 215; H. E. J. Cowdrey, "Two Studies in Cluniac History," *Studi gregoriani per la storia* 11 (1978) 178-298; G. J. Schiro, *The Career of Lamberto da Fagnana—Honorius II 1035?-1130—and the Gregorian Reform* (Ann Arbor, 1979); M. Stroll, *The Jewish Pope* (Leiden, 1987); I. S. Robertson, *The Papacy 1073-1198* (Cambridge, 1990).

LUDWIG VONES

Honorius II (antipope) (Oct. 28, 1061-May 31, 1064). Formerly *Cadalus of Parma*, born to a noble family in Verona, 1009/1010, died 1071/1072 at Parma. He became a canon of the cathedral in Parma in 1028, was ordained subdeacon in 1030 and deacon in 1034. In 1041, he was made *vicedominus* of the diocese and became bishop of Parma before May 1045. In 1061, he accepted the pleas of the Roman aristocracy and some bishops in Lombardy at the court of the German king to accept proclamation as pope. However, he was unable to get the upper hand over Alexander II and was never enthroned. At the initiative of archbishop Anno of Cologne, the synod of Mantua (1064) ended the schism and declared the election of Honorius invalid. Nevertheless, he maintained his claims and remained bishop of Parma until his death.

■ Sources: *RPR*(J) 1:593f.

■ Bibliography: *DHGE* 11:53-99; *LMA* 5:120; F. Herberhold, "Die Angriffe des Cadalus von Parma auf Rom 1062 und 1063," *Studi gregoriani per la storia* 2 (1947) 477-503; H.-G. Krause, *Das Papstwahldekret von 1059 und seine Rolle im Investiturstreit* (Rome, 1960) 129-57; V. Cavallari, "Cadalus e gli Erzoni," *Studi Storici Veronesi Luigi Simeoni* 15 (1965) 59-170; T. Schmidt, *Alexander II. (1061-73) und die römische Reformgruppe seiner Zeit* (Stuttgart, 1977) 80-88, 104-33; M. Stoller, "Eight Anti-Gregorian Councils," *AHC* 17 (1985) 252-321.

JOHANNES LAUDAGE

Honorius III (July 18, 1216-Mar. 18, 1227). Formerly *Cencio Savelli (Censius Camerarius)*, born before 1160; it is uncertain whether he came from the noble family of the Savelli. He was educated in Rome and was a canon at Santa Maria Maggiore. He became chancellor in 1188 and composed the → *Liber censuum* (1192). He was created cardinal in 1193 and headed the papal → chancellery from 1194 to 1198; after this date, he withdrew from public church life and worked as a preacher. He was already an elderly man when he was elected pope, and he carried out his office in such a way that he avoided conflicts, although he remained true to the principal concerns of his predecessor, Innocent III. He attempted to maintain the papal feudal sovereignty in England and to protect the rights of King Henry III, who was still a minor. In France, his legate Romanus was able to persuade King Louis VIII to undertake a crusade against the Albigensians in 1226.

Honorius's relations with the Sicilian and German king Frederick II were strained by the king's repeated postponements of his departure for the crusade, by the king's interventions in episcopal nominations in the Sicilian realm, and by differences of interest in the Italian realm. Nevertheless, Honorius crowned him emperor on November 22, 1220, and conceded to him the personal union of sovereignty in the empire and in the Sicilian kingdom, in the hope that the emperor's help would bring the crusade to a successful conclusion. After further delays, Frederick's expedition foundered at Mantura in the Nile delta in 1221. Despite Honorius's bitter reproaches, the emperor would not commit himself to start the crusade until 1225, setting August 1227 as the date of departure.

Honorius issued a number of ordinances concerning university studies. His most significant decrees include the recognition of the rules of the Dominicans (December 22, 1216), the Franciscans (November 29, 1223), and the Carmelites (January 30, 1226). He commissioned the collection of his decretals (*Compilatio quinta*) in 1226, probably entrusting this task to Tancred of Bologna, and was the first pope to make the application of such decretals obligatory.

■ **Sources:** C. A. Horoy, *Honorii III opera*, 5 vols. (Paris, 1879-82); *MGH.Ep* saeculi XIII, ed. C. Rodenberg (Berlin, 1883) 1:1-260; P. Pressuti, ed. *Regesta Honorii Papae III*, 2 vols. (Rome, 1888-95; repr. Hildesheim, 1978).

■ **Bibliography:** *TRE* 15:568-71; L. E. Boyle, "The Compilatio quinta and the Regests of Honorius," *Bulletin of Medieval Canon Law* 8 (1978) 9-19; W. Maleczek, *Papst und Kardinalskolleg von 1191-1216* (Vienna, 1984) 111ff., 357f.; J. E. Sayers, *Papal Government and England during the Pontificate of Honorius (1216-27)* (Cambridge, 1984); W. Stürner, *Friedrich II.* (Darmstadt, 1992) 1:227-51; G. Bakken, *Ius Imperii ad Regnum* (Cologne, 1993) 229-77; W. Maleczek, "Franziskus, Innozenz III., Honorius III. und die Anfänge des Minoritenordens," in *Il papato duecentesco e gli ordini mendicanti: Atti del XXV Convegno internazionale, Assisi 1998* (Spoleto, 1998) 23-80.

WOLFGANG STÜRNER

Honorius IV (Apr. 2, 1285-Apr. 3, 1287). Formerly *Giacomo Savelli*, born ca. 1210. His father, Luca, was a Roman senator; he was a grand-nephew of Honorius III, whose name he took. He was cardinal deacon of Santa Maria in Cosmedin and Roman senator for life (his brother Pandulph represented him). He was elected pope in Perugia, amid the desire to free the papacy from the French-Angevin embrace and to pacify the Ghibellines. He was ordained bishop and crowned in Rome on April 20; his official residence was the Savelli palace on the Aventine.

After the failure of the crusade of 1285 and the death of its principal opponents—Philip III of France (October 6, 1285) and Peter III of Aragon (November 11, 1285)—the conflict between the crown of Aragon and the house of Anjou about the throne of Sicily continued. Honorius attempted to mediate, but he was unwilling to entrust this realm, which he himself administered and reformed for a period as feudal lord (*Constitutio super ordinatione regni Siciliae*), to the Spanish king, although Charles II of Anjou had agreed to this in the Treaty of Barcelona (February 27, 1287), while he was held prisoner by the king of Aragon. Honorius excommunicated James I of Sicily (later James II of Aragon) after his coronation in Palermo, along with James's mother Constance (April 11, 1286; he intensified the terms of this excommunication on May 23). Honorius attempted to continue the policy of Gregory X vis-à-vis the German kingdom. He reached an agreement with Rudolf I about the royal rights in Italy and negotiated a date for the coronation of the emperor; however, nothing came of this, because of the opposition of the electors at the court assembly in Würzburg in March 1287. He renewed the condemnation of the sect of the *Apostolici* in 1286. He abolished the orders that had no possessions and supported the mendicant orders, confirming their privileges on November 20, 1285.

■ **Sources:** *RPR(P)* 2:1795-1824; M. Prou, *Les registres d'Honorius IV* (Paris, 1886-88); A. Paravicini Bagliani, *I testamenti dei cardinali del Duecento* (Rome, 1980) 38f., 197-207; O. Raynald, *Annales ecclesiastici* (Rome, 1646-77) XXII-XXIII.

■ **Bibliography:** *LMA* 5:121; B. Pawlicki, *Papst Honorius IV.* (Münster, 1896); S. Carocci, *Baroni di Roma* (Rome, 1993) 415-22; A. Paravicini Bagliani, *La cour des papes au XIIIᵉ siècle* (Paris, 1995).

LUDWIG VONES

Hormisdas (July 20, 514-Aug. 6, 523). Saint (feast day Aug. 6), successor to Pope Symmachus; born in Frosinone in Campagna. His election, during the Acacian schism, prompted Emperor Anastasius I, whose position was seriously threatened by the revolt of the pro-Chalcedonian general Vitalian, to take up the dialogue with Rome anew. Hormisdas was invited to a synod that was to be held in Heracleia from July 1, 515. After holding a synod in Rome and consulting King Theoderic the Great, Hormisdas sent an initial delegation of bishops to Constantinople, headed by Ennodius of Pavia. These bishops were charged to carry out Hormisdas's instructions exactly as they stood in the letter he gave them. They demanded from

Anastasius and from the bishops, as a precondition of church unity, the recognition of the decisions of Chalcedon, the approbation of all the letters of Leo I, the condemnation of Nestorius and Eutyches and their followers (including Acacius and Peter the Fuller of Antioch), the signing of a "pamphlet" containing the "Formula" or "Rule of faith of Hormisdas" (which contains all these points), and the submission of the deposition of bishops to the judgment of the pope. This legation was unsuccessful, since the defeat of Vitalian meant that the council was not held. Anastasius replied (*Collectio Avellana,* 111) that he upheld Chalcedon and Leo, but that he was not willing to take any action against Acacius. Since Hormisdas refused to change his demands in the letters he wrote in 516, the two sides did not come any closer.

Encouraged by the adoption of the Roman line by about forty bishops (mostly from the western Balkans, but some from Syria), Hormisdas repeated his demands in 517, sending a second legation and further letters (*Collectio Avellana,* 126ff.), but success continued to elude him. Only after Justin I succeeded Anastasius on July 10, 518, and both sides began to correspond and exchange new legations, was it possible to end the schism on April 22, 519 (Hormisdas's letter of thanks to Justin I: *Collectio Avellana,* 168).

Hormisdas rejected the formula propagated by Scythian monks, under the leadership of Maxentius, in the Theopaschite controversy: "One of the Trinity suffered death."

His correspondence, mostly preserved in the *Collectio Avellana,* also deals with affairs in the West, especially in Spain. It is one of the main sources for papal history in the sixth century.

■ **Editions and Sources:** Letters and rule of faith: *CPL* 1683f.; A. Thiel, ed. *Epp. Romanorum pontificum* (Braunsberg, 1867; repr. Hildesheim, 1974) 2:741-990; also in O. Guenther, ed. *Collectio Avellana, pars II* (Corpus scriptorum ecclesiasticorum latinorum 35; Vienna, 1895) nos. 106-240 (cf. Index, 830f., "Formula": ibid. no. 116b and p. 800).

■ **Sources:** V. Grümel, continued by J. Darrouzès and V. Laurent, eds., *Les regestes des actes du patriarcat de Constantinople* (Kadiköi et al., 1932) I/1, nos. 210-19.

■ **Bibliography:** *DTHC* 7:161, 76; *LMA* 5:126; *DECL* 292; W. Haacke, *Die Glaubensformel des Papstes Hormisdas im acacianischen Schisma* (Rome, 1939); A. Grillmeier and H. Bacht, eds., *Das Konzil von Chalkedon, Geschichte und Gegenwart* (5th ed. Würzburg,

1979) 2:73-94 (F. Hofmann) and passim; L. Magi, *La sede romana nella corrispondenza degli imperatori e patriarchi bizantini (VI-VII secoli)* (Rome/Louvain, 1972) 35-103; J. Speigl, "Die Synode von Heraklea 515," *AHC* 12 (1980) 47-61; A. Grillmeier, *Jesus der Christus im Glauben der Kirche* (2nd ed. Freiburg, 1991) II/1, 351-69; II/2 (1989), 336-42; M. Maccarrone, ed., *Il primato del vescovo di Roma nel primo millennio* (Vatican City, 1991) 334f. and passim; J. Speigl, "Formula Iustiniani: Kircheneinigung mit kaiserlichen Glaubensbekenntnissen (Codex Iustinianus I, 1,5-8)," *Ostkirchliche Studien* 44 (1995) 105-34; S. Ranalli, "L'epistolario di papa Ormisda, nel quadro della letteratura cristiana del VI secolo," *Studi e materiali di storia delle religioni* 61 (1995) 19-54.

GÜNTER PRINZING

Hyginus (138?-142?). Saint (feast day Jan. 11), successor of Telesphorus in the list of Irenaeus of Lyons (*Adversus haereses* 3.4.2) and thus the eighth pope; the dating of his reign here follows Eusebius (*Historia ecclesiastica* 4.10). According to the → *Liber Pontificalis,* he was a philosopher from Athens and changed the administration of the Roman community. He was probably a prominent presbyter in the group which led the church in Rome; traces of a monarchical episcopate are found there only from the time of Anicetus. The decretals transmitted under his name are not authentic. According to Irenaeus, the Gnostics Cerdo and Valentinus came to Rome during the time of Hyginus. It is uncertain whether he died as a martyr.

■ **Sources:** *LP* 1:131.

■ **Bibliography:** *DTHC* 7:356f.; *VATL* 310; T. Klauser, "Die Anfänge der römischen Bischofsliste," in *Gesammelte Arbeiten zur Liturgiegeschichte* (Münster, 1974) 121-38; J. Hofmann, "Die amtliche Stellung der in der ältesten römischen Bischofsliste überlieferten Männer in der Kirche von Rom," *Historisches Jahrbuch* 109 (1989) 1-23.

CHRISTOPH BREUER-WINKLER

Innocent I (Dec. 21, 402-Mar. 12, 417). Saint (feast day July 7), born at Alba near Rome, according to Jerome, *Ep.* 130.16, the son of his predecessor Anastasius I. His pontificate was marked by the fall of the Western empire, as Alaric I, king of the west Goths, conquered and sacked Rome in 410. In the midst of external ruin, however, Innocent never lost sight of his main goal, viz., the strengthening of the Roman → primacy. He broadened the compass of the Roman ideas and was the first to sketch them fully; alongside Siricius, Leo I, and Gelasius I, he was one of the most outstanding popes in the fourth and fifth centuries. In letters to the bishops Victricius of Rouen, Exuperius of Toulouse, Decentius of Gubbio, and others, he demanded that church discipline in the West should follow the Roman example; cases of greater moment were to be brought to the "Apostolic See." In the struggle against the Donatists, he claimed final authority in pronouncing dogmatic decisions. He made the same claim when he confirmed (without being requested to do so) the decrees of two African synods against Pelagius and Coelestius. Innocent had little success in the East when he intervened in favor of the deposed John Chrysostom; the result was a temporary rupture with the Eastern bishops and patriarchs. He was the real founder of the papal vicariate in Thessalonica, which attempted to meet the growing influence of Constantinople head-on and to bind Illyricum more securely to Rome.

■ **Sources:** *PL* 20:463-636; *LP* 1:220-24; 3, Index; *RPR*(J) 1:44-49; 2:692, 734; *Collectio Avellana:* Corpus scriptorum ecclesiasticorum latinorum 35 (Vienna, 1895) 92-98.

■ **Bibliography:** *DTHC* 7:1940-50; *LMA* 5:433; *LACL* 309; Caspar 1; W. Marschall, *Karthago und Rom* (Stuttgart, 1971) 238ff.; M.-R. Green, *Pope Innocent I* (Oxford, 1973); O. Wermelinger, *Rom und Pelagius* (Stuttgart, 1975) 116-33; C. Pietri, *Roma christiana,* 2 vols. (Rome, 1976); M. Maccarrone, *Il primato del vescovo di Roma nel primo millennio* (Vatican City, 1991); L. Datrino, "Sollecitudine pastorale di Innocenzo I: Papa di Roma, per la Chiesa sorella di Costantinopoli," *Lateranum* 64 (1998) 221-25.

GEORG SCHWAIGER

Innocent II (Feb. 14, 1130-Sept. 24, 1143). Formerly *Gregory,* from the Trastevere district in Rome. His family was given the name de Papa after him, in 1148; in the thirteenth century, they were called Papareschi. He is attested as cardinal deacon of Sant' Angelo in 1116, and he elected Gelasius II in 1118. In 1119-1120, he followed Callixtus II through France, and returned there with Petrus Pierleoni as legate in 1121 and 1123-1124. He was one of the papal negotiators who concluded the Concordat of Worms. A minority group of younger cardinals, mostly from northern Italy and France, who enjoyed the protection of the Roman Frangipani family, disregarded the compromise election that had been agreed upon

and elected him pope in a bold move against Anacletus II, who had already been elected on the same day by a majority of mostly older cardinals. This schism was caused not by church-political policies but by the relationships of the electors among themselves and vis-à-vis the cardinal chancellor Haimerich. Long-standing relationships cultivated by Innocent and his cardinals helped him attain recognition as pope in France (Etampes, May 1130) and Germany (Würzburg, October 1130); Bernard of Clairvaux and Norbert of Xanten were especially prominent in their support of Innocent, and England and the Spanish realms soon gave him their allegiance too. Innocent had lost control of Rome to Anacletus in June 1130, but he returned for a brief period in 1133 under the protection of Lothar III, whom he crowned as emperor in the Lateran on June 4. He gave Lothar the territories that Matilda had bequeathed to the papacy and accepted a more precise formulation of the Concordat of Worms. The military campaign of Lothar and Innocent in 1136-1137 against Roger II of Sicily (who supported Anacletus) was a failure, as was a renewed attempt to subdue the Norman in 1139. Innocent was taken prisoner and was forced to accept Roger's kingdom in the Treaty of Mignano (July 27, 1139) and to bestow Sicily on him. The synods that Innocent held at Clermont (November 1130), Rheims (October 1131), and Pisa (May-June 1135), like the Second Council of the Lateran (1139), mostly limited themselves to confirming older canons. One innovation in 1130 was the threat that those in major orders who failed to observe celibacy would lose their benefices; in the sphere of sacramental confession, a case reserved to the pope was first stipulated in 1131. In keeping with the increased legal business which characterized the church under Innocent, many more papal documents were issued. From now on, the cardinals regularly joined the pope in signing solemn privileges. Innocent's program of presenting himself in imperial terms found its final expression in his burial in the porphyry sarcophagus of Emperor Hadrian (in the → Lateran until 1308, thereafter in Santa Maria in Trastevere).

■ **Sources:** *LP* 2:379-85; *RPR*(J) 2nd ed. 1:840-911; *Regesta Imperii,* IV/1: *Die Regesten des Kaiserreiches unter Lothar III. und Konrad III.,* revised by W. Petke (Cologne, 1994).

■ **Bibliography:** *EC* 7:7-10; *LMA* 5:433f.; *VATL* 312f.;

P. F. Palumbo, *Lo scisma del MCXXX* (Rome, 1942); F.-J. Schmale, "Die Bemühungen Innozenz' um seine Anerkennung in Deutschland," *Zeitschrift für Kirchengeschichte* 65 (1953/54) 244-68; idem, *Studien zum Schisma des Jahres 1130* (Cologne/Graz, 1961); Mario da Bergamo (= L. Pellegrini), "Osservazioni sulle fonti per la duplice elezione papale del 1130," *Aevum* 39 (1965) 45-65; idem, "La duplice elezione papale del 1130," *Pubblicazioni dell'Università Cattolica del Sacro Cuore. Contributi,* Serie 3,10 (Milan, 1968) 265-302; D. Girgensohn, "Das Pisaner Konzil von 1135 in der Überlieferung des Pisaner Konzils von 1409," in Festschrift for H. Hempel (Göttingen, 1972) 2:1063-1100; J. Deér, *Papsttum und Normannen* (Cologne/Vienna, 1972); W. Maleczek, "Das Kardinalskollegium unter Innozenz und Anaklet II.," *AHP* 19 (1981) 27-78; T. Reuter, "Zur Annerkenung Papst Innozenz' II.," *Deutsches Archiv für Erforschung des Mittelalters* 39 (1983) 395-416; Borgolte 158-65; M. Thumser, *Rom und der römische Adel in der späten Stauferzeit* (Tübingen, 1995) 161-68; A. B. Schmidt, "Der Brief Papst Innozenz' II. an den armenischen Katholikos Gregor III.," *AHC* 31 (1999) 50-71; G. Knight, "Politics and Pastoral Care," *Revue bénédictine* 109 (1999) 359-90.

WOLFGANG PETKE

Innocent III (Jan. 8, 1198-July 16, 1216). Formerly *Lothar of Segni,* born 1160/1161 at Gavignano near Segni, died at Perugia. He studied theology in Paris and canon law at Bologna and entered curial service under Lucius III. He became subdeacon in 1187 and was created cardinal deacon of Santi Sergio e Baccho in 1190. The most widely attested of his theological works (in more than four hundred manuscripts) is his *De miseria humanae conditionis.* As the youngest cardinal, he was elected pope on the day Celestine III died. He was crowned on February 22.

Despite a number of political errors, he is one of the most significant medieval popes. He continued the tradition of the reforming papacy by calling himself "vicar of Christ" (now one of the established papal → titles) and asserted the primacy of the pope in ecclesiastical and secular matters. Within the church, he achieved a great measure of success (jurisdictional primacy, right of devolution, reservation of major cases to the pope, → *ad limina* visits), but in the secular sphere his goals remained vague, dependent as they were on political realities. The development and reorganization of the curial chancellery and administration took place during his pontificate (chancellery regulations, office of the corrector,

measures taken against forgery, keeping of a continuous register, a special register dealing with the conflict about the German throne; earliest attestations of *audientia litterarum contradictarum* [→ Rota] and the [→ Apostolic] Penitentiary). He published his legal decisions in 1210 in the first authentic collection of decretals (*Compilatio III*). His plans for a crusade were a failure: he lost control of the Fourth Crusade, which he had promoted from the beginning of his pontificate and which ended with the conquest of Constantinople in 1204, while a second crusade, proclaimed in 1213 and organized at the Fourth Lateran Council for the year 1217, ended under his successor, Honorius III, in the fiasco of Damietta (Egypt). Innocent vigorously promoted the struggle against heretics (decretal *Vergentis in senium,* 1199; ch. 3 of the decrees of the Fourth Lateran Council, where heresy is characterized as lèse majesté; the Inquisition), but this degenerated into brutal plundering of the countryside in the crusade against the Albigensians (1209-1229). On the other hand, Innocent succeeded in retaining radical reforming groups such as the Humiliati and the "poverty movement" within the church, as well as the more established communities founded by Francis of Assisi and Dominic, whose activity and way of life he officially recognized. The high point of Innocent's ecclesial influence was the Fourth Council of the Lateran (November 1215), which took up questions of politics (the crusade, the Magna Charta, Frederick II) and of faith and church reform.

On balance, Innocent was politically unsuccessful, although he had some success in claiming sovereign feudal lordship over Sicily, Aragon, Portugal, and England, and exacted the right to scrutinize the candidate for the imperial throne (decretal *Venerabilem,* 1202). His main concern was to free the papacy from exposure to the emperor, resulting from the union of the empire with the kingdom of Sicily in 1194 (Sicily had been under the feudal sovereignty of the popes since 1059). The systematic policy of restoration in central Italy after the death of Henry VI (1197) gave the pope's local sovereignty in the Patrimony of Peter a stable basis for the first time, and Innocent was able to consolidate the papal position in Rome itself. Innocent's decision for Otto IV in the conflict about the German throne (*Deliberatio de tribus electis,* 1200/1201) and the promises he exacted from the claimants were primarily intended to prevent a new union of the empire and the kingdom; the will of Empress Constance († 1198) had named the pope feudal guardian of her son, Frederick II, but the political situation made it impossible for Innocent to carry out this task. Nevertheless, Frederick's marriage to a princess from Aragon was the result of papal mediation. Trusting in the promises that had been given, Innocent—who had been disappointed in Otto IV—finally set his hopes after 1210 on the Staufer prince, although he had initially attempted to prevent him from succeeding to the imperial throne.

After a conflict about the appointment of a new archbishop of Canterbury, Innocent imposed the interdict and excommunication on England and forced King John Lackland to entrust his kingdom to the feudal sovereignty of the pope (1213/1214). On the basis of this legal situation, he declared the Magna Charta (1215) invalid. His relations to the French king, Philip II, were soured until 1213 by the question of Philip's marriage; here Innocent took the side of Ingeborg of Denmark. The French king observed the many changes in papal politics vis-à-vis Germany with skeptical reserve.

■ **Sources:** K. Langosch, ed., *Die deutsche Literatur des Mittelalters: Verfasserlexikon* (2nd ed. Berlin/Leipzig, 1981) 2:388-95; *PL* 214-17; *De miseria*, ed. M. Maccarrone (Lugano, 1955); *De miseria*, ed. E. R. Lewis (Athens, Ga., 1978); Register (years 1-2), ed. O. Hageneder et al.: *Die Register Innozenz'* (Graz et al., 1964; Rome/Vienna, 1979); *Regestum super negotio Romani imperii*, ed. F. Kempf (Rome, 1947); *The Letters of Pope Innocent concerning England and Wales*, ed. C. R. Cheney (London, 1967); *RPR(P)* 1 and 2; *Constitutiones Concilii quarti Lateranensis una cum Commentariis glossatorum*, ed. A. García y García (Vatican City, 1981).

■ **Bibliography:** *TRE* 16:175-82; *LMA* 5:434-37; *GKG* 11:196-207; *VATL* 313-17; F. Kempf, *Papsttum und Kaisertum bei Innozenz* (Rome, 1954); H. Tillmann, *Papst Innozenz* (Bonn, 1954); H. Roscher, *Papst Innozenz und die Kreuzzüge* (Göttingen, 1969); C. R. Cheney, *Innocent and England* (Stuttgart, 1976); M. Laufs, *Politik und Recht bei Innozenz* (Cologne, 1980); W. Imkamp, *Das Kirchenbild Innozenz'* (Stuttgart, 1983); W. Maleczek, *Papst und Kardinalskolleg von 1191 bis 1216* (Wiesbaden, 1984); T. Holzapfel, *Papst Innozenz, Philip II. August, König von Frankreich und die englisch-welfische Verbindung 1198-1216* (Frankfurt a.M., 1991); C. Egger, "Papst Innozenz als Theologe," *AHP* 30 (1992) 55-123; R. Foreville, *Le pape Innocent et la France* (Stuttgart, 1992); G. Baaken, *Ius imperii ad reg-*

num (Cologne/Vienna, 1993); J. E. Sayers, *Innocent III: Leader of Europe* (London et al., 1994); M. Maccarrone, ed., *Nuovi studi su Innocenzo III* (Rome, 1995); H. J. Sieben, "Basileios Pediadites und Innozenz III.," *AHC* 27/28 (1995-96) 249-74; N. Kuster, "Das Armutsprivileg Innozenz' III. und Klaras Testament: Echt oder raffinierte Fälschung?" *Collectanea Franciscana* 66 (1996) 5-95; T. M. Violante, "Innocenzo III e l'Oriente bizantino," *Nicolaus* 24 (1997) 311-52; B. M. Kienzle, "Holiness and Obedience: Denouncement of Twelfth-Century Waldensian Lay Preaching," in *The Devil, Heresy and Witchcraft in the Middle Ages*, Festschrift for J. B. Russel (Leiden, 1998) 259-78; C. M. Rousseau, "'Pater urbis et orbis': Innocent III and His Perspectives on Fatherhood," *AHP* 37 (1999) 25-37; J. C. Moore, *Pope Innocent III and His World* (Aldershot, 1999); T. Frenz, ed., *Papst Innozenz III.: Interdisziplinäre Ringvorlesung an der Universität Passau, 5.11.1997-26.5.1998* (Stuttgart, 2000); M. Menzel, "Kreuzzugsideologie unter Innozenz III.," *Historisches Jahrbuch* 120 (2000) 39-79.

THEO KÖLZER

Innocent III (antipope) (Sept. 29, 1179-Jan. 1180). Formerly *Lando of Sezze (Landus Sitinus),* the last antipope in opposition to Alexander III. The antipope Victor IV created him cardinal, and Victor's relatives chose Lando to succeed the antipope Calixtus III. He fell into the hands of Alexander III in January 1180, and was imprisoned for life in the monastery of La Cava. This brought to an end the schism that had existed since 1159.

■ **Sources:** J. B. Watterich, *Pontificum Romanorum qui fuerunt inde ab exeunte saeculo IX usque ad finem saeculi XIII vitae ab aequalibus conscriptae etc.*, Vol. 2 (1099-1198) (Leipzig, 1862) 647f.; *RPR(J)* 2:431.

■ **Bibliography:** *LMA* 5:434; B. U. Hergemöller, *Die Geschichte der Papstnamen* (Münster, 1980) 91f.; F. Liotta, ed., *Miscellanea Rolando Bandinelli papa Alessandro III* (Siena, 1986); W. Georgi, *Friedrich Barbarossa und die auswärtigen Mächte* (Frankfurt a.M., 1990) 329.

THEO KÖLZER

Innocent IV (June 25, 1243-Dec. 7, 1254). Formerly *Sinibaldo Fieschi,* born ca. 1180/1190 in Lavagna; his family, the counts of Lavagna, supported the Ghibellines. His father, Hugo, was in charge of imperial taxes. He was educated in Parma and studied civil and canon law in Bologna, where he came to the notice of the cardinal legate Hugolin (later Gregory IX). He became *auditor litterarum contradictarum* in 1226, and apostolic vice-chancellor and cardinal priest of

San Lorenzo in 1227. He was rector of the Marches of Ancona and papal legate from 1234 to 1239. After a lengthy *sede vacante,* he was elected in the first conclave to be held in → Anagni and crowned on June 28, 1243. He was immediately confronted with the struggle for supremacy between *imperium* and *sacerdotium,* and he soon disappointed Staufer expectations and made the controversy more acute by his assertion "the pope judges everyone " (*Papa iudex est omnium*). His pontificate was deeply marked by his conflict with the excommunicated emperor Frederick II. This struggle was also conducted by means of propaganda texts and culminated in the deposition of the emperor at the First General Council of Lyons on July 17, 1245, and the demand that the imperial princes elect a new king. The basis of these actions was the claim that the pope enjoyed "direct power in secular matters" (*potestas directa in temporalibus*). The emperor never recognized the election. At the same time, Innocent removed the Portuguese king Sancho II from government, suspending him as a "useless king." The Council of Lyons was the high point of the pontificate. Under the protection of King Louis IX of France, the council also discussed the crusade to win back Jerusalem, aid to the Latin empire in Constantinople, the Mongol question, and measures for church reform. The Capetians hoped for considerable political gains from a meeting in Cluny between the pope and Louis IX, but the pope did not succeed in negotiating a reconciliation— mainly because of the Sicilian question. The emperor's propaganda in the letters he wrote to the European sovereigns in defense of his standpoint (especially *Etsi cause nostre*) was answered in the manifesto *Eger cui lenia,* which employs a radical exposition of the doctrine of the two swords to justify the superiority of spiritual over secular power. The conflict escalated as a result of the pope's support of the two German anti-kings Henry Raspe and William of Holland, and was aggravated by preparations for a crusade against the Staufer; the dispute survived the deaths of Frederick II in 1250 and of Conrad IV (likewise excommunicated) in 1254.

Independently of these matters, Innocent succeeded in initiating the Dominican and Franciscan missions to the East (foundation of the Prussian dioceses of Kulm, Pomerania, Ermland, and Samland). Apart from the decrees of Lyons

relevant to canon law, which were promulgated as papal constitutions on August 25, 1245, and subsequently added with other texts to the "Liber extra," the *Apparatus in quinque libros decretalium* (printed at Strasbourg in 1477) was important. This was a commentary on the decretals of Gregory IX, which provided further support to the pope's right to depose kings. These texts, together with the further development of the inquisition of heretics (the constitution *Ad extirpandam* introduced torture by the secular arm in 1252), established his reputation as a "lawyer pope."

■ **Sources:** *RPR*(P) 2:943-1286; E. Berger, ed., *Les registres d'Innocent IV,* 4 vols. (Paris, 1884-1921); G. Abate, "Lettere secrete d'Innocenzo IV," *Miscellanea francescana* 55 (1955) 317-73; T. T. Haluscynskyj and M. M. Wojnar, *Acta Innocentii papae IV* (Rome, 1961); A. Quintana Prieto, *La documentación pontificia de Inocencio IV,* 2 vols. (Rome, 1987); *Vita Innocentii IV scripta a fr. Nicolao de Carbio,* reprinted in Melloni, *Innocenzo IV* (see bibliography below) 259-93.

■ **Bibliography:** *LMA* 5:437f.; *TRE* 16:182-85; *VATL* 317ff.; M. Pacaut, "L'autorité pontificale selon Innocent IV," *Le Moyen-âge* 66 (1960) 85-119; W. de Vries, "Innozenz IV. und die Ostkirchen," *Ostkirchliche Studien* 12 (1963) 113-31; J. A. Watt, "The Theory of Papal Monarchy in the Thirteenth Century," *Traditio* 20 (1964) 179-317; P. Herde, "Ein Pamphlet der päpstlichen Kurie gegen Kaiser Friedrich II. von 1245/46 ('Eger cui lenia')," *Deutsches Archiv für Erforschung des Mittelalters* 23 (1967) 468-538 (critical edition on pp. 508-38); E. M. Peters, "Rex inutilis: Sancho II of Portugal and Thirteenth Century Deposition Theory," *Studia Gratiana* 14 (1967) 253-305; L. Pisanu, *L'attività politica di Innocenzo IV e i Francescani* (Rome, 1969); W. Kölmel, *Regimen Christianum* (Berlin, 1970); A. Paravicini Bagliani, *Cardinali di Curia e "familiae" cardinalizie dal 1227 al 1245,* 2 vols. (Padua, 1972); A. Franchi, *La svolta politico-ecclesiastica tra Roma e Bisanzio (1249-1254)* (Rome, 1981); K.-E. Lupprian, *Die Beziehungen der Päpste zu islamischen und mongolischen Herrschern im 13. Jahrhundert* (Vatican City, 1981); L. Buisson, *Potestas und Caritas: Die päpstliche Gewalt im Spätmittelalter* (2nd ed. Cologne/Vienna, 1982); K. Pennington, *Pope and Bishops: The Papal Monarchy in the Twelfth and Thirteenth Centuries* (Philadelphia, 1984); A. Melloni, "William of Ockham's Critique of Innocent IV," *Franziskanische Studien* 46 (1986) 161-203; E. Bernal Palacios, "Repertorios del comentario de Inocencio IV a las Decretales de Gregorio IX," *Escritos del Vedat* 17 (1987) 143-72; A. Melloni, *Innocenzo IV* (Genoa, 1990); G. Baaken, *Ius imperii ad regnum* (Cologne et al., 1993); idem, "Die Verhandlungen von Cluny (1245) und der Kampf Innozenz' IV. gegen Friedrich II.," *Deutsches Archiv für Erforschung des Mittelalters* 50 (1994) 531-79;

M. Thumser, *Rom und der römische Adel in der späten Stauferzeit* (Tübingen, 1995); A. Paravicini Bagliani, *La cour des papes au XIIIe siècle* (Paris, 1995); A. Melloni, "I fondamenti del regime di cristianità al Lionese I," *Cristianesimo nella storia* 18 (1997) 61-76; D. Berg, "Papst Innozenz IV. und die Bettelorden in ihren Beziehungen zu Kaiser Friedrich II.," in *Vita religiosa im Mittelalter*, Festschrift for K. Elm (Berlin, 1999) 461-81.

LUDWIG VONES

Innocent V (Jan. 21-June 22, 1276). Blessed (feast day June 22), Dominican (1240). Formerly *Peter of Tarentaise*, born ca. 1224 at Champigny in Savoy. He studied theology in Paris from 1255 and became doctor of theology in 1259. He taught from 1259 to 1264/1265 and from 1267 to 1269; he became provincial of his order in France in 1264. Together with Albert the Great and Thomas Aquinas, he drew up the Dominican order of studies. He became archbishop of Lyons in 1272 and was in charge of the preparations for the Council of Lyons (1274). He was created cardinal bishop of Ostia in 1273 and was ordained before August 9, 1273; he was replaced by Aymar of Roussillon in April 1274. As a confidant of Gregory X, he took part in the political negotiations of the curia (at Beaucaire with Alfonso X of Castille; at Lausanne with Rudolf I of the house of Habsburg). He was elected pope by means of scrutinies at Arezzo, and crowned on February 22, 1276. His principal goal was the crusade. To this end, he continued the rapprochement with Byzantium and sought to end the conflicts which divided the Western powers; this was his intention when he crowned Rudolf I as emperor, taking account of the Angevin interests and renewing the feudal submission of Charles I of Anjou, whom he confirmed as senator of Rome and imperial vicegerent of Tuscany (1276). He composed a *Commentary on the Sentences* which bears the imprint of a transition from Augustinianism to Aristotelianism, a *Quodlibet*, and exegetical writings.

■ **Works:** T. Turco and G. B. de Marinis, eds., *Innocentius V in quattuor libros sententiarum commentaria*, 4 vols. (Toulouse, 1649-52; repr. 1964).
■ **Bibliography:** *LMA* 5:438; P. Glorieux, *Répertoire des maîtres en théologie de Paris au XIIIe siècle* (Paris, 1933) 1:104-54; H.-D. Simonin, *Les écrits de Pierre de Tarentaise* (Rome, 1943); M.-H. Laurent, *Le Bienheureux Innocent V et son temps* (Vatican City, 1947; repr. 1972); L. F. Barmann, "Peter of Tarentaise," *Revue de l'Université d'Ottawa* 31 (1961) 96-125; E. Marchisa, "Saggio sull'antropologia filosofica di Pietro da Tarentaise (Beatus I.) nel commento alle Sentenze di Pier Lombardo," *Divus Thomas* 71 (Piacenza, 1968) 210-70.

LUDWIG VONES

Innocent VI (Dec. 18, 1352-Sept. 12, 1362). Formerly *Étienne Aubert,* born in 1282 or 1295 at Les-Monts-de-Beyssac (Département of Corrèze) into a nonaristocratic family. After study of the law, leading to a doctorate (1329/1330), he was active as teacher and judge in Toulouse. He kept the seal and was the deputy of the seneschal of Toulouse and Albi. He was an official and counselor of King Philip VI, who sent him as his envoy to Benedict XII. He became bishop of Noyon in 1338 and of Clermont in 1340. Clement VI created him cardinal priest of Santi Giovanni e Paolo in 1342. He became Grand Penitentiary in 1348 and cardinal bishop of Ostia in 1352. He was elected (and crowned on December 30, 1352) after the first attested electoral capitulation in papal history, although he annulled this on July 6, 1353, as incompatible with the pope's *plenitudo potestatis.* Despite his flagrant → nepotism, he attempted somewhat half-heartedly to renew the attempts at reform begun by Benedict XII, which had been lost from view under his immediate predecessor Clement VI. Under Innocent, this took the form of moves to reform the curia (limitations on the accumulation of benefices, obligation of residence) and of the College of → Cardinals (Constitution *Ad honorem,* 1357) rather than primarily a reform of the religious orders (mendicants, Knights of St. John). Above all, he prepared the way for the return of the papacy from → Avignon to Rome; although this was financially ruinous, it was greeted by many (e.g., Petrarch and Bridget of Sweden); in view of this aim, he sent legations to Italy (Cardinal Aegiduis Alvarez Albornoz in June 1353; Cardinal Androin de la Roche in 1357/1358) to recover those territories in the → papal states that had been lost and to reestablish the administration there (*Constitutiones Aegidianae,* 1357). His endeavors to reach an understanding with Cola di Rienzo led to nothing; nevertheless, it was possible for Charles IV to be crowned emperor in Rome in 1355, although he did not supply the military support for which the pope had hoped. His attempts at mediation between England and France in the unstable Treaty of Brétigny, and between Castille and Aragon, were unsuccessful. He resumed negotiations with the Eastern church about a union, and tried in vain to initiate a crusade.

Innocent VI made the best of his limited possibilities to seek progress in church politics, but ultimately lacked the strength to achieve a genuine renewal. He was the founder of the college of St. Martial in Toulouse (1359), of the theological faculty of Bologna (1360), and of the charterhouse of Villeneuve-lès-Avignon (1356-1362), where he was buried.

■ **Sources:** É. Baluze and G. Mollat, *Vitae paparum Avenionensium* (Paris, 1916) 1:309-48; 2 (1928) 433-89; R. R. Post, *Supplieken gericht aan de pausen Clemens VI, Innocentius VI en Urbanus V 1342-66* ('s-Gravenhage, 1937); H. Hoberg, *Die Einnahmen der Apostolischen Kammer unter Innozenz VI.*, 2 vols. (Paderborn, 1955, 1972); P. Gasnault, N. Gotteri, and M. H. Laurent, *Innocent VI (1352-62): Lettres secrètes et curiales* [up to Dec. 30, 1356], 4 vols. (Paris, 1959-76); A. L. Tautu, ed., *Acta Innocentii VI* (Vatican City, 1961); J. Glénisson and G. Mollat, *L'administration des États de l'Eglise au XIVᵉ siècle: Correspondance des légats et vicaires-généraux Gil Albornoz et Androin de la Roche (1353-1367)* (Paris, 1964); J. Zunzunegui Aramburu, *Bulas y cartas secretas de Inocencio VI* (Rome, 1970); D. Williman, "Memoranda and Sermons of Étienne Aubert (Innocent VI) as Bishop (1338-41)," *Mediaeval Studies* 37 (1975) 7-41; E. Sáez und J. Trenchs Odena, eds., *Diplomatario del Cardenal Gil de Albornoz: Cancillería pontificia 1351-1353* (Barcelona, 1976); E. Sáez, M. T. Ferrer, J. Trenchs Odena et al., eds. *Cancillería pontificia 1354-56* (Barcelona, 1981); *Acta Pataviensia Austriaca: Vatikanische Akten zur Geschichte des Bistums Passau und der Herzöge von Österreich (1342-78)*, II: *Innozenz VI.* (Vienna, 1992).

■ **Bibliography:** *LMA* 5:438f.; *VATL* 319ff.; W. de Vries, "Die Päpste von Avignon und der christliche Osten," *Orientalia christiana periodica* 30 (1964) 85-128; G. Mollat, *Les papes d'Avignon* (10th ed. Paris, 1965); B. Guillemain, *La cour pontificale d'Avignon* (2nd ed. Paris, 1966); P. Colliva, *Il cardinale Albornoz, lo stato della Chiesa, le "Constitutiones Aegidianae" (1353-57)* (Bologna, 1977); N. Housley, *The Avignon Papacy and the Crusades* (Oxford, 1986); *Aux origines de l'État Moderne: Le fonctionnement administratif de la papauté d'Avignon* (Rome, 1990); B. Schimmelpfennig, ed., *Die Geschichte des Christentums* (Freiburg, 1991) VI; R. Pauler, "Die Rehabilitierung Ludwigs des Brandenburgers im Rahmen der päpstlichen Imperialpolitik," *Zeitschrift für bayerische Landesgeschichte* 60 (1997) 317-28.

LUDWIG VONES

Innocent VII (Oct. 17, 1404-Nov. 6, 1406). Pope of the Roman obedience during the Western Schism, formerly *Cosimo Gentile de' Migliorati*. Born ca. 1336 at Sulmona (Abruzzi), died in Rome, buried in St. Peter's. After studying law in Bologna, he was professor in Perugia and Padua. The Roman curia sent him to England as collector; he was also legate for Tuscany and Lombardy. He became archbishop of Ravenna in 1387, then archbishop of Bologna and cardinal in 1389. In the conclave of 1404, Innocent and the other seven cardinals of the Roman obedience swore in an electoral capitulation that they would do everything possible to end the schism, including abdication. Although he had good intentions as Pope, he lacked the strength to implement this promise. Under pressure from the German king Ruprecht, he summoned a council to meet in Rome in 1405, but nothing came of this. Innocent was forced to call King Ladislaus of Naples to his aid in Rome and became dependent on him. Although he had no success in the question of the schism, this pope carried out a valuable reorganization of the Roman university and was a supporter of early humanism.

■ **Sources:** *LP* 2:508ff., 531ff., 552ff.; L. A. Muratori, *Rerum Italicarum scriptores ab anno aerae christianae 500 ad 1500*, new ed. by G. Carducci and V. Fiorini (Città di Castello, 1900) III/2, 832-37; M. Maillard-Luypaert, ed., *Lettres d'Innocent VII* (Brussels/Rome, 1987).

■ **Bibliography:** *LMA* 5:439; *VATL* 321; G. Bolino, "Papa Innocenzo VII di G. Capogrossi," *Bolletino della Deputazione abruzzese* 70 (1980) 487-510; Borgolte 260f.; R. Russo, *Innocenzo VII: Il Papa sulmonese nel turbine del grande scisma d'Occidente* (Sulmona, 1996).

JOHANNES GROHE

Innocent VIII (Aug. 29, 1484-July 25, 1492). Formerly *Giovanni Battista Cibo*, born in 1432 in Genoa; his father subsequently became a Roman senator and a legal official at the court of Naples, where Giovanni Battista grew up. He studied in Padua and Rome and was a protégé of the cardinals Filippo Calandrini and Giuliano della Rovere. He became bishop of Savona in 1467, and of Molfetta in 1472. He was created cardinal in 1473 and became pope in 1484 as the compromise candidate of the Orsini and the Colonna; his election was probably due to simony and intrigues on the part of della Rovere. At the prompting of della Rovere, he joined the war of Neapolitan barons against King Ferrante. This, however, led to complications in foreign policy (hostility on the part of

Hungary and Milan, appeals to France for help), to the devastation of the → papal states and to further deterioration of the papal finances, which were already very weak. Innocent tried to improve the finances by selling ecclesiastical offices (some specially created for the occasion) and by a rapprochement with Florence: in 1488, he married his illegitimate son Francesc(hett)o to a daughter of Lorenzo de' Medici, whose son Giovanni (later Leo X) he created cardinal in 1489. A crusade against the Turks did not get beyond the planning stage; indeed, Innocent was the first pope to have friendly relations with the Sultan and received the Holy Lance and a sum of money in return for supporting Bayazid II against his brother Djem. The government of the church states was in the hands of local oligarchies, and the Orsini and the Colonna increased their influence. In and around Rome, Innocent exploited his available financial resources to erect buildings and to support such artists as Pollaiuolo, Pinturicchio, Andrea Mantegna, Filippo Lippi, and Perugino. His bull *Summis desiderantes affectibus* (1484), issued at the urging of the Dominicans Heinrich Institoris and Jakob Sprenger, authorized them to proceed as inquisitors against persons suspected of witchcraft; this was to have fatal consequences. In 1486, he condemned the nine hundred theses of the Neoplatonist Giovanni Pico della Mirandola. Innocent, who was often ill, found it difficult to make decisions; his office as pope made excessive demands of him, morally and politically. He did nothing to promote the urgently necessary reform of the church and the curia.

■ **Bibliography:** *DTHC* 7:2002-5; *EC* 8:18f.; *CATH* 5:1665-68; *NCE* 7:526f.; *LMA* 5:439f.; *DHGE* 25:1267; *VATL* 321ff.; K. A. Gersbach, "Onofrio Panvinio and Cybo Family Pride in His Treatment of Innocent VIII and in the 'XXVII pontificum maximorum elogia et imagines,'" *Analecta Augustiniana* 54 (1991) 115-41; R. Marino, *Cristoforo Colombo e il papa tradito* (4th ed. Rome, 1997).

HERIBERT MÜLLER

Innocent IX (Oct. 29-Dec. 30, 1591). Formerly *Giovanni Antonio Fachinetti,* born July 20, 1519, in Bologna. After studying law, he entered the service of Cardinal Alessandro Farnese (later Paul III) in Bologna. He was bishop of Nicastro from 1560 to 1575 and took part in the Council of Trent in 1562. As nuncio in Venice from 1566 to 1575, he endeavored to meet Pius V's wishes by organizing a league against Turkey. In 1576, he was appointed Latin patriarch of Jerusalem and was created cardinal in 1583. He was elected pope because the party hostile to Spain wanted to gain time; it was not yet possible to exclude the influence of Philip II. Innocent continued Gregory XIV's policy of taking the lead from Spain. He supported the French league against King Henry IV. His early death prevented him from carrying out an energetic reform of the curia. His theological and philosophical works have never been published.

■ **Bibliography:** *VATL* 323f.; Pastor 10:574-87.

GEORG SCHWAIGER

Innocent X (Sept. 15, 1644-Jan. 7, 1655). Formerly *Giambattista Pamfili,* born May 6, 1574, in Rome. After studying law in Rome, he became a consistorial advocate in 1601 and auditor of the Rota in 1604. He entered the diplomatic service of the popes as nuncio in Naples in 1621. He accompanied Cardinal Francesco Barberini, nephew of Urban VIII, on his legation to France and Spain in 1625. He was created cardinal *in petto* in 1627 and published in 1629; he was prefect of the Congregation of the Council. After the conclave had lasted thirty-seven days, and before the French veto against him reached the cardinals, he was elected pope. As pope, Innocent acted decisively against the Barberini, who were accused of lining their own pockets; however, Cardinal Mazarin forced him to pardon them. In the brief *Zelo domus Dei* (November 26, 1648), he repeated the protest made by the nuncio Fabio Chigi (later Alexander VII) against those provisions of the Peace of Westphalia which infringed on the rights of the church. He condemned five propositions in the book *Augustinus* by Bishop Cornelius Jansenius in the bull *Cum occasione* (May 31, 1653). In the conflict between France and Spain, he attempted a political balancing act. He helped Venice and Poland against the Turks, but his financial means did not allow him to help Emperor Ferdinand III. His predecessor, Urban VIII, had not been able to reach any agreement with King John IV of Portugal after Portugal was separated from Spain in 1640, and things did not improve under Innocent: while he did not issue a formal condemnation of the revolt, as Spain demanded, Innocent refused to acknowledge John as king or to accept his episcopal nominations. Innocent promoted world missions and the arts (restoration of the Lateran basilica; completion of the interior decoration of St. Peter's; construction of the splendid Villa Doria Pamfili, Gianlorenzo Bernini's fountain, the papal family palace, and Sant' Agnese on the Piazza Navona). His influential sister-in-law Olimpia Maidalchini and the papal nephews cast a negative light on his pontificate. He was buried in St. Peter's; his body was translated to Sant' Agnese in 1677.

■ **Bibliography:** M. Feuillas, "Innocent X," *Dictionnaire du Grand Siècle* (Paris, 1990) 756f.; *VATL* 324f.; Pastor 14:13-299; L. Hammermayer, "Grundlagen der Entwicklung des päpstlichen Staatssekretariats von Paul V. bis Innozenz X. (1605-55)," *RQ* 55 (1960) 157-202; A. Legrand, *La première bulle contre Jansénius: Sources relatives à son histoire (1644-53)* (Brussels/Rome, 1961-62); M. Albert, *Nuntius Fabio Chigi und die Anfänge des Jansenismus, 1639-51* (Rome et al., 1988); K. Repgen, "Die Proteste Chigis und der päpstliche Protest gegen den Westfälischen Frieden (1648-50)," in *Staat, Kirche, Wissenschaft in einer pluralistischen Gesellschaft*, Festschrift for P. Mikat (Berlin, 1989) 623-47; A. Zuccari and S. Macioce, eds., *Innocenzo X Pamphilj* (Rome, 1990); M. F. Feldkamp, "Das Breve 'Zelo domus Dei' vom 26.11.1648," *AHP* 31 (1993) 293-305 (edition); P. Blet, "Louis XIV et les papes aux prises avec le jansénisme," *AHP* 31 (1993) 109-92; 32 (1994) 65-148; K. Repgen, "Drei Korollarien zum Breve 'Zelo Domus Dei,'" *AHP* 33 (1995) 315-33; L. Nussdorfer, "Print and Pageantry in Baroque Rome," *The Sixteenth-Century Journal* 29 (1998) 439-64; R. DeMattei, "La politica della Santa Sede nel secolo XVII dalla pace di Westfalia alla 'scelta innocenziana,'" *Ricerche di storia sociale e religiosa* 55 (1999) 213-18.

GEORG SCHWAIGER

Innocent XI (Sept. 21, 1676-Aug. 12, 1689). Blessed (feast day Aug. 12). Formerly *Benedetto Odescalchi*, born May 19, 1611, into a well-to-do family of merchants at Como. After studying theology and civil and canon law, he was made apostolic protonotary and president of the → Apostolic Chamber. He was created cardinal in 1645. He was legate in Ferrara from 1646-1650, during the time of famine. He was bishop of Novara from 1650 to 1656. He was rejected by France in the conclave of 1670, but he was unanimously elected, after King Louis XIV had indicated his assent, at the close of the two-month-long conclave that followed the death of Clement X. He was an energetic leader who defended basic Christian principles and papal authority against attacks. He brought order to the administration and finances of the → papal state

and reformed curial bodies and monasteries in Rome. He kept himself free of → nepotism, and sought to ban it with a bull whose publication was prevented by the opposition of the cardinals. Like Alexander VII, he acted against tendencies toward laxism in moral theology. In 1675, he condemned sixty-five "laxist" propositions drawn from the writings of a number of Jesuits. This did not amount to a direct condemnation of moral probabilism, although Innocent personally rejected this moral system: when the Jesuit Tirso González de Santalla attacked the probabilism that was predominant in his order, Innocent supported him against all opposition and strongly promoted his election as general of the Jesuits in 1687. Innocent had already gone so far as to prohibit the Jesuits from receiving new novices for a period (1684), and he was suspected of being a Jansenist. On the other hand, he also condemned the extreme Quietism of Miguel de Molinos in 1687, and the Quietist works of Cardinal Pier Matteo Petrucci were put on the Index. In the sphere of foreign politics, Innocent had to combat the ruthless absolutism of Louis XIV, and he protested repeatedly against the illegal extension to the whole of France of the king's authority to make ecclesiastical appointments. He resisted the Gallican Articles of March 19, 1682, by refusing to confirm the king's episcopal candidates, who had signed this declaration. When Innocent abolished the right of the French ambassadors in Rome to grant asylum (1687), the French envoy Henri de Lavardin attempted to defend the liberty of his quarter by force of arms. Innocent disapproved of the persecution of the Huguenots, which began with the royal abrogation of the Edict of Nantes (1685). The conflict became even more intense in 1688, when Innocent decided in favor of Joseph Clemens of Bavaria as candidate for the archdiocese of Cologne, rejecting Cardinal Wilhelm Egon von Fürstenberg, who was the preferred candidate of Louis XIV. The only thing that prevented an open schism was the intervention by François Fénelon and the change of government in England. In international politics, the French king was always Innocent's adversary, especially on the question of the repulsion of the Turks. Innocent, supported by his nuncios, attempted to unite Europe against the Turkish menace. Despite French intrigues, he achieved an alliance between the Polish king John Sobieski and Emperor

Leopold I, so that the siege of Vienna could be raised in 1683; the victory at Kahlenberg outside Vienna ensured that the Turkish danger was definitively banished from central Europe. As a further step to repel the Turks, Innocent promoted and supported financially the Holy League of the empire, Poland, Venice, and Russia, which succeeded in liberating Hungary (1686) and recapturing Belgrade (1688). Innocent most probably knew nothing of the military campaign of William III of Orange against King James II of England (the "Glorious Revolution" of 1688), and he certainly did not support this. Innocent was the outstanding pope of his century, exemplary in his endeavor to unite the Christian peoples in peace, and this won him high esteem among non-Catholics. Leopold von Ranke saw him as an example of the "most laudable task" of the papacy, viz., mediation and peace-making. The cause of his canonization was introduced under Clement XI, but no progress was made after the pontificate of Benedict XIV, principally because of French opposition. Pius XII beatified him on October 7, 1956 (*AAS* 48 [1956] 754-59, 762-78). His tomb is in St. Peter's.

■ **Bibliography:** *BBKL* 2:1298-1303; *VATL* 325f.; Pastor 14:669-1043; P. Blet, "Innocent XI et l'assemblée du clergé de France en 1682," *AHP* 7 (1969) 329-77; idem, *Les Assemblées du clergé et Louis XIV de 1670 à 1693* (Rome, 1972); B. Neveu, ed., *Correspondance du nonce en France Angelo Ranuzi 1683-89* (Rome, 1973); P. Giani, ed., *Epistolario innocenziano* (Como, 1977); B. Neveu, "Episcopus et princeps Urbis: Innocent XI réformateur de Rome d'après des documents inédits (1676-89)," in *Römische Kurie, Kirchliche Finanzen . . . ,* Festschrift for H. Hoberg (Rome, 1979) 2:597-633; R.-J. Maras, *Innocent XI, Pope of Christian Unity* (Notre Dame, Ind., 1984); P. Giani, ed., "Celebrazioni del III centenario della morte del Beato Innocenzo XI," *Archivio Storico della Diocesi di Como* 3 (1989) 17-109; A. Lauro, *Il cardinale Giovan Battista de Luca: Diritto e riforme nello Stato della Chiesa 1676-83* (Naples, 1991); V. Sellin, "Der benutzte Vermittler: Innozenz XI. und der pfälzische Erbstreit," in *Papstgeschichte und Landesgeschichte*, ed. J. Dahlhaus and A. Kohnle, Festschrift for H. Jakobs (Cologne, 1995) 603-18.

GEORG SCHWAIGER

Innocent XII (July 12, 1691-Sept. 27, 1700). Formerly *Antonio Pignatelli,* born March 13, 1615, near Spinazzola (Basilicata), son of the prince of Minervino. He was educated at the college of the Jesuits in Rome. He entered the service of the curia under Urban VIII. He was nuncio in Florence in 1652, in Warsaw in 1660, and in Vienna in 1668. Clement X recalled him to Italy and appointed him bishop of Lecce in 1672. He was created cardinal in 1681 and was appointed bishop of Faënza and legate in Bologna. He became archbishop of Naples in 1687. His election came at the end of a five-month-long conclave, which led to riots in Rome; he was a compromise between the French and the Spanish-imperial parties. Like Innocent XI, who was his model, Innocent XII led a modest life and promoted reform. The constitution *Romanum decet pontificem* (June 22, 1692) was intended to eradicate → nepotism; in the future, all cardinals had to swear to uphold it. In 1695, he forbade the electoral capitulations which were common in the German imperial church when bishops and abbots were elected. A number of measures promoted the reform of the clergy, both secular and religious. Innocent also introduced reforms in the church states, especially limiting offices for sale (1694), without, however, damaging their finances. The religious and political conflict with France, concerning the king's right to make church appointments and the Declaration of 1682, was brought to an end, after having lasted fifty years; it was now possible to fill the many vacant French dioceses. Louis XIV proved accommodating, because he wanted papal support in the Spanish War of Inheritance, which was imminent. To begin with, Innocent had accepted the Bavarian prince as heir; but after his death, he advised Charles II of Spain to appoint Louis XIV's grandson (Philip V) as his heir. The understanding between Innocent and Emperor Leopold I, which had initially been good (support in the war against the Turks), was strained when Hanover became the ninth Electorate in 1693, and Innocent continued to favor France. The arrogant behavior of the imperial ambassador increased the tensions. In the controversy about French Quietism (Jeanne-Marie Guyon), Innocent condemned twenty-three propositions of Archbishop François Fénelon in 1699. He upheld his predecessor's decrees against Jansenism. Like Innocent XI, he supported Tirso González de Santalla against moral probabilism. He intervened in the rites controversy, but a final decision was reached only under Clement XI.

■ **Bibliography:** *BBKL* 2:1303ff.; *VATL* 326ff.; Pastor 14:1073-1166; F. Aragona Pignatelli, *Innocenzo XII e la sua famiglia* (Naples, 1946); M. Fantasia, *Innocenzo XII* (Molfetta, 1966); M. Fatica, "La reclusione dei poveri a Roma durante il pontificato di Innocenzo XII," *Ricerche per la storia religiosa di Roma* 3 (1979) 133-79; R. Leuenberger, "Die Verurteilung Fénelons durch Rom," *Zeitschrift für Theologie und Kirche* 86 (1989) 157-78; R. Ago, *Carriere e clientele nella Roma barocca* (Bari, 1990); L. M. de Palma, ed., *Studi su A. Pignatelli, Papa Innocenzo XII* (Lecce, 1992); M. Turrini, "La riforma del clero secolare durante il pontificato di Innocenzo XII," *Cristianesimo nella storia* 13 (1992) 329-59; L. Ceyssens, "Innocent XII et le jansénisme," *Antonianum* 67 (1992) 39-66; F. A. Gisondi, *Innocenzo XII, Antonio Pignatelli* (Rome, 1994); *Riforme, religione e politica durante il pontificato di Innocenzo XII: Atti del convegno di studio* (Lecce 1991; Galatina, 1995).

GEORG SCHWAIGER

Innocent XIII (May 8, 1721-Mar. 7, 1724). Formerly *Michelangelo dei Conti,* born May 13, 1655, in Poli near Palestrina, son of the duke of Poli. After studies in Ancona and under the Jesuits in Rome, he entered the service of the curia early on and worked in the administration of the church states (→ Papal States). From 1695 to 1698, he was → nuncio in Lucerne, and from 1698 to 1706 in Lisbon. He was created cardinal in 1706, and was bishop of Osimo from 1709 to 1712, and of Viterbo from 1712 to 1719. He was elected unanimously at the close of a difficult conclave. After the politics of Clement XI, Innocent sought a peaceful accommodation with the secular powers: for example, he bestowed Naples-Sicily on Emperor Charles VI in 1722, although the pope's sovereign feudal rights had been disregarded at the change of rulers in 1720 and Charles VI asserted his claim to the "Monarchia sicula." Negotiations in Vienna about the restitution of Comacchio were brought to a successful conclusion only in 1725; Innocent did not succeed in getting his sovereign feudal rights over Parma and Piacenza recognized. He disappointed the Jansenists by upholding the bull *Unigenitus.* He had been hostile to the Jesuits since his time as nuncio in Portugal. In the rites controversy, he demanded respect for the papal decrees, which had hitherto been ignored.

■ Bibliography: *VATL* 328f.; Pastor 15:392-460; *Papes et papauté au XVIIIe siècle* (Paris, 1999).

GEORG SCHWAIGER

Joan (other names such as Jutta are also found). Alleged female pope. According to the legend, she was a learned notary or teacher in Rome who dressed in male clothing, was made pope, and subsequently gave birth while mounting her horse, which then dragged her through the streets. She was stoned by the people and was buried where she died. According to another version of the story, she accompanied her lover to Athens, where she studied, and subsequently drew attention to herself in Rome as a teacher of the trivium and then became pope. Unaware that the time to give birth was approaching, she bore her child on the way from St. Peter's to the Lateran, between the Colosseum and San Clemente, but died in childbirth and was buried there. A variant sewn onto a manuscript of the fourteenth century relates that the female pope did penance for her sins in a convent and was buried there by her son, who had been created cardinal of Ostia. She is first mentioned, without a name, in the world chronicle of Jean de Mailly in Metz (ca. 1250), where we are told that she lived before the year 1100. (The autograph manuscripts of Marianus Scotus and Sigebert of Gembloux survive and disprove the assertion that she is already mentioned by these authors.) Her most important witness was Martin of Troppau, who gave her a place after Leo IV (855) as *Johannes Anglicus* from Mainz (*ut asseritur femina fuit,* "it is alleged that this pope was a woman") in the third recension of his widely read chronicle, composed ca. 1272-1277. According to Martin, she reigned for two years, seven months, and four days. Thanks to the *Flores Temporum,* to Bernardus Guidonis, and many Dominican chroniclers (perhaps in connection with the problem of incorporating the religious women's movement into the Dominican order in the mid-thirteenth century), Joan became an accepted part of history; humanists and Protestants likewise accepted the fact of her existence. The cause of this tradition is probably the misinterpretation of an inscription on a classical statue. Both the popular legend and many modern writers of fiction have woven the story of Joan around this inscription. Papal → fables.

■ Bibliography: *LMA* 5:527; I. Döllinger, *Papstfabeln des Mittelalters* (2nd ed. Stuttgart, 1890); C. d'Onofrio, *La papessa Giovanna* (Rome, 1979); A. Boureau, *La papesse Jeanne* (Paris, 1988, 1993); K. Herbers, "Die Päpstin

Johanna," *Historisches Jahrbuch* 108 (1988) 174-94; E. Gössmann, *Mulier papa* (Munich, 1994, 1998).

ANNA-DOROTHEE VON DEN BRINCKEN

John I (Aug. 13, 523-May 18, 526). Saint (feast day May 18), born in Tuscia, later deacon in Rome. Theoderic the Great summoned John to Ravenna and ordered him to undertake a diplomatic mission to Emperor Justin I on behalf of the hitherto Arian Goths of the eastern Roman empire, who were threatened with the confiscation of their churches and forcible conversion. John was the first pope to visit Constantinople. He was received with honors, but achieved at most the return of the churches. Theoderic received him ungraciously on his return and detained him in Ravenna, where John, weakened by old age, died after a few days. (It would be exaggerated to speak of his "imprisonment" or "martyrdom.") With the help of Dionysius Exiguus, John introduced the Alexandrian tables for the calculation of Easter into the Roman church; these subsequently won acceptance throughout the West.

■ Sources: *LP* 1:275-78; 3:index; *RPR*(J) 1:109f.; 2:694, 737.

■ Bibliography: *DECL* 347; *VATL* 336; Caspar 2:183-92, 766f.; H. Löwe, "Theoderich der Große und Papst Johannes I.," *Historiches Jahrbuch* 72 (1953) 83-100; P. Goubert, "Autour du voyage à Byzance du pape Jean I," *Orientalia christiana periodica* 24 (1958) 339-52; Richards 109-13.

GEORG SCHWAIGER

John II (Jan. 2, 533-May 8, 535). Formerly *Mercurius,* the Roman presbyter of San Clemente, he was the first pope to take another name. He was elected to succeed Boniface II following a dissension that had lasted almost three months. The Roman senate issued a decree that was intended to guard against such dissensions in the future; both John and Athalaric, the king of the eastern Goths, confirmed it. John gave his approval *post factum* to Emperor Justinian's decree about the faith (March 15, 533), which had put an end to the Theopaschite controversy. He increased the severity of a synodical judgment against Bishop Contumeliosus of Riez (*MGH.Ep* 3:32-35).

■ Sources: *LP* 1:285f.; *RPR*(J) 1:113; 2:694, 738.

■ Bibliography: *LACL* 356; *VATL* 337; Caspar 2:800.

GEORG SCHWAIGER

John III (July 17, 561-July 13, 574). From a noble Roman family. According to *Liber Pontificalis,* he

repaired the catacombs. Thanks to his efforts, Milan, Ravenna, and a number of churches in Africa, which had separated from Rome during the Three Chapters controversy, resumed communion with the papal see. Little information survives about this pontificate, which was overshadowed by the confusions that followed the death of Emperor Justinian I in 565 and the Langobard invasion of Italy in 568.

■ Sources: *LP* 1:305ff.; 3:index; *RPR*(J) 1:136f.; 2:695.

■ Bibliography: *DECL* 347; *VATL* 337f.; Caspar 2:350, 777; O. Bertolini, *Roma e i Longobardi* (Rome, 1972).

GEORG SCHWAIGER

John IV (Dec. 24, 640-Oct. 6, 642). From Dalmatia. After his election, but before the imperial confirmation and his episcopal ordination, John answered inquires from Irish bishops and abbots about the date of Easter (enjoining them to observe the regulations of Nicaea) and about the errors of Pelagius (see Bede, *Ecclesiastical History* 2.19). He condemned Monothelitism at the Roman synod of 641. In a letter to the sons and successors of Emperor Heraclius, he defended the orthodoxy of Honorius I (625-638) against attacks by Patriarch Pyrrhus I of Constantinople.

■ Sources: *LP* 1:330; *RPR*(J) 1:227f.; 2:698, 739; Bede, *Historia Ecclesiastica,* ed. B. Colgrave and R. A. Mynors (Oxford, 1969).

■ Bibliography: *LMA* 5:539f.; *DECL* 348; *VATL* 338f.; K. Harrison, "A Letter from Rome to the Irish Clergy, AD 640," *Peritia* 3 (1984) 222-29; S. Rizou-Couroupos, "Un nouveau fragment de la 'keleusis' d'Héraclius au pape Jean IV," (Leipzig/Berlin, 1987) 531ff.; A. Alexakis, "Before the Lateran Council of 649," *AHC* 27/28 (1995-96) 92-101.

GEORG JENAL

John V (July 23, 685-Aug. 2, 686). A Syrian. He was the archdeacon of Rome; as a deacon, he was a member of Pope Agatho's legation to the Sixth Ecumenical Council (Constantinople, 680/681). He was ordained bishop as soon as he was confirmed by the exarch of Ravenna, since Emperor Constantine IV did not insist on confirming the papal election in person. He achieved the full submission of the Sardinian bishops and received tokens of favor from Emperor Justinian II.

■ Sources: *LP* 1:366f.; *RPR*(J) 1:242; F. Dölger, *Regesten der Kaiserurkunden des oströmischen Reiches* (Munich/Berlin, 1924) nos. 252, 254ff.

■ Bibliography: *VATL* 339; Caspar 1:620f.

GEORG SCHWAIGER

John VI (Oct. 30, 701-Jan. 11, 705). A Greek. With the aid of Italian soldiers, he was able to hold his own against the exarch Theophylact in the conflict about the Byzantine throne, without breaking openly with the empire. He persuaded Duke Gisulf of Benevento not to plunder the territories south of Rome. A Roman synod in 704 discussed the case of Wilfred of York.

■ **Sources:** *LP* 1:383f.; *RPR*(J) 1:245f.; 2:700, 741.

■ **Bibliography:** *LMA* 5:539; *VATL* 339; Caspar 2:624, and frequently; P. Conte, *Regesto delle lettere dei papi del secolo VIII* (Milan, 1984) 189ff.; T. F. Noble, *The Republic of St. Peter: The Birth of the Papal State, 680-825* (2nd ed. Philadelphia, 1991) 18.

GEORG SCHWAIGER

John VII (Mar. 1, 705-Oct. 18, 707). A Greek, of noble birth. An educated man and a lover of art, he devoted attention to the building and decoration of churches in Rome. He persuaded the Langobard king Aripert II to restore church property on the Ligurian coast. Since he was afraid of Emperor Justinian II, he sent the decisions of the Trullan synod (692) back to the emperor without making any alterations, although Sergius I had refused to acknowledge them; this was interpreted as the approval even of the anti-Roman parts of the conciliar decisions, and this is why the → *Liber Pontificalis* accuses him of cowardice. There is a contemporary mosaic portrait of him in the Vatican grottoes.

■ **Sources:** *LP* 1:385ff.; *RPR*(J) 1:246f.

■ **Bibliography:** *LMA* 5:539; *VATL* 340; Caspar 2: passim; P. J. Nordhagen, *The Frescoes of John VII in Santa Maria Antiqua* (Rome, 1968); J. D. Breckenridge, "Evidence for the Nature of Relations between Pope John VII and the Byzantine Emperor Justinian II," *Byzantinische Zeitschrift* 65 (1972) 364-74; J. M. Sansterre, "A propos de la signification politico-religieuse de certaines fresques de Jean VII à Ste-Marie-Antique," *Byzantion* 57 (1987) 434-40; P. J. Nordhagen, *Studies in Byzantine and Early Medieval Painting* (London, 1990).

GEORG SCHWAIGER

John VIII (Dec. 14, 872-Dec. 16, 882). A Roman, son of Gundo. He served the Roman church for many years as deacon and was elected to succeed Hadrian II. His pontificate was marked by the struggle against the Saracens and by church-internal opposition. Emperor Louis II supported him against the Saracens, but John was unable to prevent the southern Italian princes from entering coalitions with them. After Louis's death, he decided against the east Frankish Carolingians in favor of Charles the Bald, whom he crowned emperor in Rome on December 25, 875. Although Charles renewed the pacts made by earlier emperors, he was unable to protect John against the Saracens or other enemies. John condemned Bishop Formosus of Porto and his adherents at two (?) synods in Rome because of their activities against the pope and the emperor, and had this verdict confirmed at the synod of Ponthion. When the east Frankish king Carloman invaded Italy in 877, Charles retreated before him, and died during his flight. Carloman's followers put great pressure on John, who escaped to the west Frankish kingdom. Here he sought support from the bishops at the synod of Troyes (878), but he was unable to persuade King Louis II, the Stammerer, to intervene in Italy. Since Count Boso of Vienne was not available as a candidate for the imperial crown, John had to reach an agreement with the east Frankish Carolingians. Since Carloman was ill, John crowned his brother Charles III as king of Italy at the beginning of 880, and crowned him emperor in 881. However, Charles III too proved unable to provide any help against the Saracens. John sought protection in Constantinople also and had his legates agree to the restitution of Photius at the council of 879; in return, he demanded (unsuccessfully) that Byzantium should return Bulgaria to the obedience of the Roman church. Methodius, the missionary among the Slavs, had been imprisoned by the Bavarian bishops; John freed him in 873, received him in Rome in 880 and allowed the celebration of the Slavonic liturgy, which had hitherto been forbidden. John held a number of synods, at which he asserted the papal jurisdictional → primacy vis-à-vis the archbishops of Milan and Ravenna. There is no reason to believe the statement in the Annals of Fulda that he was murdered in 882.

■ **Sources:** *LP* 2:221ff.; *MGH.Ep* 7:1-333; *RPR*(J) 1:376-422; 2:704, 746.

■ **Bibliography:** *LMA* 5:539f.; *VATL* 340f.; R. Hiestand, *Byzanz und das Regnum Italicum* (Zurich, 1964) 19-31; D. Lohrmann, *Das Register Papst Johannes' VIII. (872-882)* (Tübingen, 1968); H. Mordek and G. Schmitz, "Papst Johannes VIII. und das Konzil von Troyes (878)," in *Geschichtsschreibung und geistliches Leben im Mittelalter,* Festschrift for H. Löwe (Cologne, 1978) 179-225; W. Hartmann, *Die Synoden der Karolingerzeit im Frankenreich und in Italien* (Paderborn, 1989) 333-53; S. Scholz, *Transmigration und Translation* (Cologne, 1992)

147-62, 217f.; E. Lanne, "Le canon 34 des apôtres et son interprétation dans la tradition latine," *Irénikon* 71 (1998) 212-33.
SEBASTIAN SCHOLZ

John (VIII) (antipope) (Jan. 844). A Roman deacon. On the death of Gregory IV, he seized the Lateran with the aid of a mob. The party of the nobles made Sergius II pope; he protected John from punishment and sent him to a monastery. Louis II, son of Emperor Lothar I, was sent to Rome to investigate the matter and recognized the legitimacy of Sergius II.
- **Sources:** *LP* 2:86ff.; *RPR*(J) 1:327.
- **Bibliography:** *EC* 6:582; *LMA* 5:540; *VATL* 335.
GEORG SCHWAIGER

John IX (Apr. 898-May 900). Born in Tivoli, the son of Rampoald. During the controversy about the posthumous condemnation of Formosus, the adherents of Formosus elected him to succeed Theodore II, while the opponents of Formosus elected the former bishop of Caere, Sergius (III). With support from Emperor Lambert, John succeeded in repulsing Sergius. Together with the emperor, John held a synod at Ravenna in 898 which rehabilitated Formosus and recognized the ordinations he had carried out, while however renewing the prohibition on bishops moving from one see to another. The synod confirmed Lambert's coronation as emperor and rejected the coronation of the east Frankish emperor Arnulf; Sergius was excommunicated. In the future, the pope was to be elected by the suburbicarian bishops and the Roman clergy; emissaries from the emperor were to be present at his episcopal ordination. The consolidation of the pope and the emperor which these decrees intended came to nothing, since Lambert died in the same year. When Sergius became pope in 904, he did not recognize the pontificate of John IX.
- **Sources:** *LP* 2:232; *RPR*(J) 1:442f.; 2:705; Zimmermann *Pu* 1:13-23.
- **Bibliography:** *LMA* 5:540; R. Hiestand, *Byzanz und das Regnum Italicum* (Zurich, 1964) 52ff.; Zimmermann *Pa* 60-63; W. Hartmann, *Die Synoden der Karolingerzeit im Frankenreich und in Italien* (Paderborn, 1989) 390-95; S. Scholz, *Transmigration und Translation* (Cologne, 1992) 225-29.
SEBASTIAN SCHOLZ

John X (Apr. 914-June 928). Formerly bishop of Bologna and (from 905) archbishop of Ravenna; died in prison in 929. John owed his election—in spite of the fact that translation from one see to another was forbidden—to the Roman consul Theophylact or (according to Liutprand of Cremona) to the love of Theophylact's wife, Theodora. However, he crossed swords politically with this family, was deposed by Theophylact's daughter Marozia, and died a prisoner. John repulsed the Saracens in the battle of Garigliano in 915, in an alliance with Byzantium, Italian principalities, and Berengar I, whom he subsequently crowned emperor. In 926, the pope supported his protégé Hugo of Arles as king of Italy and relied for help in Rome on Hugo's brother Peter of Spoleto († 927). The synod of Hohenaltheim in 916 forged political links to Germany, and peace was negotiated in the Balkans, where Croatia became a kingdom in 925, with Split the seat of an archbishop. In France, John promoted missionary work among the Normans; he also intervened in the conflict about the throne in 926. During the schism of Liège, he supported the king's right to make nominations.
- **Sources:** Zimmermann *Reg;* Zimmermann *Pu* 1.
- **Bibliography:** *LMA* 5:540f.; *VATL* 343f.; T. Venni, "Giovanni X," *Archivio della Società Romana di Storia Patria* 59 (1936) 1-136; Zimmermann *J;* R. Savigni, "L'episcopato di Giovanni X," *Rivista di storia della Chiesa in Italia* 46 (1992) 1-29.
HARALD ZIMMERMANN

John XI (Mar. 931-Jan. 936). According to Liutprand of Cremona, he was a son of Sergius III and Marozia, to whom he owed his elevation to the papal dignity. When she fell at the end of 932, he too lost his power and was imprisoned. Subsequently, his (step-)brother Alberic II confined his responsibility to spiritual matters. During his pontificate, abbot Odo came to Rome and requested a privileged status for Cluny and other monasteries of the reform; this was the first such papal grant. Other papal activities involved Byzantium, Milan, and Rheims.
- **Sources:** Zimmermann *Reg;* Zimmermann *Pu* 1.
- **Bibliography:** *LMA* 5:541; L. Duchesne, "Serge III et Jean XI," *Mélanges d'archéologie et d'histoire* 33 (1913) 41-64; Zimmermann *J.*
HARALD ZIMMERMANN

John XII (Dec. 16, 955-May 14, 964). Formerly *Octavian*. He was designated for the papal office by his father, the Roman prince and senator Alberic († 954). After he assumed the government of Rome, conflicts with the principalities of Capua and Benevento in southern Italy, and with king Berengar II and his son Adalbert in northern and central Italy, led John to appeal for help in 960 to the east Frankish-German king Otto I, whom he crowned as emperor on February 2, 962. Otto guaranteed the integrity of the Patrimony of Peter by means of the "Ottonian Privilege," thus retaining imperial influence on the choice of pope. John supported Otto's plans for a church province centered on Magdeburg. He also attempted to protect the position of the papacy in Rome by fabricating the apparent "original text" of the Donation of Constantine. His renewed appeal to Adalbert, whom he received in Rome, and his plans to contact Byzantium and Hungary led to John's expulsion from Rome by Otto I in November-December 963. He was deposed from office, and a Roman synod under Otto I nominated a new pope, Leo VIII. John, however, succeeded in regaining control of Rome at the beginning of 964, and he held a synod in February of that year which condemned the measures that had been taken against him. John died in possession of the papal dignity, but the successor chosen by the Romans, Benedict V, was deposed after Otto I and Leo VIII had reconquered Rome in June 964. John was deposed for political reasons; the difficulties involved in taking legal proceedings against a pope were disguised by accusations that John's life was unworthy of a clergyman, and indeed was on the verge of apostasy and heresy, so that it was legitimate to deprive him of his office. The last synod that John held shows extensive knowledge of the papal tradition from the eighth century on and speaks against the hypothesis of a general decadence of the papacy in the mid-tenth century. John carried out building works in Rome and also supported monastic reforms in Subiaco and Farfa.

■ **Sources:** *LP* 2:246-49; Zimmermann *Reg.*

■ **Bibliography:** *LMA* 5:541f.; *VATL* 344f.; H. Fuhrmann, "Konstantinische Schenkung und abendländisches Kaisertum," *Deutsches Archiv für Erforschung des Mittelalters* 22 (1966) 63-178; Zimmermann *Pa*; Zimmermann *J*; W. Chraska, *Johannes XII.* (Aalen, 1973); H. Wolter, *Die Synoden im Reichsgebiet und in Reichsitalien von 916 bis 1056* (Paderborn, 1988) 69-86; E.-D. Hehl, "Der wohlberatene Papst: Die römische Synode Johannes' XII. vom Februar 964," in *Ex ipsis rerum documentis,* Festschrift for H. Zimmermann (Sigmaringen, 1991), 257-75; H. Hoffmann, "Ottonische Fragen," *Deutsches Archiv für Erforschung des Mittelalters* 51 (1995) 53-82.

ERNST-DIETER HEHL

John XIII (Oct. 1, 965-Sept. 6, 972). A Roman. He is attested from 961 onward as bishop of Narni and as librarian of the Roman church. He was made pope in the presence of envoys from Emperor Otto I, on whom he remained politically dependent. His collaboration with the emperor was particularly close in the synods he held: Capua was made an archdiocese in 966; Magdeburg was made the archdiocese of a church province in 967/968; Benevento was made an archdiocese in 969; preparations were made to unite the diocese of Alba with Asti.

■ **Sources:** *LP* 2:252ff.; Zimmermann *Reg;* Zimmermann *Pu* 1.

■ **Bibliography:** *LMA* 5:542; *VATL* 346; Zimmermann *J*; H. Wolter, *Die Synoden im Reichsgebiet und in Reichsitalien von 916 bis 1056* (Paderborn, 1988) 88-106; A. Landersdorfer, "Die Gründung des Erzbistums Magdeburg durch Kaiser Otto den Großen," *Münchener theologische Zeitschrift* 46 (1995) 3-20.

ERNST-DIETER HEHL

John XIV (Sept. 983-Aug. 20, 984). Formerly *Peter.* He became bishop of Pavia in 971. Emperor Otto made him his arch-chancellor for Italy in 980, and his election as pope was due to imperial influence. His choice of name was clearly intended to avoid having a pope named "Peter." After Otto's death, Pope Boniface VII overthrew John XIV at the end of April 984 and kept him a prisoner in Castel Sant' Angelo, where he died.

■ **Sources:** *LP* 2:259; Zimmermann *Reg;* Zimmermann *Pu* 1.

■ **Bibliography:** *LMA* 5:542; *VATL* 346f.; Zimmermann *J*.

ERNST-DIETER HEHL

John XV (August 985-March 996). Son of the Roman priest Leo, and cardinal priest of San Vitale. The German empress Theophanu was not involved in his elevation to the papacy, which was due to the influence of the Roman *patricius,* Johannes I Crescentius. He made the papal authority felt through interventions in response to requests from abroad: thus, he mediated in the conflict between the English king Ethelred II and the Norman duke Richard I (991); he exchanged ambassadors with Prince Vladimir of Kiev (988-994); he supported the deposed archbishop Arnulf of Rheims against the French episcopate and King Hugh Capet (991-995). The first formal papal canonization (of Ulrich of Augsburg in 993) was another expression of the papal authority.

According to a later tradition deriving from Cardinal Deusdedit, the Polish duke Meiszko I made a gift of his realm to the pope in 991/992. The family of the Crescentii set severe limitations on the pope's freedom of action in Rome, so that Gerbert of Aurillac (later Silvester II) and Abbo of Fleury judged that the papacy was in a state of paralysis. John fled from Crescentius II to Sutri and appealed to Otto III for help. The Roman nobles asked John for forgiveness, and he returned to the city, where he died just as Otto III reached Pavia.

■ Sources: *LP* 2:260; Zimmermann *Reg* nos. 641-740; Zimmermann *Pu* 1:555-635.

■ Bibliography: *LMA* 5:542; *VATL* 347f.; Zimmermann *J*, 227-54; K. Görich, *Otto III.* (Sigmaringen, 1993) 213-24, 238f.; E.-D. Hehl, "Lucia/Lucina—Die Echtheit von JL 3848: Zu den Anfängen der Heiligenverehrung Ulrichs von Augsburg," *Deutsches Archiv für Erforschung des Mittelalters* 51 (1995) 195-211.

KNUT GÖRICH

John XVI (antipope) (Feb. 997-May 998). Formerly *Philagathos,* a Greek from Rossano in Calabria, died Aug. 26 (1001?) as a prisoner in a Roman monastery. He was very well educated and was imperial chancellor for Italy from 980 to 982 and from 991 to 992. He became abbot of Nonantola in 982 and a tutor of Otto III. As "Master of the chamber" for Italy, he was one of Empress Theophanu's counselors. In 988, he became archbishop of Piacenza, which John XV had recently detached from the diocese of Ravenna. In 994, he went to Byzantium to negotiate the marriage of Otto III to the imperial princess. He was in Rome in 997, and the Roman *patricius,* Crescentius II, made him pope in place of Gregory V, who had been expelled. This breach with the emperor led to Gregory's condemnation of John's "invasion" (February 997) and to his punishment one year later, after Otto III had marched on Rome. He was formally deposed and—although Nilus the Younger of Rossano pleaded with the emperor and the pope on his behalf—he was mutilated and humiliated, being led in procession on an ass.

■ Sources: *LP* 2:261f.; Zimmermann *Reg* nos. 784-820.

■ Bibliography: *LMA* 5:542f.; *VATL* 348; P. E. Schramm, *Kaiser, Könige und Päpste* (Stuttgart, 1969) 3:214-34; Zimmermann *Pa* 105-13; A. Nitschke, "Der mißhandelte Papst," in *Gedenkschrift für J. Leuschner* (Göttingen, 1983) 40-53 (on this article, see *Deutsches Archiv für Erforschung des Mittelalters* 43 [1987] 206); K. Schreiner, "Gregor VIII. nackt auf einem Esel," in *Ecclesia et regnum,* Festschrift for F. J. Schmale (Bochum,

1989) 155-202; G. Althoff, "Warum erhielt Graf Berthold 999 ein Marktprivileg für Villingen?" in *Die Zähringer* (Sigmaringen, 1991) 3:269-74.

KNUT GÖRICH

John XVII (May 16-Nov. 6, 1003). Formerly *John Sicco,* from the Roman quarter of Biberetica. After the death of Silvester II, he was made pope by John II Crescentius, who ruled the city of Rome, and he remained dependent on him. John gave the Polish missionary Benedict, a pupil of Bruno of Querfurt, and his brethren the authorization to conduct missionary work among the Slavs. He is probably buried in the Lateran basilica.

■ Sources: *LP* 2:265; 3:132; *RPR(J)* 1:501; Zimmermann *Reg* nos. 975-79.

■ Bibliography: *VATL* 348; Zimmermann *J*; R. Poupardin, "Note sur la chronologie de Jean XVII," *Mélanges d'archéologie et d'historie* 21 (1901) 387-90; Borgolte 136.

GEORG SCHWAIGER

John XVIII (Dec. 25, 1003-June/July 1009). Formerly *John Fasanus,* a Roman and cardinal priest of St. Peter. He was the son of the priest Ursus and his wife Stephania, and was made pope by the *patricius,* John II Crescentius, and remained dependent on him. John proclaimed the papal authority when he restored the diocese of Merseburg in 1004, confirmed the diocese of Bamberg in 1007, and granted papal protection to the monastery of Fleury. Because of opposition on the part of Crescentius, he was unable to receive the German king Henry II. He achieved a temporary resolution of the latent schism between Rome and Byzantium. Following the example of John XV, he canonized five Polish martyrs in 1004 (Benedict, John, Isaac, Matthew, and Christian). It is certain that John retired as a monk to St. Paul's a short time before his death, but it is not entirely clear whether he acted freely. He died there and was buried in St. Paul's.

■ Sources: *LP* 2:266; 3:index; *RPR(J)* 1:501ff.; 2:708; Zimmermann *Reg* nos. 980-1035; Zimmermann *Pu* 2:777-842.

■ Bibliography: *LMA* 5:543; *BBLK* 3:217-20; *VATL* 348f.; Zimmermann *Pa* 114; Zimmermann *J*; A. M. Colini, "L'epitaffio del fratello di Giovanni XVIII," *Archivio della Società Romana di Storia Patria* 99 (1976) 333ff.; W. Ziezulewicz, "A Monastic Forgery in an Age of Reform: A Bull of Pope John XVIII for Saint-Florent-de-Saumur," *AHP* 23 (1985) 7-42; H. Wolter, *Die Synoden im Reichsgebiet und in Reichsitalien 916-1056* (Paderborn, 1988) 235ff.

GEORG SCHWAIGER

John XIX (Apr. 19, 1024-Oct. 20, 1032). Formerly *Romanus,* third son of Count Gregory of Tusculum. He served under his older brother and predecessor, Benedict VIII, as ruler of Rome and Campania with the titles of "consul," "duke," and "senator." He became pope as a layman, thanks to simony, and thereafter held the reins of spiritual and secular power. He was little interested in spiritual matters; his primary concern was to make money. In political matters, he prudently sought an accommodation with the Crescentii family, in order to secure his own rule. He also sought amity with Conrad II, whom he crowned emperor at Easter 1027 in the presence of King Rudolf III of Burgundy and King Canute of England and Denmark. The emperor got his way even in ecclesiastical affairs, with the result that Aquileia became a patriarchate rather than Grado. At the request of the emperor, John extended papal protection to Cluny under Abbot Odilo in 1028 and confirmed the transfer of the episcopal see of Zeitz to Naumburg. There is no reason to believe Radulf Glaber's story that John was willing to hand over the primatial rights in the East, which the patriarch of Constantinople asked of him, in return for a sum of money; but from this time on, the name of the pope was no longer mentioned in the diptychs in Byzantium.

■ **Sources:** *LP* 2:269; 3:index; *RPR*(J) 1:514-19; 2:709, 748; L. Santifaller, "Chronologisches Verzeichnis der Urkunden Johannes' XIX.," *Römische Historische Mitteilungen* 1 (1956/57) 35-76; Zimmermann *Pu* 2:1043-1126.
■ **Bibliography:** *LMA* 5:543; *BBKL* 3:220-24; *VATL* 349; A. Michel, "Die Weltreichs- und Kirchenteilung bei R. Glaber," *Historisches Jahrbuch* 70 (1951) 53-64; Zimmermann *J;* K.-J. Herrmann, *Das Tuskulanerpapsttum (1012-46)* (Stuttgart, 1973); H. Wolter, *Die Synoden im Reichsgebiet und in Reichsitalien 916-1056* (Paderborn, 1988) 325-32; H. Wolfram, "Die Gesandtschaft Konrads II nach Konstantinopel (1027/29)," *Mitteilungen des Instituts für Österreichische Geschichtsforschung* 100 (1992) 161-74.

                                        GEORG SCHWAIGER

John XX. This name is not found in the list of popes. The gap is due to the erroneous inclusion of a Pope John in the list before John XV (985-996). After this error was cleared up, the correct numerals were given to the popes in the tenth and eleventh centuries who bore this name, but the enumeration chosen by John XXI (1276-1277) and subsequent popes has been retained.

■ **Sources:** *LP* 2: xviii; 3:308; Zimmermann *Reg* no. 740.
■ **Bibliography:** *VATL* 349f.; R. L. Poole, *Studies in Chronology and History* (Oxford, 1934; repr. London, 1969) 156ff.

                                        GEORG SCHWAIGER

John XXI (Sept. 8, 1276-May 20, 1277). Formerly *Petrus Juliani,* called *Hispanus* or *Portugalensis.* He was a philosopher, theologian, and doctor. He was born in Lisbon ca. 1205, the son of a doctor, Julião. After studying philosophy and medicine in Paris from 1220 to 1229, he took his master's degree and taught in the faculty of arts there; it is possible that he undertook further studies in León, Toulouse, Montpellier, Salerno, and Siena, where he held lectures from 1245 as *doctor in phisica.* He then occupied a position at the court of Frederick II and at the papal curia, where he was the personal physician of Gregory X. After holding the posts of *Magister scholarum* and dean of Lisbon, archdeacon of Braga, and prior of Guimarães, he was elected to the see of Braga in 1272, but did not receive confirmation. In 1273, he became cardinal bishop of Tusculum. Immediately after his election, he abrogated the regulations about the conclave issued by Gregory X (papal → election), attempted to intervene in the conflict between Castille and France about Navarre and to promote negotiations for union with the Greek church at the Second Council of Lyons. The most significant act in his pontificate was his directive to seek and identify errors in the teaching imparted at the University of Paris; this was aimed against the radical Aristotelianism of the faculty of arts and resulted in the condemnation of 219 propositions on March 7, 1277. The investigators then turned their attention to the faculty of theology. John composed the *Summulae logicales,* the earliest systematization of classical logic, which was the most frequently employed manual of logic in the Middle Ages, as well as commentaries on some of Aristotle's texts. His theory of concepts (*terminus*) paved the way for later nominalism. His plan to give medicine a place in a scholastic summa between logical and natural philosophy remained largely unfulfilled (*Thesaurus pauperum*).

■ **Works:** *Exposição sobre os livros de Beato Dionisio Areopagita,* ed. M. Alonso Alonso (Lisbon, 1957); *Obras filosóficas,* ed. M. Alonso Alonso, 3 vols. (2nd ed. Barcelona, 1961); *Tractatus syncategorematum and Selected Anonymous Treatises by Peter of Spain,* ed. J. P.

Mullally and R. Houde (Milwaukee, 1964); *Tractatus Called Afterwards Summulae logicales,* ed. L. M. de Rijk (Assen, 1972); H. A. G. Braakhuis, *De 13 de eeuwse Tractaten over syncategorematische Termen,* I (Meppel, 1979); J. Pinborg, ed., "Anonymi Quaestiones in Tractatus Petri Hispani I-III traditae in codice Cracoviensi 742 (anno fere 1350)," *Cahiers de l'Institut du Moyen-Âge Grec et Latin* 41 (1982) 1-170; *On Composition and Negation,* ed. J. Spruyt (Nijmegen, 1989); M. de Asua, "Los 'Problemata' o 'Quaestiones de animalibus' de Pedro Hispano," *Stromata* 54 (1998) 267-302.

■ **Bibliography:** *Dicionário de História de Portugal* (Lisbon, 1985) 3:217f.; *LMA* 5:544; *VATL* 350f.; E. Cadier, ed., *Le registre de Jean XXI (1276-77)* (Paris, 1898); M. Grabmann, "Handschriftliche Forschungen und Funde zu den philosophischen Schriften des Petrus Hispanus," *Sitzungsberichte der Bayerischen Akademie der Wissenschaften zu München, Philosophisch-historische Klasse* 9 (1936) (a fundamental study); L. M. de Rijk, "On the Life of Peter of Spain, the author of the Tractatus, called afterwards Summulae logicales," *Vivarium* 8 (1970) 123-54; J. M. da Cruz Pontes, "A propos d'un centenaire: Une nouvelle monographie sur Petrus Hispanus Portugalensis, est-elle nécessaire?," *Recherches de théologie ancienne et médiévale* 44 (1977) 220-30; E. Brasão, "O único papa português: João XXI," *Anais da Academia Portuguesa da História* II/26 (1980) 381-404; M. A. Rodrigues, "O pensamento teológico e místico de Pedro Hispano," *Biblos* 56 (1980) 95-150; L. Bianchi, *Il vescovo e i filosofi* (Bergamo, 1990); J. Antunes, "O percurso e o pensamento político de Pedro Hispano, arcebispo eleito de Braga e papa João XXI," *IX Centenário da dedicação da Sé de Braga: Actas I* (Braga, 1990) 125-84; F. van Steenbergen, *La philosophie au XIIIe siècle* (2nd ed. Louvain/Paris, 1991) 138ff., 338ff.; H. Schipperges, *Arzt im Purpur: Grundzüge einer Krankheitslehre bei Petrus Hispanus* (Berlin, 1994).

LUDWIG VONES

John XXII (Aug. 7, 1316-Dec. 4, 1334 in Avignon). Formerly *Jacques Duèse,* born in Cahors ca. 1244 into a wealthy bourgeois family. He became a cleric and studied civil and canon law in Montpellier and Orléans, taking a doctoral degree in both. After studying theology in Paris, he taught in Toulouse and acquired a large number of benefices. He belonged to the circle around Charles II of Naples and Archbishop Louis of Anjou, before becoming bishop of Fréjus in 1300. Charles II made him chancellor in 1308; he also served as chancellor to Robert of Naples until 1313. He became bishop of Avignon in 1310. After carrying out difficult missions in connection with the legal proceedings against Boniface VIII and the Council of Vienne, he became cardinal priest of San Vitale in 1312 and cardinal bishop of Porto in 1313. At the age of seventy-two he was elected pope in Lyons by the French cardinals and crowned there on September 5, 1316; this was the outcome of pressure by the brother of the French king and brought an end to a *sede vacante* which had lasted for two years. Although he had promised to return the papacy to Rome, his actions—especially his appointments, which increased French dominance in the curia—consolidated the presence in Avignon. His entire pontificate was overshadowed by the struggle against Louis of Bavaria, since John attempted since the double election of Louis and Frederick the Fair in 1314 to win acceptance for the papal claim to a right to approve the candidate for the German throne. This brought the debate about the sovereign powers of the emperor and the pope to its final theological climax. Besides this, John consistently interpreted the papal position to mean that he had the right to bestow the office of imperial vicar in Italy; in keeping with the views of the Guelphs and Angevins, and wishing to benefit France and Anjou, he bestowed the vicariate on Robert of Naples. He even went so far as to prepare a crusade against the Visconti in Milan, who were loyal to the emperor. When Louis intervened in the imperial lands in Italy, and legal proceedings in the curia were opened (1323), there was no longer any way to avoid the conflict, in the course of which Louis was excommunicated and urged to abdicate the imperial crown. The king appealed to a general council against the pope's actions (at Nuremberg in December 1323; at Frankfurt on January 5, 1324; and at Sachsenhausen on May 22, 1324), accusing the pope of favoring heretics, and ultimately of being a heretic himself. The pope rejected Louis's title to feudal lands in the empire and to his Bavarian inheritance and finally referred to him only as "the Bavarian." The bitter literary debate between the two camps led to the composition of important theoretical works by Augustinus Triumphus, Alvaro Pelayo, and Marsilius of Padua, which gave a new and thorough definition to the relationship between *sacerdotium* and *imperium,* above all in view of the papal *plenitudo potestatis* and Rome's primatial position. Writers at Louis's court—especially the Franciscans (Marsilius's *Defensor pacis*)—prepared the ground for a secularized perspective on these questions. After marching on Rome, Louis had himself crowned emperor in the name of the Roman people on January 17, 1328, in → St. Peter's, in the absence of the pope. He proclaimed that John was deposed because of heresy and had Nicholas V elected to replace him on May 11, 1328. Nicholas crowned Louis as emperor a second time, but he could not maintain his position and submitted to John in 1330.

Apart from carrying on this struggle, John organized the administration of the curia as a fiscal centralism, with chancellery regulations which laid down the business procedures in the curia, the consolidation of the → Rota, and increased importance attached to a number of office-bearers (the confessor, secretaries, *referendarii,* clerics in the papal chamber), the organization of finances by the creation of local districts (the "collectories"), an increase in income thanks to the reservation of benefices to the pope (Constitution *Ex debito,* 1316) and the Constitution *Execrabilis* (1317), which set limits to the accumulation of benefices. John made a prominent contribution to canon law with the publication of the additional decretals up to the pontificate of Clement V (the "Clementines": bull *Quoniam nulla,* 1317), and with some decretals of his own which were added as *extravagantes* to the *Corpus Iuris Canonici.* John was also responsible for the condemnation of the writings of Petrus Johannis Olivi (1326) and twenty-eight propositions by Meister Eckhart (bull *In agro dominico,* 1329), as well as for the persecution of the Fraticelli and for the radical position taken against the "spiritual" tendency in the Franciscan order in the conflict about poverty (bull *Cum inter nonnullos,* 1323).

John's greatest problems within the church were due to the position he affirmed from 1331 onward about the beatific vision: he maintained that the righteous would enjoy this vision only after the last judgment. The cardinals and the University of Paris strongly opposed this view, and John was accused of heresy; he revoked his opinions only a short time before his death. John was a decisive defender of the sacred power of the papacy. During his pontificate, centralistic ideas in the curia reached a new level, leaving their mark on subsequent epochs. The radical fiscal policy born of these ideas was to have ominous consequences for the future of the church.

■ **Sources:** É. Baluze and G. Mollat, *Vitae paparum Avi-*

gnonensium (Paris, 1916) 1:107-94; vol. 2 (Paris, 1928) 175-98; vol. 3 (Paris, 1921) 244-478; E. von Ottenthal, *Die päpstlichen Kanzleiregeln von Johannes XXII. bis Nicolaus V.* (Innsbruck, 1888; repr. Aalen, 1968); A. Coulon and S. Clémencet, eds., *Jean XXII: Lettres secrètes et curiales relatives à la France,* 10 fascicles (Paris, 1908-12); G. Mollat, ed., *Jean XXII: Lettres communes,* 16 vols. (Paris, 1904-46); M. Dykmans, *Les sermons de Jean XXII sur la vision béatifique* (Rome, 1973); J. Tarrant, ed., *Extravagantes Johannis XXII* (Vatican City, 1983).

■ **Bibliography:** *LMA* 5:544ff.; *TRE* 17:109-12; *VATL* 351f.; E. Albe, *Autour de Jean XXII: Jean XXII et les familles du Quercy,* 2 vols. (Rome, 1902-4); G. Mollat, *Les papes d'Avignon* (10th ed. Paris, 1965); B. Guillemain, *La cour pontificale d'Avignon* (2nd ed. Paris, 1966); J. E. Weakland, "Administrative and Fiscal Centralization under Pope John XXII," *Catholic Historical Review* 54 (1968) 39-45, 285-310; idem, "John XXII before His Pontificate, 1244-1316: Jacques Duèse and His Family," *AHP* 10 (1972) 161-85; M. D. Lambert, "The Franciscan Crisis under John XXII," *Franciscan Studies* 32 (1972) 123-43; D. Unverhau, *Approbatio—Reprobatio* (Lübeck, 1973); L. Caillet, *La Papauté d'Avignon et l'Église de France: La politique bénéficiale du Pape Jean XXII en France* (Paris, 1975); J. Miethke, "Kaiser und Papst im Spätmittelalter," *Zeitschrift für historische Forschung* 10 (1983) 421-46; J. Heft, *John XXII and Papal Teaching Authority* (Lewiston et al., 1986); Z. Menache, "The Failure of John XXII's Policy toward France and England," *Church History* 55 (1986) 423-37; H.-J. Becker, *Die Appellation vom Papst an ein allgemeines Konzil* (Cologne/Vienna, 1988); *Aux origines de l'État Moderne: Le fonctionnement administratif de la papauté d'Avignon* (Paris, 1990); H. Thomas, *Ludwig der Bayer* (Regensburg, 1993); F. Accrocca, "Ancora sul caso del papa eretico," *AHP* 32 (1994) 329-42; idem, "Concerning the Case of a Heretical Pope," *Franciscan Studies* 54 (1994-97) 167-84; C. Flüeler, "Eine unbekannte Streitschrift aus dem Kreis der Münchener Franziskaner gegen Papst Johannes XXII.," *Archivum Franciscanum historicum* 88 (1995) 497-514; U. Horst, *Evangelische Armut und päpstliches Lehramt: Minoritentheologen im Konflikt mit Papst Johannes XXII.* (Stuttgart, 1996); R. Lambertini, "Usus und usura: Poverty and Usury in the Franciscans' Responses to John XXII's 'Quia vir reprobus,'" ibid., 185-210.

LUDWIG VONES

John XXIII (May 15, 1410-May 29, 1415). Formerly *Baldassare Cossa,* born ca. 1360 in Procida to a noble Neapolitan family, died Dec. 27, 1419, in Florence. In general terms, he owed his career to what Arnold Esch has called the "Neapolitan sovereignty" over the Roman papacy during the

Western Schism, and in particular to the support he received from Boniface IX, who made him a member of the Pontifical Family. After he had finished his studies in Bologna, where he became a canon, Boniface appointed him archdeacon in 1396 and cardinal legate in 1402. The success of his government was due to his military and administrative abilities. The picture of brutal ruthlessness, greed, ambition, and an immoral life that is painted in sources mostly hostile to him may indeed be exaggerated, but in the last analysis, it does describe his character (on which his family had left its mark). After renouncing the obedience of Gregory XII, he employed intrigue and spent considerable sums of money to promote a council in Pisa that would unite the cardinals of both obediences. Alexander V, who was elected in Pisa on June 27, 1409, was dominated from the outset by Cossa. His election as Alexander's successor on May 17, 1410, in a brief conclave held in Bologna, was not due to fear of the weapons he possessed, nor to simony, but rather to the interests of Florence and of Louis II of Anjou, the pretender to Naples: Cossa promised to join a common front against King Ladislaus of Durazzo and Naples, a partisan of Gregory XII who had occupied parts of the church state (→ Papal States), and the exiled opponents of Ladislaus found their rallying point in John and the Neapolitan cardinals. This meant that the overriding concern at the beginning of his pontificate was the struggle against Ladislaus; however, after the military defeat of Anjou, John reached an accommodation with Ladislaus in June 1412, which allowed him to convoke a reform synod, in accordance with the decision made at Pisa. This synod met in Rome at the end of 1412, but was a half-hearted affair. Apart from the condemnation of John Wyclif's writings, it had no further significance. When Ladislaus once again invaded, John fled to Florence in June 1413 and appealed to the German king Sigmund for help, since the civil war then raging in France meant that no support could come from that quarter. Sigmund exploited this situation to achieve the convocation of a general council, which assembled in Constance on November 5, 1414. John expected that he would win universal recognition at this council, but the king united with influential cardinals and theologians to demand the abdication of all the claimants to the papal throne. An additional factor that made John's position more difficult was the new system of national voting, since this abolished the dominance of the Italians, most of whom supported him. He had no success in his attempt to dissolve the council forcibly, when he fled on March 20/21, 1415, to his protector, Duke Frederick IV of Austria: he got no farther than Freiburg before being taken captive. The decree *Haec sancta,* promulgated at Constance on April 6, 1415, supplied the basis for suspending and "deposing" John in May of the same year. He accepted this sentence and remained for four years a prisoner of Louis III of the Palatinate in the castle of Hausen near Mannheim. After paying a large ransom, he was liberated and swore obedience to Martin V, who made him cardinal bishop of Tusculum in June 1419. John died on December 27 in Florence. His tomb in the baptistery, commissioned by Cosimo de' Medici and executed by Donatello and Michelozzo, shows him with the papal insignia.

■ **Bibliography:** *LMA* 5:546f.; *VATL* 355f.; W. Brandmüller, *Das Konzil von Konstanz 1414-18* (Paderborn, 1991) I; T. M. Buck, "Text, Bild, Geschichte: Papst Johannes XXIII. wird auf dem Arlberg umgeworfen," *AHC* 30 (1998) 37-110; W. Brandmüller, "Johannes XXIII. im Urteil der Geschichte oder die Macht des Klischees," *AHC* 32 (2000) 106-45.

HERIBERT MÜLLER

John XXIII (Oct. 28, 1958-June 3, 1963). Blessed (feast day June 3). Formerly *Angelo Giuseppe Roncalli,* born Nov. 25, 1881, at Sotto il Monte in the province of Bergamo, in modest circumstances. He studied at the Roman seminary, where he met the Redemptorist Francesco Pitocchi, who led him to draw a radical conclusion: "God is everything, I am nothing" (*Giornale dell'anima,* December 16, 1902). He was ordained to the priesthood in Rome in 1904 and was secretary to Bishop Giacomo Radini Tedeschi of Bergamo until 1919. John admired his "generosity of thought" and his pastoral sensitivity and became acquainted with liturgical, ecumenical, and social problems. He served in the army in 1918, first as a medical orderly, then as chaplain. He was spiritual director of the seminary in Bergamo from 1919 to 1921 and was in charge of the Pontifical Work for the spreading of the faith in Italy from 1921 to 1925. He was ordained bishop on March 19, 1925, and was sent by Pius XI first as apostolic visitor, then as apostolic delegate, to Bulgaria. He was apostolic delegate in Greece and Turkey from 1935 to 1944, residing in Istanbul. These years were not free of tensions, thanks to his attitude to Christians of other confessions and to the fascist government in Italy—an attitude which diverged from that of the Vatican. Proximity to Orthodox Christians made him long more strongly for the unity of the church; in Turkey, he experienced a radically lay society as well as the limitations of the Eurocentrism that was defended in ecclesiastical circles. In 1937, he moved from Istanbul to Athens; during World War II, he helped the Greeks under the German occupation and was able to prevent the deportation of Greek Jews. After Charles de Gaulle demanded that Valerio Valeri be recalled from his post as nuncio for collaborating with the Vichy regime, Roncalli became nuncio in Paris on January 1, 1945, and his years in France exposed him to new experiences: contacts with Marxists, French colonialism, the war in Algeria. The general dechristianization in France made pastoral renewal necessary. In 1953, he was appointed patriarch of Venice. The last years of Pius XII were marked by the Cold War and by rigidity in the ecclesiastical structures. John was elected as his successor in a conclave that lasted three days (October 25-28, 1958). Although he was considered a transitional pope, he developed his own ideas about his pontificate from the very start, imprinting his own style on his office. He chose a papal name that had not been used since 1415, when John XXIII was deposed by the Council of Constance. In the sermon at his coronation on November 4, 1958, he presented himself in the words of Jacob's son to his brothers: "I am Joseph, your brother." He sought to normalize life in the curia by nominating Domenico Tardini to fill the post of secretary of state, vacant since 1944, and by reintroducing the regular audiences for those holding responsibility in the various sectors of the curia. He rejuvenated and renewed the College of → Cardinals by new appointments. He emphasized the importance of his role as bishop of Rome by solemnly taking possession of the Lateran basilica, and by visiting prisons, hospitals, and Roman parishes. John prepared the way for a disentanglement of the church and the papacy from their involvement in Italian politics. He wanted a church "that serves human beings—not only those who are Catholics" (July 25, 1962). His goal was to elevate the gospel above all "views and

groups which move and shake society" (August 13, 1961). The visit of Nikita Khrushchev's daughter and son-in-law on March 5, 1963, caused a great sensation. The papal → Ostpolitik was beginning to make its presence felt.

On January 25, 1959, John announced the convocation of a new ecumenical council, a diocesan synod for Rome, and the revision of the *Code of Canon Law*. Shortly before the opening of the council (September 11, 1962), he made the emphatic point in a radio broadcast that "the church consists of everyone, and especially of the poor." The most important event of his pontificate was probably the opening address to the Second Vatican Council. Central themes were "*aggiornamento*," the desire to display mercy rather than to utter condemnations, and the rejection of the ecclesiastical "prophets of doom." John followed the work of the council, but refrained from direct intervention, apart from two instances. In mid-October 1962 he assented to a delay in voting on the membership of the conciliar commissions, in order to give the council fathers more time to exchange views; and after the vote on November 21, 1962, he supported the majority in their rejection of the proposed definition of the relationship between scripture and tradition.

The pope's vital energy had been much reduced by cancer since September 1962. He published *Pacem in terris,* the last and most important of his eight encyclicals, on April 11, 1963; it was addressed not only to Catholics but to "all persons of good will." Another important encyclical was *Mater et magistra* (May 5, 1961), which accepted the employment of an inductive methodology in the elaboration of the church's social teaching. *Pacem in terris* proclaims two fundamental principles: the impossibility "in the atomic age of using war as a means to achieve justice," and the total rejection of a "just war." With regard to collaboration between Christians and non-Christians, the pope conceded that the time was now ripe for "associations and meetings on a practical basis which would not have been opportune and fruitful yesterday." He distinguished here between the error and the one who errs, as well as between erroneous philosophical doctrines and the historical, economic, and political movements these doctrines generate. John brought the Constantinian epoch of church history to a close and gave the church a new spring. He was beatified in 2000.

■ **Works:** *Gli atti della visita apostolica di San Carlo Borromeo a Bergamo*, 5 vols. (Florence, 1936-57); *Il cardinale Cesare Baronio* (Rome, 1961); *Monsignore Giacomo Maria Radini Tedeschi, vescovo di Bergamo* (Rome, 1963); *Souvenirs d'un nonce: Cahiers de France (1944-53)* (Rome, 1963); *Discorsi, messaggi, colloqui*, 6 vols. (Rome, 1960-67); *Il giornale dell'anima*, ed. L. Capovilla (10th ed. Cinisello Balsamo, 1990; more complete ed. by A. Melloni, Bologna, 1989); *Lettere ai familiari 1901-62*, ed. L. Capovilla, 2 vols. (Rome, 1968); *Lettere 1958-63*, ed. L. Capovilla (Rome, 1978).

■ **Bibliography:** *TRE* 17:113-18; *VATL* 353ff.; G. Lercaro, *Johannes XXIII.: Entwurf eines neuen Bildes* (Freiburg, 1967); D. Aimé-Azam, *L'extraordinaire Ambassadeur* (Paris, 1967); F. M. William, *Vom jungen Angelo Roncalli (1903-07) zum Papst Johannes XXIII. (1903-63)* (Innsbruck, 1967); L. Capovilla, *Giovanni XXIII: Quindici letture* (Rome, 1970); L. Algisi, *Giovanni XXIII* (4th ed. Turin, 1981); G. De Rosa, ed., *Angelo Giuseppe Roncalli dal patriarcato di Venezia alla cattedra di San Pietro* (Florence, 1984); P. Hebblethwaite, *John XXIII, Pope of the Council* (London, 1984); G. De Rosa, ed., *Fede—Tradizione—Profezia: Studi su Giovanni XXIII e sul Vaticano II* (Brescia, 1984); G. Alberigo, ed., "L'Età di Roncalli," *Cristianesimo nella storia* 8 (1987) 1-217; F. Della Salda, *Obbedienza e pace: Il vescovo A. G. Roncalli tra Sofia e Roma 1925-34* (Genoa, 1989); S. Trinchese, *Roncalli e le missioni: L'Opera della propagazione della fede tra Francia e Vaticano negli anni '20* (Brescia, 1989); V. Conzemius, "Mythes et contremythes autour de Jean XXIII," *Cristianesimo nella storia* 10 (1989) 553-78; L. Kaufmann and L. Klein, *Prophetie im Vermächtnis* (Freiburg, 1990); M. Manzo, *Papa Giovanni vescovo a Roma* (Milan, 1991); G. Alberigo and K. Wittstadt, eds., *Ein Blick zurück—nach vorn: Johannes XXIII.: Spiritualität—Theologie—Wirken* (Würzburg, 1992); A. Melloni, "La causa Roncalli: Origini di un processo canonico," *Cristianesimo nella storia* 18 (1997) 607-36; G. Zizola, *Giovanni XXIII: Nuovi saggi 1958-1998* (Sotto il Monte, 1998); S. Gaeta, *Giovanni XXIII* (Milan, 2000); V. De Luca, *Papa Giovanni* (Venice, 2000); C. Feldmann, *Pope John XXIII: A Spiritual Biography* (New York, 2000); G. Alberigo, *Johannes XXIII.* (Mainz, 2000).

GIUSEPPE ALBERIGO

John Paul I (Aug. 26-Sept. 28, 1978). Formerly *Albino Luciani*, born Oct. 17, 1912, at Canale d'Agordo in the diocese of Belluno. His father was a worker and an anticlerical socialist. After studying in Belluno, he was ordained to the priesthood in 1935 and worked as curate and teacher of religion. He was appointed deputy rector and professor of dogmatic theology in 1937; he began higher studies at the Gregorian University in Rome in 1941. He became vicar general of the diocese of Belluno in 1944. He was appointed bishop of Vittorio Veneto in 1958, patriarch of Venice in 1969, and cardinal in 1973. He was conservative on theological questions but pastorally open. He was scarcely known outside Italy, and mostly unnoticed in the Roman curia, when he was elected in the fourth vote at the conclave. His double name, the first in papal history, proclaimed his continuity with his two immediate predecessors—who were of course very different from one another. He refused coronation and enthronement. He abandoned the "royal 'we'" and employed a language free of pious rhetoric and general appeals, speaking about problems clearly. His modesty, his relaxed piety, and his healthy common sense immediately evoked great waves of enthusiasm. His sudden death of a heart attack after only thirty-three days led to the formation of legends and rumors.

■ **Works:** *Opera Omnia* (Padua, 1988).

■ **Bibliography:** D. A. Yallop, *In God's Name* (London, 1984); V. J. Willi, *'Im Namen des Teufels?'* (Stein am Rhein, 1987); L. D'Orazi, *Impegno all'umiltà: La vita di papa Luciani* (Rome, 1987); J. Cornwall, *A Thief in the Night* (London, 1989); R. Kummer, *Albino Luciani* (Graz, 1991).

JOSEF GELMI

John Paul II (elected Oct. 16, 1978). Formerly *Karol Jozef Wojtyła*, born May 18, 1920, at Wadowice near Krakow. He studied philosophy in Krakow; during the German occupation, he worked in a factory and then studied in the secret seminary set up by Archbishop Adam Sapieha. He was ordained priest in 1946 and sent for further studies to Rome (doctor of philosophy, 1948) and Krakow (doctor of theology, 1953). He taught ethics in Lublin and Krakow from 1954, and was active as chaplain to students. He became auxiliary bishop in Krakow in 1958 and took part in the Second Vatican Council, where he was a strong supporter of *Dignitatis humanae* and participated in the final redaction of *Gaudium et spes*. He became archbishop of Krakow in 1964 and was created cardinal in 1967. From this time on, he had frequent contacts with the Roman curia and was a member of all the synods of bishops. After the unexpected death of John Paul I, he was elected pope, the first Slav and the first non-Italian since Hadrian VI (1522).

His pontificate has been marked by frequent

synods of bishops and by unparalleled travels throughout the whole world. His multilingualism has stood him in good stead in the various European countries. He has given a larger number of private and general audiences than his predecessors; these, like his visits to Roman parishes and Italian dioceses, allow him to meet a great number of people. He has had many encounters with representatives of the other Christian confessions and of non-Christian religions. John Paul II has attempted to give impetus to the ecumenical movement without compromising on fundamental Catholic positions. Although he follows traditional options in questions of doctrine and discipline, he opposed the rejection of Vatican II by the traditionalist Marcel Lefebvre. Politics have played an important role in his pontificate; his personal experience of totalitarian regimes led him to take a harder line in → Ostpolitik than his predecessor Paul VI. After a failed assassination attempt during a general audience (St. Peter's Square, May 13, 1981), he had to accept a tightening of security measures. In Poland, he encouraged Lech Walesa, the workers' leader, and the trade union Solidarity, while at the same time counseling caution after martial law was declared, in view of the threat of a Soviet invasion. The boost he gave to Polish self-awareness prepared the ground for the political breakthrough of 1989. Papal influence on the political structures of the postcommunist era has been much less than on the rejection of communism; nevertheless, one can speak of success in the East, whereas tension has marked John Paul's relations with the United States, the leading power in the West. Disagreements have arisen over questions of foreign politics and over social issues such as abortion; nevertheless, he has had an exceptionally warm welcome on his visits to Western countries also. He achieved a breakthrough vis-à-vis Israel, leading to the assumption of diplomatic relations in 1993.

He has published numerous encyclicals: *Redemptor hominis* (1979), *Dives in misericordia* (1980), *Laborem exercens* (1981), *Slavorum Apostoli* (1985), *Dominum et vivificantem* (1986), *Redemptoris mater* and *Sollicitudo rei socialis* (1987), *Redemptoris missio* (1990), *Centesimus annus* (1991), *Veritatis splendor* (1993), *Evangelium vitae* and *Ut unum sint* (1995), *Fides et ratio* (1998). He has also issued numerous Apostolic Letters and held many discourses.

Important events in his pontificate include the promulgation of the new *Code of Canon Law* (1983), the revision of the concordat with Italy (1984), a reform of the curia (Constitution *Pastor Bonus*, 1988), the promulgation of the Code of Oriental Canon Law (1990), and his discourse to the United Nations on the fiftieth anniversary of its founding (1995). The celebrations marking the Holy Year in 2000 were a high point of the pontificate; the day of reconciliation, held on the first Sunday in Lent (March 12), drew worldwide attention. On this day, the pope presented the document of the → International Theological Commission entitled "Memory and Reconciliation: The Church and the Faults of the Past." Health problems have restricted the pope's activities somewhat in recent years.

■ **Sources:** *AAS* 70 (1978–); *L'Attività della Santa Sede* (Vatican City, 1978–), a report of Vatican activities; *Insegnamenti di Giovanni Paolo II* (Vatican City, 1978–), containing discourses, etc.; International Theological Commission, *Memory and Reconciliation: The Church and the Faults of the Past* (Vatican City, 2000).

■ **Works (translated into many languages):** *The Acting Person* (Dordrecht, 1979); *Love and Responsibility* (San Francisco, 1994); *Crossing the Threshold of Hope* (London, 1994); *Gift and Mystery* (Vatican City, 1996).

■ **Bibliography:** *VATL* 357-60; M. Malinski, *John Paul II: The Life of My Friend Karol Wojtyła* (London, 1979); L. Accattoli, *Karol Wojtyła: L'uomo di fine millennio* (Milan, 1998); S. O. Horn, *Johannes Paul II.—Zeuge des Evangeliums: Perspektiven des Papstes an der Schwelle zum dritten Jahrtausend* (Würzburg, 1999); G. Weigel, *Witness to Hope: The Biography of Pope John Paul II* (New York, 1999); J. F. Crosby, *The Legacy of Pope John Paul II: His Contribution to Catholic Thought* (New York, 2000).

ERWIN GATZ

Julius I (Feb. 6, 337-Apr. 12, 352). Saint (feast day Apr. 12). The most importance source of information about Julius is his synodal letter to the leading bishops of the synod of Antioch (341), in which he granted *communio* to all those bishops and priests who had been expelled by the Arians. Since this document is transmitted only by Athanasius in his second apology against the Arians (21.1-35.8), one cannot exclude the possibility that we have a one-sided version of what Julius actually wrote; one indicator of this is the harsh treatment of Marcellus of Ancyra. Julius and the Roman synod supported Athanasius in the defense of his episcopal see and of his orthodoxy; Julius appeals with striking self-assurance to the Roman Petrine tradition as the basis of the authority he claims. He demanded that the emperors Constantius and Constans hold an imperial council, which was convoked in Serdica (Sofia) in 343. The Eastern group anathematized Julius and those Western bishops who supported Athanasius; the Western assembly decreed that bishops who were deposed should have the right to appeal to the pope. The consequence was a schism between Rome and the Eastern churches. Julius's actions culminated in the exercise of the Roman office of invigilation, which he based on arguments open to inspection by others; his aim was to achieve control over all synods that were held anywhere in the church.

■ **Sources:** *Acta SS* apr. 2:82-86.

■ **Bibliography:** *LMA* 5:805; *VATL* 360f.; P. P. Joannou, *Die Ostkirche und die Cathedra Petri im 4. Jahrhundert* (Stuttgart, 1972) 21ff., 36-105; K. M. Girardet, "Appellatio," *Historia: Zeitschrift für alte Geschichte* 23 (1974) 98-127; W. M. Gessel, "Das primatiale Bewußtsein Julius' I.," in *Konzil und Papst* (Munich et al., 1975) 63-74; K. M. Girardet, *Kaisergericht und Bischofsgericht* (Bonn, 1975) 90-93; G. Schwaiger, *Päpstlicher Primat* (Munich et al., 1977) 27, 40, 105; M. Vinzent, "Die Gegner im Schreiben Markells von Ankyra an Julius von Rom," *Zeitschrift für Kirchengeschichte* 105 (1994) 285-328.

WILHELM M. GESSEL

Julius II (Nov. 1, 1503-Feb. 20, 1513). Formerly *Giuliano della Rovere,* born 1443 at Albissola near Savona. His family was poor, but his uncle, Sixtus IV, took him under his wing, bestowing numerous bishoprics on him. He was created cardinal in 1471. During the pontificate of Alexander VI, he led the opposition against the Borgias and was forced to flee to King Charles VIII of France. Bribery played a role in his election as pope. His goal was the consolidation of the → papal states, which the family politics of the Borgias had brought to the brink of disintegration, and to use this state as the basis of a strong and independent papacy in an Italy liberated from foreign dominion. He stripped the dangerous Cesare Borgia (son of Alexander VI) of his power, and regained Perugia and Bologna for the papal state. In 1508/1509, he joined the League of Cambrai (with emperor Maximilian I, Louis XII of France, Aragon and Savoy) against Venice, which was obliged to restore to the pope the cities it had occupied in the Romagna. The pope joined Venice and Spain in the Holy League in 1511. Thanks to military support from the Swiss confederation, they succeeded at least temporarily in driving the French from Italy; the church states won back Parma, Piacenza, and Reggio Emilia. The disputes with France led to the renewal of the Pragmatic Sanction of Bourges (1510) and to the convocation by opposition cardinals in 1511 of a council, which was to assemble at Pisa in 1512. These cardinals were supported by the French king, and their project was approved by Maximilian I. In order to avoid a schism, Julius convoked the Fifth Lateran Council, to meet in May 1512. Julius promulgated a number of reforming decrees, including a prohibition of simony at papal elections.

Julius was an important patron of the arts and gave commissions to Bramante, Michelangelo, and Raphael. He laid the foundation stone of new → St. Peter's in 1506. Michelangelo created the funeral monument of Julius II (Moses) and painted the ceiling frescoes in the Sistine Chapel.

■ **Bibliography:** *LMA* 5:805; *VATL* 361-64; Pastor 3/2:659-1142; P. Pecchai, *Roma nel Cinquecento* (Bologna, 1948); G. B. Piccotti, *La politica italiana sotto il pontificato di Giulio II* (Pisa, 1949); F. Seneca, *Venezia e papa Giulio II* (Padua, 1962); C. Fusero, *Giulio II* (Milan, 1965); C. Bindi Senesi, *Giulio II* (Milan, 1967); G. de Beauville, *Jules II: Sauveur de la papauté* (Paris, 1965); C. Friess, "Die Beziehungen Kaiser Maximilians I zur Römischen Kurie und zur deutschen Kirche unter dem Pontifikat Papst Julius' II. (1508-1513)" (diss., Graz, 1974); F. Gilbert, *The Pope, His Banker and Venice* (Cambridge, Mass., 1980); J. F. D'Amico, "Papal History and Curial Reform in the Renaissance: Raffaele Maffeis 'Brevis Historia' of Julius II and Leo X," *AHP* 18 (1980) 157-210; I. Cloulas, *Jules II* (Paris, 1990); C. Shaw, *Julius II: The Warrior Pope* (Oxford, 1993).

KLAUS GANZER

Julius III (Feb. 8, 1550-Mar. 23, 1555). Formerly *Giovanni Maria del Monte,* born Sept. 10, 1487, at Rome. After studying civil and canon law in Perugia and Siena, he became chamberlain to Julius II. He was appointed archbishop of Siponto in 1513 and held a number of offices in the curia and the → papal states. He was created cardinal in 1536 and was president of the Council of Trent during the first conciliar period (1545-1547) and in Bologna (1547-1548). His election as pope was the outcome of a lengthy struggle between the imperial and the French parties, in which Julius was the compromise candidate. His electoral capitulation and pressure from the emperor forced him to summon the council to resume its activity at Trent on May 1, 1551. The suspension of the council on April 28, 1554, proved inevitable, thanks to the conspiracy of the German princes; but Julius wanted the council to promulgate the necessary dogmatic decrees and a number of general reform measures before the members departed. After the suspension, he charged a commission to draw up a bull setting out the reform; however, his death meant that this came to nothing. He became involved in a military conflict with Ottavio Farnese, whom he had appointed feudal ruler of Parma. He supported the Jesuits and entrusted to them the direction of the German College, founded in 1552. One particular success during the pontificate of Julius was the reunion of England (under Mary I) with the Catholic Church, achieved in 1554 by Cardinal Reginald Pole; this union, however, did not last. A shadow on the pontificate was cast by his adoptive nephew Innocenzo del Monte, on whom he showered favors, creating him a cardinal in 1550. Julius, in many ways a typical Renaissance prince, can truly be called a transitional figure.

■ Sources: *Concilium Tridentinum: Diariorum, Actorum, Epistularum, Tractatuum nova Collectio,* ed. Görres-Gesellschaft (Freiburg, 1901-2001) passim. The nunciature reports contain a great deal of relevant material.
■ Bibliography: *TRE* 17:445ff.; *VATL* 365f.; Pastor, vol. 6; C. Erdmann, "Die Wiedereröffnung des Trienter Konzils durch Julius III.," *QFIAB* 20 (1928/29) 238-317; H. Jedin, "Analekten zur Reformtätigkeit der Päpste Julius III. und Paul IV.," *RQ* 42 (1934) 305-32; 43 (1935) 87-156; idem, "Kirchenreform und Konzilsgedanke 1550-59," *Historisches Jahrbuch* 54 (1934) 401-31; idem, *Geschichte des Konzils von Trient* (Freiburg) I (3rd ed. 1977), II (2nd ed. 1978), III (2nd ed. 1982) passim; H. Lutz, *Christianitas afflicta: Europa, das Reich und die päpstliche Politik im Niedergang der Hegemonie Karls V. (1552-56)* (Göttingen, 1964); idem, ed., *Friedenslegation des Reginald Pole zu Kaiser Karl V. und König Heinrich II. (1553-56)* (Tübingen, 1981); H. Nova, *The Artistic Patronage of Pope Julius III* (New York, 1988); T. F. Mayer, "An Unknown Diary of Julius III's Conclave by Bartolomeo Stella, a Servant of Cardinal Pole," *AHC* 24 (1992) 345-77; W. V. Hudon, "The 'Consilium de emendanda Ecclesia' and the 1555 Reform Bull of Pope Julius III," in *Reform and Renewal in the Middle Ages and the Renaissance,* Festschrift for L. Pascoe (Leiden, 2000) 240-58.

KLAUS GANZER

Lando (end of Nov. 913-end of Mar. 914). The son of Tainus from Sabina. No documents issued by Lando survive, and the information about the length of his pontificate is contradictory. A judicial document of 1413 mentions a donation by Lando to the bishop of Vescovio (Sabina) to help rebuild the cathedral, which had been destroyed by the Saracens.

■ Sources: *LP* 2:239; *RPR*(J) 1:448; Zimmermann *Reg* 6f.
■ Bibliography: *LMA* 5:1671.

SEBASTIAN SCHOLZ

Laurence (antipope) (Nov. 22, 498-Mar. 507). Died 507/508. After the death of Anastasius II, the majority, who were dissatisfied with his conciliatory attitude during the Acacian schism, elected Symmachus pope on November 22, 498; the minority of those favorable to Byzantium, supported by the aristocracy and by the senate under Festus, immediately reacted by making the respected archpriest Laurence pope. The decision of Theoderic the Great, king of the eastern Goths, in favor of Symmachus brought only a temporary resolution to the resulting confusion. Initially, Laurence accepted this decision in February or March 499 and was made bishop of Nocera in Campania. The strife between the parties continued, and Theoderic tolerated Laurence's return to Rome, where his superior forces gave him the upper hand from 501 to 506; Symmachus remained in asylum in St. Peter's, until Theoderic's conflict with Byzantium led him to abandon Laurence in 506. Laurence submitted definitively in 507 and withdrew to a country estate belonging to Festus, where he led a severely ascetic life and died shortly thereafter.

■ Sources: *LP* 1:46ff.; *RPR*(J) 1:96-100.
■ Bibliography: *BBKL* 4:1249-52; Caspar 2:87-118, 758-61; G. B. Picotti, "I sinodi romani nello scismo laurenziano," in Festschrift for G. Volpe (Florence, 1958) 2:741-876; P. A. B. Llewellyn, "The Roman Clergy during the Laurentian Schism (498-506)," *Ancient Society* 8 (1977) 245-75; E. Wirbelauer, *Zwei Päpste in Rom: Der Konflikt zwischen Laurentius und Symmachus* (Munich, 1993); S. Vacca, *Prima Sedes a nemine iudicatur* (Rome, 1993).

GEORG SCHWAIGER

Leo I, the Great (Sept. 29, 440 [episcopal ordination]-Nov. 10, 461). Saint (feast day Nov. 10).
1. Life.—2. Pontificate.—3. Writings.—4. Significance.

1. Life

Leo came from a Tuscan family, and he is often identified with the acolyte Leo whom Augustine

83

mentions in the year 418 (*Ep.* 191.1). As archdeacon, he requested John Cassian to compose "seven books on the incarnation of the Lord against Nestorius" during the Nestorian controversy in 430. Cyril of Alexandria sought his support in 431, when Juvenal was attempting to secure the rank of patriarchate for Jerusalem. Leo is credited with decisive influence on the anti-Pelagian attitude of Rome under his predecessors. When Sixtus III died on August 18, 440, Leo was in Gaul on a political mission and was elected pope *in absentia.* He was ordained bishop in Rome on September 29, 440.

2. Pontificate

The anniversary of Leo's episcopal ordination became one of the two dates (the other in spring) for the Roman provincial synods. The imperial family visited the Vatican basilica on the occasion of the synod in February 450. Leo's primary concerns were the purity of the faith (against Pelagians and Arians, and—with help from the civil government—against Manicheans who were discovered in Rome in 443, and against Spanish Priscillians in 447) and the proper regulation of church business (Mauritania, Arles, and Vienne in Gaul; Sicily). An imperial rescript issued in 445 acknowledged the jurisdiction of the Roman bishop over all the provinces of the Western empire. In the East, Leo appointed Anastasius of Thessalonica as apostolic vicar in Illyricum. In 452, he persuaded Attila near Mantua to withdraw the Huns from Italy; when the Vandals under Geiserich plundered Rome in 455, he was able to prevent murder and arson. The christological dispute with Eutyches and Monophysitism began in 449. Leo's position is contained in the celebrated letter (the "Tome") which he addressed to Patriarch Flavian of Constantinople on June 13, 449. Dioscorus of Alexandria prevented this text from being read aloud at the synod convoked by Emperor Theodosius II in Ephesus in August 449, which Leo called "a robber synod" (*latrocinium*), but it found the official recognition demanded by the pope at the council convoked by Emperor Marcian in Chalcedon in October 451, where the central passage in the "Tome" was included in the conciliar profession of faith (DH 302). Leo delayed his assent to the council until 453 because of canon 28, which awarded Constantinople patriarchal status, because it was the residence of the emperor. In order to follow events in the East more closely, Leo appointed a chargé d'affaires in Constantinople; the first to hold this office was Julian of Chios. The Council of Chalcedon led to rioting by monks in Palestine in 452-453, and to disturbances in the church of Alexandria in 457. In this critical situation, Leo adopted the date for Easter that had been calculated in Alexandria for the year 454. The so-called "second Tome," addressed to the Palestinian monks in 453 and to the emperor Leo I in 458, is based on Leo's writings against Monophysitism.

3. Writings

Nintey-seven treatises or sermons on various occasions in the church year and 143 letters survive. Leo's contribution to liturgical texts is a matter of scholarly debate; he is not the author of the "Leonine sacramentary" which bears his name. Leo's writings, produced in the papal chancellery where Prosper of Aquitaine played a leading role, are composed in an artistic prose that has been given the name *cursus leoninus.*

4. Significance

During the reigns of weak emperors, Leo was the dominant personality who assumed responsibility for the unity of the church, which had now entered upon the inheritance of the *Imperium Romanum.* Leo was essentially a conservative, not an innovator. The central themes in his pastoral ministry are the Petrine office and the incarnation. The incarnation of God is the heart of the new world order. Whoever attacks the truth of the one Person of Christ in two natures destroys the Christian faith. Leo's insistence on the mystery of God and his realistic view of the human person and the world is ultimately born of his concern with redemption, and this is also the source of his understanding of the church, which Peter—who lives on in the Roman bishop with his confession of faith and the ministry entrusted to him—must serve. Leo has always enjoyed high esteem in the Roman Catholic Church, but the Syro-Antiochene church which came into existence after Chalcedon counts him among the Nestorians.

■ **Works:** *PL* 54-56; *Sermons,* ed. A. Chavasse, Corpus Christianorum, series latina, 138/138A (Turnhout, 1972); *Letters,* ed. E. Schwartz, *ACO* 2:1-4; ed. C. Silva-Tarouca, Textus et Documenta, Series theologica, 9, 15, 20, 23 (Rome, 1932-37); ed. O. Guenther, Corpus scriptorum ecclesiasticorum latinorum 35 (Vienna, 1895).

■ **Bibliography:** *DTHC* 9:218-301; *TRE* 19:737-41; *LMA* 5:1876f.; *DECL* 374-76; *VATL* 443f.; T. Steeger, *Die Klauseltechnik Leos des Großen in seinen Sermonen* (Haßfurt a.M., 1908); F. DiCapua, *Il ritmo prosaico nelle lettere dei papi* (Rome, 1937) 1:3-204; T. Jalland, *The Life and Times of Saint Leo the Great* (London, 1941); M. B. De Soos, *Le mystère liturgique d'après Saint Léon le Grand* (Münster, 1958; repr. 1972); E. Dekkers, "Autour de l'oeuvre liturgique de Saint Léon le Grand," *Sacris erudiri* 10 (1958) 363-98; H.-J. Sieben, "Leo der Große über Konzilien und Lehrprimat des römischen Stuhles," *Theologie und Philosophie* 47 (1972) 358-401; H. Arens, *Die christologische Sprache Leos des Großen* (Frankfurt a.M., 1982); E. P. Pepka, *The Theology of St. Peter's Presence in His Successors according to St. Leo the Great* (Ann Arbor, 1986); W. Blümer, *Rerum eloquentia: Christliche Nutzung antiker Stilkunst bei St. Leo Magnus* (Frankfurt a.M., 1991); K. I. Kang, *Ecumenical Models in the Theology of Leo the Great* (Ann Arbor, 1992); H. O. Maier, "'Manichee!': Leo the Great and the Orthodox Panopticum," *Journal of Early Christian Studies* 4 (1996) 441-60; A. S. Scarcella, *La legislazione di Leone I* (Milan, 1997); M. Parmentier, "The 'Sayings of Bishop Leo' ('Dicta Leonis episcopi') as an Anti-adoptianist Creed," *Ephemerides liturgicae* 111 (1997) 37-48; P. L. Barclift, "The Shifting Tones of Pope Leo the Great's Christological Vocabulary," *Church History* 66 (1997) 221-39; S. P. Cowe, "The Tome of Leo: Eastern and Oriental Orthodox Perspectives," *Saint Nerses Theological Review* 3 (1998) 1-21; C. Folson, "'Mysterium fidei' and St. Leo the Great," *Ecclesia orans* 15 (1998) 289-302.

HERBERT ARENS

Leo II (Aug. 17, 682-July 3, 683). Saint (feast day July 3), born in Sicily. He was educated at the Roman choir school and was respected for his eloquence, his high culture, and his knowledge of Greek and Latin. He was probably elected in January 681, but was confirmed as pope by Emperor Constantine IV only after he had recognized the Sixth Ecumenical Council of Constantinople, which had condemned Honorius I in the context of the struggle against Monothelitism (cf. Leo's letter to the emperor and letters to Spain). Although he emphasized the Roman primacy, Leo exercised his office in loyal obedience to the imperial governance of the church. He abolished Ravenna's autocephaly and began the translation of the conciliar acts into Latin. In Rome, he restored Santa Sabina and founded San Giorgio in Velabro for the Greeks. Macarius, the deposed patriarch of Antioch, and his Monothelite companions were handed over to the mild judgment of the pope.

■ **Sources:** *LP* 1:359-62, 375-79; 3:index; *RPR*(J) 1:240f.; 2:699, 741; *PL* 96:399-420; Mansi 11:713-922, 1046-58.
■ **Bibliography:** *DTHC* 9:301-4; *LMA* 5:1878; *BBKL* 4:1435f.; *VATL* 445; Caspar 2:610-19, 624f.; R. Riedinger, "Die Dokumente des Petrus Notarius Regionarius auf seiner Reise von Rom nach Spanien im Jahre 683/684," *Burgense* 29 (Burgos, 1988) 233-50; Borgolte.

GEORG SCHWAIGER

Leo III (Dec. 26, 795-June 12, 816). Saint (feast day June 12). Born into a nonaristocratic family, he was a cleric in the wardrobe of the Lateran and priest in Santa Susanna. He was elected "unanimously" on the day of Hadrian I's death. When he informed Charlemagne of his election, he sent him the keys to St. Peter's tomb and the banner of Rome, thereby acknowledging him as *patricius* and offering him an oath of loyalty. Charlemagne's reply was caesaropapist: the king's task was the protection of the church *ad extra* and the safeguarding of the faith *ad intra,* while the pope's only task was to pray. The Frankish envoys in Rome saved Leo when relatives of his predecessor, Hadrian, attacked him during a procession on Rogation Day (April 25, 799) and almost succeeded in blinding him and cutting out his tongue (which would have made it impossible for him to carry out his office). The pope visited the emperor in Paderborn and persuaded him to intervene. On his return to Rome, Leo set up a mosaic in the Triclinium of the → Lateran depicting himself as the successor of Peter and Charlemagne as the successor of Constantine. Charlemagne was received in Rome "with great honors" on November 23-24, 800: the first act of welcome, at the twelfth milestone from the city boundary, was "imperial." Charlemagne presided over a synod in St. Peter's. Since Leo as pope was not subject to the authority of any court, he took an oath of purification on December 22; this was to be significant for oaths taken by clerics in later periods. On Christmas Day, Leo crowned and anointed Charlemagne as emperor. Leo performed this epoch-making action in keeping with his own understanding of the coronation; according to Einhard, this provoked the emperor's "displeasure." Leo remained in contact with Charlemagne and visited him in Quierzy at Christmas 804. However, he opposed the emperor's intention to include the *Filioque* in the creed (808/809) and had the traditional text inscribed on bronze tablets in the Vatican. The

Liber Pontificalis praises the pope for restoring and endowing churches. At the end of his pontificate, one of the longest in history, he was once again embroiled in a revolt on the part of the nobles.

■ **Sources:** *LP* 2:1-48; 3:117-22; *RPR*(J) 1:307-16; 2:701f.; *MGH.Ep* 5:58-68, 87-104; *MGH.PL* 1:366-79.

■ **Bibliography:** *LMA* 5:1877f.; *VATL* 445f.; K. J. Benz, "'Cum ab oratione surgeret': Überlegungen zur Kaiserkrönung Karls des Großen," *Deutsches Archiv für Erforschung des Mittelalters* 31 (1975) 337-69; P. Classen, *Karl der Große, das Papsttum und Byzanz* (Sigmaringen, 1985); O. Hageneder, "Das 'crimen maiestatis,' der Prozeß gegen die Attentäter Papst Leos III. und die Kaiserkrönung Karls des Großen," in *Aus Kirche und Reich,* Festschrift for F. Kempf (Sigmaringen, 1983) 55-79; V. Peri, "Il 'Filioque' nel magistero di Adriano I e di Leone III," *Rivista di storia della Chiesa in Italia* 41 (1987) 5-25; L. E. Philipp, "A Note on the Gifts of Leo III to the Churches of Rome: 'Vestes cum storiis,'" *Ephemerides liturgicae* 102 (1988) 72-78; P. Hatlie, "Theodore of Stoudios, Pope Leo III and the Joseph Affair (808-812)," *Orientalia christiana periodica* 61 (1995) 407-23; J. Ernesti, "Paderborn, 'Ursprung und verschütteter Born des Reichs,'" *Theologie und Glaube* 89 (1999) 153-79; J. Meyer zu Schlochtern, ed., *Geistliche und weltliche Macht: Das Paderborner Treffen 799 und das Ringen um den Sinn von Geschichte* (Paderborn, 2000); K. Hengst, "Karl der Große und Papst Leo III. in Paderborn: Dichtung und Wahrheit," *Theologie und Glaube* 90 (2000) 20-38.

ARNOLD ANGENENDT

Leo IV (Apr. 10, 847-July 17, 855). Saint (feast day July 17), a Roman, son of Radoald. He was raised in the monastery of St. Martin in Rome. He was subdeacon under Gregory IV, and cardinal priest of Santi Quattro Coronati under Sergius II. He was elected in January 847 and was ordained bishop without the consent of emperor Lothar I, allegedly because of military campaigns by the Saracens. He displayed a much keener concern for the city of → Rome and for the Patrimony of Peter (laid waste by the Saracens) than most of his predecessors and followers, as can be seen in the so-called Leonine city, which he reinforced between 848 and 852, and in his policy of bestowing gifts. Leo held his own against the Saracens, with help from southern Italy, in the naval victory of Ostia in 849. Although he did not shy away from conflicts with the imperial power, Leo collaborated with Louis II (whom he crowned as emperor in 850) to increase papal authority over the eastern and western Frankish kingdoms, and over the

England of Alfred the Great. He also displayed resoluteness in the controversies with Constantinople and Archbishops Hincmar of Rheims and John VII of Ravenna, as well as with the antipope Anastasius III. Most of his letters survive only as fragments quoted in texts of canon law; in addition to questions of church politics, they also show his concern to enforce Roman ecclesiastical discipline (cf., for example, his reply to the Bretons, and the conciliar acts of December 853, which repeated and extended the reforming canons of Eugene II). He is buried in St. Peter's; his portrait can be seen in San Clemente. His feast on July 17 is no longer celebrated in the most recent calendar of the diocese of Rome.

■ **Sources:** *LP* 2:106-39; *RPR*(J) 2nd ed. 1:329-39; 2:702f., 744; *RPR.IP; RPR.GP; MGH.Ep* 5:585-612; *MGH.Conc* 3:185-93, 216, 230f., 298f., 308-46, 495-502.

■ **Bibliography:** *DTHC* 9:312-16; *HKG* 3/1:161-64; *VATL* 446f.; W. Ullmann, "Nos si aliquid incompenter . . . ," *Ephemerides iuris canonici* 9 (1953) 3-11, reprinted in *The Church and the Law in the Earlier Middle Ages* (London, 1975), no. 7; J. Osborne, *Early Mediaeval Wall-Paintings in the Lower Church of San Clemente, Rome* (London, 1978); S. Gibson and B. Ward-Perkins, "The Surviving Remains of the Leonine Wall," I and II, *Papers of the British School* 47 (1979) 30-57; 51 (1983) 222-39; K. Herbers, *Leo IV und das Papsttum in der Mitte des 9. Jahrhunderts* (Stuttgart, 1996).

KLAUS HERBERS

Leo V (Aug.-Sept. 903). Died 904(?), born near Ardea. He was probably elected as a supporter of Formosus; after thirty days, he was overthrown and imprisoned by the Roman priest (and later pope) Christopher. The circumstances and date of his death are unclear. A legendary eleventh-century *Vita* equates Leo with St. Tutwal; it is said that he was elected pope while a pilgrim in Rome.

■ **Sources:** *LP* 2:234; *RPR*(J) 2nd ed. 1:444; 2:746.

■ **Bibliography:** *BiblSS* 12:723f.; *LMA* 5:1878f.; *VATL* 447f.; Zimmermann *Pa* 68.

SEBASTIAN SCHOLZ

Leo VI (mid-June 928-beginning of January 929). A Roman, son of the *primicerius* (head of the papal chancellery) Christopher. He was cardinal priest of Santa Susanna, and was made pope after Count Vido of Tuscia had deposed John X. Leo confirmed the decisions of a synod held at Split and upheld the metropolitan rights of the archbishop of Split against Bishop Gregory of Nin.

■ **Sources:** *LP* 2:242; *RPR(J)* 2nd ed. 1:453; Zimmermann *Reg* 90-94; Zimmermann *Pu* 99f.

■ **Bibliography:** *LMA* 5:1879; *BBKL* 4:1441; Zimmermann *J* 62.

SEBASTIAN SCHOLZ

Leo VII (Jan. 936-July 939). A Roman. He was cardinal priest of San Sisto and owed his elevation to the papacy to the Roman prince Alberic II, with whom he collaborated in the reform of Roman monasteries. Odo of Cluny was summoned to Rome for this purpose. It is likely that Leo himself belonged to the Benedictine order; almost all the documents he issued concerned monasteries. He supported not only Odo's monasteries (Cluny, Déols, and Fleury) but also the reform movement of Gorze. When Archbishop Frederick of Mainz asked what he should do with Jews who were unwilling to accept baptism, Leo recommended that he expel them.

■ **Sources:** *LP* 2:244; Zimmermann *Reg* 46-60; Zimmermann *Pu* 115-65.

■ **Bibliography:** *LMA* 5:1879; *BBKL* 4:1441f.; G. Antonelli, "L'opera di Odone di Cluny in Italia," *Benedictina* 4 (1950) 19-40; Zimmermann *J* 82ff.

HARALD ZIMMERMANN

Leo VIII (Dec. 4, 963-Mar. 965). A Roman. After the deposition of John XII, a Roman synod attended by Emperor Otto I made Leo, a layman and chief treasurer, pope on December 4, 963. At the beginning of 964, John succeeded in driving Leo out of Rome and held a synod at which he deposed him. The emperor continued to support Leo, even when John XII died and the Romans elected Benedict V as his successor, and this allowed Leo to hold onto his papal office; at yet another Roman synod, which Leo and the emperor held in June 964, he had Benedict deposed, although even contemporaries who lived in the empire held that Benedict had a better claim than Leo to be the legitimate pope. At the end of the eleventh century, the well-known agreement between Leo and the emperor was the basis of a series of forged documents in which Leo restored church property to the emperor and bestowed on him the right to elect the pope and to invest bishops.

■ **Sources:** *LP* 2:250; Zimmermann *Reg* nos. 329-80; C. Märtl, *Die falschen Investiturprivilegien* (Hanover, 1986); Zimmermann *Pu* 294-333.

■ **Bibliography:** *LMA* 5:1879f.; *VATL* 448f.; H. Zimmer-

mann, "Parteiungen und Papstwahlen in Rom zur Zeit Kaiser Ottos des Großen," *Römische Historische Mitteilungen* 8/9 (1964/65-1965/66) 29-88; Zimmermann *Pa* 77ff., 235ff.; Zimmermann *J* 150ff.

ERNST-DIETER HEHL

Leo IX (Feb. 12, 1049-Apr. 19, 1054). Saint (feast day Apr. 19). Formerly *Bruno,* born June 21, 1002, in a family of Alsatian counts whose seat was in Egisheim (later in Dagsburg). He studied at the cathedral school in Toul, where he became a canon. He was court chaplain to Conrad II and was bishop of Toul from 1026 to 1051. He promoted monastic reforms and was a loyal ally of the Salic rulers, who were his relatives. Henry III nominated him to the Apostolic See in December 1048, and he was enthroned on February 12, 1049. He was the most important of the five German popes who reigned between 1046 and 1058. He made the papacy the center of church reform and increased its primatial authority. The change can be seen not so much in Leo's program (struggle against simony and Nicolaitism; promotion of the election of bishops in accord with canon law—allegedly, already when he himself was elected pope in 1048) as in the praxis of papal governance. The appointments of non-Romans as his collaborators—e.g., Frederick (later Stephen IX), Hugo Candidus, and Humbert of Silva Candida, as well as Hildebrand (later Gregory VII)—paved the way for the development of the group of cardinals in the city of Rome into the College of → Cardinals drawn from the universal church. Leo spent only a third of his pontificate in Rome; two-thirds were taken up with long journeys (three to countries north of the Alps, four to southern Italy). He summoned a large number of synods: in the Lateran (probably once a year, after Easter), in Pavia, Rheims, Mainz (1049), Salerno, Siponto, Vercelli (where Berengar of Tours was condemned in 1050), and Mantua (1053). More than 170 surviving documents (many of them forgeries) indicate the increase in papal correspondence. The privileges which Leo reorganized and signed with his own hand (*rota*) were primarily meant for monasteries, but no consistent policy vis-à-vis monastic communities can be reconstructed, since the rights of laymen too were recognized. Relations between Leo and Henry III were generally harmonious. Nevertheless, Leo marched against the Normans of southern Italy without aid from the emperor and was

87

defeated near Civitate on June 18, 1053. While he remained in Benevento for nine months (possibly as a prisoner), his legates went to Constantinople; but instead of a détente between the Latin and the Greek churches, a serious breach occurred in July 1054 (the Eastern Schism). In the meantime, Leo, a sick man, had returned to Rome, where he died. He was buried in St. Peter's and was immediately venerated as a saint.

■ **Sources:** *RPR*(J) 2nd ed. 1:529-49; 2:709f., 749; *Bibliotheca hagiographica latina antiquae et mediae aetatis,* ed. Socii Bollandiani, 2 vols. (Brussels, 1898-1901) 4818-29; M. Parisse, ed., *La vie du pape Léon IX (Brunon, évêque de Toul)* (Paris, 1997).

■ **Bibliography:** *TRE* 20:742ff.; *LMA* 5:1880f.; *BBKL* 4:1443-48; S. Weinfurter, ed., *Die Salier und das Reich* (Sigmaringen, 1991) 2:303-32; J. Dahlhaus, "Zu den Gesta episcoporum Tullensium," in *Papstgeschichte und Landesgeschichte,* Festschrift for H. Jakobs (Cologne, 1995) 177-94; idem, "Aufkommen und Bedeutung der Rota in der Papsturkunde," in P. Rück, ed., *Graphische Symbole in mittelalterlichen Urkunden* (Sigmaringen, 1996) 407-23.

JOACHIM DAHLHAUS

Leo X (Mar. 11, 1513-Dec. 1, 1521). Formerly *Giovanni de' Medici,* born in Florence on December 11, 1475, the second son of Lorenzo the Magnificent, who decided that he should have an ecclesiastical career. He received many benefices at an early age, and his father had him created a cardinal in 1489. He was educated by leading humanists. He shared the ups and downs of his family in Florence; when they were overthrown in 1494, he fled with his cousin Giulio (later Clement VII) through Germany, Flanders (where he became a friend of Erasmus of Rotterdam), and France. He returned to Rome in 1500 and devoted himself to literature and the fine arts. After the death of Alexander VI, he soon acquired political influence under Julius II. He was made legate in Bologna in 1511 and was given command of the papal-Spanish army which was meant to drive the French out of Italy. After his defeat in the battle of Ravenna (April 11, 1512), he was taken prisoner and brought to Milan, but he managed to escape and returned to Rome. Here he was successful in bringing the Medici back to Florence, which he and his brother Giulio ruled until he was elected pope; he was the de facto ruler of the city even after his election.

He was elected in a brief conclave. Since he was only a deacon, he was ordained a priest on March 15, 1513, and a bishop two days later; he was crowned on March 19. Supporters of church reform welcomed Leo with high expectations, but these were not fulfilled. In the political sphere, he endeavored to exclude French and Habsburg (German-Spanish) influence from Italy and to strengthen papal power—though with far less success than Julius II. He was guided principally by the desire to benefit his own family. After the French victory at Marignano in September 1515, Leo met Francis I of France in Bologna and was obliged to cede Parma and Piacenza to him; he did, however, obtain the abrogation of the Pragmatic Sanction of Bourges. He concluded a concordat with Francis I in 1516, which gave the king extensive sovereignty over the church and remained in force until the French Revolution. Leo's intervention in Siena led to a conspiracy against his life. In the imperial election, Leo unsuccessfully supported the candidacy of Francis I of France, and also for a time the Saxon elector Frederick the Wise. New conflicts of interest with Francis I (Ferrara) led him to form an alliance against France with emperor Charles V at the end of May 1521. Before his death, he experienced the conquest of Milan by imperial, Swiss, and papal troops. Leo called for a crusade against the Turks, but this came to nothing.

His entanglement in political business, often guided by nepotistic interests, and his delight in worldly luxuries led Leo to neglect his urgent spiritual tasks. This was obvious in the case of the Fifth Lateran Council, as it dragged on toward its inglorious end in 1517: although it issued good reforming decrees, those in charge of church government did nothing to make these effective. This meant that the last great possibility of self-reform before the Reformation had been squandered. Leo's pontificate shows little awareness of the responsibility that he bore. The sale of indulgences to finance the new construction of → St. Peter's prompted Martin Luther to publish his ninety-five theses toward the end of 1517; but the pope and the curia failed to recognize Luther's religious concern and the ominous consequences of his actions, just as they underestimated the widespread European hostility to Rome. In 1518, Leo sent Cardinal Thomas Cajetan of Vio to the imperial parliament in Augsburg to engage in a disputation with Luther, and he sent Charles of Miltitz to Saxony in 1519, bearing the → Golden Rose. It was only at the urging of Johannes Eck that he issued the bull *Exsurge Domine* against Luther on June 15, 1520, which was followed by the bull of excommunication (*Decet Romanum Pontificem*) on January 3, 1521. King Henry VIII of England wrote a book against Luther, and Leo conferred the title "Defender of the Faith" on him in 1521. Charles V defended the unity of the Catholic faith and the shattered papal authority much more effectively than did the pope himself.

Leo X was a very great patron of scholars, poets, and artists (Raphael, Michelangelo, etc.). Nevertheless, his pontificate was one of the most disastrous in the history of the church. He was buried initially in St. Peter's; his tomb has been in Santa Maria sopra Minerva since 1542.

■ **Sources:** P. Bembo, *Libri XVI epistolarum Leonis X P.M. nomine scriptarum* (Venice, 1535/36; Basel, 1539); P. Jovius, *Vita Leonis X et Adriani VI* (Florence, 1548, 1551); P. de Grassis, *Il diario di Leone X,* ed. D. Delicati and A. Armellini (Rome, 1884); M. Sanudo, *I diari XVI-LVIII* (Venice, 1886-1903); J. Hergenröther, *Leonis X P.M. Regesta,* fascicles 1-8 (1513-15) (Freiburg, 1884-91); *HCMA* 2:21; 3:13-18; S. Camerani, *Bibliografia Medicea* (Florence, 1964); P. Fabisch and E. Iserloh, *Dokumente zur Causa Lutheri (1517-21),* 2 vols. (Münster, 1988-91); L. Nanni, ed., *Epp. ad Principes,* I: *Leo X-Pius IV (1513-65), Regesten* (Rome, 1992); N. H. Minnich, *The Fifth Lateran Council (1512-17)* (London, 1993).

■ **Bibliography:** *EC* 7:1150-55; *TRE* 20:744-48; *BBKL* 4:1448ff.; *LMA* 5:1881; *VATL* 450ff.; Pastor 4/1; 4/2:3-6, 648-721; F. Nitti, *Leone X e la sua politica* (Florence, 1892; repr. Bologna, 1998); C. Falconi, *Leone X: Giovanni de' Medici* (Milan, 1987); R. Bäumer, "Leo X und die Kirchenreform," in *Papsttum und Kirchenreform,* Festschrift for G. Schwaiger (St. Ottilien, 1990) 218-99; I. Ciseri, *L'ingresso trionfale di Leone X in Firenze nel 1515* (Florence, 1990); G. Bianchini: *T. Justiniani—V. Quirini: Lettera al Papa, Libellus ad Leonem X (1513)* (Modena, 1995); H. Feld, "Wurde Martin Luther 1521 in effigie in Rom verbrannt?" *Lutherjahrbuch* 63 (1996) 11-18; N. Housley, "A Necessary Evil? Erasmus, the Crusades, and the War Against the Turks," in *The Crusades and Their Sources,* Festschrift for B. Hamilton (Aldershot, 1998) 259-79.

GEORG SCHWAIGER

Leo XI (Apr. 1-27, 1605). Formerly *Alessandro Ottaviano de' Medici,* born June 2, 1535, in Florence. He belonged to a collateral line of the ruling Medici family and was the great-nephew of Leo X. He was educated by Philip Neri. Under Pius V and Gregory XIII, he was the ambassador of the grand duke Cosimo de' Medici at the Roman curia. He became bishop of Pistoia in 1573 and archbishop of Florence in 1574. He was created cardinal in 1583 and was Clement VIII's legate in France from 1596 to 1598, where he acted prudently to ward off Huguenot influence and had a decisive share in mediating the Peace of Vervins between Spain and France. He was made cardinal bishop in 1600. His election as pope was due to French influence. He granted generous aid to Emperor Rudolf II against the Turks.

■ **Sources:** *HCMA* 3:47, 197, 275; 4:8, 36f.

■ **Bibliography:** *EC* 7:115f.; *VATL* 453; Pastor 11:45, 108, 447; 12:1-22; B. Barbiche, "Un évêque italien de la réforme catholique légat en France sous Henri IV," *Revue d'histoire de l'Église de France* 75 (1989) 45-60; G. Aranci, "Legislazione sinodale e governo pastorale dei vescovi fiorentini dopo il Concilio di Trento," *Vivens homo* 11 (2000) 131-63.

GEORG SCHWAIGER

Leo XII (Sept. 28, 1823-Feb. 2, 1829). Formerly *Annibale della Genga,* born Aug. 22, 1760, in the castle of Genga near Spoleto. After studies in Rome, he became a secret chamberlain to Pius VI, and was appointed titular archbishop of Tyre and nuncio in Cologne in 1794. Since Cologne was occupied by the French, he spent most of the following years in Augsburg and Munich. Pius VII appointed him nuncio to the imperial parliament in Regensburg in 1805, but he had no success in his endeavors to negotiate concordats with Bavaria and Württemberg, and Napoleon I put pressure on the pope to recall him. He was appointed nuncio to Paris in 1814, but the cardinal secretary of state, Ercole Consalvi, dealt with business in person, so that della Genga in effect had nothing to do. He was created cardinal in 1816 and appointed bishop of Senigallia. He was made bishop of Spoleto in 1818, and cardinal vicar of Rome and prefect of several congregations in 1820. He was elected in a difficult conclave, where the → *zelanti* outmaneuvered the liberals, whose standard-bearer was Consalvi. The papal government under Leo became increasingly rigid and reactionary, so that he was hated in the papal states; nothing remained of the moves Consalvi had made in the direction of a more democratic church politics and civil administration.

Leo endeavored to reform the curia, the Roman universities, and many religious orders. He reorganized the Roman and English colleges, reduced the number of officials, improved the educational system, and set up the Sacred Congregation for Seminaries and Universities. He supported academies and libraries, the fine arts, excavations, and world missions, especially in the East. He erected many social institutions. He took up Consalvi's policy of concordats anew and restructured church organization through "bulls of circumscription" for the kingdom of Hanover in 1824 and for the ecclesiastical province of the Upper Rhine (with the metropolitan see in Freiburg im Breisgau) in 1827. He negotiated with Louis XVIII and Charles X of France, reorganized the dioceses of Basel and Chur, and concluded a concordat with the United Netherlands in 1827. He negotiated with Spain, endeavored to secure civil freedom for Catholics in England, mediated with the Turkish sultan on behalf of the Armenians, and regulated church structures in Latin America in the aftermath of the revolutions which made these lands independent of Spain and Portugal. For a time, he was receptive to the theories of Gioacchino Ventura and Hugo-Felicité-Robert de La Mennais. The → Holy Year of 1825 was intended to re-establish contact with the people. He is buried in St. Peter's.

■ **Sources:** Barbieri, ed., *Bullarii Romani Continuatio* (Rome, 1835-40), vols. 16 and 17; A. Mercati, *Raccolta di concordati* (2nd ed. Rome, 1954) 1:402-5, 689-722; *HCMA* 6:424; 7:10f., 17-21, 439.

■ **Bibliography:** *HKG* 6/1:105f., 117-21, 813; *BBKL* 4:1450f.; *VATL* 453f.; A. F. Artaud de Montor, *Histoire du pape Léon XII*, 2 vols. (Paris, 1843); N. Wiseman, *Recollections of the Last Four Popes* (London, 1858); Schmidlin 1:367-474; R. Colapietra, *La Chiesa tra Lamennais e Metternich: Il pontificato di Leone XII* (Brescia, 1963); idem, *La formazione diplomatica di Leone XII* (Rome, 1966); C. Weber, *Kardinäle und Prälaten in den letzten Jahrzehnten des Kirchenstaates* (Stuttgart, 1978); A. J. Reinerman, *Austria and the Papacy in the Age of Metternich*, I: *Between Conflict and Cooperation, 1809-30* (Washington, 1979); G. Martina, *La Chiesa nell'età dell'assolutismo, del liberalismo, del totalitarismo*, III: *L'età del liberalismo*, 4th ed. (Brescia, 1980); K. Hausberger, *Staat und Kirche nach der Säkularisation* (St. Ottilien, 1983); L. Pásztor, *La Segreteria di Stato e il suo archivio dal 1814 al 1832*, 2 vols. (Stuttgart, 1984-85); G. Crinella, ed., *Il pontificato di Leone XII: Atti del Convegno, Genga 1990* (Urbino, 1992); G. Martina, "La prima missione pontificia nell'America Latina," *AHP* 32 (1994) 149-93.

GEORG SCHWAIGER

Leo XIII (Feb. 20, 1878-July 20, 1903). Formerly *Vincenzo Gioacchino Pecci*, born Aug. 2, 1810, in Carpineto Romano. He began his education in rhetoric, philosophy, and theology at the Roman College in 1818; he began the study of civil and canon law in 1832 and took his doctorate in 1837. He was ordained priest in the same year, and appointed domestic chaplain to the pope. After acting as delegate in Benevento, Spoleto, and Perugia, he was appointed nuncio to Belgium in 1843, where the confusions of domestic politics prevented him from having any success: the royal court demanded his recall in 1846, since he had supported the Belgian bishops in the question of the universities. He was appointed bishop of Perugia and lived far from the centers of power, although he was a resolute supporter of Pius IX and the *Syllabus*. He was created cardinal in 1853. The pastoral letters he wrote between 1874 and 1877 indicate the opening to modern culture, which was to be the great transition in his pontificate.

The conclave of 1878 was the first to be held since Rome had been declared the capital of the Italian state, and this led to disagreement about whether the papal → election should be held in Rome; Pecci was in favor of a conclave outside Italy. Sixty of the sixty-four cardinals assembled for the election in Rome on February 18, 1878, and Pecci was elected on the morning of February 20. He sent notice of his election to all the heads of state, even to those who were non-Catholics—with the exception of the Italian government. In the case of the *Kulturkampf* in Germany, it was Leo's good fortune that Otto von Bismarck himself was interested in pacification; only a few difficult problems remained to be solved in Switzerland. Despite opposition, Leo recognized the Spanish constitution of 1876. He was able to obtain a certain measure of relief for Catholics in the Slavic countries, despite the confessional and ethnic complications. The situation in Poland was especially delicate, thanks to Russian and German trends toward assimilation and the elimination of the specifically Polish elements; a somewhat similar situation existed in Ireland, where the Irish were oppressed by Great Britain. The pope appears, however, to have had a greater sympathy with antirevolutionary principles than with the Irish. Under Leo, the papacy acquired greater prestige in the Anglo-Saxon world. The President of the United States, Grover Cleveland, sent a copy of the American Constitution to the pope on the occasion of the jubilee of his priestly ordination. Leo met with bitter disappointment on the Roman Question, since neither Vienna nor Berlin was willing to act against Italy; this led him to set his hopes on a rapprochement with the French republic. Although Leo intervened personally in political matters—his secretaries of state merely carried out his instructions—he endeavored to clarify the theoretical questions in his encyclicals: *Diuturnum illud* (1881), *Immortale Dei* (1885), *Libertas praestantissimum* (1888), *Sapientiae christianae* (1890). He sets out very traditional principles, while at the same time strongly emphasizing the autonomy of the state.

Leo has been accused of opportunistic politics, and his concrete actions certainly lend some support to the charge. Nevertheless, the pope's plans worldwide cannot be reduced to this dimension. His attitude to the other churches was dictated by his hope that they would return to the Roman Catholic Church. The bull *Apostolicae curae* (1896) declared that Anglican ordinations must still be considered invalid. However, the consecration of the whole human race to the Heart of Jesus in the Jubilee Year of 1900 had a deeper motivation than all these political and confessional tendencies. Intellectually, this attitude finds its counterpart in Leo's promotion of neoscholastic philosophy and theology, both as bishop and as pope (encyclical *Aeterni Patris,* 1879). He showed his positive attitude to scholarship when he opened the Vatican Secret → Archive to scholars of all confessions. His best-known encyclical remains *Rerum novarum* (1891), which laid the foundations of Catholic social doctrine. The moral exhortations in this text—"Riches, and all other so-called 'good things,' have no significance with regard to eternal happiness"—lead to such statements as: "It is shameful to educate people for the sole purpose of making a profit out of them."

Leo had a clear consciousness of the importance of his office. He intervened in the dioceses both in political and in spiritual matters (e.g., Marian devotion), and he celebrated the history of the papacy. One of his grand gestures was the translation of the bones of Innocent III (1198-1216) in 1892 from Perugia, where he had died, to Rome. He justified this by pointing to the international importance of this pope, in whose spirit "the final

victory" could be achieved. Leo's final years show how such hopes could be imperiled. Serious reservations about democracy were expressed in the encyclical *Graves de communi* (1901), and biblical studies, which Leo had encouraged in his encyclical *Providentissimus Deus* (1893), were hampered by the narrow criticisms of the Biblical Commission. Leo was both an optimist and a pessimist.

After Pius IX, with the definition of papal → infallibility, and before Pius X, with the modernist crisis, Leo was the pope who led the Catholic Church into the world that was born of the Industrial Revolution and who attempted to reconcile the tradition in all its fullness with the modern spirit.

■ **Sources:** *ASS* 11-35 (1878-1903); *Leonis XIII Pontificis Maximi Acta,* 23 vols. (Rome, 1881-1905; repr. Graz, 1971); *Epp. encyclicae,* 6 parts (Freiburg, 1878-1904, Latin and German); *Leonis XIII Allocutiones, Epp. et Constitutiones,* 8 vols. (Bruges, 1887-1911); *Scelta di atti episcopali del card. G. Pecci ora Leone XIII* (Rome, 1879); J. Bach, *Leonis XIII Carmina, Inscriptiones, Numismata* (Cologne, 1903; German trans. ed. B. Barth, Cologne, 1904), P. de Franciscis, ed., *Discorsi* (Rome, 1882).

■ **Bibliography:** *TRE* 19:748-53; *BBKL* 4:1451-63; *VATL* 454-58; M. Spahn, *Leo XIII* (Munich, 1905); J. Févres, *Vie de Léon XIII,* 2 vols. (Paris, 1980); A. Butte, *Il Papa Leone XIII* (Milan, 1931); E. Soderini, *Il pontificato di Leone XIII,* 3 vols. (Milan, 1932-33); R. Fülöp-Miller, *Leo XIII* (Zurich, 1935); F. Hayward, *Léon XIII* (Paris, 1937); G. Monetti, *Leone XIII,* 3 vols. (Rome, 1942); E. T. Gargan, ed., *Leo XIII and the Modern World* (New York, 1961); Stanislao da Campagnola, *I Papi nella storia,* 2 vols. (Rome, 1961) II; I. E. Ward, "Leo XIII, 'the Diplomat Pope,'" *Review of Politics* 28 (1966) 47-61; P. de Laubier, "Leo XIII. und die Grundlagen des kirchlichen sozialen Denkens," in idem, *Das soziale Denken der katholischen Kirche* (Fribourg, 1982) 14-65; K. Deschner, *Ein Jahrhundert der Heils-Geschichte: Die Politik der Päpste im Zeitalter der Weltkriege* (Cologne, 1987) 37-104; G. Rambaldi, "Come Leone XIII arrivò a pubblicare la Bolla 'Apostolicae curae,'" *La civiltà cattolica* 141 (1990) 227-37, 462-77; P. Vrankic, "Kaiser Franz Joseph I. und Papst Leo XIII.," *AHP* 33 (1995) 247-73; A. Iriarte, *Dos marcos de referencia para un christianismo político: León XIII y la "Gaudium et spes"* (Vitoria, 1997); G. Miccoli, "Un'intervista di Leone XIII sull'antisemitismo," in *Cristianesimo nella storia,* Festschrift for G. Alberigo (Bologna, 1996) 577-605; M. Launay, *La papauté à l'aube du XXᵉ siècle: Léon XIII et Pie X 1878-1914* (Paris, 1997); J. M. Ticchi, "Les difficultés de l'arbitrage pontifical à la fin du 19ᵉ siècle," *AHP* 36 (1998) 183-202; F. Rodriguez Trivez, "Eclesiocentrismo de León XIII y cuestión social," in *Vivir en la*

Iglesia, Festschrift for J. Agulles (Valencia, 1999) 269-87.

OSKAR KÖHLER

Liberius (May 17, 352-Sept. 24, 366). A Roman. The course of his pontificate was determined by conflicts about Arianism. Although Liberius supported Athanasius and wanted an imperial council convoked in Aquileia, Constantius II forced through the condemnation of Athanasius at the synods of Arles (353) and Milan (355). Liberius was brought to the emperor at Milan, but when he refused to yield, he was banished to Beroea in Thrace at the end of 355, and the archdeacon Felix (II) assumed the office of bishop (antipope) in Rome. Exile broke Liberius's resistance, as four genuine letters from the spring of 357 (preserved in quotations by Hilary) bear witness: Liberius submitted to the emperor, agreed to the excommunication of Athanasius, and signed an ambiguous formula of faith (probably the first formula of Sirmium from 351/352). His assent to the second formula of Sirmium (357) cannot be proved, but he signed the third formula of Sirmium when he was brought there at the request of a group of Western bishops. This third formula contains the addition that the Son resembles the Father essentially and "in all things." Now it was possible for Liberius to return to Rome (358), where the emperor wanted him to rule jointly with Felix (II). However, Felix was expelled after rioting broke out, and could get no closer to the city than the surrounding countryside. Liberius remained a compromised figure, so that the Roman church played only a subordinate role in the church-political debates and struggles which now followed. The imperial policy, favoring the Arians and promoting a compulsory union, triumphed at the double synod of Rimini and Seleucia in 359 and in Constantinople in 360. Free theological debate became possible only when Emperor Julian (361-363) introduced a policy of toleration; his hope was that this would provoke the dissenting parties to even more violent conflicts. Liberius now reassumed his role as defender of the orthodoxy of the Council of Nicaea (325). He sent a letter of reconciliation to the Italian bishops at the close of 362, and he replied to the Eastern bishops by professing his allegiance to the Nicene faith and rejecting the heretical formulae of 359. Liberius built Santa Maria Maggiore (the "Liberian basil-

ica"). The → Chronography of 354 was written under his pontificate. Despite his policy of reconciliation, the conflict between the parties in Rome broke out anew at the election of his successor, Damasus I. Liberius was buried in the catacomb of Priscilla.

According to the Martyrology of Jerome, his feast was initially celebrated on September 23, but he is not mentioned in the Roman Martyrology. His biography was distorted, especially by legends of the sixth century where Felix (II), who had broken his oaths, appears as the legitimate pope and is celebrated as a martyr, while Liberius is presented as a traitor.

■ **Sources:** *PL* 8:1341-1410; 10:678ff.; *Collectio Avellana,* Corpus scriptorum ecclesiasticorum latinorum 35 (Vienna, 1895); letters quoted by Hilary: Corpus scriptorum ecclesiasticorum latinorum 65 (Vienna, 1916); *LP* 1:207-11; *RPR*(J) 1:32-36; 2:691.

■ **Bibliography:** *LMA* 5:1949f.; *BBKL* 5:13ff.; *DECL* 382-83; *VATL* 461f.; Caspar 1:166-96, 588-92; T. D. Barnes, "The Capitulation of Liberius and Hilary of Poitiers," in idem, *From Eusebius to Augustine* (Aldershot, 1994); J. Ulrich, *Die Anfänge der abendländischen Rezeption des Nizänums* (Berlin, 1994); Borgolte 413.

GEORG SCHWAIGER

Linus (67?-79?). Saint (feast day Sept. 23). The catalogues of popes agree that he was the first successor of Peter. Irenaeus (*Adversus haereses* 2.3.3) and Eusebius (*Historia ecclesiastica* 3.2; 4.8) identify him with the Linus mentioned in 2 Tim 4:21. According to the → *Liber Pontificalis,* Linus came from Etruria and was a pupil of Peter. The early sources date his pontificate from 64 to 79; the → Chronography of 354, followed by the *Liber Pontificalis,* dates it from 55 to 67; Eusebius dates it from 69 to 81. Linus is mentioned in the Roman canon of the Mass, but not in the Martyrology of Jerome. Because of an erroneous manuscript reading, the Venerable Bede gives October 7 as his feast day, while Florus of Lyons and Ado of Vienne celebrate him on November 26. Since the *Ordo officiorum ecclesiae Lateranensis* of prior Bernardus (1145), his martyrdom has been celebrated in Rome on September 23, in keeping with the *Liber Pontificalis.* The "Martyrdom of Blessed Peter the Apostle, Composed by Linus," a Latin version of extracts from the Greek *Acts of Peter,* was written in the sixth century.

■ **Bibliography:** *BBKL* 5:98ff.; *VATL* 462; R. Biondi, *Parliamo di San Lino* (Volterra, 1976); G. N. Verrando,

"Osservazioni sulla collocazione cronologica degli apocrifi Atti di Petro dello Pseudo-Lino," *Vetera Christianorum* 20 (1983) 391-426; J. Hofmann, "Linus—erster Bischof von Rom und Heiliger der orthodoxen Kirche," *Ostkirchliche Studien* 46 (1997) 105-41.

BÄRBEL DÜMLER

Lucius I (June 25, 253-Mar. 5, 254). Saint (feast day Mar. 4), a Roman. He was immediately expelled by Emperor Gallus, but he was soon able to return, probably when Valerian became emperor. The schism of Novatian continued. Like his predecessor Cornelius, Lucius defended the milder tendency in penitential praxis against the rigorous line taken by Novatian's adherents. Cyprian of Carthage praises his courage in confessing the faith (*Epp.* 61 and 68); but his martyrdom is first mentioned in later legends. He was buried in the catacomb of Calixtus, where a fragment of the Greek inscription bearing his name has been found.

■ Sources: *LP* 1:66ff.:, 3:75, 323; *RPR*(J) 1:19f.; 2:690, 732.

■ Bibliography: *EC* 7:1632f.; *BBKL* 5:301ff.; *DECL* 391; *VATL* 473; Caspar 12:70; W. Marschall, *Karthago und Rom* (Stuttgart, 1971).

GEORG SCHWAIGER

Lucius II (Mar. 12, 1144-Feb. 15, 1145). Formerly *Gerardo Caccianemici*, born in Bologna. He was a canon of the reformed monastery of San Frediano in Lucca, and was created cardinal priest of Santa Croce in Jerusalem in 1123. He served Honorius II and Innocent II as legate in Germany on several occasions, including the election and coronation of Lothar III in 1125. He became rector of Benevento in 1130. He was a collaborator of Cardinal Haimerich and succeeded him on his death in 1141 as papal chancellor and librarian. He was a friend of Bernard of Clairvaux, Archbishop Walter of Ravenna, and Peter the Venerable, abbot of Cluny. Lucius enforced the papal authority in Tours, Toledo, Portugal, and other places. The main concerns of his brief pontificate were the conflict with King Roger II of Sicily, with whom he sought an accommodation, and the rebellion in Rome. The autonomy that had been won under Innocent II was given the structure of a "holy senate" headed by Giordano Pierleoni, brother of the antipope Anacletus II, as *patricius*. Lucius asked the German king Conrad III for help in this conflict, but in vain; the attempt to extinguish the

Roman rebellion by military force was a failure. According to Godfrey of Viterbo (*Pantheon* 23.48), Lucius was wounded by stones that were cast down upon him while he attempted to take the capitol by storm. He died shortly afterward and was buried in the Lateran basilica.

■ Sources: *PL* 179:819-938; J. B. Watterich, *Pontificum Romanorum qui fuerunt inde ab exeunte saeculo IX usque ad finem saeculi XIII vitae ab aequalibus conscriptae etc.,* II (1099-1198) (Leipzig, 1862) 278-81; *LP* 2:385f.; *RPR*(J) 2:7-19, 717, 758.

■ Bibliography: *LMA* 5:2162; *BBKL* 5:303f.; *VATL* 473f.; F.-J. Schmale, *Studien zum Schisma des Jahres 1130* (Cologne/Graz, 1961) 48ff.; B. Zenker, *Die Mitglieder des Kardinalskollegiums von 1130 bis 1159* (Würzburg, 1964) 129; J. Deér, *Papsttum und Normannen* (Cologne/Vienna, 1972); R. Hüls, *Kardinäle, Klerus und Kirchen Roms 1049-1130* (Tübingen, 1977) 164; W. Maleczek, "Das Kardinalskollegium unter Innozenz II. und Anaklet II.," *AHP* 19 (1981) 27-78; F.-R. Swietek and T. M. Deneen, "Pope Lucius II and Savigny," *Analecta Cisterciensia* 39 (1983) 3-25; Borgolte 165f., 413.

GEORG SCHWAIGER

Lucius III (Sept. 1, 1181-Nov. 25, 1185). Formerly *Hubald* (the family name *Allucingoli* is attested at a later period), born at Lucca. He was created cardinal deacon of Sant'Adriano in 1138, cardinal priest of Santa Prassede in 1141, and cardinal bishop of Ostia in 1158. Lucius was a hard-working, impartial, and highly respected legate (e.g., in the negotiations for the Treaty of Constance, 1153). He supported Alexander III and represented him in the kingdom of Sicily in 1166-1167, in Byzantium in 1167-1168, and in the negotiations with Frederick I Barbarossa which led to the Peace of Venice in 1177. Lucius was forced to flee from the hostile Romans shortly after his election, and he spent two and a half years in southern Latium; from July 1182 onward, he resided in Verona. The synod of Verona in October 1184 helped resolve the open questions in the relations between the pope and the emperor, and made a collaboration between the two universal authorities possible for a brief time (canon *Ad abolendam* against heresies; coronation of Henry VI as joint emperor). However, there was no definitive regulation of the territorial questions in the Patrimony of Peter, and the alliance between the Staufers and Sicily soon cooled relations between the empire and the papacy. At the beginning of his pontificate, the College of → Cardinals had twenty-seven members; Lucius created fifteen additional cardinals.

■ **Sources:** *RPR(J)* 2:431-92, 766-69; *PL* 201:1071-1380; W. Holtzmann, *Papsturkunden in England,* 3 vols. (Berlin/Göttingen, 1930-52); W. Wiederhold, *Papsturkunden in Frankreich,* 7 vols. (Berlin, 1906-13); H. Meinert, *Papsturkunden in Frankreich,* new series (Berlin, 1932-33) I; J. Ramackers, *Papsturkunden in Frankreich,* new series (Göttingen, 1937-58) II-VI; idem, *Papsturkunden in den Niederlanden* (Berlin, 1933-34); C. Erdmann, *Papsturkunden in Portugal* (Berlin, 1927); P. F. Kehr, *Papsturkunden in Spanien,* 2 vols. (Berlin, 1926-28).

■ **Bibliography:** *LMA* 5:2162f.; *BBKL* 5:304-7; *VATL* 474; K. Wenck, "Die römischen Päpste zwischen Alexander III. und Innozenz III.," in *Papsttum und Kaisertum,* Festschrift for P. F. Kehr (Berlin, 1926) 442-74; B. Zenker, *Mitglieder des Kardinalskollegiums 1130-1159* (Würzburg, 1964) 22-25; G. Baaken, "Unio regni ad imperium," *QFIAB* 52 (1972) 219-97; P. Diehl, "'Ad abolendam' (X 5.7.9) and Imperial Legislation against Heresy," *Bulletin of Medieval Canon Law* 19 (1989) 1-11.

WERNER MALECZEK

Marcellinus (296?-304). Saint (feast day Jan. 16). Some uncertainty exists about the existence of this Roman bishop, since the ancient testimonies are not unambiguous. Marcellinus died during the Diocletian persecution, but there is no proof of his martyrdom. Eusebius employs an ambiguous formulation: "He was taken away by the persecution" (*Historia ecclesiastica* 7.32.1), which may refer to exile. This notice would be confirmed, if an epigram composed by Damasus I for "Marcellus" refers in fact to Marcellinus; Eusebius knows of no pope called Marcellus. The Liberian catalogue in the → Chronography of 354 mentions Marcellus as the successor to Marcellinus, but the *Depositio episcoporum* in the same work mentions only Marcellinus (buried on January 15); the Martyrology of Jerome mentions Marcellus on this date. The Donatists at the end of the fourth century accused Marcellinus of being a *traditor.* Augustine defends him against this charge (*Contra litteras Petiliani* II 92.202; *De unico baptismo* 16.27), but in his list of popes (*Ep.* 53.2) he mentions only Marcellinus. The → *Liber Pontificalis* says that Marcellinus showed weakness during the persecution, but that he repented and suffered a martyr's death. This information may derive from a lost "passion" from the end of the fourth century. Most of the lists of popes from the fourth century onward, in the West and in the East, mention a

Marcellus, while some mention Marcellinus; only the *Liber Pontificalis* mentions both. This uncertainty may be due to the fact that Marcellinus was also known as Marcellus, or else to the fact that he was a priest (not a bishop) who headed the Roman church during the *sede vacante.* During the pontificate of Symmachus (498-514), the so-called Acts of the Synod of Sinuessa (*PL* 6:11-20) were composed, a forgery intended to demonstrate the apostasy of Marcellinus. This document relates that Marcellinus confessed his guilt and uttered his own condemnation; the intention is most likely to maintain the principle that "the first see shall not be judged by anyone else" (*prima sedes non iudicabitur a quoquam*).

■ **Sources:** *LP* 1:14-41, 72, 162ff.

■ **Bibliography:** *DACL* 10:1762-73; *BBKL* 5:769; *VATL* 478; E. H. Röttges, "Marcellus," *Zeitschrift für Katholische Theologie* 78 (1956) 385-420; A. Amore, "Il preteso 'Lapsus' di Papa Marcellino," *Antonianum* 32 (1957) 411-26; R. Davis, "Pre-Constantine Chronology: The Roman Bishopric from AD 258 to 314," *Journal of Theological Studies* 48 (1997) 439-70.

ANGELO DI BERARDINO

Marcellus I (307?-309?). Saint (feast day Jan. 16), martyr. He succeeded Marcellinus (with whom he is not identical) after a lengthy *sede vacante* during the Diocletian persecution. Marcellus is said to have reorganized the diocese by introducing *tituli.* His strict attitude to those who had lapsed under persecution led to disturbances, and he was banished. He died in exile. Scholars disagree about whether Pope Marcellus is the martyr who died on January 16 (Hippolyte Delehaye; Victor Saxer), or the martyr who died on October 4 or 7 (Agostino Amore) and was buried in the catacomb of Priscilla or Balbina.

■ **Bibliography:** *DTHC* 9:1991f.; *DACL* 10:1753-60; A. Di Berardino, ed., *Dizionario patristico e di antichità cristiane* (Casale Monferrato, 1984) 2:2091 (V. Saxer); *BiblSS* 8:672-76; *EC* 8:16f.; *BBKL* 5:770f.; *VATL* 478; Caspar 1:54, 97-101; E. H. Röttges, "Marcellinus-Marcellus," *Zeitschrift für Katholische Theologie* 78 (1956) 385-420; A. Amore, "E esistito papa Marcello?" *Antonianum* 33 (1958) 57-75; W. Schwarz, "Marcellus I.," *Zeitschrift für Kirchengeschichte* 63 (1962) 327-34; R. Davis, "Pre-Constantine Chronology: The Roman Bishopric from AD 258 to 314," *Journal of Theological Studies* 48 (1997) 439-70.

JOSEF LÖSSL

Marcellus II (Apr. 9-May 1, 1555). Formerly *Marcello Cervini,* born May 6, 1501, in Montefano near Macerato, son of a noble family from the city of Montepulciano. He was a friend of those who wished to reform the Catholic Church. He was tutor to Cardinal Alessandro Farnese, the influential nephew of Paul III, and became his secretary. He was made bishop of Nicastora and cardinal in 1539, bishop of Reggio-Emilia in 1540, and bishop of Gubbio in 1544. He was sent on diplomatic missions to Germany (Emperor Charles V) and France (King Francis I). He was one of the presidents of the Council of Trent from 1545 onward. He was made cardinal librarian in 1548. Under Julius II, he worked in favor of reform in the second period of the council (1551-1552) and in Rome. He retained his baptismal name when he became pope. He resolved to carry out reforms, but died after only three weeks in office. The *Missa papae Marcelli* of Giovanni Pierluigi da Palestrina bears his name. He was buried in St. Peter's.

■ **Sources:** *NDB* Abteilung I; *Concilium Tridentinum: Diariorum, Actorum, Epistularum, Tractatuum nova Collectio*, 13 vols. (Freiburg, 1901-2001).

■ **Bibliography:** *HKG* 4:476-505; *DBI* 24:111ff.; *BBKL* 5:771-75; *VATL* 478f.; P. Polidori, *De vita, gestis et moribus Marcelli II* (Rome, 1744); Pastor 5:874f. (index); 6:317-56, 708, 715; *HCMA* 3:26, 33, 193, 256, 284; H. Jedin, *Geschichte des Konzils von Trient*, 3 vols. (Freiburg, 1977-82); M. Dykmans, "Quattre lettres de Marcel Cervini, cardinal-légat auprès de Charles Quint en 1540," *AHP* 29 (1991) 113-71; W. V. Hudon, *Marcello Cervini and Ecclesiastical Government in Tridentine Italy* (De Kalb, Ill., 1992); R. Spataro, "Il cardinale Cervini e l'argomentazione patristica durante la quarta sessione del Concilio di Trento," *Salesianum* 59 (1997) 33-49; J. I. Tellechea Idigoras, "Marcelo II y su breve pontificado, según documentos de Simancas," *Salmanticensis* 46 (1999) 411-29.

GEORG SCHWAIGER

Mark (Jan. 18-Oct. 7, 336). Saint (feast day Oct. 7), probably a Roman, who may have had a leading position in the Roman church since the time of Miltiades. He reigned briefly during the fierce controversy over Arius and Arianism. There is no reason to disbelieve the statement of the → *Liber Pontificalis* that it was decided in this period that from now on, the bishop of Ostia should be the principal consecrator at the episcopal ordination of the bishop of Rome. Mark built two basilicas, the *titulus Marci* and St. Balbina on the Via Ardeatina, where he was buried. No genuine writings by Mark have survived.

■ **Sources:** *LP* 1:80f., 202ff.; 3:index; *RPR*(J) 1:30; 2:691.

■ **Bibliography:** *LMA* 6:227f.; *BBKL* 5:781f.; *VATL* 480; Caspar 1:131, 142; L. Dolcini, *La casula di San Marco papa* (Florence, 1992); Borgolte 413.

GEORG SCHWAIGER

Marinus I (erroneously reckoned as Martin II) (Dec. 16[?], 882-May 15, 884), from Gallese. He was a subdeacon under Leo IV, a deacon under Nicholas I, and bishop of Cerveteri under John VIII. Nicholas I sent him as papal legate to Constantinople in 867 in order to carry out the deposition of Photius, and Marinus joined in the condemnation of Photius at the Council of Constantinople (869-870). He retained his responsibility for Byzantine affairs under John VIII, but did not approve of the pope's recognition of the patriarchal dignity of Photius. When he was pope, Marinus recalled Formosus, who had been banished by John VIII, and reinstalled him as bishop of Porto. Marinus met Emperor Charles III in 883 and persuaded him to act against Guido II of Spoleto (later emperor). His papal rank was disputed in Byzantium after his death, because he was already a bishop before becoming pope, thus violating the prohibition on translation from one see to another; the report that he had renounced the see of Cerveteri before becoming bishop of Rome is dubious.

■ **Sources:** *LP* 2:224; *RPR*(J) 1:425f.; 2:704; *Regesta Imperii*, ed. H. Zielinski (Vienna, 1991) I 3/1, nos. 699, 710f.

■ **Bibliography:** *LMA* 6:294; *BBKL* 5:827f.; *VATL* 479f.; F. Dvornik, *Le Schisme de Photius* (Paris, 1950) 302-16; D. Riesenberger, "Prosopographie der päpstlichen Legaten von Stephan II. bis Silvester II." (dissertation, Freiburg, 1967) 273-79; Zimmermann *Pa* 51f.; S. Scholz, *Transmigration und Translation* (Cologne, 1992) 209-16.

SEBASTIAN SCHOLZ

Marinus II (erroneously reckoned as Martin III) (end of Oct. 942–beginning of May 946). A Roman. He was cardinal priest of San Ciriaco. His election and his pontificate were strongly influenced by the Roman duke Alberic. Marinus entrusted the Roman abbey of St. Paul's to Abbot Balduin of Montecassino in 945, thereby promoting the spread of the Cluniac reform in Rome. He confirmed Archbishop Frederick of Mainz as apostolic vicar for Germany and Gaul in 946.

■ **Sources:** *LP* 2:245; *RPR*(J) 1:458f.; Zimmermann *Reg* nos. 165-67; Zimmermann *Pu* 1:172-90.

■ **Bibliography:** *LMA* 6:294f.; *BBKL* 5:828f.; Zimmermann *J* 84f.

SEBASTIAN SCHOLZ

Martin I (July 5, 649-June 17, 653 [date of deposition]). Saint (feast day Apr. 13), martyr, born in 591 at Todi in Umbria, died Sept. 16, 655, in Cherson in Crimea, and buried there. He was the apocrisiary of Pope Theodore I in Constantinople while a deacon; he was elected pope at the height of the Monothelite controversy and did not receive imperial confirmation of his election. He condemned Monothelitism at the Lateran synod in October 649. This was a highly politicized assembly, in which Maximus the Confessor and the monk Anastasius, Eastern opponents of the imperial religious politics, exercised great influence. Instead of arresting Martin, the exarch Olympius renounced his obedience to the emperor and ruled Italy as usurper until 652; this allowed Martin to remain in office unmolested. The exarch Theodore Calliopa did not succeed in seizing Martin in the Lateran basilica until June 17, 653. He gave the clergy notice that the emperor had arrested and deposed Martin, by now a sick man. Martin was brought to Constantinople (probably arriving on September 17, 653) and was kept in prison. On December 27 of that year, he was condemned to death for high treason, as a participant in the rebellion of Olympius, but the sentence was commuted at the pleading of Patriarch Paul II, and Martin was exiled to Cherson on March 26, 654. Under pressure from the emperor, the Roman clergy made Eugene I the new pope in August 654. Martin's letters from exile express his profound disappointment at his former friends.

■ **Sources:** *LP* 1:336-40; *RPR*(J) 1:230-34; 2:699, 740; *PL* 87:105-212; 129:591-604.
■ **Bibliography:** *LMA* 6:341; *BBKL* 5:907-10; *VATL* 481f.; P. Peeters, "Une vie grecque du pape S. Martin I," *Analecta Bollandiana* 51 (1933) 225-62; Caspar 2:553-78, 778ff.; P. Conte, *Il Sinodo Lateranense dell'ottobre 649* (Rome, 1989); idem, "'Consortium fidei apostolicae' tra vescovo di Roma e vescovi nel sec. VII," in *Il primato del vescovo di Roma nel primo millennio* (Rome, 1991) 363-432; O. Capitani, *Le relazioni tra le vite di Teodoro I e Martino I del Liber Pontificalis* (Rome, 1992) 5-14; *Martino I (649-653) e il suo tempo: Atti del 28 congresso storico internazionale, Todi 1991* (Spoleto, 1992); R. Riedinger, "Die lateinische Übersetzung der Ep. Encyclica Papst Martins I. und der Ep. Synodica des Sophronios von Jerusalem," *Filologia Mediolatina* 1 (Spoleto, 1994) 45-69; S. Cosentino, "Dissidenza religiosa e insubordinazione militare nell'Italia bizantina: Martino I e il suo tempo," *Rivista di storia della Chiesa in Italia* 48 (1994) 496-518; B. de Margerie, "Saint Martin I confirme la virginité corporelle de Marie dans l'enfantement," *Augustinianum* 37 (1997) 495-501.

GEORG SCHWAIGER

Martin II, Martin III. These are erroneous names given to Popes Marinus I and Marinus II in late-medieval catalogues of popes.

Martin IV (Feb. 22, 1281-Mar. 28, 1285). Formerly *Simon de Brion,* born at Mainpincien (Département of Seine-et-Marne), died at Perugia. After studies in Paris, he became treasurer of St. Martin's in Tours and was appointed chancellor of King Louis IX of France in 1260. He was created cardinal priest of Santa Cecilia in 1261 and carried out important tasks in the French-papal diplomacy. He played a central role in the negotiations between the curia and Charles of Anjou. After 1274, he was legate in France for the crusade on which the Second Council of Lyons had resolved. His election as pope in → Viterbo in 1281 was due to massive influence by Charles I of Anjou, and Martin remained very loyal to Charles throughout his pontificate. He supported Charles's plans for expansion and excommunicated Emperor Michael VIII Palaeologos in 1281, thereby ending the union between the churches which had been established by the Council of Lyons seven years earlier. Even after the Sicilian Vespers (1282), he failed to exploit the new possibilities for action which opened up when the rebels initially submitted to him. Instead, he gave one-sided support to the French-Angevin interests, excommunicating and deposing the Aragonese king Peter III of Sicily. This led to a lengthy conflict between Aragon and France about the Aragonese throne. In the church states, Martin broke with the nepotistic policy of his predecessor, Nicholas III, but the favors he lavished on his fellow countrymen contributed to polarization, making it difficult to contain the opposition which had been strengthened by the Sicilian Vespers. Nor did Martin succeed in gaining a foothold in Rome, where he had bestowed the senatorial dignity on Charles I of Anjou. Martin, whom the sources describe as a man of modest and unpretentious life, supported the pastoral activity of the Franciscans (bull *Ad uberes fructus,* 1281). He was a weak pope who failed to act energetically or display breadth of political vision in a turbulent period.

■ **Sources:** *LP* 2:459-65; *RPR*(P) 2:1756-95; F. Olivier-Martin, *Les Registres de Martin IV* (Paris, 1901-35).

■ **Bibliography:** *LMA* 6:341f.; *BBKL* 5:910ff.; *VATL* 482; N. Backes, *Kardinal Simon de Brion* (Breslau, 1910); R. Sternfeld, "Das Konklave von 1280 und die Wahl Martins IV.," *Mitteilungen des Instituts für Österreichische Geschichtsforschung* 31 (1910) 1-53; S. Runciman, *The Sicilian Vespers* (London, 1958); D. J. Geanakoplos, *Emperor Michael Palaeologos and the West 1258-82* (Cambridge, Mass., 1959); E. Pásztor, "Per la storia dell'amministrazione sotto Martino IV," *Miscellanea,* Festschrift for M. Giusti (Vatican City, 1978) 190-204; idem, "La guerra del Vespro e i suoi problem: L'intervento di Martino IV," *Quaderni catanesi di studi classici e medievali* 1 (1979) 144-76; P. Herde, *Karl I. von Anjou* (Stuttgart, 1979); A. Franchi, *I Vespri Siciliani e le relazioni tra Roma e Bisanzio* (Palermo, 1984); P. Herde, "I Papi tra Gregorio X e Celestino V," in *Storia della Chiesa* (Rome, 1994) 11:23-91; E. Biggi, "Un intervento inedito di Martino IV tra Frati Minori e clero di Piacenza nel 1282," *Archivum Franciscanum historicum* 90 (1997) 349-53.

GERALD RUDOLPH

Martin V (Nov. 11, 1417-Feb. 2, 1431). Formerly *Oddo Colonna,* born at Genazzano in 1368. He belonged to the Genazzano line of the famous Roman noble house of Colonna. He was apostolic protonotary under Boniface IX and was created cardinal in 1405. He took part in the negotiations for union between the Colleges of Cardinals in 1408 and was active (though not prominent) in the service of the Pisan obedience in the following period. He was elected by the Council of Constance in a complicated procedure (the voting lists have been preserved). His universal recognition as pope put an end to the Western Schism, which had lasted fifty years. The first reform decrees of the council, and the concordats with the participating nations, had obligated him to carry out reforms, but his priority was the return to Rome, since only there would it be possible for the papacy to reestablish its position. The council finished its business on April 22, 1418. After a lengthy stay in Florence and an arduous journey, Martin finally arrived in Rome on September 28, 1420. With skill and perseverance, he began the task of reconquering the church states (→ Papal

States) from the *condottieri* and *signori*. He restored the papal rule and its bureaucratic apparatus to a state of normality and efficiency after the continuous improvisations that had characterized the period of schism. Although he avoided the crass → nepotism of his predecessors, he necessarily relied on his own family for support in these endeavors, and he helped his relatives and their clients in the city of Rome to expand their power considerably in southern Latium. The council led to a reduction in income from ecclesiastical sources, and this made a reorganization of the papal finances necessary, with greater economic dependence on the church states. Martin, the first Roman pope in over a century, resided more in his family palace than in the Vatican. He did much to rebuild the city, which was in a completely ruinous condition, although he had no new urban concept to guide him. Despite his good will, as seen in reports about reform and a stricter praxis in the bestowal of benefices and dispensations, the reforming measures proposed at the council were realized only to a small extent. As things stood, it proved difficult to organize a successful new start in such matters as curial reform. Martin was not a man who drew up large-scale projects, but one who achieved what was possible, and his contemporaries respected him for this. In keeping with the conciliar decree *Frequens,* he convoked a reform synod at Pavia in 1423, which was transferred to Siena and soon dissolved; he convoked the Council of Basel in 1431. There are obvious tendencies to restoration in his pontificate, after the initial period when the Council of Constance set the tone. The bronze memorial slab to Martin in the Lateran church was brought from Florence in 1445.

■ **Bibliography:** *LMA* 6:342f.; *BBKL* 5:912-15; N. Valois, *Le pape et le concile* (Paris, 1909) I; K. A. Fink, "Die politische Korrespondenz Martins V nach den Brevenregistern," *QFIAB* 26 (1935/36) 172-244; P. Partner, *The Papal State under Martin V* (London, 1958); W. Brandmüller, *Das Konzil von Pavia-Siena 1423-24,* 2 vols. (Münster, 1968-74); D. Girgensohn, "Berichte über Konklave und Papstwahl auf dem Konstanzer Konzil," *AHC* 19 (1987) 351-91; M. Chiabò et al., eds. *Alle origini della nuova Roma: Martino V, Atti del Convegno Roma, 1992* (Rome, 1992); S. Weiss, *Kurie und Ortskirche: Die Beziehungen zwischen Salzburg und dem päpstlichen Hof unter Martin V.* (Tübingen, 1994); J. L. Fontes, "Cruzada e expansão: A bula 'Sane charissimus,'" *Lusitana sacra* 7 (1995) 403-20; W. Brandmüller, "Martin V.

und die Griechenunion," *Life, Law and Letters,* Festschrift for A. García y García (Rome, 1998) 133-48.

ARNOLD ESCH

Miltiades (some manuscripts have the variant *Melchiades*) (310-314). Saint (feast day Dec. 10), probably a Roman (despite what is said in the *Liber Pontificalis* 1:168). Acting on the instructions of Constantine I, he and three bishops from Gaul, together with fifteen Italian bishops, held the court of arbitration which rejected the Donatists' accusations against Caecilianus and confirmed him as bishop of Carthage.
■ **Sources:** Eusebius of Caesarea, *Historia ecclesiastica* 10.5.18ff.; Augustine, *Breviculus collationis cum Donatistis* 3.17.31ff., 18.34ff.; Optatus of Milevis, *Contra Parmenianum* 1.23.
■ **Bibliography:** *DACL* 11:1199-1203; *CATH* 8:1111; A. Di Berardone, ed., *Dizionario patristico e di antichità cristiane* (Casale Monferrato, 1984) 2:2250f.; *BBKL* 5:1537f.; *LACL* 440; *VATL* 486f.; C. Pietri, *Roma christiana* (Rome, 1976) 160-67; R. Davis, "Pre-Constantine Chronology: The Roman Bishopric from AD 258 to 314," *Journal of Theological Studies* 48 (1997) 439-470.

MARIA-BARBARA VON STRITZKY

Nicholas I (Apr. 24, 858-Nov. 13, 867). Saint (feast day Nov. 13), son of a papal official. He advanced to a leading position in the Roman clergy under Sergius II and was an influential counselor of Benedict III. After his death, Nicholas was made pope in the presence of Emperor Louis II, and he quickly developed into the most self-confident pontiff in his century. His most important adviser was Anastasius Bibliothecarius (later the antipope Anastasius III). He drew on traditions of canon law in late antiquity to assert the basic autonomy of clerical authority and its right to direct secular powers and to affirm his own → primacy in the universal church; but he also inferred unusually specific consequences from these claims for church discipline. Harsh conflicts led to limitations on the authority of John VII of Ravenna (861), and he imposed the primacy of papal jurisdiction over every metropolitan or synodical authority—drawing for the first time on the decretals of Pseudo-Isidore—when he compelled Archbishop Hincmar of Rheims to accept the rehabilitation of Bishop Rothad of Soissons, who had been deposed in 862, and to restore to office in 866 the clergy who had been ordained by the previous archbishop of Rheims, Ebo. He brought about the deci-

sive turning point in the conflict about the marriage of King Lothar II in 863, when he quashed the assent of his legates to the synod of Metz and summarily deposed the archbishops of Cologne and Trier, who were especially compromised. Although he did not succeed in holding the planned pan-Frankish synod in Rome, his authority sufficed to prevent Lothar's divorce for all time. In his relations with Byzantium, he did not shrink from disregarding the opinion of his legates and withdrawing recognition from Patriarch Photius, since his elevation to the see of Constantinople had been uncanonical. Nor did he hesitate to pave the way for the entry of the newly baptized Bulgarian prince Boris and his people into the Latin church, by sending missionaries and prescribing exact rules for the conduct of the Christian life. When a synod in Constantinople under Photius protested, Nicholas declared it abrogated; this, however, became known in Rome only after his death. Since the pressure of external events made it impossible for his successors to pursue Nicholas's energetic policies, his pontificate remained only an episode, an early high point of primatial thought and action; nevertheless, the legal texts in his numerous letters stimulated the reforming papacy of the eleventh century and the canon law of the high Middle Ages.
■ **Sources:** *LP* 2:151-72; *RPR(J)* 1:341-68; 2:703; *MGH.Ep* 6:257-690.
■ **Bibliography:** *LMA* 6:1168ff.; *BBKL* 6:860-63; *TRE* 24:535-40; *VATL* 510f.; E. Perels, *Papst Nikolaus I. und Anastasius Bibliothecarius* (Berlin, 1920); J. Haller, *Nikolaus I. und Pseudoisidor* (Stuttgart, 1936); W. Ullmann, *The Growth of Papal Government in the Middle Ages* (3rd ed. London, 1970) 190-209; H. Fuhrmann, *Einfluß und Verbreitung der pseudoisidorischen Fälschungen* (Stuttgart, 1973) 2:247-72; L. Heiser, *Die Responsa ad consulta Bulgarorum des Papstes Nikolaus I.* (Trier, 1979); J. Bakita, *Nicholas I: An Analysis of His Interpretation of Papal Primacy* (Ann Arbor, 1979); J. C. Bishop, *Pope Nicholas I and the First Age of Papal Independence* (Ann Arbor, 1984); W. Georgi, "Erzbischof Gunthar von Köln und die Konflikte um das Reich König Lothars II.," *Jahrbuch des Kölnischen Geschichtsvereins* 66 (1975) 1-33; R. Somerville, "Pope Nicholas I and John Scottus Eriugena," *Zeitschrift der Savigny-Stiftung für Rechtsgeschichte: Kanonische Abteilung* 114 (1997) 67-85.

RUDOLF SCHIEFFER

Nicholas II (Jan. 24, 1059-July 20, 1061). Formerly *Gerard*, born in Burgundy. He is attested from 1045 as bishop of Florence. After the death of Stephen IX, he was elected in summer or autumn 1058 by the cardinal bishops who had fled to Siena; Hildebrand (later → Gregory VII) had proposed his name, and Duke Godfrey the Bearded and the German court had given their assent. However, he considered himself to be pope only after he had been enthroned in Rome on January 24, 1059, and had expelled his opponent, Benedict X. The high point of his pontificate was the Lateran synod held at the end of April and beginning of May 1059, where central concerns of the Gregorian Reform were formulated. Under the influence of Hildebrand, Peter Damian, and Humbert of Silva Candida, the synod decided that the election, episcopal ordination, and enthronement of the pope should be the prerogative of the cardinal bishops. This decree about the papal election made it a matter of genuinely ecclesiastical law, without, however, diminishing the *honor* of the German king. Second, the synod forbade unchaste clergy to carry out liturgical ceremonies and allowed only those laypersons who observed the precept of monogamy to receive communion. Third, the synod corrected the rule for canons regular which had been promulgated at Aachen in 816 and obligated the clergy to follow the ideal of a canonical *vita communis* as seen in the example of the earliest Christians (Acts 2:44; 4:32-37). The synod did not expressly condemn lay investiture, but it forbade laypersons to appoint clergy to churches; it also condemned simony as a heresy, while acknowledging the validity of those ordinations which simoniacal bishops had performed free of charge. In the controversy with Berengar of Tours about the Eucharist, the synod voted against him and required him to profess the true faith with an oath; however, this profession favored the doctrine of the Capharnaites.

In the sphere of church politics, Nicholas consolidated his own position at Melfi in August 1059, when the Norman princes Robert Guiscard and Richard of Aversa, hitherto his enemies, became his vassals and accepted the obligation of preserving and extending the feudal sovereignty of the papacy. Nicholas intervened in the conflict between Archbishop Guido of Milan and the Pataria, sending Peter Damian and Anselm of Lucca as his legates. Shortly before he died in Florence, a disagreement between Nicholas and the German court lent support to the schism of Cadalus of Parma (the antipope Honorius II).

■ **Sources:** *LP* 2:280; *RPR*(J) 1:557-66; 2:711, 750; *MGH.Const* 1:537-51; J. Laudage, ed., *Der Investiturstreit: Quellen und Materialien* (Cologne/Vienna, 1989) 38-51.

■ **Bibliography:** *LMA* 6:1170; *BBKL* 6:863-67; H.-G. Krause, *Das Papstwahldekret von 1059 und seine Rolle im Investiturstreit* (Rome, 1960); F. Kempf, "Pier Damiani und das Papstwahldekret von 1059," *AHP* 2 (1964) 73-89; D. Hägermann, "Zur Vorgeschichte des Pontifikats Nicholas' II.," *Zeitschrift für Kirchengeschichte* 81 (1970) 352-61; J. Deér, *Papsttum und Normannen* (Cologne/Vienna, 1972) 63-70; R. Schieffer, *Die Entstehung des päpstlichen Investiturverbots für den deutschen König* (Stuttgart, 1981) 48-84, 208-25 (includes critical edition); J. Laudage, *Priesterbild und Reformpapsttum im 11. Jahrhundert* (Cologne/Vienna, 1984) 207-50; D. Jasper, *Das Papstwahldekret von 1059* (Sigmaringen, 1986; includes critical edition); J. Laudage, *Gregorianische Reform und Investiturstreit* (Darmstadt, 1993); E. Goetz, *Beatrix von Canossa und Tuszien* (Sigmaringen, 1995) 154-57; U.-R. Blumenthal, "The Coronation of Pope Nicholas II," *Life, Law and Letters,* Festschrift for A. García y García (Rome, 1998) 121-32.

JOHANNES LAUDAGE

Nicholas III (Nov. 25, 1277-Aug. 22, 1280). Formerly *Giangaetano di Matteo Rosso Orsini,* born 1212/1216 in Rome, died at Soriano (buried in St. Peter's). A relative of Celestine III, he was the son of the senator Matteo Rosso and Perna Caetani, who belonged to the collateral line of the Roman Orsini di Monterotondo family. He was created cardinal deacon of San Nicola in Carcere Tulliano on May 28, 1244, and was an influential member of the College of → Cardinals for thirty-three years. He headed the curial Inquisition from 1262 and played a decisive role in several papal elections before he himself was crowned pope in St. Peter's on December 26, 1277, after a *sede vacante* that had lasted more than six months. On his election, he took the name of his titular church. He had a lively awareness of his own authority and practiced → nepotism in office; Dante Alighieri banishes him to hell in the *Divine Comedy* (I 19:46-81). From the beginning of his pontificate, he took an independent course and freed the curia from its subordination to Charles I of Anjou, whom he compelled to give up the imperial vicariate of Tuscia and his dignity as Roman senator. He sought an accommodation with Rudolf I of the house of Habsburg, whom he persuaded to renounce the imperial claims to the Romagna and to bestow the feudal sovereignty of the counties of

Provence and Forcalquier on Charles of Anjou, in accordance with imperial law. It is difficult to credit the authenticity of the plan described by Bartholomew of Lucca for a transformation of the empire into four constituent states. At any rate, Nicholas's endeavors to bring France and Castille to accept peace came to nothing; nor did he succeed in consolidating the links with the Greek church which had been forged at the Second Council of Lyons in 1274. He was unable to realize his plans for a crusade, but he did prevent Charles of Anjou from attacking Byzantium. He carried out an extensive building program. He supported the Franciscan order and mediated in the controversy about poverty by means of his bull *Exiit qui seminat* (August 14, 1279).

■ **Bibliography:** *LMA* 6:1170f.; *BBKL* 6:867ff.; *VATL* 512f.; R. Sternfeld, *Der Kardinal Johann Gaëtan Orsini* (Berlin, 1905); A. Paravicini Bagliani, *Cardinali di curia e "familiae" cardinalizie dal 1227 al 1254* (Padua, 1972) 314-23; N. R. Wolf, "Die mittelalterlichen deutschen Übersetzungen der Bulle 'Exiit qui seminat' von Papst Nikolaus III.," *Franciscan Studies* 32 (1972) 242-305; B. Resmini, *Das Arelat* (Cologne, 1980) 149ff.; J. L. Heft, "Nicholas III (1277-80) and John XXII (1316-34)," *AHP* 21 (1983) 245-57; Borgolte 212ff., 220ff.; P. Herde, "Antworten des Kardinals Giangaetano Orsini auf Anfragen von Inquisitoren über die Behandlung von Ketzern und deren Eigentum," in *Ex ipsis rerum documentis*, Festschrift for H. Zimmermann (Tübingen, 1991) 345-61; H. Feld, *Franziskus von Assisi und seine Bewegung* (Darmstadt, 1994) 458ff.; A. Paravicini Bagliani, *Il corpo del Papa* (Turin, 1994); idem, *La cour des papes au XIIIᵉ siècle* (Paris, 1995); M. Thumser, *Rom und der römische Adel in der späten Stauferzeit* (Tübingen, 1995) 150ff.; P. Linehan, "A papal Constitution in the Making: 'Fundamenta militantis ecclesiae' (18 July 1278)," in *Life, Law and Letters*, Festschrift for A. García y García (Rome, 1998) 575-91.

LUDWIG VONES

Nicholas IV (Feb. 15/22, 1288-Apr. 4, 1292). A Franciscan, formerly *Girolamo d'Ascoli*, born Sept. 30, 1227, at Lisciano near Ascoli Piceno. He used the Franciscan order as a springboard for his ecclesiastical career. After his studies, he taught theology, and a commentary on the *Sentences* and sermons on the feasts of the church year and saints' days are ascribed to him. He became provincial of Dalmatia in 1272 and was papal legate in Byzantium from 1272 to 1274, where he took part in the negotiations for church union. In 1274, he succeeded Bonaventure as Minister General of the Franciscan order. He was entrusted with peace negotiations between France and Aragon from 1276 to 1279. He was created cardinal priest of Santa Pudenziana on March 12, 1278, and made cardinal bishop of Preneste on April 12, 1281, where he forged close relationships with the Colonna, who lived near the city. After a *sede vacante* of almost eleven months, he was elected as the first Franciscan pope on February 15, 1288. He declined this election, but accepted the renewed election a week later, taking the name of Nicholas, since he had been the protégé of Nicholas III. Nicholas supported the house of Anjou and crowned Charles II in Rieti on May 29, 1289, as king of Naples-Sicily, after Charles had sworn an oath of fealty to him. He attempted in vain to make the absolution of Alfons III of Aragon from the sentence of excommunication dependent on the resolution of the Sicilian question. Nor did he reach an agreement with Rudolf I of Habsburg on the imperial question. A new crusade became ever more urgent after the fall of Acre in 1291, but Nicholas met with no success here. He was more successful in his missionary endeavor in the Near East, and above all in Mongolia, when he sent John of Montecorvino to Kublai Khan in Beijing in 1289, thus preparing the foundation of an archdiocese there (1307). He strengthened the autonomy of the College of → Cardinals by granting it half of the income of the Holy See, to be administered by the chamber of the college (Constitution *Coelestis altitudo,* July 18, 1299); in making appointments, he favored the Colonna party. He attempted to furnish a legal framework for the movement of penitents who were not attached to the mendicant orders, and he both confirmed the Franciscan Third Order and gave it a rule. He concentrated his building activity on specific projects in Rome (the Lateran, Santa Maria Maggiore). He supported the universities, granting the privilege of foundation to Montpellier in 1289 and giving Paris and Bologna the right to teach both civil and canon law. His tomb, in Santa Maria Maggiore, has not survived.

■ **Bibliography:** *LMA* 6:117; *BBKL* 6:869ff.; *VATL* 512f.; N. Housley, *The Italian Crusades* (Oxford, 1982); R. Pazzelli and L. Temperini, eds., *La "Supra montem" di Niccolò IV (1289)* (Rome, 1988); A. Franchi, *Niccolò papa IV 1288-92* (Ascoli Piceno, 1990); E. Menestò, ed., *Niccolò IV, un pontificato tra Oriente e Occidente* (Spoleto, 1991); A. M. Pompei, "La 'Supra montem' di Niccolò IV e i rapporti tra Francesco e il suo Terz'Ordine," *Miscellanea francescana* 91 (1991) 439-54; F. Cardini,

Studi sulla storia e sull'idea di crociata (Rome, 1993); A. Paravicini Bagliani, *Il corpo del Papa* (Turin, 1994); idem, *La cour des papes au XIIIe siècle* (Paris, 1995); Borgolte 222f.; M. E. Capani, "Per la storia dei Minoriti nella seconda metà del Duecento: Verso il primo pontificato francescano," *Temi e immagini del medio evo*, memorial volume for L. Manselli (Rome, 1996) 85-92.

LUDWIG VONES

Nicholas V (Mar. 6, 1447-Mar. 24/25, 1455). Formerly *Tommaso Parentucelli*, born Nov. 15, 1397, at Sarzana in Liguria. He was the son of a doctor, and his father's death left him without the means to continue his study in Bologna. As a tutor in the families of the Albizzi and Strozzi, he came into contact with Florentine humanism, and after taking his master's degree in theology, he served the bishop of Bologna (and later cardinal) Niccolò Albergati. He learned much about diplomacy from accompanying him on his missions and made numerous contacts, e.g., at the councils of Basel and Ferrara-Florence and at the congress of Arras. After Albergati's death, he was appointed vice-chamberlain by Eugene IV in 1443, and bishop of Bologna in 1444. In return for serving the Roman cause so well in the struggle against the adherents of the Council of Basel, he was created cardinal in 1446. He was the compromise candidate at the election that followed Eugene's death in March 1447 and took the name of his benefactor Albergati. A man of great personal dignity, his experience and his courtesy helped to bring about the abdication of the antipope Felix V on generous conditions on April 7, 1449, and the self-dissolution of the rump council of Basel(-Lausanne) on April 25 of the same year; naturally, France played a leading role here, and the most important powers in the empire agreed with the pope. He proclaimed a Holy Year in 1450 and canonized Bernardine of Siena in a ceremony of great splendor; however, this year was overshadowed by plague and catastrophes. This jubilee marks the end of the conciliar epoch and the restoration of a papacy that intended to make renaissance Rome the center of a leading cultural power—though without tackling the unresolved problem of church reform. Extensive building projects, only some of which were completed, were meant to realize this plan. These involved the city walls and fortresses, streets and bridges, as well as the provision of water; the station churches and above all

the Leonine city and the Vatican Palace were affected. Nicholas gave commissions to artists such as Fra Angelico and supported humanist scholars such as Giovanni Francesco Poggio-Bracciolini, Lorenzo Valla, and Vespasiano Bisticci. He commissioned Latin translations of classical and patristic Greek authors; his manuscript collection of almost 1,200 volumes forms the kernel of the → Vatican Library. He attempted to stabilize the situation in the church states by means of alliances with old Roman families such as the Orsini and the Colonna and by bestowing the apostolic vicariate on the Montefeltro, the Malatesta, and the Ordelaffi. However, the opposition of the lesser aristocracy and the merchant classes led to a conspiracy headed by San Porcaro, in the tradition of Cola di Rienzo; this plot was discovered in time. When Nicholas joined the League in 1455, the church state became part of the pentarchy and shared the fragile equilibrium which held together the Italian states. Drawing on the services of outstanding cardinals such as Nicholas of Cusa, Guillaume d'Estouteville, Juan de Carvajal, Isidore of Kiev, and Bessarion, Nicholas exercised his authority on a European scale. The German legation of Cusa in 1451-1452 deserves special mention because of the reforms he undertook. Nicholas had a good relationship with King Frederick III: before the liquidation of the Council of Basel, they had agreed on the concordat of Vienna (February 17/March 19, 1483), which regulated relations between the empire and the curia until 1803/1806, and the pope blessed his marriage with Eleanor of Portugal on March 16, 1452, crowning him as emperor in St. Peter's three days later. Nevertheless, Frederick, like all the other European powers except Burgundy, refused to support the pope on the question of a crusade against the Turks, which had become especially urgent after the fall of Constantinople on May 29, 1453. Nicholas proclaimed a crusade on September 30, 1453, and commissioned John of Capistran and others to preach it, but accusations soon surfaced that he had his own reservations vis-à-vis the Greeks, and that funds for the crusade were being used for the purchase of books. On his deathbed, the pope, who had been ill since 1453, justified the major points of his pontificate in the presence of the cardinals. Both in its positive and in its negative aspects, his pontificate pointed the way to the renaissance papacy.

■ **Bibliography:** *DTHC* 11:541-48; *NCE* 10:443ff.; *GKG* 12:39ff.; *LMA* 6:1171f.; *TRE* 24:513ff.; *VATL* 514f.; *BBKL* 16:1142-48 (sources); S. Gensini, *Roma capitale (1447-1527)* (Pisa, 1994); A. Manfredi, *I codici latini di Niccolò V: Edizione degli inventari e identificazione dei manoscritti* (Vatican City, 1994); W. Brandmüller, "Die Reaktion Nikolaus' V. auf den Fall von Konstantinopel," *RQ* 90 (1995) 1-22; E. Meuthen, ed., *Acta Cusana* (Hamburg, 1996) I/3; C. Bonfigli, *Niccolò V, Papa della rinascenza* (Rome, 1997); G. L. Coluccia, *Niccolò V umanista* (Venice, 1998); B. Paolozzi Strozzi, ed. *Il parato di Niccolò V per il giubileo del 1450* (exhibition catalog, Florence, 2000).

HERIBERT MÜLLER

Nicholas V (antipope) (May 12, 1328-July 25/Aug. 25, 1330). A Franciscan, formerly *Pietro Rainalducci*, born in the last quarter of the thirteenth century at Corvaro near L'Aquila, died Oct. 16, 1333, in Avignon and buried in the Franciscan church there. He came from a humble background. He left his wife after five years' marriage and joined the Franciscan monastery of the Aracoeli in Rome. He was praised (though not universally) for the ascetic quality of his life, and he took the side of the "spirituals" in his order against John XXII in the controversy about poverty. He went over to the side of Louis the Bavarian when he came to Rome to obtain the imperial crown. After John XXII had been deposed, Louis had an electoral committee of thirteen Roman clerics elect him pope on May 12, 1328; Louis confirmed him in virtue of his imperial power, and he was crowned on May 15. Although he created nine new cardinals and appointed twenty bishops (above all from the ranks of the Franciscan and Augustinian opposition to John XXII), and endeavored to build up a curia of his own, he found little support from the emperor's immediate sphere of influence and was left to his own devices when Louis returned to the imperial territories. Their last meeting was at Pisa on January 3, 1329. When John XXII offered him a pardon and a pension of 3,000 gold florins, he renounced the papal dignity in Pisa on July 25, 1330, and submitted to John in Avignon on August 25 of that year. Thereafter, he lived as a prisoner under agreeable conditions in the papal palace until his death. He was never able to execute an autonomous policy, since he remained completely an instrument of the emperor.

■ **Bibliography:** *LMA* 6:1172f.; *BBKL* 6:871f.; *VATL* 515;

L. Lopez, "Pietro del Corvaro, antipapa Niccolò V nei manoscritti di A. L. Antinori," *Bolletino della Deputazione Abruzzese* . . . 72 (1982) 301-20; M. Berg, "Der Italienzug Ludwigs des Bayern: Das Itinerar der Jahre 1327-30," *QFIAB* 67 (1987) 142-97, esp. 179-83; Borgolte; H. Thomas, *Ludwig der Bayer* (Graz et al., 1993) 211ff.; A. Paravicini Bagliani, *Il corpo del Papa* (Turin, 1994); D. Quaglioni, ed., *Storia della Chiesa*, XI: *La crisi del Trecento e il Papato Avignonese* (2nd ed. Milan, 1995) 241ff.

LUDWIG VONES

Novatian (antipope) → **Cornelius.**

Paschal (antipope) (687). Died 692/693. The ambitious Roman archdeacon Paschal prepared his election while Pope Conon, always a sick man, was still alive. He counted on the support of the exarch John Platyn of Ravenna, to whom he promised a hundred pounds of gold. After Conon's death on September 21, 687, one Roman faction elected the archpriest Theodore, while the other faction elected Paschal; both occupied parts of the Lateran. Finally, Sergius I was recognized in October/December and was ordained bishop on December 15. Theodore accepted this situation, but force was needed in the case of Paschal, who was accused of magic, dismissed from the office of archdeacon, and banished to a monastery, where he died five years later, without having formally submitted.

■ **Sources:** *LP* 1:369-72; *RPR*(J) 1:243.
■ **Bibliography:** *LMA* 6:1753; Caspar 2:622ff.; Richards.

GEORG SCHWAIGER

Paschal I (Jan. 24, 817-Feb. 11, 824). Saint (feast day May 14), a Roman, buried in Santa Prassede in Rome. He was the abbot of St. Stephen's monastery next to St. Peter's basilica and was elected on the day Stephen IV died. He continued his predecessor's policy of close relations with the Frankish rulers and their newly founded empire. He renewed the friendly alliance in the "Pactum Hludovicianum" in 817; this text subsequently became the basis of papal rule in the church state (→ Papal States). Although he was closely tied to imperial policies and supported the mission of Archbishop Ebo of Rheims in northern Europe, Paschal conducted an autonomous policy as ruler in Rome and parts of the Patrimony of Peter, intervening in the affairs of the Frankish church. He crowned Lothar I again as emperor in Rome in 823 (perhaps also as king of the *Regnum Italiae*), emphasizing both the bond between the institution of the empire and Rome, and the validity of the *Ordinatio Imperii* of 817. This event was overshadowed by the murder of two papal office-bearers who were sympathetic to the Franks. Paschal had to take an oath of purification, and Lothar I strengthened the imperial influence by means of the *Constitutio Romana* of November 824. Paschal built and restored churches in Rome, carrying out an ambitious program that amounts to a renaissance in late antiquity. However, his energetic rule led to polarization among the Romans, and his death led to riots.

■ **Sources:** *LP* 2:52-68; *RPR(J)* 1:318ff.

■ **Bibliography:** *BBKL* 6:1567f.; *LMA* 6:1752; *VATL* 545f.; O. Bertolini, "Osservazioni sulla Constitutio Romana e sul Sacramentum cleri et populi Romani dell' 824," in *Festschrift for A. de Stefano* (Palermo, 1956) 43-78; O. Hagender, "Das crimen maiestatis, der Prozeß gegen die Attentäter Papst Leos III. und die Kaiserkrönung Karls des Großen," in *Aus Kirche und Reich,* Festschrift for F. Kempf (Sigmaringen, 1983) 55-79; T. F. X. Noble, *The Republic of Saint Peter* (Philadelphia, 1984); R. Wisskirchen, *Das Mosaikprogramm von Santa Prassede in Rom* (Münster, 1990); idem and F. Schlechter, eds., *Die Mosaiken der Kirche Santa Prassede in Rom* (Mainz, 1992); J. Fried, "Ludwig der Fromme, das Papsttum und die fränkische Kirche," in P. Godman and R. Collins, *Charlemagne's Heir: New Perspectives on the Reign of Louis the Pious* (Oxford, 1990) 231-73; J. Jarnut, "Ludwig der Fromme, Lothar I. und das Regnum Italiae," in ibid., 349-62; E. Boshof, *Ludwig der Fromme* (Darmstadt, 1996) 138f., 160-65.

PETER JOHANEK

Paschal II (Aug. 14, 1099-Jan. 21, 1118). Formerly *Rainer,* born in Bieda di Galeata in the Romagna. He entered a monastery, perhaps in the Abruzzi, as a young man. He was sent to Rome on monastery business and met Gregory VII, who gave his life a new direction by appointing him abbot of the Roman monastery of St. Laurence Outside the Walls. He was created cardinal priest of San Clemente after 1078, as the successor of the excommunicated Hugo Candidus. Urban II entrusted him with an important legation to France and Santiago de Compostela in Spain. He was a close collaborator of the reforming popes. The weakness of the imperial party helped secure his election as pope; the antipopes Theoderic, Albert, and Silvester IV, who followed Clement III, posed no serious threat to Paschal's position. He was less ready than his predecessor to make

compromises vis-à-vis Byzantium under the emperor Alexius I—indeed, he gave his approval in 1105 to the plans of Bohemund I of Taranto to lead a crusade against Byzantium. The investiture problem soon came to occupy the forefront of Paschal's church politics. He renewed the prohibition of lay investiture in 1102. He achieved acceptable resolutions to this problem with the kings of England (concordat of London, 1107) and France (at Troyes in the same year), but the conflict with the German king became more acute, and the pope issued repeated prohibitions of investiture at the synods of Guastalla (1106), Troyes (1107), Benevento (1108), and Rome (1110). In the negotiations he conducted with Henry V from 1106 onward, Paschal linked the problem of investiture to the involvement of bishops in the secular politics of the empire. In the pope's view, this was completely wrong, but it was supported by the king. In order to put an end to the "close working fellowship between the king and the bishops" (Stefan Weinfurter), Paschal made a radical proposal to the king in Santa Maria in Turi on February 4, 1111: in return for coronation as emperor, the king would renounce royal investiture, and the bishops and abbots would renounce the possessions and feudal rights that they had received from the empire. When this proposal became known, the princes reacted with indignation. Henry imprisoned the pope and the cardinals and extracted from Paschal the right to invest the bishops with ring and crozier, and the permanent prohibition of excommunicating the king (Privilege of Ponte Mammolo, April 11, 1111). Paschal was now willing to abdicate; but under pressure from the strict reforming party, who accused him of heresy, he held two synods in Rome in 1112 and 1116 at which he renewed the prohibition of investiture and repealed the contract ("privilege") with the king which had been the object of such opprobrium. Paschal was compelled to flee from Rome by the rebellion of the Romans in 1116 and by Henry's invasion of Italy in 1117. He died in → Castel Sant'Angelo shortly after his return and was buried in the Lateran basilica.

Despite all the criticism of Paschal's hesitations and his lack of success, it is important to note that he never yielded from the political positions and legal claims put forward by his distinguished predecessors.

■ **Sources:** LP 2:296-310; 3:134f., 143-56; *RPR(J)* 2nd ed.

1:702-72; *MGH.Const* 1:134-52, 564-74; U.-R. Blumenthal, "Decrees and Decretals," *Bulletin of Medieval Canon Law* 10 (1980) 15-30.

■ **Bibliography:** *LMA* 6:1752f.; *VATL* 546ff.; U.-R. Blumenthal, *The Early Councils of Pope Paschalis 1100-10* (Toronto, 1978; on this, see *AHC* 10 [1978] 279-89); C. Servatius, *Paschalis II* (Stuttgart, 1979); G. M. Cantarella, *Ecclesiologia e politica nel papato di Pasquale II* (Rome, 1982; on this, see *Zeitschrift für Rechtsgeschichte: Kanonistische Abteilung* 71 [1985] 359-62); U.-R. Blumenthal, "Bemerkungen zum Register Papst Paschalis' II.," *QFIAB* 66 (1986) 1-19; G. M. Cantarella, *La costruzione della verità: Pasquale, un papa alle strette* (Rome, 1987); C. Servatius, "Zur Englandpolitik der Kurie unter Paschalis II.," in *Deus qui mutat tempora,* Festschrift for A. Becker (Sigmaringen, 1987) 173-90; C. Morris, *The Papal Monarchy* (Oxford, 1989) 154-62; S. Beulertz, *Das Verbot der Laieninvestitur im Investiturstreit* (Hanover, 1991) 121-50; G. M. Cantarella, *Pasquale II e il suo tempo* (Naples, 1997); G. Cioffari, "Il Concilio di Bari del 1098," *Nicolaus* 26 (1999) 109-21; S. Weinfurter, "Wendepunkte der Reichsgeschichte im 11. und 12. Jahrhundert," in E. D. Hehl, ed., *Das Papsttum in der Welt des 12. Jahrhunderts* (Sigmaringen, 2000).

HUBERTUS SEIBERT

Paschal III (antipope) (1164-1168). Formerly *Guido of Crema,* died Sept. 9, 1168, in Rome, buried in St. Peter's. At the instigation of Rainald of Dassel, he was proclaimed pope in Lucca on April 22, 1164, as the successor of the imperial antipope Victor IV, and received episcopal ordination four days later. Even among the imperial party, however, this action met with objections, since it meant the prolongation of the schism. Paschal's assent legitimated the canonization of Charlemagne in Aachen on December 29, 1165. Barbarossa's fourth Italian campaign led to Paschal's enthronement in St. Peter's in Rome on July 30, 1167. Two days later, he crowned Frederick's consort Beatrix as empress in St. Peter's.

■ **Sources:** *RPR*(J) 2nd ed. 2:426-29.

■ **Bibliography:** *LMA* 6:1753f.; *VATL* 549; W. Georgi, *Friedrich Barbarossa und die auswärtigen Mächte* (Frankfurt a.M., 1990); J. Laudage, *Alexander III. und Friedrich Barbarossa* (Cologne, 1997); K. M. Sprenger, "Ein Deperditum Paschalis' III. für den gegenpäpstlichen Legaten Christian von Buch?" *Historisches Jahrbuch* 118 (1998) 261-76.

JÜRGEN PETERSOHN

Paul I (May 29, 757-June 28, 767). Saint (feast day June 28), brother of his predecessor Stephen II. He had previously worked in the papal adminis-

tration. He sent notice of his election, not to the Byzantine emperor, but to the Frankish king Pippin the Younger. The alliance concluded at Quierzy or Saint-Denis between Pippin and Stephen II had reversed previous policies. Paul consolidated this alliance, thus attaining de facto independence vis-à-vis Byzantium and guarantees in the event of a Langobard expansion. Stephen had promised Pippin a *memoria aeterna* in St. Peter's in 754, and these assurances were realized to a large extent by Paul, who brought the relics of Petronilla, the alleged daughter of St. Peter who was now venerated as patroness of the Carolingian dynasty, from the catacomb of Domitilla to a rotunda at St. Peter's, and began the practice of giving bodies of the martyrs to Frankish supplicants. He also received a mensal foundation for the tomb of St. Peter, where the imperial *Laudes* were to be sung, and guarantees of Pippin's foundations in support of St. Peter's and of the poor. The spiritual alliance was also renewed when Paul symbolically took on the role of godfather to the king's daughter, Gisela.

■ **Sources:** *LP* 1:463-67; 3:345; *RPR*(J) 1:277-83; *MGH.Ep* 3:507-58.

■ **Bibliography:** *BBKL* 7:12ff.; *LMA* 6:1823; *VATL* 552f.; D. H. Miller, "Papal-Lombard Relations During the Pontificate of Pope Paul I: The Attainment of an Equilibrium of Power in Italy 756-767," *Catholic Historical Review* 55 (1970) 348-75; idem, "Byzantine-Papal Relations during the Pontificate of Paul I: Confirmation and Completion of the Roman Revolution of the Eighth Century," *Byzantinische Zeitschrift* 68 (1975) 47-62; A. Angenendt, "Mensa Pippini Regis: Zur liturgischen Präsenz der Karolinger in Sankt Peter," *RQ* 35 (1977) 52-68; idem, "Das geistige Bündnis der Päpste mit den Karolingern," *Historisches Jahrbuch* 100 (1980) 1-94; T. F. X. Noble, *The Republic of Saint Peter* (Philadelphia, 1984); Borgolte 105-12; J. T. Hallenbeck, "King Desiderius as Surrogate 'Patricius Romanorum,'" *Studi medievali* 30 (1989) 49-64.

ARNOLD ANGENENDT

Paul II (Aug. 30, 1464-July 26, 1471). Formerly *Pietro Barbo,* born Feb. 23, 1418, into a Venetian family of merchants. His uncle, Eugene IV, made an ecclesiastical career possible for him. He became apostolic protonotary, archdeacon of Bologna, bishop of Cervia (1440), and cardinal of Santa Maria Nuova in Rome (1440). He subsequently received the bishoprics of Vicenza (1451) and Padua (1459) in addition, and became cardinal of San Marco under Nicholas V (1451). When Paul became pope, he made his chief residence the palace he had built alongside his titular church (today known as the Palazzo Venezia), a testimony to his love of splendor. The Romans appreciated the opulent feasts and elaborate ceremonies he held, beginning with his coronation. The authoritarian and aristocratic style of his government was shown when he revoked the electoral capitulation he and the other cardinals had sworn to observe, as well as in the dissolution of the College of Abbreviators, which Pius II had erected as recently as 1463, and the closure of the Roman Academy, which was headed by Pomponius Laetus. The humanists who lost their positions, above all Bartolomeo Platina, painted a picture of Paul as a barbarian who hated all the arts and sciences, and this has colored his reputation ever since. However, although Paul II displayed no great knowledge of literature, he was a prominent collector of art and classical objects, and it is probable that he moved against the "apostles of education," who were suspected of neopaganism, not because of any fundamental hostility to humanism but because of (unproved) suspicions that these scholars were involved in a conspiracy and were collaborating with the Turks. Paul sought to halt the advance of the Turks by giving aid to Hungary and to Skanderberg in Albania, as well as through an alliance with Uzun Hasan of Persia. He endeavored to create unity among the Italian states in the Pax Paulina of 1468, and renewed his efforts after the fall of Negroponte in 1470. Despite the intervention of King Matthias Corvinus, Paul had no success in the measures he took against the utraquist king of Bohemia, George of Poděbrad. The result was that George sought an alliance with Louis XI of France in order to facilitate the convocation of a general council. Although Cardinal Jean Jouffroy acted as mediator between Paul and the French king, relations were strained, partly because of the case of Jean Balue, but primarily because of the continued threats of an appeal by the University of Paris and the parliament to a general council, and of a renewal of the Pragmatic Sanction. Even Emperor Frederick III, who was a close ally of the pope, requested the convocation of a new council at Constance when he visited Paul in 1468-1469 and obtained his approval for the foundation of episcopal sees in Vienna and Wiener Neustadt. This shows that the idea of a council, attested in the electoral capitulation mentioned above, had certainly not died away. One factor encouraging this idea was the failure of the pope to carry out church reform. Although he acted against the sect of the Fraticelli, who maintained an extreme understanding of poverty, and decreed that a Holy Year should be celebrated at twenty-five-year intervals from 1475 on, there were scarcely any new or positive initiatives in his pontificate.

■ **Bibliography:** *DTHC* 12:3-9; *NCE* 11:12f.; *GKG* 12:43; *BBKL* 7:14f.; *LMA* 6:1823f.; *VATL* 553f. (all of these indicate sources and further bibliography); P. S. Gensini, ed., *Roma capitale (1447-1527)* (Pisa, 1994); W. Benziger, *Zur Theorie von Krieg und Frieden in der italienischen Renaissance* (Frankfurt a.M., 1996); C. Märtl, *Kardinal Jean Jouffroy* (Sigmaringen, 1996).

HERIBERT MÜLLER

Paul III (Oct. 13, 1534-Nov. 10, 1549). Formerly *Alessandro Farnese*, born in Feb. 1468 at Canino near Viterbo or in Rome. He received a humanist education in Rome, Florence, and Pisa. He owed his successful curial career to Alexander VI, who had been the lover of Alessandro's sister, Giulia Farnese. He was created cardinal deacon in 1493 and became dean of the College of → Cardinals in 1524. His lifestyle was no different from that of the other Renaissance popes. He had several children while a cardinal; his favorite was Pier Luigi. As pope, he practiced an excessive → nepotism: two grandsons became cardinals, while his third grandson became duke of Urbino, and his son Pier Luigi received Parma and Piacenza. Paul realized that the vacillating policies of his predecessor, Clement VII, could not be continued. Accordingly, he attempted to maintain neutrality vis-à-vis Emperor Charles V and France. Although he was personally disinclined to reform, he saw its inevitability and made men of the reforming party cardinals (e.g., John Fisher, Gasparo Contarini, Giampietro Carafa [later Paul IV], Jacopo Sadoleto, Reginald Pole, Giovanni Morone, Gregorio Cortese). He supported movements of religious renewal, both the reform of the older orders and the foundation of new orders (Theatines, Barnabites, Ursulines, Capuchins). He confirmed the Jesuit order in 1540. He set up a commission for reform in 1536, which produced the *Consilium delectorum cardinalium et aliorum praelatorum de emendanda ecclesia* in 1537. Paul was suspicious of the discussions with Protestants (Hagenau, Worms, Regensburg, 1540-1541) by means of which Charles V sought to achieve unity among the confessional parties in the empire. The spread of the ideas of the Protestant Reformation in northern Italy and the growing influence of the adherents of Juan de Valdés in Naples led to the foundation of the Inquisition in the Roman curia in 1542 (bull *Licet ab initio*) with Carafa as its leading proponent.

From the beginning of his pontificate, Paul planned to hold a council, but the first convocations (Mantua and Vicenza in 1537, Trent in 1542) led to nothing. After Charles V had won the commitment of the French king to a council in the Peace of Crépy (1544), it was finally possible to open the council at Trent on December 13, 1545. The sessions of the first period (1545-1548) produced a number of important dogmatic decrees. The legates transferred the council to Bologna when it was alleged that typhus fever had broken out; when the emperor protested, Paul ruled that no new decrees should be promulgated in Bologna. The council was suspended on September 14, 1549.

Paul had made money and an auxiliary troop of soldiers available to the emperor for the Schmalkaldic War in a treaty of 1546. In the following years, grave dissensions arose between Paul and Charles V because of the way the emperor handled the religious question and because of the pope's family politics. The proclamation of the Interim by the emperor in 1548 enraged the pope. The murder of his son Pier Luigi in 1547 brought these tensions to their high point, since Ferrante Gonzaga, the imperial vicegerent in Milan, was privy to the conspiracy.

Paul failed to persuade Charles V and the French king to end the English schism by taking military action against Henry VIII. Nevertheless, Paul gave the emperor vigorous support in his attempts to ward off the Turkish threat.

Paul was a patron of the arts and sciences. Michelangelo was appointed chief architect, sculptor, and painter in the Vatican Palace, and the *Last Judgment* in the → Sistine Chapel was painted in this period.

Paul's pontificate tends to be portrayed as a period of transition, and his character is often judged to be ambivalent. Elisabeth G. Gleason is surely not wrong to see him in her recent essay as the first pope of the Counter-Reformation. Through the changes which his appointments made to the College of → Cardinals, his introduction of reforms (*Consilium de emendanda ecclesia*), his support of the reforming orders of Jesuits and Capuchins, the foundation of the Inquisition and the convocation of the Council of Trent, he showed that he was serious in his leadership and defense of the Catholic Church.

■ **Sources:** A wealth of material will be found in the various series of nunciature reports; *Concilium Tridentinum: Diariorum, Actorum, Epistularum, Tractatuum nova Collectio,* ed. Görres-Gesellschaft, 13 vols. (Freiburg, 1901-2001).

■ **Bibliography:** *DTHC* 12:9-20; *EC* 9:734ff.; *TRE* 26:118-21; *VATL* 554f.; Pastor 5; C. Capasso, *Paolo III,* 2 vols. (Messina/Rome, 1925); L. Dores, *La cour du pape Paul III,* 2 vols. (Paris, 1932); W. Friedensburg, *Kaiser Karl V. und Papst Paul III.* (Leipzig, 1932); G. Drei, *I Farnese* (Rome, 1954); G. Müller, "Die drei Nuntiaturen Alexanders in Deutschland," *QFIAB* 39 (1959) 222-76, 328-42; H. Jedin, "Die Päpste und das Konzil in der Politik Karls V.," in P. Rassow and F. Schalk, eds., *Karl V: Der Kaiser und seine Zeit* (Cologne/Graz, 1960) 104-17; K. Repgen, *Die Römische Kurie und der Westfälische Friede,* I/1: *Papst, Kaiser und Reich 1521-1644* (Tübingen, 1962); H. Lutz, *Christianitas afflicta* (Göttingen, 1964); H. Jedin, *Geschichte des Konzils von Trient,* 3 vols. (Freiburg, 1977-82); E. G. Gleason, "Who Was the First Counter-Reformation Pope?" *Catholic Historical Review* 81 (1995) 173-84; J. S. Panzer, "The Popes and Slavery," *Homiletic and Pastoral Review* 97 (1996) 22-29 (on *Sublimis Deus*); R. Zapperi, *Die vier Frauen des Papstes: Das Leben Pauls III. zwischen Legende und Zensur* (Munich, 1997); idem, *La leggenda del Papa Paolo III: Arte e censura nella Roma pontificia* (Turin, 1998); C. Robertson, "Two Farnese Cardinals and the Question of Jesuit Taste," in J. W. O'Malley, ed., *The Jesuits* (Toronto, 1999) 134-47; M. Schmidt, "'Papst Paul wünschte, dass er die von Clemens angeordnete Arbeit fortsetzen möge': Neues zur Genese von Michelangelos 'Jüngstem Gericht' in der Sixtinischen Kapelle unter Paul III.," *Das Münster* 53 (2000) 16-29.

KLAUS GANZER

Paul IV (May 23, 1555-Aug. 18, 1559). Formerly *Giampietro Carafa,* born June 28, 1476, at Capriglio, into a noble Neapolitan family. He was a nephew of Cardinal Oliviero Carafa, to whom he owed his successful career in the curia. He became bishop of Chieti in 1505. He was nuncio in Naples in 1505-1506, in England in 1513, and in Spain in 1515, where tensions arose between Carafa and the Spanish court. He was appointed archbishop of Brindisi in 1518. He was closely connected to the "Oratory of divine love" in Rome, and he founded the order of Theatines in 1524 with Cajetan of Thiene. He was created cardinal in 1536 and became dean of the College of → Cardinals in 1553. He was appointed archbishop of Naples in 1549. He was a member of the commission for the *Consilium de emendanda ecclesia*. Cardinal Alessandro Farnese the Younger played a decisive role in his election as pope. The negative experiences during his legation in Spain and insults on the part of Charles V generated in him a deep antipathy to the Habsburgs, and he suspected the emperor of not being genuinely Catholic. He considered the Peace of Augsburg in religious matters (1555) to be invalid; the same applied to Charles's abdication and the election of Ferdinand I as emperor. Paul joined a military alliance with France against Spain in 1555, in the hope that he could destroy the Habsburg world empire. This, however, led to political disaster: Duke Fernando Alba invaded the papal states, and Paul was obliged to make a peace treaty with Spain in 1557.

After the collapse of his political ambitions, Paul turned his attention to activity within the church. His goal was to use the fullness of papal authority to introduce decisive reforms in the church; he sought to prevent a continuation of the Council of Trent. He extended the work of the Roman Inquisition, which was given a position above all other curial offices and did not shrink from confrontation with even the highest-placed officials in the church. On Paul's orders, Cardinal Giovanni Morone was imprisoned in → Castel Sant'Angelo, and the Inquisition began proceedings against him; it was also intended that proceedings be taken against Cardinal Reginald Pole. Paul published the → Index of Prohibited Books in 1559, which subsequently had to be withdrawn and revised. He also took strong measures against the Jews. → Nepotism in the old style flourished under Paul IV, who made his nephew Carlo Carafa a cardinal and entrusted all political business to him in 1555. Carlo was a man without spiritual interests or conscience, and all that he did was intended to increase the power of his family. Another nephew, Giovanni Carafa, was made Captain General of the church in the same year, and the two brothers exploited their supreme authority to the full. When Paul came to realize the extent of their crimes, he removed them from

their offices and banished them from Rome in 1559; both were executed under Pius IV.

Paul IV himself was a man of integrity, but his lack of intellectual sensibilities and his erratic character meant that his pontificate did not help the cause of reform.

■ **Sources:** A wealth of material will be found in the various series of nunciature reports.

■ **Bibliography:** *DBI* 19:497-509; *DTHC* 12:20-23; *EC* 9:736ff.; *TRE* 26:121-24; *VATL* 555f.; Pastor IV/2, V, VI; L. Riess, *Die Politik Pauls IV. und seiner Nepoten* (Berlin, 1909); P. Paschini, *S. Gaetano Thiene, Gian Pietro Carafa e le origini dei Chierici Regolari Teatini* (Rome, 1926); M. S. de Otto, *Paulo IV y la Corona de España* (Saragossa, 1943); L. Serrano, "El papa Paulo IV y España," *Hispania* 3 (1943) 295-325; T. Torriani, *Una tragedia nel Cinquecento romano: Paolo IV e i suoi nepoti* (Rome, 1951); H. Lutz, "Reformatio Germaniae," *QFIAB* 37 (1957) 222-310; R. De Maio, *Alfonso Carafa, cardinale di Napoli* (Vatican City, 1961; repr. 1981); K. Repgen, *Die Römische Kurie und der Westfälische Friede* (Tübingen, 1962) I/1; H. Lutz, *Christianitas afflicta* (Göttingen, 1964); idem, *Cardinal Morone: Il Concilio di Trento e la Riforma Cattolica* (Rome, 1965) 1:363-81; H. Jedin, "Kirchenreform und Konzilsgedanke 1550-55," *Kirche des Glaubens, Kirche der Geschichte* (Freiburg, 1966) 2:237-63; idem, *Geschichte des Konzils von Trient*, 3 vols. (Freiburg, 1977-82); P. Simoncelli, *Il caso Reginald Pole* (Rome, 1977); idem, *Evangelismo italiano nel Cinquecento* (Rome, 1979); M. Firpo and D. Marcatto, *Il processo inquisitoriale del cardinal Giovanni Morone*, 6 vols. (Rome, 1981-95); D. Chiomenti Vassalli, *Paolo IV e il processo Carafa* (Milan, 1993); A. Aubert, *Paolo IV: Politica, inquisizione e storiografia* (Florence, 1999).

KLAUS GANZER

Paul V (May 16, 1605-Jan. 28, 1621). Formerly *Camillo Borghese*, born Sept. 17, 1552, in Rome into a Sienese-Roman family of lawyers. After studying in Perugia and taking his doctorate in law in Pavia, he enjoyed a successful career in the curia. He was legate to Philip II of Spain in 1593, cardinal in 1596, bishop of Jesi from 1597 to 1599, and cardinal vicar in Rome and inquisitor in 1603. Spain prevented the election of Robert Bellarmine or of Cesare Baronius in the conclave that followed the death of Leo XI, and Paul was elected as a compromise candidate, and was crowned on May 29. He continued the Catholic reform by supporting the new orders and congregations, insisting on bishops' residental obligation in their dioceses and publishing the Roman Ritual in 1614. He supported missions, especially in India,

China, and Canada. In 1607, he abolished the *Congregatio de auxiliis gratiae,* which had been set up by Clement VIII, but without making any decision in the controversy about grace between the Jesuits and Dominicans; he did, however, forbid each side to act as censor of books published by the other. The Copernican world system was condemned in the first trial of Galileo Galilei in 1616. Paul encouraged the development of administration, health services, farming, trade, and traffic in the church state (→ Papal States). Carlo Maderno finished work on → St. Peter's during his pontificate, and the → Vatican Library was extended. He built the Palazzo and Villa Borghese and improved the Roman water supply (Acqua Paola). He was not free of → nepotism. He aimed at political neutrality between France (Henry IV) and Spain (Philip III). At the beginning of the Thirty Years' War, Paul supported Emperor Ferdinand II and the League, which was led by Maximilian I of Bavaria. Obsolete conceptions of papal supremacy led to grave political conflicts, and the pope met with no success vis-à-vis the Italian states and France. His greatest defeat came in the fundamental confrontation between the church and the republic of Venice (1605-1607). Although Paul excommunicated the senate and pronounced an interdict on the republic, these measures were basically ineffective. Paolo Sarpi defended the republic with biting literary skill. The peace that was negotiated as a compromise between France and Spain was a serious defeat for the pope. He forbade the subjects of James I in England to take the oath of loyalty that was demanded of them in the aftermath of the Gunpowder Plot (1605). He is buried in Santa Maria Maggiore.

■ **Bibliography:** *DCTH* 12:23-37; *EC* 9:738-41; *HKG* 4:650-59; Pastor 12:22-680; J. Semmler, *Das päpstliche Staatssekretariat in den Pontifikaten Pauls V. und Gregors XV.* (Rome, 1967); W. Reinhard, *Papstfinanz und Nepotismus unter Paul V.,* 2 parts (Stuttgart, 1974); M. Heckel, *Deutschland im konfessionellen Zeitalter* (Göttingen, 1983); G. Schwaiger, "Die Päpste im Zeitalter des Dreißigjährigen Krieges," *GKG* 12:103-27; K. Repgen, ed., *Krieg und Politik 1618-48* (Munich, 1988); G. Zanon, "Il Rituale di Brescia del 1570 modello del Rituale Romano di Paolo V," in *Traditio et progressio,* Festschrift for A. Nocent (Rome, 1988) 643-81; A. Kraus, "Die Geschichte des päpstlichen Staatssekretariats im Zeitalter der katholischen Reform und der Gegenreformation als Aufgabe der Forschung," *RQ* 84 (1989) 74-91; A. Fantoli, *Galileo for Copernicanism and for the Church* (Rome,

1994); Borgolte 415; S. Samerski, "Akten aus dem Staatssekretariat Pauls V. und Gregors XV.," *AHP* 33 (1995) 303-14; idem, "Das päpstliche Staatssekretariat unter L. Margotti 1609-11," *RQ* 90 (1995) 74-84; A. Antinori, *Scipione Borghese e l'architettura* (Rome, 1995); A. M. Corbo and M. Pomponi, eds., *Fonti per la storia artistica romana al tempo di Paolo V* (Rome, 1995); F. Antolín, "Un breve misional desconocido dirigido a Tomas de Jesus," *Teresianum* 47 (1996) 287-302; N. Reinhardt, *Macht und Ohnmacht der Verflechtung: Rom und Bologna unter Paul V.* (Tübingen, 2000).

GEORG SCHWAIGER

Paul VI (June 21, 1963-Aug. 6, 1978 [Castelgandolfo]). Formerly *Giovanni Battista Montini,* born Sept. 26, 1897, at Concesio in the province of Brescia, into a family of Catholic intellectuals. He was taught privately by Jesuits and Oratorians; after his ordination to the priesthood in 1920, he studied in Rome. He acted as secretary to the nunciature in Warsaw for a brief period in 1923. As organizer and chaplain to the Catholic student organization FUCI from 1923 to 1933, he came to know the concerns of coming generations of Italian laypeople. As editor of the journal *Studium* (first published in Rome in 1905), he became familiar with the political and intellectual movements of the period, and especially with French Catholicism. His political views were shaped by his parents' clear rejection of fascism. He worked in the papal secretariat of state from October 1924 on; he became secretary with the task of taking minutes in 1925, and substitute for "Ordinary ecclesiastical affairs" in 1937, with responsibility for Catholic Action and Catholic movements in various countries. After the outbreak of the Second World War, he and Domenico Tardini were the closest advisers of Pius XII. Montini's special responsibility was the organization of the information service, the Vatican relief works, and aid to refugees and prisoners of war. He became pro-secretary of state in 1952, but left the service of the curia in 1954, after being appointed archbishop of Milan (without the traditional elevation to the College of → Cardinals). As archbishop of one of the largest dioceses in the world, he endeavored to promote spiritual renewal in accord with the French model, founding pastoral centers and supporting the mission to the city. John XXIII created him cardinal in 1958. He and Cardinal Giacomo Lercaro of Bologna were the only Italian bishops who were able to draw up a concrete reform program in support of John XXIII's plan to hold a council.

He was elected pope on June 21, 1963, on the fifth round of voting, and chose the name of the apostle to the nations. He continued the Second Vatican Council, which his predecessor, John XXIII, had convoked, and outlined the direction his pontificate would take in the encyclical *Ecclesiam suam* (1964), where he sketched three great circles of dialogue: reform and dialogue *ad intra,* ecumenical dialogue with other Christian churches and communities, and the encounter with modern culture. He held fast to the Roman understanding of the primacy, reducing the college of bishops in the *Nota praevia* (November 16, 1964) to an auxiliary function in relation to the papacy. He also enforced the Roman view of primacy in his exclusion from conciliar discussion of the questions of clerical celibacy and contraception, and in his Motu proprio *Apostolica sollicitudo* (September 15, 1965), which defined the authority of the synod of bishops as exclusively consultative. He was intimately familiar with the curia, where he carried out decisive reforms in the Constitution *Regimini ecclesiae universae* (August 15, 1967) and gave impetus to the trend to internationalization above all by appointing Frenchmen such as Jean Villot, his cardinal secretary of state. (There were 1,322 curial officials in 1961, and 3,146 in 1978.) He excluded cardinals over eighty years of age from participation in the conclave (Motu proprio *Ingravescentem aetatem,* November 21, 1970) and limited the electoral college to 120 members (Constitution *Romano pontifici eligendo,* October 1, 1975). International appointments made the numerical superiority of Italian/European cardinals a thing of the past.

Paul knew how to use symbolic gestures on great occasions as bridges to reach out to new shores. He visited the holy land from January 4 to 6, 1964, and Bombay from December 2 to 5 of the same year; he visited the United Nations in New York from October 3 to 5, 1965, and met Patriarch Athenagoras in Constantinople in 1967. He took part in the eucharistic congress in Bogotà and the Latin American bishops' conference in Medellín from August 22 to 25, 1968. He visited the International Labor Office in Geneva on June 10, 1969; he traveled to Uganda from July 31 to August 2, 1970, and to Asia, Australia, and Oceania from November 26 to December 5, 1970. The abrogation of the sentences of excommunication between Constantinople and Rome on December 7, 1965, had great symbolic significance. Within the Catholic Church, a disconcerting polarization arose under the conservative slogan of "betrayal of the church" (a standard-bearer was Archbishop Marcel Lefebvre, suspended in July 1976) and the progressive slogan of "betrayal of the council." In Europe, Dutch Catholicism was severely shaken by the crisis; in Latin America, it proved difficult to refute the accusation that liberation theology had been infiltrated by Marxism. Opposition within the church reached a high point with the publication of the encyclical *Humanae vitae* in 1968. German Catholics had little taste for Paul's → Ostpolitik, which was directed by Agostino Casaroli (later cardinal secretary of state under John Paul II); this, however, aimed not at an ideological dialogue but at better living conditions for Catholics in communist countries. The arrivals in Rome of the Hungarian cardinal József Mindszenty and the Czech archbishop Josef Beran were spectacular events in this context. During the war in Vietnam, Paul VI was prepared to accept a cooling of relations with the United States. His views on society and social policy are most fully reflected in his Apostolic Letter *Octogesima adveniens* (May 14, 1971). The Apostolic Exhortation *Evangelii nuntiandi,* published in the Holy Year 1975, presented a synthesis of the church's charge to proclaim the gospel in a pluralistic world. The letter that he addressed to the Red Brigades on April 21, 1978, appealing to them to spare the life of his friend, the Italian prime minister Aldo Moro, is a moving testimony to his human qualities. He continued the practice of making concordats.

He has often been portrayed as a pope plagued by doubts and hesitations. This fails to recognize that he was an intellectual who had recognized the complexity of the situation of Christians in modern culture—and this is how he saw himself.

■ **Works:** Supplements to the periodical *Studium: Coscienza universitaria* (1930); *Via di Cristo* (1931); *Appunti per la storia della diplomazia pontificia nel secolo VIII* (Rome, 1934); *Lettere ai familiari,* 2 vols. (Brescia, 1986).

■ **Sources:** *Insegnamenti di Paolo VI,* 16 vols. (Vatican City, 1963-78); *AAS* 55-70 (1963-78); U. Morando, ed., *Regesto dei documenti ufficiali promulgati da Paolo VI* (Brescia, 1997); X. Toscani, ed., *Lettere 1915-73: Paolo Caresana, Giovanni Battista Montini* (Brescia, 1998).

■ **Bibliography:** P. Arató and P. Vian, *Elenchus biblio-*

graphicus (2nd ed. Brescia/Rome, 1981); P. Vanzan, "Una panorama bibliografica su Paolo VI," *La civiltà cattolica* 151 (2000) 258-69; *AHP* 1 (1963–). The Istituto Paolo VI in Brescia issues many publications concerning Paul VI.

■ **Secondary literature:** *DSp* 12:522-36; *VATL* 557ff.; J. Guitton, *Dialog mit Paul VI.* (Frankfurt a.M., 1969); D. A. Seeber, *Paul VI.: Papst im Widerstreit* (Freiburg, 1971); R. Aubert, "Paul VI, un 'pontificat de transition,'" *Revue nouvelle* 48 (1978) 613-28; J. Guitton, *Paul VI secret* (Paris, 1979); A. Dupuy, *La diplomatie du St. Siège après le II Concile du Vatican* (Paris, 1980); J. D. Holmes, *The Papacy in the Modern World* (London, 1981); G. Andreotti, *Meine sieben Päpste* (Freiburg, 1982) 116-80; *Paul VI et la modernité dans l'Eglise* (Rome, 1984); A. Riccardi, *Il potere del papa da Pio XII a Paolo VI* (Rome, 1988); C. Cremona, *Paolo VI* (Milan, 1991); P. Hebblethwaite, *Paul VI, the First Modern Pope* (London, 1993); A. Acerbi, *Paolo VI* (Milan, 1997); *Papst Paul VI: Zur 100. Wiederkehr seines Geburtstages 1897-1997: Vorträge des Studientages am 29.11.1997 in Aachen* (Neustadt/Aisch, 1999); C. Huber, *Paul VI. und das Kirchenrecht* (Essen, 1999).

VICTOR CONZEMIUS

Pelagius I (Apr. 16, 556-Mar. 3, 561). Born into an aristocratic family in Rome. As a deacon, he accompanied Agapitus I to Constantinople in February 536, where he was appointed apocrisiary of the Roman patriarchate and took part in the synod against Anthimus in 536. In 537, he prevented the return of Pope Silverius to Rome. He remained apocrisiary under Pope Vigilius. He supported Justinian I on questions concerning the Eastern churches and urged him to condemn Origenism (*Patrologia Graeca* 86:945-94). When he returned to Rome, he used his wealth to aid the Romans, especially during the siege and sack of the city by the Goths (546-547). King Totila sent him to Justinian in 547. He was once again in Constantinople from 551 onward, where he was Vigilius's counselor (553) when the pope rejected the condemnation of the Three Chapters. He composed the *Constitutum* for Vigilius (Corpus scriptorum ecclesiasticorum latinorum [Vienna, 1895] 35:230-50). After the condemnation of the Three Chapters, he was sent into exile, where he wrote a number of works, including the treatise *In defensione trium capitulorum* in six books, where he justified the writings of the three accused authors and recalled the ecclesiastical norm that forbade the condemnation of deceased persons. Book I and parts of books III and VI have not sur-

vived; book III defends Theodore of Mopsuestia, book IV defends Theodoret of Cyrus, and book V concerns Ibas of Edessa. Since he had no access to books in his exile, he relied above all on the *Constitutum* (which he calls the *Iudicatum*) and on Facundus of Hermiane. He criticized Vigilius severely because of the concessions he had made on the question of the Three Chapters, as well as the pope's advisers (*dictatores*), the deacons Tullianus and Petrus.

After the death of Vigilius and at Justinian's prompting, Pelagius recognized the condemnation of the Three Chapters and accepted the council (*MGH.AA* 11:204). The emperor then appointed him bishop of Rome, against the will of the clergy and the people (*PL* 68:961), and he took up his office in Rome on April 16, 556, under the protection of Byzantine troops. The Romans came to accept him because of his initiatives for rebuilding the city and because of his generosity. He was opposed by Childebert and by many Western churches, whom he attempted to win over by promises and declarations; nevertheless, the bishops of northern Italy (Milan and Aquileia) relinquished communion with Rome.

Ninety-six letters by Pelagius survive, as well as the Latin translation of a collection (*Collectio systematica*) of saints' lives (*Verba seniorum*). From his pontificate onward, each papal election required imperial confirmation.

■ **Sources:** *PL* 69:393-418; 73:855-1024; *PLS* 4:1248-69; *CPL* 1698-1703.

■ **Bibliography:** *DTHC* 23:660-69; *DECL* 475; *VATL* 559f.; Caspar 286-305; E. Sloots, *De Diaken Pelagius en de Verdediging der drie Kapitels* (Nijmegen, 1936); M. Maccarone, *Romana ecclesia, Cathedra Petri* (Rome) 1:357-431; A. Di Berardino, ed. *Patrologia* (Genoa, 1996) 4:144ff.

ANGELO DI BERARDINO

Pelagius II (579-Feb. 2, 590). Born in Rome, the son of the Goth Wunegild. He was elected pope during the Langobard siege of Rome in August 579, but it was impossible for him to obtain imperial confirmation. He received episcopal ordination on November 26. He unsuccessfully appealed for support to the Byzantines and to the three Frankish kings of Neustria, Austria, and Burgundy, who came to Italy. Pelagius endeavored to put an end to the schism with the bishops of Venetia and Istria, which had begun under Pelagius I, generated by the controversy about the

Three Chapters, but he did not succeed in re-establishing ecclesial communion. He composed a lengthy text (*ACO* IV/2:112-32) which took up all the theological questions posed in a dossier based on Leo the Great which these bishops had sent to him, and he distinguished between those conciliar statements that concern the "pure faith" and other statements that have no dogmatic status. He also examined each of the three condemned writers (Theodore of Mopsuestia, Ibas of Edessa, and Theodoret of Cyrus) and affirmed that the condemnation of the Three Chapters did not entail any diminishing of the true faith. Pelagius protested in vain when John IV Nesteutes gave himself the title "ecumenical patriarch," and he refused to acknowledge the decisions of the synod which John held in 587 (cf. Gregory the Great, *Epp.* 4.32, 34, 38; 6.41).

The → *Liber Pontificalis* and a number of inscriptions tell us that Pelagius completed many buildings in Rome. A mosaic in the basilica of St. Laurence Outside the Walls portrays him as the restorer of this church. He died of the plague and was buried in St. Peter's.

■ Sources: *PL* 72:701-60; *PLS* 4:1414f.; *LP* 1:309ff.; *RPR*(J) 1:137-40; 2:696; *ACO* IV/2, XXIIIe 105-32.

■ Bibliography: *DTHC* 12:669-75; *DACL* 13:1222ff.; *CPL* 1705ff.; *DECL* 475; *VATL* 560f.; Bertolini 225-300; G. Cuscito, "La fede calcedonense e i concili di Grado (579) e di Marano (591)," *Grado nella storia e nell'arte* (Udine, 1980) 1:207-30; A. Tuilier, "Grégoire le Grand et le titre de patriarche oecuménique," in *Grégoire le Grand* (Paris, 1986) 69-82; A. Di Berardino, ed., *Patrologia* (Genoa, 1996) 4:150f.

ANGELO DI BERARDINO

Peter, apostle (†67?). Saint (feast day June 29).
1. New Testament.—2. Later Attestation.—3. Veneration.—4. In the History of Liturgy.—5. Iconography.

1. New Testament

a. *Name.* Peter (Greek *Petros,* Aramaic *kîfâ,* translated into Greek as *Kēphas*) was not the apostle's original name, but a nickname bestowed by Jesus on *Simon* (Mark 3:16 par.; Luke 6:14; John 1:42; Matt. 16:18; "Simon Peter" is found in Matt. 16:16; Luke 5:8; John 1:40; 6:8, 68; etc.). It is no longer possible to establish when and why Jesus gave him this name, or what it originally meant, since the interpretation of *Petros* as the "rock" (*petra*) of the church (Matt. 16:18) is a play on words that makes sense only in Greek, and the obvious ecclesiological interest in this passage ("my church") presupposes the existence of a community separate from that of Israel. In other words, this interpretation came into being only after Easter (see Luz, 456). The primary meaning of *petros* and *kîfâ* is "stone," not "rock" (Lampe). As Pesch (1980) has suggested, it may be that Jesus gave Simon this name to designate the first of his disciples as the "precious stone" in the group of those who followed him.

b. *New Testament Material.* Apart from Paul, Peter is the apostle about whom the New Testament has most to say. He plays an important role in the Gospels and the Acts of the Apostles, and Paul mentions Peter/Cephas relatively often, though only in 1 Corinthians and Galatians. The two Letters of Peter are pseudepigraphical texts that claim to be composed by the apostle (1 Pet. 1:1; 2 Pet. 1:1).

c. *Biography.* Simon came from Bethsaida (John 1:44), a city influenced by Hellenism, and the Greek name of his brother Andrew shows that this influence extended to his family, which was certainly Jewish. The meaning of the epithet "Barjona," which accompanies his name once in the New Testament (Matt. 16:17), is unclear; it may signify "son of John" (John 1:42; 21:15ff.). He moved to Capharnaum when he married (Mark 1:29f.; 2:1), and worked as a fisherman (Mark 1:16ff.; John 21:3). He was one of the first disciples whom Jesus called and was later given a place by Jesus among the group of the twelve (Mark 3:16). Peter's denial of Jesus during the passion, related in all the Gospels, is most likely historical. Peter, like all the disciples, was deeply disappointed by Jesus' death on the cross, and he returned to Galilee, where he resumed work as a fisher (Mark 16:7; Matt. 28:10, 16; John 21:1-14). After Jesus' resurrection, he was the first Easter witness (1 Cor. 15:5; Luke 24:34; see also Mark 16:7). It is no doubt due to his initiative that the group of disciples soon reassembled and proclaimed the message of the resurrection. Peter returned to Jerusalem (Gal. 1:18; 2:1-10; Acts 1-12; 15:6-29). His open attitude toward the mission to the Gentiles soon brought him to Antioch (Gal. 2:11). It is a matter of scholarly dispute whether the existence of the Cephas-party in Corinth (1 Cor. 1:12; cf. 3:22) presupposes that Peter had visited this city; but one should probably rather infer from the mention of "Babylon" (= Rome) in 1 Pet. 5:13

that he had moved from Antioch to Rome. This is indicated also by the early veneration of his → tomb in that city; there are no competing traditions about his burial. John 21:18f. hints that Peter imitated the death of Jesus by being crucified (see also John 13:36). Peter mediated between the various theological tendencies among the earliest Christians. At the apostolic council (Gal. 2:1-10; Acts 15:1-33), Peter rejected the radical Jewish-Christian position, which demanded that Gentile Christians too should observe the law and circumcision, and he recognized Paul's mission to the Gentiles. His goal in the Antiochene conflict (Gal. 2:11-14) was probably to reach a compromise that would ensure unity in the community. This would have required Gentile Christians to observe a number of precepts about purity, based on James's letter, which was sent at the conclusion of the council (Acts 15:20, 29; 21:25).

d. *The Image of Peter in the New Testament Writings.* Apart from the purely historical facts, the New Testament picture of Peter allows us to draw conclusions about the significance of the apostle for the earliest Christian communities. The oldest references to Peter are found in 1 Corinthians and Galatians. Paul often speaks of Peter as the criterion, when he defends his own apostleship and his understanding of the gospel. In 1 Cor. 15:1-8, Paul places himself at the end of the list of Easter witnesses which begins with Peter, in order to emphasize that their gospel is identical and is based on their calling by the risen Lord (1 Cor. 15:11). Even when Paul develops his specific understanding of the apostolic office, and differences between him and Peter become clear, he acknowledges Peter's authority (1 Cor. 9:5; Gal. 2:7f.). Fellowship with Peter and the other apostles in Jerusalem matters to Paul (Gal. 2:9f.; cf. also Gal. 1:18). Nevertheless, he does not shrink from a dispute with Peter when the "truth of the gospel" is at stake in the Antiochene conflict (Gal. 2:11-14). It is clear that Peter was more willing to compromise than Paul (see above). Taken as a whole, Paul's letters attest the leading position of Peter and his authority among the earliest Christians, which was ultimately based on his calling by Jesus and on the risen Lord's appearance to him. The Gospels and the Acts of the Apostles confirm the outstanding role of Peter. He is one of the first to be called (Mark 1:16 par.; Luke 5:1-11; John 1:35-42). It is he who utters the fundamental profession

of faith in Christ (Mark 8:29 par.; cf. John 6:68f.), and he heads the list of the twelve called by Jesus (Mark 3:16-19 par.). Jesus gives him special promises and authority (Matt. 16:17ff.; John 21:15ff.). In contrast to his role as the disciples' spokesman, we read of his denial of Jesus (Mark 14:66-72); but he is given the task of "strengthening his brethren" after his "repentance" (Luke 22:31f.). Peter's role as initiator of a new beginning in Acts 1-2 is in keeping with these words: it is he who proposes the election of Matthias to fill the place vacated by Judas (Acts 1:15-26) and who holds the discourse which interprets the Pentecost event (2:14-36). He uncovers deceit and unhelpful developments (5:1-11; 8:18-24), confirms (together with John) Philip's mission among the Samaritans (8:14-17), and opens the church to the Gentiles (10:46ff.; see also 11:1-18; 15:6-11).

The New Testament picture of Peter is especially vivid in the Gospels of Matthew and John. In Matthew, Peter is presented both as the "typical" disciple of Jesus and as a man with his own unique and fundamental function. Peter is typical in a positive sense when he follows Jesus without any delay (Matt. 4:18ff.) and professes his faith in Jesus (16:16); he is typical in a negative sense as the "man of little faith" (14:28-31) and the one who denies Jesus (26:69-75; see also 16:21ff.). The reader of Matthew's Gospel is meant to take Peter as a model, but also to recognize in the apostle the possibility that he himself will be unfaithful. But Peter is also the unique disciple who stands at the beginning of the church and forms a point of reference for the church in every age. The much-discussed text 16:17ff. is central here. Peter is called blessed (v. 17) not because of some special achievement, but because he is the recipient of divine revelation. This "revelation" is not to be limited to the confession he has just made (v. 16), since the verb "reveal" has no object in the Greek text; rather, it embraces the entire tradition about Jesus which is preserved in the Gospel of Matthew, especially the Master's instructions (above all, the Sermon on the Mount, Matt. 5-7). Verse 18 interprets the name *Petros* as "rock" (*petra*). This makes Peter himself (not just his faith) the foundation of the entire church, that is, the guarantor of the tradition about Jesus. He promises this church, founded on Peter, that it will endure and hold out against the powers of the underworld. The image of the keys of the kingdom of heaven, and of binding and loosing (v. 19), point to Peter's doctrinal and disciplinary authority, which he exercises on earth when he hands on the instructions of Jesus and expounds these in a binding manner, thus giving access to the kingdom of heaven (unlike the Pharisees: see Matt. 23:13). Peter's function as rock is historically unique; Matthew's Gospel knows nothing of a succession to Peter in a universal ecclesial authority exercised by one single person, such as the papal office. According to 18:18, the function of binding and loosing is exercised by the community as a whole; in 28:19f., all the disciples are commissioned by the exalted Lord to teach the peoples what Jesus has commanded. Apart from this, there exists a school of Christian "scribes" in the Matthaean community (see 13:52; 23:34) with the task of preserving the tradition of the faith and bringing it up to date for each specific period. This means that Peter's ministry continues to be exercised in the community.

The specific element in the Johannine picture of Peter is his rivalry with the Beloved Disciple (John 13:21-26; 18:15f.; 20:3-9; 21:7). The latter (identified only at a subsequent stage with John the son of Zebedee) is a significant teacher in the history of the Johannine communities. In the Gospel, he symbolizes the more strongly charismatic character of the Johannine tradition, while Peter symbolizes the universal church, with its office, which was in the process of elaboration (Klauck 217f.). While John 21:15ff. (the installation of Peter as shepherd; cf. John 10:11) clearly shows that the Gospel of John does not call into question Peter's authority in the universal church, the text is concerned to ensure that its own tradition too is preserved in the church. This is surely the meaning of the affirmation that the Beloved Disciple will "remain" until the parousia (21:22); the text rejects an interpretation of this "remaining" to mean that the disciple would not die (21:23).

The two pseudepigraphical Letters of Peter both attest the outstanding importance of Peter. 1 Peter presents him, in a hint at his violent death, as a "witness to the sufferings of Christ" (5:1) who inspires confidence and hope in a community oppressed from without, while 2 Peter polemicizes under the name of Peter against opponents within the community.

We may summarize as follows. Peter appears in the New Testament as a guarantor of the tradition about Jesus, as a witness to the truth of the gospel, and as one who preserves unity in the church. The specifically Petrine ministry is seen as a historically unique apostolic service based on the fact that Peter was the first to be called by Jesus and the first to bear witness to the resurrection; on the other hand, this service must be continued, since it is always necessary in the church. The New Testament lays down criteria for such a ministry, but leaves open the question of the specific form it is to take.

■ **Bibliography:** H. R. Balz and G. Schneider, eds., *Exegetisches Wörterbuch zum Neuen Testament* (Stuttgart, 1983) 3:193-201 (R. Pesch); D. N. Freedman et al., *Anchor Bible Dictionary* (New York, 1992) 5:251-63 (K. P. Donfried); O. Cullmann, *Petrus* (Zurich, 1952; 3rd ed. 1985); Raymond Brown et al., eds., *Peter in the New Testament* (Minneapolis, 1973); F. Mussner, *Petrus und Paulus—Pole der Einheit* (Freiburg, 1976); P. Lampe, "Das Spiel mit dem Petrusnamen—Matt. XVI.18," *New Testament Studies* 25 (1979) 227-45; R. Pesch, *Simon-Petrus* (Stuttgart, 1980); A. Vögtle, "Das Problem der Herkunft von 'Mt 16,17-19,'" in idem, *Offenbarungsgeschehen und Wirkungsgeschichte* (Freiburg, 1985) 109-40; F. Hahn, "Die Petrusverheißung Mt 16,18f.," in idem, *Exegetische Beiträge zum ökumenischen Gespräch* (Göttingen, 1986) 185-200; U. Luz, *Das Evangelium nach Matthäus* (Zurich, 1986); M. Karrer, "Petrus im paulinischen Gemeindekreis," *Zeitschrift für neutestamentliche Wissenschaft* 80 (1989) 210-31; H. J. Klauck, "Gemeinde ohne Amt?" in *Gemeinde—Amt—Sakrament* (Würzburg, 1989) 195-222; P. Perkins, *Peter* (Columbia, 1994); P. Dschulnigg, *Petrus im Neuen Testament* (Stuttgart, 1996); L. Wehr, *Petrus und Paulus—Kontrahenten und Partner* (Münster, 1996); S. K. Ray, *Upon This Rock: St. Peter and the Primacy of Rome in Scripture and the Early Church* (San Francisco, 1999); C. P. Thiede, *Geheimakte Petrus: Auf den Spuren des Apostels* (Stuttgart, 2000); T. Wiarda, *Peter in the Gospels: Pattern, Personality and Relationship* (Tübingen, 2000); R. Pesch, *Die biblischen Grundlagen des Primats* (Freiburg, 2001).

LOTHAR WEHR

2. Later Attestation

The most important materials in the extrabiblical traditions about Peter are the following: (a) The disputes between Simon Magus and Simon Peter, where Peter replaces Philip (see Acts 8) and confutes Simon Magus by means of his greater thaumaturgic powers; (b) revelations of the risen Jesus to Peter in the period between the resurrection and the ascension, where Peter is often the definitive witness to revelation; (c) instructions imparted by Peter to his disciple Clement (this concept lies at the origin of the Pseudo-Clementine literature, which bears the stamp of a decidedly orthodox Catholicism); (d) the preaching of Peter, especially in Rome (the sermons attributed to him are important examples of early Christian preaching to the Gentiles); (e) the martyrdom of Peter in Rome (see *1 Clement* 5ff.) with the *Quo vadis?* legend and the tradition that Peter was crucified upside down.

The *Acts of Peter and Paul* are sometimes included in the same manuscripts. This is even more commonly the case with the accounts of their martyrdom, since they share the same feast day, June 29.

The Gnostic texts about Peter are often marked by a rivalry between Peter and women disciples of Jesus; correspondingly, texts from the period when the greater church (*die Großkirche*) was coming into being often establish a link between the apostle and the church's clergy, often portraying him directly as their teacher. The rivalry between Peter and the women disciples is connected with the survival in Gnostic circles of the older model of domestic churches, where women had greater authority. Similarly, Peter is presented as downright misogynous in the miracle tradition (the story of his daughter, of the gardener's daughter, etc.). He is frequently portrayed as well disposed to the Jews (in contrast to Paul: see Gal. 2:7, 9), especially in the Pseudo-Clementines (*Homilies, Recognitions*). Little research has been done on this literature, and only small portions have been translated into modern languages.

The revelatory texts that circulated under the name of Peter and found many readers were a response to a central hermeneutical problem: How can the contemporary interpretation of the Christian message be presented as something definitive and binding? This response recalls William Wrede's hypothesis about the "messianic secret" in the Gospel of Mark: viz., that Peter alone had received the true doctrine, which he had then transmitted secretly and in writing to certain specially chosen persons. Peter had received an extra portion of revelation; only some of this was preserved in the New Testament canon, while everything else was transmitted in secret. All who come *via* Peter to the same knowledge that he possesses are "in him." In the context of the history of religions, it thus becomes possible to employ the

system of categories found in revelation-literature to understand the Roman bishop's claim to infallibility.

Peter's role in the revelation literature of Antioch and Alexandria displays great stability over a period of many centuries. Antioch is attested in Gal. 2:11-14, while Alexandria was held to be the place where Peter's disciple Mark had worked; the Alexandrine traditions about Peter must be as old as the close relations between ancient Syrian and ancient Egyptian Christianity. Even later revelations to Schenouda are presented as Petrine revelations.

■ Bibliography: *BBKL* 7:305-20; K. Berger, "Unfehlbare Offenbarungen," in *Kontinuität und Einheit,* Festschrift for F. Mussner (Freiburg, 1981) 261-326.

KLAUS BERGER

3. *Veneration*

While theology discusses the → Petrine ministry in terms of dogmatics and canon law, the "Petrine" veneration deals with the piety that has understood Peter as present in or at his tomb and as continuing to work in his papal successors. The idea of the pope as Peter's "heir" or "successor" is the kernel of all papalist theories. According to Gerd Tellenbach, "the veneration of the vicar of Peter by the faithful . . . is an unparalleled expression of the unity of the church on earth, since it is also objectively tangible." The salvation of the world flowed forth from the see of Peter. Dioceses sought to increase their prestige by declaring that they had been founded by his disciples, and they venerated the prince of the apostles as their special patron. The most striking formulations of Peter's sovereignty came from the pen of Gregory VII, who intensified the specifically Petrine and Roman elements in the older traditions, thus emphasizing the veneration of the apostle and the papal office and making this the point of departure for subsequent historical developments: the Catholic Church is a Roman church, because Peter founded it and because it is he who leads it in each individual pope. An "authority is attributed" here to the prince of the apostles "which otherwise belongs to God alone" (Klaus Ganzer), since it is affirmed that salvation depends on obedience to Peter and his vicar. Peter is at work in the pope, proclaiming the true faith, celebrating the only correct liturgy, and deciding all controversial questions. When scholasticism introduced theological differentiations, and canon law as an academic science translated this into legal categories, the veneration of Peter, which had once enjoyed a fundamental role, was reduced to the realm of popular piety.

Peter was venerated at his → tomb on the Vatican Hill. The "trophy" erected before 200, and *a fortiori* the basilica erected by Constantine, promoted this veneration. He was also venerated at other sites in Rome. Early graffiti from the third century in the cemetery zone *ad catacumbas* attest to his veneration: *Petre et Paule petite pro . . .* ("Peter and Paul, pray for . . ."). He was venerated in San Pietro in Vincoli, where his prison chains were preserved; in the *Domine quo vadis* church on the Via Appia (where Peter had been exhorted in a vision to remain in Rome); in the Mamertine prison, San Pietro (e Paolo), which has been identified since the fourteenth century as the place of Peter's imprisonment; in San Pietro in Montorio, the alleged site of his crucifixion; and at the grave of his daughter Petronilla, who features in the apocryphal *Acts*. The tomb of Peter in the Vatican has retained its dominant position. Important official papal acts have taken place here: since the time of Greogry the Great, the episcopal ordination of the newly elected pope and his ascent of the → cathedra have been held in St. Peter's. Gregory also rebuilt the choir apse of the Vatican basilica in such a way that the altar stood immediately above the tomb of Peter (→ St. Peter's). Below the altar, in the end wall of the elevated choir, there was a *fenestella,* an opening with a short shaft leading down to the tomb, permitting pilgrims to lower cloths: these soaked up sacred power, so to speak, and served as relics. Subterranean pathways below the elevated choir gave access to the tomb, where acts with an especially binding character took place: letters, oaths, donations, and contracts were deposited here. Boniface considered himself bound for the whole of his life by the episcopal oath which he had deposited alongside the body of Peter. The → pallium, which the popes have sent to archbishops since the seventh century, is kept in a niche beside St. Peter's tomb; this suggests that the archiepiscopal office depends on a Petrine-papal authorization. Anglo-Saxon kings traveled to Rome in the late seventh and early eighth centuries in order to be baptized and receive their burial places there; the name of Santo Spirito in Sassia recalls this practice, and the → Campo Santo Teutonico is the continuation of the Frankish cemetery. The *Constitutum Constantini* describes the Constantinian Donation as a gift to Peter which has been deposited at his tomb. Charlemagne considered himself under obligation to and for St. Peter, after he had confirmed Pippin's donation in a document addressed to the apostle and written beside his tomb on Easter Wednesday 774. The Roman liturgy which was imposed in his realm was the liturgy of St. Peter; some individual details such as the tonsure were regarded as Petrine. The veneration of Peter was strengthened by the interpretation of Peter as the heavenly porter, not just as an image, but as reality: he stood with his keys at the heavenly gates, which he opened only to those who were his friends (in Scandinavian graves, the hammer of Thor was replaced after christianization by Peter's keys). Relics made Peter present everywhere, whether cloths that had touched his tomb or relics of saints from the Roman catacombs (which have been requested up to modern times). These also strengthened the ties to the see of Peter, as the city of martyrs, and requests for these relics were often accompanied by the petition to be included in the "Family of St. Peter"; the most striking example is Cluny, which had relics of Peter and enjoyed papal exemption. A continuous stream of pilgrims visited Peter's tomb to ask for his intercession and the forgiveness of their sins. After the first → Holy Year was celebrated in 1300, those in search of grace increased in numbers—as did the indulgences that were granted.

■ **Bibliography:** *LMA* 6:1957f.; W. Levison, "Die Anfänge rheinischer Bistümer in der Legende," in idem, *Aus rheinischer und fränkischer Frühzeit* (Düsseldorf, 1948) 7-27; R. A. Aronstam, "Penitential Pilgrimages to Rome in the Early Middle Ages," *AHP* 13 (1975) 65-83; N. Gussone, *Thron und Inthronisation des Papstes von den Anfängen bis zum 12. Jahrhundert* (Bonn, 1978); E. Ewig, "Petrus- und Apostelkult im spätrömischen und fränkischen Gallien," in idem, *Spätantike und fränkisches Gallien* (Munich, 1979) 2:318-54; G. Tellenbach, *Die westliche Kirche vom 10. bis zum frühen 12. Jahrhundert* (Göttingen, 1988) 65-72; A. Angenendt, "Princeps imperii—Princeps apostolorum: Rom zwischen Universalismus und Gentilismus," and R. Schieffer, "Redeamus ad fontem: Rom als Ort authentischer Überlieferung," in Angenendt and Schieffer, *Roma—Caput et Fons: Zwei Vorträge über das päpstliche Rom zwischen Altertum und Mittelalter,* ed. Gemeinsame Kommission der Rheinisch-Westfälischen Akademie der Wissenschaften und der Gerda-Henkel-Schenkung (Cologne, 1989); K. Schatz, *Der päpstliche Primat*

(Würzburg, 1990); M. Maccarrone, "'Sedes Apostolica—Vicarius Petri': La perpetuità del primato di Pietro nella sede e nel vescovo di Roma (secoli III-VIII)," *Il primato del vescovo di Roma nel primo millennio* (Vatican City, 1991) 275-362; K. Ganzer, "Das Kirchenverständnis Gregors VII.," in idem, *Kirche auf dem Weg durch die Zeit,* ed. H. Smolinsky and J. Meier (Münster, 1997) 1-15.

ARNOLD ANGENENDT

4. *In the History of Liturgy*

Like the cult of the martyrs, the cult of the apostles was originally limited in geographical terms, linked to the tomb or some other local memorial. This is why the oldest calendars indicate only one or two feasts of apostles that were celebrated in more than one place. The oldest certain attestation of the celebration of a solemn liturgy in honor of Sts. Peter and Paul in Rome on June 29 is in the *Depositio martyrum* of the Roman → Chronography of 354: *III Kalendas Iulii Petri in Catacumbas et Pauli Ostiense Tusco et Basso consulibus* (i.e., in the year 258). The entry in the earliest text of the Martyrology of Jerome for the same day reads something like this: *Romae Petri et Pauli apostolorum, Petri in Vaticano, Pauli via Ostiensi utriusque in Catacumbas (Tusco et Basso consulibus?).* The thesis proposed by Louis Duchesne, Hans Lietzmann, and others, that June 29 is the date on which the bones of the two apostles were temporarily removed from their original resting places and brought for safety to the catacombs of St. Sebastian on the Via Appia, overlooks the improbability of a translation in the third century; the consular dating is more likely connected to the introduction of a festal celebration in honor of the apostles. Since the organization of the cult of the martyrs began in the mid-third century, we must suppose that a feast day for the princes of the apostles (whose date of death was unknown) was created in 258. The three places indicated for the festal celebration in the Martyrology of Jerome—the Vatican for Peter, the Via Ostiensis for Paul, and the catacombs for both apostles—agree with other testimonies about the celebration of the feast in these three sanctuaries on June 29. Manuscripts of the Martyrology of Jerome which are already influenced by the Old Gallican liturgy mention two feasts in honor of St. Peter, the celebrations of his "Chair" on January 18 and on February 22, while the *Depositio martyrum* mentions only one feast of the

cathedra Petri, on February 22. This is probably connected to the meal that was held in memory of the dead in Rome on that day (*cathedra* denotes here a meal at which the guests sat on chairs); ecclesiastical disapproval of such celebrations in honor of the dead led in the fourth century to a reinterpretation of the feast as the memorial of the day on which Peter ascended his chair in Rome (*cathedra* denotes here the chair on which Peter sat to teach, his magisterium), but this feast disappeared ca. 500. The existence of a feast, usually celebrated on January 18, in memory of Peter's vocation as holder of the keys and foundation of the church, is securely attested in Gaul from the sixth or seventh century. In the process of osmosis between the Frankish and the Roman liturgies, this feast too was accepted in Rome, though on the traditional date, that is, February 22. Because of a mistaken interpretation of the two dates, the feast on February 22 gradually came to be a celebration of the beginning of Peter's ministry in Antioch. In 1558, Paul IV designated January 18 as the memorial of the beginning of Peter's ministry in Rome. The feast of St. Peter's chains (August 1) was originally the consecration date of a church.

■ **Bibliography:** H. Delehaye, "Tusco et Basso cons.," in *Mélanges P. Thomas* (Bruges, 1930) 201ff.; idem, *Commentarius perpetuus in Martyrium Hieronymianum,* ed. H. Quentin (Brussels, 1931); D. Mallardo, *Il calendario marmoreo di Napoli* (Rome, 1947); E. Munding, *Die Kalendarien von Sankt Gallen,* 2 vols. (Beuron, 1951); K. Mohlberg, *Colligere Fragmenta* (Beuron, 1952) 52ff.; D. Balboni, *Ephemerides Liturgicae* 69 (1954) 97-126; J. Cercopino, *De Pythagore aux Apôtres* (Paris, 1956) 231-332; A. Adam, *Das Kirchenjahr mitfeiern* (6th ed. Freiburg, 1991).

WALTER DÜRIG

5. *Iconography*

The historical and cultic starting point for representations of Peter is the probable resting place of the apostle, the → tomb of Peter. The existence of the "trophy" can be demonstrated since the second third of the second century; graffiti go back to the early third century. Old → St. Peter's, begun ca. 320, was built above this site. The oldest portrait of Peter, as far as is known, is a mural in the house church of Dura-Europos (240/250) depicting his rescue from the waves by Jesus. After Mary, Peter is the figure among Jesus' associates who has been most frequently portrayed in the course of ecclesiastical and artistic history. The earliest portraits of Peter, from the third and fourth centuries, are not distinct from those of the other apostles; generally speaking, he wears a tunic and toga. Individual traits begin to emerge from the mid-fourth century. Peter and Paul often stand on either side of Christ the Pantocrator, symbolically representing the college of apostles as a whole or the church, especially in apse mosaics (Old St. Peter's; Santa Costanza, ca. 360; the catacomb of Domitilla, 350-400; Santa Pudenziana, ca. 410). The typical image of Peter that increasingly emerges, and has remained basically unchanged until the present day, is characterized by round head with curly hair (from the late Middle Ages, a curl falls over his forehead) and a round or square beard. His attributes are a scroll (later, a book); a cross held in his hand (later a cross with two transverse beams, mounted on a staff); two (sometimes three) crossed keys, a reference to the power of binding and loosing mentioned in Matt. 16:19; and from the fourteenth century onward, the → tiara and pontifical vestments. The cock (see Mark 14 par.) sometimes appears after the Renaissance; a few earlier instances are also known. The typical colors since the high Middle Ages are blue (the tunic) and yellow (the toga). The oldest representations of scenes depict the cock crowing, Peter's imprisonment, and the miracle of the spring of water (from the apocrypha—probably meant as a symbol of baptism); this trilogy is sometimes juxtaposed to a christological trilogy. The miracle of the spring is depicted on a sarcophagus dated between the third and fifth centuries. An extensive cycle of pictures of Peter, encompassing the entire tradition about him, is attested in the transept of Old St. Peter's in the late seventh century; it probably comprised twenty-seven scenes drawn from the Gospels, the Acts of the Apostles, and apocryphal sources. Sarcophagi depicting martyrdoms from the mid-fourth century onward often portray the passions of the two apostles, as well as the scene of the *traditio legis,* the handing over of the law (which has not yet found a completely satisfactory explanation); the oldest known example is the sarcophagus fragment in San Sebastiano, from ca. 370, and the *traditio legis* is also found in mosaics (San Clemente, San Teodoro, Santa Cecilia, etc.). There is a basically continuous tradition from late antiquity to the Middle Ages of depicting Christ surrounded by the apostles, led by Peter and Paul (cf. the Cappella Palatina in

Palermo and the cathedral in Monreale, both late twelfth century). Peter is first portrayed as heavenly porter in the mosaic on the triumphal arch of Santa Prassede (ca. 800). The transformation of the classical philosopher's statue at some unknown date into a statue of Peter, which was placed above the portico door of Old St. Peter's (now the Vatican grottoes), led to the seated figure of the apostle in bronze by Arnolfo da Cambio (ca. 1300, in St. Peter's). This new category, which displays the sovereignty of Peter, inspired artists for many centuries. Peter is usually portrayed face-on. This type is found as an individual or central statue in late-medieval winged altars. The earliest German example is Peter on his throne by the Master of Erminold (Regensburg, 1280/1290); a late Gothic example is the statue by Erasmus Grasser in St. Peter's, Munich (1490). This type is also found in Italian paintings, beginning with the Stefaneschi altar by Giotto (ca. 1320, in the Vatican). Important cycles and individual scenes from the Italian Renaissance are found in the Brancacci chapel in Florence (Masaccio, Masolino, Filippino Lippi, between 1426/1428 and 1487); see also Raphael's tapestries in the Sistine Chapel in the Vatican. Michelangelo's portrait of Peter in the Cappella Paolina in the Vatican (1546) sets the tone for the following period: see Caravaggio (Santa Maria del Popolo, ca. 1600) and Peter Paul Rubens (St. Peter's, Cologne, 1635/1640). In his *Last Judgment* (Sistine Chapel, 1536-1541), Michelangelo juxtaposes Peter with Moses, as does Rubens in his *Great Last Judgment* (1615/1616, now in the Alte Pinakothek in Munich). Among artists working in Germany, Konrad Witz (remnants of a Petrine cycle, Geneva 1454) and Jan Pollack (St. Peter's in Munich, 1490) deserve mention. In paintings of the dormition of Mary, especially in late Gothic Marian cycles, Peter holds the mortuary cross (e.g., in the painting by the Master of the life of Mary, Munich). After the Renaissance, individual themes from the Petrine iconography are singled out in paintings for altars and galleries. Albrecht Dürer's painting of the apostles (Munich, 1525/1526) is particularly important. The (apocryphal) farewell of the apostles is a favorite theme in ceiling frescoes and the reredoses of high altars in southern Germany and Austria. No original ideas for portraits of Peter have been registered in the nineteenth and twentieth centuries.

■ **Bibliography:** *EC* 9:720-24; *Lexikon der christlichen Ikonographie,* founded by E. Kirschbaum, ed. W. Braunfels (repr. Freiburg, 1990) 8:158-74; *LMA* 6:1956f.; K. Künstle, *Ikonographie der christlichen Kunst* (Freiburg, 1926) 2:493, 500; E. Dinkler, *Die ersten Petrusdarstellungen* (Marburg, 1939); J. Braun, *Tracht und Attribute der Heiligen in der Deutschen Kunst* (Stuttgart, 1943; 4th ed. Berlin, 1992) 590-600; F. Gerke, "Duces in militia Christi," *Kunstchronik* 7 (1954) 95-101; E. Mâle, *Les saints compagnons du Christ* (Paris, 1958) 87-123; L. Réau, *Iconographie de l'art chrétien* (Paris, 1959; repr. Millwood, N.Y., 1983) 3:1076-1100; C. Davis-Weyer, "Das Traditio-Legis-Bild und seine Nachfolge," *Münchener Jahrbücher der bildenden Kunst* 12 (1961) 7-45; A. Weis, "Ein Petruszyklus des 7. Jahrhunderts im Querschiff der vatikanischen Basilika," *RQ* 58 (1963) 230-270; A. Pigler, *Barockthemen* (Budapest, 1974) 393-401; C. K. Carr, *Aspects of the Iconography of Saint Peter in Medieval Art of Western Europe to the Thirteenth Century* (Cleveland, 1978); J. M. Huskinson, *Concordia apostolorum: Christian Propaganda at Rome in the 4th and 5th Centuries: A Study in Early Christian Iconography and Iconology* (Oxford, 1982); *Pierre et Rome: Vingt siècles d'élan créateur* (exhibition catalog, Paris and Milan, 1997).

LAURENTIUS KOCH

Philip, Pope (?) (July 31, 768). After the overthrow of Constantine II, the priest Philip, a monk in the monastery of St. Vitus in Rome, was made pope by the Langobard party under Waldipert and was enthroned in the Lateran basilica without receiving episcopal ordination. However, on the evening of the same day, a group of nobles under the *primicerius* Christopher brought him back to his monastery. It is difficult to decide whether Philip ought to be considered a pope or an antipope.

■ **Sources:** *LP* 1:470f.; *RPR(J)* 1:284.
■ **Bibliography:** *VATL* 580f.

MANFRED HEIM

Pius I (142?-155?). Saint (feast day July 11), probably not a martyr. In the list of succession presented by Irenaeus (*Adversus haereses* 3.3.3), he is the ninth successor of Peter, between Hyginus and Anicetus. Since it was only under Anicetus that the government of the Roman church finally took the form of a monarchical episcopate, Pius was presumably a leading member of the college of priests or bishops. According to the Muratorian Fragment (2.73-77), he was the brother of Hermas. During this period, the heretics Marcion, Cerdo, and Valentinus came to Rome, as did Justin, the "philosopher and martyr."

■ **Bibliography:** *CATH* 11:251; *BBKL* 7:658f.; *VATL* 583; J. Hofmann, "Die amtliche Stellung der in der ältesten römischen Bischofsliste überlieferten Männer in der Kirche von Rom," *Historisches Jahrbuch* 109 (1989) 1-23; N. Brox, *Der Hirt des Hermas* (Göttingen, 1991); R. Minnerath, "La position de l'église de Rome aux trois premiers siècles," in M. Maccarrone, ed., *Il primato del vescovo di Roma nel primo millennio* (Rome, 1991) 139-71; R. M. Hübner, "Heis theos Iêsous Khristos: Zum christlichen Gottesglauben im 2. Jahrhundert," *Münchener theologische Zeitschrift* 47 (1996) 325-44; M. Molaroni, "Pio I e Pio II, fortuita coincidenza di un nome?" *Studi e materiali di storia delle religioni* 65 (1999) 199-218.

GEORG SCHWAIGER

Pius II (Aug. 18, 1458-Aug. 14, 1464). Formerly *Enea Silvio de' Piccolomini,* an important humanist; born Oct. 18, 1405, at Corsignano near Siena into an impoverished noble family, died at Ancona (tomb initially in St. Peter's, in Sant'Andrea della Valle since 1614). He studied law in Siena under Antonio Roselli and Mariano de' Sozzi, acquiring at the same time a profound education in letters, with Filelfo in Florence as one of his teachers. He took part in the Council of Basel in 1432 as a member of the suite of Cardinal Domenico Capranica, where he belonged to a curial group with ties of friendship to Germany. He occupied the office of *scriptor* and carried out legations to Arras and Scotland. He defended the conciliarist line and was one of those who elected Felix V in 1439, becoming his secretary in 1440. He was crowned as poet by King Frederick III at the imperial diet in Frankfurt in 1442 and joined the royal chancellery in 1443. Here he had a career both as diplomat (embassies to Eugene IV, accepting obedience to him, 1445-1447, etc.) and as poet. He became "the leading figure of the humanist movement" in central Europe (Paul Weinig). He was ordained priest and became bishop of Trieste in 1447 and of Siena in 1450. He prepared the marriage and imperial coronation of Frederick III between 1450 and 1452, and played a decisive role at the three imperial diets that examined the Turkish question (1454-1455). In summer 1455, he returned definitively to Italy, where he was created cardinal in 1456 and elected pope (coronation on September 3, 1458). His papal name is a literary allusion to Virgil's *pius Aeneas.*

This turning point in his life had little effect on his activity or his character.

The idea of a European crusade against the Turks runs like a missionary leitmotif through Pius's years as pope. The poorly attended congress of princes at Mantua in 1459, and the subsequent refusal of the princes to act, disappointed the papal hopes. The period of the Western Schism had made the pope more dependent on the → papal states and Italian territorial politics, and he exploited the available possibilities in the relationships between the states (the "pentarchy"), e.g., in the struggle against the Malatesta dynasty. He sought a rapprochement with Naples already in 1458, and acknowledged Ferrante as king; from then on, his policies were marked by closeness to Naples-Aragon and to Milan under the Sforzas, by coolness vis-à-vis Venice and Florence, and by hostility to France (since the house of Anjou claimed the throne of Naples). He succeeded only partly in holding on to papal supremacy; the bull *Execrabilis* (January 1460) forbade appeals from the pope to a council, and Louis XI abrogated the Pragmatic Sanction in 1461. Conflicts with imperial princes whom Pius excommunicated (Diether von Isenburg, archbishop of Mainz; Duke Sigismund of Tirol with his procurator, Gregor von Heimburg) and with the Bohemian king Gregory of Poděbrad (abrogation of the Compact Acts of Prague, 1462) came to a head in a crisis that harmed the prestige of the curia in Germany.

Pius did not succeed in reforming the curia. His conduct of office was not brilliant, but he consciously chose his priorities in the spirit of the Renaissance, with his pontificate as his "work of art," and his speeches were outstanding. He changed the name of his birthplace to "Pienza" and developed it into the first model city. He was one of the most highly educated and most colorful of all the popes. He died after having spent the last of his strength on building up a fleet of ships for the crusade.

He produced work that is exceptionally versatile and vital. The large number of manuscripts, printed versions, and translations attest to the wide readership Pius II found. This applies especially to his letters, poems, discourses and educational treatises, the short story *Eurialus and Lucretia,* and the satire *De curialium miseriis.* He is the founder of source-critical local history (*Historia Bohemica, Historia Austrialis*). His *Commentarii* (1460-1463) remain unparalleled both as an individual picture of his age and as a papal self-portrait. Although he was not given to speculation, many of his works discuss theological themes, e.g., his writings on the Council of Basel, the puzzling *Epistula ad Mahometem* on the conversion to Christianity of the Turkish sultan, *Germania* with its defense of the curia (1458), the disputation *De sanguine Christi,* prayers he composed, and the great bull against the Turks (*Ezechielis,* October 22, 1463) and the bulls of excommunication.

■ **Sources:** *Opera* (Basel, 1551; repr. 1967); I. D. Mansi, ed., *Pii II P.M. orationes...*, 3 vols. (Lucca, 1755-59); R. Wolkan, ed., *Der Briefwechsel des Eneas Silvius Piccolomini,* 4 parts, Fontes rerum Austriacarum 61-62, 67-68 (Vienna, 1909-18); D. Hay and W. K. Smith, eds., *De gestis concilii Basiliensis* (2nd ed. Oxford, 1992); A. van Heck, ed., *De viris illustribus* (Vatican City, 1991); idem, ed., *Carmina* (Vatican City, 1994); idem, ed., *Commentarii* (Vatican City, 1994; other editions: F. Totaro, ed. [Rome, 1984]; I. Bellus and I. Boronkai, eds. [Budapest, 1993-94]). *Biographies:* L. A. Muratori, *Rerum Italicarum scriptores ab anno aerae christianae 500 ad 1500* (Milan, 1724) 3:967-92.

■ **Bibliography:** *Die deutsche Literatur des Mittelalters: Verfasserlexikon* (2nd ed. Berlin, 1989) 7:634-69; *CATH* 11:251ff.; *LMA* 6:2190ff.; *BBKL* 7:659ff.; *TRE* 26:649-52; *Repertorium Germanicum,* ed. Deutsches Historisches Institut in Rome (Berlin/Tübingen, 1993) VIII; G. Voigt, *Enea Silvio de' Piccolomini als Papst,* 3 vols. (Berlin, 1856-63; repr. 1967); D. Maffei, ed., *Enea Silvio Piccolomini Papa Pio II* (Siena, 1968); Pastor XXIII-XXIV; D. Brosius, "Die Pfründen des Enea Silvio Piccolomini," *QFIAB* 54 (1974) 271-327; idem, "Breven und Bullen Pius' II.," *RQ* 70 (1975) 180-224; idem, "Das Itinerar Papst Pius' II.," *Mitteilungen des Instituts für Österreichische Geschichtsforschung* 55/56 (1976) 421-32; K.-M. Setton, *The Papacy and the Levant* (Philadelphia, 1978) 2:196-270; A. Esch, *Enea Silvio Piccolomini als Papst Pius: Lebenslehren und Weltenwürfe...,* ed. H. Boockmann et al. (Göttingen, 1989) 112-40; Borgolte 272f., 276-81; L. Rotondi Secchi Tarugi, ed., *Pio II e la Cultura del suo tempo* (Milan, 1991); J. Helmrath, "Die Reichstagsreden des Enea Silvio Piccolomini" (dissertation, Cologne, 1994); E. Meuthen, "Ein 'deutscher' Freundeskreis an der römischen Kurie," *AHC* 27/28 (1995/96) 487-542, esp. 498f., 508-14; A. Tönnesmann, *Pienza* (2nd ed. Munich, 1996); C. Märtl, *Kardinal Jean Jouffroy (†1473)* (Sigmaringen, 1996); L. Schmugge et al., *Die Supplikenregister der päpstlichen Pönitentiarie aus der Zeit Pius' II.* (Tübingen, 1996); P. J. Weinig, *Aeneam suscipite, Pium recipite: Die Rezeption eines humanistischen Schriftstellers im Deutschland des 15. und 16. Jahrhunderts* (Wiesbaden, 1998); M. Molaroni, "Pio I e Pio

II, fortuita coincidenza di nome?" *Studi e materiali di storia delle religioni* 65 (1999) 199-218; B. Neidiger, "Papst Pius II. und die Klosterreform im Deutschland," *Vita religiosa im Mittelalter,* Festschrift for K. Elm (Berlin, 1999) 629-52.

JOHANNES HELMRATH

Pius III (Sept. 29-Oct. 18, 1503). Formerly *Francesco de' Piccolomini Todeschini,* born in 1439 at Sarteano near Siena. After his studies in Perugia, his uncle, Pius II, appointed him bishop of Siena and cardinal in 1460. He also held the see of Pienza from 1495 to 1498. He was cardinal protector of the German nation and attended the "great diet of Christians" as papal legate in Regensburg in 1471. When King Charles VIII of France invaded Italy in 1494, he was sent as envoy to negotiate with him. He was the only cardinal who protested when Alexander VI expropriated territory belonging to the church state and bestowed it on his son Juan. As a cardinal, Pius was a generous benefactor of artists and scholars. He was already severely ill with gout when he was elected pope. His bones were translated to Sant'Andrea della Valle along with those of his uncle in 1614.

■ **Bibliography:** *DTHC* 12:1632f.; *CATH* 11:253; *BBKL* 7:661-64; *VATL* 586; Pastor III/2:659-78; E. Piccolomini, "La famiglia di Pio III," *Archivio della Società Romana di Storia Patria* 26 (1903) 146-64; idem, "Il pontificato di Pio III," *Archivio storico italiano* 32 (1903) 102-38; J. Schlecht, *Pius III. und die deutsche Nation* (Munich, 1914); A. A. Strnad, "F. Todeschini-Piccolomini: Politik und Mäzenatentum im Quattrocento," *Römische Historische Mitteilungen* 8/9 (1964/65-1965/66) 101-423; idem, "Pius III. und Österreich," *Theologisch-praktische Quartalschrift* 116 (1968) 175-89.

KLAUS GANZER

Pius IV (Dec. 25, 1559-Dec. 9, 1565). Formerly *Gian Angelo de' Medici* (not related to the Medici of Florence), born Mar. 31, 1499, in Milan. After studies in medicine and jurisprudence, he came to Rome in 1526 and held various offices in the church state. In 1542-1543, he was apostolic commissioner to the troops whom Paul III sent against the Turks, and his career began to prosper under this pope. He received major orders when he was appointed archbishop of Ragusa in 1545. He was general commissioner to the papal auxiliary troops in the Schmalkaldic war in Germany. He was created cardinal in 1549, but had no important offices during this period, since he did not

sympathize with Paul IV's desire for reform. He was elected in the difficult conclave in 1559 as a candidate of last resort, and he immediately changed the political course, endeavoring to establish good relations with Emperor Ferdinand I and King Philip II of Spain. Within the church, he toned down the harsh measures taken by Paul IV; for example, he rehabilitated Cardinal Giovanni Morone. He pronounced sentence on the two nephews of Paul IV, who were executed; he himself, however, showered favors on a large number of his relatives. His favorite nephew, Charles Borromeo, was created cardinal and administrator of the archdiocese of Milan in 1560, receiving the post of secretary of state. He honored the obligation he had accepted in his electoral capitulation, and after overcoming numerous political difficulties, summoned the council to meet at Trent again. It opened on January 18, 1562. When the controversies about the residential obligation of bishops, the papal → primacy, and the character of the episcopal office almost led to the collapse of the council, he appointed Morone its president. Thanks to Morone's skill, it proved possible to bring the council to a positive conclusion on December 3/4, 1563. Pius confirmed the decrees of the council as a whole by word of mouth on January 26, 1564, and in a solemn manner by the decree *Benedictus Deus* on June 30, 1564. He published the → Index of Forbidden Books in March 1564 and the Tridentine Profession of Faith in November 1564, after he had reorganized the → Rota, the → Apostolic Penitentiary, and the → Apostolic Chamber. Under pressure from Emperor Maximilian II and the Bavarian dukes, Pius gave permission in 1564 for communion to be administered under both kinds in Germany, Austria, Bohemia, and Hungary. He promoted the arts and sciences. Discontent among the populace in the church state (→ Papal States) led to an unsuccessful conspiracy.

Pius was a transitional figure. Although he was personally marked by the Renaissance mentality—he had several illegitimate children before becoming pope—he could not close his eyes to the necessity of reforming the church. At the same time, he sought to save as much as possible of the old structures of the Roman curia.

■ **Sources:** *Concilium Tridentinum: Diariorum, Actorum, Epistularum, Tractatuum nova Collectio,* ed. Görres-

Gesellschaft, 13 vols. (Freiburg, 1901-2001); *NBD*(G) 2:1-4.

■ **Bibliography:** *DTHC* 12/2:1633-47; *EC* 9:1496; *CATH* 11:253f.; *BBKL* 7:665; *TRE* 26:652-55; *VATL* 589ff.; T. von Sickel, *Zur Geschichte des Konzils von Trient* (Vienna, 1872); Pastor VII; J. Susta, *Die römische Kurie und das Concil von Trient unter Pius IV.,* 4 vols. (Vienna, 1904-14); F. Häfele, "Papst Pius IV. und seine Nepoten," *Vierteljahresschrift für Geschichte und Landeskunde Vorarlbergs* 5 (1921) fascicle 1; M. Constant, *Concession à l'Allemagne de la Communion sous les deux espèces,* 2 vols. (Paris, 1923); P. Paschini, *Il primo soggiorno di S. Carlo Borromeo a Roma* (Rome, 1935); H. Jedin, *Krisis und Wendepunkt des Trienter Konzils (1562/63)* (Würzburg, 1941); idem, *Geschichte des Konzils von Trient* (Freiburg, 1976) IV/1-2; R. Rezzaghi, "Cronaca di un conclave: L'elevazione di Pio IV," *Salesianum* 48 (1986) 539-81; K. Ganzer, "Das Konzil von Trient—Angelpunkt für eine Reform der Kirche?," *RQ* 84 (1989) 31-50; idem, "Aspekte der katholischen Reformbewegungen im 16. Jahrhundert," *Abhandlungen der geistes- und sozialwissenschaftlichen Klasse der Akademie der Wissenschaften und der Literatur in Mainz* (Wiesbaden, 1991) n. 13.

KLAUS GANZER

Pius V (Jan. 7, 1566-May 1, 1572). Saint (feast day Apr. 30), Dominican (from 1518). Formerly *Michele Ghislieri*, born Jan. 17, 1504, in Bosco near Alessandria. After studies in Genoa, he was ordained priest in 1528 and taught philosophy and theology in Pavia. As inquisitor of the diocese of Como, he came to the appreciative notice of Giampietro Carafa (later Paul IV); under Julius III, he became general commissioner of the Inquisition in Rome. He was appointed bishop of Sutri and Nepi in 1556 and created cardinal in 1557. He was appointed Grand Inquisitor of the Roman church in 1558, and bishop of Mondovì in 1560. Charles Borromeo played the decisive role in his election as pope. Pius entrusted the most important curial offices to men of the school of Paul IV. His twenty-five-year-old great nephew, the Dominican Michele Bonelli, became Cardinal Nephew. The Council of Trent had left a number of tasks to be completed by the pope: the Roman Catechism was published in 1566, the Roman Breviary in 1568, and the Roman Missal in 1570. The → Apostolic Penitentiary was reorganized and its authority limited to the *forum internum*. Pius insisted on the clergy's residential obligation and promoted the foundation of seminaries. He was especially zealous for the Inquisition—every tendency to deviate from the faith was to be pursued with the strictest measures, and numerous persons were condemned to death. Pius proposed to take up afresh the inquisitial investigation of Cardinal Giovanni Morone, whom Pius IV had rehabilitated. In the so-called controversy about grace, Pius condemned seventy-six propositions of Michael Bajus and his adherents. In France, where Calvinism was spreading, Pius aimed to destroy the Huguenots completely, and he objected to the Peace of San Germano (1570). In the case of England, he resolved to act resolutely against Elizabeth I, and he declared her guilty of heresy in the bull *Regnans in excelsis* (February 2, 1570). This meant that she was excommunicated and lost her right to the English throne; her subjects were freed from their oath of loyalty to her. This, the very last sentence of deposition pronounced by a pope against a ruler, was a grave mistake, which made the situation of the English Catholics worse. Pius was dissuaded from making a formal protest against the Peace of Augsburg (1555). The development of much stronger royal control of the church in Spain put a strain on relations between Pius and Philip II, but the pope succeeded in realizing the Holy League between Spain and Venice against the Turks. After the victory of the armada under Don John of Austria in the gulf of Lepanto on October 7, 1571, Pius established the feast of Our Lady of Victories (later renamed the feast of the rosary).

Pius was completely uninterested in classical art, and the cardinals had great difficulty in dissuading him from getting rid of the precious antiquities ("pagan images of the gods") which belonged to the papacy. He supported new editions of the works of Bonaventure and Thomas Aquinas. Pius was a man of great religious zeal and ascetic strictness, whose overriding priority was always the reform of the church. His narrowness of spirit made him the embodiment of the intransigent Catholic reformer of the sixteenth century, a man with no understanding of the kind of religious intellectual attitude, inspired by humanism, that one finds in such figures as Gasparo Contarini and Reginald Pole.

■ **Sources:** *Biographies:* G. Catena, *Vita del gloriosissimo papa Pio V* (Rome, 1582, often reprinted); J. A. Gabuzzi, *De vita et rebus gestis Pii V P.M. libri VI* (Rome, 1605); F. Goubeau, ed., *Epp. Apostolicae* (Antwerp, 1640); W. E.

Schwarz, *Der Briefwechsel Maximilians II. mit Pius V.* (Paderborn, 1889); L. Serrano, *Correspondencia diplomatica entre España, Venecia y la Santa Sede durante el pontificado de S. Pio V,* 4 vols. (Madrid, 1914); *NBD*(G) 2:5-7.

■ **Bibliography:** *DTHC* 12:1647-53; *EC* 9:1498ff.; *CATH* 11:255-58; *BBKL* 7:665ff.; *TRE* 26:655-59; *VATL* 580ff.; B. Hilliger, *Die Wahl Pius' V. zum Papste* (Leipzig, 1891); L. Serrano, *La Liga de Lepanto entre España, Venecia y la Santa Sede (1570-73),* 2 vols. (Madrid, 1918-20); C. Hirschauer, *La politique de S. Pie V en France (1566-72)* (Paris, 1926); B. de Meester, *Le Saint-Siège et les troubles des Pays-Bas 1566-70* (Louvain, 1934); L. Browne-Oll, *The Sword of St. Michael: St. Pius V* (Milwaukee, 1943); E. van Eijl, "Les censures des universités d'Alcalà et de Salamanque et la censure du Pape Pie V contre Michel Baius (1565-67)," *Revue d'histoire ecclésiastique* 48 (1953) 719-76; idem, "L'interprétation de la bulle de Pie V portant condamnation de Baius," *Revue d'histoire ecclésiastique* 50 (1955) 499-542; G. Grente, *Le pape des grands combats, S. Pie V* (2nd ed. Paris, 1956); K. M. Setton, *The Papacy and the Levant* (Philadelphia, 1984) IV; A. d'Andigne, "Saint Pie V et la victoire de Lépante," *Pensée catholique* 248 (1990) 74-86; E. García Hernán, "Pio V y el Mesianismo profetico," *Hispania sacra* 45 (1993) 83-102; N. Lemaitre, *Saint Pie V* (Paris, 1994).

KLAUS GANZER

Pius VI (Feb. 15, 1775-Aug. 29, 1799). Formerly count *Giovanni Angelo Braschi,* born Dec. 25, 1717, in Cesena. After legal studies in Ferrara, he entered the service of the cardinal legate Tommaso Ruffo. He was ordained priest in 1758 and became an apostolic chamberlain in 1766. He was elected pope as the candidate of the → *zelanti;* he received episcopal ordination on February 21, 1775, and was enthroned on the following day. His pontificate was one of the longest in church history. Its beginning was overshadowed by the controversies about the Jesuit order. The revocation by Johann Nikolaus von Hontheim in 1778 meant a partial success in the question of Febronianism; but even a journey by Pius in person to Vienna in 1782 could not alter Emperor Joseph II's zeal for reforming the state church. Elector Karl Theodore of Palatinate-Bavaria gave the pope a friendly welcome in Munich, as did Clemens Wenzeslaus in Augsburg.

The Emser congress, held in 1786 as a result of the controversy around the nunciature in Munich, gave expression to the episcopalist endeavors of the German archbishops. The French Revolution displaced these questions from the agenda. The bull *Auctorem fidei* (August 28, 1794) condemned the errors of the synod of Pistoia (1786), but political considerations led Pius to wait until 1791 before he condemned the French Revolution itself, the civil constitution of the clergy and the constitutional church, in the Briefs *Quod aliquantum* (March 10) and *Caritas* (April 13). His participation in the first coalition against Napoleon ultimately led, in the Peace of Tolentino (February 19, 1797) to the loss of Avignon, Venaissin, Ferrara, Bologna, and later Ancona. He was also obliged to pay large sums of money in reparation and to hand over valuable works of art. Repeated disturbances in Rome, and events such as the shooting of the French general Duphot on December 28, 1797, led to the occupation of Rome and the church state by the French. The proclamation of the Roman republic on February 15, 1798, put an end for the time being to the existence of the church state (→ Papal States). Pius was arrested and brought first to Siena and Florence, then to Briançon, and finally to Valence, where he died. His body was returned to Rome only in February 1802; the sculptor Antonio Canova created his tomb.

The pontificate of Pius, which saw the return of → nepotism on a large scale, was marked by great building projects in Rome and the church states. The sacristy of St. Peter's was built, the Museo Pio-Clementino (→ Vatican Museums) was finished, and a part of the Pontine marshes was drained. Pius had already issued emergency regulations for the next papal election on November 13, 1798. He was a man of high culture, pleasant and dignified, but he lacked breadth of political vision and strength of will.

■ **Bibliography:** *CATH* 11:258-61; *BBKL* 7:667-70; *VATL* 591-93; A. Latreille, *L'Église catholique et la révolution française,* 2 vols. (Paris, 1946-50); E. Piscitelli, *La riforma di Pio VI e gli scrittori economici Romani* (Milan, 1958); G. Schwaiger, "Pius VI. in München," *Münchener theologische Zeitschrift* 10 (1959) 123-56; E. Kovacs, *Der Pabst in Teutschland* (Vienna, 1983); J. Gelmi, *Die Päpste in Lebensbildern* (Graz, 1989) 243-47; D. Menozzi, ed., *La chiesa italiana e la rivoluzione francese* (Bologna, 1990); P. Blet, "Pie VI et la Révolution française," in O. de la Brosse, ed., *La France et le Saint-Siège* (Rome, 1995) 215-40; P. Stella, *La bolla "Auctorem fidei" nella storia dell'ultramontanismo* (Rome, 1995); C. Semeraro, "Bibliothece papali tra rivoluzione e restaurazione (1775-1823)," *Super fundamenta apostolorum,* Festschrift for A. M. Javier Ortas (Rome, 1997) 273-313;

B. Plongeron, "La silence de la papauté devant la Révolution française," *Papes et papauté au XVIIIᵉ siècle* (Paris, 1999) 299-317.

JOSEF GELMI

Pius VII (Mar. 14, 1800-Aug. 20, 1823). A Benedictine (from 1756). Formerly *Barnaba Chiaramonti* (religious name: *Gregorio*), born Aug. 14, 1742, in Cesena in the Romagna; ordained priest in 1765. He was professor of theology in Parma from 1766 to 1775, and in Rome from 1775 to 1782. He was open to modern culture and supported reform. He became bishop of Tivoli in 1782, and bishop of Imola and cardinal in 1785. During the "three Jacobin years," he elaborated a modern program covering the relationship between the political power and Christian requirements, a reorganization of civil society, and the possibilities of adopting the values proclaimed by the French Revolution and giving these a Christian interpretation (see his homily at Christmas 1797 on "the church and democracy"). After a conclave lasting four months, he was elected pope as a compromise candidate and entered Rome on July 3, 1800. His priorities were doctrine and pastoral work, and he was well able to distinguish between the spiritual concerns of the church and political problems. He refused to appoint as secretary of state a cardinal who was wholly subservient to Austria, choosing instead Ercole Consalvi, a conservative reformer who knew when to be firm and when to yield. Resistance on the part of the reactionary majority in the curia prevented the necessary rejuvenation of the institutions in the church state (→ Papal States). Pius soon succeeded in regulating the ecclesiastical-religious situation in France. Although most of the College of → Cardinals expressed great reservations, he made important concessions in the concordat that he concluded with Napoleon I in 1801, thereby ensuring significant privileges for the French church. By demanding the resignation of all the French bishops of the "ancien régime," he increased awareness of the papal primacy. He was, however, unable to prevent Napoleon from promulgating the "Organic articles" without any prior consultation of Rome. Pius concluded a similar concordat with the Italian republic in 1803. He attempted in vain to reorganize the ecclesiastical structures in Germany after secularization. Despite all his reservations, Pius went to Paris for Napoleon's coronation as emperor in 1804; he hoped to achieve concessions vis-à-vis the church states and the abolition of the "Organic articles," but he had little success. When Pius declined to take part in France's continental blockade against England, Napoleon occupied Rome on February 2, 1808, and united the remnant of the church state with France on May 17, 1809. Pius replied by excommunicating the "man who has stolen the Patrimony of Peter" (June 10, 1809). He was taken to Savona, where he remained until 1812, then to Fontainebleau, where he was separated from all his advisers. After Napoleon's fall, Pius returned to Rome on May 25, 1814.

Pius had won moral authority for himself through his resistance to Napoleon, and he made good use of this in the following period of restoration. The Vienna Congress fully reestablished the papal state. Consalvi reorganized the church state, but his isolation within the reactionary curia prevented him from carrying out necessary reforms. Pius conducted the ecclesiastical restoration in Europe in a flexible spirit, but also was guided by the conviction that it was necessary to oppose the rationalist tendencies of the Enlightenment. He renewed the condemnation of the Freemasons in a bull issued on September 21, 1821; and the Protestant origin of the Biblical Societies led to the suspicion that they were propagating indifferentism. Pius endeavored to give new impetus to the spiritual life of the people through missions in the parishes, days of recollection for the clergy, the encouragement of confraternities and pilgrimages, an increase in the number of Marian feasts, and the resumption of canonization processes. His character was conciliatory, and he concentrated on essential matters. Despite his respect for tradition, he was able to accept a number of modern movements. In church politics, he largely followed the line represented by Consalvi, but he was open to other influences, where he held that this was demanded by the interests of the church. He negotiated a number of concordats with German and Italian states; an agreement about Poland was signed with Russia, and discussions were held with the Swiss confederation. After initial hestiations, he recognized the newly independent states in Latin America.

In summary, it can be said that Pius led the Catholic Church—which was threatened with collapse at the beginning of his pontificate—along a path of renewal.

■ **Sources:** Barbieri, ed., *Bullarium Romanum, Continuatio XI-XV* (Rome, 1846-53); A. Mercati, *Raccolta di Concordati* (2nd ed. Rome, 1954) 1:561-88; *Documenti relativi alle contestazioni insorte fra la S. Sede ed il governo francese*, 6 vols. (Rome, 1833-34); E. Consalvi, *Memorie* (Rome, 1951); B. Pacca, *Memorie*, 3 vols. (Rome, 1830).

■ **Bibliography:** *General accounts:* DTHC 12:1670-83; EC 9:1504-8; CATH 11:261-68; TRE 26:659ff.; BBKL 7:670-73; VATL 593f.; C. Wunderlich, *Der Pontifikat Pius' VII. in der Beurteilung der deutschen Mitwelt* (Leipzig, 1913); H. de Mayol de Lupé, *La captivité de Pie VII*, 2 vols. (2nd ed. Paris, 1916); E. Hocks, *Napoleon und Pius VII* (Freiburg, 1949); P. Bastgen and H. Tüchle, "Pius VII und Consalvi: Zur Geschichte des Konklaves in Venedig," *Historisches Jahrbuch* 79 (1960) 146-74; L. Pásztor, "Ercole Consalvi, prosegretario del conclave di Venezia," *Archivio della Società Romana di Storia Patria* 83 (1960) 99-187; idem, "Le 'Memorie sul Conclave tenuto in Venezia' di Ercole Consalvi," *AHP* 3 (1965) 239-308; L. Dal Pane, "Le riforme economiche di Pio VII," *Studi Romagnoli* 16 (1965) 257-76.

Individual questions: A. Roveri, *La Missione Consalvi e il Congresso di Vienna*, 3 vols. (Rome, 1970-73); idem, *La S. Sede tra Rivoluzione e Restaurazione: Il cardinale Consalvi 1813-15* (Florence, 1975); *Atti del Convegno di storia del Risorgimento: Pio VII e il cardinale Consalvi, un tentativo di riforma nello Stato Pontificio* (Viterbo, 1981); M. Chappin, *Pie VII et les Pays-Bas* (Rome, 1984); M. M. O'Dwyer, *The Papacy in the Age of Napoleon and the Restoration: Pius VII, 1800-23* (Lanham, 1985); I. Spada, *La Rivoluzione francese e il papa* (Bologna, 1989); C. Semeraro, "Bibliothece papali tra rivoluzione e restaurazione (1775-1823)," *Super fundamentum apostolorum*, Festschrift for A. M. Javier Ortas (Rome, 1997) 273-313; *Roma fra la Restaurazione e l'elezione di Pio IX* (Rome, 1997); A. de la Hera, "La Iglesia y la emancipación iberoamericana," in Gedenkschrift for W. Schulz (Frankfurt a.M., 1999) 173-90; L. F. Maschietto, "Relazione del conclave tenito in S. Giorgio Maggiore di Venezia, 14 marzo 1800," *Benedictina* 47 (2000) 91-137.

ROGER AUBERT

Pius VIII (Mar. 31, 1829-Nov. 30, 1830). Formerly *Francesco Saverio Castiglioni*, born Nov. 20, 1761, in Cingoli (Ancona). After studies, primarily in canon law, at Bologna, he was ordained priest in 1785. He was appointed bishop of Montalto in 1800 and was imprisoned by Napoleon I in 1808 when he refused to swear an oath of allegiance. In 1816, he was appointed cardinal and bishop of Cesena; in 1821, he was made Peniten-

tiary and bishop of Frascati, and became prefect of the Congregation of the Index in 1822. He belonged to the party of the → *zelanti*, but he was a learned man, much appreciated by Ercole Consalvi and Pius VII. In the conclave of 1823, he was the main rival to Leo XII. He was already ill when he was elected in 1829, as the candidate of the moderate party. In the administration of the → papal states, he lessened the harshness of the police and introduced measures to promote economic and social renewal, but he was not open to the problems of the modern world in the aftermath of the French Revolution. In general, he left politics to his secretary of state, Giuseppe Albani. He recognized Louis-Philippe as king of France immediately after the revolution of July 1830. He set up an archiepiscopal see in Constantinople for the Uniate Armenians.

■ **Sources:** Barbieri, ed. *Bullarium Romanum, Continuatio XVIII* (Rome, 1856).

■ **Bibliography:** DTHC 12:1683-86; CATH 11:268-71; BBKL 7:673-77; VATL 594f.; C. Vidal, "La Monarchie de Juillet et le Saint-Siège au lendemain de la Révolution de 1830," *Revue d'histoire diplomatique* 46 (1932) 497-517; R. Moscati, "Il governo napoletano e il conclave di Pio VIII," *Rassegna storica del Risorgimento* 20 (1933) 257-74; G. Malazampa, *Una gloria delle Marche, Pio VIII* (Alba, 1933); Schmidlin 1:474-510; E. Vercesi, *Tre pontificati* (Turin, 1936) 115-80; P. de Leturia, "Pio VIII y la independencia Hispanoamericana," *Saggi storici intorno al papato* (Rome, 1959) 387-400; R. Colapietra, "Il diario Brunelli del Conclave del 1823," *Archivio storico italiano* 120 (1962) 76-146; idem, "Il diario Brunelli del Conclave del 1829," *Critica storica* 1 (1962) 517-41, 636-61; O. Fusi-Pecci, *La vita di Pio VIII* (Rome, 1965); A. Pennacchioni, *Il papa Pio VIII Francesco Castiglioni* (Cingoli, 1994); S. Bernardi, ed., *La religione e il trono: Pio VIII nell'Europa del suo tempo, Convegno di studi, Cingoli, 1993* (Rome, 1995).

ROGER AUBERT

Pius IX (June 16, 1846-Feb. 7, 1878). Blessed (feast day Feb. 7). Formerly *Giovanni Maria Mastai-Feretti*, born May 13, 1792, in Senigallia, into a family of the landed aristocracy who were open to modern ideas. He studied at the college of the Piarists in Volterra from 1802 to 1809, then at home from 1809 to 1814 because of an epileptic illness. Although he recovered, he retained a great irascibility all his life. He was in Rome from 1814, where he came under the influence of spiritual reformers among the Roman clergy (Vincent Pallotti, Gaspare del Bufalo); although his theological studies were insufficient, he was ordained to the priesthood in 1819. He was auditor on a papal legation to Chile from 1823 to 1825, and became president of the Hospice of San Michele in Rome in 1825. He was appointed archbishop of Spoleto in 1827 and bishop of Imola in 1832. He was a vigorous pastor and acquired the unjustified reputation of being a liberal, because he called for administrative reforms in the church state (→ Papal States) and displayed sympathies with representatives of Neo-Guelphism. He was created cardinal in 1840 and was elected pope in a brief conclave in 1846; his main rival was Luigi Lambruschini.

Pius at once gained great popularity through limited concessions, but the myth of the "liberal pope" soon lost all its substance as it became clear that Pius refused to transform the Patrimony of Peter into a modern constitutional state and to join in the Italian war of independence against Austria, which he saw as incompatible with his role as father of all the faithful (discourse of April 29, 1848). Finally, the economic crisis of the church state and Pius's lack of political skills led to a crisis, and the pope had to flee from a revolt on November 24, 1848. He remained in Gaeta while the republic was proclaimed in Rome. With the help of a French expeditionary corps and the support of the European powers, he was able to return to Rome on April 12, 1850. The ensuing political restoration under the leadership of the secretary of state, Giacomo Antonelli, brought administrative improvements, but the intelligentsia were embittered toward a regime that granted its citizens no political freedom. Camillo Benso Cavour easily exploited this situation to the advantage of his plans for Italian unification. After the annexation of the Romagna in March 1860 and the Marches and Umbria after the defeat of Castelfidardo in September of the same year, the pope did succeed for another ten years in holding on to Rome and the surrounding areas with French support, but in the end, the war between Germany and France gave the Italian troops the opportunity to occupy Rome on September 20, 1870. Pius, who felt that his responsibilities vis-à-vis all Catholics obliged him to defend the church state, refused to accept the fait accompli, rejecting the law of guarantees which Italy offered him. From now on, he considered himself a prisoner in the Vatican.

Pius was a failure in the political and diplomatic sphere, since the solutions to the problems he faced demanded greater intellectual acumen than he possessed. Nevertheless, his pontificate was marked by some success in religious matters (irrespective of how one may wish to judge specific tendencies). Although he was not very active in the missionary activities, he was able to reestablish the hierarchy in England (1850) and the Netherlands (1853), and to conclude concordats and conventions with Russia (1847), Spain (1851), Austria (1855), Portugal (1857), and several states in Central and South America. The Roman centralism, which extinguished the particularism that still existed in the national churches, was systematically promoted, culminating in the solemn declaration of papal → infallibility and the papal jurisdictional → primacy at the First Vatican Council (December 8, 1869-October 20, 1870). Pius himself exerted repeated pressure to obtain the definitions in chs. 3 and 4 of the Dogmatic Constitution *Pastor aeternus.* Resistance to these tendencies came above all from the Eastern Catholic churches, which saw them as a threat to their own traditions, but also from some of the German and French clergy, who were afraid that the Roman curia would deprive them of all possibility of independent action. Pius succeeded in evoking a genuine "veneration of the papacy" which made it easier to achieve a close unity between the mass of the faithful and the lower ranks of the clergy on the one hand, and the new role of the pope in the church on the other. His strong encouragement of these tendencies was not prompted by personal considerations, but rather by pastoral motives: he believed that this was the necessary precondition for the renewal of Catholic life, especially in states where governmental interventions placed limits on the activity of the local churches, and the most suitable instrument to unite all the vital forces of Catholicism against the rising wave of secularism. Pius endeavored to renew religious life, to raise the spiritual level of the clergy, and to promote Catholic life in general. He encouraged eucharistic adoration and devotion to the sacred Hearts of Jesus and Mary; Marian piety was promoted above all by the definition of the Immaculate Conception of Mary in the bull *Ineffabilis Deus* (December 8, 1854). Pius's belief in the inevitable success of his work of religious renewal led him to adopt an intransigent attitude:

he ceaselessly repeated a list of principles that he saw as the basis of a Christian restoration of society. Convinced that a secular state endangered the eternal salvation of the faithful, Pius protested incessantly against the revolutionary principles of 1789; the most spectacular expression of such protests is found in the encyclical *Quanta cura* (1864) and the *Syllabus,* a clumsy document appended to this text. Pius was incapable of distinguishing between ideologies that compromised the Christian spirit and the positive value in his contemporaries' desire for a secularization of public life, or of seeing what would give a deeper spiritual dimension to the Catholic apostolate in the long term. He saw liberalism only as an ideology that denied the supernatural. He did indeed acknowledge the distinction between rejecting religious freedom as an ideal and accepting it as the lesser of two evils; but he himself inclined to the thesis of an officially Christian society, which excluded religious tolerance, as we see especially in his disapproval of the Spanish constitution of 1876, which admitted a certain degree of tolerance. His efforts to check the onward march of liberalism generated hostility to Rome in large sectors of public opinion, especially among scientists, and his own person—as living proof of a failure to understand modern culture—only increased this trend. The final years of his pontificate were marked by controversies, especially with the Armenian Catholics, who objected to Roman decrees which limited their freedom to elect their own bishops, and with Germany, where Otto von Bismarck, who disliked the movement for Catholic emancipation, unleashed the *Kulturkampf.*

In all that he did, Pius was hampered by a superficial education, which prevented him from grasping the complexity of the problems with which he was confronted, as well as by the mediocrity of his advisers, who judged questions with the intransigence of abstract theorists and had no contact with contemporary intellectual life. On the other hand, Pius possessed a practical mentality and the courage to complete what he saw as his tasks. He wished always to act as priest and pastor, and he had a profound piety. The cause of his canonization, promoted by some persons soon after his death, was opened under Pius X in 1907, but was suspended "for lack of sufficient documentation" in 1922. It was reopened under Pius XII in 1954. The heroicness of his virtues was recognized in 1985, and Pope John Paul II beatified him together with John XXIII on September 3, 2000. The beatification of Pius IX was greeted by controversy in the media.

■ **Sources:** *Acta Pii IX,* 9 vols. (Rome, 1854-78); *Atti,* 2 vols. (Rome, 1857); P. De Franciscis, ed., *Discorsi . . . ,* 4 vols. (Rome, 1872-78); G. Maiole, ed., *Pio IX: Lettere al cardinale L. Amat 1832-48* (Modena, 1949); P. Pirri, *Pio IX e Vittorio Emanuele II dal loro carteggio privato,* 3 vols. (Rome, 1944-61); A. Mercati, *Raccolta di concordati* (2nd ed. Rome, 1954) 751-1000, [3]-[71]; A. Marcone, *La parola di Pius IX,* 2 vols. (Genoa, 1964); J. Gorricho, *AHP* 4 (1966) 281-348; G. Martina, *Pio IX e Leopoldo II* (Rome, 1967); G. Cittadini, *Il carteggio privato di Pio IX e il rè Ferdinando di Napoli* (Macerata, 1968); L. Pásztor, *Pio IX* 12 (1982) 3-85; V. Cárcel Ortí, *AHP* 21 (1983) 131-81; G. Cittadini, *G.M. Mastai (Pio IX): Lettere,* 4 vols. (Naples, 1990-94); *AAS* 92 (2000) 439ff.

■ **Bibliography:** *DTHC* 12:1686-1716; *EC* 9:1510-23; *CATH* 11:271-79; *Dizionario storico del Movimento cattolico in Italia* (Casale Monferrato, 1982) 2:480-86; *TRE* 26:661-66; *BBKL* 7:677f.; *VATL* 595-99; E. E. Y. Hales, *The Catholic Church in the Modern World* (London, 1954); N. Blakiston, *The Roman Question 1858-70* (London, 1962); N. Miko, *Das Ende des Kirchenstaats,* 4 vols. (Vienna, 1962-70); *Atti del Convegno . . . sulla figura e sull'opera di Pio IX* (Senigallia, 1974); A. B. Hasler, *Pius IX.,* 2 vols. (Stuttgart, 1977); *Pio IX arcivescovo di Spoleto* (Florence, 1980); *Atti del II Convegno . . .* (Florence, 1981); C. Falconi, *Il giovane Mastai . . . 1792-1827* (Milan, 1981); A. Polverari, *Vita di Pio IX,* 3 vols. (Vatican City, 1986-88); L. Brogoglio, *Pio IX, profilo spirituale* (Vatican City, 1989); G. Martina, *Pio IX,* 3 vols. (Rome, 1974-90, a fundamental study); K. Schatz, *Vaticanum I,* 3 vols. (Paderborn, 1992-94); Y. Chiron, *Pie IX pape moderne* (Paris, 1995); A. Marani, "Tra sinodi e conferenze episcopali: La definizione del ruolo degli incontri collettivi dei vescovi fra Gregorio XVI e Pio IX," *Cristianesimo nella storia* 17 (1996) 47-93; P. K. Hennessy, "The Infallibility of the Papal Magisterium as Presented in the Pastoral Letters of the Bishops of the United States After Vatican I," *Horizons* 23 (1996) 7-28; G. Martina, "Verso il sillabo," *AHP* 36 (1998) 137-81; C. Langlois, "Lire le 'Syllabus,'" *Problèmes d'histoire des religions* 9 (1998) 75-103; H. Euler, "'Den Papst nach Jerusalem schicken': Ein Streit zwischen Papst und Kaiser im 19. Jahrhundert," *Forschungen zur Reichs-, Papst- und Landesgeschichte,* Festschrift for P. Herde (Stuttgart, 1998) 941-63; I. Gobry, *Pie IX, le pape des tempêtes* (Paris, 1999); A. Paita, *Pio IX* (Milan, 2000); L. Coutois, "La liberté comme mal: L'Eglise et le monde moderne au XIXᵉ siècle," *Imaginaires du mal* (Paris, 2000) 221-36; F. Martí Gilabert, "La misión en Chile del futuro Papa Pio IX," *Anuario de historia de la iglesia* 9

(2000) 235-58; V. Conzemius, "Seligsprechung im Widerstreit," *Herder Korrespondenz* 54 (2000) 452-56; K. Schatz, "Fragen zur Seligsprechung Pius' IX.," *Stimmen der Zeit* 218 (2000) 507-16; *Periodical: Pio IX* (Rome, 1972–).

ROGER AUBERT

Pius X (Aug. 4, 1903-Aug. 20, 1914). Saint (1954; feast day Aug. 21). Formerly *Giuseppe Sarto,* born June 2, 1835, in Riese (Treviso) into a family of modest means. He was ordained priest in 1858. In 1875, he was appointed chancellor and spiritual director of the seminary in Treviso, and became bishop of Mantua in 1884, where he created a model diocese. In 1893, he became patriarch of Venice and cardinal. Here, he supported an alliance of Catholics and liberals against the socialists. He had great organizational talents and resoluteness of will. He distrusted innovations and had a very authoritarian understanding of his role in leading the clergy and Catholic Action. After Austria had vetoed Mariano Rampolla in the conclave of 1903, he was elected pope.

He held that his predecessor, Leo XIII, had been insufficiently cautious in his policy of openness vis-à-vis the modern world, so that a new approach was necessary. His attitude of "Catholic defense," supported by his cardinal secretary of state, Raffaele Merry del Val, was evident in three main fields. In church politics, Pius X returned to the intransigence that had characterized the pontificate of Pius IX. This led to new tensions with Russia and Germany (encyclical on Charles Borromeo, disapproval of confessionally mixed trade unions) and the United States, where the "liberal" bishop John Ireland fell from favor, and Pius refused to grant an audience to President Theodore Roosevelt. Diplomatic relations with Spain were broken off in 1910. The laws of separation in Portugal led to an open conflict in 1911, as had already happened after the separation of church and state in France in 1905, when Pius condemned the new law about cultic associations.

In the social field, although he sympathized with endeavors to do something about the "undeserved wretchedness of the workers," he accused the Christian Democrats of pushing the moral and religious aspects of the social problem into the background and giving too much priority to the workers' material claims. The main point of his accusation, however, was that they dared to act with excessive autonomy vis-à-vis the ecclesiastical hierarchy. The rejection of democratic ideas in the Vatican, in favor of paternalistic solutions, can be seen in the measures taken against the adherents of Romolo Murri, in the dissolution of the "Opera dei Congressi" in Italy, the different treatments of the "Sillon" movement and "Action française" in France, and the support for the confessional trade unions in Germany (the "Berlin tendency"), as well as in the encyclical *Singulari quidam* (1912) and the proposal that the Christian trade union movement be condemned.

In the academic field, Pius acted energetically against modernism. He believed that insufficiently mature assimilations of theological and ecclesiastical doctrine to modern science must be prevented at all costs, since this entailed the loss of essential values. To this end, many books were placed on the → Index, and he published the decree *Lamentabili* on July 3, 1907, and the encyclical *Pascendi dominici gregis* on September 8 of the same year. The strict surveillance of professors of theology and philosophy led to unjustified suspicions of a doctrinal integralism directed against scholarly research. The pope was guided here by members of his entourage whose unenlightened conservatism gave the antimodernist measures an ugly tone and hampered the development of theological studies, especially in exegesis, patristics, and early church history. In the view of recent scholars such as Bedeschi, Poulat, and Snider, it must be recognized that Pius gave his personal support on more than one occasion to a kind of ecclesiastical secret police—something that can scarcely be considered acceptable behavior today.

Nevertheless, it would not be fair to limit our assessment of Pius's pontificate to these negative aspects. He improved relations with Austria, and especially with Italy, on the basis of a more realistic evaluation of the Roman Question and of his fear that socialism would make even more progress. He was also concerned to promote a Christian restoration of the social order (*instaurare omnia in Christo,* "to restore all things in Christ": see his encyclical of October 4, 1903, and his Motu proprio of March 19, 1904). Not only did he reject errors; he also took positive steps toward a pastoral goal. Drawing on his forty years of experience in pastoral work and supported by devoted collaborators, Pius disregarded all the routine procedures of the bureaucracy and introduced reforms that had been needed for centuries. He sought to improve the ascetical and academic formation of the clergy (Pastoral Letter of August 4, 1908; encouragement to read the Bible and to engage in study, amalgamation of the tiny Italian seminaries; regulations governing the examination of candidates for ordination; regulations for the diocesan seminaries in Italy). He encouraged Catholic Action, especially in Italy (encyclical *Il fermo proposito*, June 11, 1905), although it was given a structure that made the action of the laity appear a mere extension of the action of the clergy, and it remained very conservative (see encyclical *Vehementer nos*, 1905). He promoted instruction in the catechism and preaching and issued decrees allowing more frequent (even daily) communion and lowering the age of first communion. He introduced liturgical reforms, restructuring the breviary and the missal and restoring Gregorian chant. He began the process of simplification and new codification of Latin canon law, contributing not only juridically but also morally to the improvement of church discipline. Finally, he reorganized the curia, modernizing its administration and its working methods, so that it could better tackle its tasks, which had been made more difficult by the increasing centralization of the church (which Pius too promoted). Although Pius did not appear to his contemporaries to be particularly modern, these measures certainly made him a reforming pope. Like other popes of this period, he was at one and the same time an innovator and a traditionalist.

■ **Sources:** *ASS* 36-41 (1903-8); *AAS* 1-6 (1909-14); N. Vian, ed., *Lettere* (2nd ed. Padua, 1958); R. Sartoretto and F. da Riese, eds., *Scritti inediti (1858-64)*, 2 vols. (Padua, 1971-74); F. Crispolti, *Ricordi* (Milan, 1932); R. Merry del Val, *Pio X: Impressioni e ricordi* (Padua, 1949); L. v. Pastor, *Tagebücher*, ed., W. Wühr (Heidelberg, 1950) 414-611; *Positio super introductione causae* (Rome, 1942); *Positio super virtutibus* (Rome, 1949); *Disquisitio circa quasdam obiectiones* (Rome, 1950).

■ Bibliography: *DTHC* 12:1716-40; *EC* 9:1523-30; *DSp* 12:1429-32; *CATH* 11:279-87; *TRE* 26:667-70; *BBKL* 7:679f.; *VATL* 599ff.; I. Daniele, "La formazione di S. Pio X nel Seminario di Padova," *Studia Patavina* 1 (1954) 286-317; M. Landrieux, "Le conclave de 1903," *Etudes* 299 (1958) 157-83; E. Poulat, *Intégrisme et catholicisme intégral* (Tournai, 1969); idem, "La dernière bataille du pontificat de Pie X," *Rivista di storia della Chiesa in Italia* 25 (1971) 83-107; R. Brack, *Deutscher Episkopat und Gewerkschaftsstreit 1910-14* (Cologne, 1976); M. Bartolucci, *Il ministero catechistico di S. Pio X* (Rome, 1976);

Schwaiger 49-77; C. Snider, *L'episcopato del cardinal Ferrari* (Vicenza, 1982) II; D. Agasso, *L'ultimo papa Santo Pio X* (Turin, 1985); E. Cattaneo, "Il diario per il conclave di Pio X scritto dal cardinale Ferrari," *Ricerche storiche sulla Chiesa Ambrosiana* 56 (1985) 91-122; *Sulle orme di Pio X: Giuseppe Sarto dal microcosmo veneto alla dimensione universale* (exhibition catalog, Venice, 1986); F. Martín Hernandez, "El conclave de 1903," *Salmanticensis* 36 (1989) 192-207; G. Romanato, *Pio X* (Milan, 1992); A. Haquin, "Les décrets eucharistiques de Pie X," *La Maison Dieu* 203 (1995) 61-82; G. Vian, "Sviluppi ed esiti dell'antimodernismo durante il pontificato di Pio X," *Rivista di storia e letteratura religiosa* 32 (1996) 591-615; M. Launay, *La papauté à l'aube du XXᵉ siècle: Léon XIII et Pie X 1878-1914* (Paris, 1997); E. Cabello, "San Pio X y la renovación de la vita cristiana," *Anuario de la historia de la iglesia* 6 (1997) 45-60; Y. Chiron, *Saint Pie X* (Versailles, 1999).

ROGER AUBERT

Pius XI (Feb. 6, 1922-Feb. 10, 1939). Formerly *Achille Ratti*, born May 31, 1857, in Desio near Monza, into a well-to-do family. He studied at the seminary in Milan and the Gregorian University in Rome and was ordained to the priesthood in 1879. He became professor of dogmatic theology at the seminary in Milan in 1882, and was appointed librarian of the Ambrosian library in Milan in 1888, and prefect of the library in 1907. He became pro-prefect of the → Vatican Library in 1912 and prefect in 1914. In 1918, he was appointed apostolic visitor to Poland, and nuncio to Poland in 1919. He was appointed titular archbishop of Lepanto on October 28, 1919. He was sent in 1920 as commissioner for the regions of Upper Silesia where a referendum was to be held, but the difficult situation led to his recall. He was appointed archbishop of Milan in 1921, and created cardinal on June 13 of that year. After seven months as archbishop, he was elected pope as the compromise candidate.

As the monarchies collapsed, Pius pointed to the kingship of Christ, making this the theme of the Jubilee Years (1925, 1929, and 1933). He instituted the liturgical feast of Christ the King and consecrated the human race to the Heart of Jesus. He attached great importance to the consolidation of Catholic Action, which was propagated with particular vigor in Italy, and dedicated his first encyclical to this theme (*Ubi arcano*, 1922). Other important encyclicals were *Quas primas* (1925), *Miserentissimus Redemptor* (1928), *Casti connubii* (1930), *Quadragesimo anno* (1931), and *Ad catholici sacerdotii* (December 20, 1935). He beatified and canonized a large number of persons and proclaimed Peter Canisius, John of the Cross, and Albert the Great doctors of the church. He indicated new paths for missionary work by setting up missionary seminaries, training indigenous clergy, and founding new ecclesiastical circumscriptions. Although he was favorably disposed to the Eastern churches, he was hesitant about the ecumenical movement. He was a great promotor of the arts and sciences. Faculties for church history and missiology were erected at the Gregorian University, which was given new premises; the Biblical Institute and the Institute for Oriental Studies were aggregated to the Gregorian. The Constitution *Deus scientiarum Dominus* laid down a new structure of studies for the whole world in 1931. In 1925, he founded the Institute for Christian Archeology, in 1929 the Russian seminary, and in 1930 the Academy of Sciences. He also gave support to the Vatican Library, the Catholic University of Milan, and church art. With the help of his cardinal secretaries of state, Pietro Gasparri (1922-1930) and Eugenio Pacelli (from 1930, later Pius XII), concordats were concluded with Latvia (1922), Bavaria (1924), Poland (1925), Rumania and Lithuania (1927), Prussia (1929), Baden (1932), and Austria (1933). Other agreements were reached with Czechoslovakia in 1926, with France and Portugal in 1928, and with Ecuador in 1937. In 1926, he condemned the chauvinistic "Action française," the movement led by Charles Maurras. This led to violent protests from French Catholics, who disagreed on this issue. After the fascists seized power in Italy in 1923, Pius withdrew his support from the "Partito Popolare Italiano" and its founder, Luigi Sturzo. An outstanding event in church politics was the resolution of the Roman Question, which had festered since 1870, through the so-called → Lateran Treaties (February 11, 1929). When a violent dispute broke out in 1931 with Benito Mussolini about the education of the young, Pius wrote the encyclical *Non abbiamo bisogno*, which condemned the fascist understanding as a pagan deification of the state; however, it was not yet possible to resolve these difficulties in 1931. When Mussolini conquered Abyssinia in 1935, in defiance of international law, the Vatican made no protest. An accommodation with National Socialism in Germany became possible when solemn assur-

ances on the part of Adolf Hitler led the bishops to abandon their negative stance in 1933. Negotiations for a concordat began in Rome on April 10 and were concluded on July 20, 1933. In the concordat with the German Reich, which was a great success for Hitler in the realm of foreign politics, the Holy See attempted to compel the regime to observe formal law; but in the encyclical *Mit brennender Sorge* (March 14, 1937), written by Cardinal Michael von Faulhaber and revised by Pacelli, the pope attacked the Nazi ideology head-on and condemned the repeated infringements of the concordat. Pius sharply rebuked the Viennese cardinal, Theodor Innitzer, when he enthusiastically greeted Hitler after the Austrian *Anschluss.* After initial negotiations, Pius adopted a decidedly anticommunist stance, which culminated in the encyclical *Divini Redemptoris* (March 19, 1937). He died shortly before the outbreak of the Second World War and was buried in St. Peter's.

In a phrase drawn from the *Dies Irae,* Paul VI called Pius *rex tremendae maiestatis,* a "king of tremendous majesty." He succeeded in uniting a down-to-earth sobriety, firm trust in God, and bold optimism.

■ **Sources:** *AAS* 14-31 (1922-39); DH 3660-3776; D. Bertetto, *Discorsi di Pio XI,* 3 vols. (Turin, 1960-61).

■ **Bibliography:** *CATH* 11:287-300; *TRE* 26:674-77; *BBKL* 7:680ff.; *VATL* 602ff.; A. Fitzek, ed., *Pius XI. und Mussolini, Hitler, Stalin* (Eichstätt, 1987); J. Gelmi, *Die Päpste in Lebensbildern* (Graz, 1988) 292-302; M. F. Feldkamp, "Pius XI. und Paul Fridolin Kehr," *AHP* 32 (1994) 293-327; J. Schasching, *Zeitgereicht—zeitbedingt: Nell-Breuning und die Sozialenzyklika Quadragesimo anno nach dem Vatikanischen Geheimarchiv* (Bornheim, 1994); G. Passelecq, *L'encyclique cachée de Pie XI* (Paris, 1995); J. Daujat, *Pie XI: Le pape de l'Action catholique* (Paris, 1995); *Pape Pie XI: Actes du Colloque organisé par l'Ecole française de Rome, 1989* (Rome, 1996); D. Menozzi, "Liturgia e politica: L'introduzione della festa di Cristo Re," in *Cristianesimo nella storia,* Festschrift for G. Alberigo (Bologna, 1996) 607-56; J. Escudero Imbert, "El pontificado de Achille Ratti, papa Pio XI," *Anuario de historia de la iglesia* 6 (1997) 77-111; H. Petit, *L'église, le Sillon et l'Action française* (Paris, 1998); L. Crippa, "Per un accostamento storico-dottrinale alla personalità e alla attività magisteriale di Pio XI," *Benedictina* 45 (1998) 183-203; idem, "Nel sessantesimo della morte: Per un approfondimento dell'ecclesiologia di Pio XI," *Benedictina* 46 (1999) 5-23; J. Lenzenweger, "Papstwahlen 1914 und 1922," in *In factis mysterium legere,* Festschrift for I. Rogger (Bologna, 1999) 187-94.

JOSEF GELMI

Pius XII (Mar. 2, 1939-Oct. 9, 1958). Formerly *Eugenio Pacelli*, born Mar. 2, 1876, in Rome, in a family of distinguished lawyers. After brilliant studies at state schools, at the Gregorian University, and at Sant'Apollinare, he entered the service of the secretariat of state in 1901 and became a close collaborator of Pietro Gasparri in 1904. He was professor of ecclesiastical diplomacy from 1909 to 1914. He became undersecretary of the *Sacra Congregatio pro Negotiis Ecclesiasticis extraordinariis* in 1912, and pro-secretary in 1914. He was appointed titular archbishop of Sardis and apostolic nuncio in Munich in 1917, and charged to persuade the German government to accept the pope's proposal for peace. The brief Soviet government in Munich in 1919 left him terrified all his life of a communist seizure of power. He was appointed nuncio to Germany in 1920, and after the concordat with Bavaria was concluded, he moved to Berlin in 1924. He was created cardinal in 1929 and succeeded Gasparri as secretary of state in 1930. He played a decisive role in the conclusion of the Austrian and German concordats in 1933, and he undertook journeys to France, Hungary, North and South America.

He was elected pope in a conclave that lasted just one day, and he endeavored to continue the concordatory policy of his predecessor. He concluded agreements with Portugal (1940), Spain (1953), the Dominican Republic (1954), and Bolivia (1957). He attempted through diplomatic activity to prevent the outbreak of the Second World War. Once the war had begun, his primary concern was to remain strictly neutral, although he spared no pains to send humanitarian aid to prisoners of war and refugees. He also provided special support to Jews, but he was unwilling to make any public protest on the question of the treatment of the Jews, believing that his silence would ward off "worse things" and would allow him to organize aid more effectively. When Rome was occupied on September 10, 1943, Pius gave asylum in the Vatican to innumerable refugees. Democracy was the theme of his Christmas message in 1944. He considered communism a greater danger than National Socialism, and a decree of the Holy Office (July 1, 1949) inflicted the penalty of excommunication on all who promoted communism; this was especially significant in the Italian context.

In forty encyclicals, numerous messages, and discourses, Pius addressed most of the fundamental religious questions of his time. He gave especial support to Catholic education, to the clarification of questions in Catholic moral teaching, and to the defense of the dignity of the human person. In the theological realm, he promoted Mariology, above all by the dogmatic definition of Mary's assumption into heaven (Apostolic Constitution *Munificentissimus Deus*, 1950) and by the encyclical *Ad coeli Reginam* on Mary's dignity as queen (1954). He left open the questions of her role as mediatrix and co-redemptrix. In the encyclical *Mystici Corporis* (1943), he presented a profound ecclesiological study; he did justice to modern exegesis in the biblical encyclical *Divino afflante Spiritu* (1943). The encyclical *Mediator Dei* (1947) was a moderate acceptance of the liturgical movement, and his liturgical reforms culminated in the reduction of the fast before communion and in the reordering of Holy Week. The encyclical *Humani generis* (1950) was directed against the *Nouvelle Théologie*. The encyclical *Provida Mater* (1947) gave ecclesiastical recognition to secular institutes. The encyclical *Haurietis aquas* (1956) was devoted to the veneration of the Heart of Jesus. Although Pius did not write a social encyclical, his statements on social questions fill nearly 4,000 pages. He was more favorably inclined to the ecumenical movement than his predecessor. Pius XII canonized thirty-three persons, including Pius X in 1954. He greatly increased the number of ecclesiastical circumscriptions, and he erected the local hierarchies in China (1946), British West Africa (1950), South Africa (1951), British East Africa (1953), French Africa, and Burma (1955). In 1946 and 1953, he created a total of fifty-six new cardinals; the nomination of three German bishops (Josef Frings, Konrad von Preysing, and Clemens August von Galen) was a sensation at the time. He rejected the idea of a collective guilt on the part of Germans. As a great admirer of German virtues, he surrounded himself with German collaborators such as Ludwig Kaas, August Bea, Robert Leiber, and Gustav Gundlach. His authoritarian temperament led him to leave the office of secretary of state vacant after the death of Luigi Maglione in 1944. Pius died in → Castelgandolfo and is buried in St. Peter's.

He was a man of acute intellect, with an exceptional memory, a great gift for languages, and a vigorous appetite for work. He won high international prestige for the papacy through his charisma. After his death, however, he was criticized for his authoritarian style of government, his theatrical gestures, and his irritating → nepotism. Above all, questions have been raised about his silence in the face of the crimes committed by National Socialism.

■ **Sources:** *AAS* 33-50 (1939-58); DH 3780-3928; *Discorsi e Radiomessaggi di Sua Santità Pio XII,* 20 vols. (Vatican City, 1941-59); *Herder Korrespondenz* 1-13 (1946-59); A. F. Utz and J. F. Groner, eds., *Aufbau und Entfaltung des gesellschaftlichen Lebens: Soziale Summe Pius' XII.,* 3 vols. (Fribourg, 1954-61); P. Blet et al., eds., *Actes et Documents du Saint-Siège relatifs à la Seconde Guerre Mondiale,* 11 vols. (Vatican City, 1965-81).

■ **Bibliography:** *CATH* 11:300-311; *TRE* 26:674-77; *BBKL* 7:682-99; *VATL* 604-7; H. Schambeck, ed., *Pius XII. zum Gedächtnis* (Berlin, 1977); L. Papeleux, *Les silences de Pie XII* (Brussels, 1980); M. P. Lehnert, *"Ich durfte ihm dienen"* (Würzburg, 1982); J. Chelini, *L'Église sous Pie XII: La tourmente (1939-45)* (Paris, 1983); A. Riccardi, ed., *Le Chiese di Pio XII* (Bari, 1986); J. Gelmi, *Die Päpste in Lebensbildern* (Graz, 1988) 302-12; J. Chelini, *L'après-guerre (1945-58)* (Paris, 1989); S. Samerski, "Die Aufnahme diplomatischer Beziehungen zwischen dem Heiligen Stuhl und dem Deutschen Reich (1920)," *AHP* 34 (1996) 325-68; P. Blet, *Pie XII et la Seconde Guerre Mondiale d'après les archives du Vatican* (Paris, 1997); J. Cornwell, *Hitler's Pope* (New York, 1999); K. Braun, *Anzeiger für die Seelsorge,* fascicle 8 (2000) 379f.; E. Nassi, *Pio XII e il comunismo* (Florence, 1999); G. Arboit, "Le Saint-Siège et la question juive en Europe Central pendant la Seconde Guerre Mondiale," *AHP* 37 (1999) 161-90; A. Heinz, "Liturgische Reform vor dem Konzil," *Liturgisches Jahrbuch* 49 (1999) 3-38; M. Marchione, *Pope Pius XII: Architect for Peace* (New York, 2000); M. F. Feldkamp, *Pius XII. und Deutschland* (Göttingen, 2000); H. Hürten, *Pius XII. und die Juden* (Cologne, 2000); G. Miccoli, *I dilemmi e i silenzi di Pio XII* (Milan, 2000).

JOSEF GELMI

Pontian (July 21, 230-Sept. 28, 235 [abdication]). Saint (feast day Aug. 13), celebrated as a martyr. According to the → *Liber Pontificalis,* he was a Roman. Origen had been deposed from the clerical state at the instigation of Bishop Demetrius of Alexandria, and a Roman synod gave its assent to this. After Alexander Severus, who had practiced toleration in religious matters, Maximinus Thrax became emperor in March 235 and immediately took harsh action against the leadership of the Roman church, forcibly putting an end to the schism that had begun under Calixtus I (see Euse-

bius of Caesarea, *Historia Ecclesiastica* 6.28). According to the → Chronography of 354, Pontian and his rival bishop, Hippolytus, were deported from Rome to Sardinia. Pontian renounced his office on September 28, 235 (the first certain date in papal history); his successor was Anterus. Pontian and Hippolytus soon succumbed to their hardships in Sardinia. Both were buried on August 13 in Rome, in an undated year during the pontificate of Fabian. Pontian was buried in the papal crypt of the catacomb of Calixtus, which had just been completed, and the inscription on his tomb was discovered in 1909.

■ **Sources:** *LP* 1:XCIVf., 4; 3:74, 354.

■ **Bibliography:** *DECL* 495; *BBKL* 7:829f.; *VATL* 610; Caspar 1:43-46, 48; R. Minnerath, "La position de l'église de Rome aux trois premiers siècles," in M. Maccarrone, ed., *Il primato del vescovo di Roma nel primo millennio* (Rome, 1991) 139-71; Borgolte 416.

GEORG SCHWAIGER

Romanus (end of July/beginning of Aug. 897-Nov. 897 [†?]). Born in Gallese, he was cardinal priest of San Pietro in Vincoli. It is uncertain whether he was a supporter of Formosus. According to an eleventh-century catalogue of popes, Romanus was a monk before becoming pope. If this is historically accurate, it is possible that he was deposed by supporters of Formosus for failing to promote Formosus's rehabilitation with sufficient resoluteness.

■ **Sources:** *LP* 2:230; *RPR*(J) 1:441; 2:705; Zimmermann *Pu* 1:9-12.

■ **Bibliography:** *LMA* 7:1002; *VATL* 660; Zimmermann *Pa* 59.

SEBASTIAN SCHOLZ

Sabinian (Sept. 13, 604-Feb. 22, 606). Born in Volterra. Under Gregory I, Sabinian was deacon and apocrisiary in Constantinople. It is clear that his election in March 604 was a reaction by the Roman deacons to the preference shown by Gregory I to monks and clergy who lived under a religious rule. Sabinian was held in ill-repute among the populace because of his alleged lack of compassion in the distribution and purchase of grain during a famine.

■ **Sources:** *LP* 1:315; *RPR*(J) 1:220.

■ **Bibliography:** *BBKL* 8:1148ff.; *VATL* 680f.; Caspar 2:805 (index); J. Richards, *Gregor der Große* (Graz et al., 1983) 315; Borgolte 416.

MANFRED HEIM

Sergius I (Dec. 15, 687-Sept. 8, 701). Saint (feast day Sept. 9), born in Palermo of Syrian stock. He was a priest in Rome and was elected in preference to two other candidates. His emphasis on papal primacy was expressed in the reburial of Leo I in → St. Peter's on June 8, 688, and in his refusal to obey Emperor Justinian II by signing the decrees of the Synod of Constantinople (the Quinisext, 691/692) which contradicted the Western tradition. The troops in Rome, Ravenna, and the Pentapolis likewised refused to obey the emperor's orders to arrest Sergius, and this rebellion is considered the beginning of the separation of the West from Byzantium. In Italy, Sergius succeeded in establishing the primacy of Rome by conferring episcopal ordination on Archbishop Damian of Ravenna and by ending the schism in Aquileia shortly before 700. He bestowed the → pallium on Archbishop Brithwald of Canterbury in 699 and acceded to the request of Pippin II by ordaining Willibrord as archbishop of the Frisians in 695. He baptized the English king Caedwalla in Rome in 689.

■ **Sources:** *LP* 1:371-82; 3:97f.; *RPR*(J) 1:244f.; 2:639, 741.

■ **Bibliography:** *BBKL* 9:1436-41; *LMA* 7:1786f.; *VATL* 722f.; Caspar 1:631-36; Richards 208-11; Borgolte 96f.; R. Wisskirchen, "Zur Apsisstirnwand von Ss. Cosma e Damiano," *Jahrbuch für Antike und Christentum* 42 (1999) 169-83.

SEBASTIAN SCHOLZ

Sergius II (Jan. 844-Jan. 27, 847). A Roman. He was an archpriest in the city and was chosen in a divisive election. He was ordained bishop without first obtaining the imperial assent, in contravention of the *Constitutio Romana* of Emperor Lothar I. When the emperor sent his son Louis II to Rome to investigate the matter, he recognized Sergius, who promised to observe the rights of the emperor and crowned Louis king of the Langobards on June 15, 844. Sergius appointed Drogo of Metz his vicar for Gaul and Germany, and refused to restore to office the deposed archbishops Ebo of Rheims and Bartholomew of Narbonne. According to one version of the biography of Sergius in the → *Liber Pontificalis*, his brother Benedict, bishop of Albano, usurped power in Rome at the beginning of 846. The resulting disorders and the simony which dominated church affairs in Rome favored the attack by the Saracens in August 846.

■ **Sources:** *LP* 2:86-105; 3:123f.; *RPR*(J) 1:327ff.; 2:702,

744; H. Zielinski, *Regesta Imperii* (Cologne, 1991) I, 3/1, 21-41; K. Herbers, 1/4/2/1 (Cologne, 1999) 1-64.

■ **Bibliography:** *LMA* 7:1787; *VATL* 723; K. Herbers, *Leo IV. und das Papsttum in der Mitte des 9. Jahrhunderts* (Stuttgart, 1996) 99-104, 577.

SEBASTIAN SCHOLZ

Sergius III (Jan. 29, 904-Sept. 911). A member of a noble Roman family. He was bishop of Cerveteri from 893 to 896, then returned to the order of priesthood. After a divisive election in 898, Sergius could not maintain his position against John IX, but was expelled, deposed, and excommunicated. With the help of the opponents of Formosus, he returned to Rome in 904, removed his predecessors Leo V and Christopher, and declared all the popes since John IX illegitimate. Sergius reinstated the decisions of Stephen VI concerning Formosus and declared his pontificate illegitimate and the ordinations he had performed invalid. This unleashed a literary controversy. Sergius found support in the Roman senator Theophylact and margrave Alberic of Spoleto. In the controversy about the fourth marriage of the Byzantine emperor Leo VI, Sergius gave permission for this marriage.

■ **Sources:** *LP* 2:236ff.; 3:128; *RPR*(J) 1:445ff.; 2:705, 746; Zimmermann *Pu* 1:31-57.

■ **Bibliography:** *LMA* 7:1787; *VATL* 724; Zimmermann *Pa* 63-73; S. Scholz, *Transmigration und Translation* (Cologne, 1992) 225-40.

SEBASTIAN SCHOLZ

Sergius IV (July 31, 1009-May 12, 1012). Formerly *Petrus* (with the nickname *Buccaporca* or *Os porci*, "pig's snout"), son of the cobbler Petrus. He became bishop of Albano in 1004. The circumstances in which he became pope are unclear; during his pontificate, he was completely dependent on John II Crescentius. His death, shortly before the end of the domination of the Crescentian family in Rome, may have been violent. Sergius sought a rapprochement with Henry II and confirmed privileges which John XVIII had granted to Bamberg, as well as the possessions of the reestablished diocese of Merseburg. The report that, after the church of the Holy Sepulcher in Jerusalem was destroyed, he appealed in 1010 for a crusade seems plausible.

■ **Sources:** *LP* 2:267; 3:132, 371; *RPR*(J) 1:504f.; 2:708; Zimmermann *Reg* nos. 1036-74; Zimmermann *Pu* 2:443-63.

■ **Bibliography:** *LMA* 7:1787f.; *BBKL* 9:1441f.; *VATL* 724f.; Zimmermann *J*; Borgolte 417; H. M. Schaller, "Zur Kreuzzugsenzyklika Papst Sergius' IV.," *Papsttum, Kirche und Recht,* Festschrift for H. Fuhrmann (Tübingen, 1991) 135-53 (with critical edition).

GEORG SCHWAIGER

Severinus (May 28-Aug. 2, 640). A Roman from the lower classes, son of Avienus. He was already elderly when elected. Since Rome refused to assent to the Monothelite positions adopted in the *Ekthesis* of patriarch Sergius, the Byzantine emperor Heraclius initially withheld his assent to the papal → election. Finally, the imperial court was satisfied with the assurance of the papal envoys that the *Ekthesis* would be presented to Severinus for his signature. This allowed the episcopal ordination to go ahead on May 28, 640— only two months before the death of the candidate. The brevity of his pontificate explains why Severinus made no statement about the *Ekthesis.* He was buried in St. Peter's.

The badly paid soldiers in the city of Rome exploited the delay between Severinus's election and his ordination to cause disturbances—clearly without any direct connection to the dogmatic and church-political conflicts about the *Ekthesis.* After an initial unsuccesful military intervention, the military commander (*cartularius*) in the city, Maurice, sealed the stores that were kept for charitable purposes in the Lateran, and informed Isaac, the *patricius* and exarch of Ravenna, who arrived with his soldiers, spent a week in the Lateran palace, and finally confiscated all that the church possessed. He acted according to proper legal forms, although the → *Liber Pontificalis* says that he "stole" church property.

■ **Sources:** *LP* 1:n. LXXIII, 328f.; *RPR*(J) 1:227.

■ **Bibliography:** *BBKL* 9:1510f.; *VATL* 725; E. Caspar, "Die Lateransynode von 649," *Zeitschrift für Kirchengeschichte* 51 (1932) 114, n. 87; Caspar 2:526ff., 536f.; Bertolini 317f.; H. Foerster, *Liber Diurnus Romanorum Pontificum* (Bern, 1958), index; Zimmermann *Pt* 42-45.

GEORG JENAL

Silverius (June 1[8?], 536-Mar.[?] 11, 537 [deposition] or Nov. 11, 537 [abdication]). Saint (feast day June 20), born in Frosinone in Campania, died Dec. 2, 537, on the island of Ponza or Palmaria in the gulf of Gaeta; he was the son of Pope Hormisdas. After the sudden death of Agapitus I in Constantinople, the Roman subdeacon Sil-verius was made pope under pressure from Theodahad, king of the east Goths, and the Roman clergy were compelled to accept him. In December 536, Silverius surrendered Rome without a struggle to the Byzantine general Belisarius. Under the influence of his wife, who was a friend of Empress Theodora I, Belisarius accused Silverius of high treason and had him arrested in March 537. He was deposed and brought to Patara in Lycia; Vigilius, a favorite of Theodora, was ordained pope in Rome on March 29, 537. On the instructions of Emperor Justinian I, Silverius was brought back to Rome for an investigation of what had happened. He was handed over to Vigilius, persuaded to abdicate, and banished to Ponza. He was subsequently venerated as a martyr.

■ **Sources:** Liberatus of Carthage, *Breviarium causae Nestorianorum et Eutychianorum,* 22; Procopius, *De bello Gothico* 1:25f.; 3:15, *Anecdota* 1; *LP* 1:290-95; *RPR*(J) 1:115f.; 2:694, 738.

■ **Bibliography:** *BBKL* 10:336ff.; *LMA* 7:1904; *VATL* 729; Borgolte.

GEORG SCHWAIGER

Silvester I (314-335). Saint (feast day Dec. 31). He was the successor to Miltiades. No genuine texts from his hand have survived. He did not attend the synod of Arles (314), about which Optatus informed him; he was represented by the priests Victor and Vincentius at the Council of Nicaea (325). This meant that Silvester played virtually no role in Constantine's politics, although the Roman church too benefited from the emperor's donations. From the fifth century on, legends declared that Silvester had been a confessor of the faith under Diocletian and that he had influenced Constantine to convert and accept baptism; this legend was one of the foundations for the Constantinian Donation, which like the *Canon Sylvestri* (*Constitutum Silvestri*), is a forgery.

■ **Bibliography:** *BBKL* 10:338-41; *DECL* 537; *VATL* 730; E. Ewig, "Das Bild Constantins des Großen," *Historisches Jahrbuch* 75 (1956) 10-37; R. J. Loenertz, "'Actus Sylvestri': Genèse d'une légende," *Revue d'histoire ecclésiastique* 70 (1975) 426-39; C. Pietri, *Roma christiana* (Rome, 1976) 1:168-87; R. P. C. Hanson, *The Search for the Christian Doctrine of God* (Edinburgh, 1988) 154, 184.

THOMAS BÖHM

Silvester II (Apr. 9, 999-May 12, 1003). Formerly *Gerbert of Aurillac,* born 940/950 in the Auvergne. He was educated in the monastery of Aurillac and taught at the cathedral school in Rheims. Silvester was one of the most important medieval popes. His contemporaries prized him above all for his outstanding knowledge of the *quadrivium,* and he also wrote detailed studies of the branches of the *trivium,* especially rhetoric and dialectic. This reputation explains the myths that began to form around his person soon after his death, although the predominantly negative portrait of Silvester is due primarily to the generally negative evaluation up to the present day of the tenth-century papacy. Pierre Riché was the first to present a biography that does justice to Silvester's person. On the other hand, German scholarship has tended to evaluate Silvester skeptically, against the background of the brief reign of Otto III.

Silvester's life and work were decisively affected by the Ottonian rulers even before he was called to the see of Peter. He owed to Otto II his nomination as abbot of Bobbio; lack of political support and opposition in the monastery itself forced him to relinquish this post in 983, after only one year as abbot, and he returned to Rheims, where he and his mentor, Archbishop Adalbero, remained devoted to the Ottonian family. After Archbishop Arnulf (989-991) had been deposed in a legally dubious procedure instigated by the French king Hugh Capet, Silvester became archbishop of Rheims in 991. His seven years in this office were filled with controversies, both literary and conciliar. He had a decisive meeting with Otto III in Rome, who offered him a new perspective as "intellectual" at the imperial court, since papal intervention in the conflict between rival candidates for the see of Rheims made it impossible for him to return to France. Scholars in an earlier period (see Percy E. Schramm) held that Silvester exercised a dominant influence on the policies of Otto III, but this picture must be nuanced, since it is no longer possible to maintain that the emperor's primary goal can be described in the somewhat classicist concept of a "renewal of the empire of the Romans." Rather, Otto's priority was a program of church reform, and Silvester, who had many years' experience of conflicts with an official and papal church that was unwilling to reform, was the obvious person to put this program into action. Silvester's elevation to the *cathedra Petri* and his programmatic choice of name must also be seen as the expression of the imperial and papal intention to reform the church, since

the name "Silvester" evoked for their contemporaries the Council of Nicaea (325), at which the pope and the emperor had united to promote ecclesiastical "reform." Recent scholarship (see Hans-Henning Kortüm) has attempted to show that Silvester as pope did not abandon his understanding of the papal office, marked by concern for church reform and by a positive evaluation of councils. This is indicated by the famous Diploma of Otto III from the year 1001, with its criticism of the pope: it is highly probable that it was drawn up by Silvester himself.

■ **Bibliography:** *LMA* 4:1300-1303; *VATL* 730ff.; P. E. Schramm, *Kaiser, Rom und Renovatio* (3rd ed. Düsseldorf, 1962); U. Lindgren, *Gerbert von Aurillac und das Quadrivium* (Wiesbaden, 1976); W. Bergmann, *Innovationen im Quadrivium des 10. und 11. Jahrhunderts* (Stuttgart, 1985); M. Tosi, ed., *Gerberto: Scienza, storia e mito, Atti del Gerberto Symposium* (Bobbio, 1985); P. Riché, *Gerbert d'Aurillac* (Paris, 1987); O. Guyotjeannin, ed., *Autour de Gerbert d'Aurillac: Le pape de l'an mil* (Paris, 1996); N. Charbonnel, ed. *Gerbert l'Européen: Actes du colloque d'Aurillac, 1996* (Aurillac, 1997); O. Engels, "Überlegungen zur ottonischen Herrschaftsstruktur," in B. Schneidmüller, ed., *Otto III—Heinrich III: Eine Wende?* (Sigmaringen, 1997) 267-325; F. G. Nuvolone, *Vis amicitiae: Nel millenario dell'elezione pontificia di Gerberto, ex abate di Bobbio* (Piacenza/Bobbio, 1999); H.-H. Kortüm, "Gerbertus qui et Silvester," *Deutsches Archiv für Erforschung des Mittelalters* 55 (1999) 1-26.

HANS-HENNING KORTÜM

Silvester III (antipope) (1045-1046). Formerly *Johannes,* died 1062/1063. He was made pope in opposition to Benedict IX in January 1045, but was forced in March of that year to return to the diocese of Sabina, where he had been bishop since 1012. He probably renounced his claim to the papacy in March 1046 in favor of Gregory VI, in whose favor Benedict IX too had abdicated on May 1, 1045. At the synod of Sutri on December 20, 1046, Silvester was definitively deposed from the papal dignity. He was bishop of Sabina until his death. He was one of the signatories to the decree about papal elections in 1059.

■ **Sources:** *LP* 2:270ff., 331f.; *RPR*(J) 2nd ed. 1:523f.
■ **Bibliography:** *BBKL* 10:341f.; *LMA* 7:1908; *VATL* 732; Zimmermann *Pa* 119-31; K.-J. Hermann, *Das Tuskulanerpapsttum (1012-1046)* (Stuttgart 1973) 151-65; H. Wolter, *Die Synoden im Reichsgebiet und in Reichsitalien von 916-1056* (Paderborn, 1988) 379-94.

ERNST-DIETER HEHL

Silvester IV (antipope) (Nov. 11, 1105-Apr. 12/13, 1111). Formerly the archpriest *Maginulf;* the dates of his birth and death are unknown. He was made pope by Roman nobles, but he was obliged to flee from Paschal II to Osimo a few days later. Margrave Werner of Ancona protected him in Osimo. Silvester had adherents among the Latin clergy in Constantinople, who were in contact with Simeon II, the former Greek patriarch of Jerusalem. Emperor Henry V finally compelled him to abdicate.

■ **Sources:** *RPR*(J) 1:773f.

■ **Bibliography:** *LMA* 7:1908; C. Servatius, *Paschalis II.* (Stuttgart, 1979) 43, 71f., 251; P. Plank, "Patriarch Symeon II. und der 1. Kreuzzug," *Ostkirchliche Studien* 43 (1994) 275-327, esp. 289-98.

AXEL BAYER

Simplicius (Mar. 3, 468-Mar. 10, 483). Saint (feast day Mar. 2), born at Tivoli. He broke with his predecessor, Hilary, by making relations with the East the primary concern of his pontificate, in the period when the Western Roman empire was disintegrating. He opposed the attempts of Patriarch Acacius of Constantinople to translate can. 28 of the Council of Chalcedon (defining the precedence of the patriarch of Constantinople over the other Eastern patriarchs) into reality. In the growing conflict in the East over Monophysitism, he was a resolute defender of the Chalcedonian definition (451). However, the letters he sent to Emperor Basiliscus and (after his overthrow) to Emperor Zeno and Patriarch Acacius had no effect; the Acacian schism was not resolved until 519, under Pope Hormisdas and Emperor Justin I. Nor was he successful in the action he took to defend the orthodox faith in Alexandria, where Peter III Mongus was made patriarch on the death of the Monophysite patriarch Timothy Aelurus in 477, while the defenders of the Chalcedonian definition restored Timothy Salophaciolus to office. The emperor confirmed Timothy, but after he died in 482, Emperor Zeno followed the advice of Acacius and political calculations and rejected Timothy's successor, John Talaia. Against the will of Simplicius, Zeno now gave his support to Peter Mongus. The emperor and his patriarch in Constantinople disregarded the Roman objections. Simplicius probably died before news of the emperor's *Henotikon* could reach him; the task of protesting fell to his successor, Felix II.

Simplicius appointed Bishop Zeno of Seville as apostolic vicar of Spain and improved the quality of church life in Rome, *inter alia* by means of some remarkable buildings such as San Stefano Rotondo. He died after a long illness and was buried in the vestibule of St. Peter's.

■ **Sources:** *PL* 58:35-62; *ActaSS mar.* 1:133-38; A. Thiel, *Epp. Romanorum Pontificum* (Braunsberg, 1878) 1:174-214; *LP* 1:249ff.; *RPR*(J) 1:77-80; 2:693; Liberatus of Carthage, *Breviarium causae Nestorianorum et Eutychianorum,* 16ff.; *Collectio Avellana,* Corpus scriptorum ecclesiasticorum latinorum 35/1 (Vienna, 1895) 124-54; E. Schwartz, *Publizistische Sammlung zum Akazianischen Schisma* (Munich, 1934) 119-22.

■ **Bibliography:** *DTHC* 14:2161-64; *BBKL* 10:482ff.; *DECL* 539; Caspar 2:14-25, 746-49; H. H. Anton, "Kaiserliches Selbstverständnis in der Religionsgesetzgebung der Spätantike und päpstliche Herrschaftsinterpretation im 5. Jahrhundert," *Zeitschrift für Kirchengeschichte* 88 (1977) 38-84; Borgolte.

GEORG SCHWAIGER

Siricius (Dec. 384-Nov. 26, 399). Saint (feast day Nov. 26). A Roman. He had been in the service of the Roman church since the time of Pope Liberius. He was unanimously elected to succeed Damasus I and was confirmed by Emperor Valentinian II on February 25, 385, doubtless with the intention of putting an end to the intrigues of the antipope Ursinus. Although Jerome portrays Siricius as a simple man, he had experience and self-confidence. Although he was overshadowed by Ambrose, the bishop of Milan, he defended the claims of the Roman church more strongly than Damasus. The writings of the Roman bishops up to this time had mostly breathed the spirit of exhortation, instruction, and consolation, but Siricius went further than Damasus in employing the chancellery style of imperial edicts, characterized by the use of commandments or prohibitions and pathos, and with no appeal to juridical texts to justify what is said. Conscious of his "care for all the churches," Siricius issued *decreta generalia* on questions of church discipline and liturgy, with a legal force equal to that of synodal canons. He employed this style in replying on February 12, 385, to Bishop Himerius of Tarragona, who had sent Damasus fourteen questions about church discipline. Siricius forbade the rebaptism of Arians who returned to the true faith; the only acceptable dates for adult baptisms were Easter and Pentecost; he reduced the severity of peniten-

135

tial discipline; he laid down regulations about the age of candidates for ordination and about the chastity and celibacy of clergy and monks. Since Himerius was instructed to communicate these answers to the other Spanish bishops too, this must count as the oldest surviving papal → decretal. Siricius sent the nine canons of the Roman synod of 386 (including a prohibition of episcopal ordination by one bishop alone and without the consent of the Apostolic See, and insistence on the observance of celibacy) to the church in Africa, and probably to other churches also. Inquiries by bishops from Gaul were also answered in the form of canons. In order to guarantee Roman influence in the East, he made the bishop of Thessalonica responsible for the bishops of that region in 385; this was the beginning of the later apostolic vicariate there. Siricius disapproved of the execution of Priscillian and sought to make it easier for his adherents to return to the Catholic Church. He condemned Jovinian and Bishop Bonosus of Naissus. Siricius consecrated the new building of the basilica of St. Paul's Outside the Walls in 390.

■ **Sources:** Jerome, *Ep.* 127; Paulinus of Nola, *Ep.* 5:14; *Collectio Avellana, Ep.* 40: Corpus scriptorum ecclesiasticorum latinorum 35 (Vienna, 1895) 90f.; *PL* 13:1131-96; *LP* 1:86f., 216f.; *RPR*(J) 1:40ff.; 2:691, 734.

■ **Bibliography:** *DTHC* 14:2171-74; *BBKL* 10:530f.; *DECL* 539; *VATL* 732f.; Caspar 1:257-85, 599f.; L. M. García y García, "El papa Siricio (†399) y la significación matrimonial," *Hispania christiana,* Festschrift for J. Orlandis Rovira (Pamplona, 1988) 123-37; Borgolte; D. Jasper, "Die canones synodi Romanorum ad Gallos episcopos—die älteste Dekretale?" *Zeitschrift für Kirchengeschichte* 107 (1996) 319-326; N. Adkin, "Pope Siricius' 'Simplicity,'" *Vetera christianorum* 33 (1996) 25-28; M. F. Connell, "Did Ambrose's Sister Become a Virgin on December 25 or January 6?" *Studia liturgica* 29 (1999) 145-58.

GEORG SCHWAIGER

Sisinnius (Jan. 15-Feb. 4, 708). A Syrian. He was probably elected in October 707, but confirmed only three months later by the Byzantinian exarch in Ravenna. During his pontificate, which lasted only twenty days, the ordination of a bishop for Corsica is recorded, as well as measures for the rebuilding of the city wall around Rome.

■ **Sources:** *LP* 1:388; *RPR*(J) 1:247.
■ **Bibliography:** *LMA* 7:1939; *VATL* 733.

MANFRED HEIM

Sixtus I (Xystus) (116?-125?). Saint (feast day Apr. 6). In the list of succession presented by Irenaeus of Lyons (*Adversus haereses* 3.3.3), he is the sixth successor of Peter, coming after Alexander I. According to the → *Liber Pontificalis*, he was a Roman. He probably had a prominent role in the corporate leadership of the Roman community. He was later venerated as a martyr.

■ **Sources:** *LP* 1:54-57; 3:index.
■ **Bibliography:** *DTHC* 14:2193f.; *BBKL* 10:575ff.; *VATL* 740f.; Caspar 1:8-16.

GEORG SCHWAIGER

Sixtus II (Xystus) (257-Aug. 6, 258). Saint (feast day Aug. 7), probably of Greek origin. He was elected bishop of Rome in 257, at the outbreak of Emperor Valerian's persecution of the Christians; the first imperial edict was issued in August of that year. As a consequence of the second edict (summer 258), which imposed the death penalty on those who refused to sacrifice and was especially directed against the clergy, Sixtus was arrested with four deacons in the catacomb of Calixtus on August 6, 258, after celebrating a forbidden liturgy, and was probably beheaded at once (Cyprian, *Ep.* 80.1; Eusebius of Caesarea, *Historia ecclesiastica* 7.27.1, gives the wrong date; Caspar 1:71f.), not crucified as Prudentius asserts (*Peristephanon* 2.21-24). He was buried in the papal crypt in the catacomb of Calixtus.

Sixtus continued the negative attitude of his predecessor Stephen in the question of the rebaptism of converted heretics. Although Cyprian of Carthage was in favor of rebaptism, Sixtus agreed with Dionysius of Alexandria, who often sought advice in Rome in this difficult pastoral matter. Nevertheless, Sixtus resumed contact with the bishops of northern Africa and Asia Minor which Stephen had broken off. Cyprian praised him as "a good priest, a man who made peace, and therefore a most blessed martyr" (Pontius of Carthage, *Vita Cypriani* 14). Ambrose quotes his Passion (*De officiis ministrorum* I 41:204ff.). In the course of his restoration of the catacombs, Pope Damasus I honored him in two inscriptions, at the place of execution and above his tomb. The person and martyrdom of St. Laurence are closely linked to Sixtus, and both saints are mentioned in the Roman canon. The only text by Sixtus that survives is a fragment of a letter to Dionysius in which he says that baptism must be conferred anew on those who have been baptized invalidly, i.e., not in the name of the Trinity (Bienert 44). He is not the author of the so-called Sentences of Sextus (*Analecta Bollandiana* 67 [1949] 247f.; *Liber Pontificalis* 1:155: *Xystus philosophus*).

■ **Sources:** *LP* 1:6f., 11, 68f., 155f.; *ActaSS aug.* 2:124-42.

■ **Bibliography:** *Lexikon der christlichen Ikonographie,* founded by E. Kirschbaum, ed. W. Braunfels (Freiburg, 1990) 8:378f.; *DACL* 15:1501-15; *BiblSS* 11:1256-61; *BBKL* 10:578-82; *DECL* 539-40; *LMA* 7:1942; *VATL* 741; P. F. de'Cavalieri, "Un recente studio sul luogo del martirio di S. Sisto II," *Studi e Testi* 33 (1920) 145-78; H. Delehaye, "Recherches sur le légendier romain," *Analecta Bollandiana* 51 (1933) 43-49; W. A. Bienert, *Dionysius von Alexandrien: Das erhaltene Werk* (Stuttgart, 1972); G. Schiller, *Ikonographie der christlichen Kunst* (Gütersloh, 1980) IV/2, 213f.; G. N. Verrando, "Alla base e intorno alla più antica Passio dei santi Abdon e Sennes, Sisto, Lorenzo ed Ippolito," *Augustinianum* 30 (1990) 145-87; D. Mazzoleni, "San Sisto, il Santo e la sua Basilica," *Studi e materiali di storia delle religioni* 59 (1993) 151-90.

STEFAN HEID

Sixtus III (July 31, 431-Aug. 19, 440). Saint (feast day Mar. 23), a Roman. While active as a priest in Rome, he was initially looked on as an ally of Pelagius, but after Pope Zosimus condemned the British monk in 418, Sixtus vigorously attacked the heresy (see the letters addressed to Sixtus by Augustine: *Epp.* 191 and 194). In the controversy about Nestorianism, Sixtus supported the attempts by Emperor Theodosius II to achieve a peaceful resolution, which led to the unification formula of 433 and reconciliation between Patriarchs John of Antioch and Cyril of Alexandria. In Illyria, Sixtus maintained the rights of the apostolic vicariate of Thessalonica against Patriarch Proclus of Constantinople. He erected many buildings in Rome, in order to repair the damage inflicted by the western Goths in 410. These included the baptistery in the Lateran; according to Theodor Klauser, Sixtus did not build Santa Maria Maggiore, but merely contributed two inscriptions to the basilica. During the pontificate of Sixtus, Emperor Valentinian III came to Rome bearing precious gifts. A number of works attributed to Sixtus III are not genuine (*De divitiis; De malis doctoribus; De castitate*). The same is true of the *Gesta de Xysti purgatione,* part of the Symmachian forgeries, which tells how Sixtus took an oath to purify himself of the accusation of sexual immorality. Leo I, his successor, already exercised considerable influence during Sixtus's pontificate as a deacon.

■ **Sources:** *PL* 50:581-619; *PLS* 3:21f.; *ActaSS mar.* 3:714-18; *LP* 1:232-37; 3:index; *RPR*(J) 1:57f.; 2:692.

■ **Bibliography:** *BBKL* 10:583f.; *DECL* 540; *VATL* 742; Caspar 1:416-22; H. Ulbrich, "Augustins Briefe zur entscheidenden Phase des Pelagianischen Streits (415-418)," *Revue des Etudes Augustiniennes* 9 (1963) 51-75; T. Klauser, "Rom und der Kult der Gottesmutter," *Jahrbuch für Antike und Christentum* 15 (1972) 120-35; C. Pietri, *Roma christiana,* 2 vols. (Rome, 1976); Borgolte 417.

GEORG SCHWAIGER

Sixtus IV (Aug. 9, 1471-Aug. 12, 1484). Formerly *Francesco della Rovere,* a Franciscan, born July 21, 1414, in Celle near Savona. After studies at several houses of his order and universities in Italy, he taught theology in Padua and Bologna. It was probably here that he came to the attention of Cardinal Bessarion, not only as an esteemed professor but also as a preacher of rhetorical brilliance. He became provincial of Liguria in 1460 and general of his order in 1464. Sixtus continued his endeavors to reform the order and to achieve a reconciliation between the Conventuals and the Observants even after he was created a cardinal in 1467 (possibly at the suggestion of Bessarion). He led a monastic life in the vicinity of his titular church, San Pietro in Vincoli, remained general until 1469, and composed several theological treatises. His election as pope was supported both by the duke of Milan and by his own nephew Pietro Riario, whose generous promises persuaded the majority of the cardinals to vote for his uncle. Sixtus disregarded his electoral capitulation and made Riario and another nephew, Giuliano della Rovere, cardinals in December 1471, thus marking the beginning of a consistently nepotistic government which aimed at improving the social standing of his relatives (the Riario, Basso, and Giuppo families) and making up for the della Rovere family's lack of dynastic power in Rome and in the church state (→ Papal States). In keeping with this policy, an increasing number of men from Genoa and Liguria were appointed to swell the ranks of the curia, and the necessary financial resources were found by doubling the number of offices for sale, extending the sale of indulgences, and increasing taxes in the church state (which amounted to 69 percent of all income). This revenue also financed the pope's generous patronage of the arts. The papal court became a center of humanist learning and arts, and when the Roman Academy was reopened, it attracted scholars such as Pomponius Laetus and Bartolomeo Platina, who was appointed to head the → Vatican Library. Artists such as Perugino, Sandro Botticelli, and Domenico Ghirlandaio decorated the → Sistine Chapel, which—alongside Santa Maria del Popolo, Santa Maria della Pace, and the Santo Spirito hospital—is the most celebrated example of the building projects, supported also by the cardinals, which made Rome the metropolis of the Renaissance. The streets of the city were repaired and extended, and the Ponte Sisto was constructed. Although Sixtus sought to enhance the spiritual profile of the papacy by bestowing privileges on the mendicants, especially the Franciscans (bull *Mare magnum*, 1474), promoting the doctrine of the Immaculate Conception of Mary and celebrating a Jubilee Year in 1475, as well as through the persecution of heretics and the reintroduction of the Inquisition in Spain, the papacy lost moral authority because of its involvement in the conspiracy of the Pazzi: Sixtus's close friend Girolamo Riario was the man behind the attack on the brothers Lorenzo and Giuliano de' Medici, which cost the life of the latter. Florence, which had opposed Sixtus's bestowal of the county of Imola on Girolamo Riario, now supported disturbances in the papal cities in Umbria and the Romagna, and became the ally of Sixtus's most powerful foe, Louis XI of France. This war spread to the other Italian states, but it soon ended, thanks to the Turkish conquest of Otranto. The papal fleet led the relief of this city. The pope himself was more than willing to engage in a crusade, even welcoming the participation of the grand prince of Moscow, but although he urged the Italian powers to take further action against the Turks after the death of Mehmet II, they did not follow him. The hostilities that broke out afresh in 1482 involved the Orsini and Colonna families, thus affecting Rome too. Finally, they led to the Peace of Bagnolo (August 7, 1484), which was a disappointment for Sixtus. The appeal for a new council made by archbishop Andreas Jamometič of Krajna in 1482 in the Minster in Basel (seat of the last universal council) reflected—apart from all personal dissensions and political calculations that were involved—the widespread dissatisfaction with a pontificate marked by → nepotism, fiscalism, and disastrous politics in Italy. At the

same time, this pontificate had immense importance for the culture of the Renaissance.

■ **Bibliography:** *DTHC* 14/2:2199-2217; *NCE* 13:272f.; *LMA* 7:1944; *BBKL* 10:584-99; *VATL* 742ff.; L. DiFonzo, *Sisto IV, carriera scolastica e integrazioni biografiche (1414-1484)* (Rome, 1987); *Sisto IV e Giulio II, mecenati e promotori di cultura: Atti del convegno internazionale di Studi, Savona 1985* (Savona, 1989); F. Benzi, *Sisto IV, renovator urbis* (Rome, 1990); S. Schüssler, *Das Grabmal Sixtus' IV. in Rom* (Mainz/Munich, 1998); L. Miglio, "Libri, alchimia e medicina nella Roma di Sisto IV," *Roma, magistra mundi*, Festschrift for L. E. Boyle (Louvain-la-Neuve, 1998) 2:597-613; A. Ippoliti, *Il complesso di San Pietro in Vincoli e la committenza della Rovere 1467-1520* (Rome, 1999).

HERIBERT MÜLLER

Sixtus V (Apr. 24, 1585-Aug. 27, 1590). Franciscan Conventual (since 1534). Formerly *Felice Peretti* (as cardinal: *Montalto*), born Dec. 13, 1521, in Grottamare (Marches of Ancona) into a poor family. He studied in Ferrara and Bologna. He became vicar general of the order of Friars Minor and was appointed bishop of Sant' Agata dei Goti in 1566. He was created cardinal in 1570 and was bishop of Fermo from 1571 to 1577. Thanks to earlier tensions, he was excluded from church politics under Gregory XIII. When he became pope, Sixtus acted with severity against the banditry in the church state (→ Papal States). He endeavored to improve living conditions in the church state in general and established a healthy financial situation by making rigorous savings in the budget of the papal court and by greatly increasing the number of curial offices for sale. He was also active as patron of the arts and sciences, and he put up many buildings in Rome (Acqua Felice, Via Sistina; he erected the obelisk and completed the dome of St. Peter's). His reorganization of the curia included the limitation of the number of cardinals to seventy and the setting up of fifteen congregations of cardinals which were directly responsible to the pope (Constitution *Immensa aeterni*, 1588). His headstrong conduct with regard to the new edition of the Vulgate caused great embarrassment, and the text had to be reissued under Clement VIII. Sixtus's policies were born of the conviction that secular rulers were subordinate to the pope both in spiritual and in temporal matters. In France, the course of events indicated that Henry of Navarre, who had Calvinist sympathies, would gain the throne, and Philip

II of Spain put pressure on Sixtus to join an alliance against Henry. The pope did indeed declare in 1585 that, since he was a heretic, Henry had forfeited all claims to the throne, but he attempted to avoid a total dependence on Spain. The collapse of his attempts to regain England for the Catholic Church (execution of Mary Queen of Scots in 1587, defeat of the Spanish Armada in 1588) disappointed Sixtus.

Sixtus possessed exceptional talents and was highly skilled in administration and in financial matters. He had an exaggerated idea of his own papal dignity, and he had no hesitations in showering favors on his own family. Nevertheless, he is one of the most important popes of the sixteenth century.

■ **Bibliography:** *DTHC* 14/2:2217-38; *EC* 11:782-87; *BBKL* 10:599-609; *VATL* 744ff.; M. de Bonard, "Sixtus V., Heinrich IV. und die Liga," *Revue des questions historiques* 60 (1932) 59-140; A. von Hübner, *Der eiserne Papst* (Berlin, 1932); J. Grisar, "Päpstliche Finanzen . . . ," *Miscellanea Historiae Pontificiae* 7 (Rome, 1943) 205-366; F. Sarazani, *La Roma di Sisto V, "er papa tosto": Potere assoluto e grandezza irrazionale di un personaggio entrato nella fantasia popolare* (Rome, 1979); N. Del Re, "Sisto V e la sua opera di organizzazione del governo centrale della Chiesa e dello Stato," *Idea* 36 (1980) 41-53; R. Schiffmann, *Roma felix: Aspekte der städtebaulichen Gestaltung Roms unter Papst Sixtus V.* (Frankfurt a.M., 1985); I. De Feo, *Sisto V* (Milan, 1987); *Studia Sixtina nel IV centenario del pontificato di Sisto V* (Rome, 1987); M. L. Madonna, ed., *Roma e Sisto V: Le arti e la cultura* (Rome, 1993); I. Polverini Fosi, "Justice and Its Image: Political Propaganda and Judicial Reality in the Pontificate of Sixtus V," *Sixteenth Century Journal* 24 (1993) 75-96; *Celebrazioni del IV centenario del pontificato di Sisto V: Atti del Convegno di studi "Montalto e il Piceno in età sistina"* (Ascoli-Piceno, 1994); E. García Hernán, "La curia romana, Felipe II y Sixto V," *Hispania sacra* 46 (1994) 631-50; L. J. Villalon, "San Diego de Alcalá and the Politics of Saint-Making in Counter-Reformation Europe," *Catholic Historical Review* 83 (1997) 691-715; R. B. Trabold, "Soziales Mäzenatentum im Frühbarock: Betrachtungen zur päpstlichen Kunstförderung unter Sixtus V. . . . ," in *Im Gedächtnis der Kirche neu erwachen,* Festschrift for G. Adriányi (Cologne, 2000) 621-28.

KLAUS GANZER

Soter (166?-174?). Saint (feast day Apr. 22). In the ancient lists of bishops, he is the twelfth successor of Peter, coming after Anicetus. According to the → *Liber Pontificalis,* he was a Roman from Campania. Soter wrote a letter to Corinth, accompany-ing a generous donation. The fragments of a reply by Bishop Dionysius give a moving account of this action (Eusebius of Caesarea, *Historia ecclesiastica* 4.23.9-12). He is not the author of the so-called *Second Letter of Clement,* and it is probable that he did not compose a letter against Montanism (*Praedestinatus* 1.26; cf. Tertullian, *Adversus Praxean* 1). Under Soter, the date of Easter was fixed for the first Sunday after 14 Nisan. He was later venerated as a martyr, but there is no certain evidence of this.

■ **Sources:** *LP* 1:135; *ActaSS apr.* 3:4ff.

■ **Bibliography:** *DTHC* 16:2422f.; *BBKL* 14:1492f.; *DECL* 543; *VATL* 746; Caspar 1:627.

GEORG SCHWAIGER

Stephen I (May 12, 254-Aug. 2, 257). Saint (feast day Aug. 2). A Roman. Stephen's pontificate was a time of external calm between the persecutions of the Christians by Emperors Decius and Valerian, but intense controversies raged within the church about whether mildness or rigor should be shown toward heretics and *lapsi* (those who had betrayed the faith during persecution) when these persons wished to return to the communion of the church. The conflict over the question of baptism by heretics was especially acute. Stephen emphasized Roman primacy very strongly and demanded that the entire church accept the Roman practice of forbidding the rebaptism of *lapsi.* He proclaimed the principle *nihil innovetur, nisi quod traditum est* ("let no innovations be made, keep to what has been handed down"). This led to severe dissensions with the churches in Africa and Asia Minor, but there is no absolutely clear evidence of excommunications. Attempts at mediation by Bishop Dionysius of Alexandria bore fruit only under Sixtus II, after the deaths of Stephen and Cyprian of Carthage. Stephen's awareness of the special position of the bishop of Rome was displayed also in the disciplinary measures he took against bishops in Spain and Gaul. Although he was not a victim of the persecution under Valerian, Stephen was later venerated as a martyr. He was buried in the papal crypt in the catacomb of Calixtus.

■ **Sources:** Cyprian, *Ep.* 67-75; Eusebius of Caesarea, *Historia ecclesiastica* 7.2-9; *LP* 1:68f., 154; 3:index; *RPR*(J) 1:20f.; 2:690, 732.

■ **Bibliography:** *DHGE* 15:1183f.; *BBKL* 10:1350f.; *DECL* 546; *VATL* 764; Caspar 1:627; H. Kirchner, "Der Ketzerstreit zwischen Karthago und Rom," *Zeitschrift für Kirchengeschichte* 81 (1970) 290-307; W. Marschall,

Karthago und Rom (Stuttgart, 1971); S. G. Hall, "Stephen of Rome and the One Baptism," *Studia Patristica* 17 (1982) 796ff.; idem, "Stephen I of Rome and the Baptismal Controversy of 256," in B. Vogler, ed., *Miscellanea Historiae Ecclesiasticae* (Brussels/Louvain, 1987) 8:78-82; J. Srutwa, "The Gospel of Matthew 16:16-19 as an Argument of Pope Stephen I for the Roman Primacy," *Analecta Cracoviensia* 27 (1995) 323-28.

GEORG SCHWAIGER

Stephen (II) (Mar. 752). A Roman priest. He was elected to succeed Zachary, but died four days later, before receiving episcopal ordination. He was included until 1960 in the official list of popes in the *Annuario Pontificio* as "Stephen II," so that the numerals of the following popes with this name were one unit higher.

■ **Sources:** *LP* 1:440; 3:102; *RPR*(J) 1:270.
■ **Bibliography:** *DHGE* 15:1184; *VATL* 764.

SEBASTIAN SCHOLZ

Stephen II (Mar. 752-Apr. 26, 757). Previously a Roman deacon. Under Stephen, the papacy turned definitively to the Franks, after Byzantium failed to send aid in 752 in the conflict with Aistulf, king of the Langobards, who claimed sovereignty over Rome. Stephen looked for help to the Frankish king Pippin III the Younger and was the first pope to cross the Alps when he journeyed to meet Pippin at Ponthion in January 754. Pippin performed the ministry of *strator* for the pope and promised to protect the Roman church. They concluded an "alliance of mutual love" at Quierzy in April 754, and Pippin promised to bestow territories in central Italy on the pope (the so-called Donation of Pippin). Stephen anointed Pippin in Saint-Denis on July 28, 754, and accorded him the title of *patricius Romanorum,* in order to strengthen the dynasty against the Frankish opposition and bind it more closely to Rome; this was also the purpose of the spiritual relationship between Stephen and Pippin which was established in Quierzy. After Pippin's victory over the Langobards in 755, Stephen once again called on him for help against Aistulf in 756. The territories that the Langobards had conquered since 749 now came into the possession of the pope (rather than of Byzantium) and formed the basis of the later church states (→ Papal States).

■ **Sources:** *LP* 1:440-62; 3:102f.; *RPR*(J) 1:271-77; 2:701; *MGH.Ep* 3:487-507.
■ **Bibliography:** *BBKL* 10:1351-54; *LMA* 8:116f.; *VATL*

765; A. Angenendt, "Das geistliche Bündnis der Päpste mit den Karolingern (754-796)," *Historisches Jahrbuch* 100 (1980) 1-94; J. T. Hallenbeck, *Pavia and Roma* (Philadelphia, 1982), 55ff.; M. Kerner, "Die frühen Karolinger und das Papsttum," *Zeitschrift des Aachener Geschichtsvereins* 88/89 (1982) 5-41; O. Engels, "Zum päpstlich-fränkischen Bündnis im 8. Jahrhundert," in *Ecclesia et regnum,* Festschrift for F.-J. Schmale (Bochum, 1989) 21-38; R. Schieffer, *Die Karolinger* (Stuttgart, 1992) 60-65; W. Hartmann, "Zur Autorität des Papsttums im karolingischen Frankenreich," in *Mönchtum—Kirche—Herrschaft 750-1000* (Sigmaringen, 1998) 113-32.

SEBASTIAN SCHOLZ

Stephen III (Aug. 7, 768-Jan. 24, 772). A Roman priest of Sicilian origin. Pope Constantine II was removed from office by the *primicerius* Christopher, with Langobard help, in 768, but Philip, the Langobard candidate, could not hold onto office. Under the influence of Christopher, Stephen was elected pope. With the aid of his patron, he conducted an anti-Langobard policy. A Roman synod in April 769, which was also attended by some Frankish bishops, declared the pontificate of Constantine II illegitimate and issued new regulations for the papal election. At the same time, the iconoclastic attitude of the Byzantine emperor was condemned. Stephen's pontificate was strongly influenced by the power struggle of the Frankish kings Charlemagne and Carloman. When Charlemagne wished to marry the daughter of a Langobard king in 770, Stephen threatened him with excommunication and made Carloman the offer of *compaternitas*. After reaching an accommodation with Charlemagne, Stephen sought a rapprochement with the Langobards too, and the Roman party that was hostile to the Langobards and supported Carloman lost its power. However, Carloman's death at the end of 771 changed the situation radically, so that Stephen's successor, Hadrian I, introduced a new policy.

■ **Sources:** *LP* 1:468-85; *RPR*(J) 1:285-88; 2:701; *MGH.Ep* 3:558-67.
■ **Bibliography:** *BBKL* 10:1354f.; *LMA* 8:117; *VATL* 765f.; Zimmermann *Pa* 16-25; J. T. Hallenbeck, *Pavia and Rome* (Philadelphia, 1982) 106ff.; T. F. X. Noble, *The Republic of Saint Peter* (Philadelphia, 1984) 112-27; W. Hartmann, *Die Synoden der Karolingerzeit im Frankenreich und in Italien* (Paderborn, 1989) 83-86; J. Jarnut, "Ein Bruderkampf und seine Folgen: Die Krise des Frankenreiches (768-771)," in *Herrschaft, Kirche, Kultur,* Festschrift for F. Prinz (Stuttgart, 1993) 165-76; W. Hartmann, "Zur Autorität des Papsttums im

karolingischen Frankenreich," in *Mönchtum—Kirche—Herrschaft 750-1000* (Sigmaringen, 1998) 113-32.

SEBASTIAN SCHOLZ

Stephen IV (June 22, 816-Jan. 24, 817). A member of the Roman nobility, he was a deacon when made pope without the assent of the emperor. He made the Romans swear an oath of allegiance to the Frankish emperor and soon journeyed into the Frankish realm in order to preserve the peace and unity of the church, which were threatened by older tensions and by the church reform of Emperor Louis I the Pious. Stephen renewed the alliance of friendship between the papacy and the Franks and clarified the legal questions, which were given definitive form in the *Pactum Hludovicianum* in 817, under Paschal I. Louis, who had been emperor since 813, was crowned and anointed by Stephen on October 5, 816, using a crown that had allegedly belonged to Constantine the Great. However, this coronation had no constitutive significance.

■ **Sources:** *LP* 2:49ff.; 3:121; *RPR*(J) 1:316ff.; 2:702.

■ **Bibliography:** *BBKL* 10:1355f.; *VATL* 766f.; T. F. X. Noble, *The Republic of Saint Peter* (Philadelphia, 1984); J. Fried, "Ludwig der Fromme, das Papsttum und die fränkische Kirche," in P. Godman and R. Collins, eds., *Charlemagne's Heir* (Oxford, 1990) 231-73; E. Boshof, *Ludwig der Fromme* (Darmstadt, 1996) 135-40; W. Hartmann, "Zur Autorität des Papsttums im karolingischen Frankenreich," in *Mönchtum—Kirche—Herrschaft 750-1000* (Sigmaringen, 1998) 113-32.

SEBASTIAN SCHOLZ

Stephen V (Aug./Sept. 885-Sept. 14, 891). A priest who belonged to the Roman nobility. He was elected pope without imperial assent, but soon persuaded Emperor Charles III, who had been angered, to recognize him. Since Charles took no action against the Saracens, Stephen asked Byzantium for help in 885. Only Duke Guido II of Spoleto provided active support. Stephen adopted Guido, thereby designating him as the future emperor. When Charles III died in 888, Guido—who in the meantime had been crowned king of Italy—demanded the imperial crown. Stephen felt himself threatened, but his appeal to the east Frankish king Arnulf for help went unheeded, and he was compelled to crown Guido as emperor on February 21, 891. In the mission to the Slavs, Stephen recognized Bishop Wiching of Neutra as the successor to Methodius and forbade the celebration of the liturgy in the Slavonic language, although he did allow preaching in Slavonic.

■ **Sources:** *LP* 2:191-98, 226; 3:126f.; *RPR*(J) 1:427-35; 2:705; *MG.Ep* 7:334-65.

■ **Bibliography:** *LMA* 8:117f.; *VATL* 767; E. Dümmler, *Geschichte des ostfränkischen Reiches* (2nd ed. Leipzig, 1888) 3:248-58, 367f.; R. Hiestand, *Byzanz und das Regnum Italicum im 10. Jahrhundert* (Zurich, 1964) 29f., 45-53; V. Peri, "Il mandato missionario e canonico di Metodio e l'ingresso della lingua slava nella liturgia," *AHP* 26 (1988) 9-69.

SEBASTIAN SCHOLZ

Stephen VI (end of Apr./beginning of May 896-Aug. 897). A Roman, bishop of Anagni. He was probably elected pope with the assent of Farold, the representative of Emperor Arnulf, who was ill. Stephen soon recognized Lambert of Spoleto as emperor. In December 896 or January 897, Stephen held a synod in the presence of the exhumed corpse of Pope Formosus, who was accused of illegitimately leaving his diocese of Porto to become bishop of Rome ("translation" was forbidden by canon law). Formosus's pontificate and the ordinations he had carried out were declared invalid, with the intention of weakening the position of his adherents. Stephen was taken captive at the end of July 897 in a rebellion in Rome and was later murdered.

■ **Sources:** *LP* 2:229; *RPR*(J) 1:439f.; Zimmermann *Pu* 1:3-9.

■ **Bibliography:** *LMA* 8:118; *VATL* 767f.; Zimmermann *Pa* 55-59; W. Hartmann, *Die Synoden der Karolingerzeit im Frankenreich und in Italien* (Paderborn, 1989) 388ff.; S. Scholz, *Transmigration und Translation* (Cologne, 1992) 219-24.

SEBASTIAN SCHOLZ

Stephen VII (mid-Jan. 929-end of Feb. 931). A Roman, cardinal priest. Like his predecessor, Leo VI, he was made pope under the influence of Vido of Tuscia and Marozia while John X was still alive. John was murdered in prison during the pontificate of Stephen. Stephen, obviously an elderly man, had no power and was perhaps only "keeping the seat warm" for his successor, John XI, the illegitimate son of Marozia.

■ **Sources:** *LP* 2:242; 3:129; *RPR*(J) 1:453f.; 2:706; Zimmermann *Reg* nos. 95-100.

■ **Bibliography:** *BBKL* 10:1356f.; *LMA* 8:118; *VATL* 768.

SEBASTIAN SCHOLZ

Stephen VIII (July 939-end of Oct. 945). A Roman, cardinal priest. He was made pope by Alberic II, a son of Marozia, and was completely dependent on him. The support he gave to the Cluniac reform in and around Rome was also prompted by Alberic. Stephen intervened in the conflict between the west Frankish king Louis IV and his vassals and exhorted the princes and all the inhabitants of France and Burgundy to recognize Louis under pain of excommunication. According to a later source, Stephen took part in a conspiracy against Alberic, who threw him into prison and had him mutilated.

■ **Sources:** *LP* 2:244; 3:129; *RPR*(J) 1:457f.; Zimmermann *Pu* 1:165-72; Zimmermann *Reg* nos. 154-64.

■ **Bibliography:** *BBKL* 10:1357; *LMA* 8:118; *VATL* 768.

SEBASTIAN SCHOLZ

Stephen IX (Aug. 2/3, 1057-Mar. 29, 1058). Formerly *Frederick of Lorraine,* a Benedictine. He died in Florence and is buried in the cathedral there. He was the son of Duke Gozelo I and brother of Duke Gottfried the Bearded. He was canon (perhaps also archdeacon) of the cathedral in Liège, and in 1049 also became dean of St. Alban's in Namur. Before October 1050, he came to Rome at the request of Leo IX. He is attested as chancellor in Rome from March 9, 1051, and also as deacon and librarian of the Roman church from June 10 of the same year. In 1054, he went to Constantinople as papal legate with Humbert of Silva Candida and Archbishop Peter of Amalfi, thereby contributing to the outbreak of the Eastern Schism; it is, however, unclear to what extent he took part in literary invectives against the Greeks. In order to evade tensions with Emperor Henry III, he entered Montecassino in 1055, where he was elected abbot on May 23, 1057. Pope Victor II created him cardinal priest of San Crisogono on June 14 and personally conferred the abbatial benediction on him on June 25. His election to the papacy on August 2, with the aid of his brother Gottfried, had something of the character of a surprise military action, although the customary rites were observed; he was crowned one day later. He did not regard it as necessary to get the subsequent assent of the German court (*RPR*[J] 1:4372); in any event, this was obtained without problems by his legates Anselm (later Alexander II) and Hildebrand (later Gregory VII) in the winter of 1057-1058. In Italy, Stephen furthered the worldly ambitions of Gottfried the Bearded and planned a joint military campaign with his brother against the Normans. He also fought against marriage within the forbidden degrees of relationship and against the marriage of priests. He made Humbert of Silva Candida chancellor and librarian of the Roman church, promoted Peter Damian to the office of cardinal bishop of Ostia, and enabled Hildebrand to become the archdeacon of Rome. This signaled a new phase of the Gregorian Reform.

■ **Sources:** C. Will, ed., *Acta et scripta* (Leipzig/Marburg, 1861) 93-153; A. Michel, *Humbert und Kerullarios I* (Paderborn, 1924) 97-111 (the attributions are uncertain: cf. *Deutsches Archiv für Erforschung des Mittelalters* 32 [1976] 54f.); *PL* 143:865-84; J. B. Watterich, *Pontificum Romanorum qui fuerunt inde ab exeunte saeculo IX usque ad finem saeculi XIII vitae ab aequalibus conscriptae etc.* (Leipzig, 1862) 1:188ff.; *RPR*(J) 1:553-56; *LP* 2:278; 3:133; *MGH.SS* 34:351ff.

■ **Bibliography:** *DHGE* 15:1198-1203; *BBKL* 10:1357-60; *LMA* 8:118f.; *VATL* 769f.; A. Michel, "Die Accusatio des Kanzlers Friedrich von Lothringen (Papst Stephan) gegen die Griechen," *RQ* 38 (1930) 153-208; G. Despy, "La carrière lotharingienne du pape Étienne IX," *Revue belge de philologie et d'histoire* 31 (1953) 955-72; R. Hüls, *Kardinäle, Klerus und Kirchen Roms 1049-1130* (Tübingen, 1977) 168f., 248; J. Dahlhaus, "Aufkommen und Bedeutung der Rota in den Urkunden des Papstes Leos IX.," *AHP* 27 (1989) 7-84; J. Laudage, *Gregorianische Reform und Investiturstreit* (Darmstadt, 1993); W. Peters, "Papst Stephan und die Lütticher Kirche," in *Papstgeschichte und Landesgeschichte,* Festschrift for H. Jakobs (Cologne, 1995) 157-76; F. Goez, *Beatrix von Canossa und Tuszien* (Sigmaringen, 1995).

JOHANNES LAUDAGE

Symmachus (Nov. 22, 498-July 19, 514). Saint (feast day July 19), born in Sardinia. After the death of Anastasius II, the majority—who had been unhappy with his conciliatory attitude in the schism of Patriarch Acacius of Constantinople—made the deacon Symmachus pope, and he was ordained bishop in the Lateran. The minority of those friendly to Byzantium, supported by the aristocracy and by the senate under Festus, reacted by making the archpriest Laurence pope; he was ordained bishop in Santa Maria Maggiore. Only a temporary respite to the confusion was achieved when Theoderic the Great, king of the east Goths, decided in favor of Symmachus, and Laurence was made bishop of Nocera in Campania. Symmachus held a synod on March 1, 499, to lay down rules for the election of future popes (*MGH.AA* 12:399-415). After accusations were made against Symmachus, a synod of Italian bishops in Rome refused to condemn him, on the grounds that Symmachus as pope was not subject to any human court, but only to the judgment of God (ibid. 416-37). The schism reflected the contentious issues that divided the Roman clergy and the senate, and Rome and Constantinople, as well as the endeavor of the Roman see to achieve independence vis-à-vis both Theoderic and Constantinople. With Theoderic's support, Laurence was able to return to Rome; the greater military power available to him allowed Laurence to exercise the papal office from 501 to 506, while Symmachus was restricted to asylum in St. Peter's (on the synod he held in 502, see *MGH.AA* 12:438-55). The confusions and conflicts ended only when Theoderic's conflict with Constantinople led him to abandon his support for Laurence in 506. Symmachus was restored to his full rights and proved a defender of the faith against Eastern church politics, which insisted on retaining the *Henotikon*. He bestowed the → pallium on Bishop Caesarius of Arles and issued a decree laying down the primatial rights of Arles in the church in Gaul and Spain.

■ **Sources:** A. Thiel, *Epp. Romanorum Pontificum* (Braunsberg, 1868) 1:639-738; *MGH.AA* 12:399-455; *LP* 1:43-46, 260-68; *RPR*(J) 1:96-100; 2:693f., 736.

■ **Bibliography:** *DTHC* 14:2984-90; *BBKL* 11:359-63; *DECL* 548; *VATL* 775; Caspar 2:87-129, 758-61; G. P. Picotti, "I sinodi romani nello scisma laurenzio," in *Studi storici*, Festschrift for G. Volpe (Florence, 1958) 2:741-86; C. Pietri, "Le Sénat, le peuple chrétien et les partis du cirque à Rome sous le pape Symmaque (498-514)," *Mélanges d'archéologie et d'histoire* 78 (1966) 123-39; P. A. B. Llewellyn, "The Roman Clergy during the Laurentian Schism (489-506)," *Ancient Society* 8 (1977) 245-75; C. Pietri, "Aristocratie et société cléricale dans l'Italie chrétienne au temps d'Odoacre et de Théodoric," *Mélanges de l'Ecole Française de Rome, Antiquité* 93 (1981) 417-67; Borgolte; M. Maccarrone, ed., *Il primato del vescovo di Roma nel primo millennio* (Rome, 1991); J. Gaudemet, "Aux origines de la 'libertas ecclesiae' dans la Rome symmaquienne," in *Histoire et société*, Festschrift for G. Duby (Aix-en-Provence, 1992) 113-25; S. Vacca, *Prima Sedes a nemine iudicatur* (Rome, 1993); E. Wirbelauer, *Zwei Päpste in Rom: Der Konflikt zwischen Laurentius und Symmachus* (Munich, 1993); J. D. Alchermes, "Petrine Politics: Pope Symmachus and the Rotunda of St. Andrew at Old St. Peter's," *Catholic Historical Review* 81 (1995) 1-40; T. Sardella, *Società, Chiesa e Stato*

nell'età di Teodorico: Papa Simmaco e lo scisma laurenziano (Soveria Mannelli, 1996).

During the trial of Symmachus, his adherents composed the *Symmachian forgeries*, which relate invented trials of popes in the attempt to demonstrate that the pope cannot be judged by any court on earth. The trials are first, *Sinuessanae Synodi Gesta de Marcellino papa*; second, *Constitutio (Canon) Silvestri*; third, *Gesta Liberii*; fourth, *Gesta de Xysti purgatione et Polychronii accusatione*. The form and language of these texts is clumsy, their ideas a dim reflection of Pope Gelasius I.

The intention of the narrative of these invented trials is to correct the trial of Symmachus by taking up critical points of papal history (Marcellinus, Liberius, Sixtus III, Silvester I). These forgeries found many readers and became very influential, thanks above all to their inclusion (in selective and abbreviated form) in the → Liber Pontificalis.

■ **Sources:** *Text:* P. Coustant, *Epp. Romanorum Pontificum* (Paris, 1721) 1:appendix, 2ff.; *LP* 1:CXXVI ff.

■ **Bibliography:** *LMA* 4:246-51; I. von Döllinger, *Die Papstfabeln des Mittelalters* (2nd ed. Stuttgart, 1890) 57ff.; Caspar 2:107-10; W. Speyer, *Die literarischen Fälschungen im heidnischen und christlichen Altertum* (Munich, 1971); P. V. Aimone, "Le falsificazioni simmachiane," *Apollinaris* 68 (1995) 205-20.

GEORG SCHWAIGER

Telesphorus (125?-138?). Saint (feast day Jan. 5). According to the list of bishops presented by Irenaeus of Lyons (*Adversus haereses* 3.3.3), who mentions his martyrdom, he was the seventh bishop of Rome. This list anachronistically projects the monarchical episcopate, which had become established by Irenaeus's time, back into the first half of the second century. Historically speaking, Telesphorus probably belonged to the group of leading priests or bishops in Rome. His name was remembered (perhaps because of his martyrdom?) and was therefore available for inclusion in the list of "bishops of Rome." In his letter to Bishop Victor of Rome (ca. 195), Irenaeus mentions Telesphorus as one of the "priests" who held office "before Soter" and displayed tolerance in questions of church discipline vis-à-vis Christians from other communities (Eusebius, *Historia ecclesiastica* 5.24.14). Later information about the "pontificate" and activity of Telesphorus (e.g.,

143

Eusebius 4.5.5, 10; *Liber Pontificalis* 9) have no historical value.

■ **Bibliography:** *BiblSS* 12:188f.; *BBKL* 11:625; *VATL* 777; L. Hertling, "Namen und Herkunft der römischen Bischöfe der ersten Jahrhunderte," in *Saggi storici intorno al papato* (Rome, 1959) 1-16; T. Klauser, *Die Anfänge der römischen Bischofsliste* (Münster, 1974) 121-38; N. Brox, "Probleme einer Frühdatierung des römischen Primats," *Kairos* 18 (1976) 81-99; idem, "Das Papsttum in den ersten drei Jahrhunderten," *GKG* 11:25-42.

FRANZ DÜNZL

Theodore I (Nov. 24, 642-May 14, 649). Born in Jerusalem, the son of a bishop; buried in St. Peter's. The dominating issue in the pontificate of the first Byzantine pope was the Monoenergetic-Monothelite controversy. After the equivocation of Honorius I, Theodore conducted a vigorous struggle against Monothelitism and excommunicated Pyrrhus I and Paul II, patriarchs of Constantinople. Theodore had initially rejected Paul and recognized Pyrrhus as patriarch, since he had abjured the heresy, but then he relapsed; Paul had spoken openly in defense of Monothelitism. Theodore, who enjoyed the continuous support of Maximus the Confessor, sent Bishop Stephen of Dor as papal legate to the church of Palestine, which was lacerated by the controversies. He also prepared the Lateran synod which was held in October 649. He died before he could respond to the *Typos* of Emperor Constans II.

■ **Sources:** *LP* 1:331-35; *RPR*(J) 1:228ff.; 2:698; Mansi 10:699-708.

■ **Bibliography:** *LMA* 8:629; *BBKL* 14:1544f.; *VATL* 778; Richards 184ff.; O. Capitani, "Le relazioni tra le vite di Teodoro I e Martino I del LP," *Studi e Ricerche sull'Oriente Cristiano* 15 (1992) 5-14.

MANFRED HEIM

Theodore (antipope [?]) (end of 687). Archpriest in Rome. After the death of John V in 686, Theodore was the candidate of the Roman military forces. After the death of Conon on September 21, 687, he was made pope; the opposing candidate this time was the archdeacon Paschal. In the course of the conflicts that ensued between the two rival claimants, however, it was Sergius I who won election in October/December 687. Theodore, who had not yet received episcopal ordination, submitted at once. The designation "antipope" is therefore inexact.

■ **Sources:** *LP* 1:368-72; *RPR*(J) 1:243f.

■ **Bibliography:** *LMA* 8:630; *BBKL* 11:860f.; *VATL* 778; Caspar 2:621ff.; Richards 206ff.

MANFRED HEIM

Theodore II (Dec. 897). A Roman priest. During his pontificate, which lasted only twenty days, Theodore convoked a synod that restored to honor Formosus, who had been posthumously deposed by Stephen VI, and recognized the ordinations he had carried out. Theodore had Formosus's body reburied in St. Peter's.

■ **Sources:** *LP* 2:231; 3:128; *RPR*(J) 1:441; Mansi 17:221.

■ **Bibliography:** *LMA* 8:629f.; *BBKL* 11:859f.; *VATL* 778; Zimmermann *Pa* 59f.; W. Hartmann, *Die Synoden der Karolingerzeit im Frankenreich und in Italien* (Paderborn, 1989) 390; S. Scholz, *Transmigration und Translation* (Cologne, 1992) 225.

SEBASTIAN SCHOLZ

Theodoric (antipope) (Sept. 1100-Jan. 1101). Died 1102 at La Cava. He was created cardinal deacon of Santa Maria in Via Lata in 1084 and was one of the most important partisans of the antipope Clement III, who made him cardinal bishop of Albano. After Clement's death, he was made pope and was enthroned at once. He was taken prisoner by the followers of Paschal II in January 1101 while he was on his way to meet Emperor Henry IV and was brought back to Rome. Theodoric died in 1102, a prisoner in the abbey of the Trinity at La Cava.

■ **Sources:** *LP* 2:298.

■ **Bibliography:** *LMA* 8:624; *VATL* 778f.; R. Hüls, *Kardinäle, Klerus und Kirchen Roms* (Tübingen, 1977) 92; C. Servatius, *Paschalis II. (1099-1118)* (Stuttgart, 1979) 69-72, 339.

MANFRED HEIM

Urban I (222-230). Saint (feast day May 25). Because of the paucity of sources, we know little about the personality and the pontificate of Urban I. According to Eusebius's church history, he was the successor to Calixtus I. The dates for Urban's reign given in the list of Roman bishops in the Liberian Catalog (in the → Chronography of 354) do not agree with the other information given there. He was pope for eight or nine years during the reign of Emperor Alexander Severus, who practiced tolerance in religious matters; there was no further persecution of Christians in Urban's pontificate. The schism of Hippolytus continued. The Adoptianist and Montanist movements seem to have been less active in Rome during his pontificate. Otherwise, there is no certain information about his period in office. According to the → *Liber Pontificalis*, he was of Roman origin. There is no reason to accept the historicity of an order by Urban that only silver be used for cultic vessels, or of a Letter to All Christians in his name; similarly, a decretal of Urban in the Pseudo-Isidorian collection is unhistorical. Affirmations about his martyrdom are based on the legendary *Passion of St. Cecilia* (fifth century) and apocryphal acts of martyrs. The Martyrology of Jerome records his burial in the catacomb of Calixtus, where a funeral slab with his name and his episcopal office in Greek has been found.

■ **Sources:** Eusebius of Caesarea, *Historia ecclesiastica* 6.21.2; 6.23.3; *MGH.AA* 9:74; *LP* 1:XCIII f., 4f., 62f., 143f.; *ActaSS nov.* 2/2:206f.

■ **Bibliography:** *ActaSS mai.* 6:5-23; *BiblSS* 12:837-41; *BBKL* 12:924f.; Caspar 1:32-57; Richards; E. Dal Covolo, *I Severi e il cristianesimo* (Rome, 1988).

STEPHAN C. KESSLER

Urban II (Mar. 12, 1088-July 29, 1099). Blessed (feast day July 29). Formerly *Odo of Châtillon*, born ca. 1035 into a noble family, probably near Châtillon-sur-Marne. After studies in Rheims under Bruno the Carthusian, he became canon and archdeacon of Rheims, and later monk and prior in Cluny. He was created cardinal bishop of Ostia in 1080 and sent to Germany as legate in 1084-1085. The beginning of his pontificate was overshadowed by the menace of Emperor Henry IV and the imperial antipope Wibert of Ravenna (Clement III). Nevertheless, Urban succeeded in overcoming the crisis that had affected the reforming papacy since the death of Gregory VII and in ensuring the historic breakthrough of the Consistory. His policies and the reform he undertook were primarily determined by the papal schism, which the emperor supported; Urban did not succeed in solving this problem. Nor was it possible to resolve the investiture problem; Urban did not follow his predecessors in making this a priority, although he did intensify the prohibition of investiture by forbidding clergy to swear oaths of feudal allegiance, at the Councils of Clermont (1095) and Rome (1099). No peace was reached in the conflict with the emperor or in the German conflict about investiture. Relations with England remained very tense, despite the pope's de facto acceptance of the Norman subordination of the church to the state. Despite his conflict with Philip I of France (concerning the king's marriage), Urban avoided a breach and paved the way for the future alliance between the papacy and the French kingdom. His pontificate had the greatest effect in the Iberian peninsula and southern Europe, where Urban supported the Christian reconquest of Spain and church restoration; he developed a theology of history (following Daniel 2:21) which spoke of a "change in the times" willed by God. In Spain, he reorganized the church and detached the Spanish church from Narbonne in Gaul. In southern Italy and Sicily, the cooperation between the papacy and the Normans led to the legation-privilege for Count Roger I in 1089 (*Monarchia Sicula*). Nothing came of attempts to reach an understanding with the Greek church (negotiations with the Byzantine emperor Alexius I Commenus and Patriarch Nicholas III Grammaticus in 1089; the Council of Basri in 1098). When imperial legates asked for help against the Turks at the Council in Piacenza in 1095, Urban linked the concepts of Christian reconquest and restoration with aid to Byzantium and Christians in the East, and initiated the movement of the crusades with the appeal he launched at Clermont in November 1095. His concentration of the episcopal structure of the church on the papal primacy, development of the College of → Cardinals, strengthening of the judicial powers of the papacy, extension of the curia, the → Apostolic Chamber and the papal → chancellery indicated the direction that the Roman church of the twelfth century would take in ecclesiology, canon law, and administration.

■ **Sources:** *LP* 1:293ff.; 3:65; J. B. Watterich, *Pontificum Romanorum qui fuerunt inde ab exeunte saeculo IX usque ad finem saeculi XIII vitae ab aequalibus conscriptae, etc.*, I *(972-1099)* (Leipzig, 1862) 571-620, 744ff.; *RPR*(J) 2nd ed. 1:657-701; 2:713, 752f.; *RPR.GP; RPR.IP; PL* 151:9-266; R. Somerville, *The Councils of Urban II, Decreta Claromontensia* (Paderborn, 1972); idem, *Pope Urban II, the Collectio Britannica and the Council of Melfi* (Oxford, 1996).

■ **Bibliography:** *LMA* 8:1282ff.; *BBKL* 15:1391-94; *VATL* 792f.; H. Fuhrmann, *Papst Urban II. und der Stand der Regularkanoniker* (Bayerische Akademie der Wissenschaften, Philosophisch-historische Klasse, Sitzungsberichte, Munich, 1984); E. Mazza, "Il prefazio della Vergine Maria istituito da Urbano II," *Marianum* 57 (1995) 269-89; R. Somerville, "Pope Urban II, 'To the Beloved Sons in Christ J. and His Brothers,'" in *Roma, magistra mundi*, Festschrift for L. E. Boyle (Louvain-la-

Neuve, 1998) 2:843-53; C. Capizzi, "Il concilio di Bari (1098)," *Nicolaus* 26 (1999) 69-90; G. Cioffari, "Il concilio di Bari del 1098," *Nicolaus* 26 (1999) 109-21; A. Becker, "Urbain II et l'Orient," *Nicolaus* 26 (1999) 123-44; G. Andenna, "Urbano II e la questione dell'unità delle Chiese cristiane d'Oriente e d'Occidente," *Nicolaus* 26 (1999) 317-26; R. Somerville, "Pope Urban II, a Pseudo-Council of Chartres, and 'Congregatio' (c.16, q.7, c.2 'Palea')," in *Reform and Renewal in the Middle Ages and the Renaissance,* Festschrift for L. Pascoe (Leiden, 2000) 18-34.

ALFONS BECKER

Urban III (Nov. 25, 1185-Oct. 20, 1187). Formerly *Humbert Crivelli,* born in a Milanese family, died and buried at Ferrara. He studied civil and canon law and was the teacher of Peter of Blois. He became a canon regular, archdeacon of Bourges and of Milan, and bishop of Vercelli. He was created cardinal priest of San Lorenzo in Damaso at the beginning of September 1182 and was papal legate in Lombardy from 1183 to 1184. He was appointed archbishop of Milan in early January 1185 and was elected pope in Verona the day his predecessor, Lucius III, died. As pope, he retained possession of his diocese but did not leave Verona. Initially, Urban declared his (feigned?) readiness to continue Lucius's negotiations with Emperor Frederick I Barbarossa about the Patrimony of Peter, but an implacable enmity toward the emperor was caused by the marriage of Henry VI with Constance of Sicily in Milan on January 27, 1186 (at which Urban was represented by two cardinals) and the surprising coronation of Henry by the patriarch of Aquileia, after Lucius had strictly refused to crown him; from now on, Henry was known as *caesar.* Urban complained to the imperial parliament about the emperor's refusal to hand back church property and to renounce his rights to booty and to feudal sovereignty. Urban went back on his original promise and ordained the papal candidate in the schism of Trier as archbishop on June 1, 1186—probably after consulting the archbishop of Cologne, Philip of Heimsberg, who was appointed papal legate and made a strong appeal for support for the papal candidate in June and July. Urban also supported the revolt in Cremona. Henry VI was sent at once to Italy by his father and demanded that all the cities take an oath of loyalty to the emperor, while Barbarossa remained in Germany and

assured himself of the support of the bishops in the empire at the imperial parliament of Gelnhausen on November 28, 1186. Negotiations, which were started only after many complications had been overcome, led to nothing, since Urban fled to Ferrara, which was hostile to the emperor.

■ **Bibliography:** *LMA* 8:1284; *BBKL* 15:1934f.; *VATL* 793ff.; K. Ganzer, *Die Entwicklung des auswärtigen Kardinalats im hohen Mittelalter* (Tübingen, 1963) 134ff.; F.-J. Heyen, "Über die Trierer Doppelwahlen von 1183 und 1242," *Archiv für mittelrheinische Kirchengeschichte* 21 (1969) 21-28; *Urbano III nell'ottavo centenario della morte (1187-1987)* (Ferrara, 1987[?]); C. Reisinger, *Tankred von Lecce* (Cologne, 1992) 42-45, 63f., 117; O. Engels, *Stauferstudien* (2nd ed. Sigmaringen, 1996) 194ff.; L. Falkenstein, "Urbans III. Dekretale JL 15746 [WH 280] und der Streit um die Einkünfte der Kirche in Brieulles-sur-Meuse," *Zeitschrift der Savigny-Stiftung für Rechtsgeschichte, Kanonistische Abteilung* 117 (2000) 185-261.

ODILO ENGELS

Urban IV (Aug. 29, 1261-Oct. 2, 1264). Formerly *Jacques Pantaléon,* born before 1200 (probably ca. 1185) at Troyes, died at Perugia. His origins were humble (his father repaired shoes), and he was educated in the abbey of Notre-Dame-aux-Nonnains. He studied the arts, canon law, and perhaps also theology in Paris, where he took the degree of Master. He became a canon in Laon, and was archdeacon in Liège. He was appointed papal legate in Livonia, Pomerania, and the empire in 1247. He was made bishop of Verdun, then patriarch of Jerusalem in 1255; in this latter office, he attempted to resolve the conflict between Venice and Genoa. He was elected by seven cardinals as a compromise candidate and was crowned on September 4, 1261, in Viterbo. He made his residence in Viterbo and Orvieto and never entered Rome. He enlarged the College of Cardinals by appointing Frenchmen. After the end of the Latin empire of Constantinople, he sought an accommodation with Byzantium. He acted as arbiter in the conflict about the German throne and in the controversy between the English king and his barons. He laid the foundations of the end of the power of Manfred the Staufer in Sicily, by supporting Charles of Anjou and making a treaty on August 15, 1264, which initiated Charles's assumption of sovereignty in the Sicilian kingdom. In the bull *Transiturus* (August 11, 1264), he prescribed the feast of Corpus Christi for the universal church.

■ **Bibliography:** *Dictionnaire Encyclopédique du Moyen Âge* (Cambridge et al., 1997) 2:1556; *BBKL* 15:1395-98; *LMA* 8:1284; *VATL* 795; S. Martinet, *La Fête-Dieu, Jacques de Troyes et l'école de théologie de Laon* (Laon, 1965); A. Paravicini Bagliani, "Gregorio da Napoli, biografo di Urbano IV," *Römische historische Mitteilungen* 11 (1969) 59-78; I. Rodríguez and R. de Lama, *La documentación pontificia de Urbano IV* (Rome, 1981); J. Foviaux, "Les sermons donnés à Laon en 1242 par le chanoine Jacques de Troyes, futur Urbain IV," *Recherches Augustiniennes* 20 (1985) 203-56; E. Pispisa, *Il Regno di Manfredi* (Messina, 1991) esp. 286ff.; B. Berg, "Manfred of Sicily and Urban IV: Negotiations of 1262," *Mediaeval Studies* 55 (1993) 111-36; M. Rubin, *Corpus Christi: The Eucharist in Late Medieval Culture* (Cambridge, 1991; repr. 1994); I. Grobry, *Deux papes champenois, Urbain II et Urbain IV* (Troyes, 1994); J. Lamberts, "The Origin of the Corpus Christi Feast," *Worship* 70 (1996) 432-46; *Fête-Dieu (1246-1996): Actes du Colloque de Liège, 1996* (Louvain-la-Neuve, 1999: numerous essays).

LUDWIG VONES

Urban V (Sept. 28, 1362-Dec. 19, 1370). Blessed (feast day Dec. 19), formerly *Guillaume Grimoard,* a Benedictine, born ca. 1310 in the castle of Grisac (Gévaudan) into a family belonging to the southern French aristocracy; died in Avignon and is buried in St. Victor's church in Marseilles. He entered the Benedictine priory of Chirac, perhaps after studying civil law in Toulouse. He became prior of Saint-Mau in the diocese of Auch. After further studies of the arts and canon law in Montpellier, Toulouse, and Paris, he became doctor in civil and canon law and bachelor in canon law. He then taught in Montpellier, Paris, and Avignon. After acting as procurator-general of the Cluniac order, papal legate in Italy, vicar general in Clermont and Uzès, as well as prior of a number of other monasteries, he became abbot of St. Germain in Auxerre in 1352, and abbot of St. Victor's in Marseilles in 1361. He was elected pope as a compromise candidate while still abbot, thanks to the support of influential families of cardinals, and was crowned in Avignon on November 6, 1362. Urban was a deeply pious man who had a high vision of his papal office and was profoundly inspired by the idea of a church reform in keeping with the Benedictine spirit, closely akin to the idea of *ordo* in the high Middle Ages, which demanded collaboration between the pope and the emperor. His reforming measures and the goals of his church politics were guided by high ideals. He fought against the amassing of benefices and issued important reform Constitutions on this issue; he also acted against heresy and the huge armies of mercenaries, taking extensive defensive measures in Provence and Languedoc; he acted to restore the great congregations of monks and canons regular. He supported the universities where priests were trained; Krakow, Pécs, and Vienna were founded at this time. He also took action to recover the church states, sending Cardinals Aegidius Albornoz, and Androin de la Roche on missions to Italy, and fighting against Bernabò Visconti. The return of the papacy to Rome was a major issue between 1367 and 1370; Urban had contacts with Petrarch and Bridget of Sweden on this subject. The intention was to make Rome once again the center of Christendom; Charles IV's visit in 1368 must be seen in this context. Urban also supported the idea of a crusade and attempted to mediate a peace in the Hundred Years War. He tried to reestablish unity between the Eastern and the Western churches, and John V Palaeologos made a personal profession of faith in Rome in 1369. He could not extricate himself from nepotism, making his brother Anglic Grimoard bishop of Avignon and cardinal; but although he called many of his fellow countrymen from Gévaudan and members of the Benedictine order to be his close associates in the curia, he did not succeed in setting his own stamp on it and reforming it. His retreat from Italy has been the object of much criticism, but it made political sense. Despite all this, he was certainly a reforming pope, and soon after his death he was venerated in Provence and in Gévaudan. His canonization process was interrupted during the Western Schism and was never brought to a successful conclusion. His cult as "Blessed" was confirmed in 1870.

■ **Bibliography:** *LMA* 8:1284f.; *Dictionnaire Encyclopédique du Moyen Âge* (Cambridge et al., 1997) 2:1556f.; *VATL* 795f.; *BBKL* 19; R. Pauler, *Die Auseinandersetzungen zwischen Kaiser Karl IV. und den Päpsten* (Neuried, 1996); B. Galland, *Les Papes d'Avignon et la Maison de Savoie (1309-1409)* (Rome, 1998); E. Delaruelle, "La translation des reliques de Saint Thomas d'Aquin à Toulouse (1369) et la politique universitaire d'Urbain V," *Bulletin de littérature ecclésiastique* 100 (1999) 299-317; L. Vones, *Urban V. (1362-70)* (Stuttgart, 1999); idem, "Papsttum und Episkopat im 14. Jahrhundert: Probleme der avignonesischen Päpste mit den Bistümern des Deutschen Reiches unter besonderer Berücksichtigung des Pontifikats Urbans V (1362-70)," *RQ* 94 (1999) 149-82; P. N. Zutshi, "The Registers of the Common Letters of Pope Urban V and Pope Gregory XI," *Journal of Ecclesiastical History* 51 (2000) 497-508.

LUDWIG VONES

Urban VI (Apr. 8, 1378-Oct. 15, 1389). Formerly *Bartolomeo Prignano*, born ca. 1318 into a respected Neapolitan family. He was a canon lawyer, and after a career at the university (rector in 1350) and in the church (vicar general) in Naples, he became archbishop of Acerenza in 1363 and was called to the curia in Avignon, where he gained a wide administrative experience in the papal chancellery under Cardinal Pierre de Monteruc. When Gregory XI returned to Rome in 1377, he appointed him head of the chancellery and archbishop of Bari. He was elected in tumultuous circumstances, in a conclave that was under pressure by the Romans to elect a Roman, or at least an Italian, pope; nevertheless, his election should be considered valid, especially in view of reactions in contemporary ecclesiastical correspondence and of the universal recognition accorded to Urban in the first weeks of his pontificate. In August 1378, a group of cardinals, mostly French, declared his election invalid on the grounds that the Romans had forced them to elect Urban; they elected Clement VII at Fondi on September 20. This was the outcome of the bitter collision course which Urban had taken against those who had elected him. He wounded them with such harsh attacks on their lifestyle and their errors that they retaliated by accusing him of being incapable of performing the duties of his office; moreover, he was extremely arrogant and obstinate. This was also a reflection of the conflict between an Italian papacy and a College of Cardinals where Frenchmen formed the majority; the aftereffects of the epoch of the Avignon papacy under French domination could still be felt. This meant that the discussion about the legitimacy of the two papal claimants soon shifted from the level of canon law to politics: in the Western Schism which now broke out, two "obediences," that of Rome and of Avignon, were formed. After Clement was expelled from Italy by military force, Urban, convinced of his own legitimacy, refused all negotiations and appeals to a universal council and called for a crusade against his rival. As feudal sovereign of the kingdom of Naples, he deposed Queen Joan I, who belonged to the French branch of the house of Anjou and supported Clement. He had crowned Charles III of Durazzo, of the Hungarian branch of the house of Anjou in 1381, but now he quarreled with him too, when Charles demanded that he make his nephew duke of Capua and Amalfi; he accused Charles of involvement in a plot by cardinals who wanted to put him under restraint, and he proclaimed a crusade against Charles too. He had five cardinals executed in Genoa, the city to which he had fled in the course of his year-long struggles against the king. After Charles was murdered in Hungary, the plan to occupy Naples failed, principally because Urban failed to pay the wages of the mercenaries. When he returned to his see in 1388, he quarreled with the Romans and may have died a victim of poisoning. He is buried in St. Peter's.

The election of Urban signaled the beginning of Neapolitan domination in the curia. Everything seemed to augur well at the beginning of Urban's pontificate, bearing in mind his former conduct of life, his desire to reform the church, and his administrative talent. He pursued reform with an excessive rigor; his psychopathic traits appeared only after he had assumed office. These included an obsessive hatred of the College of Cardinals, of which he had never become a member, despite his many years of service in the curia. His behavior weakened the Roman position in the schism, since many office-bearers went over to the obedience of Avignon; the papal finances were in a catastrophic state; and the church state sank into anarchy. His election was no doubt legitimate, but the same cannot necessarily be said for his pontificate itself. Only a few truly ecclesial acts can be recorded during this time: the extension of the Franciscan feast of the Visitation of Mary to the universal church; the celebration of every thirty-third year as a → Holy Year; and privileges of foundation for the universities of Heidelberg, Cologne, Erfurt, and Lucca.

■ **Bibliography:** *GKG* 12:8ff.; *BBKL* 12:925-28; *LMA* 8:1285f.; *VATL* 796ff.; L. Tacchella, *Il pontificato di Urbano VI a Genova (1385-86) e l'eccidio dei cardinali* (Genoa, 1976); *Genèse et débuts du Grand Schisme d'Occident (1362-94)* (Paris, 1978); M. Jacoviello, "Un papa napoletano nello scisma d'occidente: Bartolomeo Prignano (1378-89)," *Campania Sacra* 21 (1990) 72-95; W. Brandmüller, "Zur Frage nach der Gültigkeit der Wahl Urbans VI." (first published 1974), in *Papst und Konzil* *im Großen Schisma* (Paderborn, 1990) 3-41; A. M. Voci, "Alle origini del Grande Scisma d'Occidente . . . ," *Bullettino dell'Istituto Storico Italiano* 99 (1994) 297-339; idem, "Giovanna I d'Angio e l'inizio del Grande Scisma d'Occidente," *QFIAB* 75 (1995) 178-255; J.-Y. Tilliette, "Les leçons de l'histoire: Un document inédit sur le conclave mouvementé de 1378," in *Milieux naturels, espaces sociaux,* Festschrift for R. Delort (Paris, 1997) 635-51.

HERIBERT MÜLLER

Urban VII (Sept. 15-27, 1590). Formerly *Giambattista Castagna,* born Aug. 4, 1521, in Rome, member of a noble Genoese family. He studied civil and canon law in Perugia, Padua, and Bologna, where he became doctor in both laws. He was archbishop of Rossano from 1553 to 1573 and took part in the last period of sessions of the Council of Trent. He was nuncio in Spain from 1565 to 1572, and in Venice from 1573 to 1576. He attended the Diet of Pacification at Cologne in 1578-1579, which met to resolve the conflict about Flanders, and he was created cardinal in 1583. Although he was already *papabile* in 1585, he led an existence out of the limelight under Sixtus V. He was elected in 1590 as the candidate of the Spanish-Tuscan party, but died only twelve days later of malaria.
- Sources: *NBD* III 2:197-202, 223-370; A. Buffardi, *Nunziature di Venezia* (Rome, 1972) XI.
- Bibliography: *BBKL* 12:928f.; *VATL* 798; L. Arrighi, *Vita Urbani VII* (Bologna, 1614); Pastor 10:503-18; E. García Hernán, "Urbano VII: Un papa de trece dias," *Hispania sacra* 47 (1995) 561-86.

ALEXANDER KOLLER

Urban VIII (Aug. 6, 1623-July 29, 1644). Formerly *Maffeo Barberini,* born Apr. 5, 1568, in Florence. He attended the Collegium Romanum and studied civil and canon law in Pisa, where he became doctor in both laws. He was *referendarius* in the two Signatura courts in 1589 and became governor of Fano in 1592. He purchased a position as clerical chamberlain in 1597 and was sent to Paris in October 1601. He was appointed titular archbishop of Nazareth and nuncio in France in November 1604; he held this position until 1607. He was created cardinal in 1606 and was bishop of Spoleto from 1608 to 1617. He was legate in Bologna from 1611 to 1614, then prefect of the Signatura court of Justice. He was celebrated as a Latin poet and a friend of the sciences. As pope, he leaned toward France, altering the politics of his predecessor, Gregory XV. He stopped paying subsidies to the emperor and the League and accepted the expulsion of papal troops by France in Veltlin (1624-1625). Francesco Barberini's legation to France and Spain in 1625 was a failure, and the pope did not take part when the Treaty of Monzón was signed in 1626. Urban's aims in the Mantuan War of Succession (1628-1630) were the weakening of the house of Habsburg, political equilibrium in Italy, and the indirect furthering of French interests; an initiative of the nuncio in Paris, Giovanni Francesco Guidi di Bagno, led to the conclusion of a secret alliance between Bavaria and France in the spring of 1631. Despite Spanish threats, Urban accepted the alliance between France and Sweden in 1631, as he had earlier accepted the peace between France and England in April 1629. In view of the Swedish military successes and the risk that the imperial Catholic position in the empire might collapse, Urban resolved to send financial aid to the emperor and the League; this subvention ended with the Peace of Prague in 1635. The special nuncios whom he sent to the Catholic princes in 1632, in the attempt to persuade them to make peace, had no success. French entry into the war in 1635 caused confusion in Rome; subsequently, cardinal Marzio Ginetti was sent as legate to Cologne to negotiate a peace. The nuncio in Cologne, Fabio Chigi (later Alexander VII), worked from 1643 onward as a neutral mediator for the Peace of Westphalia. (His instructions made it virtually impossible for him to protect Catholic interests, and the protests made by Chigi in 1648 and Innocent X in 1649 against the regulations about confessional politics in the Peace of Münster and Osnabrück were the logical outcome of this situation.) Apart from the preservation of the political equilibrium in Italy, Urban's main concerns were to ensure the stability of the → papal states (to which Urbino was returned between 1623 and 1631) and to promote his own family. Urban's excessive → nepotism provided the backdrop to the War of Castro against the Farnese dynasty (1641-1644), which ruined the papal finances. The external splendor of this pontificate, with magnificent works of art (e.g., by Giovanni Lorenzo Bernini), cannot conceal its negative aspects: the struggle against Gallicanism and Jansenism met with no success; the Institute of the Blessed Virgin Mary, founded by Mary Ward, was dissolved in 1631; and the disciplinary condemnation of Galileo Galilei on June 22, 1633, had particularly grave consequences for the relation of the church to modern science.

■ Sources: A. Cauchie and R. Maere, *Recueil des instructions générales aux nonces de Flandres 1596-1635* (Brussels, 1904); A. Leman, *Recueil des instructions générales aux nonces ordinaires de France de 1624 à 1634* (Paris/Lille, 1920); K. Repgen, "Fabio Chigis Instruktion für den Westfälischen Friedenskongreß (1636)," *RQ* 48 (1953) 79-116; idem, "Die Hauptinstruktion Ginettis für den Kölner Kongreß (1636)," *QFIAB* 34 (1954) 250-87; B. de Meester, *Correspondance du nonce Giovanni Francesco Guidi di Bagno (1621-27),* 2 vols. (Brussels/Rome, 1938); G. Incisa della Rocchetta and V. Kybal, *La Nunziatura di Fabio Chigi (1640-51)* (Rome, 1943-46) I/1-2; W. Brulez, *Correspondance de Martino Alfieri (1634-39)* (Brussels/Rome, 1956); P. Blet, *Correspondance du nonce en France Ranuccio Scotti (1639-41)* (Rome, 1965); W. Goetz and D. Albrecht, *Briefe und Akten zur Geschichte des Dreißigjährigen Krieges,* new series (Munich, 1907-64) Part II/1-5; Q. Aldea, "España, el Papado y el Imperio durante la Guerra de los Treinta Años: Instrucciones a los Embajadores de España en Roma (1631-43)," *Miscelánea Comillas* 27 (1957) 291-437; H. Tüchle, ed., *Acta Sacrae Congregationis de Propaganda Fide Germaniam spectantia 1623-49* (Paderborn, 1962); *NDB(G)* 7/1-4.

■ Bibliography: *BBKL* 12:929-33; *VATL* 798ff.; Pastor XIII; J. Grisar, "Päpstliche Finanzen, Nepotismus und Kirchenrecht unter Urban VIII.," *Miscellanea historiae pontificiae* 14 (1943) 205-366; K. Repgen, "Finanzen, Kirchenrecht und Politik unter Urban VIII.," *RQ* 56 (1961) 62-74; D. Albrecht, *Die auswärtige Politik Maximilians von Bayern 1618-35* (Göttingen, 1962); A. Kraus, *Das päpstliche Staatssekretariat unter Urban VIII 1623-44* (Freiburg, 1964); G. Lutz, *Kardinal G. F. G. di Bagno: Politik und Religion im Zeitalter Richelieus und Urbans VIII* (Tübingen, 1971); G. Lutz, "Rom und Europa während des Pontifikats Urbans VIII.," in R. Elze et al., eds., *Rom in der Neuzeit* (Vienna, 1976) 72-167; P. Surchat, *Die Nunziatur, von Ranuccio Scotti in Luzern 1630-39* (Rome et al., 1979); K. Jaitner, ed., *Die Hauptinstruktionen Clemens' VIII. für die Nuntien und Legaten an den europäischen Fürstenhöfen, 1592-1605* (Tübingen, 1984) 1:LXIX-CLXXII; 2:725-749; J. B. Scott, *Images of Nepotism: The Painted Ceilings of Palazzo Barberini* (Princeton, 1991); L. Nussdorfer, *Civic Politics in the Rome of Urban VIII* (Princeton, 1992); A. Kraus, "Das päpstliche Staatssekretariat unter Urban VIII.," *AHP* 33 (1995) 117-67; L. Nussdorfer, "Print and Pageantry in Baroque Rome," *Sixteenth Century Journal* 29 (1998) 439-64; F. Beretta, "Le procès de Galilée et les archives du Saint-Office," *Revue des sciences philosophiques et théologiques* 83 (1999) 441-90.

KLAUS JAITNER

Ursinus (antipope) (Sept. 24, 366-Nov. 16, 367). Died after 384. Immediately after the death of Liberius on September 24, 366, a minority who had been profoundly dissatisfied with the installation of the antipope Felix (II) made the Roman deacon Ursinus pope, and he received episcopal ordination at once from Bishop Paul of Tribur. The aristocratic majority elected Damasus I, who was ordained bishop on October 1, 366, in the Lateran basilica. After bloody conflicts, Damasus succeeded with help from the emperor in establishing his claim. Ursinus was banished in October 366, but was able to return to Rome on September 15, 367. However, the emperor compelled him to leave Rome two months later, on November 16. His adherents maintained their position in northern Italy, and Damasus was the object of their fierce polemic, while Ursinus was banished to Cologne. After Damasus died on December 11, 384, Ursinus reappeared on the scene, but the election of Siricius definitively removed him from the arena of church politics.

■ Sources: *LP* 1:212f.; 3:index; *RPR(J)* 1:36.

■ Bibliography: *LMA* 8:1330; *BBKL* 122:951ff.; *VATL* 800f.; Caspar 1:196-201, 628; A. Lippold, "Ursinus und Damasus," *Historia, Zeitschrift für Alte Geschichte* 14 (1965) 105-28; C. Pietri, *Roma christiana* (Rome, 1976) 1:408-18.

GEORG SCHWAIGER

Valentine (Aug.-Sept. 827). A Roman. He ascended the ranks of the Roman clergy under Paschal I and Eugene II and became archdeacon. He was unanimously elected pope after the death of Eugene II, but he died forty days after his episcopal ordination. No official acts of his pontificate are recorded.

■ Sources: *LP* 2:71f.; 3:122; *RPR(J)* 1:322f.

■ Bibliography: *LMA* 8:1389; *VATL* 802.

SEBASTIAN SCHOLZ

Victor I (189?-198?). Saint (feast day July 28), probably not a martyr. According to Jerome (*De viris illustribus* 53), he was a Latin, while according to the → *Liber Pontificalis* he came from Africa. This vigorous bishop gave greater prominence to the Latin element in the Roman community. Victor sought to achieve acceptance of the Roman claims to leadership of the church, especially in the controversy about the date of Easter. He ordered synods to be held, and he himself held a synod in Rome; apart from the province of Asia under the leadership of Bishop Polycrates of Ephesus, most of these synods spoke in favor of the Roman custom of celebrating Easter on a Sunday. Victor behaved harshly in the Easter controversy and "attempted" to exclude the Quartodecimans (who celebrated Easter on Nisan 14) from church communion (Eusebius of Caesarea, *Historia ecclesiastica* 5.24.9). This provoked considerable opposition, especially from Irenaeus of Lyons (ibid., 5.24.15ff.). Victor deposed the Gnostic Florinus from the priestly office and excommunicated Theodotus the Elder because of his Monarchian theology. His writings, mentioned by Eusebius and Jerome, have not survived. The Roman bishop who issued letters of peace for the Montanists, then withdrew these when Praxeas told him what the Montanists actually believed (see Tertullian, *Adversus Praxean* 1), was probably not Victor, but his successor, Zephyrinus.

■ **Sources:** *LP* 1:137f.; 3:index; *RPR*(J) 1:11f.; 2:689, 731.
■ **Bibliography:** *TRE* 25:517-30; *VATL* 825f.; M. Richard, "La lettre de S. Irénée au pape Victor," *Zeitschrift für die neutestamentliche Wissenschaft* 66 (1965) 260-82; W. Huber, *Passa und Ostern* (Berlin, 1969); N. Brox, "Tendenzen und Parteilichkeiten im Osterfeststreit des 2. Jahrhunderts," *Zeitschrift für Kirchengeschichte* 83 (1972) 291-324; A. Strobel, *Ursprung und Geschichte des frühchristlichen Osterkalenders* (Berlin, 1977); idem, *Texte zur Geschichte des frühchristlichen Osterkalenders* (Berlin, 1983); A. Hamilton, "Easter Communion," *Pacifica* 8 (1995) 245-73; E. Lanne, "Reception in the Early Church," *The Jurist* 57 (1997) 53-72.

GEORG SCHWAIGER

Victor II (Apr. 13, 1055-July 28, 1057). Formerly *Gebhard*, born ca. 1020, died at Arezzo (tomb in the mausoleum of Theoderic the Great in Santa Maria Rotonda in Ravenna). He was of Swabian origin and may have been related to the counts of Calw. He was a pupil at the cathedral school in Regensburg, where he became a canon and a close associate of Bishop Gebhard III, who successfully proposed him to King Henry III as bishop of Eichstätt on December 25, 1042. From ca. 1050 onward, he was an important counselor of the emperor, an opponent of Leo IX's policy vis-à-vis the Normans and the supporter of a modern reform of the church. It was probably for this reason that Henry III recommended to a Roman delegation led by Hildebrand (later Gregory VII) that

he should be elected pope. However, Gebhard accepted the papal office only when he was assured at the beginning of March 1055 in Regensburg that he could retain his diocese and that the territories forming the Patrimony of Peter would be restored to him. His enthronement in St. Peter's in Rome on Holy Thursday of 1055 introduced a phase of collaboration between church and state. Pope and emperor held a synod jointly in Florence in 1055, at which the boundaries of the church possessions in the Romagna were adjusted; Victor assumed the administration of the duchy of Spoleto and the county of Fermo. At the beginning of 1056, he granted the monastery of Vallombrosa exemption and papal protection. He compelled Abbot Peter of Montecassino to renounce his office and held discussions with Henry III about southern Italy in September of that year. He was present at the emperor's deathbed in Bodfeld in October 1056 and was made protector of the young emperor Henry IV. He buried the emperor in Speyer and brought about an accommodation between the royal court and the imperial princes, encompassing also Duke Gottfried the Bearded of Lorraine and Count Baldwin of Flanders. He returned to Italy in February 1057 and held synods in the Lateran and in Arezzo.

■ **Sources:** *LP* 3:390; J. B. Watterich, *Pontificum Romanorum qui fuerunt inde ab exeunte saeculo IX usque ad finem saeculi XII vitae ab aequalibus conscriptuae etc.* (Leipzig, 1862) 1:177-88; *RPR*(J) 1:549-53; 2:710f., 750; F. Heidingsfelder, *Regesten der Bischöfe von Eichstätt* (Erlangen, 1915) I/1, 66-76; Mansi 19:833-62.
■ **Bibliography:** *LMA* 8:1665; *BBKL* 12:1337ff.; *VATL* 826f.; R. M. Kloos, "Päpste aus Bamberg und Eichstätt," in L. Schrott, ed., *Bayerische Kirchenfürsten* (Munich, 1964) 84-88; W. Goetz, "Papa qui et episcopus," *AHP* 8 (1970) 27-59; idem, "Gebhard I., Bischof von Eichstätt als Papst Victor II. (ca. 1020-57)," *Fränkische Lebensbilder* 9 (Würzburg, 1980) 11-21; S. Weinfurter, *Die Geschichte der Eichstätter Bischöfe des Anonymus Haserensis* (Regensburg, 1987, with edition); G. Frech, "Die deutschen Päpste—Kontinuität und Wandel," in S. Weinfurter, ed., *Die Salier und das Reich* (Sigmaringen, 1991) 2:311f.; G. Martin, "Der salische Herrscher als 'Patricius Romanorum,'" *Frühmittelalterliche Studien* 28 (1994) 257-95; E. Goez, *Beatrix von Canossa und Tuszien* (Sigmaringen, 1995) 148-51; J. Laudage, "Heinrich III. (1017-1056): Ein Lebensbild," in J. Rathofer, ed., *Das salische Kaiserevangeliar, Kommentar-Band* (Münster/Madrid, 1999) 1:85-145.

JOHANNES LAUDAGE

Victor III (May 24, 1086/May 9, 1087-Sept. 16, 1087). Blessed (1887; feast day Sept. 16). A Benedictine (1048/1049), formerly *Dauferius*, born ca. 1027; died and buried at Montecassino. After a period as a hermit, Victor entered the monastery of Santa Sofia in Benevento and took the religious name *Desiderius*. In 1055, he moved to Montecassino, where he became abbot on April 10, 1058. He remained abbot until 1087 and helped the monastery to flourish greatly: seventy volumes were added to the library; the monastery's possessions were extended; and the abbey was rebuilt on a grand scale. Between 1076 and 1079 Victor composed a treatise on the miracles of St. Benedict. His contacts with Nicholas II, Alexander II, and Gregory VII show that he was a supporter of the Gregorian Reform and the papal feudal policy. He acted in keeping with these ideas both as cardinal priest of Santa Cecilia and as papal vicar in southern Italy, where he negotiated the alliance with the Normans on June 24, 1059. He succeeded in reconciling Robert Guiscard with the pope in 1080. He incurred the displeasure of Gregory VII by meeting King Henry IV in 1082, although a breach was avoided: as abbot, he welcomed the pope to Montecassino in 1084 and was present at his deathbed in the following year.

Although Victor was elected pope in Rome on May 24, 1086, he was not one of his predecessor's favorite candidates, and he was opposed by Wibert of Ravenna (the antipope Clement III), Hugh of Dié, and the Normans. Accordingly, he fled four days after his election to Montecassino and accepted his election only on March 7, 1087, at the synod of Capua. The Normans' change of coalition partners made it possible for him to be enthroned in Rome on May 9, 1087, but Victor soon returned to Montecassino. He held a synod in Benevento in August 1087, which took a relatively moderate line: the excommunication of Henry IV was not renewed, and apart from the condemnation of Wibert and Hugh, only the customary prohibitions of simony and lay investiture are recorded. Urban II owed his election as pope to Victor III.

■ **Works:** *Dialogi de miraculis s. Benedicti auctore Deside-rio abbate Casinensi, MGH.SS* 30/2:1111-52.

■ **Sources:** *ActaSS sep.* 5:400-434; *LP* 2:292; J. B. Watterich, *Pontificum Romanorum qui fuerunt inde ab exeunte saeculo IX usque ad finem saeculi XII vitae ab aequalibus conscriptae etc.* (Leipzig, 1862) 1:549-71;

RPR(J) 1:655f.; 2:713; *Chronica monasterii Casinensis: MGH.SS* 34:358-457; Mansi 20:629-38.

■ **Bibliogaphy:** *BiblSS* 12:1286-89; *BBKL* 12:1339-42; *LMA* 8:1665f.; *VATL* 827f.; R. Hüls, *Kardinäle, Klerus und Kirchen Roms 1049-1130* (Tübingen, 1977) 154ff.; G. A. Loud, "Abbot Desiderius of Montecassino and the Gregorian Papacy," *Journal of Ecclesiastical History* 30 (1979) 305-326; H. Dormeier, *Montecassino und die Laien im 11. und 12. Jahrhundert* (Stuttgart, 1979); H. E. J. Cowdrey, *The Age of Abbot Desiderius* (Oxford, 1983); F. Avagliano and O. Pecere, eds., *L'età dell'abate Desiderio*, 3 vols. (Montecassino, 1989-92); S. Beulertz, *Das Verbot der Laieninvestitur im Investiturstreit* (Hanover, 1991); J. Laudage, *Gregorianische Reform und Investiturstreit* (Darmstadt, 1993); M. Gude, "Die 'fideles sancti Petri' im Streit um die Nachfolge Papst Gregors VII.," *Frühmittelalterliche Studien* 27 (1993) 290-316; H. E. J. Cowdrey, *Pope Gregory VII 1073-85* (Oxford, 1998); W. D. MacCready, "The Incomplete 'Dialogues' of Desiderius of Montecassino," *Analecta Bollandiana* 116 (1998) 115-46; idem, "Dating the 'Dialogues' of Abbot Desiderius of Montecassino," *Revue bénédictine* 108 (1998) 145-68.

JOHANNES LAUDAGE

Victor IV (antipope) (Mar.-May 1138). Date and place of death unknown. *Gregory of Ceccano*, an official in the Roman church, was created cardinal priest of Santi XII Apostoli by Paschal II (first attested on February 18, 1107). He was removed from his post as cardinal at the Lateran council in 1112 because of his opposition to Paschal, but after he made a written request to Calixtus II in 1119, he was restored to office by the Lateran council of 1123. He was a supporter of the intransigent line of the Council of Vienne (1112) and an elector of Anacletus II. After the latter's death, he was elected by his fellow cardinals as Anacletus's successor, but he could not make good his claim to the papacy: according to the Chronicle of Montecassino (4:130: *MGH.SS* 34:607), Innocent II bribed the adherents of Victor with gifts of money to abandon their allegiance to him, so that Victor soon had to resign (end of May 1138).

■ **Bibliography:** *BBKL* 13:1342f.; *LMA* 8:1666; *VATL* 828f.; C. Servatius, *Paschalis II., 1099-1118* (Stuttgart, 1979) 49, 53, 58, 301; B. Schilling, *Guido von Vienne—Papst Calixt II.* (Hanover, 1998) 552, 557.

ODILO ENGELS

Victor IV (antipope) (Sept. 7, 1159-Apr. 20, 1164). Formerly *Octaviano de Montecello*, member of a lateral branch of the Crescentii family. He was created cardinal deacon of San Nicola in Carcere Tulliano in 1138 and made cardinal priest of Santa Cecilia in 1151. He was frequently sent as legate to the imperial court, since he belonged to the group of cardinals who did not agree with Hadrian IV's Italian politics. During the sack of Milan in 1159, Frederick I Barbarossa bestowed the county of Terni on Victor and his brothers. He emerged from a difficult conclave as the imperial pope, since—unlike Alexander III—he declared himself in favor of the collaboration between *imperium* and *sacerdotium*. In concrete terms, this meant that the emperor had a right, in virtue of his office, to sovereignty over the city of Rome. Both claimants were men of personal integrity and could put forward arguments drawn from canon law to support their position; hence it is impossible to understand the schism of 1159 without this political background. Frederick Barbarossa wanted the matter to be decided by the synod which he had convoked in Pavia for the beginning of 1160, but this plan did not succeed: the synod confirmed Victor, but Alexander solemnly excommunicated the emperor on Holy Thursday. Victor's "obedience" remained restricted to the imperial sphere; at the synod of Beauvais in July 1160, Louis VII of France and Henry II of England declared their support for Alexander, and Spain and the Christian East likewise recognized him before January 1161. A renewed attempt of the emperor in favor of Victor at Saint-Jean-de-Losne in August 1162 was unsuccessful, because the French king was unwilling to change his "obedience." The imperial court met the protests in Western Europe at the arrogance of imposing a pope whom no one wanted, by arguing that each monarch decided independently on the appointment to episcopal sees in his realm. This makes it readily understandable that a new imperial antipope (Paschal III) was elected as soon as Victor died at Lucca on April 20, 1164. He was buried in Lucca.

■ **Bibliography:** *LMA* 8:1666f.; *VATL* 829; P. Kehr, "Zur Geschichte Victors IV. (Octavian von Monticelli)," *Neues Archiv der Gesellschaft für Ältere Deutsche Geschichtskunde zur Beförderung einer Gesamtausgabe der Quellenschriften deutscher Geschichten des Mittelalters* 46 (1926) 53-85; H. Schwarzmaier, "Zur Familie Victors IV. in der Sabina," *QFIAB* 48 (1968) 64-79; T. A. Reuter, "The Papal Schism, the Empire and the West 1159-1169" (dissertation, Exeter, 1975); H. Mayr, "Der Pontifikat des Gegenpapstes Victor IV." (dissertation,

Vienna, 1977); W. Madertoner, "Die zwiespältige Papstwahl des Jahres 1159" (dissertation, Vienna, 1978); W. Goez, "Imperator advocatus Romanae ecclesie," in *Aus Kirche und Reich,* Festschrift for F. Kempf (Sigmaringen, 1983) 320-26; W. Georgi, *Friedrich Barbarossa und die auswärtigen Mächte 1159-80* (Frankfurt a.M., 1990); J. Laudage, *Alexander III. und Friedrich Barbarossa* (Cologne, 1997), esp. 103-54; O. Engels, *Die Staufer* (7th ed. Stuttgart, 1998) 74-86.

ODILO ENGELS

Vigilius (Mar. 29, 537-June 7, 555). Died at Syracuse. He came from an aristocratic family and was already designated by Boniface II for a short time as his successor in 531. He established good relations with the empress Theodora in Constantinople in 535-536; shortly afterward, with the support of Byzantine troops, he became pope after the controversial deposition of Silverius. At the beginning of the conflict about the Three Chapters, in November 545, Emperor Justinian I summoned him to Constantinople in order to ensure the assent of the West to the imperial edict against the Three Chapters (M. Geerard, *Clavis Patrum Graecorum* [Turnhout, 1983] 6881). After long hesitation, Vigilius condemned the Three Chapters in April 548 in his *Iudicatum* (fragment: *Collectio Avellana* 83:299-302: Corpus scriptorum ecclesiasticorum latinorum 35/1 [Vienna, 1895] 316f.), while at the same time maintaining the doctrinal definition of Chalcedon. This led to massive Western protests, including Vigilius's excommunication by a synod in northern Africa in 550 (*MGH.AA* 11:202). Vigilius refused to sign a further imperial edict (*Clavis Patrum Graecorum*, 6885). Isolated and without any influence, he did not accept the presidency at the synod of 553 (the fifth ecumenical council), nor did he take part in its meetings. When Justinian exposed secret agreements that Vigilius had made, his name was removed from the diptychs. A compromise proposal which the papal chancellery had prepared in advance—*Constitutum* I (*Collectio Avellana* 83:230-320)—had no effect. Vigilius gave up the struggle and composed two documents (*Ep. II ad Eutychium* [December 8, 553]: ACO 4/1:245ff.; *Constitutum* II [February 23, 554]: ACO 4/2:138-68) in which he accepted the condemnation of the Three Chapters and engaged in self-criticism. Vigilius also renewed the apostolic vicariate in Spain and repaired damage to the Roman catacombs. He died in Syracuse, on his return journey to Rome. Despite the weaknesses of his character, his political misjudgments, and his unsuccessful tactics, Vigilius endeavored to ensure that the Roman church enjoyed its rightful place in the Byzantine empire, which was growing in strength. This was the reason for his acceptance of a number of dubious compromises.

■ **Sources:** *CPL* 1694-97; H. J. Frede, *Kirchenschriftsteller* (4th ed. Freiburg, 1995) 788ff. (especially letters and documents connected with the Three Chapters).

■ **Bibliography:** *BBKL* 12:1383-87; *LMA* 8:1658; *VATL* 829f.; E. Schwartz, "Vigilius-Briefe," *Sitzungsberichte der Bayerischen Akademie der Wissenschaften zu München, Philosophisch-Philologische (und Historische) Klasse* (Munich, 1940) 2; E. Zettl, *Die Bestätigung des V. ökumenischen Konzils durch Papst Vigilius* (Bonn, 1974); A. Grillmeier, *Jesus der Christus im Glauben der Kirche* (Freiburg, 1989) II/2, 439-84; J. Speigl, "Leo quem Vigilius condemnavit," in *Papsttum und Kirchenreform*, Festschrift for G. Schwaiger (St. Ottilien, 1990) 1-15; C. Sotinel, "Autorité pontificale et pouvoir impérial sous le règne de Justinien: le pape Vigilius," *Mélanges de l'École Française de Rome, Antiquité* 104 (1992) 439-63; C. Capizzi, *Giustiniano I tra politica e religione* (Soveria Manelli, 1994) esp. 68-74, 104-31.

JOSEF RIST

Vitalian (July 30, 657-Jan. 27, 672). Saint (feast day Jan. 27), born in Segni, the son of Anastasius. He endeavored to restore good relations with Constantinople, and therefore gave emperor Constans II immediate notification of his election and episcopal ordination. He shifted attention away from the dogmatic decisions of the Lateran synod of 649 against Monothelitism. Constans visited Rome in 663, but the Langobard menace compelled him to abandon his plans to move the center of his empire westward. The emperor detached the church of Ravenna from the Roman patriarchate in 666, declaring it autocephalous. Vitalian encouraged the abandonment of Irish-Scottish practices in England, as decided by the synod of Whitby (664), and he ordained the highly educated Greek monk Theodore of Tarsus as archbishop of Canterbury in 668, sending him to England with Abbot Hadrian and Benedict Biscop to reorganize the church. After Constans was murdered, Vitalian gave his support to his son, Constantine IV. He greatly extended the choir school that Gregory I had founded in the Lateran.

■ **Sources:** *PL* 87:999-1010; *LP* 1:343ff.; 3:index; *RPR*(J) 1:235ff.; 2:699, 740.

■ **Bibliography:** *BBKL* 12:1515ff.; *LMA* 8:1761f.; *VATL*

833f.; Caspar 2:580-87, 678-82; Bertolini 355-64; V. Monachini, "I tempi e la figura del papa Vitaliano," in *Storiografia e storia*, Festschrift for E. Dupré Theseider (Rome, 1974) 2:573-88; R. Schieffer, "Kreta, Rom und Laon: Vier Briefe des Papstes Vitalian vom Jahre 668," in *Papsttum, Kirche und Recht im Mittelalter*, Festschrift for H. Fuhrmann (Tübingen, 1991) 15-30.

GEORG SCHWAIGER

Xystus → Sixtus.

Zachary (Dec. 3, 741-Mar. 15, 752). Saint (feast day Mar. 22), of Greek origin. He was the last of a line of Italo-Greek and Greco-Syrian popes. He was born in 679(?) in Siberena in Calabria or in Athens (?); we have virtually no information about his life before 741. According to the → *Liber Pontificalis*, he may be identical to Zachary the "deacon of the holy Roman church," who was one of the signatories to the decrees of the Roman synod in 732. Zachary achieved a number of valuable goals in the political and diplomatic sphere. He met king Liutprand in Terni and Pavia, concluded a peace treaty with the Langobards, and improved relations between Rome and Constantinople, although he continuously opposed the iconoclastic policy of Constantine V Copronymus. Boniface frequently asked his advice on matters of religious discipline, and Zachary instructed him to support the reform of the Frankish church and to improve canonical legislation; he also supported the convocation of the "council of Germany" in 742 or 743. He issued regulations at the Roman synod of 743 to improve the prestige of the clergy, not neglecting questions concerning clerical marriage. He declared the legitimacy of the Carolingian dynasty, founded by Pippin the Younger in 747. He persuaded the Langobard king Ratchis to lift the siege of Perugia, but he could not prevent the king's brother, Aistulf, from conquering Ravenna in 751. As a capable administrator of the Patrimony of Peter, Zachary organized agrarian policy by means of the system of *domuscultae*. He founded organizations to provide material support to the clergy and help for the needy, pilgrims and refugees. He bestowed numerous privileges on the abbey of Montecassino and subsequently extended these to the monastery of Fulda. Zachary restored the Lateran palace and churches such as Santa Maria Antiqua (where his portrait is preserved). He also translated the *Dialogues* of Gregory the Great into Greek. This was destined primarily for Greek monks and laity in Rome and southern Italy, but it soon found many readers in the East too.

■ **Sources:** *LP* 1:426-39.

■ **Works:** *PL* 66:125-204; 77:127-432; G. Ricotti, ed., *Gregorio Magno, 'Vita di San Benedetto'; Il libro dei 'Dialoghi' nella versione greca di papa Zaccaria* (Alexandria, 2001).

■ **Bibliography:** *The Oxford Dictionary of Byzantium* (New York/Oxford, 1991) 3:2218; F. L. Cross, ed., *The Oxford Dictionary of the Christian Church* (3rd ed. London, 1997) 1776; *LMA* 9:435f.; *VATL* 842; D. Bartoluni, *Di San Zaccaria Papa e degli anni del suo pontificato* (Regensburg, 1879); Bertolini 479-513, 770f., 828f.; N. Brox et al., eds., *Die Geschichte des Christentums* (Freiburg, 1994) vol. 4, ch. 3/3-4.

GIANPAOLO RIGOTTI

Zephyrinus (198?-217?). Saint (feast day Aug. 26). According to the author of the "Little Labyrinth," he took action against the Theodotians. According to Hippolytus of Rome, his profession of faith—"I know only one God, Christ Jesus, and other than him, no God who is begotten and passible"—favored the Monarchianism of Noëtus of Smyrna, i.e., the doctrine that was the common teaching of the church at that period, not only in Rome and Asia Minor but everywhere, before it "became the heresy" of Sabellianism (to use Hübner's phrase). According to Hippolytus (*Refutatio omnium haeresium* 9.7.3), Zephyrinus simultaneously professed that "it was not the Father who died, but the Son." This indicates the necessity of a distinction in the dispensation of salvation, which would have to find its basis "in God himself." This is especially true if this formula was intended as polemic against Praxeas.

■ **Sources:** So-called Little Labyrinth; Eusebius of Caesarea, *Historia ecclesiastica* 5.28; Hippolytus of Rome, *Refutatio omnium haeresium* 9.7.1; 11.1-3.

■ **Bibliography:** *DECL* 605; *VATL* 843f.; G. Bardy, "Les écoles romaines," *Revue d'histoire ecclésiastique* 28 (1932) 501-32, esp. 529f.; H. Jedin, *Geschichte des Konzils von Trient* (3rd ed. Freiburg, 1977) 291-96; M. Decker, "Die Monarchianer: Frühchristliche Theologie im Spannungsfeld zwischen Rom und Kleinasien" (dissertation, Hamburg, 1987); R. M. Hübner, "Heis theos Iêsous Khristos: Zum christlichen Gottesglauben im

2. Jahrhundert—ein Versuch," *Münchener theologische Zeitschrift* 47 (1996) 325-44, esp. 338, 341f.; W. A. Löhr, "Theodotus der Lederarbeiter und Theodotus der Bankier—ein Beitrag zur römischen Theologiegeschichte des 2. und 3. Jahrhunderts," *Zeitschrift für die neutestamentliche Wissenschaft* 87 (1996) 101-25, esp. 101, 105, 117.

KARL-HEINZ UTHEMANN

Zosimus (Mar. 18, 417-Dec. 26, 418). Of Greek, perhaps of Jewish, origin, he served as a priest under Innocent I. His short pontificate was marked by maladroit actions and the difficulties to which these led. His first mistake was the nomination of the ruthless bishop Patroclus of Arles—perhaps because he had helped Zosimus become bishop of Rome—as metropolitan over the provinces of Vienne and Narbonensis I and II, with extensive rights over the clergy in Gaul. Another mistake was the acceptance of the appeal by the North African priest Apiarius and his rehabilitation. Whereas his predecessor, Innocent I, had confirmed the condemnations pronounced by African synods against Pelagius and Caelestius, Zosimus declared them both to be orthodox in faith. It was only African opposition and a rescript by Emperor Honorius that persuaded him to condemn Pelagianism in 418. Zosimus is buried in the basilica of San Lorenza on the Via Tiburtina in Rome.

■ **Sources:** *PL* 20:642-86, 693, 704; *LP* 1:225f.; *RPR*(J) 1:49ff.; *PLS* 1:797.

■ **Bibliography:** *BiblSS* 12:1493-97; *BBKL* 14:589-93; *DECL* 606; *VATL* 845; Caspar 1:344-60; F. Floeri, "Le pape Zosime et la doctrine augustinienne du péché originel," *Augustinus magister* (Paris, 1954) 2:755-61; G. Langgärtner, *Die Gallienpolitik der Päpste* (Bonn, 1964) 24-52; W. Marschall, *Karthago und Rom* (Stuttgart, 1971); C. Pietri, *Roma christiana* (Rome, 1976) 2:1000-1021, 1101-5, 1212-54; O. Wermelinger, "Das Pelagiusdossier in der 'Tractoria' des Zosimus," *Freiburger Zeitschrift für Philosophie und Theologie* 26 (1979) 336-68; M. Wojtowytsch, *Papsttum und Konzile von den Anfängen bis zu Leo I.* (Stuttgart, 1981); D. Frye, "Early fifth-century Gaul," *Journal of Ecclesiastical History* 42 (1991) 349-61; M. Lamberigts, "Augustine and Julian of Aeclanum on Zosimus," *Augustiniana* 42 (1991) 311-30.

STEFAN HEID

Academies, Pontifical. In the tradition of the academies established in Italy from the period of humanism onward, similar organizations were founded in papal Rome.

1. The most important today is the *Pontificia Accademia delle Scienze.* This body traces its origin to the Accademia dei Lincei (founded 1603), which was given a new form by Pius IX in 1847 as the Accademia dei Nuovi Lincei. In 1922, Pius XI gave it the "Casina" of Pius IV in the Vatican Gardens as its seat, and he gave it its current name in 1936. It is responsible to the pope in person, has an international character and eighty ordinary members (as well as several honorary members) drawn from the fields of mathematics, the natural and the human sciences. Its membership is not limited to Catholics. It holds congresses in these sciences at irregular intervals. Its goal is the honoring and promotion of research.

2. The *Pontificia Accademia di Teologia,* given papal approbation in 1718 and refounded in 1956, promotes the authentic Catholic faith.

3. The *Accademia Romana di Archeologia,* founded in 1810 (and bearing the title *Pontifical* since 1829), promotes Christian archaeology and the history of Christian art. From 1871 to 1894, its president was Giovanni Battista de' Rossi, who did much to develop Christian archaeology.

4. The *Insigne Accademia di Belle Arti e Lettere dei Virtuosi al Pantheon,* founded in 1542-43 (and bearing the title *Pontifical* since 1861), seeks to study, cultivate, and perfect the fine arts.

5. The *Accademia dell'Immacolata,* founded in 1835 (and bearing the title *Pontifical* since 1864), promotes and coordinates studies of Marian dogma.

6. The *Pontificia Accademia di S. Tommaso d'Aquino,* founded by Leo XIII in 1879, was united in 1934 with the *Accademia di Religione Cattolica,* which had been founded in 1801. It promotes the study of Thomism.

7. The *Pontificia Accademia Mariana Internazionale,* founded in 1946, serves to promote Mariology.

8. The *Pontificia Accademia delle Scienze Sociali,* founded in 1994, promotes social, economic, political, and legal sciences in the light of the church's social teaching.

9. The *Pontificia Accademia per la Vita,* likewise founded in 1994, seeks to promote and defend life.

10. The *Collegium Cultorum Martyrum,* founded in 1879 and since 1995 the *Pontificia Accademia "Cultorum Martyrum,"* promotes the veneration of the martyrs and the study of the catacombs.

Despite its name, the *Pontificia Accademia Ecclesiastica* is not an academy in the sense meant here, but is one of the Roman colleges.

■ **Bibliography:** *EC* 1:165-83; *VATL* 10-16, 147f.; G. B. Marini-Bettòlo, *The Activity of the Pontifical Academy of Sciences 1936-86* (2nd ed. Vatican City, 1987); C. Pietrangeli, "La Pontificia Accademia di Archeologia," in P. Vian, ed., *Speculum mundi: Roma centro internazionale di ricerche umanistiche* (Rome, 1992); R. Ladous, *Des Nobel au Vatican: La fondation de l'Académie Pontificale des Sciences* (Paris, 1994); *AnPont* (2000) 1876-93, 2018-24.

ERWIN GATZ

Acta Apostolicae Sedis (*AAS*); subtitle: "Commentarium officiale." The official organ of the Apostolic See is published by the Secretariat of State (see John Paul II, Apostolic Constitution *Pastor Bonus,* June 26, 1988, art. 43, n. 1: *AAS* 80 [1988] 871). It was founded by Pius X (Apostolic Constitution *Promulgandi,* September 29, 1908: *AAS* 1 [1909] 5f.; "Ordo servandus in moderatione et administratione Commentarii Officialis," January 5, 1910: *AAS* 2 [1910] 37ff.), to replace the *Acta Sanctae Sedis* as the Holy See's organ of promulgation and publication. In addition to laws and other decrees, it publishes → pronouncements of the Apostolic See and records personal events such as appointments.

■ **Bibliography:** *CATH* 1:84f., 94; *EC* 1:253f.; *DizEc* 1:29; *DMC* 1:39f.; *NCE* 1:94; *VATL* 3; W. Plöchl, *Geschichte des Kirchenrechts* (2nd ed. Vienna 1970) 3:96f.; L. Wächter, *Gesetz im kanonischen Recht* (St. Ottilien, 1989) 321ff.; H. Socha, *MKCIC* can. 8; W. Aymans and K. Mörsdorf, *Kanonisches Recht: Lehrbuch aufgrund des CIC* (13th ed. Paderborn et al., 1997) 1:157f.; *AnPont* (2000) 1241, 1935.

FRANZ KALDE

Acta Romanorum (RR.) Pontificum. Collective term for papal decisions in matters of doctrine and of discipline, when these are issued in writing. In a broader sense, embracing authoritative dispositions taken by the Holy See (can. 361 CIC), the documents of the Roman curial authorities likewise belong under this heading. Depending on their contents, jurisdiction, their external form, etc., the Acta Romanorum Pontificum have been given various designations in the course of church history. The birth of canon law studies in the twelfth century led to a juridically clearer survey of the papal legislative right, and this also influenced the legal terminology used in papal decrees. Alongside conciliar canons and patristic texts, the Acta Romanorum Pontificum constitute a major element in the canonists' collections up to the Decretal of Gratian. When the decretal came to enjoy a virtual monopoly in the process of developing law from the twelfth century onward, the Acta Romanorum Pontificum formed by far the largest part in the collections of decrees. These collections of papal bulls have been published from the sixteenth century onward; from 1865, this was done in the → Acta Sanctae Sedis, and from 1908 in the → Acta Apostolicae Sedis.

■ **Bibliography:** DDC 6:166-71; A. van Hove, *Commentarium Lovaniense in Codicem Iuris Canonici, Prolegomena* (2nd ed. Mechlin, 1945); A. M. Stickler, *Historia iuris canonici latini*, I: *Historia fontium* (Turin, 1950); P. Landau, *L'evoluzione della nozione di "legge" nel diritto canonico classico: "Lex et Iustitia" nell'utrumque ius: radici antiche e prospetti attuali* (Vatican City, 1989) 263-79; P. Erdö, *Introductio in historiam scientiae canonicae* (Rome, 1990); H. Dondorp, "Review of Papal Rescripts in the Canonists' Teaching," *Zeitschrift der Savigny-Stiftung für Rechtsgeschichte, Kanonistische Abteilung* 76 (1990) 172-253; 77 (1991) 32-110; T. Frenz, *Papsturkunden des Mittelalters und der Neuzeit* (2nd ed. Stuttgart, 2000).

HERBERT KALB

Acta Sanctae Sedis (*ASS*). This Roman periodical was founded by Pietro Avanzini in 1865 for the publication and explanation of → pronouncements by the Apostolic See. Initially, it had only a private character. The original title, *Acta ex iis decerpta quae apud Sanctam Sedem geruntur in compendium opportune redacta et illustrata*, was replaced by *ASS* from vol. 6 (1870) onward. From this date, the Apostolic See used the *ASS* de facto as its medium of proclamation, and Pius X declared it the official organ of publication of the

Holy See on May 23, 1904 (*ASS* 37 [1904] 4), replacing it on January 1, 1909 with the → *Acta Apostolicae Sedis*. The *ASS* appeared in forty-one volumes; a general index was published in 1909.

■ **Bibliography:** DDC 1:158; CATH 1:85; EC 1:254f.; DMC 1:44f.; VATL 3f.; W. Plöchl, *Geschichte des Kirchenrechts* (2nd ed. Vienna, 1970) 3:96; (1969) 5:297f.

FRANZ KALDE

Ad Limina Visit (the correct Latin term is *visitatio liminum* or *ad limina Apostolorum*) is the designation of the "visit to the graves" of the princes of the apostles Peter and Paul in Rome, which all Catholic Ordinaries are required to make at regular intervals. In the course of this visit, they present an account of the state of their diocese, have an audience with the pope, and contact the Roman curia (cf. canons 399-400 CIC). The *ad limina* visit primarily serves to promote the dialogue between the Apostolic See and the local churches—a dialogue that has its theological basis in the *communio ecclesiarum*. It also helps the pope in the fulfillment of the universal pastoral guidance which is entrusted to him as Peter's successor.

The legal institution of the *ad limina* visit developed from indications in the Bible (see Gal. 1:18; 2 Cor. 11:28). Many texts from the fourth century onward testify that bishops were obliged to visit Rome. Gregory the Great laid down in 597 that the bishops of Sicily must come to Rome every fifth year (*PL* 77:875). In 743, Pope Zachary obligated the bishops who lived close to Rome to a yearly *ad limina* visit (*Distinctio* 93 c. 4). The Gregorian Reform led to a strengthening of the papal rights of inspection. The decretals of Gregory IX (1234) prescribed a universal obligation to a yearly *ad limina* visit; it was possible for bishops to be represented by another, or to be dispensed (X 2, 24, 4). In the aftermath of the Council of Trent, the *ad limina* visit took on great significance, once Sixtus V had reformed the relevant legal ordinances in the Constitution *Romanus Pontifex* (1585). Significant revisions, above all with regard to the structure of the bishops' reports, were undertaken by Benedict XIII, Benedict XIV, and Pius X. The Congregation of Bishops confirmed the five-yearly plan for the bishops' reports from January 1, 1976 onward (decree of June 29, 1975: *AAS* 67 [1975] 674ff.).

Canon 400 §1 *CIC* prescribes that diocesan bishops shall make the *ad limina* visit every fifth year (in the year in which their report is due), according to an established cycle beginning from January 1, 1976, unless the Apostolic See makes other provisions (see can. 341 §§1 and 2 of the 1917 *Code*). If a diocesan bishop or apostolic vicar cannot come, regulations cover his representation; an apostolic prefect is not obliged to make the *ad limina* visit (can. 400 §§ 2 and 3). A military Ordinary is obliged to make the *ad limina* visit (see John Paul II, Apostolic Constitution *Spirituali militum curae,* April 21, 1986, no. 12; *AAS* 78 [1986] 485). On the *ad limina* visit in the Eastern Catholic churches, see cann. 206 §2 and 208 §2 *CCEO*.

■ **Primary Sources:** John Paul II, Apostolic Constitution *Pastor Bonus,* June 28, 1988 (*AAS* 80 [1988] 841-934); Congregation for Bishops, *Direttorio per la visita "ad limina"* (Vatican City, 1988).
■ **Bibliography:** F. M. Cappello, *De visitatione liminum Apostolorum,* 2 vols. (Rome, 1912-13); J. Hirnsperger, "Der Ad-Limina-Besuch des Bischofs: Zur neueren Entwicklung der rechtlichen Grundlagen," in *Pax et Iustitia,* Festschrift for A. Kostelecky (Berlin, 1990) 337-55; W. Aymans and K. Mörsdorf, *Kanonisches Recht: Lehrbuch aufgrund des CIC* (13th ed. Paderborn et al., 1997) 2:351f.; V. Cárcel-Ortí, "La visita 'ad limina' nel Magistero di Giovanni Paolo II," in *Ius in vita et in missione Ecclesiae* (Venice, 1994) 337-51; *Comentario exegético al Código de Derecho Canónico* (2nd ed. Pamplona, 1997) II/1, 799-811.

JOHANN HIRNSPERGER

Affectio Papalis denotes the capacity of the pope, by virtue of the universality and immediacy of his primatial authority (can. 331 *CIC*), to deal according to his own free choice with all matters that lie outside the sphere of those things reserved to him by law (*manus appositio;* see can. 595 §1 *CIC*), thereby eliminating the competence of the subordinate authority (which per se has the right to deal with such matters). Correspondingly, each one of the faithful has the right to appeal at any time to the pope. The *affectio papalis* was elaborated in the high Middle Ages. From the twelfth century onward, it covered the fields of appointment to ecclesiastical offices and the conduct of legal cases (e.g., X 2, 28, 41). Today the *affectio papalis* is relevant mainly in the law governing administration and legal cases: on the one hand, the pope can take any case into his own hands

(cann. 1405 §1 n. 4, 1417 §2 *CIC*: *advocatio causae*), and on the other, each of the faithful may bring his case before the pope.
■ **Bibliography:** *DDC* 1:260; J. Häring, "Die Affectio papalis," *Archiv für katholisches Kirchenrecht* 109 (1929) 127-77.

GEORG MAY

Anagni. This city in the Italian province of Frosinone is called the "city of the popes" because popes often took refuge here from rebellions in the city of Rome and ruled from here. Innocent III, Gregory IX, Alexander IV, and Boniface VIII all came from Anagni; the last-named pope was humiliated here by the Colonna and the French in 1303. It was incorporated into the papal states from the fifteenth century onward.
■ **Bibliography:** R. Ambrosi De Magistris, *Storia di Anagni,* 2 vols. (Anagni, 1889); P. Zappasodi, *Anagni attraverso i secoli,* 2 vols. (Veroli, 1908; Anagni, 1985); A. Vauchez, "L'Eglise d'Anagni au XIIIe siècle," *AHP* 36 (1998) 11-17.

MARIA LUPI

Annuario Pontificio, the Papal Yearbook, is the official work of reference containing up-to-date (and historical) information about popes, cardinals, patriarchs, bishops, local churches (including titular sees), organs and officers of the Roman curia and the Vatican City state, papal orders of chivalry, papal nunciatures, the Diplomatic Corps accredited to the Holy See, institutes of the consecrated life, papal and Catholic institutes of education, Latin place-names employed by the curia, and an index of persons (including holders of honorary papal titles). The *Annuario* began as the "Notizie per l'anno . . ." in 1716; the present name has been in use from 1860 to 1870, and again from 1912.
■ **Bibliography:** *CATH* 1:607f.; *EC* 1:1381f.; *DizEc* 1:159; *DMC* 1:241f.; *VATL* 33f.; *AnPont* (2000) 1241, 1935.

FRANZ KALDE

Antipope designates an illegitimate pope, rival of the legitimate pope (→ Papacy). Fully satisfactory criteria of illegitimacy do not exist, partly because the papal → election was slow to develop a legally guaranteed form and partly because the deposition of a pope never had an absolutely certain legal basis. This means that the list of antipopes has been continually revised up to very recent times. After the papal election of 1059, popes who were regarded by their contemporaries as illegitimate were no longer enumerated "III, IV," etc. when a new pope was designated. The concept of *antipapa* is first found in 1127 (Hugh of York, *Chronicon pontificium ecclesiae eboracensis,* ed. C. Johnson [London, 1961] 84f.) and was used as a polemical term which evoked associations with *antichristus.*

■ **Bibliography:** *EC* 1:1483-89; *VATL* 240ff.; M. E. Stoller, "The Emergence of the Term Antipapa in Medieval Usage," *AHP* 23 (1985) 43-61.

ODILO ENGELS

Apostolic Administration (*Administratio Apostolica*) is a local church similar to a diocese (can. 368 *CIC*), which for grave reasons is not (or not yet) erected as a diocese. It is entrusted to an Apostolic Administrator who governs it in the name of the pope with ordinary, representative jurisdiction (can. 371 §2). This form of organization is chosen when reasons of church politics do not allow the definitive demarcation of the borders of a diocese (examples are Görlitz, that part of the archdiocese of Breslau which remained in German territory after World War II, from 1972 to 1994; Innsbruck-Feldkirch from 1921 to 1968; Burgenland in Austria from 1922 to 1960).

■ **Bibliography:** *HKKR* 335; *AnPont* (2000) 1148ff., 1924.

JOSEPH LISTL

Apostolic Almonery (*Eleemosinaria Apostolica*). From the sixth century on, the *Saccularius* ("keeper of the bag") in Rome had the duty of distributing alms. From the twelfth century, the administration of the papal charity was institutionalized in the Roman curia in the Apostolic Almonery. In Avignon, the office of *Eleemosinarius secretus* was set up to deal with the private charity of the pope. The modern Apostolic Almonery depends directly on the pope and administers his charitable giving.

■ **Bibliography:** *VATL* 26ff.; Apostolic Constitution *Pastor Bonus,* no. 193 (*AAS* 80 [1988] 841-934); *AnPont* (2000) 1392, 1989.

HERBERT KALB

Apostolic Chamber (*Camera Apostolica*) designates a papal financial bureaucracy introduced in the twelfth century, following the promising model of Cluny. The name (a "chamber" is a treasury surrounded by a wall) and the system (centralized bookkeeping) are probably of Norman origin. After the return from Avignon, control by the papal exchequer took on particular significance, and the Apostolic Chamber administered both the sovereign and the private income of the → Holy See. For a time, it was the highest governing body of the → papal states. Since the loss of these territories in 1870, it has enjoyed only a limited competence in the financial administration of the Apostolic See. Its head, the Camerlengo ("Chamberlain"), retains the rights of the Apostolic See during a → *sede vacante* and exercises the supreme jurisdiction to a certain extent; this may reflect ideas about the rights connected to benefices. The expression "chamber" (e.g., "chamber of commerce") is derived from the collegial character of the jurisdiction exercised by the Apostolic Chamber in financial and other matters.

■ **Primary Sources:** *AAS* 67 (1975) 609f.; 80 (1988) 841f., nn. 171f.

■ **Bibliography:** *DDC* 3:388f.; *HDRG* 2:570f.; *VATL* 367f.; J. Barbarič, *Camera apostolica: Obligationes et solutiones camerale primo (1299-1560)* (Zagreb, 1996); *AnPont* (2000) 1337, 1960.

HELMUT SCHNIZER

Apostolic Datary. This was one of the offices in the Roman → curia which administered requests for dispensations in the *forum externum* (the external legal sphere). The exact date of its foundation is not known. It probably had its origin in the papal → chancellery, the fruit of a separation of the two tasks of writing the papal letters and giving advice before such letters were written. It became completely independent of the chancellery under Martin V (1417-31) at the latest. The name "datary" comes from the *datarius,* whose office emerged from the distinction between the signing of Apostolic Letters by the pope and the dating of these letters by a delegate. Before the reform by Leo XIII, the decisive norms governing this praxis were the chancellery rules, the brief *Decet Romanum Pontificem* of Sixtus V (1588), and the Constitution *Gravissimum* of Benedict XIV (1745). It was the *datarius* who had the task of definitively resolving all matters that called for a decision (apart from trivial matters or questions that could be resolved by rule of thumb). This office, a *munus praelatitium,* was so important that even cardinals (called *Pro-datarius*) held it; other officials were the *sub-datarius,* the *officialis* *per obitum* and subordinates. The Apostolic Datary prepared the decision for the pope (*papa, non datarius concedit gratias*). Only when the concession had been granted and the *datarius* had set the date on the rescript and registered it, did the petitioner receive a *ius quaesitum*. With respect to the pope's decisions, the *datarius* possessed official credibility (*fides*), not universal jurisdiction. The competence of the Apostolic Datary was continuously extended, covering especially the task of setting and collecting the fees for appointments to ecclesiastical offices. It embraced the following sectors: the granting of dispensations (from irregularities, from the prohibition of certain activities on the part of clergymen, from all diriment impediments to marriage except cases involving *principes supremi*), the granting of indults, exemptions, and privileges, extension or limitation of privileges and concessions already granted, appointments to benefices reserved to the Holy See (with the exception of those offices bestowed by the Consistory or the Propaganda Congregation) and the bestowal of *beneficia affecta*, as well as financial administration. Special rules applied where a cumulative competence involved other dicasteries of the Holy See as well. Pius X's reform of the curia (*Sapienti consilio*, 1908) limited the competence of the Apostolic Datary to the bestowal of offices that were not reserved to the Consistory and a number of matters concerning benefices. Since it had lost its significance, it was abolished under Paul VI. It was mentioned in the → *Annuario Pontificio* for the last time in 1967.

■ **Bibliography:** *VATL* 172f.; G. B. De Luca, *Relatio Curiae Romanae* (Cologne, 1683); G. Moroni, *Dizionario di erudizione storico-ecclesiastica* (Venice, 1843) 19:109-59, 159-61; J. H. Bangen, *Die Römische Kurie* (Münster, 1854) 396ff.; P. Hinschius, *Das Kirchenrecht der Katholiken und Protestanten in Deutschland* (Berlin, 1869) 1:422ff.; N. Del Re, *La Curia Romana* (2nd ed. Rome, 1970) 443ff.

RICHARD PUZA

Apostolic Penitentiary (*Paenitentiaria Apostolica*) is one of the three highest papal courts in the church. However, since it is responsible for the granting of indults and for indulgences, it is not an ecclesiastical court in the strict sense of the term; as the papal body responsible for granting favors, it is an administrative body concerned primarily with matters of conscience in the church. Its com-

petence lies in the *forum internum,* the inner legal sphere of the church, and includes the issue of indulgences, without infringing on the competence of the Congregation for the Doctrine of the Faith with regard to dogmatic teaching (Apostolic Constitution *Pastor Bonus,* June 28, 1988, nos. 117-20). In the sacramental sphere (in connection with the sacrament of penance) and in the nonsacramental legal sphere, the Apostolic Penitentiary grants absolutions, dispensations, transmutations of obligations, validations, the reduction of penalties, and other favors (see also cann. 64, 1048, 1082 *CIC*). It has the obligation of providing sufficient priests to hear confessions in the patriarchal basilicas of the city of Rome and of giving these the appropriate faculties. It is headed by the Cardinal Major Penitentioner, supported by a regent and five other prelates as his advisers. Officials take care of the cases submitted to the Penitentiary.

■ **Bibliography:** *CATH* 10:1168-72; *VATL* 608ff.; J. Provost, "Pastor bonus: Reflections on the Reorganization of the Roman Curia," *Jurist* 48 (1988) 532; L. De Magistris and U. M. Todeschini, "La Penitenzeria Apostolica," in P. A. Bonnet and C. Gullo, eds., *La Curia Romana nella Costituzione Apostolica "Pastor Bonus"* (Vatican City, 1990) 419-30; "Penitenzeria Apostolica," in *L'attività della Santa Sede nel 1990* (Vatican City, 1990) 1201f.; F. Tamburini, "La Sacrée Pénitencerie apostolique et les pénitenciers mineurs pontificaux," *Studia canonica* 31 (1997) 449-59; John Paul II, "Em.mo P.D. paenitentiario maiori missus," *AAS* 90 (1998) 608-13; *AnPont* (2000) 1295, 1947.

ILONA RIEDEL-SPANGENBERGER

Apostolic See → Holy See.

Apostolic Signatura (*Supremum Tribunal Signaturae Apostolicae*) was set up in its present form in 1908 as the highest court of the Roman → curia. Its origins can be traced to the body commissioned by the pope to sign the petitions that were directed to him (*referendarii*): when the sources speak of a "signature," they refer to the act of signing. The separation of the *Signatura gratiae* from the *Signatura iustitiae* probably took place under Alexander VI. The *Signatura gratiae* was a body concerned with pardon, the *Signatura iustitiae* a genuine court that consisted of judges ("voters") and *referendarii*. It ceased to exist with the demise of the papal states.

In 1968, Paul VI set up a second section within

the Apostolic Signatura, a court to deal with matters of administration; this was maintained in the 1983 *CIC* and the Apostolic Constitution *Pastor Bonus* (1988). The members of the Apostolic Signatura are cardinals and bishops. This body has three sections, which have the following competencies: (1) a section dealing with legal processes (appeals; declarations of nullity; *restitutio in integrum,* the renewed examination of a case against judgments of the → Rota, either against its refusal to undertake a reexamination or against its judges when they are accused of failing to maintain impartiality; and the resolution of conflicting claims to competence); (2) a court for questions of administration (appeals when a specific administrative act of a dicastery of the Roman curia infringes a law; decisions about conflicting claims to competence on the part of the Roman dicasteries); (3) a section dealing with administrative matters (prorogations of competence; delegation of third instances; the faculty to contract civil marriages). We may summarize the functions of the Apostolic Signatura as follows: the first section functions as a court of cassation, the second section as a ministerial council or administrative court, and the third section as a ministry of justice. While its decisions are not published, the Apostolic Signatura reports its activities annually in the *Attività della Santa Sede.*

■ **Bibliography:** *VATL* 728f.; I. Gordon, "De Signaturae iustitiae competentia," *Periodica de re morali canonica liturgica* 69 (1980) 351ff.; R. Puza, "Rescriptum und commissio," *Zeitschrift der Savigny-Stiftung für Rechtsgeschichte, Kanonistische Abteilung* 97 (1980) 354-70; J.-B. d'Onorio, *Le Pape et le gouvernement de l'Église* (Paris, 1992) 394ff.; G. Agustoni, "Supremum Signaturae Apostolicae Tribunal," *Periodica de re canonica* 87 (1998) 613-22; U. Navarrete, "Commentarium," *Periodica de re canonica* 87 (1998) 623-41; *AnPont* (2000) 1296f., 1948.

RICHARD PUZA

Archive, Vatican Secret. From the earliest centuries, the popes ensured that important documents (acts of the martyrs, conciliar proceedings, etc.) were kept safely. The importance of the pontifical → chancellery and the increasing differentiation of curial tasks led to the creation of a number of papal archives with varied contents, significance, and organization. The Vatican Secret Archive developed from 1612 onward, through the collection of archives from the Bibliotheca Secreta, → Castel Sant' Angelo and the → Apostolic Chamber. Napoleon I had the archives brought to Paris in 1810; they were restored and returned to Rome, though with serious losses, in 1815-1817.

When Leo XIII opened the Vatican Archive to scholarly research in 1880, it retained its main task, that of serving the pope and his curia as an administrative archive. The name *Archivio Segreto Vaticano* recalls the narrower function of the archive until the eighteenth century; although it has been increasingly opened (most recently through the release of documents up to January 22, 1922, by John Paul II), even today it is not a public archive in the strict sense. Both its universal character and the immense quantity of official books and files which it contains—e.g., 7,365 registers of pleas for the years 1342-1899—make it the most important central archive of the universal church. There also exist other comprehensive archives, e.g., in the Congregation for the Evangelization of the Peoples.

A school of archivist studies (Scuola Vaticana di Paleografia, Diplomatica e Archivistica) has been attached to the Vatican Archive since 1884. A number of foreign institutes have conducted specialized research since the opening of the Archive, e.g., the Austrian Historical Institute (founded 1881), the German Historical Institute (founded 1888 as the Prussian Historical Institute), and the Historical Institute of the Görres Society (founded 1888).

■ **Bibliography:** *VATL* 242f.; K. A. Fink, *Das Vatikanische Archiv* (2nd ed. Rome, 1951); A. Palestra and A. Ciceri, *Lineamenti di Archivistica Ecclesiastica* (Milan, 1965); S. Duca and S. and S. Familia, *Enchiridion Archivorum Ecclesiasticorum* (Vatican City, 1966); S. Duca and B. Pandižić, *Archivistica Ecclesiastica* (Vatican City, 1967); J. Gadille, *Guide des archives diocésaines en France* (Lyons, 1971); L. E. Boyle, *A Survey of the Vatican Archives and Its Medieval Holdings* (Toronto, 1972); M. Giusti, "Das Vatikanische Geheimarchiv," in *Der Vatikan und das christliche Rom* (Vatican City, 1975) 335-53; L. Chudoba, "Gli archivi ecclesiastici in Austria," *Archiva Ecclesiae* 18-21 (1975-78) 85-106; E. G. Franz, *Einführung in die Archivkunde* (3rd ed. Darmstadt, 1990); *Führer durch die Bistumsarchive der katholischen Kirche in Deutschland* (2nd ed. Siegburg, 1991); S. M. Pagano, "Una discutibile 'guida' degli Archivi Vaticani," *AHP* 37 (1999) 191-201; *AnPont* (2000) 1374, 1983.

TONI DIEDERICH

Avignon, Papal Palace

Ground Floor

Upper Floor

Avignon, a city in southern France, at the confluence of the Rhône and Durance rivers, papal residence from 1309 to 1376.

The assault on Boniface VIII at → Anagni (September 7, 1303) imperiled the political power of the papacy and endangered the pope's exercise of office. The election of Clement V on June 5, 1305, under French influence, led to a gradual transfer of the focus of curial activity away from Italy and the → papal states, although it was never doubted that → Rome was the real seat of the papacy. John XXII (1316-1334), who had been bishop of Avignon from 1310 to 1313, took up residence as pope in the episcopal palace there, but did not succeed in getting the curia to move even as far as Bologna. He and his successor Benedict XII (1334-1342) were the first popes who made Avignon their residence on a permanent basis, in view of the impossibility of returning to Rome. Clement VI (1342-1352) bought the city from Queen Joan I of Naples, an Anjou, and succeeded in getting Charles IV to renounce his sovereign legal rights over the city; but he was not able to take over its governance.

Whereas Clement V had lived in the Dominican

monastery in Avignon, John XXII made the episcopal palace with St. Stephen's church his residence. The full reconstruction of the palace began under Benedict XII. The architect Pierre Poisson erected a fortresslike building defended by towers, with a cloister and rooms for the curia (the Palais vieux). The sober severity of this building was in contrast to the splendid new building raised by Clement VI to the south (the Palais neuf, with Jean de Louvres as architect). Innocent VI (1352-1362), who surrounded the city of Avignon with a rampart, largely completed his building activities with the erection of the tower of St. Laurence. Military activities during the Western Schism damaged the palace, which was the residence of the papal legation from 1433 onward. It became a prison during the French Revolution and was used as barracks in the nineteenth century. It was restored in the twentieth century and turned into a museum.

■ **Bibliography:** *LMA* 1:1303; L. H. Labande, *Le palais des papes et monuments d'Avignon au XIVe siècle,* 2 vols. (Marseille, 1925); G. Colombe, *Le palais des papes d'Avignon* (3rd ed. Paris, 1939); S. Gagnière, *Le palais des papes d'Avignon* (Paris, 1965); F. Enaud, *Les fresques du palais des papes à Avignon* (Paris, 1971) 1-139; V. G. Wetterlöf,

Les Ymagiers à la cour des papes d'Avignon et à la cour des rois de France (Lund, 1975); *Le fonctionnement administratif de la papauté d'Avignon: Actes de la table ronde (Avignon, 23-24 janvier 1988) organisée par l'Ecole Française de Rome* (Rome, 1990); P. Hutton, *The Palais des Papes d'Avignon and the Crisis in Papal Ideology* (Evanston, Ill., 1995); D. Vingtain and C. Sauvageot, *Avignon, le Palais des Papes* (La Pierre-Qui-Vire, 1998).

MARCEL ALBERT/LUDWIG VONES

Bene Valete ("Fare ye well") is the expression of blessings in the eschatocol (closing section) of a papal privilege. Originally written in capital letters, it is found from 1049 as the counterpart of the *rota* in the form of a monogram before the comma (until 1092). It is sometimes absent (e.g., under Gregory VII); it is not found again after Urban V.

■ **Bibliography:** *VATL* 67; M. Kordes, *Der Einfluß der Buchseite auf die Gestaltung der hochmittelalterlichen Papsturkunden* (Hamburg, 1993) 201f., 207-13; T. Frenz, *Papsturkunden des Mittelalters und der Neuzeit* (2nd ed. Stuttgart, 2000) 18f.

ODILO ENGELS

Biblical Commission → Commissions, Pontifical.

Biblical Institute, Pontifical → Institutes, Pontifical.

Blessings, Papal.

1. *History*

The first papal blessing of the people was imparted by Boniface VIII in 1300, when he celebrated the first → Holy Year. Clement VII attached a plenary jubilee indulgence to this blessing in 1525. Since that date, it has been imparted in a solemn form from the balcony of St. Peter's as the → *urbi et orbi* blessing ("for the city of Rome and the world") at Christmas and Easter. Apart from this, archbishops and bishops impart it in a simple form twice a year (according to the ruling by Clement XIII in 1761) or three times a year (according to the ruling by Pius XII in 1943).

Until 1967 priests had the authority to impart the papal blessing in particular circumstances (e.g., at the conclusion of retreats and popular missions). Benedict XIV gave priests permission to impart it when they administer viaticum.

■ **Bibliography:** G. Moroni, *Dizionario di erudizione storico-ecclesiastica* (Venice, 1840) 5:74-77; A. Adam and R. Berger, *Pastoralliturgisches Handlexikon* (5th ed. Freiburg, 1990) 399f.; *VATL* 719f.

ANTON THALER

2. *Canon Law*

The pope imparts the papal blessing (*benedictio apostolica seu papalis*), to which a plenary indulgence is attached, either solemnly *urbi et orbi* or (e.g., on the occasion of audiences) in a simple form. Diocesan bishops and other heads of local churches can impart it three times a year (*Enchiridion indulgentiarum,* norm 10 §2). Since 1967, it has been possible to receive the papal blessing and the indulgence via radio; this was extended to cover television in 1985. Priests can impart the papal blessing with the indulgence only to the dying (can. 530 no. 3 *CIC*); the reform of indulgences in 1967 abolished other faculties for priests (papal blessing on the occasion of popular missions and retreats) and privileges accorded to priests who belonged to an order (can. 915 *CIC* 1917).

■ **Bibliography:** *VATL* 719f.; *MKCIC.*

HEINRICH J. F. REINHARDT

Bullarium, a collection of the most important papal bulls and briefs (from the Latin *bulla,* a capsule, here denoting the metal seal used by sovereigns; it was made sometimes of precious metals, sometimes of lead; from the twelfth century on, papal lead bulls bore the name of the pope and on the reverse the portraits of Peter and Paul). The only official *Bullarium* is vol. 1 (1746) of the *Bullarium* of Benedict XIV; all others are private works, e.g., the *Bullarium* of Laertius Cherubini (1586-88) or the *Magnum Bullarium Romanum* of Hieronymus Mainardi and Carolus Cocquelines (18 vols., Rome, 1732-62, with documents from Leo I to Benedict XIV), with two continuations by other scholars (A. Barbieri, A. Spetia, and R. Segreti, 19 vols. [Rome, 1835-57, repr. 1963-64; 9 vols., Prato, 1840-56]).

■ **Bibliography:** *VATL* 96; L. Santifaller, *Neuere Editionen mittelalterlicher Königs- und Papsturkunden* (Vienna, 1958); H. Bresslau, *Handbuch der Urkundenlehre für Deutschland und Italien,* 2 vols. (3rd ed. Leipzig, 1958); P. Sella, *I Sigilli dell'Archivio Vaticano,* 3 vols. (Rome, 1937-64); P. Herde, *Beiträge zum päpstlichen Kanzlei- und Urkundenwesen im 13. Jahrhundert* (2nd ed. Lassleben, 1967).

DIETER A. BINDER

Campo Santo Teutonico is the name of a complex of buildings on Vatican territory to the south of → St. Peter's which is today the seat of three institutions: the Archconfraternity of Our Lady of Sorrows in the Campo Santo of the Germans and Flemings (which owns the site), the Collegio Teutonico, a college of priests who live in the building owned by the Archconfraternity, and the Roman Institute of the Görres Society.

During the Roman imperial period, the circus of Caligula and Nero stood on this site; according to Tacitus (*Annales* 15), Roman Christians died as martyrs here. After St. Peter's was built, a cemetery was founded here; the name "Campo Santo" is attested from the fourteenth century. It is probable that this was the site of the "Schola Francorum," whose existence has been demonstrated from the eighth century onward. About 1450, Germans living in Rome united to form the Confraternity, which still exists (as an Archconfraternity since 1579), in order to remember the dead and to aid pilgrims. The chapter of St. Peter's gave them the cemetery, for which they have cared ever since. The church they built beside this cemetery (whose architect was probably Giovanni de' Dolci, the builder of the → Sistine Chapel) was consecrated in 1501, and they adorned it with many works of art.

With the intensification of German interest in Rome in the nineteenth century, the Campo Santo Teutonico acquired a new task: the Archconfraternity welcomed German priests and made it possible for them to undertake higher studies in Rome. During the long rectorate of Anton de Waal (1872-1917), who guided the ancient institution on its path into the modern period, this led to the foundation of a college of priests (1876). It began modestly with little money, but over the years it built up a significant collection of small works of ancient Christian art and an important scholarly library. It has given many scholars the opportunity to spend time in Rome. After the Vatican opened its Secret → Archives to researchers in 1881, de Waal extended his interest to church history. In 1887, he founded the *Römische Quartalschrift* (95 vols. and 53 supplements up to 2000). In 1888, the Roman Institute of the Görres Society was founded, concentrating primarily on Christian archaeology and church history. Significant projects include the edition of the Acts of the Council of Trent and of the nunciature in

Cologne; the most recent undertaking, in conjunction with the German Archeological Institute and the Mainz Academy of Sciences, is a study of the paintings in the Roman catacombs. The college and the institute have produced many university professors and scholars, e.g., Joseph Wilpert, Stephan Ehses, Theodor Klauser, and Hubert Jedin. When a sovereign → Vatican state was erected in 1929, the Campo Santo Teutonico remained Italian territory but was given extraterritorial status; this meant that it was able to give numerous political refugees asylum in the closing phase of the Second World War.

■ **Bibliography:** A. de Waal, *Der Campo Santo der Deutschen in Rom* (Freiburg, 1896); P. M. Baumgarten, *Cartularium Vetus Campi Sancti Teutonicorum in Urbe* (Rome, 1908); A. Schmidt, *Das Archiv des Campo Santo Teutonico* (Freiburg, 1967); E. Gatz, ed., *Hundert Jahre deutsches Priesterkolleg beim Campo Santo Teutonico* (Freiburg, 1977); idem, *Anton de Waal (1837-1917) und der Campo Santo Teutonico* (Freiburg, 1980); idem, ed., *Der Campo Santo Teutonico in Rom,* I: A. Weiland, *Der Campo Santo Teutonico in Rom und seine Grabdenkmäler;* II: A. Tönnesmann and U. V. Fischer Pace, *Santa Maria della Pietà. Die Kirche des Campo Santo Teutonico* (Freiburg, 1988); "Deutsche im Rom des 15. und 19. Jarhunderts," *RQ* 86 (1991), various essays; E. M. Schaffer, "Kommentierter Katalog zur Ausstellung '1200 Jahre Campo Santo Teutonico,'" *RQ* 93 (1998) 108-36 (this volume includes various other essays on the history of the Campo Santo).

ERWIN GATZ

Canonization.

1. Concept.—2. History.—3. Legal Basi.s—4. Procedure.—5. Theology.

1. *Concept*

Canonization (on the Latin term *canonizatio,* see 4 below) denotes the solemn judgment by the pope about the happy outcome of the lives of servants of God "who have followed Christ their model in a particular way and borne outstanding witness to the kingdom of heaven by the shedding of their blood (the martyrs) or by the heroic exercise of the virtues (the confessors)" (*AAS* 75 [1983] 349). "By canonizing some of the faithful, i.e., by solemnly proclaiming that they practiced heroic virtue and lived in fidelity to God's grace, the church recognizes the power of the Spirit of holiness within her and sustains the hope of believers by proposing the saints to them as models and intercessors" (*Catechism of the Catholic Church*, 828). This official certainty justifies the public cult of the saints.

2. History

The origins of canonization lie in the early Christian veneration of the martyrs. From the second half of the fourth century onward, the public cult of the saints was also extended to those who had achieved a reputation for holiness, confirmed by extraordinary signs accomplished after their deaths, which were interpreted as miracles. Thus, even without shedding one's blood, it was possible by the heroic exercise of the virtues to attain the merits of martyrdom. Subsequently, those great bishops and teachers who had fought against heresies and professed the true faith were also honored as *confessores*. Important hermits, cenobites, ascetics, monks, and missionaries soon shared in this honor as well. The common factor in all these cases was veneration by the faithful, and the external sign of the acknowledgment of this veneration was the exhumation of their bones in the presence of the local bishop, so that they might be placed anew in an altar. Apart from this "elevation" or "translation" of the body, the canonization of a martyr or confessor consisted in the approval of the cult by the local bishop; one part of this ceremony was the public reading to the faithful of the life story (*vita*) of the candidate for canonization, including the tortures he had endured or the great deeds he had performed. Such elevations to "the honor of the altars" often occurred on the occasion of a synod, when the assembled bishops gave their solemn consent to the public cult. No distinction was made between those called "blessed" and those called "saints."

Because of the occurrence of abuses, and in order to bestow greater weight on the episcopal approval of the cult, recourse was had, initially only in some cases, to the bishop of Rome. The first canonization carried out by a pope was that of Bishop Ulrich of Augsburg by John XV on June 11, 993. The universal reservation of canonization to the pope goes back to the decretal *Audivimus* of Alexander III (1159-1181), which became binding only in 1234 when it was included in the decretals of Gregory IX (c.5 1 X 3,45). Despite this, bishops continued to approve the public cult of Servants of God. Gradually, the use of the attributes *beatus* and *sanctus* led to the emergence of a distinction

between episcopal beatification and papal canonization. No instrument existed to translate the exclusive papal right into practice until Sixtus V founded the Congregation of Rites in 1588 and gave it the relevant competence.

The canonization process, as laid down in the 1917 *Code of Canon Law*, goes back to Urban VIII and Benedict XIV. Urban VIII reversed the existing procedure, so that it no longer involved the approbation by the legitimate authority of an existing cult: now, a servant of God could be officially venerated only after his heroic striving for virtue and his exemplary character had been demonstrated in a legal process. This presupposes the investigation (still required today) of the absence of any cult (*processus super non cultu*), an obvious antithesis to the equally essential requirement that the candidate be the object of veneration by the faithful. Paul VI responded in the Motu proprio *Sanctitas clarior* (March 19, 1969) to requests by the bishops at the Second Vatican Council that the undue length of the process be shortened.

3. Legal Basis

In the Apostolic Constitution *Divinus perfectionis Magister* (January 25, 1983), John Paul II restructured the process of canonization in keeping with the directives of the norm of can. 1403 §1 *CIC*. Following on this Constitution, the Congregation for Causes of the Saints issued special guidelines for the bishops with regard to investigations in canonization processes (February 7, 1983). A transitional decree published on the same day governed the procedure in cases that were already under consideration. Statutes approved by the pope on March 21, 1983, regulate the internal procedures of this dicastery.

4. Procedure

After a formal beatification, which concerns only a limited papal approval of the cult, e.g., for one local church, one religious family, or one particular country, canonization refers to the inclusion of the name in the list of saints, or "canon" (hence the noun *canonizatio*). The canonization process basically follows the rules of the beatification process. Apart from a sufficient degree of veneration, one miracle is required, performed at the intercession of the *beatus* in the period following the beatification; this must be investigated in a separate process. After this, the pope alone decides whether he will proceed to the canonization. The fact that a process has been successfully concluded entails no legal right to canonization. Unlike all other canonical processes, which aim at the execution of a legal judgment, the particularity of the beatification and canonization process is that it only presents conclusions for a possible papal judgment; the pope makes his judgment freely, on the basis of his own evaluation of the results of the process. Thus, he can either confirm it or reject these results; and both happen.

No obligatory liturgical rite for canonization has been promulgated until the present date. At present, canonizations follow a liturgy created for each specific instance.

5. *Theology*

By means of canonization, the church does not primarily acknowledge the striving for personal perfection on the part of Christ's followers, although this element is present; from the perspective of a theology that does not focus narrowly on the salvation of the individual human person, canonization represents more than the attainment of the heroic degree of virtues, or the incitement to imitate a model.

Ecclesiologically speaking, canonization is a process of the church's own self-recognition: the Second Vatican Council deals with canonization when speaking of the link between the eschatological character of the pilgrim church and its unity with the heavenly church (*Lumen Gentium*, 48-51). Thus, every canonization is a reflection of the church about itself, expressing the eschatological consciousness that empowers concrete persons by name as "saints." This means that the saints are not "happy accidents" in an abstract institution (the church) whose primary function is to provide the means of salvation, such that their heroic degree of virtue makes them models set apart from the sinful daily life of "normal" Christians and entitles them to special veneration as saints. On the contrary, the saints are the realization of the specific promise of salvation which Christ made to his church. When the church guarantees the holiness of the saints, it confesses its faith in itself as "indestructibly holy" (*Lumen Gentium*, 48); and at the same time, it affirms its own history.

Accordingly, holiness is not realized as the abstract ideal of a supernatural obligation, which follows an invariable pattern with a fixed catalogue of criteria for establishing the heroic degree of virtue. (This idea could certainly find support in the highly structured procedure followed up to now in the canonization process.) Rather, holiness takes on new and specific forms that are historically unique and cannot be forced into the Procrustean bed of ready-made schematizations. The great saints of the church confirm this.

■ **Primary Sources:** Benedict XIV, *De servorum Dei beatificatione et beatorum Canonizatione*, 4 vols. (Prato, 1839-42).

■ **Bibliography:** K. Rahner, *Schriften zur Theologie* (Einsiedeln et al., 1956) 3:111-26; W. Schamoni, *Inventarium Processuum Beatificationis et Canonizationis* (Hildesheim et al., 1983); A. Casieri, *Postulatorum Vademecum* (2nd ed. Rome, 1985); W. Schulz, *Das neue Selig- und Heiligsprechungsverfahren* (Paderborn, 1988); Congregatio de Causis Sanctorum, *Index ac Status Causarum* (Vatican City, 1999); R. Rodrigo, *Manuale per istruire i processi di canonizzazione dei Santi* (Vatican City, 1992); A. Eszer, "Il concetto della virtù eroica nella storia," in *Sacramenti, Liturgia, Cause dei Santi*, Festschrift for G. Casoria (Naples, 1992) 605-36; A. Royo Mejia, "Evolución histórica de la prueba de la heroicidad de las virtudes en las causas de los Santos en los siglos anteriores a Benedicto XIV," *Archivo teológico Granadino* 56 (1993) 25-61; L. Gerosa, "Heiligkeit und Kirchenrecht," *Theologie und Glaube* 87 (1997) 177-91; R. Latourelle, "Miracle et sainteté dans les causes de béatifications et de canonisation," *Science et esprit* 50 (1998) 265-77; R. Rusconi, "La santità dell'età contemporanea tra agiografia e biografia," *Rivista di storia e letteratura religiosa* 35 (1999) 567-86; A. Vauchez, "Les origines et le développement du procès de canonisation (XII.-XIII. siècles)," in *Vita religiosa im Mittelalter*, Festschrift for K. Elm (Berlin, 1999) 845-56; L. Gerosa, "Die Heiligsprechungspraxis der Kirche und die theologischen Grundlagen des kanonischen Prozessrechts," in *Winfried Schulz in Memoriam* (Frankfurt a.M. et al., 1999) 327-41.

WINFRIED SCHULZ

Cappella Papale (*cappella papalis*).
1. This term designates the liturgy celebrated, normally by the pope himself as "head of the Catholic religion," on great solemnities and particular occasions (e.g., canonizations), in which particular persons take part (see no. 2 below). The elaborate liturgy, which has remained almost unchanged since the fifteenth century, was strongly marked by elements of courtly ceremonial (e.g., princes as assistants to the → throne, the use of silver trumpets, a preliminary tasting of the

wine before the offertory). In the aftermath of the Second Vatican Council, the *cappella papale* was reformed, and its rite no longer differs from that of other Masses celebrated by the pope.

2. This term also designates a section of the Pontifical → Household, a precisely defined group of bishops, priests, and laymen, who have particular places in these liturgies. The composition of this group was established anew by Paul VI in the Motu proprio *Pontificalis Domus* (March 28, 1968). The current list is published in the → *Annuario Pontificio*.

■ **Bibliography:** *VATL* 111f.; Motu proprio *Pontificalis Domus, AAS* 60 (1968) 305-15; A. Bugnini, *La riforma liturgica (1948-1975)* (Rome, 1983) 778-89; *AnPont* (2000) 1344f., 1964.

MARC RETTERACH

Cardinal, College of Cardinals. After the pope, the cardinals are the highest dignitaries in the Catholic Church. They are the "senate" of the pope, whom they elect and whom they assist in the government of the universal church.

1. History

The Latin word *cardinalis* (from *cardo,* "hinge") originally designated a cleric who belonged to the bishop's church. This title was given at first only to the deacons of the ecclesiastical districts of Rome; later it was extended to the highest-ranking priests of the → titular churches and to the seven bishops of the suburbicarian dioceses. About 1100, the development of the three orders of cardinal bishops, cardinal priests, and cardinal deacons was completed. They elected the pope jointly for the first time in 1130 (Papal → Election). In 1179, Alexander III definitively gave the cardinals the exclusive right to elect the pope. From the end of the twelfth century onward, bishops outside Rome have been members of the college as cardinal priests and deacons; the rank held by cardinals is independent of their ordination. Until the reform by Sixtus V in 1586-1587, which raised the number of cardinals to seventy (six bishops, fifty priests, fourteen deacons), the College of Cardinals had immense influence on the government of the church, as can be seen in the electoral capitulations, the consistories, and the signing of papal documents. The → nepotism of the sixteenth century in the papal senate gives the impression that personal interests often played the dominant role.

By creating fifteen → congregations of cardinals in 1588, Sixtus V reduced the influence of the college as a whole.

Since the pontificate of Pius XII, the College of Cardinals has become increasingly international. John XXIII was the first to exceed the number of seventy cardinals. After the Second Vatican Council, wide-reaching changes in the rights of the cardinals were made by Paul VI, beginning in 1965; these changes were enshrined in canon law.

2. Present-day Law

(Cf. esp. cann. 349-59, 883 2°, 967 §1, 1242; 1405 §1 2°, 1558 §2 *CIC.*) The three classes of the College of Cardinals have been retained, although the class of bishops has been numerically strengthened by the inclusion of those Eastern patriarchs who are created cardinals. Cardinal priests and cardinal deacons can "opt" for other titular churches or deaconries; after ten years, cardinal deacons can become cardinal priests. The one created cardinal must be a priest distinguished for faith and the conduct of his life, for piety and prudence in matters of administration. Apart from exceptional cases, one who is not already a bishop is ordained to the episcopate. The pope nominates cardinals freely, although it is customary for the bishops of some dioceses and the holders of certain offices in the curia to become cardinals. A secret nomination ("*in petto*") also exists; here the obligations and rights remain in suspense until the publication. The honorific rights of cardinals include the red habit and the title "Eminence." Apart from this, they are entitled to administer the sacrament of penance everywhere in the world and to be buried in their own church; they are answerable only to the judgment of the pope, and if they are to be heard as witnesses, they have the right to specify where their testimony will be given. Cardinals exercise no jurisdiction of any kind in their titular churches or dioceses, although a function as protector and counselor does exist. Outside Rome, they are exempt. Curial cardinals must live in Rome; all others are obliged to come to Rome whenever the pope summons them. During the → *sede vacante*, all the offices of the curial cardinals are extinguished, with the exception of those of the Camerlengo of the Roman church, the Major Penitentioner, and the cardinal vicar of the diocese of Rome. When cardinals reach the age of seventy-five, they are asked to resign from their offices; at eighty, they lose their curial offices and the right to elect the pope. This means that the body of papal electors and the College of Cardinals are no longer identical.

The cardinal dean presides over the College of Cardinals as first among equals. He is elected by the cardinal bishops from among their number, and he adds the title of the diocese of Ostia to his own title. Like the subdean, who is elected in the same way, he must reside in Rome, and he has the right to ordain the pope to the episcopate, if the newly elected pope is not yet a bishop.

The College of Cardinals acts as a ceremonial or genuine consultative organ of the pope, especially in the ordinary → consistories (which may be "public," i.e., solemn) and in the extraordinary consistories. During the *sede vacante,* the government of the church is entrusted to the College of Cardinals, in order that ordinary or very urgent business (e.g., the preparation of the papal election) may be expedited. The civil authority in the → Vatican state is entrusted to the College of Cardinals during the same period. Precise regulations are laid down by the Apostolic Constitution *Romano Pontifici eligendo.*

■ **Primary Sources:** Paul VI, Motu proprio *Ad purpuratorum patrum, AAS* 57 (1965) 295f.; idem, Motu proprio *Sacro cardinalium consilio, AAS* 57 (1965) 296f.; idem, Motu proprio *Ingravescentem aetatem, AAS* 62 (1970) 810-13; idem, Apostolic Constitution *Romano Pontifici eligendo, AAS* 67 (1975) 609-45.

■ **Bibliography:** *TRE* 17:628-35; *VATL* 372-75; C. G. Fürst, *Cardinalis* (Munich, 1967); G. Alberigo, *Cardinalato e Collegialità* (Florence, 1969); G. May, "Das Papstwahlrecht in seiner jüngsten Entwicklung," in *Ex aequo et bono,* Festschrift for W. Plöchl (Innsbruck, 1977) 231-62; *HKKR* 277-81; W. Imkamp, "Praestantia et efficientia: Anmerkungen zur Entwicklung des Kardinalates unter Papst Paul VI.," *Divinitas* 37 (1993) 128-47; A.-G. Martimort, "L'évolution du Collège des Cardinaux dans l'Église de la seconde moitié du XXᵉ siècle," *Bulletin de littérature ecclésiastique* 98 (1997) 251-60; *MKCIC,* introduction to cann. 349-59/2.

RUDOLF MICHAEL SCHMITZ

Cardinal Secretary of State presides over the Secretariat of State in the Roman → curia and is thus the highest official in today's curia, the official counselor of the pope in political and general church matters. From the time of Martin V onward, the papal Secretaries of the Secret Chamber (an office which developed from the medieval institution of princely secretaries) dealt with diplomatic correspondence and documents of the chancellery. In 1487, Innocent VIII appointed the Private Secretary (*secretarius domesticus*) to head the twenty-four Apostolic Secretaries. Leo X subordinated the *secretarius intimus* (called "Secretary of State" from 1605) to the Cardinal Nephew (who was in charge of papal politics), but after 1644 the Secretary of State was always a cardinal and subordinate only to the pope; this order of things became definitive in 1692. The responsibilities of this office were revised by Pius X in 1908. The competence of the Cardinal Secretary of State was extended after the Second Vatican Council, above all in the two curial reforms by Paul VI (1967) and John Paul II (1988), both of which strengthened the position of the Secretariat of State and made it definitively the highest authority in the curia.

As required by the pope, the Cardinal Secretary of State summons the plenary assembly of cardinal prefects of the curial bodies, and he presides over the council of cardinals, which deals with the organizational and economic matters of the → Holy See. With the consent of the pope, he decides when to summon meetings of individual cardinal prefects. In the absence of the pope, he enjoys special powers, and he is the representative of the pope in the civil government of the → Vatican state.

■ **Primary Sources:** Paul VI, Apostolic Constitution *Regimini Ecclesiae universae, AAS* 59 (1967) 885-928; John Paul II, handwritten letter *Quoniam in eo, AAS* 71 (1979) 256; idem, handwritten letter *Le sollicitudini crescenti, AAS* 76 (1984) 495-96; idem, Apostolic Constitution *Pastor Bonus, AAS* 80 (1988) 841-934; *Regolamento della Curia Romana, AAS* 84 (1992) 201-53.

■ **Bibliography:** *VATL* 752ff.; A. Kraus, "Secretariatus und Sekretariat: Der Ursprung der Institution des Staatssekretariats," *RQ* 55 (1960) 43-84; K. Mörsdorf, "Der Kardinalstaatssekretär: Aufgabe und Werdegang eines Amtes," *Archiv für katholisches Kirchenrecht* 131 (1962) 193-211, also in idem, *Schriften zum Kanonischen Recht,* ed. W. Aymans et al. (Paderborn et al., 1989) 391-99; L. Chiapetta, *Prontuario* (Rome, 1994), 1121ff.

RUDOLF MICHAEL SCHMITZ

Castelgandolfo, a small Italian town in Latium by Lake Albano in the province of Rome, 426 m above sea level, 15 km southeast of Rome, with ca. 5,000 inhabitants. The emperor Domitian had a villa here in the Roman period. In the twelfth century, the noble family Gandolfi, who bestowed their name upon the place, built a house which came into the possession of the Savelli family in the thirteenth century. In 1596, the → Apostolic Chamber purchased the property, and Urban VIII commissioned Carlo Moderno to build the papal palace. Giovanni Bernini built the domed church dedicated to St. Thomas of Villanova, which was decorated with paintings by Carlo Maratta and Peter of Cortona. Clement XIV increased the papal possessions by acquiring the Villa Cibo. With the → Lateran Treaty of 1929, the papal palace and garden, as well as the neighboring Villa Barberini (where ruins of the emperor Domitian's buildings may be seen), became the extraterritorial possession of the → Holy See. Since 1936, the papal palace has been the site of a famous observatory. Castelgandolfo has been the summer residence of the popes since the seventeenth century; it was here that Pius XII (1958) and Paul VI (1978) died.

■ **Bibliography:** *DHGE* 11:1417f.; *VATL* 831f.; E. Bonomelli, *I Papi in Campagna* (Rome, 1953); R. Lefevre, "Castel Gandolfo tra Medioevo e Barocco," *Urbe* 51 (1988) 24-37.

JOSEF GELMI

Castel Sant'Angelo was built with great splendor in 139 C.E. as the mausoleum of the emperor Hadrian, his family, and successors, and was used until 217. A cylinder (64 meters in diameter) is constructed on a quadratic base (ca. 87 meters wide), with central chambers in tiers, surrounded by spiral galleries; above these there was a mound of earth, once planted with shrubs, and at the highest point a four-horsed chariot with a statue of Hadrian. Virtually all the sculptures that once adorned the building and the clothing in marble and travertine stone are lost. The Bridge of the Angel (Ponte Sant'Angelo) from the same period stands in axial relation to the building.

It took on strategic importance as a reinforcement of the bridgehead, after it was included in the Aurelian city walls in 271. Only after 1379 did it become papal property on a permanent basis. Under Nicholas V and above all Alexander VI, it was developed into an impregnable fortress in which the popes resided for certain periods; it was connected to the Vatican by a corridor along which they could flee in danger. It was also used as a treasury, an archive, and a prison. It was deco-rated under Julius II, Leo X, and above all Paul III; the baroque garlands were placed on the ramparts under Urban VIII. Restorations in the twentieth century changed its appearance; today it is used as a museum.

The name and the statue of an angel seen at its highest point today recall the vision of Gregory the Great during a procession in time of plague (590), when the archangel Michael appeared to him above the building and said that the plague would soon end.

■ **Bibliography:** *LMA* 3:1921f.; M. Borgatti, *Castel Sant' Angelo in Roma* (2nd ed. Rome, 1931); M. De' Spagnolis, "Contributi per una nuova lettura del Mausoleo di Adriano," *Bolletino d'Arte* 61 (1976) 62-68; C. D'Onofrio, *Castel Sant'Angelo e Borgo tra Roma e Papato* (Rome, 1978); R. Mertzenich, *Der Alexander-Zyklus der Sala Paolina in der Engelsburg zu Rom* (Aachen, 1990); P. Spagnesi, *Castel Sant'Angelo: La fortezza di Roma* (Rome, 1995).

GEORG GATZINGER

Cathedra designates the seat of the bishop in his cathedral, where he leads the liturgy, proclaims the Word, and carries out ordinations; it is the sign of his teaching office and of his pastoral authority, as well as of unity in the faith which the bishop proclaims (*Caeremoniale Episcoporum* 42). From ancient times, it has been taken for granted that the teacher sits: the seat is the distinguishing mark of the charge committed to him (cf. Jesus' words about the "chair of Moses" [Matt. 23:2]). From the second century on, the "apostolic" or "episcopal chair" was used as a metonym for the episcopal office (Muratorian Fragment 75f.; Tertullian, *De praescriptione haereticorum* 36; Cyprian, *Ep.* 55.8). In the basilicas, the chair is located at the vertex of the apse, elevated above the seats of the priests on either side, which in many places (cf. Torcello, Poreč) took the form of a semicircular *synthrōnon*. Later, probably because of the desire to pray and celebrate Mass facing east, the *cathedra* and the priests' seats (as choir stalls) moved to the side of the altar. In the Middle Ages, in keeping with the position of bishops in the imperial church, the cathedra increasingly took the form of a princely throne, a chair adorned with steps, a baldachin, and silk hangings. In Mediterranean lands, the artistic elaboration of the *cathedra* itself was preferred: often, instead of wood, precious marble was used, adorned with ivory (see the *cathedra* of Maximinus in Ravenna, eighth century), and the chair was provided with a back and armrests. Today, the *cathedra* is placed in such a way that the bishop is not seated higher than necessary; it is easy for him to make contact with the entire assembled congregation. A baldachin is no longer prescribed, but ancient and valuable works of art are to be preserved. The *cathedra* is always reserved to the local bishop (with the exception of the president of a synod); other bishops are given a seat in an appropriate place, but not in the form of a *cathedra.*

The term *cathedra* was also employed for the chair that was set in place for the deceased person at the exequial meal. We find such chairs in the catacombs, and this is the origin of the feast of "Peter's Chair" (*cathedra Petri*), which was later understood as the celebration of the beginning of his ministry (*natale de cathedra*). A similar veneration of the cathedra of the founder-bishop is also attested in the case of James in Jerusalem (Eusebius of Caesarea, *Historia ecclesiastica* 7.19). The *cathedra Petri* venerated in Rome in the apse of St. Peter's is a wooden chair made for Charlemagne and then given to the pope as the throne for his coronation; remnants of an older oaken throne are fastened to this, and it received its baroque covering under Giovanni Lorenzo Bernini.

■ **Bibliography:** *DACL* 3:19-75; *LMA* 2:175; *Nuovo Dizionario di Liturgia,* ed. D. Satore and A. Triacca (Rome, 1984), 789-97; *VATL* 383ff.; E. Stommel, "Die bischöfliche Cathedra im christlichen Altertum," *Münchener theologische Zeitschrift* 3 (1952) 17-32; P. E. Schramm, *Herrschaftszeichen und Staatssymbolik,* I, (Stuttgart, 1954) 316-25; II (1956) 694-707; E. Stommel, "Bischoffstuhl und Hoher Thron," *Jahrbuch für Antike und Christentum* 1 (1958) 52-78; E. Dyggve, "La SS. Cattedra di San Pietro," *Analecta Romana Instituti Danici* (Rome, 1959/60) 13-32; J. Emminghaus, *Gestaltung des Altarraums* (Leipzig, 1976); Rituale Romanum: *De Benedictionibus* (Rome, 1984) 339-45; M. Maccarone, "La 'Cathedra Sancti Petri' nel medioevo: Da simbolo a reliquia," *Rivista di storia della Chiesa in Italia* 39 (1985) 349-447.

RUPERT BERGER

Chamberlains, Papal. The reordering of the Pontifical Household by Paul VI in the Motu proprio *Pontificalis Domus* (March 28, 1968) abolished or gave new titles and functions to the various classes of papal chamberlains that had existed up to that date: priests could be "genuine chamberlains," "secret chamberlains," "honorary chamberlains,"

and "chamberlains outside Rome," while laymen could be "genuine secret chamberlains," "secret chamberlains," and "honorary chamberlains." The priestly service in the Pontifical Household is now undertaken by two "prelates of the antechamber," and the titles "domestic prelate" and "supernumerary secret chamberlain" were changed to "honorary prelate of His Holiness" and "chaplain to His Holiness" (Papal → Orders); the function performed by laymen lives on in the "Gentlemen of His Holiness." These persons are nominated because of particularly meritorious services rendered to the Holy See (i.e., independently of their family background) and constitute a college under the Prefecture of the Pontifical Household, with specific functions in the papal liturgy and in the reception of those admitted to private audiences. They are members of the Pontifical → Family.

■ **Bibliography:** *VATL* 189f., 244f.

MARTIN HÜLSKAMP

Chancellery, Pontifical (*Cancelleria Apostolica*). This is to be considered the oldest dicastery of the Roman → curia, going back to the *notarii Sanctae Romanae Ecclesiae* headed by the "Primicerius" and his deputy, the "Secundicerius," in the fourth century. They were responsible for the production of papal letters and documents; as *scrinarii,* they looked after the archives.

The first certain evidence of the apostolic chancellery comes from the thirteenth century, when Innocent III reorganized this body and extended its responsibilities. A lead seal was usually employed for papal letters; the pontifical chancellery was also given the task of keeping the → fisherman's ring. The chancellery lost some of its responsibilities with the erection of the Secretariat for Letters in the fifteenth century.

With the curial reform of Pius X, it was given responsibility for Apostolic Letters (can. 260, *CIC* 1917). Those with leading functions in the pontifical chancellery were made cardinals with the official titles of Librarian, Chancellor, and Vice-Chancellor; the last of these, Luigi Traglia, relinquished office on March 31, 1973. After the Second Vatican Council, Paul VI initially widened the competence of the pontifical chancellery in his curial reform (*Regimini Ecclesiae Universae*), with the erection of an office responsible for sending Apostolic Letters, but he subsequently abolished it

(*Quo aptius,* Feb. 27, 1973). Before its abolition, the Pontifical Chancellors had the following officials: the cardinal and his deputy (called the regent), the college of Apostolic Protonotaries, two adjutants, an archivist and secretary, and three clerks (one of whom was responsible for the seals). The pontifical chancellery had its seat in the Palazzo della Cancelleria, to which it gave its name. After the abolition, an office in the Secretariat of State was erected, called "Cancelleria Litterarum Apostolicarum," but this too now belongs to the past.

In his curial reform of 1988 (*Pastor Bonus,* 42-43), John Paul II entrusted the classical tasks of the pontifical chancellery to the → Secretariat of State, where they are carried out by the first Section for General Affairs. It is here that the lead seal and the Fisherman's ring are kept.

■ **Primary Sources:** *Regimini Ecclesiae Universae, AAS* 59 (1967) 885-928; Motu proprio *Quo aptius, AAS* 65 (1973) 113-16; *Pastor Bonus, Constitutio Apostolica de Romana Curia, AAS* 80 (1988) 841-934; "Regolamento generale della Curia Romana," *AAS* 84 (1992) 201-67.
■ **Bibliography:** *VATL* 369f.; N. Del Re, *La Curia Romana* (Rome, 1970); P. A. Bonnet and C. Gullo, *La Curia Romana nella Costituzione Apostolica "Pastor Bonus"* (Vatican City, 1990).

JOHANNES O. RITTER

Chronography of 354. This is the name given by scholars since Theodor Mommsen to a richly illustrated Roman state calendar (Codex Luxemburgensis, the original text, is lost; the reconstruction is based on eight manuscripts, the oldest of which is from the Carolingian period). The author and illustrator may be Dionysius Filocalus, who is mentioned at the beginning and may be identical with the calligrapher of the same name.

Contents: (1) A calendar with pictures (cf. *DACL*) with indications about days when games are held and the senate meets, and the *natales Caesarum* (without pagan or Christian feasts). (2) Consular chronicles from 509 B.C.E. to 354 C.E.; the birth and death of Christ are mentioned. (3) The table of dates for Easter for one hundred years from 312. (4) A list of the city prefects of Rome from 254 to 354, and the list of consuls. (5) A list of the dates of death and places of burial of the twelve Roman bishops from Lucius (255) to Julius (352). (6) A list of the dates of death and places of burial of the Roman martyrs (the later martyrologies developed from such lists). (7) A list of the

Roman bishops from Peter to Liberius (Liberian Catalogue) with dates of their reigns and important events (the first part, up to 230, contains many inaccuracies; the second part is more reliable). This is also called the "Bouchier catalogue," after the first editor, Gilles Bouchier. It is the basis of the → *Liber Pontificalis.* (8) A chronicle of world history from Adam to 354, based in the first part on the chronicle of Hippolytus (234). (9) A chronicle of the city of Rome from the period of the kings to the death of Licinius in 325. (10) A description of the fourteen regions of Rome (*notitia*). Scholars disagree about whether pagan elements in this Chronicle are only the expression of nostalgia (Mommsen), or indications of historical reality (Henri Stern, Michele R. Salzman).

■ **Bibliography:** *PRE* 3:2477-81; *DACL* 3:1555-60; 9:527-30; *DECL* 126f.; C. Nordenfalk, *Der Kalender vom Jahre 354 und die lateinische Buchmalerei des 4. Jahrhunderts* (Göteborg, 1936); H. Stern, *Le calendrier de 354* (Paris, 1953); idem, *ANRW* II, 12/2 (1981) 431-75; M. R. Salzman, *On Roman Time* (Berkeley, 1990).

THEODORA HANTOS

Coat of Arms, Papal. The first pope whose coat of arms is preserved in contemporary depictions is Boniface VIII. Until 1969, the → *Annuario Pontificio* published the papal coats of arms from Innocent III onward; these were mostly later attributions to the popes of their family arms. It is characteristic of papal coats of arms (as for ecclesiastical heraldry in general) that they usually have no crest. The following elements have become standard heraldic style since the fifteenth century: two crossed keys, united by a red tasseled cord either above or behind the shield; the → tiara is suspended above the shield. The key on the heraldic left (i.e., on the viewer's right) is the key for loosing, and is golden; that on the heraldic right is the key for binding, and is silver.

■ **Bibliography:** *LMA* 4:2145; 8:2034; *VATL* 837; B. B. Heim, *Heraldry in the Catholic Church* (2nd ed. Gerrards Cross, 1981).

TONI DIEDERICH

Collegiality, Episcopal. The Second Vatican Council gave new force to the "collegiate character and structure of the episcopal order" (*Lumen Gentium* 22), which is the primary form of the apostolic ministry: "Just as, by the decree of the Lord, Saint Peter and the rest of the apostles form one college, so for a like reason the Roman Pontiff, the successor of Peter, and the bishops, the successors of the apostles, are united together in one" (ibid.; *CIC* can. 330). This makes collegiality constitutive of the episcopal office itself, not merely of the exercise of this ministry; it is this that entitles the bishops to take part in an ecumenical council (*Christus Dominus* 4). Since the pope, as head of the college of bishops, can never *exist* without collegiality—although he can *act* without an explicit reference to the college of bishops (the *actus collegialis*)—the papal office too finds its theological locus, basis, and structure in the collegiality of the bishops. The necessity of the apostolic succession shows the constitutive character of collegiality diachronically or through time. Far from contradicting the personal or local dimensions of the episcopal office, collegiality is expressed precisely in these dimensions. "This college, in so far as it is composed of many members, is the expression of the variety and universality of the People of God; and of the unity of the flock of Christ, in so far as it is assembled under one head" (*Lumen Gentium* 22).

According to *Presbyterorum Ordinis* 7 and 8, the collegiality of priests must find stronger expression than hitherto in the presbyterate of the local church.

■ **Bibliography:** *Lumen Gentium* 22f.; K. Rahner and J. Ratzinger, *Episcopate and Primacy* (New York, 1962); G. Baraúna, ed., *De Ecclesia: Beiträge zur Konstitution "Über die Kirche" des II Vatikanischen Konzils* (Freiburg, 1966) 2:44-70 (J. Ratzinger) 71-165; W. Henn, *The Honor of My Brothers: A Short History of the Relation between the Pope and the Bishops* (New York, 2000).

JOSEF FREITAG

Commissions, Pontifical. At the present date, the Roman → curia includes five Pontifical Commissions among its dicasteries, as well as some commissions incorporated in Congregations.

1. *Pontifical Commission for the Cultural Goods of the Church.* This was erected by John Paul II on March 25, 1993, as an autonomous commission, replacing the Pontifical Commission for the Maintenance of the Artistic and Historical Patrimony. It is headed by a president with the rank of archbishop.

2. *Pontifical Commission for Church Archaeology,* founded by Pius IX on January 6, 1852. It is responsible for cemeteries and Christian catacombs in Italy and for early Christian memorial sites.

3. *Pontifical Biblical Commission,* set up under Leo XIII on October 30, 1902, to promote biblical studies, and reorganized under Paul VI. Its president is the Prefect of the Congregation for the Doctrine of the Faith.

4. *Pontifical Commission for the Revision and Emendation of the Vulgate,* erected by Pius X on November 21, 1907, with the task of producing a new critical edition of the Vulgate. On January 15, 1984, John Paul II entrusted it with the task of producing a new text of the entire Old Testament.

5. *Pontifical Commission "Ecclesia Dei,"* erected by John Paul II on July 2, 1988, in order to lead adherents of Marcel Lefebvre back to communion with the pope and with the Roman Catholic Church.

■ **Primary Sources:** *"Pastor Bonus,"* Constitutio Apostolica de Romana Curia, *AAS* 80 (1988) 841-934.

■ **Bibliography:** *VATL* 389-401; *AnPont* (2000) 1353-60, 1976ff.

JOHANNES O. RITTER

Conclave → Election, Papal.

Concordat.
1. Concept.—2. History.—3. Legal Nature.—4. Contract Partners, Agreement and Termination.

1. *Concept*

This term designates a mutual contract in international law between the → Holy See and a state, with the aim of establishing the permanent ordering of all (or some) of the ecclesiastical matters and questions of state-church law which concern both partners to the concordat.

The term concordat (as *conventio sollemnis*) is given only to those contracts between the Holy See and a state which establish a comprehensive ordering, or at least an ordering that covers several significant areas of church–state relations. Additional regulations or provisional orderings are called "agreements" (*conventio, accordo, accordo concordatario,* exchange of notes, protocol, or sometimes *modus vivendi*). Irrespective of the terminology used and of the degree of solemnity with which the treaty is concluded, all these concordatary agreements, which are summarized by the term "agreements" (*conventiones,* cf. can. 3 *CIC*), have the same degree of validity, obligation, and permanent force. Agreements between a state and the bishops of a country are not concordats in the strict sense of the term; these can be signed only with the consent of the Holy See.

2. *History*

In the history of concordats a distinction is made between *concordata pacis,* representing a peace treaty between state and church—the historical prototype of which is the Concordat of Worms in 1122 between Pope Calixtus II and Emperor Henry V, which put an end to the investiture conflict—*concordata amicitiae,* which confirm an already existing relationship of friendship, and finally *concordata defensionis iurium et libertatis ecclesiae* (concordats for the defense of the rights and freedom of the church), when a rupture of the relations between state and church must be prevented, or a fundamentally new ordering of the relationship is to be agreed upon.

Historically significant concordats include those concluded by Pope Martin V in 1418 at the Council of Constance with the conciliar nations in the form of papal bulls; the so-called German princely concordats of 1447, and the Vienna concordat of 1448 about the bestowal of church offices; and the French concordats of 1472 and 1516, which were influenced by Gallicanism. The concordat concluded between Pius VII and Napoleon on July 15, 1801, was defensive; its authority was greatly restricted by the so-called organic articles subsequently issued unilaterally by the French state. The Bavarian concordat of June 5, 1817, followed the same pattern: its authority was later restricted by the religious edict later issued unilaterally by the kingdom of Bavaria. So-called bulls of circumscription ordered church life anew in the period after Napoleon in Prussia (1821), the states of the church province of the Upper Rhine (1821/27) and in Hanover (1824): these were agreed between the Holy See and the states, then promulgated by the pope and published by the states in their legal gazettes as laws of the state. A comprehensive concordat with Austria was agreed to in 1855; this was terminated by the state during the *Kulturkampf,* but remained de facto valid until the end of the Habsburg monarchy in 1918. After the First World War, in the "era of concordats" that began under Pius XI (1922-1939), church life was ordered anew by means of concordats concluded with Latvia (1922), Poland (1925), Rumania,

Lithuania, and Czechoslovakia (1927). The Roman Question, which had simmered since 1870, was resolved by the → Lateran Treaties (state treaty, financial treaty, and concordat) concluded between the Holy See and the kingdom of Italy on February 11, 1929. The Bavarian concordat of March 29, 1924, was the prototype of a new kind of concordatary regulation of the relationship between church and state in Germany; this model was followed in the concordats with Prussia (1929) and Baden (1932). The concordat between the Holy See and Hitler's Germany (July 20, 1933) had a very clearly defensive character; despite all the persecutions and state hostilities during the period of National Socialism (1933-1945), it offered the Catholic Church a legal basis for the defense of its rights, even though this gave weak support in the face of the systematic injustice of the Nazi state. This concordat with the German Reich was acknowledged by the Federal Constitutional Court in a judgment dated March 26, 1957, as validly concluded, and is still in force; given the change in the "constitutional background" within Germany, the concordat concluded with Hitler's Reich became a "concordat of friendship" in a country governed by a stable constitution. As a consequence of the Second World War, only a few concordats were concluded under Pius XII (1939-1959), viz., with Portugal (1940), a comprehensive concordat with Spain (August 27, 1953), and one with the Dominican Republic (1954).

The Second Vatican Council entailed a significant caesura for the concordatary politics of the Holy See. The church successfully demanded that the state give up all its rights to exercise influence on episcopal nominations and other ecclesiastical offices. States were also urged to renounce their rights to propose or nominate candidates for episcopal sees. In the era after the Council, concordats were concluded with Venezuela (1964), Argentina (1966), Columbia (1973), Spain (1976), Peru (1980), Haiti, and Italy (1984). A *modus vivendi* to protect the religious freedom of Catholics was reached with two states which at that time had communist governments—Hungary (1964) and Yugoslavia (1966)—as well as with Tunisia (1964) and Morocco (1986). Twenty-six concordats were concluded under John Paul II between 1978 and January 1, 1996, more than under any previous pope. The "fundamental agreement" between the Holy See and Israel was signed on December 30,

1993, paving the way for the assumption of mutual diplomatic relations (*AAS* 86 [1994] 716-29). Recent developments indicate that concordats remain the best way to establish a permanent peaceful ordering in those countries in which, thanks to the historical development and the situation with regard to state-church law, it is possible to establish by treaty the cooperation between state and church.

3. *Legal Nature*

Today it is agreed that concordats are international treaties between the Holy See and a state. The so-called curialist theory of privilege, which the church maintained in the Middle Ages—taking its point of departure from the idea of the church's superiority to the states of the world, under which concordats were understood as revocable privileges granted by the pope—has been abandoned, even as a theory, since Leo XIII (1878-1903) at the latest. The same is true of the so-called legal theory maintained on the part of states, which had developed from the absolutist state-church system of the period of the Enlightenment, where the local sovereign governed the church: this theory understood concordats, even as late as in the nineteenth century, as a unilateral law of the state, which it could revoke at any time. This view was maintained in the period of the *Kulturkampf* (and even later) by Protestant professors of civil and church law, e.g., Paul Hinschius, Rudolph Sohm, and Ulrich Stutz. By contrast, it is universally held today, in theory and in praxis, that concordats are treaties in international law in the strict sense, concluded between church and state. The view that, because of their specific contents, concordats are treaties of a wholly particular kind has not won acceptance in praxis; as a reaction to attempts to equate all agreements made between the state and religious groups, this interpretation saw concordats as a unique phenomenon in the special legal sphere of the relations between state and church.

Today the following view prevails: "It must be insisted, in agreement with the praxis on the part of states, that concordats belong to the sphere of international law" (U. Scheuner, in *Handbuch des Staatskirchenrechts,* 333), although one may not overlook the particular characteristics of concordats vis-à-vis the Agreement of Vienna about the law of contracts (May 23, 1969)—since the contract partner on the church's side is not a "state" but the Holy See (as a designation for the totality of the Catholic Church).

4. *Contract Partners, Agreement and Termination*

The rules of international law govern the agreement, the validity, and the termination of concordats. The regulations of the universal international law of contracts, as stipulated in the Vienna Convention on the Law of Treaties (May 25, 1969) for contracts between states, apply to concordats, governing the following points: the negotiation of the contract; in the case of agreement, the initialing (with abbreviated signatures of the delegated negotiators); signature (concluding the contract); assent by parliament (normally in the form of a law); ratification by the competent representative or executive organ (head of state, government; in the case of the Holy See, by means of the pope's signature); exchange of declarations that both sides accept the contract (documents of ratification).

All concordats include a so-called friendship clause, which obligates the partners, in the case of subsequent disagreements about the interpretation or application of a regulation in the contract, to reach an amicable solution by common consent (cf. art. 33, par. 2 of the concordat with the German Reich).

Clauses concerning a temporal limitation and termination (as in art. 20 of the 1922 concordat with Latvia, or art. 23 par. 2 of the 1927 concordat with Rumania) are unusual. The normal way for a concordat to be terminated is by mutual agreement; in exceptional cases, the concordat can expire when one of the contract partners ceases to exist, when customary law develops in opposition to the concordat, or when it fails to be applied over a long period ("desuetude"). The breach of a concordat (i.e., the conscious infringement of one or all contractual obligations) is an illegal dissolution, which offends against the natural law principle that "agreements are to be kept." This does not lead to the automatic extinction of the concordat, but it frees the other contractual partner from all obligations, giving this partner at the same time the right to terminate the contractual relationship. In practice, there have been many unilateral terminations of concordats by states, e.g., France's termination of the Napoleonic concordat in 1905.

■ **Primary Sources:** A. Mercati, *Raccolta di concordati su* *materie ecclesiastiche tra la Santa Sede e le Autorità Civili,* I, *1098-1914,* II, *1915-1954* (Vatican City, 1954); L. Schöppe, ed., *Konkordate seit 1800: Originaltext und deutsche Übersetzung* (Frankfurt a.M., 1964); idem, *Neue Konkordate und konkordatäre Vereinbarungen: Abschlüsse in den Jahren 1956 bis 1969* (Hamburg, 1970); C. Corral Salvador and J. Giménez y Martínez de Carvajal, eds., *Concordatos vigentes,* 2 vols. (Madrid, 1981).

■ **Bibliography:** E. Friesenhahn et al., eds., *Handbuch des Staatskirchenrechts der Bundesrepublik Deutschland* (Berlin, 1975) 2:299-344; 2nd ed., ed. J. Listl and D. Pirson, *Handbuch des Staatskirchenrechts der Bundesrepublik Deutschland* (Berlin, 1995) 2:217-50; *HKG* 7:179-229; *TRE* 19:462-71; U. Stutz, *Konkordat und Codex* (Berlin, 1930); J. Heckel, "Der Vertrag des Freistaates Preußen mit den evangelischen Landeskirchen vom 11.5.1931: Zu seiner Ratifikation am 29.6.1931," *Theologische Blätter* 11 (1932) 193-204; H. Wagnon, *Concordats et droit international* (Gembloux, 1935); H. Barion, "Konkordat und Codex," in Festschrift for U. Stutz (Stuttgart, 1938) 371-88; idem, "Über doppelsprachige Konkordate," *Deutsche Rechtswissenschaft* 5 (1940) 226-49; J. H. Kaiser, *Die politische Klausel der Konkordate* (Berlin, 1949); A. Ottaviani and I. Damizia, *Institutiones Iuris Publici Ecclesiastici,* 2 vols. (4th ed. Vatican City, 1958-60); D. Pirson, "Der Kirchenvertrag als Gestaltungsform zwischen Staat und Kirche," in Festschrift for H. Liermann (Erlangen, 1964) 177-95; A. Hollerbach, "Die neuere Entwicklung des Konkordatsrechts," *Jahrbuch des öffentlichen Rechts der Gegenwart,* new series 17 (1968) 117-63; H. Reis, "Konkordat und Kirchenvertrag in der Staatsverfassung," *Jahrbuch des öffentlichen Rechts der Gegenwart,* new series 17 (1968) 165-394; G. Lajolo, *I Concordati moderni* (Brescia, 1968); H. E. Feine, *Kirchliche Rechtsgeschichte,* I, *Die katholische Kirche* (5th ed. Weimar, 1972); U. Scheuner, "Kirchenverträge in ihrem Verhältnis zu Staatsgesetz und Staatsverfassung," in *Schriften zum Staatskirchenrecht* (Berlin, 1973) 355-72; idem, "Evangelische Kirchenverträge I und II," in *Schriften zum Staatskirchenrecht,* 347-54; H. F. Köck, *Die völkerrechtliche Stellung des Heiligen Stuhls* (Berlin, 1975); H. E. Cardinale, *The Holy See and the International Order* (London/Worcester, 1976); R. Minnerath, *L'église et les états concordataires (1846-1981)* (Paris, 1983); H. F. Köck, *Rechtliche und politische Aspekte von Konkordaten* (Berlin, 1983); J. Listl, *Die Konkordate und Kirchenverträge in der BRD* (Berlin, 1987), I, Introduction, 3-23; J.-N. D'Onorio et al., eds., *Le Saint-Siège dans les relations internationales* (Paris, 1989).

JOSEPH LISTL

Congregations are part of the Roman → curia and number among those organs with responsibilities for the governance of the universal church in accordance with the special laws which go beyond what is laid down in the Code (can. 360).

1. History.—2. Present-day Law.

1. *History*

The practice of discussing and deciding all matters of importance with the papal → Consistory (a practice dating to the twelfth century) encountered practical difficulties with the increasing amount of work involved, making a division of labor within the congregation based on competencies necessary. Initially, an ad hoc commission of cardinals was charged with preparing more difficult matters for the Consistory; from the beginning of the sixteenth century onward, they were entrusted with decisions in certain standard cases. These commissions, which now met regularly, were already called "congregations"; they had their own officials, but were not yet set up on a permanent basis. The decisive step here was taken by Paul III in 1542 with the foundation of the *Congregatio Romanae et universalis Inquisitionis,* later called Holy Office and renamed *Congregatio pro doctrina fidei* (Congregation for the Doctrine of the Faith) by Paul VI in 1965; this congregation is the highest authority in matters of faith, and as such has remained both a court and an administrative body until the present day.

The tasks entailed in the execution and interpretation of the reform decrees of the Council of Trent led under Pius IV in 1564 to the establishment of the *Congregatio super executione et observatione Sancti Concilii Tridentini* (later simply called *Sacra Congregatio Concilii*). The next congregation to be founded, under Pius V in 1571, was that of the Index (*Congregatio indicis librorum prohibitorum*), which existed until 1917.

On the basis of these organizational acts, Sixtus V created in the Constitution *Immensa aeterni* (January 22, 1588) a comprehensive system of fifteen congregations, each with limited sectorial reponsibilities (six for the papal states, the others for matters concerning the universal church, Italy, and Rome). To begin with, special importance attached to the *Congregatio pro erectione ecclesiarum et provisionibus consistorialibus* (later: *Sacra Congregatio Consistorialis*), which prepared the matters to be decided in the Consistory; however, the Consistory soon declined into a matter of formality, and the traditional curial offices were increasingly overshadowed by the powerful rise of the congregations. These came to rival even the papal courts, since the congregations became more and more involved in legal cases, employing for this purpose the summary court procedure created by Clement V (chapter 2 in the Clementines 2.1); this meant that they were superior to the courts, which were required to follow the normal court procedure. The Sacred Congregation of the Council became the main rival of the → Rota Romana.

Among the new institutions established after Sixtus V, the *Congregatio de Propaganda Fide*, erected by Gregory XV in 1622 stands out; after *Pastor Bonus* (1988), it is now called *Congregatio pro Gentium Evangelizatione*. The origins of this congregation are to be found at a still earlier period, linked to the missionary concerns of the Apostolic See. In 1862, under Pius IX, a *Congregatio de propaganda Fide pro negotiis ritus orientalis* was set up, and put under the authority of the Prefect of Propaganda Fide; Benedict XV established the present-day *Congregatio pro Ecclesiis Orientalibus* as an autonomous congregation (Motu proprio *Dei providentia*, May 1, 1917).

Pius X established the Congregation for Religious, with responsibilities for the consecrated life, and detached the Congregation for the Sacraments from the Sacred Congregation of the Council. The total number of congregations has varied greatly in the course of time: in the mid-nineteenth century, they numbered almost thirty, and there were twenty-one at the beginning of Pius X's pontificate. He reduced them to eleven. The characteristic element of this concentration (apart from the consequences of the loss of the papal states) is that some congregations, whose competence had hitherto been limited to Rome or Italy, now became responsible for the entire Latin church.

2. Present-day Law

Today's organization of the congregations is based on the curial reform by John Paul II in the Apostolic Constitution *Pastor Bonus* (June 28, 1988) and the executive regulations *Regolamento Generale della Curia Romana* (February 4, 1992); special organizational acts concerned individual congregations. The congregations have a collegial constitution. Their members are cardinals and (diocesan) bishops; the pope nominates them and determines their number. Each congregation is

headed by a cardinal prefect (called pro-prefect if not yet a cardinal). The secretary, who is an archbishop, and the higher-ranking full-time collaborators discharge important functions; each congregation has consultors (theologians, canon lawyers, or other specialists) on whose advice it draws.

The congregations are primarily organs at the highest administrative level; they have legislative competence only in individual cases, with the specific approval of the pope. Some congregations also possess judicial competence. All decisions of greater importance must be presented to the pope for his ratification (with the exception of those matters for which a special mandate has been given); this takes place in regular audiences. The form of papal ratification is either general or special (*in forma specifica*). Within the congregation, a plenary assembly, to which all members are invited (usually once a year), discusses fundamental questions. All members resident in Rome are summoned to the ordinary meetings. The leaders and most important collaborators form the "congress." Apart from this, it is envisaged that the various dicasteries will collaborate, and "standing inter-dicasterial commissions" are erected to meet specific needs (according to *AnPont* [2000] 1292ff., five such commissions existed in 2000). The pope brings the leading cardinals together for consultations several times a year. When the Holy See is vacant, the prefects and members of the congregations lose their offices; the secretaries carry on the day-to-day business. According to the dispositions of *Pastor Bonus,* there are nine congregations, with the following responsibilities:

(a) *Congregation for the Doctrine of the Faith (Congregatio pro Doctrina Fidei),* with the duty of promoting and protecting the truth of doctrines concerning faith and morals. It is responsible for the *privilegium fidei* and has the judicial power to inflict penalties in cases of offenses against the faith and grave scandals in the field of morals or in the celebration of the sacraments.

(b) *Congregation for the Eastern Churches (Congregatio pro Ecclesiis Orientalibus),* with responsibility for administrative matters concerning the Eastern Catholic churches, e.g., the nomination of bishops, organization of structures in the local churches, quinquennial reports and → *ad limina* visits.

(c) *Congregation for Divine Worship and the*

Discipline of the Sacraments (Congregatio de Cultu Divino et Disciplina Sacramentorum), which deals with liturgical matters and the celebration of the sacraments, nullity of ordination, dispensation from the obligations of the diaconate and priesthood, and dispensations in cases of *matrimonium ratum et non consummatum.*

(d) *Congregation for the Causes of the Saints (Congregatio de Causis Sanctorum),* which supports the diocesan bishops in causes of beatification and canonization and examines whether such requests deserve support.

(e) *Congregation for Bishops (Congregatio pro Episcopis),* with responsibility for the local churches and bishops, for nominations of bishops, the episcopal ministry, and apostolic visitations; it is also responsible for personal prelatures.

(f) *Congregation for the Evangelization of Peoples (Congregatio pro Gentium Evangelizatione),* which guides and coordinates the missionary activity of the Catholic Church.

(g) *Congregation for the Clergy (Congregatio pro Clericis),* with responsibility for the life and ministry of the diocesan clergy (priests and deacons), for religious instruction, and for questions concerning the administration of property.

(h) *Congregation for the Institutes of Consecrated Life and for Societies of the Apostolic Life (Congregatio pro Institutis vitae consecratae et Societatibus vitae apostolicae),* which decides on questions concerning members of religious orders and congregations, secular institutes, societies of apostolic life, hermits, and consecrated virgins.

(i) *Congregation for Catholic Education (Congregatio de Institutione Catholica),* with three departments responsible for (1) seminaries, (2) ecclesiastical and Catholic universities and faculties, and (3) Catholic schools and other educational institutions.

■ **Primary Sources:** Apostolic Constitution *Pastor Bonus de Romana Curia,* AAS 80 (1988) 841-934; *Regolamento generale della Curia Romana,* AAS 84 (1992) 201-67.
■ **Bibliography:** *VATL* 401-22; *HKKR,* 2nd ed.; N. Del Re, *La Curia Romana* (Rome, 1970); P. A. Bonnet and C. Gullo, *La Curia Romana nella Costituzione Apostolica "Pastor Bonus"* (Vatican City, 1990); *AnPont* (2000) 1245-91, 1936-46.

JOHANNES O. RITTER

Consistory. The papal Consistory is closely linked to the history of the College of → Cardinals. From

the eleventh century, the cardinals became an influential institution in the universal church, collaborating in the governmental acts of the pope. A "consistory" originally denoted a solemn, public judicial trial, in which cardinals and others took part; in the broader sense, it designates the consultation by the pope of the assembly of curial cardinals. With the institutionalization of the → congregations of cardinals in the sixteenth century, the Consistory was pushed into the background, serving now as a solemn forum for papal governmental acts and for publishing decisions that had already been made. The *CIC* envisages a plenary consultative assembly of the cardinals, with the pope presiding, in the form of an ordinary Consistory at which all the cardinals resident in Rome are present, to discuss grave matters and to promulgate certain solemn acts. An extraordinary Consistory is also envisaged, at which all the cardinals of the world are present, to treat especially grave matters. Consistories with a purely ceremonial significance are public; not only cardinals but also prelates, ambassadors, and invited guests may be present at these (can. 353).

■ **Bibliography:** *DDC* 4:353-56; *VATL* 428f.; W. Maleczek, *Papst und Kardinalskolleg von 1191 bis 1216* (Vienna, 1984); *Código de derecho canónico* (4th ed. Valencia, 1993) 184-89.

HERBERT KALB

Council, Ecumenical.
1. Historical Development.—2. Canon Law.

1. Historical Development
(a) *Form and Nature*
Councils have been a part of the church's life from the earliest times (in Asia Minor and Rome from the end of the second century, in connection with the controversy about the date of Easter and with Montanism; in North Africa from the mid-third century, as a consequence of the controversy about baptism by heretics). Their external form has been largely determined by the specific cultural context. In the learned city of Alexandria, the council at the time of Origen consisted in a doctrinal dispute between a bishop suspected of heresy and the "teacher" *(didaskalos)* of the church; in Cyprian's Africa, the council bears the imprint of the procedures of the Roman senate; among the Germanic peoples, their special ideas about law affect the council; in the fifteenth century in the

West, the corporative governing bodies of the Italian city-states and universities become the model (idea of representation). Modern parliamentary ideas too have influenced the concrete mode of holding a council.

Despite external changes, however, it is possible to discern a common character. Cyprian's phrase *in unum convenire* designates not only an external but also an inner "coming together" brought about by the Holy Spirit, the *unanimitas* which is both vertical and horizontal, i.e., a consensus embracing both the councils of the past and present. Vincent of Lérins calls this the *consensio antiquitatis et universitatis* (*Commonitorium* 33). The patristic idea of the council as consensus was taken over by medieval canon law and inspired the explicit reflection of the conciliarists in the fifteenth century about the nature of councils (Nicholas Cusanus, John of Segovia, John of Ragusa). The basic idea has survived until the present day, irrespective of the disputes that raged in subsequent centuries about the precise modalities of the consensus that constituted a council (voting by individuals or by classes of participants or by nations; majority voting or unanimity; the role of the pope in the council, etc.).

(b) *Comprehensiveness and Authority*

Born of the necessity to find a solution in common to questions of faith or of church order, councils reflect the degree of the organization of the church in each respective period of its history. Initially, we find informal meetings of neighboring bishops; when larger church provinces were formed, provincial synods came into being. In Africa, the "plenary council" was held, embracing all the African church provinces. The development of patriarchates led to patriarchal synods, and the emergence of the imperial church under the emperor Constantine the Great led to imperial or ecumenical synods. The spread of Christianity in the Germanic kingdoms led to synods which met under the presidency of the king, later called national synods. Councils were also held on the lowest level of the ecclesiastical hierarchy; these were later called diocesan synods.

When inquiring into the specific authority of these various synods, one must avoid anachronisms: for example, the idea that ecumenical and particular councils comprise two essentially different categories, viz., ecumenical and particular

or local, is not attested in the East before the sixth century and is not genuinely found in the West before the twelfth century. The ecumenical council was essentially the highest authoritative body of the church, summoned by the emperor to decide questions of the faith. The new feature introduced by the first ecumenical council was that the claim which all councils tended to make, viz., that they taught the truth bestowed by the Spirit, now became a matter of theological principle, though of course this claim was not acknowledged at once in the case of the Council of Nicaea (325). This was the outcome of a lengthy process in which the conviction grew that the church must be capable of defending the faith from distortion, not only once and for all (as at Nicaea), but whenever necessary. The ancient church did not yet employ the concept of → "infallibility" for this capacity, which it came to attribute to ecumenical councils; this ambiguous term is applied to councils only in the fourteenth century, in the course of the debates about the specific authority of the pope, with the polemical intention of subordinating the pope to the council. In formal terms, the infallibility of the ecumenical councils was defended primarily by the conciliarists at Basel. As a reaction to Martin Luther's explicit rejection of this doctrine, it became a fundamental axiom of Catholic theology.

(c) *Ecumenicity and Reception*

While not a few of the so-called particular synods of the ancient church were received ecumenically, a number of synods that were held in an ecumenical manner were not in fact accepted by the church. The list of ecumenical councils accepted in the Roman Catholic church today (see [g] below) attests to the dominant role played by the see of Rome in their reception. In the ancient church, only those councils were included in this list which had won the assent of the pope (at least subsequently); at a later period, the inclusion in the list was the result of a consensus of historians and theologians, under papal leadership, that a council merited the rank of "ecumenical council," or else the result of a direct decision by the pope to hold an ecumenical council. After the schism with the East, the Western church long hesitated to include any of its own general synods in the list of the ecumenical councils which had been held together with the Greeks; this happened first at the

Council of Constance, which went beyond the list of the ancient church and included Lateran IV, Lyons II, and Vienne as ecumenical. Historians and theologians of the Counter-Reformation made various attempts at drawing up a complete list of the ecumenical councils; finally, Robert Bellarmine's list won acceptance, and this is essentially the list accepted today.

(d) Pope and Council

The debates in the second and third centuries between Roman bishops and the so-called particular synods of other churches (concerning the date of Easter and baptism by heretics) contain in embryonic form the conflict about church leadership which was bound to break out openly, as soon as both the council and the papacy had fully developed. Clear indications of a rivalry between the two can already be seen at the imperial councils of Ephesus (431 and 449) and Chalcedon (451), but the leading role of the emperor within the ancient church was able to preserve the unstable equilibrium between papal and conciliar governance. After the papacy became emancipated, first from the Greek and then from the Western emperor, it was no longer possible to evade the question about where the highest authority in the church lay. Very different answers were given to the questions about the summoning and presidency of an ecumenical council, about the right to confirm its decisions, and indeed about the whole concept of an ecumenical council, depending on whether one came down on the side of the pope or of the council. The theological literature of the last two centuries concerning councils has been mainly concerned with problems of this kind.

(e) Frequency and Necessity

An adequate assessment of the phenomenon of councils looks beyond the so-called ecumenical councils: a flourishing conciliar life existed long before these came into being in the fourth century. Despite all the significance that some of them have for the church's life, ecumenical councils are exceptions and represent only a small segment of the total conciliar reality. The high number of historically attested councils and the repeated insistence of ecumenical councils that synods on lower levels should be held regularly show that councils on levels below that of the ecumenical councils are a part of normal church life.

The stipulation of the Council of Constance (in the decree *Frequens*) that ecumenical councils too should be held on a regular basis, i.e., every ten years, foundered not only because of papal resistance but also thanks to its own impracticability. Pro-papal theologians always maintained a merely relative necessity of ecumenical councils, against the Gallicans who maintained an absolute necessity.

(f) Orthodox and Protestant Views

With the loss of church unity, a unified understanding of councils was lost as well. The Eastern church did indeed hold a number of extraordinary patriarchal councils after 1054, but no additional ecumenical synods, so that the number of ecumenical councils remained seven. Vis-à-vis the Roman church, the Orthodox always insisted on the fundamental equality in rank of all the five patriarchs who participated in a council (pentarchy); until the end of the Byzantine empire, they also insisted on the right of the emperor to convoke a council, and on the necessity of holding ecumenical councils to decide important questions.

While both Luther and Calvin dismissed the infallibility of councils, they did not themselves reject councils in principle, but only the form in which they were dominated by the pope. Synodal structures existed in the Reformed church, and some councils were held (Synod of Dordrecht, 1618-19), but after a single conciliar assembly (Synod of Homberg, 1526) no more synods were held by the Lutherans. Lutheran orthodoxy does indeed have a theology of synods (*locus de synodis*), but this theory has never been put into practice.

(g) Ecumenical Councils Recognized by the Roman Catholic Church

(1) Nicaea I (325), (2) Constantinople I (381); (3) Ephesus (431); (4) Chalcedon (451); (5) Constantinople II (553); (6) Constantinople III (680-681); (7) Nicaea II (787); (8) Constantinople IV (869-870); (9) Lateran I (1123); (10) Lateran II (1139); (11) Lateran III (1179); (12) Lateran IV (1215); (13) Lyons I (1245); (14) Lyons II (1274); (15) Vienne (1311-12); (16) Constance (1414-18); (17) Basel-Ferrara-Florence-Rome (1431-45); (18) Lateran V (1512-17); (19) Trent (1545-63); (20) Vatican I (1869-70); (21) Vatican II (1962-65).

■ **Bibliography:** On (a) to (e): B. Botte, ed., *Das Konzil und die Konzile* (Stuttgart, 1962); H. J. Sieben, *Die Konzilsidee der alten Kirche* (Paderborn, 1979); M. Woytowytsch, *Papsttum und Konzile von den Anfängen bis zu Leo I. (440-461)* (Stuttgart, 1981); H. J. Sieben, *Traktate und Theorien zum Konzil* (Frankfurt a.M., 1983); idem, *Die Konzilsidee des lateinischen Mittelalters* (Paderborn, 1984); idem, *Die katholische Konzilsidee von der Reformation bis zur Aufklärung* (Paderborn, 1988); idem, *Die Partikularsynode* (Frankfurt a.M., 1990); idem, *Katholische Konzilsidee im 19. und 20. Jahrhundert* (Paderborn, 1993); J. Helmrath, "Locus concilii," *AHC* 27/28 (1995-96) 593-622; H. J. Sieben, *Vom Apostel-Konzil bis zum Ersten Vatikanum* (Paderborn, 1996); K. Schatz, *Allgemeine Konzilien—Brennpunkte der Kirchengeschichte* (Paderborn, 1997); J. Laudage, "Ritual und Recht auf päpstlichen Reformkonzilien (1049-1123)," *AHC* 29 (1997) 287-334; N. H. Minnich, "The Voice of Theologians in General Councils from Pisa to Trent," *Theological Studies* 59 (1998) 420-41; H. J. Sieben, "Von angeblich oder wirklich gefälschten, von erfundenen und vorfabrizierten Konzilien," *Theologie und Philosophie* 74 (1999) 17-47; *Periodical: AHC* 1 (1969) ff.; On (f): *Oxford Dictionary of Byzantinum,* 3 vols. (New York/Oxford, 1992) 1:540-43; *Evangelisches Kirchenlexikon,* 3 vols., ed. H. Brunnotte and O. Weber (2nd ed. Göttingen, 1985–) 2:1430-40; H. J. Margull, ed., *Die ökumenischen Konzilien der Christenheit* (Stuttgart, 1961); P. Meinhold, *Konzile der Kirche in evangelischer Sicht* (Stuttgart, 1962); J. Meyendorff, *Die orthodoxe Kirche gestern und heute* (Salzburg, 1963) 35-46; C. Tecklenburg-Johns, *Luthers Konzilsidee in ihrer historischen Bedingtheit und ihrem reformatorischen Neuansatz* (Berlin, 1966); On (g): C. J. von Hefele, *Geschichte der ökumenischen Konzilien,* 12 vols. (Mainz, 1963-87); W. Brandmüller, ed., *Konziliengeschichte,* 2 series, I ff. (Paderborn, 1980f.); H. Jedin, *Kleine Konziliengeschichte* (5th ed. Freiburg, 1991); G. Alberigo, ed., *Geschichte der Konzilien* (Düsseldorf, 1993); K. Schatz, *Allgemeine Konzilien* (see above). N. Tanner, *The Councils of the Church: A Short History* (New York, 2001).

HERMANN JOSEF SIEBEN

2. *Canon Law*

The prevailing norms for an ecumenical council are to be found in the section of the Code dealing with the "college of bishops" (cann. 336-41). The Code affirms that the college of bishops, together with the pope, possesses "supreme and full authority" in the church (can. 336), and that the ecumenical council is one form in which the episcopal college "in solemn form" exercises this "power over the universal church" (can. 337 §1). Accordingly, "all bishops, but only bishops, who are members of the college of bishops, have the right and the obligation to be present at an ecumenical council with a deliberative vote" (can. 339 §1). Nonbishops too may be summoned to take part in an ecumenical council, but their role must be defined more precisely (can. 339 §2). Without a pope, there can be no ecumenical council (can. 340): only he can summon it, interrupt it, continue it, and dissolve it, and only he can approve its decrees (can. 338 §1).

The Code issues norms not only for the ecumenical council but also for the "plenary council for all the particular churches of the same Episcopal conference" (can. 439 §1) and for the "provincial council for the various particular churches of the same ecclesiastical province" (can. 440 §1). As in the case of the ecumenical council, so here too it is only the bishops who have the right to vote (can. 443 §1); all others take part as counselors (can. 443 §3).

■ **Bibliography:** HKKR 266-272; MKCIC, Introduction to cann. 336-41 and 439-46.

LUDWIG SCHICK

Council, Pontifical.

The Roman → curia includes eleven Councils, initially erected as autonomous Secretariats, Councils, and Commissions. The Apostolic Constitution *Pastor Bonus* (July 28, 1988) uses the Latin term *consilium* for all of these (see nos. 131-70).

1. *Pontifical Council for the Laity* (*Pontificium Consilium pro Laicis,* nos. 131-34), founded by Paul VI on January 6, 1967, in accordance with the conciliar text *Apostolicam Actuositatem* (Motu proprio *Catholicam Christi Ecclesiam*). Its president is a cardinal, aided by a vice-president with the rank of bishop. Apart from prelates, members include distinguished laypersons from all parts of the world. Their task is to encourage and support the laity and lay organizations in carrying out their tasks in the church and the world, above all in interpenetrating secular structures with the spirit of the gospel; they are also to coordinate the activities of the laity in the various countries. The Pontifical Council for the Laity has the authority to found international lay associations, to approve these and give their statutes formal recognition. It publishes a periodical and has a service of information and documentation (first issue, 1983).

LUDWIG SCHICK

2. *Pontifical Council for Promoting Christian Unity* (*Pontificium Consilium ad Unitatem Christianorum fovendam*), founded in 1960 as the "Secretariat for Christian Unity" and given the status of an independent dicastery in the Roman curia in 1988. Among other things, the Council is to undertake appropriate initiatives in the ecumenical field and to put into practice the decrees of the Second Vatican Council with reference to ecumenism; it publishes a service of documentation in three languages (*Information Service, Service d'information, Dokumentationsdienst*).

3. *Pontifical Council for the Family* (*Pontificium Consilium pro Familia*), founded in 1973 as a committee with the same name and given the status of an independent dicastery in the Roman curia in 1988. The broad field of its activities includes the pastoral care, theology, catechesis, and spirituality of the family, as well as the promotion and protection of the rights of families and children.

4. *Pontifical Council "Iustitia et Pax"* (*Pontificium Consilium de Iustitia et Pace*), founded in 1967 at the same time as the Council for the Laity (see no. 1 above) as a Study Commission for "Justice and Peace"; the present juridical form dates from 1988. The main goal of this Council is the promotion of justice and peace in accordance with the gospel and with the church's social teaching.

5. *Pontifical Council "Cor Unum"* (*Pontificium Consilium "Cor Unum"*), founded in its present form in 1971 and given the status of an independent dicastery in the Roman curia in 1988. The important tasks of this Council include the furthering of Christian love of neighbor and witness to the gospel, especially for those in need and the victims of catastrophes and disasters. The Council supervises two Foundations, "John Paul II Foundation for the Sahel Zone" and "Foundation Populorum Progressio."

6. *Pontifical Council for the Pastoral Care of Migrants and Itinerant People* (*Pontificium Consilium de Spirituali Migrantium atque Itinerantium Cura*), founded as a Commission in 1970 and given the status of an independent dicastery in the Roman curia in 1988. It has responsibility for immigrants, persons seeking asylum, refugees, and in a wider sense for all those who must travel, including pilgrims and tourists.

7. *Pontifical Council for Pastoral Health Care Workers* (*Pontificium Consilium pro Valetudinis Administris*), founded in 1985 as a Commission in the Pontifical Council for the Laity (see no. 1 above), and made an independent Council in 1988. Its responsibilities include presenting statements on questions of the health sector and health policies, as well as contact with the various Catholic groups and organizations that are active in the health sector.

8. *Pontifical Council for the Interpretation of Legislative Texts* (*Pontificium Consilium de Legum Textibus*), founded in 1917 as the "Commission for the Authentic Interpretation of the *CIC*" and given the new task in 1963 of a "Pontifical Commission for the Revision of Canon Law," then transformed again after the promulgation of the new *CIC* in 1983 into the "Pontifical Commission for the Authentic Interpretation of the Codex." This Commission was given the status of a Council in 1988. In addition to the interpretation of the *CIC* and (after 1990) of the *CCEO*, it must also decide whether decisions taken by subordinate bodies are in agreement with the universal laws of the church (*Pastor Bonus,* no. 158). The Council publishes the periodical *Communicationes,* which also contains documents and official texts.

9. *Pontifical Council for Interreligious Dialogue* (*Pontificium Consilium pro Dialogo inter Religiones*), founded in 1964 as the "Secretariat for Non-Christians" and given its present juridical form in 1988. Its tasks include the promotion and regulation of contacts with non-Christian religions. The "Commission for Religious Relationships with Muslims," founded in 1974, is attached to this Council.

10. *Pontifical Council for Culture* (*Pontificium Consilium de Cultura*), founded in 1993 through the fusion of the dicastery of the same name (founded in 1982) with the "Secretariat for Non-Believers" (founded in 1965 and placed under this Council in 1988). It has two sections, "Faith and Culture" (with the task of coordinating the cultural activities and initiatives of the Holy See, local churches and Catholic organizations) and "Dialogue with the Cultures" (with the tasks of studying atheism and engaging in dialogue with nonbelievers). The "Council for Coordinating the Papal Academies" has been attached to this Council since 1995.

11. *Pontifical Council for Social Communication* (*Pontificium Consilium de Communicationibus*

Socialibus). The origins of this Council lie in foundations made in 1948 and 1952, and in the "Pontifical Commission for Social Commission" erected in 1964, which was given its present juridical form in 1988. Its responsibilities include the exercise of influence on the media of communication (print, film, radio, television), including Catholic media.

■ **Primary Sources:** Apostolic Constitution *Pastor Bonus, AAS* 80 (1988) 841-912.

■ **Bibliography:** *VATL* 642-50; L. A. Dorn, *Der Papst und die Kurie* (Freiburg, 1989); A. Bonnet and C. Gullo, eds., *La Curia Romana nella Costituzione Apostolica "Pastor Bonus"* (Vatican City, 1990); F. Gioia, ed., Pontifical Council for Interreligious Dialogue, *Interreligious Dialogue: The Official Teaching of the Catholic Church (1963-95)* (Boston, 1997); *AnPont* (2000) 1302-36, 1951-59.

BRUNO STEIMER

Couriers, Pontifical (Latin *cursores*). These lay servants of the pope were members of the → *Cappella papale* and had the task of bringing the members of the Pontifical → Household their invitations to the consistories and the solemn Masses of the pope. In the course of his curial reform, Paul VI abolished the pontifical couriers (Motu proprio *Pontificalis Domus,* March 28, 1968, art. 6 §4).

■ **Bibliography:** *DizEc* 1:797.

JOSEPH WEIER

Curia, Roman.
1. History.—2. Present Situation.—3. Structure.

The Roman curia is the totality of the bodies and institutions which assist the pope in the discharge of his supreme pastoral office, to the benefit and service of the universal church and the local churches, thus strengthening unity in faith and the fellowship of the people of God, and furthering the church's specific mission in the world (art. 1 of the Apostolic Constitution *Pastor Bonus*). The pope and the Roman curia together constitute the Apostolic See (*Sedes Apostolica*), which of its very nature is a juridical subject (can. 361 *CIC*).

1. *History*
In the earliest period, the Roman bishop was assisted by the clergy and the regional deacons. The system of *iudices de clero* gradually developed. The papal court and central administration

moved from the *episcopium* to the *patriarchium* and the Lateran Palace. From the eleventh century on, the suburbicarian bishops acquired a more prominent position as collaborators of the pope, soon joined in this task by the other cardinals; these were the permanent counselors in the papal Consistory. The → Apostolic Chamber came into being to administer finances. The term *curia* has been the usual designation of the central papal administration since Urban II.

In the following period, the curia grew and took on a differentiated structure. The → *Cappella papale* came into being from the end of the eleventh century; the Pontifical → Family served the pope in his own living quarters. The most important body in the Roman curia was the papal → chancellery. Under Innocent III, the → Apostolic Penitentiary was founded. The → Rota (*Audientia sacri palatii*) has existed as judicial authority since Clement IV. Alexander IV attempted to ensure the financing of the Roman curia by introducing the *servitium commune* or *minutum*. In → Avignon, the Camerlengo became the most influential official. In the fifteenth century, the → apostolic datary was detached from the Chamber. In 1542, Paul III instituted a Commission of cardinals which became a permanent institution and received the name "Congregation of the Holy Inquisition" under Sixtus V; other permanent Roman → congregations followed. Sixtus V brought this development to an initial conclusion with the creation of fifteen congregations in 1588. The → Secretariat of State worked alongside these bodies. Two more congregations were erected in the seventeenth century, Propaganda Fide and the Congregation for Indulgences and Relics.

At the beginning of the twentieth century, Pius X reorganized the Roman curia. His aim was to tighten up the structures, clarify responsibilities, and separate the judicial and administrative functions. The Congregation for Extraordinary Ecclesiastical Affairs, founded in 1814, received wider responsibilities. In the course of the Second Vatican Council, unsuccessful attempts were made to have the curia understood as the instrument not only of the pope but also of the college of bishops. Paul VI extended the Roman curia by setting up Secretariats and Councils and made the Secretariat of State the most important body. He decreed that bishops of local churches should become members of the congregations. With the Apostolic Constitution *Pastor Bonus* (June 28, 1988), John Paul II carried out the most recent reorganization of the Roman curia.

2. *Present Situation*

The Roman curia consists of the bodies ("dicasteries") of the Secretariat of State, the congregations, the courts, the councils, and offices. These enjoy equal status in law, and each has its own statutes.

The Secretariat of State is the central dicastery of the Roman curia. The first department deals with everything concerning the daily ministry of the pope that lies outside the ordinary competence of the Roman curia and the other institutions of the Holy See; it is responsible for relations with the other bodies in the Roman curia. The second department has responsibility for relations between the church and the various states, for concluding concordats and other treaties, and for the nomination of bishops in particular circumstances.

The nine congregations are responsible for the doctrine of the faith; the Eastern Catholic churches; worship and the sacraments; canonization; bishops; the spreading of the faith; the clergy; institutes of consecrated life and societies of apostolic life; seminaries and institutes of education. These bodies have a collegial structure.

The eleven councils ($\rightarrow$ Council, Pontifical) are primarily concerned with information and the exchange of ideas, cultivating contacts and giving advice, but they are also able to posit administrative acts within the sphere of their competence. The Council for the Interpretation of Legislative Texts gives the authentic interpretation of all the laws issued by the supreme ecclesiastical authority and ensures that executive and administrative regulations issued by the other curial bodies or by episcopal conferences are in conformity with the law. The pope is advised on financial matters pertaining to the Holy See by a commission of cardinals independent of the Roman curia; this had thirteen members in 2000.

The Apostolic Penitentiary is usually included among the courts, although it is in fact a monocratically structured body which issues dispensations; the other courts are the $\rightarrow$ Apostolic Signatura (the highest ecclesiastical court and supreme administrative legal instance) and the Roman Rota, the ordinary papal court of appeal.

The Apostolic Chamber, the Administration of the Patrimony of the Holy See ($\rightarrow$ Finances), and the Prefecture for the Economic Affairs of the Holy See are monocratic offices. The Prefecture of the Pontifical Household and the Office for the Liturgical Celebrations of the pope, the Central Labor Office and the Office of Statistics are "offices," i.e., not dicasteries. The Vatican Secret $\rightarrow$ Archive, the $\rightarrow$ Vatican Library and the pontifical $\rightarrow$ academies are merely connected to the Holy See, not integral parts of the curia.

3. *Structure*

Most of the departments of the Roman curia are headed by a cardinal prefect or archbishop-president, with a group of cardinals and bishops, assisted by a secretary; consultors, higher officials, and minor officials complete the picture. The members (i.e., cardinals and bishops), the secretary, and the higher officials and consultors are appointed for five years. The cardinals who head the dicasteries must offer their resignation when they reach the age of seventy-five; the other heads of departments and the secretaries lose their membership of the body when they reach seventy-five, and the members when they reach eighty. On the death of a pope, all heads of office and members automatically lose their offices, with the exceptions of the Camerlengo of the Roman church and the Great Penitentioner. Day-to-day business is carried on by the secretaries.

As advisers of the pope, the $\rightarrow$ cardinals are members of the Roman curia, and they are appointed as heads of the most important bodies. The College of Cardinals as such, however, has lost virtually all its role in the government of the universal church: the $\rightarrow$ Consistory is no longer the place where controversial subjects must be discussed.

The service carried out by the Roman curia is a participation in the mission of the pope. It is the necessary instrument he employs to carry out his tasks as shepherd of the universal church. There is a relationship of representation between the Roman curia and the pope; curial bodies act within the framework of their competence in the name and with the authority of the pope. The ordinary authority of the dicasteries of the Roman curia is vicarious: it possesses only that authority which the pope gives it. It may not develop a will of its own independently of the pope or against

him. Not all the dicasteries share in the jurisdictional authority of the pope. Offices that
demand the exercise of jurisdictional authority are
reserved to those in holy orders. Apart from the
courts and the Congregation for the Doctrine of
the Faith, the curial bodies have only administrative competence. During the → *sede vacante,* the
College of Cardinals governs the Roman curia,
with an authority limited to ordinary and urgent
business.

The dicasteries handle matters that are reserved
to the Holy See either because of their particular
significance or on the basis of canon law; matters
which exceed the competence of individual bishops or groups of bishops; and matters laid before
the dicasteries by the pope or brought to the Holy
See by the faithful. The most important business
of each dicastery is reserved to the plenary assembly, which takes place once a year; only those
members resident in Rome are invited to the ordinary meetings, which are held more frequently.
The competence of the dicastery is determined in
principle by the matter to be treated; matters that
concern the competence of several dicasteries
must be examined in common. Where mutual
consultation is frequently required, interdicaster-
ial commissions may be set up. The cardinals who
head the dicasteries meet several times a year, in
order to examine important questions, to coordinate work, and to exchange information. Documents addressed to the universal church must be
sent before publication to the dicasteries involved;
more important decisions (apart from those made
by the courts) must be submitted to the pope for
his approval. Laws and general decrees with the
effect of laws need the *specifica approbatio* of the
pope. Conflicts about authority among the dicasteries are settled by the Apostolic Signatura. Procedures in the Roman curia follow the *Ordo
servandus* of the curia as a whole and of each
dicastery.

The Roman curia promotes hierarchical and
ecclesial *communio.* It depends on close collaboration with the local churches and episcopal conferences. When the bishops make their → *ad limina*
visits to Rome, they make contact with the curial
dicasteries.

■ **Primary Sources:** *Ordo servandus in SS. Congregatio-
nibus, Tribunalibus, Officiis Romanae Curiae,* September
29, 1908: *AAS* 1 (1909) 36-108; Apostolic Constitution
Sapienti consilio, June 29, 1908: *AAS* 1 (1909) 7-19;

cann. 242-64 *CIC/1917; Lumen Gentium* 8 and 18-27;
Christus Dominus 9-10; Apostolic Constitution *Regi-
mini Ecclesiae universae,* August 15, 1967: *AAS* 59 (1967)
885-928; Apostolic Constitution *Pastor Bonus,* June 28,
1988: *AAS* 80 (1988) 841-934; *Ordinatio Officii Laboris,*
September 30, 1994: *AAS* 84 (1992) 841-55; Apostolic
Constitution *Universi Domini gregis,* February 22, 1996:
AAS 88 (1996) 305-43; *Regolamento generale della Curia
Romana: AAS* 60 (1968) 129-76; 84 (1992) 201-67; 91
(1999) 630-99.

■ **Bibliography:** *DTHC* 3:1931-83; *LMA* 5:1583-88; *TRE*
20:343-52; *HKKR* 2nd ed. *VATL* 433-38; H. Schmitz,
Kurienreform, 2 vols. (Trier, 1968-76); I. Gordon, "De
curia romana renovata: Renovatio 'desiderata' et renovatio 'facta' conferuntur," *Periodica de re morali canonica liturgica* 58 (1969) 59-116; P. Herde, *Audientia
litterarum contradictarum,* 2 parts (Tübingen, 1970); G.
Delgado, *La Curia romana: El gobierno central de la Iglesia* (Pamplona, 1973); A. Therme, "Le Synode des
Evêques et la Curie romaine," *L'année canonique* 27
(1983) 55-66; L. Pásztor, *La Segreteria di Stato e il suo
archivo,* 2 vols. (Stuttgart, 1984-85); C. Suchard, *Die
Deutschen an der päpstlichen Kurie im späten Mittelalter
(1378-1447)* (Tübingen, 1987); J. I. Arrieta, "La reforma
de la Curia Romana (Commentario a la Constitución
Apostólica 'Pastor bonus')," *Ius Canonicum* 29 (1989)
186-204; idem, "Principios informadores de la Constitución Apostólica 'Pastor bonus,'" *Ius Canonicum* 30
(1990) 59-81; A. Viana, "La potestad de los dicasterios
de la Curia Romana," *Ius Canonicum* 30 (1990) 83-114;
A. Cattaneo, "Der ekklesiologische Ort der Römischen
Kurie nach der Apostolischen Constitution 'Pastor
bonus,'" in *Fides et Ius,* Festschrift for G. May (Regensburg, 1991) 109-18; F. J. Urrutia, "Quondam habeatur
approbatio 'in forma specifica,'" *Periodica de re canonica*
80 (1991) 3-17; A. Viana, "El regolamento generale de la
Curia Romana (4.2.1992)," *Ius Canonicum* 32 (1992)
501-29; G. May, *Ego N.N. Catholicae Ecclesiae Episcopus*
(Berlin, 1995); F. d'Ostillo, *Il diritto amministrativo della
chiesa* (Vatican City, 1995); F. Zanchini DiCastigli-
onchio, "Neue Tendenzen der Kompetenz in der römischen Kurie," *Concilium* 32 (1996) 454-461; E.
Meuthen, "Reiche, Kirchen und Kurie im späten Mittelalter," *Historische Zeitschrift* 265 (1997) 597-637; N. Del
Re, *La Curia Romana* (4th ed. Rome, 1998); E. Pásztor,
*Onus apostolicae sedis: Curia Romana e cardinalato nei
secoli XI-XV* (Rome, 1999); A. Viana, "'Approbatio in
forma specifica': El regolamento general de la Curia
Romana de 1999," *Ius Canonicum* 40 (2000) 209-28.

GEORG MAY

Decretals (*Litterae* or *Epistolae decretales*) are letters in which the pope responds to questions
about canon law or church discipline, usually
addressed to individual persons. From a formal

perspective, they obligate only the persons or regions to which they are addressed, but in practice they also denote a norm to be followed in similar cases. They have been collected since the fifth century; from the twelfth century, with the increase of papal influence on administration, judicial sentencing, and legislation, they acquired preeminent significance for the development of classical canon law.

The first compilations of decretals were appendixes to the *Decretum Gratiani;* after 1175, these compilations stood on their own. The "primitive" compilations mostly present the decretals without any order or divisions; in the systematic collections, they tend to be grouped under various headings according to the matters treated. Bernard of Pavia created the standard categories in five books with many headings, in his *Breviarium extravagantium* (ca. 1190). His compilation of decretals later formed the first of the so-called "Quinque compilationes antiquae," the main foundation of the decretals of Gregory IX in 1234.

■ **Bibliography:** *LMA* 3:623-26; E. Friedberg, *Quinque compilationes antiquae* (Leipzig, 1882); idem, *Die Canones-Sammlungen zwischen Gratian und Bernhard von Pavia* (Leipzig, 1897); S. Kuttner, *Repertorium der Kanonistik* (Rome, 1937), 272-385; A. M. Stickler, *Historia iuris canonici latini,* I: *Historia fontium* (Turin, 1950) 18f., 217-72; G. Fransen, *Les décrétales et les collections de décrétales* (Turnhout, 1972); W. Holtzmann and C. R. and M. G. Cheney, *Studies in the Collections of Twelfth-Century Decretals* (Vatican City, 1979); P. Landau, *Kanones und Dekretalen: Beiträge zur Geschichte der Quellen des kanonischen Rechts* (Goldbach, 1997); C. Duggan, *Decretals and the Creation of "New Law" in the Twelfth Century* (Aldershot, 1998).

RUDOLF WEIGAND

Diplomatic Corps Accredited to the Holy See.
1. History.—2. Systematic Reflections.—3. Statistics.

1. *History*

As long as Italy was an integral part of the Roman-Byzantine empire, the emperor could conduct business with the pope via local officials; this made it unnecessary to have imperial ambassadors at the Holy See. East-Roman ambassadors were sent to the Holy See from the first half of the fifth century onward, but solely for the purpose of guaranteeing the canonical election of a new pope; this practice was often interrupted and died out in

the eighth century. In the following period, the pope received ambassadors not only from the new Frankish power which protected him, but also from other newly established kingdoms such as Bulgaria and Hungary. After the renewal of the empire in the West in 800, the emperors and their ambassadors had the primary functions of protecting the popes and maintaining order; these functions ceased with the reformed papacy in the eleventh century, and the imperial embassies, like those of other kings, princes, and states, represented political interests. Their meetings and cooperation during the medieval councils can be considered an early form of multilateral diplomacy.

There is evidence that some powers maintained permanent embassies at the papal court from the beginning of the thirteenth century; from the mid-fifteenth century, this became the rule for the Italian city-states and soon afterward became general practice. In the sixteenth century, such permanent embassies became the usual institutional form of diplomacy, although those states that became Protestant tended for a long time to have only occasional contacts with the Holy See. At this period, both priests and laymen were nominated as ambassadors to the Holy See.

The state-church systems employed by the Catholic powers above all in the seventeenth and eighteenth centuries (Gallicanism, Febronianism, Josephinism, etc.) often entrusted their embassies in Rome with the mediatory function between the church of the realm and the Holy See, which they would not allow the apostolic → nuncios to carry out. These tendencies died out in the nineteenth century. The definitive loss of the → papal states in 1870 entailed a far-reaching change, since the ambassadors to the Holy See now were concerned primarily with a religious-political rather than a purely political agenda. Since states continued to have a diplomatic representation at the Holy See, a "double" diplomatic corps came into being in Rome when the capital of Italy was transferred there from Florence. While the privileges and immunities of the diplomatic missions accredited to the Holy See were meant to be protected by the Italian law of guarantees (1871), the inadequacy of this arrangement became obvious during the First World War, when those states hostile to Italy were obliged to move their embassies to the Holy See onto the soil of neighboring neutral countries.

185

Even the solution offered by the Lateran Treaty in 1929, viz., the erection of the → Vatican state and the guarantee of the rights of the foreign missions accredited to the Holy See, proved to be inadequate during the Second World War; those states hostile to Italy had to move their diplomatic representations into Vatican City, and this meant a considerable reduction in staff, viz., two persons per mission.

In 1870, fourteen states were represented at the Holy See, and in 1929, thirty. After the Second World War, the number of missions accredited to the Holy See increased greatly (Islamic states, new states created in the decolonization process, successor states of the U.S.S.R. and Yugoslavia).

2. *Systematic Reflections*
(a) *The Basis:* The embassies to the Holy See are the expression of the passive right to embassies; the active right to embassies is expressed in the papal → legations. The period from 1870 to 1929, when no church-state existed, showed that this right belongs to the Holy See as a spiritual sovereign, independently of any secular sovereignty.

(b) *Form:* The passive right to embassies on the part of the Holy See is exercised according to the *universal forms of international law,* as codified, for example, in the Vienna Convention on Diplomatic Relations of 1961.

(c) *Structures:* (1) *Substantial issues.* The Holy See's passive right to embassies covers all matters that concern the power which sends the embassy in its relationship to the Holy See. Apart from questions of the relations between church and state, this may cover issues of general political significance (e.g., world peace, development). (2) *Personnel.* The power that sends the embassy must obtain the *agrément* of the Holy See for its head of mission; this can be refused without any reasons being given, and any member of the diplomatic mission can be declared *persona non grata* at any time. In order to demonstrate that its competence includes not only religious matters but also political issues, the Holy See has not accepted any priests as head of mission since 1870. A third-world state appointed a woman as head of mission for the first time in 1975, against the opposition of the Roman curia; this praxis is now universally accepted. (3) *Institutional questions.* The desire to save money leads many countries today to appoint one and the same diplomat to several countries. This means that almost a third of the embassies to the Holy See are conducted from missions in other countries, above all in Paris, Bonn, Bern, Brussels, and London. But in order to demonstrate its independence from Italy, the Holy See does not accept any double representation by a mission accredited to the Quirinal. (4) *Special Cases.* Because of the special character of the Holy See as a religious institution, a number of exceptional cases in the course of its bilateral diplomatic relationships past and present deserve mention here. Great Britain was represented by a mission to the Holy See from the time of the First World War onward, but it was only in 1982 that a nunciature could be set up in London; on the other hand, it was only in 1992 that Switzerland appointed an ambassador "on special mission" to the Holy See, although there has been a nunciature in Bern since 1920. The United States has sent a "personal representative of the President" to the Holy See as needed (e.g., during the Second World War) but full diplomatic relations were adopted only in 1984. Other examples of special forms are Poland in 1988-1989 ("Delegation for permanent working contacts"), the U.S.S.R. in 1990 ("representatives," a system continued by Russia), Mexico since 1991 ("permanent personal representative of the president"), and Israel since 1994 ("special representative").

3. *Statistics*
At present, 172 states, the Palestinian Liberation Organization, and the Sovereign Maltese Order have diplomatic missions to the Holy See; the United Nations Organization is represented by an "information center" (AnPont [2000] 1426-57).

■ **Bibliography:** *LMA* 4:1371f.; *VATL* 182; R. A. Graham, *Vatican Diplomacy* (Princeton, N.J., 1959); I. Cardinale, *Le Saint-Siège et la diplomatie* (Paris et al., 1962); H. F. Köck, *Die völkerrechtliche Stellung des Heiligen Stuhls* (Berlin, 1975); I. Cardinale, *The Holy See and the International Order* (London, 1976); A. Dupuy, *La Diplomatie du Saint-Siège* (Paris, 1980); M. Merle and C. de Montclos, *L'Église catholique et les relations internationales* (Paris, 1988); J.-B. D'Onoria, ed., *Le Saint-Siège dans les relations internationales* (Paris, 1989); P. C. Kent, *Papal Diplomacy in the Modern Ages* (Westport, 1994); G. Barberini, *Chiesa e Santa Sede nell'ordinamento internazionale: Esame delle norme canoniche* (Turin, 1996).

HERIBERT FRANZ KÖCK

Documents, Papal.

1. *Papal Documents*

The bishops of Rome have composed letters and issued documents from earliest times, but these documents are preserved only in copies; the most ancient documents to be preserved in the original are from 788 to 819. The Roman $\rightarrow$ curia modeled itself on the state bureaucracy from the Peace of Constantine at the latest, which allows us to assume the existence of a papal $\rightarrow$ register from a very early date; the oldest register preserved in the original is that of Gregory VII. The subjects and the number of the documents issued reflected the historical development of the papacy in the church; the church reform of the eleventh century, the elaboration of canon law from the twelfth century on, and the centralizing tendencies of the Avignon period led to a continuous increase in activity, which reached its high point in the late fifteenth century, but has diminished somewhat in the modern period. Throughout this time, the body which issued the documents underwent great changes, and the procedure involved became steadily more complex, although the external and internal characteristics of the documents remained astonishingly stable.

The lead bull ($\rightarrow$ *Bullarium*) was employed as a seal, attached either with bundles of silk threads (for solemn and simple privileges, *litterae cum serico,* bulls, consistorial bulls) or with hemp threads (*litterae cum filo canapis, litterae clausae*). The choice of thread entailed differences in the external characteristics, and was in part dictated by the legal contents of the document. Gold seals have been used very seldom in the modern period. The seal of the $\rightarrow$ fisherman's ring, impressed on wax, served to authenticate secret letters in the late Avignon period and papal briefs (attested from 1390); in the nineteenth century, the colored seal was introduced as an alternative. No seal is attached to Motu proprios (since the late fifteenth century) or to pleas.

Papyrus was used for documents until 1057 and was replaced by parchment (in use since 1007). Paper was usually employed for the pleas. The so-called Roman curial handwriting, which is difficult to read, was used until 1123; from 971, it had been replaced by the curial (Carolingian) minuscule, and then gothic script in the fourteenth century and degenerated to the *scrittura bollatica* from the seventeenth century onward (abolished in 1878 by Leo XIII). Briefs were written in humanistic script from Eugene IV onward. The rules of the "curial style," prescribing particular forms of address and honorific adjectives, dictated the formulations in the documents, and many booklets with advice on correct formulation survive.

The documents can be divided into various groups, from the following perspectives. (a) Their genesis: some documents were issued by the curia on its own initiative (*litterae de curia*), while others respond to petitions by supplicants (*litterae communes*). (b) Their contents: some documents grant a favor or a permission (*litterae gratiae*), while others pronounce a judgment or issue a command (*litterae justiciae*). (c) In the twelfth and thirteenth centuries, the manner of authorization: some documents were read aloud in the presence of the pope (*litterae legendae*), while in other cases, this was unnecessary (*litterae dandae*). (d) The dues: some documents were taxed, while others were issued free of charge.

There is no evidence of a genuine papal $\rightarrow$ chancellery in the earliest period. Various prelates of the papal court served as dataries, and Roman notaries were the scribes. The librarian took on a leading role in the ninth and tenth centuries. The chancellor became the central figure in the eleventh century, until he was replaced by the vice-chancellor after 1216; the title of "Chancellor" fell into desuetude until Pius X reintroduced it. The leader of the chancellery was assisted by notaries, flanked from the thirteenth century on by assistants (*abbreviatores* and *scriptores*), who were originally employed on a private basis. The petitioners' procurators also played an important role. The assistants gradually became official employees of the chancellery and were hired by the vice-chancellor, or even by the pope in person. The secretaries had a special role from the late Avignon period onward; their main task was to issue briefs, and their work is the origin of the secretariats (see especially the $\rightarrow$ Secretariat of State), while the $\rightarrow$ Apostolic Signatura and the $\rightarrow$ Apostolic Datary have their origins in the officials who were charged with examining the pleas. The chancellery personnel greatly increased in numbers in the fourteenth and fifteenth centuries; toward the close of the fifteenth century, ca. five hundred persons worked there. From the fifteenth century, and especially from the reign of Sixtus IV on, all the chancellery positions were transformed into purchasable offices (*officia venalia vacabilia*) and grouped into colleges. From the sixteenth century on, the secretariats and the datary increased in importance, at the expense of the chancellery; the datary was abolished by Paul VI in 1973.

The procedure when a document was to be issued was a matter of custom, with a mixture of organization and improvisation. Only a few questions were settled by the popes, as need arose, and most of these concerned the removal of abuses; even larger-scale reform constitutions, such as that of John XXII, had only a limited effect. Comprehensive "regulations" did not exist before the twentieth century (the so-called chancellery regulations govern the ecclesiastical praxis of approbation, not the actual procedure). The most important sources for establishing the procedure are the chancellery notes on the documents; next in importance are the formulae of the employees' oaths and the regulations of their service.

Two stages were involved in the expedition: the approval of the request and the issuing of the document. Until 1216, petitions had to be brought in person and expressed orally; after this date, representation by a procurator was allowed. Written pleas became customary in the fourteenth century; these were approved ("signed") with a handwritten note by the pope, the vice-chancellor, or (from Eugene IV onward) a clerk. Pleas that were approved were recorded in the register of pleas; these have been preserved from 1342 onward. The → Apostolic Penitentiary likewise approved pleas, which were recorded in separate registers. In some cases, from the fifteenth century onward, the plea served as a substitute for the document: here the plea was valid *sola signatura,* and it was not necessary to issue a document with seal. When dioceses and abbeys were bestowed, the consistorial note and its counterpart served the same function as pleas.

The issuing of a document involved five steps: the draft, the finished version, examination of the finished version, sealing, and registration. Depending on the manner of expedition, different officials saw to the first and the third steps. Registration was initially voluntary, but became obligatory in the fourteenth century; in the case of the simple *litterae iusticiae,* it was not required until the sixteenth century. When the finished version was produced, four taxes (in exceptional cases, five), of equal amounts, were stipulated. Two of these taxes reimbursed the personnel (the draft and the finished version), two were paid to the → Apostolic Chamber (the seal and the registration); in addition, extra charges and tips were paid. Poor petitioners were freed from paying some of these taxes. There were many possibilities of speeding up the expedition and sidestepping the regulations. The documents issued by the personnel of the Penitentiary in the name of the pope followed the same procedure.

Papal documents are preserved in almost all the archives in the world. They are made available to scholars in semiofficial collections (*Bullaria*) and publications which group them according to their period, their contents, or the regions concerned. Large-scale projects study the period up to 1198 (the "Pius Foundation," also called the "Göttinger Papsturkundenwerk") and the period from 1198 to 1417 (the "Censimento"). Historical institutes in Rome study the tradition of registers in the Vatican Secret → Archive: the Austrian institute investigates the reign of Innocent III, the French institute the registers up to the end of the Avignon period, and the German institute the "Repertorium Germanicum."

2. *Conciliar Documents*

The reform councils of the fifteenth century (Pisa, Constance, Basel, Pisa II) issued documents in their own names. These were modeled on papal documents, but displayed characteristic changes in the formulae used. The Council of Basel built up its own chancellery, which expedited several thousands of documents and kept its own registers.

3. *Documents of Curial Bodies*

From the fifteenth century onward, curial bodies—especially the Apostolic Chamber—issued documents in their own names, following the papal model in style and form. The seals of the curial head of the department or of the department itself were different from the papal seal: oval pointed wax seals were employed, often attached by strips of parchment. We have no information about the procedures involved in issuing these documents. The Apostolic Chamber also issued documents by means of notarial instruments. As yet, little research has been done into the documents of the Inquisition.

4. *Documents of Cardinals*

Cardinals sometimes issued documents as a college, during the *sede vacante*. Both in the Avignon period and in the fifteenth century, groups of cardinals issued representative documents concerning indulgences, which were used to promote the sale of indulgences and were often decorated by artists. In their form and style, these imitate the papal documents, but bear the seal of each individual cardinal. The documents of cardinal legates likewise follow the model of the papal documents. Sometimes a legate was accompanied by a chancellery of his own, with an organization modeled on that of the papal chancellery.

■ **Bibliography:** T. Frenz, *Papsturkunden des Mittelalters und der Neuzeit* (Stuttgart, 1986; 2nd ed. 2000); *General studies: DHP* 39-46; *LMA* 6:1688-91; H. Bresslau, *Handbuch der Urkundenlehre für Deutschland und Italien*, I (2nd ed. Berlin, 1911; 3rd ed. 1958; 4th ed. 1969); II (2nd ed. Berlin, 1915/1931; 3rd ed. 1958; 4th ed. 1968); III (index) (3rd ed. Berlin, 1960); L. Schmitz-Kallenberg, "Die Lehre von den Papsturkunden," in A. Meister, *Grundriß der Geschichtswissenschaft*, I/2 (2nd ed. Berlin, 1913) 56-116; A. de Bouard, *Manuel de diplomatique française et pontificale*, 2 vols. (Paris, 1929-48); P. Herde, *Beiträge zum päpstlichen Kanzlei- und Urkundenwesen im 13. Jahrhundert* (2nd ed. Kallmünz, 1967); P. Rabikauskas, *Diplomatica Pontificia* (2nd ed. Rome, 1968; 3rd ed. 1972; 4th ed. 1980); T. Frenz, *Die Kanzlei der Päpste der Hochrenaissance 1471-1527* (Bibliothek des Deutschen Historischen Instituts in Rom 63) (Tübingen, 1986). *On individual questions:* G. Ueding and W. Jens, eds., *Historisches Wörterbuch der Rhetorik* (Tübingen, 1998) 4:1536-41; H. Burger, "Beiträge zur Geschichte der äußeren Merkmale der Papsturkunden im späteren Mittelalter," *Archiv für Urkundenforschung* 12 (1931-32) 206-43; K. A. Fink, "Untersuchung über die päpstlichen Breven des 15. Jahrhunderts," *RQ* 43 (1935) 55-86; P. Rabikauskas, *Die römische Kuriale in der päpstlichen Kanzlei* (Rome, 1958); P. Herde, *Audientia litterarum contradictarum*, 2 vols. (Tübingen, 1970); L. Santifaller, *Liber Diurnus* (Stuttgart, 1976); T. Frenz, "Littera Sancti Petri: Zur Schrift der neuzeitlichen Papsturkunden 1550-1878," *Archiv für Diplomatik, Schriftgeschichte, Siegel- und Wappenkunde* 24 (1978) 443-515; idem, "Die Urkunden des Konzils von Basel," *Lectiones eruditorum extraneorum in facultate philosophica universitatis Carolinae Pragensis factae, Fasciculus* 2 (1993) 7-26; S. Weiss, *Die Urkunden der päpstlichen Legaten von Leo IX. bis Coelestin III. (1049-1198)* (Cologne, 1995); L. Schmugg, P. Hersberger, and B. Wiggenhauser, *Die Supplikenregister der päpstlichen Pönitentiarie aus der Zeit Pius' II. (1458-64)* (Tübingen, 1996). *Illustrations:* A. Brackmann, *Papsturkunden* (Leipzig/Berlin, 1914), drawing on G. Seeliger, *Urkunden und Siegel in Nachbildungen für den akademischen Gebrauch,* II (Leipzig, 1914); G. Battelli, *Acta Pontificum* (2nd ed. Vatican City, 1965). *Editions:* see T. Frenz, *Papsturkunden* (above); Zimmermann *Pu*; *Repertorium Poenitentiariae Germanicum: Verzeichnis der in den Supplikenregistern der Pönitentiarie . . . vorkommenden Persone, Kirchen und Orte des Deutschen Reiches* (Tübingen, 1996ff.).

THOMAS FRENZ

Election, Papal.

1. *History*

Catholics hold that Christ himself installed the apostle → Peter as supreme pastor of all Christians, and that he was the first bishop of Rome. The oldest sources show that, as was customary when bishops were chosen at that period, the successor of Peter was elected by the clergy and the people of the imperial capital. Only seldom (as in the case of Boniface II) did a pope give indications about who should succeed him. No one who was already a bishop could be chosen; usually deacons of the city of Rome were elected, and then consecrated by the neighboring bishops. The bishop of Ostia was most commonly the consecrator in the early period. From the fourth to the early eighth century, the Roman emperor claimed a right of confirmation, often exercised by his representative, the exarch of Ravenna. The emperor Lothar I was the first to demand that the one chosen swear an oath of fidelity to him before his consecration (*Constitutio Romana*, 824). De facto, it was usually the aristocracy of the city of Rome who decided the election in the early and early high Middle Ages, although Otto I made the Romans promise in 962 not to make anyone pope without the imperial consent. On many occasions, he, Otto III, and especially Henry III decided who became pope.

A normative regulation of the papal election began with the much disputed "Decree Concerning Papal Elections " issued by Nicholas II in 1059. This decree was motivated by the need to show the legitimacy of his own election, which had taken place outside Rome, but it was never fully put into practice. Nevertheless, it indicated the direction that would be taken in the future: the election of a non-Roman as pope is legitimate, even when it takes place outside Rome and the one chosen is already a bishop; the election is made by the cardinal bishops, and the cardinal priests, the clergy, and the people of Rome must give their assent. Although hostility to the crown was not a central concern of this decree, it marginalized in the long term the participation of king or emperor in the election. After a forgery was produced by supporters of the antipope Clement III, listing the cardinal deacons (not mentioned specifically in 1059) among the electors, the papal election became the exclusive right of the College of → Cardinals; this was an important factor in the consolidation of the college. It exercised this exclusive right for the first time in 1130.

The schism of 1130, and especially that of 1159, pointed out all the more strongly the need for legal clarification, particularly since it was necessary to interpret the concept of *pars melior et sanior,* which was viewed as decisive for settling a disputed papal election. This led Alexander III to issue the decree *Licet de vitanda* in 1179 (Third Lateran Council): the one elected by at least two thirds of the cardinals (whose number was not yet regulated by norm) is pope. This rule proved its worth, although it often took a long time to form the requisite majority. This led to the first papal election in a conclave in 1241, when the Roman senator Matteo Rosso Orsini forcibly locked the cardinals into the ruins of the Septizonium. On the basis of similar experiences, Gregory X issued the decretal *Ubi periculum maius* at the Second Council of Lyons, establishing the conclave as a legal requirement: after the lapse of a certain period of time, the cardinals are shut up in a suitable room, if possible in the place where the last pope has died; their food is progressively reduced, until they have made the election. Despite (or because of) this rigid ordinance, which could sometimes become life-threatening in the Roman summer, the conclave was repeatedly broken, with the result that the *sede vacante* could be intolerably lengthy, lasting more than twenty months (1241-1243, 1268-1271).

In the period of the reform councils, the exclusive right of the cardinals was criticized, but the changes that were introduced, especially with regard to a widening of the group of papal electors, proved unsuccessful. On the other hand, a number of papal elections were decided by "accession," i.e., when cardinals who had originally voted for another candidate subsequently joined the majority among the electors, so that the two-thirds majority could be reached. Three modes of

election, finally regulated by Gregory XV in 1621, were valid: voting by word of mouth or by paper ballot (*electio per scrutinium,* first attested unambiguously in 1198); a choice made by electors who constituted an authoritative commission among the College of Cardinals (*electio per compromissum*); and an informal, spontaneous election through a quasi-Pentecostal unanimity on the part of the electors (*quasi per inspirationem*). The *ius exclusivae*—whereby a state charged a cardinal to exclude certain candidates from the papal election as *personae non gratae*—was never acknowledged as valid, but it was claimed by some Catholic states and was in fact practiced in 1823 and 1903. The *ius exclusivae* was forbidden by the Apostolic Constitution *Commissum Nobis* (1904), which also forbade accession, since this risked opening the door to simony or to elections that sought to win personal favors.

■ Bibliography: *LMA* 6:1691ff.; *VATL* 422ff.; P. Hinschius, *System des katholischen Kirchenrechts,* I (Berlin, 1869; repr. Graz, 1959) 217-94; H. Fuhrmann, "Die Wahl des Papstes," *Geschichte in Wissenschaft und Unterricht* 9 (1958) 762-80; H. Krause, *Das Papstwahldekret von 1059 und seine Rolle im Investiturstreit* (Rome, 1960); H. E. Feine, *Kirchliche Rechtsgeschichte,* I: *Die katholische Kirche* (5th ed. Weimar, 1972); G. May, "Das Paptswahlrecht in seiner jüngsten Entwicklung," in *Ex aequo et bono,* Festschrift for W. M. Plöchl (Innsbruck, 1977) 231-62; P. Herde, "Die Entwicklung der Papstwahl im 13. Jahrhundert," *Österreichisches Archiv für Kirchenrecht* 32 (1981) 11-41; D. Jasper, *Das Papstwahlrecht von 1059* (Sigmaringen, 1986); B. Schimmelpfennig, "Papst und Bischofswahlen seit dem 12. Jahrhundert," in R. Schneider and H. Zimmermann, eds., *Wahlen und Wählen im Mittelalter* (Sigmaringen, 1990) 173-95; L. Schmugge, "Bischofs- und Papstwahlen im Mittelalter," *Communio* 25 (1996) 116-22; J. Lenzenweger, "Papstwahlen von 1914 und 1922," in *In factis legere,* Festschrift for I. Rogger (Bologna, 1999) 187-94; F. A. Burkle-Young, *Papal Elections in the Age of Transition (1878-1922)* (Lanham, Md., 2000).

WERNER GOEZ

2. *Canon Law*

When the Holy See becomes vacant through the death or abdication of the pope (see can. 332 §2 *CIC*; can. 44 §2 *CCEO*), a papal election becomes necessary, and this is regulated by the Apostolic Constitution *Universi dominici gregis* of John Paul II (Feb. 22, 1996: *AAS* 88 [1996] 305-43). Here, as in can. 349 *CIC,* the exclusive right of the College of Cardinals to elect the pope is maintained (no.

33); thus, endeavors to widen the group of electors, e.g., by including the members of a synod of bishops, have not won acceptance. This Constitution is largely identical in terms of substance with the regulations for the papal election laid down by Paul VI in the Apostolic Constitution *Romano Pontifici eligendo* (Oct. 1, 1975: *AAS* 67 [1975] 609-45).

During the → *sede vacante*, the College of Cardinals exercises particular functions of government, but nothing may be altered in the government of the universal church (nos. 1-4, can. 335 *CIC*; can. 77 *CCEO*). Only those cardinals who are under eighty when they enter the conclave are eligible to vote. The cardinals meet for the election in the conclave, which is held in the → Sistine Chapel (no. 50). In order to exclude influence by secular powers and to keep all the ballots secret, a number of penalties are stipulated, and the cardinals are forbidden to have any contact with the outside world (cf. nn. 55-61, 78-83). A two-thirds majority is necessary for the election of the pope; if the number of cardinal electors is not divisible by three, one extra vote must be added (n. 62). After thirty-three unsuccessful ballots, the College of Cardinals may decide that from now on, an absolute majority suffices, or else that a runoff between the two leading candidates should be held (nn. 74f.). The 1975 regulations are changed to exclude an election by acclamation or inspiration, or by empowering a smaller electoral commission (cf. n. 62).

If the one elected pope is already a bishop, he possesses the plenitude of papal authority as soon as he accepts his election (n. 88). If one who is not a bishop is elected pope, he must immediately receive episcopal ordination (can. 332 §1 *CIC*; can. 44 §1 *CCEO*), and he receives the plenitude of papal authority only when this is done. This makes it clear that the papal ministry is rooted in the episcopal ministry and cannot be detached from this.

■ **Bibliography:** P. Krämer, *Kirchenrecht* (Stuttgart et al., 1992) 2:103ff.; J. J. Foster, "The Election of the Roman Pontiff," *The Jurist* 56 (1996) 691-705; W. Aymans and K. Mörsdorf, *Kanonisches Recht: Lehrbuch aufgrund des CIC* (13th ed. Paderborn et al., 1997) II, §63 BI b; G. Ghirlanda, "Accettazione della legittima elezione e consecrazione episcopale del romano pontefice secondeo la Cost. Ap. 'Universi dominici gregis' di Giovanni Paolo II," *Periodica de re canonica* 86 (1997) 615-56; K. Schlaich, "Einige Beobachtungen zum Recht der Papst-

wahl," in Festschrift for M. Heckel (Tübingen, 1999) 237-50.

PETER KRÄMER

Encyclicals. Encyclicals, since Benedict XIV (1740-1758), have been announced and printed circular letters of the popes, addressed to the whole episcopate of the church or to a portion of it, as well as through them to the faithful, and on occasion to all people of good will. Their contents are subjects of doctrine on faith and morals, philosophy, and teachings on society, state, and economy, as well as on discipline and church policy. *Litterae encyclicae* (encyclical letters) are distinguished from the (seldom employed) *epistolae encyclicae* (encyclical epistles) mainly by the importance of the topic, which is often embodied in the first two or three words of the official text, which also serve as the title. Encyclicals are normally published in Latin; increasingly they are provided with official translations into other languages. Encyclicals contain no norms of canonical legislation. They are usually conditioned by specific timely questions or particular situations, and serve as a means for exercising the ordinary general magisterium of the pope, and (ever since Leo XIII) have been a primary source of the church's preaching. As a rule they contain many doctrines that already have been put forth as dogmas. Encyclicals always oblige obedient acceptance, yet gradations are possible depending on their propositional content and the degree of authority. If they state a judgment about questions that until then have been in dispute, their content is withdrawn from free debate of theologians (DH 3885).

■ **Bibliography:** F. M. Gallati, *Wenn die Päpste sprechen: Das ordentliche Lehramt des Apostolischen Stuhles und die Zustimmung zu dessen Entschiedungen* (Vienna, 1960); A. Pfeiffer, *Die Enzykliken und ihr formaler Wert für die dogmatische Methode*, in Studia Friburgensia NF 47 (Freiburg, 1968). J. A. Komonchak, "Ordinary Papal Magisterium and Religious Assent," *Contraception: Authority and Dissent*, ed. C. E. Curran (New York, 1969) 101-26.

GEORGE MAY

Encyclicals, Social. This term refers to the body of papal social teaching dealing with issues of economic and political justice beginning with Pope Leo XIII's encyclical *Rerum novarum* in 1891. Subsequent papal encyclicals, were most often issued on anniversaries of the previous ones, including: *Quadragesimo anno* (Pius XI, 1931), *Mater et magistra* and *Pacem in terris* (John XXIII, 1961 and 1963), *Populorum progressio* (Paul VI, 1967), and three encyclicals by John Paul II: *Laborem exercens* (1981), *Sollicitudo rei socialis* (1987), and *Centesimus annus* (1991). Together with other documents, usually including *Gaudium et spes* (Vatican Council II, 1965), *Octogesima adveniens* (Apostolic Letter of Paul VI, 1971), *Iustitia in mundo* (International Synod of Bishops, 1971), and *Evangelii nuntiandi* (Apostolic Letter of Paul VI, 1975), they form the body of Catholic social teaching (some add a number of discourses on social topics by Pius XII to this group).

The earlier social encyclicals dealt primarily with problems arising from the Industrial Revolution stressing the dignity of the worker, the need for unions, and the intervention of the state to protect the rights of workers. Subsequent documents deal with the various social problems facing modern society, recognizing (since the early 1960s) that the social problem is now worldwide.

From the beginning, these documents have rested on an anthropology based on the innate and God-given dignity and social nature of the human person called to live with others in community and relationship. This papal teaching has thus opposed the extremes of one-sided individualism as in laissez faire capitalism and one-sided collectivism as in radical socialism and communism. The state has a limited but very positive function to play in working for the common good. Justice involves not only individuals but the relationship of society to individuals and individuals to society. Recent documents have stressed human (civil and economic) rights and also the preferential option for the poor.

The early social encyclicals followed a natural law approach (human reason reflecting on creation and human nature can achieve true moral knowledge) and employed a deductive methodology. Since Vatican II a greater role has been given to Scripture and theological concerns as directly related to human society, but the insights of natural law continued to be emphasized. Post-Vatican II documents, as best illustrated in *Octogesima adveniens*, have used a more inductive methodology, but John Paul II has generally pulled back from the more inductive approach of his predecessor.

The papal social encyclicals constitute authoritative teachings of the Roman Catholic church. According the the formula first used in *Quadragesimo anno* (41) and often repeated, the competence of the church in social, political, economic and trade questions refers, "not to question of a technical kind," i.e., to evaluations of empirical facts, causal connections, and the effectiveness of solutions), but only to all that is "related to the moral law." This helps explain their somewhat general character since the popes deal with moral norms and issues rather than economic and political aspects as such. In the light of the complexity of concrete issues and the differing application of principles, Catholics will, and often do, disagree on specific proposals and legislation. Catholic theoreticians likewise often disagree about the general interpretation of these documents precisely because of their generality. In the United States, for example, neoconservative theologians have often disagreed with the interpretation of the papal teaching in the documents of the U.S. bishops. The natural law methodology of the earlier documents and the explicit salutation of the later documents indicate that the popes are also addressing the entire world and trying to contribute to solving the problems facing human society.

The authoritative nature of the social encyclicals, together with the commentaries on and citations of earlier documents in the series, bolsters the understanding strongly proposed by John Paul II that the documents constitute a whole often known as Catholic social teaching. However, there is more discontinuity than the authors themselves will explicitly acknowledge as pointed out above, for example, in the methodological shifts that have occurred or in the growing importance given to the freedom, equality, and participation of the person.

National conferences of bishops came into existence after Vatican II. *Octogesima adveniens* (n. 4) called for churches to analyze the situation in their own countries and to propose approaches based on the gospel and the social teaching of the church. The United States bishops in 1983 and 1986 wrote two very influential pastoral letters: *The Challenge of Peace: God's Promise and Our Response* and *Economic Justice for All*. In 1996, the bishops of England and Wales issued *The Common Good and the Catholic Church's Social Teach-*

ing. These national documents complement the papal documents but usually give more specific direction while recognizing that Catholics can disagree on complex specific issues.

Catholic scholars have negatively criticized various aspects of the social encyclicals. The papal encyclicals have been drafted by a small unknown group whereas the very nature of documents intended for the whole world and the ecclesiology of a post-Vatican II church call for a very broad and public consultation. Other negative criticisms include: the encyclicals too often cite only "predecessors of happy memory" and fail to dialogue with contemporary realities; the concept of teaching found in these documents fails to recognize many different forms of teaching such as the heroic witness of many Catholic lay people as well as the failure to recognize that the church itself is not only a teacher but also a learner; discontinuities and differences within the body of teaching are not acknowledged; the popes fail to point out past mistakes in Catholic theory and practice.

However, all recognize the important contribution the social encyclicals and Catholic social teaching have made to the life of the Catholic Church and to the broader human society. The social encyclicals have made Catholics themselves more conscious that action on behalf of justice is a constitutive dimension of the preaching of the gospel and the redemptive mission of Jesus and the church.

Earlier encyclicals reflected the Western European world from which they came, but the later documents have had a significant influence throughout the whole world. The encyclicals' recognition of innate personal human dignity and rights, together with solidarity with all others, has ramifications in all parts of the world. The pontificate of John Paul II (1978) shows the church universal has become a significant voice throughout the world in the struggle for human rights and human solidarity especially for the poor and the oppressed.

■ **Sources:** D. J. O'Brien and T. A. Shannon, *Catholic Social Thought: The Documentary Heritage* (Maryknoll, N.Y., 1992).

■ **Bibliography:** D. Dorr, *Option for the Poor: A Hundred Years of Vatican Social Teaching,* rev. ed. (Maryknoll, N.Y.:, 1992); G. Weigel and R. Royal, eds., *Building the Free Society: Democracy, Capitalism, and Catholic Social Teaching* (Grand Rapids, 1993); J. A. Dwyer, ed., *The New Dictionary of Catholic Social Thought* (Collegeville,

Minn., 1994); A. Anzenbacher, *Christliche Sozialethik* (Paderborn, 1997); M. L. Krier Mich, *Catholic Social Teaching and Movements* (Mystic, Conn., 1998); C. E. Curran, *Catholic Social Teaching, 1891 to the Present: An Historical, Theological, and Ethical Analysis* (Washington, D.C., 2002).

CHARLES E. CURRAN

Enthronement. The enthronement of the pope usually took place after his consecration (or benediction) in St. Peter's, when he ascended the → *cathedra Petri.* Until the decree of Nicholas II regulating the papal election (1059), the pope could exercise acts pertaining to his office only after this enthronement. During the exile in Avignon, an enthronement was impossible; after the return of the popes to Rome, the practice was not resumed.

Today, the pope assumes "full and supreme authority in the church" as soon as he accepts his election (or, if he is not already a bishop, after his episcopal ordination: can. 332 §1, *CIC*). The solemn eucharistic celebration at the beginning of his pontificate has no legal significance.

■ **Bibliography:** *VATL* 333f.

AUGUST HAGEN AND THADDÄUS A. SCHNITKER

Ex cathedra → Infallibility.

Fables, Papal. This designation applies to materials concerning traditions about the popes of the first millennium, first collected by Ignaz von Döllinger. The fables include the unhistorical Englishman → Cyriacus, who renounced the papal office in the third century in order to share in the martyrdom of the 11,000 virgins; → Marcellinus, who denied the Christian faith and then deposed himself at a (fictitious) synod in Sinuessa in 393; Silvester I, who baptized the emperor Constantine the Great in Rome and received the Constantinian Donation from him; the allegedly orthodox Felix II, the opponent of Liberius, who was in reality an Arian; Anastasius II (496-498), Gelasius's successor, who endeavored to achieve a balance during the Acacian schism and was therefore depicted as a heretic; Gregory II, who allegedly renounced his obedience to the iconoclastic Byzantium; above all, Pope → Joan (allegedly ca. 855), whose existence is attested from the thirteenth century on; and Silvester II, who is said to have made a pact with the devil.

The fact that Döllinger also includes the lack of attention paid to the cause of Honorius I in the

Middle Ages indicates that traditional materials of this kind contained a great deal of hidden potential for later interconfessional controversy about the papacy; and the controversies did in fact draw on these fables.

■ **Bibliography:** *LMA* 6:1685f.; I. von Döllinger, *Die Papstfabeln des Mittelalters* (2nd ed. Munich, 1890); Zimmermann, *Das Papsttum im Mittelalter.*

ANNA-DOROTHEE VON DEN BRINCKEN

Family, Pontifical. This term designates a group of clergy and laity whose origins go back to the papal court; it was radically reformed by Paul VI in the Motu proprio *Pontificalis Domus* (Mar. 28, 1968). Along with the *Cappella Papalis* and the *Cappella Musicale Pontificia*, it is under the authority of the Prefecture of the Pontifical → Household, and renders certain services, mostly to the pope. The members of the Pontifical Family are the Substitute of the Secretariat of State, the Secretary for Relations to States, the Almoner of His Holiness, the President of the Pontifical Diplomatic Academy, the Theologian of the Pontifical Household, the seven ordinary protonotaries and the honorary protonotaries, the honorary prelates of His Holiness, the chaplains to His Holiness, and the preacher of the Pontifical Household. Lay members of the Pontifical Family include the Assistants to the → Throne, the Special Delegate of the Papal Commission for the State of Vatican City, the commander of the Pontifical Swiss → Guard, the president of the Pontifical → Academy of the Sciences, the papal → chamberlains, the members of the Pontifical Household, and those who work in the antechamber.

■ **Bibliography:** *VATL* 221f.; *AnPont* (2000) 1346ff., 1966-72.

MARTIN HÜLSKAMP

Finances of the Apostolic See.
1. *The Holy See*
The "Administration of the Patrimony of the Apostolic See" (APSA) has responsibility for the financing of the administration of the universal church, with an Ordinary Section for cash liquidity and administration of real estate, and an Extraordinary Section for capital (stocks and shares). The consolidated balance of the → Holy See includes the individual budgets of the Roman → curia and the government organs (printing press,

publishing house, and bookstore, → *Osservatore Romano*, → Vatican Radio). Half of the annual financial framework of more than 300 billion lire (1992) comes from income on capital; one third comes from → Peter's Pence and other donations to the Holy Father; one sixth comes from contributions by dioceses, religious orders, and other sources of income. The balance in 1992 was 1,300 billion lire; the real estate has only sentimental value.

2. *Vatican City*
The secular responsibilities of the Vatican City are those of any municipal administration, in addition to some of the sovereign functions of a state (coinage, post, customs). The yearly financial framework is 150 billion lire (1992), the balance 160 billion lire (1992); it is scarcely possible to put a price on real estate and the artworks in the museums.

3. *Financial Inspection*
The "Prefecture for the Economic Affairs of the Holy See" has the responsibility of setting up and inspecting the budget proposals and yearly balance sheets of the Holy See and of the → Vatican state, as well as the preliminary inspection of transfers of real estate and building projects. Its authority extends to virtually all other Vatican bodies as well.

4. *Council of Cardinals*
The "Council of Cardinals for Organizational and Economic Affairs of the Apostolic See" (fifteen members, three from each continent) meets twice a year to study budget proposals and yearly balance sheets and gives an account of these matters to the diocesan bishops.

5. *The "Institute for the Works of Religion" (IOR)*
The IOR is often called the "Vatican Bank," although it is more like a savings bank for church organizations and employees and is in fact the administration of a Foundation. It is organized according to Vatican civil law, under the guidance of a commission of cardinals led by an administrative council of five professional bankers. A general director executes the directives of this council.

■ **Bibliography:** *VATL* 329-32, 622f., 824; C. Pallenberg, *Die Finanzen des Vatikans* (Munich, 1973); E. Gatz, ed., *Römische Kurie, Kirchliche Finanzen, Vatikanisches*

Archiv, Festschrift for H. Hoberg, 2 vols. (Rome, 1979); H. Benz, *Finanzen und Finanzpolitik des Heiligen Stuhls* (Stuttgart, 1993); *AnPont* (2000) index.

EUGEN HILLENGASS

Fisherman's Ring (*anulus piscatoris*) has been the official papal ring since the fourteenth century and forms part of the papal → insignia. It is so called because its stone bears the name of the pope and a picture of St. → Peter drawing the fisherman's net into his boat. It is first mentioned under Clement IV (1265-1266). It was used regularly to seal papal briefs from the time of Nicholas V (1447-1455) until it was replaced in 1843 by a seal bearing the same image; this is the source of the formula *datum sub anulo piscatoris.*
■ **Bibliography:** *EC* 1:1217-21; *LMA* 1:739; *VATL* 222; K. A. Fink, "Untersuchung über die päpstlichen Breven des 15. Jahrhunderts," *RQ* 43 (1935) 55-86.

RUPERT BERGER

Golden Rose. On the fourth Sunday in Lent, very likely under the inspiration of the Byzantine veneration of the cross in mid-Lent (*PL* 143:635) or of popular spring customs, the pope bore a rose in his hand in the stational procession to the church of Santa Croce. This was originally a real rose; later, a rose of gold was carried. Still later, it was filled with balsam and musk ("It delights with its color, it refreshes with its fragrance, it fortifies with its taste": Innocent III, *PL* 217:393). He then gave this to the city prefect (this is first mentioned under Leo IX in 1049 as a custom already ancient at that date). Later, the rose was brought to meritorious persons; the first of these was Fulques of Anjou in 1096, for the First Crusade, and the same was done to Don John of Austria in 1576 for the victory of Lepanto. It was also bestowed on cities such as Venice and on Roman basilicas. After 1759, it was given exclusively to women rulers (hence the name "rose of virtue"). It was given for the last time by Pius XI in 1937 to Queen Elena of Italy; since then the custom has fallen into desuetude.
■ **Bibliography:** *LMA* 4:1545; *VATL* 660f., 790; J. Krebs, "La rose d'or," *Questions liturgiques et paroissiales* 11 (1926) 71-104, 149-78; E. Cornides, *Rose und Schwert im päpstlichen Zeremoniell von den Anfängen bis zum Pontifikat Gregors XIII.* (Vienna, 1967); C. Burns, *Golden Rose and Blessed Sword: Papal Gifts to Scottish Monarchs* (Glasgow, 1971); G. Sacchi Lodispoto, "La rosa d'oro," *Strenna dei Romanisti* 45 (1984) 467-83.

RUPERT BERGER

Guard, Pontifical Noble. This body was founded in 1801 by Pius VII in succession to a cavalry corps that had ceased to exist in 1798. It consisted mostly of aristocrats from the papal states and was responsible for the protection of the pope and for honorary duties. It was reformed on various occasions, most recently under John XXIII. Paul VI renamed it the Honorary Pontifical Guard and subsequently abolished it on September 14, 1970, along with the Pontifical Palace Guard and the Pontifical → Police, since the "corps which exist today no longer correspond to the needs for which they were founded" (*AAS* 61 [1970] 587).
■ **Bibliography:** *VATL* 187ff.; U. Nersinger, *Eine kleine Geschichte der Päpstlichen Garden* (Vienna, 1996).

MARTIN HÜLSKAMP

Guard, Swiss. The Pontifical Swiss Guard (*Cohors Helvetica*) consists exclusively of Swiss who form a papal bodyguard, palace guard, and guard of honor. The popes in the fifteenth century had often taken Swiss troops into their service, and Julius II erected a permanent guard of two hundred men in 1506. The number of guards has varied in the course of history, but has never exceeded 250; today there are 100. Their baptism of fire came when they defended Clement VII during the sack of Rome in 1527 and made it possible for him to flee to → Castel Sant'Angelo. One hundred forty-seven guardsmen died with their commander, Kaspar Röist, while forty-two reached safety in the fortress.

Paul III reestablished the Swiss Guard toward the end of his pontificate, by means of a treaty with the oldest group of Swiss cantons under the leadership of Lucerne, whereby these agreed to provide guardsmen. For a long time, the soldiers came exclusively from the oldest, German-speaking cantons, but today they come from all parts of Switzerland. Apart from short intervals in the nineteenth century, they have existed continuously from Paul III to the present day. Paul VI abolished the Papal Noble → Guard, the Palatine Guard, and the Gendarmerie Corps in 1970, but the Swiss Guard still exists. The guardsmen today stand on duty at the main entrances to the → Vatican state and in the Apostolic Palace, as well as in → Castelgandolfo; they are on duty in papal audiences and Masses and provide a guard of honor when important visitors are received. They serve for a minimum of two years. They must first have completed the basic military training in the Swiss recruits' school; they must be male and single (only officers are allowed to enter the Swiss Guard as married men). The uniform they wear on solemn days, in red, gold, and blue, recalls the heraldic colors of the Medici popes.

■ Bibliography: *DHP* 718f.; *VATL* 715ff.; P.-M. Krieg, *Die Schweizer Garde in Rom* (Lucerne, 1960); *AnPont* (2000) 1371, 1981.

ERWIN GATZ

Historiography, Papal. Given the position and significance of the papacy in Western history, this is a part of church historiography and historiography generally. Initially, we find lists and catalogues of episcopal succession in Hegesippus, Irenaeus of Lyons, Eusebius of Caesarea, and others: a theological concern in the debate with gnosis and heresy was to demonstrate the orthodoxy of the tradition in the "apostolic churches" (Tertullian, *De praescriptione haereticorum* 36.1; Irenaeus, *Adversus haereses* 3.1.1) in the apostolic succession (*diadochē, paradōsis*), which were governed by the bishops, with Rome at the head. Irenaeus transmits the oldest list of Roman bishops, which may go back to Hegesippus (*Adversus haereses* 3.3.1ff.).

The elaboration of catalogues of succession into lists of bishops was the work of Christian chronography from the third century onward. This involved the attempt, by means of synchronous lists of rulers, consuls, Olympiads, etc., to establish a pattern of historical succession, and hence to arrive at more precise dates for pontificates (Sextus Julius Africanus, Hippolytus of Rome, and especially Eusebius). A complete chronology of the Roman bishops (without any value derived from tradition, until the first third of the third century) is first furnished by the Liberian Catalogue (in the → Chronography of 354), employing synchronization with the annals of Roman consuls. This formed the oldest part of the → *Liber Pontificalis*, transmitted in many manuscripts, which had the rank of a kind of semiofficial papal historiography in the Middle Ages. The numerous lists of popes in manuscripts of chroniclers and canon lawyers in the high and late Middle Ages have not yet been systematically investigated.

During the Middle Ages (with few exceptions),

until the period of the humanists, the constitutive document of papal sovereignty was the Donation of Constantine and the legend of Pope Silvester. It was only after the church reform of the eleventh and twelfth centuries, with an ecclesiology more strongly centered on Rome, that the papacy looked positively on the forgeries of Pseudo-Isidore. Theological reflection on the church became more common in the West only in the high and late Middle Ages, after the contest between the "two powers" in the investiture conflict. This reflection was now linked to the papal → primacy. In accordance with the new significance of the *sacerdotium,* church history in John of Salisbury (†1180), Martin of Troppau (†1278), Bartholomew of Lucca (†1326/27), and others is now largely papal history; this is true also in the case of Bartholomew Platina (*Liber de vita Christi et pontificum* [Venice, 1479]), a partisan author who displays little originality and whose work is a humanist conclusion to the medieval papal historiography.

Where the medieval chronicles ventured beyond an exclusive adherence to the *Liber Pontificalis,* they remained bound to the edifying, salvation-historical scheme of the ages of the world, and they were uncritically open to fables (Papal → Fables) and legends. Apart from the semiofficial historiography, we also find a few examples of critical papal historiography in the Middle Ages, e.g., in the polemical pamphlets, often dictated by partisan passion in the struggles between the "two powers," and in the sometimes radical writings of the late Middle Ages on the authority and the reform of the papacy. The most significant works of church history in the fourteenth and fifteenth centuries addressed themes that moved their contemporaries deeply (conciliarism, the Western Schism, and reform councils), and these works too belong to papal historiography. Doubt was cast only rarely on the foundations of the papacy in sacred scripture (e.g., by Marsilius of Padua, died ca. 1343), but this made little impact.

A fundamental change came only with the Reformation. Protestantism not only rejected the idea that the papacy was of divine origin; many Protestants also looked on it as endangering the salvation of souls, as we see in Martin Luther's late book *Against the Papacy in Rome, Founded by the Devil* (1545), and in Matthias Flacius and the *Historia ecclesiastica* of the Centuriators of Magdeburg. They were opposed by Caesar Baronius in his *Annales ecclesiastici,* covering the period up to 1198 (1st ed. Rome, 1588-1607, with many subsequent editions). A literary exchange never took place—in the following centuries, one-sided polemics and apologetics dominated both Catholic and Protestant historiography, essential parts of which were papal historiography (Robert Bellarmine, Francisco Torres, David Blondel, etc.). No histories of the popes worthy of the name were written until the nineteenth century. Alonso Chacón and Onofrio Panvinio were among those who wrote church histories with emphasis on papal historiography; the church histories of Sébastien Le Nain de Tillemont and Claude Fleury were influenced by Gallicanism and Jansenism; we may add to these the *chef d'oeuvre* of Etienne Baluze, the *Vitae paparum Avenionensium* (Paris 1693; ed. G. Mollat in 4 vols., Paris, 1914-27).

Nevertheless, critical acumen and philological interests led to the beginnings of a critical papal historiography in the modern period. For Catholic scholars, this meant initially the critical study of the sources and of hagiography, involving the systematic collection and manuscript investigation of the sources themselves, especially by the monks of St. Maur and the Bollandists. Notable fruits of these endeavors were the *Conatus chronico-historicus ad catalogum Pontificum* by Daniel Papebroch (Antwerp, 1685), the collection of the *Pontificum Romanorum Epistulae* by Pierre Coustant (Paris, 1721), which was often republished (lastly by Andreas Thiel, Braunsberg, 1868), and the various editions of the → *Bullarium Romanum.* Here belong also the *Vitae Pontificum Romanorum ab coaequalibus conscriptae,* ed. in 2 vols. by Johannes Matthias Watterich (Leipzig, 1862).

Many new sources for the history of the papacy and its relationships to particular countries were published in major editions in the nineteenth century, especially after Leo XIII opened the Secret → Archive in the Vatican in 1881 (at present, this is accessible up to the death of Benedict XV in 1922; see Primary Sources, below). Paul Fridolin Kehr began in 1896 the collection and publication of medieval papal → documents (covering the period before 1198, after which we have a continuous transmission in registers) relevant to individual countries. He was the first director of this task, and Pius XI set up for him in 1931 the "Pius Foundation for the Study of Papal Documents

and the Study of Medieval History," which publishes the *Regesta Pontificum Romanorum (RPR),* with sections dealing with *Italia Pontificia (RPR.IP), Germania Pontificia (RPR.GP), Gallia Pontificia, Anglia Pontificia, Hispania Pontificia, Hungaria Pontificia, Africa Pontificia (America Pontificia),* and *Oriens Pontificius.* A yearly account appears in the *Deutsches Archiv für Erforschung des Mittelalters,* and the edition of the papal → registers (from 1198 onward) is prepared (and published since 1884) by the Austrian Cultural Institute in Rome or by the Library of the French Schools of Athens and Rome. The publication of the → nunciature reports was particularly important for the period of the Reformation and Counter-Reformation.

The official list of popes in the → *Annuario Pontificio* (from 1947 onward) was one of the beneficiaries of the newly kindled scholarly consciousness, which has increasingly helped to dismantle the confessional polemics and false apologetics or panegyrics that had marked church and papal historiography. The decisive transition was begun by Leopold von Ranke (*Die römischen Päpste,* 3 vols. [Berlin, 1834-39]), who was able to use the great European archives (though not yet the Vatican archive). In the words of Herman Tüchle, "Although his work, which emphasizes the Roman Counter-Reformation, covers only three centuries and lays far too much emphasis on the diplomatic-political role of the popes, it is a masterpiece of psychological historiography, objective endeavor and artistic form—and it has not been matched since." It is not possible for a single scholar to write an academic history of the papacy, and significant Protestant and Catholic scholars have mastered only parts of it.

■ **Primary Sources (editions):** *MGH; RPR*(J)*; RPR*(P)*; ACO; LP;* P. Fabre and L. Duchesne, eds., *Liber censuum Ecclesiae Romanae,* 3 vols. (Paris, 1889-1952); T. Sickel, ed., *Liber diurnus Romanorum Pontificum* (Vienna, 1889, ed. H. Forster [Bern, 1958]); J. von Pflugk-Harttung, *Acta Pontificum Romanorum,* 3 vols. (Tübingen, 1881-88).

■ **Bibliography:** *Histories of the popes* (see also the select bibliography, p. 13*f.); Caspar (to the mid-eighth century: a torso compiled from the papers he left at his death: *Das Papsttum unter fränkischer Herrschaft* [Darmstadt, 1956 (up to 800)]); Haller (a work of significant creative power; anti-Roman); Seppelt (the most comprehensive Catholic work; based on available printed sources; sober and reliable; see the brief presentation: F. X. Seppelt and G. Schwaiger, *Geschichte der Päpste: Von den Anfängen bis zur Gegenwart* [Munich, 1964]); Pastor (with rich material from archives; many reprints and translations); valuable documentary supplement to this work: A. Haidacher, *Geschichte der Päpste in Bildern* (Heidelberg, 1965); Schmidlin (continuation of Pastor, but with less creative force); Zimmermann *Pa*; Zimmermann *Pt*; G. Barraclough, *The Medieval Papacy* (London, 1968; repr. 1979); M. Pacault, *La papauté, des origines au concile de Trente* (Paris, 1976); Richards; H. Fuhrmann, *Von Petrus zu Johannes Paul II.* (Munich, 1980; 2nd ed. 1984 [sources, bibliography, current state of research]); B. Schimmelpfennig, *Das Papsttum von der Antike bis zur Renaissance* (Darmstadt, 1984; 4th ed. 1996); M. Greschat, ed., *Das Papsttum,* 2 vols. (Stuttgart, 1985 [revised and partly changed: M. Greschat and E. Guerriero, eds., *Storia dei papi* (Milan, 1994)]); C. Morris, *The Papal Monarchy: The Western Church from 1050 to 1250* (Oxford, 1989); I. S. Robinson, *The Papacy 1073-1198: Continuity and Innovation* (Cambridge, 1990); K. Schatz, *Der päpstliche Primat* (Würzburg, 1990); *Il primato del vescovo di Roma nel primo millennio* (Rome, 1991); M. Maccarrone, ed., *Romana ecclesia: Cathedra Petri,* 2 vols. (Rome, 1991). *Series:* Miscellanea Historiae Pontificiae (Rome, 1939–); *PuP. Periodical:* AHP (1963–); *Dictionaries:* J. N. D. Kelly, *The Oxford Dictionary of Popes* (Oxford, 1986); DHP (contributions by international experts). *On the subject of papal historiography:* T. Frenz, *Papsturkunden des Mittelalters und der Neuzeit* (2nd ed. Stuttgart, 2000); H. Fuhrmann, "Papstgeschichtsschreibung: Grundlinien und Etappen," in A. Esch and J. Petersen, eds., *Geschichte und Geschichtswissenschaft in der Kultur Italiens und Deutschlands* (Tübingen, 1989) 141-91 (best overview and introduction). The most comprehensive bibliographies are continually updated in *AHP, Revue d'histoire ecclésiastique,* and *Deutsches Archiv für Erforschung des Mittelalters.* → Papacy, Pope.

GEORG SCHWAIGER

Holy See (Sancta Sedes) has been synonymous with the "Apostolic See" since the 1917 *Code of Canon Law* (can. 7). It is the legally defined designation for the pope and/or the organs of the Roman → curia which act in his name (can. 361 CIC 1983). Originally, this was a designation of episcopal sees that had been founded by apostles; "Holy" or "Apostolic" is applied today only to the → cathedra Petri, the office of the bishop of Rome. The linguistic and conceptual formation of this objectifying designation of the highest pastoral authority takes up the very ancient symbol of the throne of the judge or king as an expression of his sovereign power. Because of its quality as a moral person, positive law (can. 113) attributes the character of a legal subject to the Holy See.

This observation is declared to be a deduction from the divine order—in other words, in a legal culture in which the historically developed concept of juridical person is a central structural element, it is logically necessary to attribute this status to the highest ecclesiastical authority; here we must note the ideas of the *ius publicum ecclesiasticum* and the doctrine of the *societas perfecta* (see also cann. 1254, 1255, 1259, 1271, 1273). The Holy See is also the legal subject of the property that belongs to the highest church authority (→ Apostolic Chamber). The praxis and the dominant doctrine of international law acknowledge the Holy See as a subject of international law both antecedent to and in addition to the → Vatican state which came into being in 1929 (→ Lateran Treaty). The status of the Holy See in international law is based on the customary law that developed after the Middle Ages, thanks to the efficient exercise of spiritual sovereignty. In official dealings with the United Nations, only the designation "Holy See" is to be used (exchange of notes on October 29, 1957). This is why one must inquire whether specific documents of international law concern the Holy See, the Vatican state, or both legal subjects. Special importance attaches to the status of the Holy See in international law today because of efforts to promote world peace.

On the ecclesiological significance of the legal concept "Holy See," see → Primacy; Power of the → Keys; Roman → Curia.

■ **Bibliography:** *VATL* 297f.; H. Oechslin, *Die Völkerrechtssubjektivität des Apostolischen Stuhls und der katholischen Kirche* (Freiburg, 1974); H. Köck, *Die völkerrechtliche Stellung des Heiligen Stuhls* (Berlin, 1975); *HKKR* 263f.; W. Aymans and K. Mörsdorf, *Kanonisches Recht: Lehrbuch aufgrund des CIC* (13th ed. Paderborn et al., 1997) 1:131; J. Abbass, *Apostolic See in the New Eastern Code of Canon Law* (Lewiston et al., 1994); C. García Martín, "El estatuto jurídico de la Santa Sede en las Naciones Unidas," *Ius canonicum* 38 (1998) 237-89; S. Gatzhammer, "Vorschläge zur Lösung der 'Quaestio Romana' in Bezug auf die päpstliche Souveränität von 1848 bis 1928," in *Winfried Schulz in Memoriam* (Frankfurt a.M. et al., 1999) 285-309; J. Joblin, "Il ruolo internazionale della Santa Sede," *La civiltà cattolica* 151 (2000) 158-62.

HELMUT SCHNIZER

Holy Year. A "Holy Year" is meant to contribute in a special manner to the sanctification of the faithful, above all through the pilgrimage to the main churches in Rome, which expresses the willingness to practice repentance, sealed in the devout celebration of the sacraments (primarily confession and communion) and in the indulgence linked to this. When innumerable pilgrims streamed to Rome in 1300, the first year of a new century, Pope Boniface VIII granted a special plenary indulgence, to be repeated every hundred years; Clement VI reduced the recurrence in 1343 to every fifty years ("Jubilee Years"), Urban VI in 1389 to every thirty-three years, and Paul II in 1470 to every twenty-five years. Traditionally, the pope inaugurates the Holy Year by opening the Golden Door of St. Peter's; simultaneously, cardinal legates do the same in the Lateran, Santa Maria Maggiore, and St. Paul's Outside the Walls. From 1500 onward, the jubilee indulgence was extended in the following year to the entire world. An innovation in 1975 was the celebration of the Jubilee Year in the dioceses in the preceding year as a time of repentance closely following the "path of salvation" in the church year, with penitential celebrations in Lent and a special week of reconciliation; this concluded with the pilgrimage to Rome in 1975. Two special eucharistic canons on the theme of reconciliation were composed for this occasion. The extraordinary Holy Year in 1983, celebrating the 1,950th anniversary of the redemption, was celebrated from the outset in the whole world. Above all, the sacrament of penance was meant to allow the faithful to experience Christ's redeeming action, but works of mercy were also to play an important role: basically, it was "an ordinary year celebrated in an extraordinary way" (John Paul II, bull *Aperite portas* 3). Most recently, the year 2000 was celebrated as a Holy Year throughout the world.

■ **Bibliography:** *EC* 6:678-86; *DDC* 6:191-203; *VATL* 298-303; A. de Waal, *Das Heilige Jahr* (2nd ed. Münster, 1900); P. Bastien, *Tractatus de anno sancto* (Münster, 1901); F. X. Kraus, *Essays* (Berlin, 1901) 2:217-336; H. Thurston, *The Roman Jubilee: History and Ceremonial* (London, 1925); A. Laici, *Gli Anni Santi e le basiliche giubilari* (Rome, 1925); G. Castelli, *Gli Anni Santi* (Rocca San Casciano, 1949); H. Schmidt, *Bullarium anni sancti* (Rome, 1950); *Ordo Anni Sancti celebrandi in ecclesiis particularibus* (Rome, 1973); M. Sievernich, "Das 'Heilige Jahr': Symbolische Bedeutung und theologische Deutung," *Praktische Theologie* 34 (1999) 97-104;

A. Cuva, "I giubilei degli anni 'centesimi,'" *Rivista liturgica* 86 (1999) 769-83; R. Trisco, "The First Jubilees Celebrated in the United States," *Catholic Historical Review* 86 (2000) 85-94.

RUPERT BERGER

Household, Pontifical (*Casa Pontificia*). In the Motu proprio *Pontificalis Domus* (March 28, 1968) Paul VI reintroduced this term for the papal court, whose roots date to the Constantinian period. The *Liber Pontificalis*, in the vita of Pope Julius I, provides information about its members: the first notary (*primicerius notariorum,* distantly related to the present-day office of the → Cardinal Secretary of State) together with the archdeacon and archpriest form the viceregents of the Holy See (*servantes locum Sanctae Sedis Apostolicae*). In addition, there is the second notary (*secundarius notarium*), the sacristans (*ararius* and *sacellarius*), the first archivist (*protoscriniarius*), the vestiary (*vestarius*), private chamberlain (*cubiclarius*), and the librarian (*bibliothecarius*). Even after 1870, the papal court remained essentially the same as from the time of Nicholas II, with the members of the Pontifical → Family increasingly gaining importance, and it served the pope in his dual role as head of the church and political sovereign. The functions within the Pontifical Household, which includes both priests and laity, and to which the *cappella papale* and the Pontifical Family belong, are coordinated by the Prefecture of the Pontifical Household, who is responsible for all not strictly liturgical functions of the pope, such as travel and audiences.

■ **Primary Sources:** *AAS* 60 (1968) 305-15
■ **Bibliography:** *VATL* 114-15.

MARTIN HÜLSKAMP

Index of Forbidden Books (*Index librorum prohibitorum*). A list of explicitly forbidden writings. Following the example of governmental lists, Paul IV first set up the *Index* in 1559. It contained three alphabetical lists: those of authors whose entire work was banned, those of authors some of whose works were banned, and titles of anonymously written books. After the advent of printing, Pius V assigned the censorship of books to the newly established (1571) Congregation of the Index. Pope Benedict XV dissolved this congregation on March 25, 1917, and handed over its charge to the Holy Office (renamed the Congregation for the Doctrine of the Faith in 1965).

The 1917 Code of Canon Law regulated the banning of books after publication (cann. 1395-1405). Titles of books banned by the Holy See were published in the *Acta Sanctae Sedis* and at the same time placed on the Index. They were not allowed to be published, read, kept, sold, translated or made accessible to others. The ban was issued as either absolute or "donec corrigatur" (until the improved new edition). The constitution *Sollicita ac provida* of July 9, 1753, definitively regulated the procedure for putting books on the *Index*. Apart from the legal exemptions, permission for special exemptions from the book ban could be obtained (*CIC*/1917, cann. 1400-1404). In certain narrowly defined situations, violators were threatened with excommunication (cann. 2318).

In the wake of the Second Vatican Council, significant changes took place with respect to the Index. Archbishop Josef Cardinal Frings of Cologne criticized the Holy Office during the council; subsequently a declaration was made to the press by the Proprefect of the Holy Office, Cardinal Alfredo Ottaviani, that the Index no longer had any legal standing, and the Index and the legal bans on books (can. 1399) were annulled through the decrees of the Congregation for the Doctrine of the Faith of June 14 and November 15, 1966. Punishments that had been incurred were lifted. In place of the legal prescriptions that were supposed to protect faith and morals, but that were also used and misused as an instrument of reprimand, a legal free space was created for the personal responsibility of the individual Christian believer. Here as ever, every Christian is called to responsibility before his or her conscience. The 1983 Code of Canon Law contains no regulations on a ban on books, but it does mention their previous scrutiny and judgment.

As far back as Alexander III, the pope had ordered a prior censorship of books for four German church provinces. At the Fifth Lateran Council this was declared binding for the entire church, and was explicitly confirmed by the Council of Trent. The reorganization undertaken by Leo XIII through the constitution *Officiorum et munerum* on January 25, 1897, was by and large adopted in the *CIC*/1917 (cann. 1385-1394). It underwent a fundamental change through the decree of the Congregation for the Doctrine of the Faith *De ecclesiae pastorum vigilantia circum libros* of March 19, 1975. The 1983 Code of Canon Law has extended the regulations on oversight of books (cann. 822-832) through legal statements on other means of mass communication. The right to freely express one's opinion (can. 212 §3) and freedom of research (can. 218) is limited by the need to safeguard the intactness of faith and morals. Only in this way can the church do justice to the charge of its Lord Jesus Christ.

■ **Primary Sources:** *Index Librorum Prohibitorum Sanctissimi Domini Nostri Pii PP XII issu editus anno 1948* (Rome, 1948). 1917 Code of Canon Law (*Codex Iuris Canonici*); 1983 Code of Canon Law.

■ **Bibliography:** DHGE 25, 1054ff.; F. H. Reusch, *Der Index der verbotenen Bücher*, 2 vols. (Bonn, 1883-1885); J. Hilgers, *Der Index der verbotenen Bücher* (Freiburg, 1904); G. May, "Die Aufhebung der kirchlichen Bücherverbot," *Ecclesia et ius*, Festschrift for A. Scheuermann (Munich et al., 1968) 547-71; H. Paarhammer, "*Sollicita ac provida*. Neuordnung von Lehrbeanstandung und Bücherzensur in der katholischen Kirche im 18. Jahrhundert," in *Ministerium Iustitiae*, Festschrift for H. Heinemann (Essen, 1985) 343-61; W. Rees: "Der Schutz des Glaubens- u. Sittenlehre durch kirchliche Gesetze," *Archiv für katholisches Kirchenrecht* 160 (1991) 3-24; ibid., *Die Strafgewalt der Kirche* (Berlin, 1993) 231ff.

WILHELM REES

Infallibility.

1. Biblical Data.—2. History of Theology and Dogma.—3. Systematic Theology.

The term "infallibility" (*infallibilitas*) formally designates the epistemological aspect of faith in the indefectibility (*indefectibilitas*) of the church of Jesus Christ, which is guided by the Holy Spirit so that it may proclaim the gospel. In material terms, it designates the charism that is bestowed under defined circumstances on the entire church and on particular members of the church (the pope, and the bishops together with the pope), so that affirmations about doctrine may be made that are free of error ("inerrancy") and hence "irreformable."

1. Biblical Data

The New Testament does not use this term, but infallibility is hinted at in Matt. 16:18; 28:20; John 16:13. These passages express the conviction that the church cannot be destroyed, since it is rooted in the divine plan of salvation (cf. the New Testament images of "people of God," "body of Christ," "temple of the Holy Spirit"). Since its essential task is to hand on the testimony to Christ, the church must be the "bulwark of the truth" (1 Tim. 3:15) and must proclaim the faith (above all its christological foundations) without any error (cf. 1 John 2:22; 4:2, 15; 5:1, 5). Paul is convinced that he can do this without falling into error (Gal. 1:6ff.,11f.), since his message is based on the word of Christ himself (Rom. 10:10, 17; cf. 1 Cor. 9:15f.). What the community hears in preaching is not a human word, but the word of God (1 Tim. 2:13; cf. 2 Tim. 2:19).

2. *History of Theology and Dogma*

Until the fourteenth century, the concept of "infallibility" was used of God alone. The conviction of the inerrancy of the universal church refers to the *regula fidei* of the church, to the decrees of the first four ecumenical councils (see DH 265) and to the faith that is rooted in synchronous and diachronic consensus (Irenaeus of Lyons, *Adversus haereses* 3.4.1; Vincent of Lérins, *Commonitorium* 2.3). The faith is preserved in the universal church, despite all divisions (Thomas Aquinas, *Summa theologiae* II-II 1,2.10; *Quodlibet* 9,1; Martin Luther, *De servo arbitrio*, WA 18, 649f.; *Lumen Gentium*, 12). No agreement exists about whether and to what extent inerrancy can be made concrete in institutional-juridical terms. From a very early date, a special fidelity to the faith is ascribed to the church of Rome (e.g., Theodoret of Cyrus, *Ep.* 116: Hormisdas's profession of faith: DH 363ff.), *inter alia* (especially from the seventh century on) as a supporting pillar of the pentarchy. This fidelity was not ascribed to the bishop of Rome, whose fall into heresy and schism was regarded as a possibility.

From the twelfth century onward, the controversy about the mendicant orders led theologians and canon lawyers (especially from these orders themselves) to define the active, determinative and ultimately decisive role of the pope in matters of the faith. This is his role because he proclaims the faith as head of the church—otherwise, he would cease to be pope (Bonaventure, *De perfectione evangelica* 2.2.5; Thomas Aquinas, *Summa theologiae* II-II 1,10; *Decretum Gratiani* II 24,11,12; Petrus Johannis Olivi). According to Hervaeus Natalis and Antoninus of Florence (*Summa* III 22,3), the pope can err *ex proprio*

motu ("when he acts of his own accord"), but not *utens consilio* (a variant reads: *concilio*) *et requirens adiutorium universalis ecclesiae* ("when he makes use of the counsel [or: council] and requests the help of the universal church").

In the conciliarist controversy, infallibility was concentrated on the pope as the sole guarantor of truth. This reversed the order of previous arguments: now it was argued not that the pope is infallible because the church is infallible, but rather that the church is infallible because of the pope. Episcopalist tendencies (Episcopalism, Gallicanism, Johann Nicolaus of Hontheim, Jansenism) continued the conciliarist tradition by affirming the infallibility of the universal church. When Gallicanism disappeared as a result of the French Revolution, ultramontanist concern for security led to attempts in the nineteenth century to strengthen the sovereignty of the pope by means of a dogmatic definition of his infallibility (e.g., Joseph-Marie de Maistre; Bartolomeo Alberto Cappellari, subsequently Gregory XVI; Henry Edward Manning; Ignaz von Senestrey). One main reason for this was the hope for quick and obligatory decisions when the community of faith was disturbed. At the First Vatican Council, this question was excerpted from the comprehensive ecclesial constitution and was the object of lively debates. Infallibility was declared to be a matter of faith on July 18, 1970 (*Pastor aeternus*, DH 3065-74); 140 minority bishops (ca. 20 percent of the total) were absent. The council declared that the pope possesses the prerogative of infallibility when he speaks *ex cathedra* (i.e., exercising the highest teaching authority in matters of faith and morals in a manner that obligates the entire church; he must have the explicit intention of making a definition and of pronouncing a definitive judgment). The relationship to the universal church is expressed indirectly: in the past, popes have employed all available means to ensure that their teaching accords with divine revelation (DH 3069). The *relatio* by Bishop Vinzenz Gasser (July 11, 1870) provided an important key to the interpretation of this definition.

A process of "creeping infallibility" began after the council. With the growth of papal teaching authority (Papal → Encyclicals) there was an increasing tendency to attribute a definitive character to the pope's words. The Second Vatican Council (DH 4131, 4149f.) integrates papal infallibility more clearly into the universal church (via the episcopal college). Postconciliar developments in magisterial teaching (the declaration *Mysterium fidei* of the Congregation for the Doctrine of the Faith, 1973; can. 749 *CIC*; Profession of Faith and oath of loyalty, 1989; instruction *Donum veritatis* of the Congregation for the Doctrine of the Faith, 1990; Motu proprio *Ad tuendam fidem,* with commentary by the same congregation, 1998) make a clear distinction between the primary object of infallibility (viz., the truths contained in revelation) and its secondary object (logically or historically linked with the primary object, and interpreting it or guaranteeing it: DH 4536), and widen the infallible teaching authority of the pope and the ordinary magisterium to encompass "definitive" teachings from the secondary doctrinal sphere, even when the formal designation of such teachings does not go beyond their actual presentation, so that their link to the primary object is not in fact made explicit (second addition to the Profession of Faith).

The bishops possess infallibility only in unity with and under the pope (*communio hierarchica*), either when they assemble in council and address the universal church as teachers and judges, or in the daily exercise of their teaching office when they authoritatively and definitively declare that a doctrine belongs to the deposit of the faith or to the exposition of this faith. Thus, a general agreement concerning a doctrine is not enough; it must be presented as "definitively binding" (*tamquam definitive tenendam,* DH 4149). The pope does not possess an "infallible" ordinary magisterium; if, however, he proclaims a doctrine with the intention to define it and meets no objection on the part of the bishops, the impression can arise that the episcopacy agrees with the contents of the doctrine and with its definitive quality, considering it to belong to their own ordinary magisterium—such a doctrine would de facto count as infallible, and the pope would only need to confirm that this was the case. In general, however, the principle is that a doctrine can be defined as "infallible" only "when this is unambiguously the case" (*manifesto constiterit,* can. 749 §3 *CIC*).

3. Systematic Theology

If the church as a whole is the sacrament that creates unity between God and human beings, as well as among human beings, precisely by reason of the proclamation of the gospel (*Lumen Gentium* 1), it requires the "inerrant charism of truth and faith" (DH 3071) to equip it for this salvific task. Only so can the church present the message of faith in an absolutely reliable manner, free from error; for if this message were to prove to be substantially in error, it would no longer be salvific. This protection is serviceable only if it is linked to concrete structures and institutions within the church, e.g., sacred scripture (*Dei Verbum* 11) and tradition (ibid. 9), elements belonging to the past that have a specific share in infallibility; and elements active in the present, viz., the *sensus fidelium* (*Lumen Gentium* 12), which gives assent to the faith, paying particular heed to academic theology (*Dei Verbum* 24), and the magisterium of pope and bishops (*Lumen Gentium* 25). Hence, in this dialogical-communal process of deciding upon and accepting the substance of faith (including the moral doctrines that give this substance life), the church shares in the prophetic preaching office of Christ.

Since the ultimate guarantor is the Holy Spirit, infallibility is not the same thing as the gift of the fullness of truth and the perfect expression of this truth: the Spirit blows where and when it wills, so that saving truth exists even outside the church (*Unitatis Redintegratio* 3; *Nostra Aetate* 2). The church remains capable of error and conditioned by history in those insights and decisions that do not essentially concern its sacramental tasks (DH 4539); consequently, the formulations of infallible judgments are capable of improvement and amendment. They remain in need of interpretation and are therefore dependent on the reception by the community of faith. Such definitions can err, where the community of faith cannot recognize the church's faith in them, or finds this faith badly or insufficiently expressed. An infallible decision always remains open to deeper insight in the further course of history; it is without error, formally speaking, but it always reflects the state of knowledge in the situation in which it was formulated. Naturally, the acknowledgment of infallibility implies no judgment about the moral or intellectual status of the subject of infallibility; it is limited to the sphere of faith.

The clearest claim to infallibility is made by church officials, with particular emphasis on the → primacy of the pope, since he is explicitly aware of his ministry to service the unity of Christendom and ensure the reliability of the faith. This service is thus the criterion for his exercise of authority; and this authority is relative in that it is subject to the faith of the universal church. Since a church office-holder does not possess special illuminations and sources of knowledge, he may do nothing other than explain the faith of the church in an obligatory manner which remains faithful to tradition (*Dei Verbum* 10). The structure of this authority is conservative (not creative), limited to responding precisely to specific circumstances where the substance of the faith is at risk. This is why the magisterium must employ all available means to discern what the faith of the church actually is.

In this context, papal infallibility has a representative necessity as the final decisive authority within the unity of the one church and of the magisterium, a unity articulated in various structures. "In 'personal' concreteness, the pope represents nothing other than the 'universal' inerrancy of the church, which the bishops embody together with him in a 'collegial' fashion" (Kehl 365). This cannot be done by making one decision after another in response to daily events; it must be thought of as an emergency regulation designed to meet grave threats to the unity and faith of the church (DH 3115f.), and the highest authority must act on behalf of the whole community of faith—i.e., it is not the action of the pope as a private theologian, as patriarch of the West, primate of Italy, or bishop of Rome, nor addressing only individual persons and groups in the church. This is why the infallibility of the pope cannot be linked to juridical conditions but is valid *ex sese, non autem ex consensu ecclesiae* ("of itself, not because of consent on the part of the church," DH 3074: this is directed against the Gallican thesis that would accord legal validity to papal decision on the basis of subsequent ratification by the college of bishops). This does not, however, affect the pope's obligation to agree with the faith of the entire church—this is the epistemological basis of his decision.

The papal right to make obligatory decisions finds its response in the obedience of the faithful. If the pope claims that his decisions are put forward infallibly, the obedience is expressed in the *fides divina* (giving assent to the word of God) *et catholica* (through the testimony of the church: DH 3011). Assent to doctrines from the secondary sphere is based on the doctrine of the infallibility

of the church and the belief that the Holy Spirit assists the magisterium in a particular manner (commentary on *Ad tuendam fidem* by the Congregation for the Doctrine of the Faith); such doctrines are *de fide tenendae.* According to can. 750 §2, inserted in the *CIC* in 1998, one who "rejects" such propositions, which are to be held in a definitive manner, "opposes . . . the doctrine of the Catholic church." Nevertheless, obedience cannot be unconditional, since even infallible decisions have a conditional character: "Where there is no unanimity in the universal church, nor a clear testimony in the sources, a binding decision is not possible. If such a decision were to be taken, its formal conditions would not exist, and one would therefore have to question whether it was legitimate." This question makes the right to "criticize papal utterances . . . both possible and necessary" (Ratzinger 144).

■ **Bibliography:** W. Kern, H. J. Pottmeyer, and M. Seckler, eds., *Handbuch der Fundamentaltheologie* (Freiburg, 1988) 4:153-78; J. Ratzinger, *Das neue Volk Gottes* (Düsseldorf, 1969); H. Küng, *Unfehlbar? Eine Anfrage* (Zurich, 1970); B. Tierney, *Origins of Papal Infallibility 1150-1350* (Leiden, 1974); F. X. Bantle, *Unfehlbarkeit der Kirche in Aufklärung und Romantik* (Freiburg, 1976); G. Thils, *Primauté et infaillibilité du Pontife Romain à Vatican I* (Louvain, 1980); U. Horst, *Unfehlbarkeit und Geschichte* (Mainz, 1982); F. A. Sullivan, *Magisterium* (Dublin, 1983); J. R. Dionne, *The Papacy and the Church* (New York, 1987); P. Granfield, *The Limits of the Papacy* (New York, 1987); M. O'Gara, *Triumph in Defeat: Infallibility, Vatican I, and the French Minority Bishops* (Washington, D.C., 1988); K. Schatz, *Der päpstliche Primat* (Würzburg, 1990); G. Thils and T. Schneider, *Glaubensbekenntnis und Treueeid* (Mainz, 1990); M. Kehl, *Die Kirche* (Würzburg, 1992); J. P. Boyle, *Church Teaching Authority* (London, 1994); L. J. Welch, "The Infallibility of the Ordinary Magisterium: A Critique of Some Recent Observations," *Heythrop Journal* 39 (1998) 18-36; G. Calabrese, "L'infallibilità del Papa," *Ricerche teologiche* 10 (1999) 209-54; P. Knauer, "Nicht unfehlbare Glaubenlehre, aber doch definitive kirchliche Lehre?," *Zeitschrift für katholische Theologie* 122 (2000) 60-74.

WOLFGANG BEINERT

Insignia, Papal. These are special versions of the episcopal insignia, including the papal throne, the → tiara, the papal crosier (a ferrule that is not curved), the → fisherman's ring (*anulus piscatoris),* and special papal vestments.

BRUNO STEIMER

Institutes, Pontifical. These centers of teaching and research are either independent or attached to ecclesiastical academic institutions.

1. *Biblical Institute (Pontificio Istituto Biblico,* "Biblicum")

It was founded by Pius X (May 7, 1909) to give worldwide impetus to Catholic biblical scholarship in the face of the progress made by Protestant exegesis. It was entrusted to the guidance of the Jesuits under Leopold Fonck. A branch was founded in Jerusalem on July 1, 1927; in the academic year 1932-1933, a faculty for Middle Eastern Studies was erected in addition to the biblical faculty. As a result of the Second Vatican Council (Constitution *Dei Verbum,* 1965), the number of students rose by almost 100 percent (200 in 1959; 380 students from all parts of the world in 1969). In keeping with the Apostolic Constitution *Sapientia christiana* (April 15, 1979), special emphasis is laid on teaching the biblical languages and auxiliary sciences (history of the biblical period, archaeology, etc.). The two faculties have the right to confer all academic degrees; between 1909 and 2000, more than 6,500 students have successfully completed biblical studies at the university, which is immediately responsible to the pope (bachelor's degree, licentiate, doctorate, *laurea* [corresponding to the German *Habilitation*]). The international fame of the professors has increased over the years: Augustin Bea (1881-1968), Stanislas Lyonnet (1902-1968), Max Zerwick (1901-1975), Carlo Martini (born 1929, appointed archbishop of Milan in 1979), Ignace de la Potterie, Albert Vanhoye.

The Biblical Institute publishes the periodicals *Biblica* (1920–), *Verbum Domini* (1921–), and *Orientalia* (1920-30; new series, 1932–). The *Elenchus Bibliographicus Biblicus* (1920–; from 1984, *Elenchus of Biblical Bibliography*) by Peter Nober (1912-80) and Robert North has particular scholarly importance.

■ **Bibliography:** *Acta Pontificii Instituti Biblici* (Rome, 1909f.); A. Bea, *Pontificii Instituti Biblici prima quinque lustra* (Rome, 1934); "75° anniversario della fondazione del Pontificio Istituto Biblico," *Biblica* 65 (1984) 429-37; G. Martina, "A novant'anni dalla fondazione del Pontificio Istituto Biblico," *AHP* 37 (1999) 129-60; *AnPont* (2000) 1835.

HUBERT RITT

2. *Oriental Institute (Pontificio Istituto Orientale)*

This was founded by Benedict XV (October 15, 1917) as an institute for the advanced study of ancient Near Eastern Christianity; it had the same goal as the Congregation for the Eastern Churches, which the same pope founded. It was given the faculty of conferring academic degrees in 1920. In 1922, Pius XI entrusted it to the Jesuit order, first at the seat of the Pontifical Biblical Institute (see above), and from 1926 independently in its present seat (Piazza Santa Maria Maggiore). The first Jesuit to serve as rector was Bishop Michel-Joseph d'Herbigny. Pius XI was a great benefactor of the unique library collection; he supported Cyrille Korolevsky and Eugène Tisserant on their journeys to purchase books (1923-1924). The faculty of oriental (Eastern) canon law was erected in 1971.

Publications: *Orientalia Christiana,* separated in 1935 into *Orientalia Christiana Periodica* and *Orientalia Christiana Analecta;* also the series *Kanonika* (1992–). Important professors include the following. Theology: Martin Jugie, Bernhard Schultze, Theophilus Spačil, Georges Dejaifve; liturgy: Alfons Raes; spirituality: Irénée Hausherr; canon law: Emil Herman; Christian archaeology: Guillaume de Jerphanion; Syriac studies: Ignacio Ortiz de Urbina; the edition of the Acts of the Council of Florence (monographs: Georg Hofmann, Joseph Gill, Johannes Krajcar, Wilhelm de Vries).

■ **Bibliography:** *DHGE* 25:1333-36; *Orientalia Christiana Periodica* 33 (1967) 5-46 (C. Korolevskij), 303-50 (A. Raes); E. Farrugia, ed., *The Pontifical Oriental Institute: The First Seventy-five Years 1917-92* (Rome, 1993); R. Taft and J. L. Dugan, eds., *Il 75° anniversario del Pontificio Istituto Orientale: Atti delle celebrazioni guibilari 15-17 ottobre 1992,* Orientalia Christiana Analecta 244 (Rome, 1994); V. Poggi, *I primi professori del PIO,* Orientalia Christiana Analecta 251 (Rome, 1996) 217-44; V. Poggi, *Per la storia del Pontificio Istituto Orientale,* Orientalia Christiana Analecta 263 (Rome, 2000); *AnPont* (2000) 1835.

VINCENZO POGGI

3. *Missionary Institute (Pontificio Istituto Missioni Estere, P.I.M.E.)*

This was founded in 1926 by uniting the Missionary Institutes of Milan (founded by Msgr. Angelo Ramazzotti and erected in 1850 by the bishops of Lombardy under the name Lombard Seminary for Foreign Missions) and Rome (founded in 1871 by

Msgr. Pietro Avanzini and canonically erected in 1874 by Pius IX under the name Pontifical Seminary of the Holy Apostles Peter and Paul for Foreign Missions). Both of these institutes had the same goal, viz., the preparation of diocesan priests to be sent out to the missions, and they were under the authority of the Sacred Congregation of Propaganda. The Milan institute also accepted laymen, and the secular priests remained incardinated in their own dioceses.

The missionaries from Milan worked initially in Melanesia and Micronesia, where Bl. John Mazzucconi was martyred in 1855 on Woodlark Island; later they worked in India, Bengal, Hong Kong, Burma, and China. The missionaries from Rome evangelized southern Shensi in China, where Bl. Alberic Crescitelli suffered martyrdom in 1900; many of them went to local churches which already existed in America, Australia, and Europe, in order to assist where there was a shortage of priests. After the fusion in 1926, the P.I.M.E. widened its apostolic activities to embrace Africa, Brazil, and countries in Asia. At the present day, it works in fifteen nations.

Today, the P.I.M.E. is a Society of Apostolic Life with the goal of missionary work in accordance with *Ad Gentes* and *Redemptoris missio*. Its members are priests and laymen who bind themselves by a promise to work as missionaries for the whole of their lives. Priests and laymen who commit themselves for a specific period to work as missionaries are "associate" members of P.I.M.E. The institute is international. It has a long tradition of activity in the cultural field and in giving new impetus to missionary work; here, Paolo Manna, founder of the Unione Missionaria del Clero, and Giovanni Battista Tragella, historian of the missions, deserve special mention.

■ Bibliography: G. B. Tragella, *Le Missioni Estere di Milano nel quadro degli avvenimenti contemporanei,* 3 vols. (P.I.M.E. Milan, 1950-1963); C. Suigo, *Pio IX e la fondazione del primo Istituto missionario italiano* (P.I.M.E. Rome, 1978); P. Gheddo, *PIME, una proposta per la missione* (Bologna, 1989); *AnPont* (2000) 1570f.

DOMENICO COLOMBO

4. *Pontifical Institute of Mediaeval Studies*
This has its seat on the campus of St. Michael's College at the University of Toronto. It was originally founded in 1929 as the Institute of Mediaeval Studies by Etienne Gilson, Gerard Phelan, and Henry Carr, C.S.B., and was canonically erected as a pontifical institute by Pius XII on October 18, 1939. As an institute of pontifical right, it confers the academic degrees of licentiate (MSL) and doctorate (MSD) in medieval studies. Its library, with 100,000 volumes, is one of the most prominent collections in its field in North America. With around two hundred publications from all areas of medieval research, the publishing house of the Institute is the second largest university press in Canada. Its publication *Mediaeval Studies* appears annually.

STEPHEN D. DUMONT

5. *Other Institutes*
The *Annuario Pontificio* for 2000 lists the following additional institutes: (a) Pontificio Istituto di Musica Sacra (Rome, founded 1911); (b) Pontificio Istituto di Archeologia Cristiana (Rome, founded 1925); (c) Pontificio Istituto di Spiritualità "Teresianum" (Rome, founded 1935); (d) Pontificio Istituto di Studi Arabi e d'Islamistica (Rome, founded 1960); (e) Pontificio Istituto Superiore di Latinità (Rome, founded 1964); (f) Pontificio Istituto "Regina Mundi" (Rome, founded 1970); (g) Pontifical Institute of Theology and Philosophy (Alwaye in India, founded 1972); (h) Pontifical Oriental Institute of Religious Studies (Kottayam in India, founded 1982); (i) Pontificio Istituto "Giovanni Paolo II" per Studi su Matrimonio e Famiglia (Rome, founded 1982); (j) St. Peter's Pontifical Institute (Bangalore in India, founded 1985).

BRUNO STEIMER

International Theological Commission. This commission, attached to the Congregation for the Doctrine of the Faith, was set up by Paul VI in 1969 on the basis of a proposal made at the Synod of Bishops in 1967. The final version of the statutes is dated August 6, 1982 (Motu proprio *Tredecim anni iam: AAS* 74 [1982] 1201-5; art. 55 of the Apostolic Constitution *Pastor Bonus,* June 28, 1988: *AAS* 80 [1988] 841-912).

The task of the International Theological Commission is to investigate doctrinal questions of special importance, as well as questions that present new aspects, thus aiding the church's magisterium, in particular the Congregation for the Doctrine of the Faith, whose cardinal prefect is president of the Commission. The members, numbering thirty at most, should be drawn from various theological schools and nations. The commission has a secretary, appointed by the pope; his name is proposed by the president after consulting the members. A plenary meeting should be held at least once a year, but it is also possible to consult the members in writing only. The International Theological Commission is directed to discuss specific questions. Serious structural deficiencies were improved by the new ordering in 1982, but the International Theological Commission should have a representative president chosen by the members from among their own ranks. It must be able to decide for itself which questions to discuss.

■ Bibliography: *VATL* 779; *AnPont* (2000) 1361f. 1979.

HERIBERT SCHMITZ

Keys, Power of the.

1. *History.*—2. *Systematic Theology.*

1. *History*

The "power of the keys" (Latin *potestas clavium* or *claves*—parallel: *potestas ligandi et solvendi,* the "power to bind and loose") is a metaphor for the authority in spiritual matters exercised on various levels and by various office-holders in the church. It derives from the classical and biblical idea of realms in the next world (heaven and hell) which are closed per se, but are made accessible by an authoritative holder of keys. According to Rev. 1:14, this is Christ himself, the promised Messiah in the dynasty of David, who held the keys (3:7f.; cf. Isa. 22:22). In Matt. 16:19, Christ entrusts to Peter "the keys of the kingdom of heaven" and the authority to bind and loose, which he also entrusts to the other disciples (Matt. 18:18). This means that Peter not only guards the entrance to the kingdom of God as the "heavenly porter," but can also regulate entry. In Luke 11:52, Jesus speaks of the "keys of knowledge," but it is unclear whether this is an objective genitive (i.e., the keys which give access to knowledge) or a subjective genitive (i.e., knowledge is itself a key). In the course of the history of the church and theology, the metaphor of "power of the keys" was employed in the development of theological reflection on the spiritual authority that exists in the community of faith: sacramental authority (penance and indulgences), judicial competence (excommunication), author-

ity to teach and govern (office), and the mutual relations of the faithful ("brotherly correction").

(a) *In the patristic period.* Since Matt. 16:19 was initially interpreted on the basis of John 20:23, the power of the keys was understood as the power to forgive sins, entrusted to spiritual persons (Augustine, *Treatise on John* 50.12; 121.4; 124.5; *Sermon* 295.2f.). This led to a tension between the spiritual and the judicial elements, on which the fathers often comment (e.g., Origen, *Commentary on Matthew* 12.14; Jerome, *Commentary on Matthew* 16.19; Ambrose, *De paenitentia* 7.33). Tertullian asserted that only those who possess the Spirit have the power of the keys (*De pudicitia* 21.9f.); Cyprian's response (*Ep.* 33.1), which concentrates the power of the keys on the bishop and his presbyters, won universal acceptance. The "power of the keys" now covers both sacramental and nonsacramental authority, and it finds its main synthesis from the fourth century onward in the Petrine prerogative of the pope, who now understands himself as the direct successor of Peter and hence also of Peter's power of the keys. (The first pope to make this claim was Stephen I: see Cyprian, *Ep.* 75.17.) The explicit "document of legitimation" for the interpretation of the power of the keys as the primatial plenitude of authority is the affirmation in the pseudepigraphical *Letter of Clement to James* that when Peter handed over the office of Roman bishop to Clement, he also gave him the authority mentioned in Matt. 16:18ff. Leo I interprets the power of the keys as the pastoral authority which reveals Christ's salvific working in the Petrine representation (*Ep.* 10; *Sermones* 4.3).

(b) *In the Middle Ages.* The lines laid down in the patristic period are developed further. (1) The power of the keys is understood as the judicial authority exercised in the sacrament of penance (Peter Lombard, *Sentences* 4.18). The doctrine elaborated by Thomas Aquinas (*Summa theologiae* III 17ff.) is received and defined by the Council of Trent: when they absolve, bishops and priests exercise a *potestas* (DH 1670, 1703). In order that the power of the keys may be exercised, a specific knowledge (*discretio,* with reference to Luke 11:52) of the individual sinful acts is required (cf. Gratian, *Decretum* I, *distinctio* 22.2: this is why there are *two* keys). Medieval theologians disagreed about whether the power of the keys was declaratory and made God's forgiveness manifest (as early scholasticism held), or shared in this act of forgiveness as its sacramental instrument (as Thomas held). John Duns Scotus's theory of the two paths of forgiveness (sacramental, and by means of perfect contrition outside the sacrament) called the universality of the power of the keys into question. (2) As the theology of the papal office developed, the power of the keys came to embody the "fullness of power" (*plenitudo potestatis*) enjoyed by the Roman bishop in the universal church. He comes to be seen as the author of all forms of power of the keys, including the authority (from the eleventh century on) to depose sinful rulers and to absolve their subjects from their oath of loyalty (cf. Gregory VII's verdict of deposition against Henry IV in 1076). Theologians in the fourteenth century discussed whether this "world monarchy" (the term used by Franciscus de Maironis) is genuinely derived from the biblical power of the keys.

(c) *In the modern period.* During the Reformation, the power of the keys in both its forms played an important role in the theological debate. For Luther, the power of the keys is a mark of the church, together with baptism and the Lord's Supper: the keys are "office and power" (*officium et potestas*) bestowed by Christ for the forgiveness of all sins, even secret sins (Schmalkald Articles III 7). According to Philip Melanchthon, they are bestowed on all the members of the church (*De potestate papae*). The Council of Trent confirmed the traditional Catholic teaching (see above) and laid special emphasis on the right of those who held the power of the keys to "bind," in virtue of their authority (DH 1692, 1715). Neoscholasticism understood the power of the keys as the unlimited papal authority in legislation, government, and jurisdiction, which includes the power to forgive sins (cf. D. Palmieri, *De Romano Pontifice* [Rome, 1891]). The metaphor has lost much of its significance since the nineteenth century; it played no role in the Second Vatican Council, and it is mentioned only once in passing in the 1983 Code (can. 988 §1, in the context of penance).

2. Systematic Theology

Although the theological concept of the power of the keys is virtually absent from handbooks of canon law—as was the case well into the nineteenth century—the problems to which it once referred have lost nothing of their theological significance. These include the ecclesial constitution and offices, the relationship between the authority of the primacy and of the episcopate, the competence of all members of the church and their right to collaboration in the fellowship of faith, the sacramental intercession of the church in the work of salvation, church order and discipline, procedures by which doctrine is defined, and disciplinary practice in matters of doctrine (procedures when theologians are accused of doctrinal error).

We may make the following affirmation about the aspects of the ecclesial constitution to which this term refers: the "power of the keys" is an *analogous* concept which reminds us that Christ is the only one who truly has the right to exercise this power. This means, first, that all authority which is exercised in the church is only secondary: it always remains linked to the primary bearer of the keys (i.e., Christ). Provided that it does remain so linked, however, it possesses ecclesiological legitimacy de facto. Second, the members of the church share in the power of the keys to the extent that this is necessary, on the basis of this link to Christ; hence, in certain circumstances, those who are not office-bearers may have this power, in order to impart spiritual consolation. Third, when this power is employed, its goal must be identical with the goal of Christ's working: i.e., it must aim at giving access to God and accomplishing the salvation of human beings, even when it "binds." This goal and the necessity of the official institutional character of the church dictate the necessity and the extent of the power of the keys.

■ **Bibliography:** E. Fahlbusch et al., eds., *Evangelisches Kirchenlexikon* (3rd ed. Göttingen, 1996) 4:81ff.; L. Hödl, *Die Geschichte der scholastischen Literatur und Theologie der Schlüsselgewalt* (Marburg, 1960); H. von Campenhausen, *Kirchliches Amt und geistliche Vollmacht* (2nd ed. Tübingen, 1963); B. Tierney, *Origins of Papal Infallibility* (Leiden, 1972); S. E. Hansen, "Forgiving and Retaining Sin: A Study of the Text of John 20:23," *Horizons in Biblical Theology* 19 (1997) 24-32.

WOLFGANG BEINERT

Lateran

1. Basilica.—2. Baptistery.—3. City Palace.

The area in southeast Rome by the Aurelian Wall was called "Lateran" after the city palaces of the Laterani, a noble Roman family, which stood here until the late fourth century.

1. The *basilica* of St. John Lateran, "mother and head of all churches" (*mater et caput omnium ecclesiarum*), is the episcopal cathedral of the pope and Christendom's highest-ranking patriarchal basilica. The name *basilica Lateranensis* (e.g., Jerome, *Ep.* 77.4) derives from its location. It was the first official Christian cultic building to be founded by the Emperor Constantine as the Roman bishop's church, and it was dedicated to the Savior in thanksgiving for his victory over Maxentius at the Milvian Bridge (312). The emperor gave the Roman church the barracks of a troop of the imperial guards on the eastern edge of the Caelian Hill, so that they could build their church there (remains of the original building can be seen under the present-day church). Thus the location of the cathedral is determined above all by the imperial domains, which stretched as far as the Sessorian Palace of the emperor Severus in the eastern part of Rome. The "Constantinian basilica" (as late classical sources call it), which was retained to a large extent when the baroque architect Francesco Borromini rebuilt St. John Lateran, was a hall with five naves, surrounded by columns; as was customary in ancient cultic buildings, it was oriented from east to west, thus determining the layout of today's basilica. The Lateran basilica shows how the profane Roman basilica, a hall for assemblies, was adapted to the Christian cult; this remained the standard type for Christian church buildings.

The central nave, ninety meters in length, with an architrave colonnade of sixteen pillars on each side, is flanked to the right and to the left by two lower aisles, which are separated by arched colonnades of twenty-one pillars. A uniform paneled roof covers the two side aisles. The inner aisles have the same length as the central nave, but the shorter external aisles end in the west at a diagonal, chapel-like annex which extends beyond the alignment of the church. The transept which stands at this point today is medieval. Today's apse, built in 1886, with the choir brought forward, replaces the ancient apse, which was directly joined to the central nave. An ambulatory was constructed around this apse, probably in the fifth century, giving access to the baptistery, which Constantine had built to the northwest of the basilica. A bright light shone into the hall through the great windows in the clerestory of the nave, set above each arch which linked the pillars. There

were also windows in the apse. Windows in the external walls of the basilica gave light to the side aisles, which had no direct internal light. Thus the illumination made a distinction between the various parts of the hall. The eastern façade probably had three great windows and three portals leading into the central nave; there may have been an atrium before the entrance.

The walls, only eighty centimeters in breadth, were built in keeping with Roman architectural tradition and supported a wooden ceiling; this followed the example of the great functional buildings of the late imperial period, such as the baths. The Constantinian basilica also imitates the functional buildings of late antiquity in the structuring of the building, with a differentiated interior design expressed in the relations between the *volumina* in the external building. Unlike its exterior, the interior of the basilica was sumptuously decorated: sixteen columns of red granite with white marble capitals stood in the central nave and twenty-one green marble columns on plinths of white marble stood in the side aisles. The floor and walls were covered in bright marble. Fifth-century sources speak of murals on the clerestory walls with typologically related scenes from the Old Testament and the New. In this way, the Constantinian basilica continued the custom of luxurious decoration of the great buildings of the imperial and late-classical periods. The splendid interior also included gilded beams on the open ceiling, or gilded coffered ceilings. The crown of the apse was decorated by a golden mosaic, perhaps initially without pictorial motifs; these probably did not exist before the renovation of the mosaic by the military commander Flavius Felix in 428-430. One can still recognize the basic classical substance (the throne of Christ, the victorious cross, jubilant apostles), even after medieval renovations (under Leo III [796-816] and by Iacopo Torriti and Camerino in 1288-94), in the mosaic which was repositioned in the new apse in 1884-1886.

The bases, shafts, and capitals of the Constantinian church were taken from older buildings of the imperial period; these so-called spoils were placed in pairs, following the alternation of the different types of capital, at an angle to the longitudinal axis of the central nave. The classical principle of form, the traditional arrangement of equally important elements in the colonnade, is

The Lateran in the Thirteenth Century

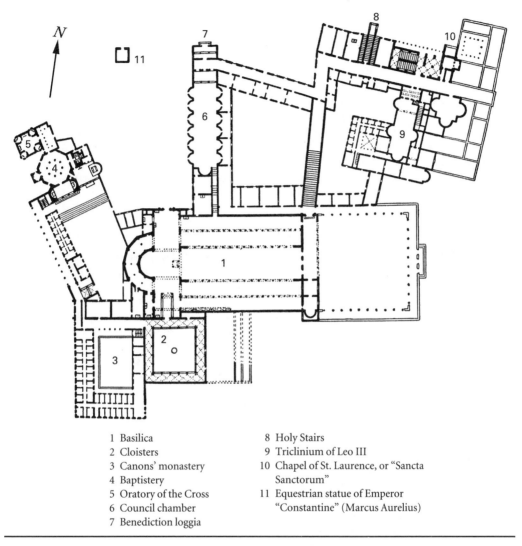

1 Basilica
2 Cloisters
3 Canons' monastery
4 Baptistery
5 Oratory of the Cross
6 Council chamber
7 Benediction loggia

8 Holy Stairs
9 Triclinium of Leo III
10 Chapel of St. Laurence, or "Sancta Sanctorum"
11 Equestrian statue of Emperor "Constantine" (Marcus Aurelius)

superseded in the Christian basilica by an arrangement that accentuates particular elements. Barricades in the central nave cleared a path about three meters in breadth for the solemn liturgical entrance and exit of the bishop: thus, the basilica offered the monumental space for the solemn liturgy which developed by means of borrowings from the forms of state and imperial representation. Correspondingly, the *presbyterium* occupies almost one-fifth of the building and is given special emphasis by the chapel-like annexes at the west end. This is where the golden incense stands donated by Constantine stood, as well as the silver *fastigium*, a monumental gabled construction

with statues of Christ, the apostles, and angels, which separated the *presbyterium* from the central nave. Four bronze columns and a gilded bronze capital from the imperial period, which belonged to this *fastigium*, were included in the altar of the Blessed Sacrament which Clement VIII (1592-1605) built in the first transept. In the diagonal chapels at the edge of the space of the congregation, seven silver altars donated by Constantine were used for the offertory rite.

The basilica was often damaged by earthquakes and fires and then restored, above all by Leo the Great in the mid-fifth century, Hadrian I (eighth century), Sergius III (905), and Clement V (1308).

In 1291, Nicholas IV erected a transept in the basilica, on the model of → St. Peter's. According to Francesco Petrarca, the building was without a roof from 1362 to 1369; it was restored by Urban V (1362-1370). Between 1370 and 1378, Gregory XI built a façade before the northern transept; this was completed under Pius IV (1562-1567). The gilded coffered roof, designed by Pirro Logorio, was installed under Pius IV. The basilica was restored again from 1431 to 1437 with frescoes by Gentile da Gabriano and Pisanello. In 1650, Innocent X commissioned Francesco Borromini to carry out a thorough renovation of the building. The classical pillars, some of which had already been buttressed in the Middle Ages, were clothed with double buttresses, and the green columns from the colonnades in the aisles in the Constantinian basilica were moved into the niches of these buttresses. The façade we see today was erected in 1735 under Clement XII. The bronze doors of the central nave come from the Curia in the Roman Forum.

2. The Constantinian *baptistery* was restored by Sixtus II (432-440). In the ambulatory of this octagonal building, which is still standing today, there are eight columns of porphyry with capitals taken from other buildings; these columns bear the clerestory. In the vestibule, which has two apses, there are remains of the ancient marble wall paneling and an apse mosaic with entwined vines (green and gold on a blue background). Pope Hilary (461-468) added the chapels of John the Evangelist (with a fifth-century mosaic in the vault and bronze doors from 1196) and John the Baptist (with ancient bronze doors and columns of porphyry). In 640, John IV built the chapel of St. Venantius, which has mosaics from the seventh century.

3. The idea that Constantine gave the Roman bishop the *city palace* of his wife Faustina is based on a misinterpretation of a passage in Optatus of Milevis (*Contra Parmenianum* 1.21). Archaeological criteria do not permit the identification of the ancient city palaces that have been uncovered in this region of Rome with the bishop's palace. The *patriarchium* north of the basilica is not mentioned before the early Middle Ages, and its ruins are no earlier than that period: at the end of the eighth century, Leo III erected reception halls and

the great *triclinium*, sixty-eight meters in length. Remains are found in and under the Scala Sancta (formerly the palace chapel) to the north of the present-day palace; the mosaic depicting Christ and apostles, Charlemagne and Christ, and Pope Sylvester and Constantine is now on the south façade. From the ninth century onward, the palace was extended to include buildings with various functions, on the model of the imperial palaces in Constantinople. During the exile in Avignon (1305-1376), both the palace and the basilica burned down. The palace was demolished by Sixtus V in 1586 and was rebuilt by Domenico Fontana on the model of the Palazzo Farnese; this work was completed in 1598. Since the popes moved into the Vatican in 1377, the palace has been the home of canons (from 1603), then a hospital (from 1623), papal museums (from 1844), and the vicariate of the diocese of Rome (from 1967).

■ **Bibliography:** *VATL* 440f., 665-70; P. Lauer, *Le palais du Latran* (Paris, 1911); W. Buchowiecki, *Handbuch der Kirchen Roms* (Wiesbaden, 1967) 1:61-88; E. Nash, "Convenerunt in domum Faustae in Laterano S. Optati Milevitani," *RQ* 71 (1976) 1-21; J. Wilpert and W. N. Schumacher, *Die römischen Mosaiken der kirchlichen Bauten vom IV.-XIII. Jahrhundert* (Freiburg, 1976) 19-30, 38, 45, 91-95 (illustrations 25-27), 321 (illustrations 80-81); R. Krautheimer et al., *Corpus Basilicarum Christianarum Romae* (Vatican City, 1977) 5:1-92; H. Brandenburg, *Roms frühchristliche Basiliken des 4. Jahrhunderts* (Munich, 1979) 22-54; R. Krautheimer, *Rom* (Munich, 1987); C. Pietrangeli, *Il Laterano* (Frankfurt, 1989); V. Santa Maria Scrinari, *Il Laterano imperiale, I: Dalle Aedes Laterani alla Domus Faustae* (Vatican City, 1991); H. Brandenburg, "Die konstantinischen Kirchen in Rom," in *Mousikos anēr*, Festschrift for M. Wegner (Bonn, 1992) 33-39; F. Lombardi, *Chiese, Conventi, Chiostri: Inventario* (Rome, 1993) 38f.; P. Liverani, "Note di topografia lateranense," *Bolletino della Commissione Archeologica Comunale di Roma* 95 (1993) 143-53; S. de Blaauw, *Cultus et Decor* (Vatican City, 1994) 1:110-331; H. Brandenburg, "Kirchenbau und Liturgie," in *Divitiae Aegypti,* Festschrift for M. Krause (Wiesbaden, 1995) 36-43; idem, in J. Poeschke, *Antike Spolien in der Architektur des Mittelalters* (Munich, 1996) 18f.; P. Liverani, "Dalle aedes Laterani al patriarchio Lateranense," *Rivista di archeologia cristiana* 75 (1999) 521-49.

HUGO BRANDENBURG

Lateran Treaties. These were concluded on February 11, 1929, between the → Holy See and Italy, and ended the Roman Question, which had arisen when the → papal states ceased to exist in 1870. The basis of the negotiations was worked out in 1919, and the substance of the Lateran Treaties was elaborated between 1926 and 1929. Three elements were involved.

First, the state treaty founded the state of Vatican City (→ Vatican State), which serves to guarantee the pope the independence of his pastoral ministry. This treaty acknowledged the sovereignty of the Holy See in the international sphere, confirmed the Catholic religion as the religion of the Italian state, and gave Rome the title of capital of Italy.

Second, the concordat regulated the relationships between church and state, guaranteeing the free exercise of spiritual authority, state protection of Christian marriage and religious communities, and the position and payment of the clergy.

Third, the financial agreement gave the Holy See 750 million lire in cash and 1 billion lire in state bonds in compensation for the loss of the papal states and as the basis of the Holy See's own economic activity.

A concordat revised the Lateran Treaties in 1984. This document established the legitimacy of religious pluralism and ordered anew the contributions made by the state to priests and to ecclesiastical institutions.

■ **Primary Sources:** *AAS* 21 (1929) 209-25, 77 (1985) 521-78; F. Pacelli, *Diario della Conciliazione* (Vatican City, 1959).

■ **Bibliography:** P. Scoppola, *La Chiesa e il fascismo* (2nd ed. Bari, 1971); G. Spadolini, *La questione del Concordato* (Florence, 1976); L. Carlen, "50 Jahre Lateranverträge," *Civitas* 34 (1978-79) 273-80; K. Repgen, "Pius XI. und das faschistische Italien," in W. Pöls, ed., *Staat und Gesellschaft im politischen Wandel* (Stuttgart, 1979) 331-59; M. Morgante, *Il Concordato tra la Santa Sede e la Repubblica Italiana* (Milan, 1988).

HARTMUT BENZ

Legations, Papal.

1. History.—2. Canon Law.

1. *History*

From among the world's religions, only the Christian church—more specifically the Roman Catholic Church—developed a system of legations. This preceded the development of a similar system between states; it accompanied the growth of the jurisdictional primacy of the bishop of Rome, and its primary significance initially related to the interior life of the church, although the bishops of Rome had their legates at the imperial court in Constantinople or at the residence of the exarch in Ravenna as early as the fifth to the seventh centuries. These were called apocrisiaries (*apocrisiarii,* also *responsales* or *responsores,* since it was their duty to transmit "answers").

From the fourth century onward, legates *a latere* (literally, "from the side" of the bishop of Rome), whose commission was limited, represented his interests at the synods of local churches and at councils.

A third form of church legates in the early period is seen in the apostolic vicar, who governed a large ecclesiastical area as supermetropolitan, with the bishop of Rome's authority: in the early Middle Ages this developed into the missionary legate (e.g., St. Augustine, the apostle to England; Boniface; Willibrord; Ansgar; etc.), whose mission in non-Christian territories was usually carried out from an established see, with the help of missionaries whom they commissioned. This type of legate was sometimes continued in the *legatus natus.* These were usually primates or bishops of preeminent sees (Canterbury, Gnesen, Cologne, Lund, Rheims, Salzburg, York; at certain periods also Mainz, Trier, Toledo alternating with Tarragona, Pisa [for Corsica], Torres [for Sardinia and Corsica], as well as the Latin patriarchs of Constantinople, Antioch, and Jerusalem). The designation as *legatus natus,* to which the king of Hungary was also entitled, was purely honorific; the Norman princes in southern Italy and later the Spanish kings claimed this title. The legal texts in the decretals distinguish between *legati a latere* and *legati nati,* who were always bishops. We also find the *legatus missus,* an envoy sent by the Holy See to carry out specific tasks. Often he was a simple priest. Since the law enshrined in the decretals gave legates an ordinary vicarious authority ("titulus de officio legati": X 1.30 and VI 1.15), they intervened in all the areas where the bishop had supreme authority (the so-called "concurrent jurisdiction").

During the Western Schism, the legates once again carried out a variety of functions, since both popes and antipopes sent them as envoys to secular rulers. From the mid-fifteenth century onward, commercial-political interests—especially those of the republic of Venice—led to the establishment of permanent legations between the city-states and small independent territories in Italy; the growth of national states favored the same development in western Europe at this period. The popes were slow to replace their old and well-proven system of legates with the new system of permanent legations. The new kind of permanent papal envoys were called → nuncios (*nuntii*), and the representative legation itself was designated a "nunciature." It is a matter of dispute which papal legation first deserves this name, that in Spain (from 1450) or that in Venice (from 1500). Nor is it clear whether the popes followed the example of the other Italian states here, or whether the so-called *collectores* (collectors of papal dues from the beginning of the thirteenth century on) were a preliminary form of nuncio; it is at any rate clear that diplomatic tasks were seldom entrusted to the *collectores*.

The popes supported permanent nunciatures in numerous lands before the Council of Trent, which clarified a number of questions relating to concurrent jurisdiction, although the measures taken by the council seem vitiated at the outset by the declaration that bishops were delegates of the pope. The council also decreed that the papal legates should intervene in the jurisdiction of the local bishop only in exceptional, urgent cases. Trent laid down the tasks of the nuncio within the church (informing the curia; collaborating in investigating the suitability of candidates for the episcopal office), and this norm is still valid today. In 1572, there were papal legations in Florence, Naples, Turin, and Venice, as well as in France, Portugal, and Spain; there were also representatives at the imperial court and in Poland. Shortly after this date, as the Counter-Reformation progressed, further nunciatures were erected in the Rhineland (Cologne), in the Alpine countries (Upper German nunciature, Graz, Lucerne) and in Brussels. The nuncios' responsibilities within the church, as set out above, led in practice to repeated conflicts in various countries about the judicial authority of the nunciature, especially in the seventeenth century, and to debates in the eighteenth century about the whole idea of papal legations (nunciature controversy in Munich, 1784-1785; Punctation of Ems, 1786).

The three kinds of legate continued to exist after nuncios were introduced, and since only these three were mentioned in the written canon

law of the period, scholars produced detailed commentaries on them. After Trent, *legati ordinarii* (most probably a development from the *legati missi*) were appointed as papal vicars to administer the districts in the papal states.

After 1560, the following ranking among the nunciatures developed: the "great" nunciatures were those in Madrid, Paris, and at the imperial court, while the others were regarded as "small" nunciatures. This had no effect on the rights of the nuncios, but it became customary for the nuncios in the "great" nunciatures to be created cardinals when their term of office expired; they were then called "pro-nuncios." (This term has been used since 1965 to designate the papal envoys in states in which they do not automatically assume the role of doyen of the diplomatic corps.) In the sixteenth century, the "internuncio" was the temporary head of a nunciature; later this term designated an envoy to an autonomous region, and it has been used since the nineteenth century for envoys in a narrower sense. In the regulations of the Congress of Vienna (1815) about diplomatic rank, legates and envoys were given the same status as the ambassadors of secular powers, and the so-called permanent status of doyen, bestowed on the nuncio in Catholic countries, was also acknowledged. Both of these regulations were confirmed by the Convention of Vienna in 1961. The *CIC* of 1917 mentions the *legatus a latere* (can. 266) and legates with the title of nuncio and internuncio (can. 267 §1; there is also an inappropriate mention of apostolic delegates in can. 267 §2). *Legati nati* are mentioned indirectly in can. 270.

■ **Bibliography:** J. Höfer and K. Rahner, eds., *Lexikon für Theologie und Kirche* (2nd ed. Freiburg, 1960) 4:766-73; W. Plöchl, *Geschichte des Kirchenrechts* (2nd ed. Vienna, 1960-70) I-III; P. Gerbore, *Formen und Stile der Diplomatie* (Reinbek, 1964); K. Walf, *Die Entwicklung des päpstlichen Gesandtschaftswesens in dem Zeitabschnitt zwischen Dekretalenrecht und Wiener Kongreß (1159-1815)* (Munich, 1966); H. E. Feine, *Kirchliche Rechtsgeschichte,* I: *Die katholische Kirche* (5th ed. Weimar, 1972); P. Blet, *Histoire de la Représentation diplomatique du St-Siège* (Vatican City, 1982).

KNUT WALF

2. *Canon Law*

In accordance with no. 9 of the conciliar decree *Christus Dominus,* Paul VI reorganized the papal legations in the Motu proprio *Sollicitudo omnium ecclesiarum* of June 24, 1969 (*AAS* 61 [1969] 473-84). The programmatic exordium to this text is a detailed presentation of the pope's care for the local churches and of the links between the pope and the bishops. The second part is the main source of cann. 362-67 (*CIC* 1983); in accordance with can. 20 and can. 6 §1 no. 3, this Motu proprio is a special law that remains in force. The primary task of the legations is their function of service within the church; the stipulations of international law enter only at a secondary stage, when the papal envoy enjoys diplomatic status. Diplomatic recognition, which is particularly important for new states, is accorded by the → Holy See through a mutual act of accreditation, both in the name of the church (can. 362) and on the basis of the status of the → Vatican state as a sovereign subject in international law.

(a) The principal *tasks within the church* are the following. The legates must report on the state of the local church; they are to support the bishops, while maintaining the independence of their authority in government; although it is explicitly stated that they are not themselves members of the episcopal conference, they must maintain close contact with this body (can. 450 §2); in accordance with can. 377 §3 and the norms laid down in *AAS* 64 (1972) 386-91, they are to direct the informative process about suitable candidates for the episcopal office; they are to bear witness to the pope's concern for the land in question and to cultivate good relationships with the other Christian communities and with non-Christian religions.

(b) Papal envoys have *diplomatic tasks* when they represent the Holy See in accord with international law. Unlike apostolic delegates and visitors, whose legation concerns only the local church, the → nuncio, pro-nuncio and internuncio (and where appropriate, also the chargé d'affaires) normally assume the office of representative vis-à-vis the state when they hand over their letter of accreditation to the head of state. Their primary duty is to foster relations between the Holy See and the governing authorities and to improve the relations between church and state through the conclusion of concordats and similar agreements, and by putting these into practice. They should consult the local bishops on these matters, and keep them informed of the state of negotiations. Art. 3 of the fundamental law of the Vatican City state (June 7, 1929) declares that the papal legates also are the diplomatic representatives of the Vatican state vis-à-vis the host state. The Holy See is represented in international organizations and participates in international conferences either as the highest governing organ of the church or in the name of the sovereign Vatican state, or else on the basis of a dual juridical status.

In the year 2000, the Holy See was represented by an apostolic nunciature in 169 states, as well as at the European Union and in fifteen other international governmental organizations and nine nongovernmental organizations.

■ **Bibliography:** Görres-Gesellschaft, ed., *Staatslexikon: Recht—Wirtschaft—Gesellschaft* (7th ed. Freiburg, 1988) 4:288ff.; K. Ganzer and H. Schmitz, *Motuproprio über die Aufgaben der Legaten des römischen Papstes,* Nachkonziliare Dokumentation 21 (Trier, 1970); M. Oliveri, *Natura e fundazioni dei Legati Pontifici nella storia e nel contesto ecclesiologico del Vaticanum II* (Turin, 1979); W. Schulz, *Leggi e disposizioni usuali dello Stato della Città del Vaticano,* 2 vols. (Rome, 1981-82); *MKCIC* cann. 362-67; *AnPont* (2000) 1399-1430, 1995f.; *New Commentary on the Code of Canon Law,* ed. J. P. Beal, J. A. Coriden, T. Green (New York, 2000) 490ff.

WINFRIED SCHULZ

Letters, Papal. From earliest times, papal letters have given expression to the popes' endeavor to exercise spiritual authority beyond the limits of the city of Rome and its environs. They are frequently a reaction to juridical and theological questions from other churches. They correspond in form to the style employed for letters in general; in time, this developed into the various kinds of papal → documents. There is no clear distinction between the simpler genres, i.e., the *litterae,* the *litterae cum filo canapis* or *litterae clausae* with a papal bull of lead from the twelfth and thirteenth centuries, and the secret letters (or briefs) validated by the fisher's seal (→ Fisherman's Ring) from the late fourteenth century onward.

Until the late Middle Ages, papal letters are seldom preserved in the archives of their recipients; mostly they are attested by the inclusion of a note of their contents or of a copy in the papal → register. Above all, however, they were collected from the late fourth century onward, so that they could serve as model juridical decisions (collections of → Decretals), or for purposes of historical and church-political documentation (examples are the *Collectio Avellana* and the *Codex Carolinus*). Formally speaking, the forgeries of Pseudo-Isidore likewise consist largely of papal letters. Only in the modern period do we find general doctrinal letters in the form of → encyclicals.

■ **Bibliography:** P. Rabikauskas, *Diplomatica Pontificia* (4th ed. Rome, 1980); G. May, *Ego N.N. Catholicae Ecclesiae Episcopus* (Berlin, 1995); T. Fren, *Papsturkunden des Mittelalters und der Neuzeit* (2nd ed. Stuttgart, 2000).

RUDOLF SCHIEFFER

Liber Censuum Ecclesiae Romanae. A collection of various texts concerning the Roman church, employing older drafts made by the apostolic chamberlain Cencio Savelli (later Honorius III) in 1192. The title comes from the list of regular payments to the Holy See. In the original manuscript, these include *inter alia* the list of exemptions for dioceses and monasteries; the *Liber de mirabilibus urbis Romae;* the *Ordo Romanus;* the ritual for the coronation of the emperor; chronicles of the popes; a list of documents issued by the Holy See. Subsequent additions show that the original and copies were in use at the curia until the time of Eugene IV.

■ **Edition:** P. Fabre and L. Duchesne, 2 vols. (Paris, 1889-1910); 3rd ed., ed. G. Mollat (Paris, 1952).

■ **Bibliography:** *LMA* 5:1941f.; *VATL* 458f.; P. Fabre, *Etude sur le Liber censuum de l'Église romaine* (Paris, 1892); V. Pfaff, "Die Einnahmen der römischen Kurie am Ende des 12. Jahrhunderts," *Vierteljahrschrift für Sozial- und Wirtschaftsgeschichte* 40 (1953) 97-118; idem, "Der Liber censuum von 1192," *Vierteljahrschrift für Sozial- und Wirtschaftsgeschichte* 44 (1957) 78-96, 105-20, 220-42, 325-51; R. Elze, "Der Liber censuum des Cencius (Codex Vaticanus latinus 8486) von 1192-1228," *Bullario dell'Archivio paleografico italiano,* new series 2-3 (1956-57) 251-70; T. Schmidt, "Die älteste Überlieferung von Cencius' Ordo Romanus," *QFIAB* 60 (1980) 511-22; T. Montecchi Palazzi, "Cencius Camerarius et la formation du Liber censuum de 1192," *Mélanges de l'Ecole Française de Rome. Moyen-âge, Temps modernes* 96 (1984) 49-93.

UTA-RENATE BLUMENTHAL

Liber Diurnus Romanorum Pontificum. This is the oldest collection of formulae (ca. 100) for papal documents. It survives in three parchment codices written in Carolingian minuscule letters (V, C, and A); the collection of canons by Deusdedit (the counselor of Gregory VII and Urban II) includes larger excerpts. There is no agreement among scholars about the date of compilation, the provenance of the text, the structure of its composition, the extent and degree to which it was actually used, and its function (as a "schoolbook" for training papal notaries or as a book of formulae for practical use).

■ **Bibliography:** *LMA* 5:1946f.; *VATL* 459f.; H. Foerster, *Liber diurnus Romanorum pontificum* (Bern, 1958); H. Zimmermann, ed., *Liber diurnus: Studien und Forschungen von L. Santifaller* (Stuttgart, 1976); H.-H. Kortüm, *Zur päpstlichen Urkundensprache im frühen Mittelalter* (Sigmaringen, 1995) 312ff.

HERBERT KALB

Liber Pontificalis. Most manuscripts transmitted this collection of biographical sketches of the popes under the designation *Gesta* or *Chronica pontificum;* since it is preceded by an exchange of letters between Damasus I and Jerome, it was often attributed by early writers to the former. The *Liber Pontificalis* (*LP*) remained a fundamental source until the end of the Middle Ages and enjoyed official character for a time. Its sections follow the principle of a stereotype construction (name of the pope, provenance, length of pontificate, legal acts, building activity, ordinations, important events of the period, death, place of burial, *sede vacante*) which intends to promote the idea of an uninterrupted succession of popes who carried out one and the same office. This made it a model for the historiography of other ecclesiastical institutions. With some pontificates, however, the influence of political propaganda (e.g., in Stephen II's conflict with the Langobards, in the case of popes who promoted church reform, or during the Western Schism) or the negative portrait of a pope (e.g., Sergius II) led to the composition of detailed and indeed partisan biographies that went far beyond the limitations of this pattern.

The *Liber Pontificalis* was not composed in one block, but was a serial compilation; in its final, fifteenth-century form, it was a historical compendium consisting of numerous sequential narratives and additions. In Louis Duchesne's view, the oldest part may have covered the period up to the pontificate of Felix IV (526-530); Theodor Mommsen held that it went as far as the beginning of the seventh century. This was the work of one author, relying for the chronography on already existing lists of popes (→ Chronography of 354 and the so-called Index). The next part covered the period up to Felix V; its authors were members of the curia, probably belonging to the papal *vestiarium*. Initially, they updated the *Liber Pontificalis* with groups of biographies; later, contemporary accounts (sometimes begun during the pontificate in question) were added to these. After the quasi-official character of the *Liber Pontificalis* had made it known throughout the whole of Western Christianity, these continuous additions ceased in the tenth century, until Pandulf, cardinal deacon under Anacletus II, took up the *Liber Pontificalis* once again and continued it, both shortening the text and inserting new sections, at least until the time of Honorius II; all that remains of this text, however, is a further redaction by Petrus Guillelmus, librarian in Saint Gilles, in 1142.

Like the *Gesta pontificum Romanorum* of Cardinal Boso, which likewise continued the *Liber Pontificalis* up to 1178, this work too was soon forgotten; but Petrus Boherius, bishop of Orvieto, took it up anew at the beginning of the Western Schism and provided it with excellent footnotes, mostly from the perspective of canon law and church politics. In addition to Boherius's work, the *Liber Pontificalis* was continued, initially up to John XXII (Codex Vallicellianus C 79), in the form of an appendix drawn from the works of Martin of Troppau and Bernard Guidoni, which had meanwhile established themselves as leading historical texts. Finally, the *Liber Pontificalis* was continued during the pontificate of Eugene IV, until the reign of Martin V, on the basis of these elaborations; some textual traditions display extensive additions. For the period from Benedict XII to Innocent VI, however, an already existing continuation of Bernard Guidoni (Codex Vaticanus latinus 2040) was employed; an independent and detailed (and partisan) account was composed only for the epoch of the Western Schism. At the end of the fifteenth century, the *Liber Pontificalis* was replaced by the papal history of Bartholomew Platina (→ Historiography), composed in keeping with humanist tastes.

■ **Edition:** T. Mommsen, *MGH: Gesta pontificum* I (Berlin, 1898); L. Duchesne and C. Vogel, *Le Liber Pontificalis*, 3 vols. (2nd ed. Paris, 1955-57); U. Prerovský, *Il Liber Pontificalis nella recensione di Pietro Guglielmo e del cardinale Pandolfo, glossario da Pietro Bohier*, 3 vols., Studia Gratiana 21-23 (Rome, 1978).

■ **Bibliography:** *LMA* 5:1946f.; *VATL* 460f.; G. Billanovich, *Gli umanisti e le cronache medioevali: Italia medioevale e umanistica* (Padua, 1958) 1:103-37; A.

Brackmann, "Der Liber Pontificalis," in idem, *Gesammelte Aufsätze* (2nd ed. Darmstadt, 1967) 382-96; O. Bertolini, *Il "Liber Pontificalis": La storiografia altomedioevale* (Spoleto, 1970) 387-455; G. Melville, "De gestis sive statutis Romanorum Pontificum," *AHP* 9 (1971) 377-400; H. Geertmann, *More veterum* (Groningen, 1975); Zimmermann *Pt*; D. M. Deliyannis, "A Biblical Model for Serial Biography: The 'Book of Kings' and the Roman 'Liber Pontificalis,'" *Revue bénédictine* 107 (1997) 15-23; P. Schreiner, "Der Liber Pontificalis und Byzanz," in *Forschungen zur Reichs-, Papst- und Landesgeschichte*, Festschrift for P. Herde (Stuttgart, 1998) 33-48.

GERT MELVILLE

List of Popes. The oldest list of Roman bishops, which may go back to Hegesippus (ca. 160), is transmitted ca. 180 by Irenaeus of Lyons (*Adversus haereses* 3.3.1-3); it ends with Eleutherus (174?-189?) and probably recalls the names of the leading bishops in the Roman church in the period before the practice of having only one bishop in a city won full acceptance in Rome, ca. 150. Hegesippus's concern is with the Roman "guarantors of the apostolic tradition and of pure doctrine" (Eusebius of Caesarea, *Historia ecclesiastica* 4.22.2f.). The list of popes used by Eusebius probably goes back to Sextus Julius Africanus. The elaboration of lists of succession into lists of bishops was the work of Christian chronographers from the third century onward, as they attempted to employ synchronizations to establish more precise dates for the pontificates (Sextus Julius Africanus, Hippolytus of Rome, and especially Eusebius); the first complete chronology of the Roman bishops is supplied by the Liberian Catalogue (in the → Chronography of 354), synchronizing the pontificates with the annals of the Roman consuls. (This work has little historical value, since the dates up to 235 are artificial.) Later lists of popes continue this work, e.g., Epiphanius of Salamis (*Adversus haereses* 27.6), Optatus of Milevis (*Contra Parmenianum Donatistam* 2.3), Jerome (*Chronicon ad annum post natum Abraham*), Augustine (*Ep.* 53.2), Prosper Tiro of Aquitaine (list of popes up to Leo I), Theodoret of Cyrus (almost complete list of popes from Marcellinus to Celestine I), and Socrates (names and dates of reigns from Damasus I). The Liberian Catalogue formed the oldest part of the → *Liber Pontificalis*. The lists of popes in manuscripts of chronicles and canon law texts in the high and late Middle Ages have not yet been systematically examined. In general, the list of popes in the *Liber Pontificalis* remained standard; the lists of popes by Martin of Troppau (†1278) and Bartholomew Platina (†1481), which were often adopted and extended, reflect the state of their own historical periods.

There has been no consensus, either in the medieval period or in modern times, about a number of popes and antipopes, nor about the two (or three) lines of popes during the Western Schism (1378-1417). Historical-critical research since the sixteenth and seventeenth centuries has brought greater certainty in many cases, but dogmatic and apologetic interpretations are not lacking even today. The medallions in the Roman basilica of St. Paul's Outside-the-Walls, first mounted in the second half of the fifth century and restored after the fire of 1823, offered a very influential list of "legitimate" popes (including the two popes of the Pisan line during the Western Schism); for example, *La Gerarchia cattolica* printed this list from 1873 to 1903. Franz Ehrle drew up a new list for the editions in 1904 and 1905, in keeping with Louis Duchesne's edition of the *Liber Pontificalis* but with dogmatically determined changes. The → *Annuario Pontificio* reproduced the list of popes from St. Paul's in its editions from 1913 to 1946. Since 1947, it has printed the list revised by Angelo Mercati ("with the corrections deemed opportune in keeping with the findings of historical science up to the present date," *AnPont* [2000] 7*), but this list remains in need of improvement based on historical-critical research.

A church historian must abandon the idea of determining precisely the number of indubitably "legitimate" popes, and this is why the popes in our list are not enumerated (1, 2, 3 . . .). Sometimes it is impossible to decide whether a particular pope should be counted among the popes, the → antipopes, or neither of these categories. The main reason for this difficulty is that, at certain periods of history, it is impossible to reach a completely unambiguous and universal agreement about the conditions of validity for the election and ordination of the bishop of Rome, or about the end of his pontificate. Many popes were installed and removed from office under irregular circumstances (sometimes by secular powers); sources about the election procedures are often scanty or one-sided. At least until Nicholas II's decree about the papal → election (1059), the decisive date for the assumption of office is that of the episcopal ordination and papal enthronement, not the date of the election as such (whatever form this may have taken).

The asterisk (*) following a name in the list of popes indicates those who should not be regarded as legitimate bishops of Rome. For the precise dates and some particular difficulties, see the articles on the individual names mentioned in this list, all of which (with the exception of a few antipopes) are included in the first part of this dictionary.

■ **Primary Sources.** *LP* 1:13-18; 2:IX-XXIII; 3 (index).

■ **Bibliography:** See the various presentations of papal history as a whole: *EC* 9:751-68; *VATL* 535-40; K. A. Fink, "Zur Beurteilung des Großen Abendländischen Schismas," *Zeitschrift für Kirchengeschichte* 73 (1962) 335-43; Zimmermann, *Pt* 211-19; H. Grotefend, *Taschenbuch der Zeitrechnung des deutschen Mittelalters und der Neuzeit* (12th ed. Hanover, 1982) 122-29; M. E. Stoller, "The Emergence of the Term Antipapa in Medieval Usage," *AHP* 23 (1985) 43-61; Borgolte; *AnPont* (2000) 7*-24*. → Papacy; → Historiography.

GEORG SCHWAIGER

The list of popes can be found at the front of this book (pp. xvii–xviii).

Mass, Papal. The solemn *Missa papalis* was distinguished from a pontifical Mass by elaborate special ceremonial, some of which came from royal courts (→ Tiara; → *Sedia Gestatoria;* prostrations; tasting of the gifts before the offertory; communion from the chalice by means of a metal *fistula* or drinking straw). After Vatican II, it took the form of a solemn pontifical Mass (cf. *Caerimoniale Episcoporum*, 1984, part II); the only specifically papal ceremonies retained were (on some occasions) the proclamation of the Gospel in Greek, and the custom of elevating the Host and the chalice in three directions.

■ **Bibliography:** *VATL* 543f.; A. Hudal, *Missa papalis* (Rome, 1925); J. Brinktrine, *Die feierliche Papstmesse* (2nd ed. Rome, 1950); V. Fantuzzi, "Celebrazioni liturgiche pontificie, radio e TV," *La civiltà cattolica* 150 (1999) 168-80; J. Castellano Cervera, "Il cammino delle celebrazioni liturgiche pontificie," *Rivista liturgica* 87 (2000) 85-102.

ANDREAS HEINZ

Names, Papal. The first popes to assume a new name on their election were those whose previous names were pagan (Mercurius = John II), politically disadvantageous (Octavianus = John XII), or vulgar (Os Porci [pig's snout] = Sergius IV). Peter was frowned upon as a papal name. From the mid-eleventh century, as greater emphasis was placed on the worldwide responsibilities of the papacy, a change of name became customary, initially to mark the contrast to the episcopal office outside Rome, which some popes from Clement II onward retained; later, in order to emphasize that they had become "new men" through their elevation to the see of Peter. It is improbable that there is any link to monks' change of name upon entering religious life. The proclamation of the papal name seems to have been initially a privilege reserved to the archdeacon. Usually the choice of name appeals to a predecessor's conduct of office and understanding of the papal role, or else a link to a previous pope (his relative or benefactor); sometimes it invokes the saint on whose feast the election took place. Since 1046, only three popes have kept their baptismal names: Julius II, Hadrian VI, and Marcellus II.

■ **Bibliography:** *LMA* 6:1686f.; *VATL* 544; R. L. Poole, *The Names and Numbers of Medieval Popes: Studies in Chronology and History* (Oxford, 1934) 156-71; F. Krämer, "Über die Anfänge und die Beweggründe der Papstnamensänderung im Mittelalter," *RQ* 51 (1956) 148-88; W. Goez, "Zur Erhebung und ersten Absetzung Papst Gregors VII.," *RQ* 63 (1968) 134-39 (the pope did not choose his own name); idem, "Papa qui et episcopus," *AHP* 8 (1970) 27-59; B.-U. Hergemöller, *Die Geschichte der Papstnamen* (Münster, 1980); M. Guerra Gomez, *Los nombres del Papa: Estudio filológico-teológico de varios nombres del Papa en los primos siglos del cristianismo* (Burgos, 1982); M. Molaroni, "Pio I e Pio II: Fortuita coincidenza di un nome?" *Studi e materiali di storia delle religioni* 65 (1999) 199-218.

WERNER GOEZ

Nepotism. (Latin *nepos*: nephew, descendant). This polemical term was applied in the seventeenth century to relatives of the pope, then for the practice of favoritism based on kinship. Today it is used in general when rulers bestow positions and advantages on those close to them. While the practice was legitimate in a society organized by family and client relationships, it became corrupt in a society that rewarded achievement and was based on abstract principles of organization. Thomas Aquinas saw it as a matter of justice that rulers looked after their own relatives (*Summa*

theologiae II-II *quaestio* 101); where candidates had qualities of equal value, it was legitimate to bestow offices on one's relatives, since they were held to be more reliable (II-II *quaestio* 63). Thus the nepotism of the late Middle Ages and the early modern period was an exercise of the ruler's sovereignty, allowing him to provide for his relatives in varying degrees; it was something normal and useful, not at all an "ulcer" that kept breaking out afresh in the course of papal and church history.

The only point of criticism concerned the threat to church property, especially when nepotism became excessive. While celibacy was intended to prevent passing on church benefices by inheritance, nepotism meant that nephews possessed informal rights; the popes' "plenitude of power" permitted them to indulge in excesses at the cost of the College of Cardinals, since they simply appealed to their supreme authority in order to ignore the prohibition of nepotism by the Council of Trent (session 25 *de reformatione* 1). On the other hand, cardinals and church chapters accepted nepotism, since they hoped that they would have a chance to benefit from it.

The critical discussion of this system began with the political and financial crisis of the papal sovereignty under Urban VIII. This led to the abolition of institutionalized nepotism with the bull *Romanum decet Pontificem* of Innocent XII (1692); only now were the cardinals willing to obligate themselves for the future not to engage in nepotism. It lived on, however, in an informal and limited manner, although it reached new and relatively excessive heights under Pius VI, Leo XIII, and once again under Pius XII.

■ **Bibliography:** *LMA* 6:1093f.; G. Leti, *Il nipotismo di Roma* (Amsterdam, 1667); (C. Sfondrato), *Nepotismus theologice expensus,* published without date or place (1692); J. Grisar, "Päpstliche Finanzen, Nepotismus und Kirchenrecht unter Urban VIII.," *Miscellanea Historiae Pontificiae* 7/14 (1943) 205-366; W. Reinhard, *Papstfinanz und Nepotismus,* 2 vols. (Stuttgart, 1974); idem, "Nepotismus," *Zeitschrift für Kirchengeschichte* 86 (1975) 145-85; A. I. Menniti, *Il tramonto della Curia nepotista. Papi nipoti e burocrazia curiale tra XVI e XVII secolo* (Rome, 1999); S. Carocci, *Il nepotismo nel medioevo* (Rome, 1999).

WOLFGANG REINHARD

Nunciature Reports. Originally a concept applied in the nineteenth century to papal diplomats' reports about the Reformation, it designates today the entire correspondence between ordinary → nuncios and extraordinary emissaries (e.g., legates; → legations, papal) and the Secretariat of State and other Roman bodies (especially the → congregations), including both the principal instruction and the jurisdictional authority given at the beginning of the mission and the final report. From the late sixteenth century onward, weekly dispatches consisting of several letters dealing with different matters were exchanged; those with greatest political importance were in code. The nunciature reports are essential sources for our knowledge of the Reformation and the post-Tridentine renewal, especially in Brussels, Graz, Cologne, and Lucerne; from the seventeenth century on, they provide information primarily about the relations between church and state. Their value as sources tends to decline between the sixteenth and nineteenth centuries, in keeping with their increase in volume. This is why there are numerous full editions of the reports from the sixteenth and early seventeenth centuries, whereas the later period is represented only by selected editions of key documents (the principal instructions) and texts dealing with specific topics, or collected chronicles.

The study and edition began when the Vatican archives were opened in 1881. Scholars divided the work in 1888, according to the nations involved, among the Prussian, later German, Historical Institute (*NBD*: Kaiser 1530-59, 1572-85, 1629ff.), the Austrian Historical Institute (Kaiser 1560-72, Graz), and the Görres Society (*NBD[G]*: originally 1585-1605, Cologne from 1584). Swiss editions have been published since 1895, and Czechoslovakian editions since 1923 (Kaiser 1592-1628); Belgian chronicles have been edited since 1924 (Brussels and Cologne). The "Nunziature d'Italia," "Acta Nuntiaturae Gallicae," and "Acta Nuntiaturae Polonae" are also important. Belgian, French, Portuguese, and Spanish scholars have continued the work into the nineteenth century. The new series *Instructiones Pontificum Romanorum* opens up a promising new path for the study of the nunciature reports of the seventeenth and eighteenth centuries: so far the principal instructions under Clement VIII, Paul V, and Gregory XV (1592-1623) have been published.

■ **Editions:** *NBD*; *NBD(G)*; A. Bues, "Acta Nuntiaturae Polonae," *Zeitschrift für Ostforschung* 41 (1992) 386-98.
■ **Bibliography:** H. Lutz et al., "Nuntiaturberichte und Nuntiaturforschung," *QFIAB* 53 (1973) 152-275, separate publication Tübingen, 1976; G. Lutz, "Die Nuntiaturberichte und ihre Editionen," in R. Elze and A. Esch, eds., *Das Deutsche Historische Institut in Rom 1888-1988* (Tübingen, 1990) 87-121, 271ff.; M. F. Feldkamp, "Die Erforschung der Kölner Nuntiatur," *AHP* 28 (1990) 201-83; A. Koller, *Kurie und Politik: Stand und Perspektiven der Nuntiaturberichtsforschung* (Tübingen, 1998).

WOLFGANG REINHARD

Nuncio → Legations, papal.

Orders, Papal. The pope bestows orders on laypersons for special merit; in the exchange of diplomatic courtesies, orders of knighthood and lesser honors are also bestowed, according to the following ranking.

1. *Order of Christ*, founded by John XXII on March 14, 1319.

2. *Order of the Golden Spur*, founded at an unknown date and renewed by Pius X on February 7, 1905. Orders 1 and 2 are bestowed only in one single class.

3. *Order of Pius* (in four classes), founded by Pius IX on June 17, 1847, reorganized by Pius XII on November 11, 1939, and December 21, 1957.

4. *Order of St. Gregory the Great* (in three classes), founded by Gregory XVI on September 1, 1831, and renewed by Pius X on February 7, 1905.

5. *Order of St. Silvester* (in three classes), founded by Gregory XVI on October 31, 1841, and renewed by Pius X on February 7, 1905. Since June 2, 1993, the Orders of Pius, Gregory, and Silvester have also been bestowed on women, in three classes: (a) Dama, (b) Dama di Commenda con Placca, and (c) Dama di Gran Croce. The lesser honors are the cross "Pro Ecclesia et Pontifice," founded by Leo XIII, and the "Benemerenti" medal for meritorious persons.

Honorary titles are bestowed on priests, according to the following ranking: (a) apostolic supernumerary protonotary, (b) honorary prelate, and (c) chaplain to His Holiness. Holders of all three titles are addressed in English as "Monsignor" (see also Pontifical → Family).

■ **Bibliography:** *VATL* 659f.; *AnPont* (2000) 1372f., 1982.

WINFRIED SCHULZ

Oriental Institute → Institutes, Pontifical.

Osservatore Romano (Italian: *L'Osservatore romano,* "The Roman Observer"). The Vatican daily newspaper for political and religious questions is directly subordinate to the Holy See (see Apostolic Constitution *Pastor Bonus,* art. 191). It began publication on July 1, 1861; after the Second World War, weekly publications began in six languages (1949 French; 1950 Italian; 1968 English; 1969 Spanish; 1970 Portuguese; 1971 German), and a monthly edition in Polish began in 1980.

■ **Bibliography:** *EC* 9:422f.; *NCE* 10:808f.; *CATH* 10:319f.; *VATL* 520ff.; D. Hansche, "Zur Geschichte des Osservatore Romano," *Communicatio Socialis* 3 (1970) 13-23, 99-109; *L'Attività della Santa Sede nel 1996* (Vatican City, 1997) 1064-69; *AnPont* (2000) 1381f., 1985.

FRANZ KALDE

Ostpolitik, Papal. This German term designates the efforts under John XXIII and Paul VI to begin a dialogue with the communist states of Eastern Europe. These popes wished to achieve a greater measure of freedom for the local churches in these states, but without making any ideological concessions.

Since the time of Pius XI, the Holy See had been confronted with communist policy vis-à-vis religion in the Soviet Union. The pope hoped initially that it would be possible to conclude a concordat ensuring legal guarantees for Catholics, but he abandoned this plan and took the offensive under Stalin's violent rule, from 1930 onward. In 1937, his encyclical *Divini Redemptoris* condemned the communist worldview. The communist policy toward religion had a more incisive effect on the Catholic Church after the Second World War, when communist regimes under the aegis of the Soviet Union were established in all the occupied countries (with the exception of Austria). Their long-term goal was the elimination of the church and Christianity in the communist sphere of influence, although tactics varied from brutal repression to attempts to instrumentalize the church. With the end of Stalinism, pressure became less severe, but the situation of the church remained generally precarious. Pius XII attacked the communist persecution of the church and of Christians and made it clear that Christianity and communism were incompatible; he maintained this standpoint in the face of the persecutions and infringements of human rights in Eastern bloc countries, which persisted throughout his pontificate.

Papal Ostpolitik changed under John XXIII, in the context of the general easing of tensions between East and West, and Paul VI took up the diplomatic offensive, without abandoning the basic policy of his predecessors. The main point of his strategy was no longer demarcation, but dialogue. He attempted to achieve greater freedom for church action, without making ideological concessions. His closest collaborator in this task was Agostino Casaroli. The pope's first goal was to appoint diocesan bishops where there were none and to ensure that they were free to contact the Holy See; he also wished to revitalize church life. Agreements were reached first with Hungary (1964) and with Yugoslavia (1966), which adopted full diplomatic relations with the Holy See in 1970. Negotiations with the other states, especially Czechoslovakia, proved more difficult; the states continued their repression in an unobtrusive manner, while practicing a politics of stalling. There was little need for action in Poland and East Germany, where church structures remained intact under the firm leadership of Cardinals Stefan Wyszynski and Alfred Bengsch. Critics of Paul VI's Ostpolitik alleged that he made excessive concessions to the governments in question. The Holy See succeeded in securing respect for fundamental human rights (and hence for religious freedom too) included in the concluding acts of the "Conference for Security and Cooperation in Europe" in 1975.

When the archbishop of Cracow, Cardinal Karol Wojtyła, was elected pope in October 1978 and took over the leadership of the Catholic Church as John Paul II, the power of the Soviet Russian empire was to all appearances still unbroken. Thanks to his long experience in dealing with the communist system and to his insight into its weakness, papal Ostpolitik under John Paul broadly reverted to a fundamental opposition to communist doctrine. He was less interested in coming to an agreement with communism; rather, he emphasized the importance of fundamental changes, judging that the time for these had come. During his first visit to his native land in 1979, millions of Poles thronged to see him, and this was a psychological preparation for the strike of the shipyard workers in Danzig in 1980 and the foundation of the free trade union, Solidarity, under Lech Wałesa. This time the Soviet Union did not react as in previous years, when uprisings in East Germany (1953), Hungary (1956), and Czechoslovakia (1968) were brutally smashed; it left this to the government of the Polish state under General Wojciech Jaruzelski, who declared martial law in Poland in December 1980 and imprisoned the leaders of Solidarity—without, however, crushing the resistance.

In this period, the vigorous diplomatic initiative of John Paul II succeeded in bringing both the Solidarity movement and the Soviet and Polish governments to act with moderation. From 1985 onward, the process of *détente* was promoted by the policy of Michael Gorbachev; this led after 1989 to free elections and to the end of communist rule in Eastern Europe, to German reunification in 1990, and to the dissolution of the Soviet Union in 1991 with the concomitant collapse of the Soviet regime. The contribution of papal Ostpolitik here was primarily the diplomatic support of the freedom movement.

Since the end of the communist era, papal Ostpolitik has concentrated on the reestablishment of the hierarchy and the negotiation of legal guarantees for church activity; the Holy See has given up the idea of a return to the *status quo ante*. The pope himself has sought to encourage Catholics by means of his pastoral visits to almost all the formerly communist countries.

■ **Bibliography:** *DHP* 1237ff.; A. Riccardi, *Il Vaticano e Mosca* (Rome, 1992); A. Stehle, *Geheimdiplomatie im Vatikan: Die Päpste und die Kommunisten* (Zurich, 1993); H. J. Hallier, "Der Heilige Stuhl und die deutsche Frage," *RQ* 90 (1995) 237-55; K.-J. Hummel, ed., *Vatikanische Ostpolitik unter Johannes XXIII. und Paul VI.* (Paderborn et al., 1999); J. Pilvousek, "Katholische Bischofskonferenz und Vatikan," *Kirchliche Zeitgeschichte* 12 (1999) 488-511; H. Meier, "Bemerkungen zur vatikanischen Ostpolitik 1958-1978," in Festschrift for M. Heckel (Tübingen, 1999) 151-57; E. Gatz, ed., *Kirche und Katholizismus seit 1945,* II (Paderborn et al., 1999 [articles studying the various countries in question]).

ERWIN GATZ

Pallium. This name originally designated the cloaklike wrap favored above all by philosophers in Rome. It was often rolled up to form a sash, which was worn draped around the shoulders. The clothing regulations of the emperor Theodosius in 382 (Codex Theodosianus XIV 10,1) laid down that officials who exercised functions in the name of the emperor should wear *pallia discolorata.* It seems that the emperor also bestowed this symbol of sovereignty on the pope, who in turn bestowed it on preeminent bishops in his patriarchate. Since the ninth century, it has been the insignia of all archbishops.

Today it is a woolen stole in the form of a ring worn over the chasuble (in the past, it was attached to this vestment by means of three needles). An end-piece weighted with lead hangs down in front and behind. It is decorated with six crosses in black silk. It is blessed on the vigil of the feast of Sts. Peter and Paul and is kept in the *Confessio* of → St. Peter's. Within the borders of their metropolitan district, archbishops wear it during solemn celebrations of the Mass and some acts of ordination and consecration held during the Mass, as a sign of their communion with the Holy See.

■ **Bibliography:** *LMA* 6:1643f.; *VATL* 533f.; J. Braun, *Die liturgische Gewandung im Occident und Orient* (Freiburg, 1907) 620-76; L. Duchesne, *Les origines du culte chrétien* (5th ed. Paris, 1925) 404-10; O. Engels, "Der Pontifikatsantritt und seine Zeichen," *Settimane di studio* (Spoleto, 1987) 2:707-66; M. Basso, "La nicchia dei palli," *Notitiae* 230/231 (1985) 497-519.

RUPERT BERGER

Papacy, Pope.
1. Concept and Origin.—2. Ancient Church.—3. Middle Ages.—4. Modern Period.

1. Concept and Origin

"Pope" (Greek *pappas,* Latin *papa*) is the usual designation today of the bishop of Rome as the one who exercises the → Petrine ministry in the universal church and as head of the Catholic Church. The title comes from the Greek linguistic sphere, where it originally also designated abbots and bishops; from the fifth century onward, it has designated both the bishop of Rome and the other patriarchs. In Rome, it is found first on a tombstone from the second half of the fourth century (*sub Liberio papa,* "when Liberius was pope"); since the fifth century, it has been reserved in the West for the Roman bishop. From the period of the Gregorian Reform onward, other terms joined *papa* in common use as brief titles for the one who exercised the Petrine ministry (*Pontifex Maximus, Servus servorum Dei;* in the Middle Ages, also *Apostolicus;* from Innocent III onward, *Vicarius*

Christi; → Titles, Papal); in the strictly theological language of the magisterium, however, "bishop of Rome" (*pontifex romanus*) remains the official designation. The term *papatus,* "papacy," has been used for the institution since the eleventh century.

The Catholic faith holds firmly that the papacy is based on the promises and affirmations that Jesus made to Simon → Peter in the New Testament (Matt. 16:16-19; Luke 22:31f.; John 21:15-19) and on the succession of the Roman bishops in this ministry of Peter; the classic dogmatic definition of this conviction was formulated at the First Vatican Council. Naturally, it is not possible to understand the "institution" of the papacy by Jesus Christ and the succession in the Petrine ministry in an ahistorically rigid manner; an explicit consciousness that the bishop of Rome is Peter's successor is attested even in Rome no earlier than the mid-third century (Cyprian of Carthage, *Ep.* 75), but this did not determine the way in which the Roman bishops understood their ministry until the fourth and fifth centuries. Elsewhere in the church, this understanding gained ground even more slowly; in the East, it was accepted only sporadically and in individual cases. In addition to this, it is probable that the office of a single bishop, as distinct from a college of presbyters, did not exist in Rome before Anicetus (ca. 155-166; cf. *1 Clement* and Ignatius's *Letter to the Romans*).

It may indeed be accepted as probable that Peter came to Rome and suffered martyrdom (by crucifixion) in the persecution of Christians by the emperor Nero (64-67), in which Paul too died; but the only certain fact—demonstrated above all by the excavations under → St. Peter's—is that the Roman church venerated the → tomb of Peter on the Vatican Hill no later than the mid-second century. This Petrine tradition (which had not yet developed into the concept of the Roman bishop as Peter's successor) was one of several essential factors in the slow and indirect emergence of the central position held by the Roman community within the *communio* of all the churches in the patristic period; together with the equally significant Pauline tradition, it constitutes the dual apostolicity of the Roman church, with Peter and Paul as the two preeminent leaders who handed the testimony of their faith over to the Roman church in their martyrdom. Another vital factor was the de facto central position of Rome as imperial capital. Besides this, events experienced from the fourth century onward made a center of ecclesiastical unity appear necessary. The concrete Petrine ministry was born of the totality of these factors.

This means that the appeal to the passages about Peter in the New Testament (especially Matt. 16:18) is made only at a later stage. This does not, however, make such an appeal "ideological": the church is a historically existing reality, and when historical experience indicates that certain institutions are necessary and "essential," these are not simply created *ex nihilo* but are "discovered" as already implicitly present in the New Testament and church tradition. This is true *a fortiori* of a ministry of unity for the whole church: the recognition of the historical necessity of this office presupposes a long historical process over the course of many centuries. Only then was it possible to understand the Petrine texts in the New Testament as "relevant" to the present-day ministry of the bishop of Rome.

2. Ancient Church

To begin with, one cannot speak of a papal office or of a "superiority" of the Roman community vis-à-vis other churches. Nevertheless, there is evidence of the religious and spiritual significance of the Roman church as far back as our sources take us. This is not described in juridical categories, but is expressed in a special fraternal responsibility and concern for other churches, which includes exhortation (*1 Clement;* Ignatius of Antioch, *Letter to the Romans;* Eusebius of Caesarea, *Historia ecclesiastica* 4.23; inscription of Avircius, ca. 200). The episcopal office, and in particular the "apostolic churches (sees)," played a prominent role in the struggle against gnosis, as guarantors of the apostolic *paradōsis.* In this context, and by virtue of its dual tradition (Petrine and Pauline), Rome and its bishop acquired a particular significance from the end of the second century onward, though this naturally did not imply any exclusive competence for determining the correct transmission of the faith (Irenaeus of Lyons, *Adversus haereses* 3.3.1-2; Tertullian, *De praescriptione haereticorum* 36.1-4). When Roman bishops appealed to this privileged tradition and sought to establish the Roman position even against divergent "apostolic" traditions, as in the paschal controversy (ca. 195) and in the controversy about baptism by heretics (255-256), this did not succeed, at any rate in the short term; but the Roman doctrinal tradition had a significant effect in the long term and almost always won the day.

From the third century onward, especially when divisions arose, communion with the Roman church became particularly important. Within the network of the *communio,* Rome assumed a prominent rank, rooted in a special responsibility that had its origin in the Petrine-Pauline charism, but not different in principle from the general solidarity and fraternal responsibility which bound all the churches and bishops together (see, e.g., Cyprian, *Ep.* 68.3; Julius of Rome takes the same line as late as 341: Athanasius, *Apologia contra Arianos* 35). Besides this, Rome shared this function to a large extent with the two other "main churches" (later patriarchates) of Antioch and Alexandria. The fact that the Roman bishops maintained a decisive anti-Arian line in the fourth century (with the exception of vacillations under Liberius) strengthened their position in the eyes of those who upheld Nicene orthodoxy. On the other hand, the rigid "strictly Nicene" policy, especially in the case of Damasus, who showed no comprehension for the "young Nicenes," led to opposition and anti-Roman resentment in the East (Basil of Caesarea, *Ep.* 239.2), especially in the see of Constantinople, which was raised to patriarchal rank by the council of 381.

The transfer of the imperial capital to Constantinople in the East by Constantine the Great (330) meant that the popes were freed in the long term from imperial pressure, so that they could take an independent position vis-à-vis state authority. This also meant, however, that the bishop or patriarch of the new capital became a dangerous rival, especially once the other Eastern patriarchs were no longer capable of presenting a counterweight to Constantinople's authority.

From the second half of the fourth century, above all under the decisive and vigorous Popes Damasus I (366-384), Siricius (384-399), Innocent I (402-417), and Leo the Great (440-461), a massive shift occurred in the Roman bishops' understanding of their ministry and in the claims they made. The idea of primacy had hitherto tended to be spiritual-charismatic, or determined by the concept of *paradōsis.* Now a more juridical view was asserted. The concept of the Roman bishop as Peter's successor—his heir and (as Leo puts it) his "vicar," i.e., holding Peter's authority—was now detached from the total complex of ideas about Petrine-Pauline apostolicity. Appeal was made to this concept in support of the claim to lead the universal church (*sollicitudo omnium ecclesiarum*); Peter was portrayed emphatically as the lawgiver, the Moses of the new covenant. Behind this lies the introduction of specifically Roman imperial concepts of leadership into the church, as a consequence of the christianization of Rome and of its governing classes from the fourth century on: instead of the Rome of the *paradōsis,* which bears witness, we now have Rome as *caput mundi,* which gives the world its laws. This met a need on the part of the growing missionary church of the West for leadership: it had only one "apostolic church," viz., Rome.

At this period, the realization of the Roman claims to primacy was much more a program than a reality, even in the West. One cannot speak of any genuine papal government of the church outside the Roman church province (*Italia suburbicaria*). The Council of Serdica (342) did indeed appeal to the *memoria Petri* and acknowledge Rome as the authority to which recourse (more precisely, appeals) could be made when bishops were deposed; but it took seven hundred years for this to become the universal rule in the West. Questions about faith and church discipline were not seldom sent to Rome from the areas of northern Italy, France, Illyricum, and Greece (which belonged to the Roman patriarchate until the eighth century), but this never occurred regularly. Even definitions of the faith were made independently of Rome in local councils. This was even more true of the North African church, which accepted a greater *auctoritas* of Rome (as the older sister) in matters of doctrine, but not a juridically superior *potestas.* Above all, this church claimed jurisdictional autonomy (the Councils of Carthage in 419 and 424 forbade recourse to Rome).

The exercise of the primacy in relation to the East is basically coterminous with Rome's relationship to the councils. The Roman bishop was represented by presbyters at the First Ecumenical Council in Nicaea (325), but the sources do not allow us to discern any attribution of a special role to Rome. In the course of the Arian disputes and the struggle to establish the authority of Nicaea, Rome made the claim (first in 371 or 372) that councils were valid only with the consent of the Roman bishops. From now on, the main thrust of papal politics vis-à-vis the councils is a clear "continuity line," i.e., the consistent upholding of those councils which had already been acknowledged (initially, Nicaea) and of their decisions, together with the rejection of councils and decisions that contradicted these. Pope Celestine I played a significant role at the Council of Ephesus (431), where Rome in union with Alexandria (Cyril) supported a one-sided unification Christology against Constantinople and Antioch. Leo, who was theologically more independent and took more account of the concerns of the other party, rejected the Second Council of Ephesus (the "Robbers' synod," 449), at which Alexandria (now with Dioscorus as bishop), despite Roman protests, presented an even more radical version of the position of the first council in 431. Leo, or rather his legates, were authoritative participants in the Council of Chalcedon (451), which was the high point of the acknowledgment of Roman doctrinal authority in the East. Leo's doctrinal epistle (the "Tome") was acknowledged as the kerygma of the *cathedra Petri*, which is present in the Roman see. As far as jurisdiction was concerned, however, can. 28 of this council revealed the limits of the primacy: appealing to the principle of political rank, it elevated Constantinople to the second see in the church. Leo protested, appealing to the unalterable ranking of the "three Petrine sees" (Rome, Alexandria, Antioch), but he could not get this decision annulled. Constantinople became the second see.

■ **Bibliography:** W. Marschall, *Karthago und Rom* (Stuttgart, 1971); P P. Joannou, *Die Ostkirche und die Cathedra Petri im 4. Jahrhundert* (Stuttgart, 1972) (on this, see the criticisms in the essay by W. de Vries with the same title, *Orientalia christiana periodica* 40 [1974] 114-44); W. Grotz, "Die Stellung der Römischen Kirche anhand frühchristlicher Quellen," *AHP* 13 (1975) 7-64 (on this, see the criticism by P. Stockmeier, "Romische Kirche und Petrusamt im Licht frühchristlicher Zeugnisse," *AHP* 14 [1976] 357-72); C. Pietri, *Roma christiana,* 2 vols. (Rome, 1976); M. Wojtowych, *Papsttum und Konzile von den Anfängen bis zu Leo I.* (Stuttgart, 1981) (on this, see the critical essay with the same title by S. O. Horn, *AHC* 17 [1985] 9-17); V. Twomey, *Apostolikos Thronos: The Primacy of Rome . . . in the Church History of Eusebius and . . . Athanasius the Great* (Mün-

ster, 1982) (on this, see the critical review by H. J. Sieben, *Theologie und Philosophie* 58 [1983] 257-60); S. O. Horn, *Petrou Kathedra: Der Bischof von Rom und die Synoden von Ephesus (449) und Chalcedon* (Paderborn, 1982); M. Maccarrone, ed., *Il primato del vescovo di Roma nel primo millennio* (Vatican City, 1991); R. Minnerath, *De Jérusalem à Rome: Pierre et l'unité de l'église apostolique* (Paris, 1994); R. Davis, "Pre-Constantinian Chronology: The Roman Bishopric from AD 258 to 314," *Journal of Theological Studies* 48 (1997) 439-70.

KLAUS SCHATZ

3. *Middle Ages*

Until the mid-eighth century, Rome belonged to the Eastern empire. Following a decree of Justinian I, Gregory I declared that the four ecumenical councils were equivalent to the four Gospels. Conflicts with emperors led to the elaboration of important doctrines (doctrine of the "two powers" in 494, the Symmachian forgery in 502), and the martyrdom of several popes (John I, Martin I). Popes who made too many concessions were regarded for a time as heretics (Vigilius, Pelagius I, Honorius I); but in the eyes of Agatho and other popes, the Roman church had never abandoned the truth faith, and Peter was the guarantor of this church vis-à-vis the whole Christian world. The separation from Byzantium began under Gregory II, as a reaction to measures taken by the emperors (the taxation and confiscation of Roman patrimonies, the subordination of southern Italy, Sicily, and Illyricum to the patriarch of Constantinople; the iconoclastic controversy). Despite all the Eastern influence (the diaconal churches, feasts and art, the provenance of the upper classes), the Latin element predominated in Rome—in the collections of liturgical and legal texts, in church music ("Gregorian chant"), in the → *Liber Pontificalis,* and in papal writings, especially those of Gregory I.

Gregory I opened up a new field for papal activity with the mission to the Anglo-Saxons, which became particularly important after the synod of Whitby in 664: it was now possible for the papacy to realize its claims at least in the West, in a period in which it was no longer necessary to pay attention to Byzantium or (after the Islamic conquest) the formerly autonomous churches in northern Africa and Spain. The Anglo-Saxon mission and reform in the Frankish kingdom followed Roman directives, and the detachment of the pope from Byzantium led to a new alliance, this time between Rome and the Franks (from 750/751). A phenomenon that recurs throughout papal history into the modern period can be observed clearly even as early as this, viz., the election of a new pope from among the opposition to the pope who has just died. Despite the discontinuity from one pope to the next, this is nevertheless an indication of the continuity of the office.

Until the mid-eleventh century, Frankish and then German emperors dominated Rome and the papacy, intervening even in questions concerning matters of doctrine (iconoclastic controversy; *Filioque*), although the Donation of Constantine (ca. 760) had intended to propagate a papacy that was independent of the emperor. On the other hand, the Carolingians ensured the physical safety of the papacy (→ Papal States; Leonine city) and increased its prestige by dividing up their imperial church into provinces headed by archbishops who required the pallium from the pope in order to exercise their office. The Pseudo-Isidorian decretals were composed in France ca. 850, with the intention of strengthening the suffragans and reducing the power of the archbishops. The ultimate effect was to strengthen the position of the pope in the church, as this collection was held to be genuine, despite its many forgeries, and it provided important evidence in favor of the papal claims, especially from the eleventh century onward. These claims were also promoted by translations of Roman relics to France and the French adaptation and reworking of Roman collections of liturgical and canon-law texts. Already in the later Carolingian period, and increasingly from the tenth century on, papal legates and synods (sometimes held under the joint presidency of pope and emperor), as well as the granting of privileges of protection and exemption to monasteries strengthened papal influence. Nicholas I already held a view of the papal primacy which implied a claim to the position that Gregory VII was to emphasize at a later date; from the Ottonian period on, organizational measures and church reform were impossible without the pope. Nevertheless, the pope could intervene only in Italy, France (and Catalonia), and Germany and its sphere of influence (Bohemia, Poland, Hungary). In Rome itself, the older self-understanding of the papacy, harking back to the Byzantine epoch, lived on; no pope was canonized after the mid-eighth century, and Franks and Germans were unpopular.

But Rome too changed: greater emphasis was now laid on the → Lateran as the center of Rome and of the papal state. At the same time, Roman families gained more influence, so that specifically Roman interests now guided the papacy and → nepotism became a constant element of its history. The so-called corpse synod of 896/897 was marked by these factors; the ensuing struggle between adherents and opponents of Formosus in the "dark century" *(saeculum obscurum)* led to a break with older canon law, so that it became possible for a bishop, notwithstanding his spiritual "marriage" to his local church, to ascend the episcopal throne of Rome as pope.

Until the early fourteenth century, the popes were heads of the "universal church," but in reality this comprised only the Latin church, since the schism that had grown out of the events of 1054 became firmly established from the early twelfth century on. The crusades did not alter this situation, since the Eastern Christians could not accept the new Latin patriarchs who were installed there. The claim to be head of all Christians was made all the more vigorously, although it could not be put into practice, and reached its apex in the Constitution *Unam sanctam* of Boniface VIII (1302). The so-called investiture conflict had helped to increase papal authority, not least because many attempts at reform could be realized only after they had found allies in Rome, which took on the task of propagating them effectively. One should not overestimate the importance of Gregory VII's *Dictatus papae* (1075), but many of his claims were (or later became) reality. From the time of Urban II, the doctrine of the "two powers" was interpreted in favor of the papacy. It was intensified from the twelfth century onward by the theory of the two swords (given definitive form in *Unam sanctam*). Popes governed the church in practice through their dispensations from norms and judgments given in response to appeals, as well as the nomination and transfer of bishops (from the thirteenth century); the same can be said of councils, legates, and nuncios or delegated judges. This led to the new collections of canon law, but it also prompted criticism—a criticism prompted by the many popes who mixed church politics with family interests. The attack on Boniface VIII at Anagni in 1303 seemed the just reward for such papal hubris.

From 1316, the popes lived for sixty years in so-called exile in → Avignon, developing the city into an impressive residence. For the first time since the investiture conflict, there was an administrative continuity in local government, which provided a special incentive to use the church as a source of tax revenues. This in turn increased criticism of the curia. Problems of doctrine (controversies about poverty and about the beatific vision) likewise provoked criticism, as well as did the conflict with the emperor Louis the Bavarian and the often pro-French position of the popes in the Hundred Years' War. This led even prior to the Western Schism of 1378 to conciliarist ideas; naturally the schism intensified these, until finally the supremacy of the council over the pope was declared at Basel. One success of the Council of Constance was the reduction of the papal tax revenues. The schism and the councils lent impetus to the tendency to form national churches.

The church union agreed to at Florence (1439) and the end of the Council of Basel (1447-1449) with its excessive ideas about the constitution of the church led to a pendulum swing in favor of the papacy. Although conciliar ideas about reform were preserved and transmitted even in Rome (a fact that was later to prove important for the Council of Trent), the dominant tendency there was restoration. Rome was developed into a residence on the model of Avignon, with the Vatican as its center; the popes made the → papal states secure and extended their territory, and, in their capacity as local sovereigns, encouraged humanism and the Renaissance.

Outside the papal states, rulers restricted the popes' activities. Lack of zeal for reform, the sale of offices, indulgences, and Roman privileges, as well as a frequently immoral lifestyle, provoked criticism. Consequently, at the end of the Middle Ages, the pope was indeed acknowledged as head of the Latin church, but he could make his claims a reality only vis-à-vis recipients of privileges, priests who sought an ecclesiastical career, and his own subjects in the papal states.

■ **Bibliography:** Caspar; Bertolini; P. Brezzi, *Roma e l'impero medioevale (774-1252)* (Bologna, 1947); Zimmermann *Pt*; Zimmermann *J*; M. Pacaut, *La papauté, des origines au concile de Trente* (Paris, 1976); W. Ullmann, *Kurze Geschichte des Papsttums im Mittelalter* (Berlin, 1978); G. Barraclough, *The Medieval Papacy* (London, 1968; repr. 1979); Richards; *GKG* vol. 11; C. Morris, *The Papal Monarchy: The Western Church from 1050 to 1250* (Oxford, 1989); I. S. Robinson, *The Papacy 1073-1198: Continuity and Innovation* (Cambridge, 1990); R. Schieffer, "Die Beziehungen karolingischer Synoden zum Papsttum," *AHC* 27/28 (1995-96) 147-63; Borgolte; B. Schimmelpfennig, *Das Papsttum von der Antike bis zur Renaissance* (4th ed. Darmstadt, 1996); T. Prügl, "Der häretische Papst und seine Immunität im Mittelalter," *Münchener theologische Zeitschrift* 47 (1996) 197-215; A. Melloni, "I fondamenti del regime di cristianità al Lionese I (13. Luglio 1245)," *Cristianesimo nella storia* 18 (1997) 61-76; W. Hartmann, "Zur Autorität des Papsttums im karolingischen Frankenreich," in *Mönchtum—Kirche—Herrschaft* (Sigmaringen, 1998) 113-32; B. Guillemain, *Les papes d'Avignon 1309-1376* (Paris, 1998); S. Cavallotto, "Concilio e papato," *Protestantesimo* 54 (1999) 367-72; P. G. Caron, "L'interpretazione della Lettera gelasiana nel pensiero e nell'azione dei papi del duecento," in Festschrift for P. Bellini (Catanzaro, 1999) 161-74; P. Delogu, "The Papacy, Rome, and the Wider World in the Seventh and Eighth Centuries," in *Early Medieval Rome and the Christian West*, Festschrift for D. A. Bullough (Leiden et al., 2000) 197-220; J. Miethke, *De potestate papae: Die päpstliche Amtskonzeption im Widerstreit der politischen Theorie von Thomas von Aquin bis Wilhelm von Ockham* (Tübingen, 2000).

BERNHARD SCHIMMELPFENNIG

4. *Modern Period*

In the transition period from the Middle Ages to the modern period, the popes and the Roman → curia were blind to the extent of alienation from Rome that had been growing over centuries in many areas of Western Christendom. In this simmering atmosphere of crisis, Martin Luther's actions in late 1517, in reaction to the scandalous proclamation of the issuance of indulgences to finance the building of the new St. Peter's in Rome, unleashed the greatest catastrophe for the papacy and the church, namely, the hostile separation of the Germanic North and large parts of central and eastern Europe from Rome in the Protestant Reformation. This meant the end of the universal authority of the papacy.

Initially, the strongest advocate of the old Roman church and the papacy was Emperor Charles V, who was hindered rather than helped by the popes, especially when he attempted to have a council summoned. The decisive and irrevocable secession of almost half of Europe occurred under Clement VII and at the beginning of the pontificate of Paul III. After the early failure of Hadrian VI, it was Paul III whose reign brought a turning point. Ultimately, the tremendous shock brought a breakthrough for renewal in the church, even in the worldly curia. The Council of Trent (1545-1563), under the leadership of presidents appointed by the pope, furnished the main foundations of the Catholic reform, which went hand in hand with the Counter-Reformation. Under the reforming Popes Pius V, Gregory XIII, and Sixtus V, the papacy resolutely took on the leadership of the renewal. This work was continued by Clement VIII, Paul V, and Gregory XV, who found special support in new orders (Jesuits, Capuchins) and in old orders which underwent a process of regeneration, and who worked closely with the Catholic political powers. Until the Peace of Westphalia (1648), none of the parties in the confessional struggle hesitated to employ political means, often brutally, to achieve their ends.

The post-Reformation, post-Tridentine church had become smaller in every respect. As a reaction to the attack by the Reformers, Roman centralization was extended in a church that was now more "Latin" than ever (permanent nuntiatures [→ Legations, Papal]; → *Ad limina* visits). This was the period in which the doctrine of the distinguishing "marks" of the true church was also elaborated. With the erection of the Congregation of Propaganda in 1622, the papacy assumed the leadership of the flourishing world missions, which were supported especially by the great orders (Jesuits, Dominicans, Franciscans, Capuchins) and the patronal powers of Spain and Portugal. However, the increasing political weakness of the papacy, evident as early as the Thirty Years' War (Urban VIII, Innocent X, Alexander VII), was confirmed in all its peace treaty negotiations in the seventeenth and eighteenth centuries.

In the period between the Peace of Westphalia and the French Revolution, as the Western world became increasingly secularized, the papacy—despite the inner solidity and the high prestige it had attained—could do nothing to prevent its declining influence even in Catholic countries. The Baroque period displayed religious vitality in many spheres, but there were also harsh confrontations with absolutism on the part of rulers and states, with Enlightenment tendencies to hostility to the church and the papacy, with Gallicanism in France, episcopalism (Febronianism) in the

German imperial church, and Josephinism in the Habsburg territories; conflicts also arose because of Jansenism, systems of moral theology, and missionary methods. In order to avoid political conflicts, the cardinals elected popes who were honest, but mostly kept a low profile. The great exceptions were Innocent XI, Benedict XIV, and in a certain sense also Innocent XII. The suppression of the Jesuits by Clement XIV in 1773, in response to powerful political pressure, and the de facto useless visit of Pius VI to plead with the emperor Joseph II in Vienna in 1782 demonstrated to all the world the political powerlessness of the papacy.

The nineteenth century (or the period between the French Revolution and the outbreak of war in 1914) began with the collapse of the old order. This brought a profound humiliation of the papacy by the Revolution and by Napoleon (loss of the papal states, imprisonment of Pius VI and Pius VII). These hardships were borne with dignity and won the papacy a new respect. A renewal took place within the church in the nineteenth century, initially supported by the politics of restoration and the Romantic movement, and this increased the papacy's importance within the church. Various intellectual and political tendencies (liberalism, ultramontanism, neoscholasticism) led to passionate political, ecclesiastical, and also theological debates as early as the pontificate of Leo XII; these became more acute under Gregory XVI and Pius IX. The strongly centralizing church politics of these popes, viewed by many as reactionary, put a strain on relations with European constitutional governments and increased tensions in the papal states (which had been restored in 1815) and among the intellectual classes. A great number of educated Catholics were alienated from the papacy and the church precisely in the Romance countries. The theological and church-political debates reached their peak in the controversy about the *Syllabus* of Pius IX (1864) and about the First Vatican Council (1869-70), which focused on the definition of the papal primacy. As the secular power of the pope disintegrated with the loss of the papal states in 1870, the church displayed a unified front to the outside world—in the papacy. The clarification of the relationship between pope and bishops remained on the theological agenda. Leo XIII, with his diplomatic and conciliatory manner, succeeded in pacifying much of this turbulence and in laying the foundations of appropriate relationships to the modern world and its problems. Nevertheless, the debate about Christian witness in the modern world continued to smolder, and it broke out anew at the turn of the nineteenth and twentieth centuries. The conflict became public in the pontificate of Pius X (who was interested not in politics but in religious renewal and reform within the church): the key terms here are Reform Catholicism, modernism, and integralism.

After grave diplomatic blunders and inner-church turbulences under Pius X, the pontificate of Benedict XV brought a period of necessary calm, but was completely overshadowed by the First World War and its consequences. The edition of the *Code of Canon Law* in 1917-1918 (emphasizing centralization) and the break with the Europeanization of world mission (encyclical *Maximum illud,* 1919), were pointers to the future. Pius XI endeavored to consolidate the church in those lands that had been shattered by war and revolutions (numerous → concordats; in particular, the resolution of the Roman Question, which had remained open since 1870, through the → Lateran Treaties of 1929, which created the sovereign Vatican state). The confrontation with totalitarian systems hostile to Christianity (communism and Bolshevism, fascism, Nazism) brought him many difficulties; these only increased under his successor, Pius XII, as a result of the Second World War and its aftermath.

The pontificates of John XXIII and his successor, Paul VI, are characterized by a clear attempt to develop an understanding of Petrine office that is appropriate to the modern world, especially in the promotion of the unity of all Christians, in the achievement of peace and social justice, and in an unambiguous testimony to the Christian faith and Christian responsibility in the world. The clearest expression of this endeavor was the Second Vatican Council (1962-1965). Despite various tendencies and some setbacks, the goals set by the council remain determinative (John Paul I, John Paul II).

■ Bibliography: *TRE* 25:647-76; Pastor; Schmidlin; *GKG* vol. 12; H. Fuhrmann; on papal historiography: A. Esch and J. Petersen, eds., *Geschichte und Geschichtswissenschaft in der Kultur Italiens und Deutschlands* (Tübingen, 1989) 141-91; G. Zizola, *Les papes du XXe siècle* (Paris, 1996); J. I. Saranyana, "Balance de los pontificados del siglo XX," *Anuario de historia de iglesia* 6 (1997) 23-28; F. J. Coppa, *The Modern Papacy since 1789* (London, 1998); M. Lienhard, "Les réformateurs protestants du XVIe siècle et la papauté," *Positions luthériennes* 46 (1998) 157-73; G. Schwaiger, *Papsttum und Päpste im 20. Jahrhundert von Leo XIII. bis zu Johannes Paul II.* (Munich, 1999); P. Koeppel, ed., *Papes et papauté au XVIIIe siècle* (Paris, 1999); *Il ministero del Papa in prospettiva ecumenica* (Milan, 1999); A. D. Wright, *The Early Modern Papacy from the Council of Trent to the French Revolution, 1564-1789* (London, 2000).

GEORG SCHWAIGER

Papal State(s).
1. Origin.—2. History.—3. Problematical Aspects.

The term "papal state(s)" in the broad sense refers to the extensive territorial domains which the popes acquired after the Peace of Constantine; in the narrower sense, it refers only to those areas of central Italy in which the popes were the local sovereigns (or laid claim to such sovereignty) from the mid-eighth century to 1859/1870. This territory, with → Rome as its capital, included the Roman countryside, the Patrimony of Peter, Umbria, the Marches, and Romagna and stretched from the Tyrrhenian Sea to the Adriatic. Besides this, the exclaves of Pontecorvo and Benevento in southern Italy, the city of → Avignon in southern France, and the county of Venaissin belonged to the papal state. The fortunes of the papal states were closely linked to the development of the papacy as a spiritual elective monarchy and the leading power of Western Catholic Christianity, in which the spiritual and the secular spheres of administration interlocked closely. Since many pontificates were brief, the papal states were exposed to numerous changes and breaks in continuity.

1. *Origin*
From the fourth century onward, thanks to donations by emperors and nobles, the Roman church became the greatest landowner in Italy; its territory was called the "Patrimony of Peter" from the sixth century. Most of this territory lay around Rome; other possessions were in southern Italy, Sicily, Corsica, and Sardinia, as well as in northern Africa. Pope Gregory the Great played a particularly important role in establishing an efficient administration; revenues helped to provide for the poor in Rome. As the power of Byzantium

declined, Italian antipathy to the Byzantine tax burdens and the Byzantine hostility to icons resulted in the papacy assuming more governmental tasks. Thus its position became ever stronger, although there was initially no questioning of the formal sovereignty of the emperor. This changed only when Byzantium proved incapable of mounting any effective resistance to the threat that loomed from the Langobards. In this situation, Stephen II followed up earlier contacts by going in person to the Frankish kingdom in 754. Shared interests led him to enter the alliance of Ponthion/Quierzy with King Pippin the Younger and the rising Frankish dynasty. This dynasty

agreed to protect the papacy, and the pope bestowed on Pippin the honorific title of *patricius Romanorum*. In three campaigns (754, 756, and 774-775), Pippin and Charlemagne subdued the Langobards. In 754, Pippin promised to return the duchy of Rome and other areas to the pope, but he received only the heartland of the later papal state. In 800, as a result of the coronation of Charlemagne as emperor, this area was incorporated in the Carolingian empire as an autonomous region under papal sovereignty. This is the latest date for the composition (probably in Rome) of the Donation of Constantine, which was produced as evidence in favor of the papal claims

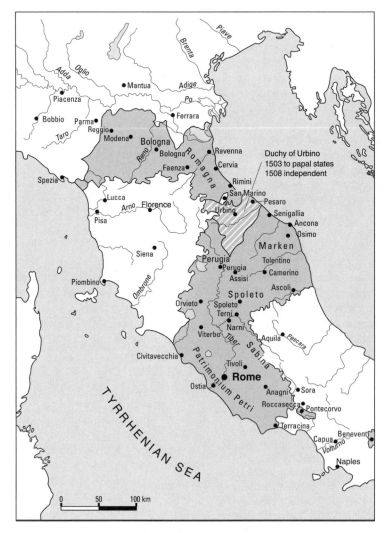

The Papal States ca. 1500

from Leo IX until the late Middle Ages; only in the fifteenth century was it recognized as a forgery.

2. History

The alliance between the popes and the Franks was renewed in each new change of political office from the eighth century on, confirming the papal possession of further territories and guaranteeing protection from enemies. With the decline of Carolingian power, however, this protective function disappeared, and Rome was ruled by noble families from the late ninth century onward. This led to the nadir of papal history in the tenth century ("the dark century"), and the papal state was reduced to the duchy of Rome. The renewal of the Carolingian donations by Otto the Great on the occasion of his imperial coronation in 962 brought no changes here; only when the papacy regained its strength under German influence, through the acceptance of the ideas of the Gregorian Reform, did a temporary consolidation succeed. After Nicholas II had entered an alliance with the Normans, the papal state was ruled for more than a century by a series of different parties. Nevertheless, the popes received new donations in the eleventh and twelfth centuries, e.g., by Countess Matilda of Tuscany ca. 1079.

A thoroughgoing stabilization of the papal sovereignty in the papal states occurred only after the death of Emperor Henry VI (1197) under Celestine III and Innocent III. The latter pope was resolute in his intentions and saw full sovereignty over the worldly possessions of the Roman church as the presupposition for its spiritual activity. Accordingly, he nominated a senator as head of the Roman communes and required an oath of loyalty from him and from the barons in the Patrimony. Like other sovereign powers (i.e., lords and cities) Innocent was encouraged by the promises of Otto IV to begin extensive recuperations of imperial possessions, taking over the duchy of Spoleto, the Marches, and southern Tuscany. He did indeed lose these soon afterward, but he received a renewed promise from Frederick II in 1213; at the same time, the papal state seceded from the empire. The territory of the papal state was confirmed after Charles of Anjou defeated the Staufers in 1266, with the borders that had existed in 1213, but the de facto sovereignty of the popes was reduced after this date by the emergence of the free cities where nobles ruled; these were often at enmity with one another.

The absence of the popes during the exile in Avignon had far-reaching effects on the papal state. Their absence led in effect to the extinction of papal sovereignty, so that income from the papal state dried up: this in turn led to the creation of a novel system with income derived from levying ecclesiastical taxes. In 1347, Cola di Rienzo attempted to set up a secular sovereignty in Rome without the pope; the cardinal legate and vicar Aegidius Alvarez Albornoz succeeded only in 1353 in reconquering the papal state, which had disintegrated into many smaller sovereign entities. He ensured its territorial unity by constructing fortresses. In 1353, he gave the Marches of Ancona the "Aegidian Constitutions," which were extended to the papal states as a whole from the fifteenth century. These constitutions remained in force, with numerous additions, until 1816.

Although Martin V wished to return to Rome soon after his election in 1417, in order to avoid being influenced by secular powers and to escape the domination of the Council of Constance, he was not yet able to take up residence in Rome, since the papal state existed in name only. The real ruler of central Italy at this period was Brancaccio of Montone, the first great *condottiere*. There were obstacles to be overcome before the papal sovereignty could be reestablished (as even the council wished). Only in 1420, after making a great many concessions, could Martin V move from Florence to Rome; but he was unable to assert his rule until Brancaccio died during the siege of L'Aquila in 1424. Not even the flight of Eugene IV from Rome in 1434 could any longer pose a serious threat to papal sovereignty.

Papal → nepotism caused grave problems from the end of the fifteenth century to the seventeenth. Cesare Borgia brought many smaller territories under his control ca. 1500, but his empire collapsed on the death of Alexander VI. Julius II reestablished the direct authority of the Holy See over these areas and concentrated on regaining the territories of the Roman church that had been lost and on expelling foreigners from Italian soil. After numerous campaigns, the expulsion of the local tyrants from Perugia and Bologna, and his victory over Venice, the papal states reached their greatest territorial extension under Julius II. He created a principality for his nephew Francesco

Maria della Rovere, not by granting land belonging to the papal state but by arranging for his nephew to be adopted by the childless duke of Urbino, Guidobaldo of Montefeltre. The Sack of Rome in 1527 seemed to imperil the continued existence of the papal states, but they were confirmed in the Peace of Barcelona.

During the Thirty Years' War, when Urban VIII sought to preserve both the dignity of the papal office and the independence of the papal states, and his fear of involvement in war moved him to build powerful fortresses to defend Rome, it became clear that the papal state no longer enjoyed any political importance. Urban was unsuccessful in his attempts to imitate Julius II and Paul III in spending vast sums of money to create an independent principality which he might bestow on his own family. In military terms, the papal state was wholly insignificant thereafter; however, the city of Rome rose to the rank of a leading European metropolis of art in the baroque period.

The lengthy demise of the papal states began with the French Revolution. In 1796, the legations of Ferrara and Bologna declared their independence of the papal state and joined with Modena and Reggio to form the Cispadane Republic. In 1796, the French occupied Rome, proclaimed the republic, and carried off Pius VI into captivity. Pius VII returned to Rome in 1800. The French occupied the papal states a second time in 1806, and Rome in 1808. In 1809, Napoleon revoked the donation by Charlemagne. The papal state was incorporated into the kingdom of Italy.

The papal state was the only former spiritual state to be reestablished by the Congress of Vienna in 1815, though without the territories north of the Po, and without Avignon and Venaissin. The French institutions were abolished, and the prerevolutionary order reestablished. A limited reordering of the public administration and the legal system took place in 1816, but without reconciling the traditions of the papal states with the new requirements. The beginnings of reform by the Cardinal Secretary of State, Ercole Consalvi, met with resistance on the part of the conservatives, and most of them were revoked after the death of Pius VII. It was still the case that only clergymen could hold the higher offices of state, and this led to the formation of secret opposition societies (the *carbonari*), who plotted the overthrow of the regime. In this period, the papal state was one of the most backward societies in Europe; this judgment applies also to agriculture and trade. There were scarcely any industries, so that the state budget was permanently in the red. The city of Rome remained economically unproductive, a monument to its own history. Only the service branch expanded, thanks to the growing number of pilgrims and tourists.

Despite repeated attempts, the conservatives who held power did not succeed in putting needed reforms into practice, and general dissatisfaction with this led, after to the French (July 1830) and Belgian revolutions, to the erection in 1831 of a provisional government in Bologna and to a revolt that affected most of the papal states. This revolt was crushed by Austria. Difficulties were increased by Gregory XVI's rejection of the Italian unity movement. This was indeed antihierarchical after 1830, but there was also a Catholic branch, inspired by the writer Alessandro Manzoni and the philosopher Vincenzo Gioberti, which sought to mediate between authority and freedom and to promote the national movement of the Risorgimento not against the pope but together with him. These "Neo-Guelphs" hoped that the Italian states would join to form a federation under the pope. After the outmoded line taken by Gregory XVI, there was initially a wide approval of Pius IX, who seemed to be sympathetic to the liberals and the unity movement; this approval was increased by measures such as entrusting a government ministry to a layman in 1847. But he could not countenance the transformation of the papal states into a constitutional monarchy or embrace the ideas of 1789. Genuinely incisive reforms did not take place, and this soon led to a cooler assessment of the pope. The mood worsened in April 1848, when he rejected the plea to enter the war against Austria on the side of Piedmont, which was increasingly taking over the leadership of the unity movement. After his prime minister, Pellegrino Rossi, was murdered, Pius IX yielded to the insistence of Giacomo Antonelli and left Rome for Gaeta in the kingdom of Naples, while Antonelli appealed to the European powers to restore the papal states by means of military intervention. This meant that Antonio Rosmini-Serbati, who argued for a reconciliation with modern ideas, was no longer a voice that counted.

A republic was proclaimed in Rome but was

crushed in 1849 through a military action by Austria, Spain, Naples, and France, so that the pope could now return. Pius IX, convinced that the papal state was absolutely necessary for his religious task, now took a reactionary course and did not carry out the reforms recommended by France. After the defeat of Austria in 1859, the latent dissatisfaction led to the revolt of the Romagna, which came under the rule of Piedmont. The Roman Question was to absorb the attention of the Catholic world for decades. Pius IX, influenced by Antonelli, rejected every compromise and heeded the urging of Xavier de Mérode that he should build up a volunteer army. Despite this, the irregulars of Giuseppe Garibaldi pressed forward, and the papal state lost all its territories to Piedmont in 1860, with the exception of the Patrimony of Peter. The political realism of Camillo Cavour, who endeavored to get the pope to renounce his sovereignty over the papal state in return for a guarantee of freedom for the church in a united Italy ("a free church in a free state"), led nowhere. The papal troops succeeded in repulsing Garibaldi at Mentana in 1867, but the military collapse of France at Sedan made it possible for the Italian troops to occupy Rome on September 20, 1870, after only a token resistance by the papal soldiers. Despite the protests of Pius IX, the annexation of the papal state by the kingdom of Italy was inevitable. This took place shortly after the city was occupied and was later confirmed by a referendum. Rome became the capital of Italy in 1871. The Roman Question long remained problematic for the united state of Italy; it was resolved only in 1929, with the founding of the → Vatican state through the → Lateran Treaties.

3. Problematical Aspects

The papal state has always been criticized by those authors who rejected in principle the exercise of secular sovereignty by the church; others such as Aegidius Alvarez Albornoz described the papal state as necessary for salvation. It is a matter of dispute whether the papal state did in fact guarantee the spiritual independence of the popes, but this certainly seems probable if one makes a comparison with the patriarchs of Byzantium, who had no state of their own: of the 122 patriarchs nominated between 379 and 1451, 36 were compelled by the emperor to renounce their see. It remains true, of course, that the use of spiritual discipline to maintain secular power compromises spiritual integrity, and the endeavor to keep hold of the papal states—which ultimately were basically a political burden, with a balance sheet permanently in the red—absorbed the energies of the papacy and of the Catholic Church in the final phase, until the close of the nineteenth century, in a very negative manner. In the light of this, the foundation of the Vatican state in 1929 appears an ideal and workable compromise.

■ Bibliography: TRE 19:92-101; LMA 5:1180-83; DHP 624-32; V. Reinhardt, ed., Die großen Familien Italiens (Stuttgart, 1992); M. Miele, "Note sui concilii provinciali dello Stato della Chiesa in età post-tridentina," AHC 26 (1994) 119-26; M. Tosti, "Vescovi e Rivoluzione nello Stato della Chiesa," Rivista di storia della Chiesa in Italia 49 (1995) 43-65; L. Fiorani, La rivoluzione nello Stato della Chiesa 1789-99 (Pisa et al., 1998); F. Marazzi, I Patrimonia Sanctae Romanae Ecclesiae nel Lazio (secoli 4-10) (Rome, 1998); E. Menestò, ed., Dal patrimoni di San Pietro allo Stato pontificio; La Marca nel contesto del potere temporale: Atti del Convegno di Studio, Ascoli Piceno, 14-16 settembre 1990 (repr. Spoleto, 2000).

ERWIN GATZ

Peter's Pence (obulus, denarius, or census Sancti Petri). This collection is taken up on the feast of Sts. Peter and Paul (June 29) or on the previous or following Sunday in all the parishes of the world, to permit the → Holy See to carry out its tasks (→ Finances of the Apostolic See). It is not mentioned in the CIC and is to be distinguished from the gifts of the dioceses made on the basis of can. 1271. It is mentioned in the "Directory of the Pastoral Ministry of Bishops" issued by the Congregation for Bishops on February 22, 1973 (no. 46).

Peter's Pence was paid to the Holy See in England in the eighth century, and later in regions such as Scandinavia and Poland; these payments ceased in the Reformation period. The French journalist Charles-René de Montalembert organized a collection of the faithful for the pope in 1859; similar initiatives followed in other countries, including Germany and Austria.

■ Bibliography: DDC 4:1121ff.; RGG 3rd ed. 5:243; DMC 1:86ff.; NCE 11:235; HKKR 879f.; HDRG 3:1638f.; E. Fahlbusch et al., eds., Evangelisches Kirchenlexikon (3rd ed. Göttingen, 1992) 3:1142; LMA 6:1942; VATL 568f.; H. Benz, Finanzen und Finanzpolitik des Heiligen Stuhls (Stuttgart, 1993) 79-85; F. Kalde, Kirchlicher Finanzausgleich (Würzburg, 1993) 78ff.

FRANZ KALDE

Petrine Ministry.
1. Biblical Theology.—2. Systematic Theology.—
3. Ecumenical Perspectives.

1. Biblical Theology

When modern scholars speak of a "Petrine ministry," they already presuppose a "Petrine succession" in the sense of a pastoral ministry on behalf of the universal church (see John 21:15ff.), whereas the New Testament speaks neither of Petrine succession nor of a Petrine ministry in this sense. One must therefore distinquish between this fact and the later apologetic appeal to the Petrine tradition of the New Testament, especially Jesus' words to Peter in Matt. 16:17ff., which were used to prove the existence of a ministry of → Peter's successor, exercised by the bishop of Rome. In accord with a historical-critical understanding, however, one cannot employ the New Testament texts about the Petrine ministry without paying attention to their original meaning. This is why in the current theological discussion we must ask whether these texts provide support for the idea of a Petrine ministry, in view of (a) the particular position held by Peter in the group of Jesus' disciples before and after Easter, and (b) the influence they may have continued to exercise even after Peter's death.

(a) The Gospels agree that the vocation of Simon Bar-Jona (Matt. 16:17) to follow Jesus was linked very early with the bestowal of the Aramaic name *Cephas* (John 1:42, *Petros* in Greek). He has an outstanding importance among the group of disciples of the earthly Jesus: Simon is one of the first to be called, and his name is mentioned first in the list of the Twelve. He is the disciples' spokesman in decisive situations, especially when he confesses that Jesus is the Messiah (Mark 8:29 and parallels; cf. John 6:68f.). Jesus tells Peter that he will deny Jesus during the passion, but he also speaks of Peter's repentance and calls him to "strengthen his brothers" (Luke 22:31-34). In keeping with this position, the risen Lord appears to Simon (Peter) (Luke 24:34; cf. 1 Cor. 15:5), and he emerges as spokesman in the group of disciples after Easter, or in the "earliest community" (Acts 1:15-26; 2:14-42, etc., esp. 15:6-29; cf. Gal. 1:18; 2:6-10). This indicates the special authority that Peter enjoyed on the basis of his vocation and commissioning by Jesus; this found its most important expression in the logion in Matt.

16:17ff. The foundation of the church upon "Petros"—emphasizing the metaphorical significance of this name—and the power to bind and loose which is entrusted to him (though cf. Matt. 18:18) suggest his importance for the *one* universal church in the fellowship of the various communities, as early Christian history developed, even though an institutional office at the service of the unity of the church did not yet exist.

(b) The fundamental importance of Peter for the church of Jesus Christ and for its internal and external unity is indirectly attested as early as Paul's account of his first meeting with Cephas (Gal. 1:18) and especially of the so-called Antiochene controversy (2:11-14), where Paul reproached Peter for having "yielded" to "those of the circumcision party" (2:12) and thus calling into question the fellowship between Jewish and Gentile Christians. He expects that Peter, more than anyone else, will stand firm in the "truth of the gospel" (2:14). Paul's text fails to mention that Peter's role here, as earlier at the apostolic council, was what Luz (p. 470) calls "a mediatory role." In keeping with this, Peter was remembered in the postapostolic period not primarily as a theological teacher; that role was primarily Paul's. Rather, Peter's role was that of exhortation and preaching. The ancient church preserved two Letters attributed to Peter, encouraging the church in the Diaspora in his name (1 Pet. 1:1), so that it might stand firm in its "trials" (1:6; 4:13). 2 Peter is an explicitly "catholic" exhortation, addressed to all Christians and urging them to preserve the vocation they have received. Finally, according to the tradition handed on by Papias, Peter was the guarantor of Mark's Gospel, which was based on Peter's teaching and preaching in Rome (Eusebius of Caesarea, *Historia ecclesiastica* 3.39.3ff.; Irenaeus of Lyons, *Adversus haereses* 3.1.1).

■ **Bibliography:** H. R. Balz and G. Schneider, *Exegetisches Wörterbuch zum Neuen Testament* (Stuttgart, 1992) 2:193-201; *TRE* 26:263-73; G. Denzler et al., *Zum Thema Petrusamt und Papsttum* (Stuttgart, 1970); W. Trilling, "Zum Petrusamt im Neuen Testament," *Theologische Quartalschrift* 151 (1971) 110-33; A. Vögtle, "Messiasbekenntnis und Petrusverheißung," in *Das Evangelium und die Evangelien* (Düsseldorf, 1971) 137-70; R. E. Brown et al., eds., *Peter in the New Testament: A Collective Assessment by Protestant and Roman Catholic Scholars* (Minneapolis, 1973); J. Blank, "Neutestamentliche Petrus-Typologie und Petrusamt," *Concilium* 9 (1973) 173-79; P. Hoffmann, "Der Petrusprimat im

Matthäusevangelium," in *Neues Testament und Kirche,* Festschrift for R. Schnackenburg (Freiburg, 1974) 94-114; F. Mussner, *Petrus und Paulus—Pole der Einheit* (Freiburg, 1976); R. Pesch, *Simon-Petrus* (Stuttgart, 1980); J. Blank, "Petrus und Petrusamt im Neuen Testament" (1979) in idem, *Vom Urchristentum zur Kirche* (Munich, 1982) 89-146; J. Gnilka, *Das Matthäusevangelium* (Freiburg, 1988) 2:71-80; U. Luz, *Das Evangelium nach Matthäus* (Zurich, 1990) 2:467-83; D. O'Brian, "Thou art Peter," *Cross Currents* 46 (1996) 379-87; U. Wilckens, "Joh 21,15-23 als Grundtext zum Thema 'Petrusdienst,'" in *Wege zum Verständnis,* Festschrift for C. Demke (Leipzig, 1997) 318-33; M. Diefenbach, "Ökumenische Probleme infolge johanneischer Auslegung: Eine wirkungs- und rezeptionsgeschichtliche Betrachtung des johanneischen Petrusbildes," *Catholica* 52 (Münster, 1998) 44-66; M. Benedetti, "Petrus und das Papstamt," in *Semiotica biblica,* Festschrift for E. Güttgemanns (Hamburg, 1999) 109-24; J. M. van Cangh, "Le rôle de Pierre dans le Nouveau Testament," in P. Tihon, ed., *Changer la papauté?* (Paris, 2000) 441-62.

KARL KERTELGE

2. *Systematic Theology*

The term "Petrine ministry" (or service or function) denotes that task within and on behalf of the universal church based on Christ's promises to Peter which emphasizes the unique position of Peter among the apostles and constitutes an authority that goes beyond his historical person. Thus, the Petrine ministry is a fundamental ecclesial aspect of the church linked to its essence (*de iure divino*) and is therefore to be defined in ecclesiological terms. Historically speaking, this Petrine ministry is contained, realized, and unfolded in the papacy, which takes concrete form in the bishop of Rome. While Petrine ministry and the papacy are indissolubly linked, they are not identical, since not all the cultural and legal interpretations of the papacy necessarily reflect the historical exercise of its Petrine ministry; in a community of faith that is permanently in need of reform, the possibility of a defective exercise of this ministry cannot be ruled out. In this respect, the Petrine ministry is itself a critical standard against which its holder is to be judged; it is in principle legitimate to criticize a pontificate by appealing to the Petrine ministry.

Materially, structural succession means that the bishop who sits on the Roman *cathedra* possesses jurisdictional → primacy, which includes the highest teaching authority (→ Infallibility), vis-à-vis the universal church. Both primacy and infallibility are formally determined by the theological-ecclesiological limits contained in their definition as well as the acknowledgment of the existence and competence of the episcopal college, the preservation of the principle of the local church, and the necessity that the pope share in the faith of the universal church and the apostolic tradition. The exercise of the Petrine ministry is primarily a pastoral task and duty, which is realized in concern for doctrinal truth, the handing on of the gospel in its totality, the preservation and acknowledgment of the "plentitude" of the Catholic faith, the unity of local Roman Catholic churches on the basis of one and the same faith, the unification of all Christian churches, and the dialogue with other religions. The authority mentioned at the beginning of this paragraph is a fundamental presupposition for the exercise of these tasks; equally fundamental is the obligation of the one who carries out the Petrine ministry to observe the principles of catholicity, synodality, and subsidiarity, which belong just as much to the essence of the church.

■ **Bibliography:** G. Denzler et al., *Zum Thema Petrusamt und Papsttum* (Stuttgart, 1970); R. E. Brown et al., eds., *Peter in the New Testament* (Minneapolis, 1973); A. Brandenburg and H. J. Urban, eds., *Petrus und Papst,* 2 vols. (Munich/Zurich, 1982); "Das Papsttum als Petrusdienst," *Münchener theologische Zeitschrift* 38 (1987) 3-109; J. A. Möhler-Institut, ed., *Das Papstamt: Anspruch und Widerspruch* (Paderborn, 1996); → Primacy.

WOLFGANG BEINERT

3. *Ecumenical Perspectives*

The strict refusal to accept the papal ministry was long the bond that united non-Roman churches, and it appeared that any possibility of agreement had been quashed once and for all by Vatican I's dogmatic declarations about the universal jurisdictional → primacy and → infallibility of the pope. The situation has been changed since Vatican II by the participation of the Roman Catholic Church in the ecumenical movement and by shared exegetical and historical insights. Consequently, the question of the Petrine ministry has been discussed in various bilateral ecumenical dialogue commissions (especially Catholic–Lutheran and Catholic–Anglican dialogue), in the larger context of the understanding of church and ministry.

Ecumenical rapprochement on the Lutheran side has been aided by growing awareness of the necessity of a ministry for the unity of the universal church, coupled with the possibility of acknowledging this ministry in the Petrine service of the bishop of Rome—assuming that it undergoes a fundamental renewal in theology and praxis under the gospel. On the Catholic side, a distinction is made between the → papacy as the historical expression of the Petrine ministry, and the Petrine ministry as the theological substance of the papacy (see 2 above); this has led to an examination and reform of the historical form of the papacy in the light of its biblical and patristic origins. John Paul II has officially confirmed this willingness to reform in his offer to engage with the non-Catholic churches in a dialogue about his ministry (*Ut unum sint*, 1995, nos. 95f.).

If the Petrine ministry is to become transparent and acceptable to all churches in the future as a service for the unity of the universal church, it must be shaped anew on the basis of the ancient *communio* ecclesiology which regained prominence at Vatican II, realizing the principles involved in such an understanding of the church, i.e., recognition of the legitimate plurality of life in the local churches and of collegial and synodal structures, and putting into practice the principle of subsidiarity. In addition to this, one must distinguish and separate the functions that have accrued to the bishop of Rome apart from the specifically Petrine ministry (e.g., patriarch of the West or bishop of the local Roman church). This appears essential, if agreement is to be reached with the Orthodox churches, who recognize a primacy of the bishop of Rome as "primacy of honor" among patriarchates which enjoy juridical equality.

■ Bibliography: *TRE* 25:676-95; J. Ratzinger, ed., *Dienst an der Einheit* (Düsseldorf, 1978); V. von Aristi et al., *Das Papstamt—Dienst oder Hindernis für die Ökumene?* (Regensburg, 1985); W. Klausnitzer, *Das Papstamt im Disput zwischen Lutheranern und Katholiken* (Innsbruck, 1987); P. Hünermann, ed., *Papstamt und Ökumene* (Regensburg, 1997); J. Puglisi, ed., *Petrine Ministry and the Unity of the Church: "Toward a Patient and Fraternal Dialogue": Symposium Celebrating the 100th Anniversary of the Foundation of the Society of the Atonement, Rome, December 4-6, 1997* (Collegeville, 1999); J. R. Quinn, *The Reform of the Papacy* (New York, 1999).

MICHAEL KAPPES

Police, Papal. The papal police force was founded under Pius VII in 1816 as the "Corpo dei Carabinieri" to ensure public order in the → papal state. It initially numbered 2,800 men. Under Pius IX, it was renamed the "Gendarmeria Pontificia" in 1851. It continued in existence after 1870 but was abolished in 1970. Today, the "Corpo di Vigilanza" is responsible for law and order in the Vatican City (*AAS,* supplement 62 [1991] 9ff.).

■ Bibliography: *VATL* 835f.; *AnPont* (2000) 1647.

MARTIN HÜLSKAMP

Primacy.

1. History of Theology.—2. Systematic Theology.—3. Canon Law.—4. Ecumenical Perspectives.

1. *History of Theology*

The existence of a Roman bishop is attested with certainty only from the year 235, when Pontian renounced this office, but early texts clearly express a preeminence of the Roman church—as the only apostolic see in the West, the guardian of the tombs of Peter and Paul, and the site of John's suffering "before the Latin Gate"—in establishing and protecting the faith (*1 Clement* 5:3-7; Ignatius of Antioch, heading of *Letter to Romans;* Irenaeus of Lyons, *Adversus haereses* 3.3.1). This preeminence was buttressed by the claims to authority made by its local bishops (Stephen I, Miltiades) in the third century, and it received support in the fourth century from the political and cultural importance of the imperial capital. It was further developed by reference to the pope as Peter's successor, and was recognized as decisive in disputes about the faith. The decisive doctrinal developments of the early period, however, are the work not of Roman bishops but of the ecumenical councils in which papal legates took part. These were summoned by the East-Roman emperor and adjudicated even papal doctrines (Chalcedon, 451) and actions (trial of Honorius, 681).

It is only from the second half of the fourth century that one can truly speak of a claim to primacy, with Damasus I (366-384), then above all with Leo I (440-461: theological) and Gelasius I (492-496: political). This primacy was definitively established, as far as the West was concerned, with Gregory I (590-604). Supported by the Germanic peoples' veneration of Peter and by the reform movements of the tenth and eleventh centuries, the early medieval popes claimed and acquired—often thanks to the lack of unity among the bishops—prerogatives both in canon law (the system of privileges, appeals to the pope, the erection of dioceses) and in politics (the coronation of the emperor from 800 to 1530, the support of the Patrimony of Peter by the Carolingian rulers). From the time of Leo IX (1049-1054), they were supported by the College of → Cardinals, an instrument of church government that became the body of papal electors in 1059, and by the Roman → curia (the central bureaucracy).

The concept of primacy reached an initial high point in the Middle Ages with the *Dictatus Papae* of Gregory VII (1075), which categorically laid down the universal jurisdictional → primacy (*plenitudo potestatis*) over the partial ecclesiastical authority of the bishops, who met with little success in the claims they later made to a (relative) autonomy (see 2 below). This text also affirmed the "freedom of the church" (*libertas ecclesiae*) vis-à-vis secular powers (the emperor and princes), but these succeeded even in the high Middle Ages in emancipating themselves from church control to a rudimentary extent; in the modern period, this emancipation became complete. The mendicant orders of the thirteenth century were decisive defenders of the primatial claims of the pope, who from the twelfth century on (Innocent III) was understood as the "vicar of Christ" (and no longer as "vicar of Peter": → Titles, Papal). In 1302, Boniface VIII declared that the acknowledgment of papal primacy was necessary for salvation (*Unam sanctam*).

In the late Middle Ages, the effects of increased papal centralism and the Western Schism led to a desire for a "reform in head and members" (William of Occam, John Wyclif, Jan Hus, Martin Luther, John Calvin). Such reform often entailed questioning papal primacy, leading the popes to mistrust the substance of the theological claims involved; with the Counter-Reformation, this stance strengthened absolutist tendencies (unification of the liturgy, the institution of nuncios, the Roman catechism, the Holy Office, → *ad limina* visits). As a reaction to the French Revolution and modern secularization, reform groups in the church were primarily concerned with attaining certainty; this led in a definitive manner in the nineteenth century to a concern with visibility of the church, centering on the primacy of the pope

(B. A. Cappellari, later Gregory XVI, *Il trionfo della Santa Sede* [Venice, 1799]; J. de Maistre, *Du Pape* [Lyons, 1819]; the ultramontanist veneration of the pope). A second peak in the history of the idea of primacy was the dogmatic definition of the jurisdictional principle by the First Vatican Council (DH 3053-64) and its rigorous application in practice (condemnations of modernism in 1907 and 1910; the same position was already manifested in the *Syllabus* of 1864).

John XXIII (1958-1963) was the first to attempt to develop a new understanding of the primacy, involving a high esteem for the college of bishops and a magisterium understood in pastoral terms. Although Vatican II introduces the principle of collegiality as a theology of the episcopal office complementing Vatican I, it recalls and intensifies the doctrine of papal primacy (DH 4146f.; cf. the "Nota praevia," DH 4353-59). This has been given juridical form in the 1983 Codex, and has been theologically and practically realized in the pontificate of John Paul II, although his encyclical *Ut unum sint* (1995) declares that the form of the exercise of papal primacy is subject to change.

■ **Bibliography:** TRE 25:647-96; LMA 6:1667-85; 7:210f.; G. Thils, *La primauté pontificale* (Gembloux, 1972); G. Schwaiger, *Päpstlicher Primat und Autorität der Allgemeinen Konzilien im Spiegel der Geschichte* (Paderborn, 1977); A. Carrasco-Ruoco, *Le primat de l'évêque de Rome* (Fribourg, 1990); K. Schatz, *Der päpstliche Primat* (Würzburg, 1990); M. Maccarrone, ed., *Il primato del Vescovo di Roma nel primo millennio* (Vatican City, 1991); A. Garuti, *S. Pietro unico titolare del primato: A proposito del decreto del S. Uffizio del 24 gennaio 1647* (Bologna, 1993); P. Rodriguez, "La constitución dogmática 'Pastor aeternus' leida desde la encíclica 'Ut omnes unum sint,'" *Analecta Cracoviensia* 29 (1997) 319-36; A. T. Hack, "Zur römischen Doppelapostolizität," *Hagiographica* 4 (1997) 9-33; R. Weigand, "Rom und Konstantinopel," in *Forschungen zur Reichs-, Papst- und Landesgeschichte,* Festschrift for P. Herde (Stuttgart, 1998) 201-10; *Il primato del successore di Pietro: Atti del Simposio Teologico, Roma, dicembre 1996* (Vatican City, 1998); A. Carrasco Ruoco, "Der päpstliche Primat und das Zweite Vatikanum," *Communio* 27 (1998) 310-29; V. Peri, "Sinodi, patriarcati e primato romano dal primo al terzo millenario," in *Il ministero del Papa in prospettiva ecumenica: Atti del colloquio Milano 16-18 aprile 1998* (Milan, 1999) 51-97; S. K. Ray, *Upon This Rock: St. Peter and the Primacy of Rome in Scripture and the Early Church* (San Francisco, 1999); W. Henn, *The Honor of My Brothers: A Short History of the Relation between the Pope and the Bishops* (New York, 2000).

2. Systematic Theology

The primacy is a part of the constitutional reality of the Roman Catholic Church, founded on theology and regulated by canon law. The structural principles of this church, in the framework of ecclesial *communio,* also include the episcopal hierarchy with its collegial constitution, the synodal principle, the principle of the local church, and the shared responsibility of all the baptized. This means that the primacy must be exercised and understood within and subject to this ecclesial structure, since both derive from the will of Jesus Christ, the founder of the church (in other words, both are *iure divino*).

The primacy can be defined as the highest, universal, full, and immediate ordinary governmental authority over the entire church and each of the faithful (Jurisdictional → Primacy, *primatus iurisdictionis*); it must be distinguished from the task of a mere superior overseer (*primatus inspectionis* or *directionis*) and from an honorific precedence (*primatus honoris*) in the church. Historically speaking, the bearer of this authority is the pope (→ Papacy), thanks to his position as bishop of Rome. As the successor of the first apostle, Peter, he claims to possess all the privileges that Christ bestowed on Peter for his special service in and for the church. The primacy received its definitive dogmatic definition at Vatican I (DH 3053-64); this was stated with greater precision at Vatican II (DH 4164f., to be read jointly with the "Nota praevia" which belongs to the conciliar Acts: DH 4353-59). The primacy includes the → infallibility of the magisterium in questions of faith and morals (DH 3074).

It is scarcely possible to justify papal primacy in a strict historical-critical sense, since a historical continuity between the biblical Peter and the Roman bishop as his successor cannot be proved. It can, however, be integrated into an ecclesiology that infers from the dynamics of the historical development (see 1 above) that a structural identity exists between the Petrine ministry and the essential form as realized in the historical papacy. This means that the papacy does in fact derive from the christologically given fundamental form of the church and is "of divine right." Since the elaboration of this fundamental form necessarily takes place in history, the primacy is manifested in various ways, which are "of human right"; the extent to which these are in conformity with the Petrine ministry depends exclusively on their conformity with all the data of ecclesiology and of existential reality, on ethical values, and on the demands made by the office itself. There is no form of primacy laid down once and for all, but only an abiding task, viz., "to return again and again to the origin in order to measure the concept and reality of the primacy" (J. Ratzinger, *Lexikon für Theologie und Kirche,* 761).

Theologically speaking, the primacy serves to guarantee and manifest church unity: this is the goal that directs its exercise. This unity is not primarily administrative but spiritual, seeking to maintain the people of God in the fellowship of the body of Christ under the inspired word of God. Naturally, the primacy can be exercised in this world only as regulated by canon law; but this spiritual reality determines the manner of its exercise. In concrete terms, the promotion of unity must include the preservation of catholicity: and this means the preservation of the principles of collegiality, subsidiarity, and the plurality of forms of life and theological thought, since both unity and catholicity are essential qualities of the church. Accordingly, the jurisdictional primacy encounters its limits not only in the fact that it must observe the faith of the church but also in the duties and rights of all the faithful, including the laity (cann. 208-31 *CIC*), and in the episcopal college, which likewise exists "of divine right" and serves unity. This is why the episcopal college possesses the highest authority to govern and teach—though only together with the pope—in such a way that while the pope can exercise the primacy in autonomous acts of his own, he always does so as representative of the entire church, i.e., not in opposition to or wholly prescinding from the bishops (cf. DH 3050, 4146f.).

■ **Bibliography:** J. Höfer and K. Rahner, eds., *Lexikon für Theologie und Kirche* (2nd ed. Freiburg, 1963) 8:761ff.; H. J. Urban and H. Wagner, eds., *Handbuch der Ökumene* (Paderborn, 1987) III/2, 131-47; P. Eicher, ed., *Neues Handbuch theologischer Grundbegriffe* (2nd ed. Munich, 1992) 4:167-83; E. Fahlbusch et al., eds., *Evangelisches Kirchenlexikon* (3rd ed. Göttingen, 1992) 3:1016-33; Arbeitsgemeinschaft ökumenischer Universitätsinstitute, ed., *Papsttum als ökumenische Frage* (Munich/Mainz, 1979); J. Tillard, *L'évêque de Rome* (Paris, 1982); P. Granfield, *Das Papsttum* (Münster, 1984); K. Lehmann, ed., *Das Petrusamt* (Münster, 1984); P. Granfield, *The Limits of Papacy* (New York, 1987); W. Beinert, ed., *Glaubenszugänge* (Paderborn,

1995) 1:131-55; 2:560-73; P. Collins, *Papal Power: A Proposal for Change in Catholicism's Third Millennium* (London, 1997); J. R. Quinn, *The Exercise of the Primacy* (New York, 1998); M. J. Buckley, *Papal Primacy and the Episcopate* (New York, 1998); H. J. Pottmeyer, *Die Rolle des Papsttums im dritten Jahrtausend* (Freiburg, 1999).

WOLFGANG BEINERT

3. Canon Law

In current canon law, "primacy" denotes the preeminent position of the pope in the church. Although this concept itself is not employed, the primacy is described in cann. 331-33 *CIC* and 43-45 *CCEO*: as pastor of the universal church, the pope possesses in virtue of his office supreme, full, immediate, and universal authority, which he may freely exercise at all times. The pope has authority not only over the universal church but also over all individual local churches and groupings of local churches, with the intention of strengthening and protecting the legitimate, ordinary, and immediate authority which the bishops possess in the local churches that are entrusted to them. The concept of primacy is found explicitly in can. 591 *CIC* (the right of the pope to withdraw religious institutes from episcopal authority), as well as in can. 1273 *CIC* and can. 1059 *CCEO* (highest administrative level, with power to dispose of church goods) and in can. 1417 §1 *CIC* (the right of the faithful to bring disputed matters or questions of penal sanctions directly to the Holy See). Canon 361 makes it clear that, when the code speaks here and elsewhere of the Holy or Apostolic See (*Sancta Sedes, Sedes Apostolica*), this refers not only to the pope but also to various institutions of the Roman → curia.

The primacy is rooted in a sacramental dimension, since episcopal ordination is the absolute precondition of exercising the papal ministry. It is only together with episcopal ordination that the acceptance of a legitimately conducted papal → election gives the newly elected pope full and supreme authority in the church; if one who is not a bishop is elected pope, he must immediately receive episcopal ordination (see can. 332 §2 *CIC*; can. 44 §2 *CCEO*); it follows that he is not pope before this ordination. The sacramental basis of the primacy can also be seen in the definition of papal authority as "genuinely episcopal" (*vere episcopalis:* can. 218 §2 *CIC* 1917). It is as bishop of one particular local church, that of Rome (can.

331 *CIC* 1983; can. 43 *CCEO*), that the pope has primatial authority. This link is not mere chance, but is ultimately the fruit of the doctrine that the church is no monad, but consists "in and of many local churches" (see can. 368 *CIC*; *Lumen Gentium* 23.1).

The primacy of the pope must be protected against two erroneous interpretations. On the one hand, it is more than a mere primacy of honor (see can. 218 §1 *CIC* 1917): it is a juridically relevant preeminence that is exercised above all in the authentic and ultimately binding proclamation of the faith (see can. 749 *CIC* 1983) and in various functions of government, viz., legislation, administration, and the pronouncing of legal verdicts. On the other hand, the plenitude of power that the pope has acquired de facto in the course of history is not necessarily linked with the primacy. Papal primacy is inherently subject to the danger of an excessive centralism. A decentralization seems necessary and is legally possible, as we see in the different elaborations of the relationship between the universal and the local church in the Latin and the Eastern codes. The fundamental sphere of papal primatial authority consists in guaranteeing the authenticity of Word and sacraments, thereby creating unity in the ecclesial *communio*. This will be best attained if the legal system presupposes a graduated approach which gives the individual local churches and groupings of local churches greater autonomy. Although the pope has the right, thanks to his primatial authority, to decide in keeping with the demands of circumstances when he acts personally and when collegially (see can. 333 §2 *CIC*; can. 45 §2 *CCEO*), the primacy is oriented to the collaboration of all the bishops and the local churches' responsibility for their own life.

■ **Bibliography:** K. Mörsdorf, *Schriften zum Kanonischen Recht,* ed. W. Aymans et al. (Paderborn et al., 1989) 241-55, 322-38; P. Krämer, *Kirchenrecht* (Stuttgart et al., 1992) 2:99-103; H. J. Reinhardt, "Zur Frage der (Selbst-)Beschränkung des päpstlichen Jurisdiktionsprimats im Hinblick auf die nichtkatholischen Christen," *Catholica* 57 (Münster, 1997) 255-63; J. I. Arrieta, "Primado, episcopado y communión eclesial," *Ius canonicum* 38 (1998) 59-85; J. MacAreavey, "The Primacy of the Bishop of Rome: A Canonical Reflection in Response to 'Ut unum sint,'" *Studia canonica* 34 (2000) 119-54.

PETER KRÄMER

4. Ecumenical Perspectives

(a) The Orthodox Church

It was only in the twelfth and thirteenth centuries, when the crusades showed what Rome's jurisdictional → primacy over all of Christendom meant in concrete terms, that it became a theme of theological controversy. The Greek and oriental churches have always acknowledged that certain episcopal sees enjoy a particular dignity, based on special local apostolic traditions, but this did not lead to the growth of dominant hierarchical centers, as one might have expected in such cases as Jerusalem or Ephesus. Rather, the erection of these centers followed changing geopolitical structures (Alexandria, Antioch, Constantinople). The late recourse to apostolic aetiologies in Alexandria (Peter's disciple Mark) or Constantinople (Andrew the "first-called") function as flowery rhetoric or rather weak replies to the verbal metaphor whereby Rome justified its primacy by appealing to Peter.

It was quite unproblematic to accord the Roman community and its bishop a primacy within the universal church on the basis of Rome's unique political position—but not a supremacy above all others—in the first three centuries. Even after this period, there is a readiness to acknowledge the primacy of Rome in canon law and synods, and to define it (can. 3 of Constantinople I; can. 28 of Chalcedon); indeed, this readiness still exists today, if unity in faith and church life were to be restored. This, however, has nothing to do with recognizing a special and exclusive succession to Peter on the part of the Roman bishops; this idea was already rejected by Bishop Firmilian of Caesarea in Cappadocia in his letter to Cyprian of Carthage (*Ep.* 75.17). Rather, John Chrysostom explicitly says that every bishop exercises the → Petrine ministry in his own local church (*De sacerdotio* 2.1f.), while Augustine emphasizes in his debates with the Donatists that Catholic Christians everywhere must have a primary care for their unity with the church of Jerusalem, where the preaching of salvation began (*Homily* 2.2f. on 1 John).

■ **Bibliography:** M. Jugie, *Theologia dogmatica Christianorum orientalium ab ecclesia catholica dissidentium* (Paris, 1931) 4:320-423; N. Afanassieff et al., *La primauté de Pierre dans l'Église Orthodoxe* (Neuchâtel, 1960); F. Dvornik, *Byzance et la primauté Romaine* (Paris, 1964); J. Darrouzès, "Les documents byzantins du XIIᵉ siècle sur la primauté Romaine," *Revue des études byzantines* 23 (1965) 42-88; J. Spiteris, *La critica bizantina del primato romano nel secolo XII* (Rome, 1979); Bishop Vasilios (Tsiopanas) of Aristi et al., *Das Papstamt: Dienst oder Hindernis für die Ökumene?* (Regensburg, 1985); A. Rauch and P. Imhof, eds., *Das Dienstamt der Einheit in der Kirche. Primat—Patriarchat—Papsttum* (St. Ottilien, 1991); D. Papandreou, "Petrusdienst und Primat," *Theologische Quartalschrift* 178 (1998) 97-111; A. Garuti, "Primato del Vescovo di Rome e dialogo Catolico-Ortodosso," *Antonianum* 73 (1998) 3-42; C. Davey, "Statements on Primacy and Universal Primacy by Representatives of the Orthodox Church," *One in Christ* 35 (1999) 378-82; E. MacManus, "Aspects of Primacy according to Two Orthodox Theologians (Afanassieff, Zizioulas)," *One in Christ* 36 (2000) 234-50.

PETER PLANK

(b) The Lutheran Church

The Reformation did not begin with an attack on the primacy as such, although its opponents often represented it in this way: Martin Luther's declared willingness to obey the pope gave place to a critique with a more radical stance only when it became clear that the concerns of the Reformers met with rejection in Rome. He soon formulates the idea—at first (from December 1518) as the expression of his concern, then (from October 1520) of his conviction—that the pope is "Antichrist" (2 Thess. 2:4). From that time on, this verdict is a constant element of Reformation polemics, and it was included in the Lutheran confessional texts.

The kernel of this apocalyptic-eschatological verdict is basically formed by three accusations: the pope makes himself "judge over scripture"; he formulates "new articles of faith"; and obedience to the pope is declared to be "necessary for salvation." Nevertheless, we repeatedly see in Luther, and even more clearly in Philipp Melanchthon, a certain openness vis-à-vis a papacy that "the gospel would allow," a papacy that would no longer incur those verdicts.

The dogma of primacy and infallibility proclaimed in 1870 was understood by evangelical theology as the definitive confirmation of the Reformation polemics. In the question of primacy, "the key has now turned in the lock" (P. Brunner, *Kerygma und Dogma* 13 [1967] 182).

This is not the view taken by today's Catholic–Lutheran dialogue, which has discussed the question of primacy on several occasions (United States; Germany). The question of papal primacy as a "service of the universal unity of the church" is once again open. The deepest hope on the evangelical side is that the primacy may "be subordinated to the primacy of the Gospel through theological reinterpretation and a restructuring in practice" (Malta Report, 1972).

■ **Bibliography:** J.-J. von Allmen, *La primauté de l'Église de Pierre et de Paul* (Fribourg/Paris, 1977); H. H. Scott, *Luther and the Papacy* (Philadelphia, 1981); W. Klausnitzer, *Das Papstamt im Disput zwischen Lutheranern und Katholiken* (Innsbruck/Vienna, 1987); H. Meyer, "Das Papsttum bei Luther und in den lutherischen Bekenntnisschriften," in W. Pannenberg, ed., *Lehrverurteilungen—kirchentrennend?* (Freiburg/Göttingen, 1990) 3:306-28; Johann-Adam-Möhler-Institut, ed., *Das Papstamt: Anspruch und Widerspruch: Zum Stand des ökumenischen Dialogs über das Papstamt* (Münster, 1996); P. Hünermann, ed., *Papstamt und Ökumene: Zum Petrusdienst an der Einheit aller Getauften* (Regensburg, 1997); H. Döring, *Ökumene vor dem Ziel* (Neuried, 1998); M. Lienhard, "Les réformateurs protestants du XVIᵉ siècle et la papauté," *Positions luthériennes* 46 (1998) 157-73; W. Pannenberg, "Evangelische Überlegungen zum Petrusdienst des römischen Bischofs," *Communio* 2 (1998) 345-58; O. H. Pesch, "Petrusdienst im 21. Jahrhundert: Eine ökumenische Perspektive," *Communio viatorum* 40 (1998) 145-62; V. Leppin, "Luthers Antichristverständnis vor dem Hintergrund der mittelalterlichen Konzeptionen," *Kerygma und Dogma* 45 (1999) 48-63; A. Garuti, "Primato del Vescovo di Roma e dialogo Cattolico-Luterano," *Antonianum* 74 (1999) 379-430, 587-626.

HARDING MEYER

(c) The Reformed Churches

As with Lutheran Churches, the central figures of what emerged as the Reformed tradition did not begin with an attack on papal primacy but sought a Reformed church and papacy in the light of the Word of God. John Calvin, arguably *the* systematic theologian of the Reformation and the one whose theology influenced the major Confessions of Faith of the Reformed Churches, saw that the claims of the papacy to universal temporal and spiritual jurisdiction belonged neither to Christ's institution nor to the practice of the ancient church (*Institutes of the Christian Religion* Bk IV, Lausanne Articles, and Two Discourses on the Articles). His most systematic treatment of the papacy occurs in his respectful correspondence with Cardinal Sadolet, where he concludes that even if a claim to the succession to Peter could be established, obedience to the pope would only be due if fidelity to Christ and the priority of the gospel was maintained. Peter, it was asserted, was accorded honor, not power, by Jesus.

In the Reformed Confessions of Faith, two attitudes are evident—that of Calvin's view (e.g., First Helvetic Confession, French Confession 1559, Belgic Confession 1561); or the papacy is not mentioned directly (e.g., Heidelberg Catechism, Geneva Confession 1536). However, because of persecution and the predominant influence of Roman Catholics in a variety of countries, polemical language and attitudes flourished.

For Reformed Churches, a more positive appreciation of the role and place of Peter has been induced by Oscar Cullmann's New Testament study *Peter: Disciple—Apostle—Martyr.* This marked the beginning of a reassessment of the papacy. The U.S. bilateral dialogue between Reformed and Roman Catholics saw the rejection of sixteenth-century papal jurisdiction as a "protest against the scope and character of jurisdiction and authority which had come to be asserted by the papacy" and saw the need for visibly manifesting the essential oneness of the universal church noting the possibility of this being exercised by a personal office in conjunction with collegial and communal structures. The report does note the difficulty even here of claims to primacy and universal jurisdiction and to infallibility in teaching and is aware of the resistance to the acknowledgement of such an office. In other contexts, and in the international dialogue, it has not yet been possible to discuss this issue.

■ **Bibliography:** John Calvin, *Institutes of the Christian Religion* (London: SCM, 1960); John Olin, ed., *A Reformation Debate: John Calvin and Jacobo Sadoleto* (New York: Harper, 1966); Arthur Cochrane, ed., *Reformed Confessions of the Sixteenth Century* (Philadelphia: Westminster Press, 1961); Oscar Cullmann, *Peter: Disciple—Apostle—Martyr* (2nd ed. London: SCM, 1962); Roman Catholic–Presbyterian/Reformed Consultation, *Ministry in the Church* (Richmond, Va., 30 October 1971); J.-J. von Allmen, *La Primauté de l'Église de Pierre et de Paul* (Paris, 1977).

ALAN D. FALCONER

(d) The Anglican Communion

The first phase of the English Reformation was essentially jurisdictional, stimulated by King Henry VIII's desire for a male heir and the consequent divorce of wives who failed to provide him with a successor: this was the King's Great Matter. Under Henry VIII, papal jurisdiction was repudiated by Parliament and administrative and financial links with the papacy severed, though catholic faith was explicitly maintained. The Convocations of Bishops and Clergy acknowledged the king as supreme head on earth of the Church of England (1531-1535). But the sixteenth-century conflict can be seen as the culmination of a long series of conflicts between the English Crown and the papacy going back over centuries and not unique to England, as witnessed in the investiture controversies from the eleventhth century. Significantly, Henry VIII caused the name and shrine of St. Thomas Beckett of Canterbury (martyred 1170) to be obliterated.

Papal jurisdiction was restored briefly under Mary I in 1555; to be repudiated under Elizabeth I in 1558. In the second and more doctrinal phase of the English Reformation confessional expression of the Anglican position on the papacy is found in the final form of the Articles of Religion (1562). Article XIX states that "the Church of Rome hath erred" and XXXVII says that "the Bishop of Rome hath no jurisdiction in this Realm of England."

Theological opinion in the sixteenth and seventeenth centuries varied between high church divines such as Archbishop Laud or Bishop Cosin, who regarded the bishop of Rome as Patriarch of the West. Others were less positive, such as the Puritan Cartwright, who regarded the pope as Antichrist. Newman in his early evangelical days held this view. No Popery had become a patriotic political creed with consequences to this day in Northern Ireland. Between 1717 and 1720 William Wake, Archbishop of Canterbury, conducted a serious but private correspondence about unity with theologians of the Paris theological faculty: the project was Gallican in content. By the end of the nineteenth and the early twentieth centuries some Anglicans began to view the primacy of Rome in a more positive light, notably the lay ecumenist Lord Halifax. It was discussed during the informal Malines Conversations (1921-25). The visits of Archbishops Fisher, Ramsey, Coggan, Runcie, and Carey (1960-) to successive popes keeps the question of the role of the bishop of Rome on Anglican agendas, as did Pope John Paul II's visit to Canterbury Cathedral in 1982. These exchanges have been consolidated with the work of the Anglican Roman Catholic International Commission (ARCIC). The final report of ARCIC included two statements and an elucidation dealing with the bishop of Rome and his ministry. These texts claimed agreement on the basic principles of universal primacy, recording persisting differences on papal supremacy. This convergence was accepted by the Lambeth Conference of 1988 after generally positive responses from most of the Provinces of the Anglican Communion. The response of the Congregation for the Doctrine of the Faith in 1991 was ambivalent. The Church of England's House of Bishops responded positively to the papal encyclical *Ut Unum Sint* inviting other Christians to critically interrogate the office of bishop of Rome (1995 and 1997). ARCIC has since produced a further statement *The Gift of Authority* (1995). It builds on the earlier work of the Commission and offers agreement about the pope's role with that of the whole people of God as gift. It is before the churches at the present time.

■ **Bibliography:** J. H. Blunt, *The Reformation of the Church of England: Its History, Principles, and Results (Part I. A.D. 1514-1547)* (Oxford/Cambridge, 1878); T. M. Parker, *The English Reformation to 1558* (London, 1950); *Anglicanism*, ed. P. E. More and F. L. Cross (London, 1951); T. G. Jalland, *The Church and the Papacy: An Historical Study* (London, 1944); B. Barlow, *"A brother knocking at the door": The Malines Conversations 1921-1925* (Norwich, 1996); *Anglican/Roman Catholic Dialogue: The Work of the Preparatory Commission*, ed. A. C. Clark and C. Davey (London, 1974); *Anglicans and Roman Catholics: The Search for Unity*, ed. C. Hill and E. J. Yarnold (London, 1994); J.-M. Tillard, *L'Évêque de Rome* (Paris, 1982); J. de Satgé, *Peter and the Single Church* (London, 1981); *Ut Unum Sint*, Papal Encyclical (Rome, 1995); *May They All Be One: A Response of the House of Bishops of the Church of England to Ut Unum Sint*, House of Bishops Occasional Paper (London, 1997); J. R. Quinn, *The Reform of the Papacy: The Costly Call to Christian Unity* (New York, 1999); *The Final Report of the Anglican-Roman Catholic International Commission* (London, 1982; reprinted in *Anglicans and Roman Catholics: The Search for Unity*); *The Gift of Authority: Authority in the Church III, An Agreed Statement by the Anglican-Roman Catholic International Commission* (London/Toronto/New York, 1999).

CHRISTOPHER HILL

Primacy, Jurisdictional. Jurisdictional primacy denotes the full, supreme, and universal authority of the pope (→ Primacy) over the church: "But in order that the episcopate itself might be one and undivided, Christ set Blessed Peter at the head of the other apostles and established in him a perpetual and visible principle and foundation of the unity in faith and communion" (*Lumen Gentium* 18), a principle that remains established in the successor of Peter, the bishop of Rome: "By virtue of his office as Vicar of Christ and shepherd of the entire church, the Roman pontiff has full, supreme and universal power over the church, which he is always able to exercise freely" (ibid., 22). This is how the Second Vatican Council summarizes the decree of the Dogmatic Constitution *Pastor aeternus* of the First Vatican Council (1870) about the jurisdictional primacy of the pope (DH 3050-75; on the history, see Schatz, 1990).

This primacy, bestowed directly by Christ, is considered a truly episcopal authority vis-à-vis pastors and faithful of all rites and ranks in matters concerning faith and morals, discipline and the government of the entire church. It does not restrict the ordinary and immediate authority of episcopal jurisdiction, but rather strengthens and protects it (DH 3060f., 3064). This means that it is not the exclusive source of ecclesiastical jurisdiction, but its plenitude. It is not possible to appeal to any higher body against judgments of the bishop of Rome, not even to an ecumenical → council (DH 3063). The jurisdictional primacy contains the "highest authority of the magisterium," viz., the → infallibility of the pope (DH 3065, 3074). The Second Vatican Council complemented the already existing doctrine about the primacy by means of its teaching about the episcopal office and the college of bishops: "The order of bishops, which is the successor of the apostolic college in the office of teachers and pastors, and in which the fellowship of the apostles continues to exist in all ages, is likewise—together with its head, the bishop of Rome, and never without this head—the bearer of the highest and full authority over the entire church" (*Lumen Gentium* 22). In ecumenical dialogue, the jurisdictional primacy is the object of intense study as both a hindrance to the unity of all Christians and a source of hope for this unity.

■ **Bibliography:** G. Greshake, "Das Dienstamt des Papstes," in G. Greshake, *Gottes Heil—Glück des Menschen* (Freiburg, 1983) 323-53; *Dokumente wachsender Übereinstimmung: Sämtliche Berichte und Konsenstexte interkonfessioneller Gespräche auf Weltebene* I (Paderborn et al., 1983; 2nd ed. 1991; 3rd ed. 1993) 164-69,

176-88, 351ff., 466; II (Paderborn, 1992), 517-25, 565, 664ff., 747ff.; K. Schatz, *Der päpstliche Primat* (Würzburg, 1990); H. Döring, "Das Dienstamt der Einheit des Bischofs von Rom in der neueren ökumenischen Literatur," in A. Rauch and P. Imhof, eds., *Das Dienstamt der Einheit in der Kirche* (St. Ottilien, 1991) 449-505; K. Schatz, *Vaticanum I*, III (Paderborn, 1994); John Paul II, encyclical *Ut unum sint* (1995).

JOSEF FREITAG

Pronouncements of the Apostolic See. This is the collective term for a variety of statements, announcements, proclamations, and decrees issued by the pope himself, by the → Holy See, or the Roman → curia in written texts, *viva voce,* or images, which vary in content, form, and obligatory force. They are addressed to various persons, not only within the church (to the entire church or to a part of it such as a particular diocese, or to a more narrowly defined group of persons) but also outside the church (to all human persons, or to the whole world).

In terms of content, one can distinguish the following types: "simple" statements which give information, explanations, or reactions; public and private, sovereign and nonsovereign statements; doctrinal statements (on questions of faith and morals) of the authentic ordinary or extraordinary magisterium in a solemn or simple form; obligatory infallible statements (see cann. 749-50 *CIC*) or obligatory but noninfallible statements (see cann. 752-54 *CIC*); legal proclamations of the Apostolic See (legal norms of various degrees, proclamations concerning the administration of law, similar proclamations, or legal documents concerning other matters).

The proclamations of the Apostolic See have a variety of names: *Constitutio Apostolica* (usually a proclamation of greater significance), *Litterae decretales, Litterae apostolicae* (sometimes *sub plumbo datae, motu proprio datae;* Motu proprio), *Epistulae*—these groups are mentioned explicitly in *Pastor Bonus,* art. 42. We also find *Litterae encyclicae* and *Epistula encyclica, Adhortatio Apostolica* (with the adjective *postsynodalis,* as the definitive papal assessment of the fruits of a synod of bishops); *Decretum, Instructio, Ordinatio, Normae, Regulae, Directorium (generale), Declaratio, Notificatio, Communicatio, Litterae circulares; Rescriptum (ex Audientia SS.mi), Responsum (ad propositum dubium), Dubium, Monitum, Notae directivae,*

Epistula; Homilia (sermon), *Allocutio* (address, especially the weekly general audiences, speeches made during papal journeys and to bishops visiting Rome); *Nuntius* (message, sometimes *gratulatorius* [congratulations], *televisificus* or *scripto datus*); *Conventio* (*Concordatum, Modus vivendi, Litterae mutuo datae* [exchange of Notes]).

The proclamations of the Apostolic See have a variety of external forms: Bull, Brief, *Epistula, Litterae simplices, Chirographum seu litterae autographae* (handwritten).

Since there is no official definition of the precise valency of these terms, nor any unified terminology, the name and form employed do not permit any direct inference about the weightiness or obligatory character of a proclamation; the decisive factor is the matter in question. The sequence followed in the indexes of the → *Acta Apostolicae Sedis* (*Index generalis actorum; Index documentorum chronologico ordine digestus*) says little about the importance of these proclamations.

The pronouncements of the Holy See are not always published. Some are also published in a translation (usually nonofficial); normally, it is the Latin text that is authentic and binding. The organs of publication employed are the *AAS* and the → *Osservatore Romano* (daily newspaper covering religious and political matters), as well as the → *Annuario Pontificio, L'Attività della Santa Sede,* and *Annuarium Statisticum Ecclesiae* (yearly statistics). Some proclamations of the Holy See are communicated in press conferences (Press Office of the Holy See).

The vigor of tradition can be seen in the maintenance of the numerous designations inherited from the past. This is why all attempts at creating a uniform typology have failed.

■ **Bibliography:** G. Michiels, *Normae generales Juris Canonici: Commentarius libri I CIC* (2nd ed. Paris et al., 1949) 1:213-20; L. Wächter, *Gesetz im kanonischen Recht* (St. Ottilien, 1989); F. G. Morrisey, *Papal and Curial Pronouncements: Their Canonical Significance in Light of the 1983 Code of Canon Law* (2nd ed. Ottawa, 1995); H. Grote, *Was verlautbart Rom wie? Eine Dokumentenkunde für die Praxis* (Göttingen, 1995); J. Gehr, *Die rechtliche Qualifikation der Beschlüsse des Zweiten Vatikanischen Konzils* (St. Ottilien, 1997).

HERIBERT SCHMITZ

Radio Vatican. In the aftermath of the → Lateran Treaties, Pius XI commissioned the Italian radio pioneer Guglielmo Marconi in 1929 to construct a Vatican transmitter, and this was inaugurated on February 12, 1931. The first director was the Jesuit Giuseppe Gianfranceschi, and the Society of Jesus has provided the general director and the technical and program directors throughout the history of Radio Vatican. Until 1939, there were no programs, merely occasional discourses and messages of the popes and transmissions of worship and other celebrations. Today, Radio Vatican produces programs in thirty-eight languages. The three basic elements are up-to-date information about daily events in church life throughout the world, theological and ecclesiastical education, and spiritual help for the faithful. The → Secretariat of State has responsibility for the contents of Radio Vatican, which is financed by the Financial Administration of the Vatican. There is no advertising and no license fees are collected.

About four hundred persons, from the various lands to which Radio Vatican broadcasts, are involved in this work. The programs can be heard on three wavelengths, short, medium, and VHF. Programs have also been broadcast via satellite since 1993.

■ **Bibliography:** *VATL* 634f.; R. Tucci, "50 Jahre Radio Vatikan," *Funk-Korrespondenz* 7 (Feb. 11, 1981), Beilage Kirche und Rundfunk, pp. B1-B10; *AnPont* (2000) 1385-88, 1986.

WOLFGANG PÜTZ

Register, Papal. Following the example of the Roman, especially the imperial, authorities (*commentarii, gesta, regesta*), the popes began at a very early date to keep copies of the → Letters they sent out; these were initially ordered according to the year of indiction, and are attested as early as the mid-fourth century. They served canon lawyers and others as sources for their collections. Incoming correspondence, notes, and other materials were sometimes also preserved in papyrus rolls, later in parchment codices; paper was used increasingly from the fourteenth century onward. The continuous series, albeit with some gaps, is preserved only from Innocent III (1198) on; it covers more than twenty thousand volumes down to most recent times, and most of this material is in the Vatican Secret → Archive. Apart from an eleventh-century copy in the Beneventana of a register of John VIII (Registra Vaticana 1; 876-882), and what is probably an original register of Gregory VII (Registra Vaticana 2), the early original registers were probably lost in the confusion of thirteenth-century Rome.

Registrations were made either at the request of the petitioner or because of curial interest (curial letters), mostly on the basis of drafts but sometimes using the original texts. In the thirteenth century, the sequence is roughly chronological, following the years of each pontificate, with supplements and summaries of particular groups of letters, since it was common for months to pass before bundles of drafts were copied together onto calligraphic codices. At that period, fewer than 10 to 20 percent of outgoing documents were registered; important curial letters are often missing; and the practice varied from one pontificate to the next. From the time of Innocent IV, the curial letters were preserved in special registers separate from the "common letters" (*Litterae communes*). There were also special registers (especially that of Innocent III about the conflict over the German throne: Registra Vaticana 6) and some "chamber registers" which dealt primarily with the business of the papal states and papal finances.

Important changes took place in Avignon. The chancellery register was initially committed to paper, then ordered chronologically and thematically and copied onto parchment; from the middle of the pontificate of Innocent VI, such copies were made only in part, and this ceased altogether later on. From John XXII on, secret registers on parchment were also produced in the "secret chamber" of the pope; from the time of Gregory XI, these were the work of the secretaries. The → Apostolic Chamber produced its own parchment registers from the fourteenth century on; these too were the work of the secretaries, so that they overlap with the secret registers. The basis of these registers was usually provided by the originals in the case of the "common letters," and drafts in the case of the chamber and secret registers. From Benedict XII on, petitioners' requests were registered on paper in the suppliants' registers. We have similar registers of the → Apostolic Penitentiary from the beginning of the fifteenth century, but none of the outgoing letters has been preserved. After the close of the Western Schism, the registers were written on paper.

According to the modern classification, the Registra Vaticana comprise the parchment registers from their beginnings, the secret and the chamber registers; the Registra Avenionensia con-

sist primarily of chancellery registers on paper from the Avignon period. The chancellery registers from Boniface IX (1389) were kept in the Lateran in the nineteenth century, so that they are called the Registra Lateranensia. We have registers of briefs from Paul II (1470) onward, and from 1575 we also have Registra contradictarum (*sc.* Litterarum). The different series of registers, especially after the fifteenth century, often correspond to the different procedures involved in issuing the documents.

■ **Edition:** L. Santifaller, *Neueditionen mittelalterlicher Königs- und Papsturkunden* (Vienna, 1958) 37-43.

■ **Bibliography:** *LMA* 6:1687f.; *VATL* 652f.; H. Bresslau, *Handbuch der Urkundenlehre für Deutschland und Italien* (2nd ed. Leipzig, 1912) 1:104-24; F. Bock, "Einführung in das Registerwesen des avignonischen Papsttums," *QFIAB* 31 (1941; with illustrations); K. A. Fink, *Das vatikanische Archiv* (2nd ed. Rome, 1951) 34-45, 80; M. Giusti, *Studi sui registri di bolle papali* (Vatican City, 1968); E. Pásztor, "Per la storia dei registri pontifici nel Duecento," *AHP* 6 (1968) 71-112; H. Diener, *Die großen Registerserien im Vatikanischen Archiv (1378-1523)* (*QFIAB* 51) 305-8; separate publication, Tübingen, 1972; L. E. Boyle, *A Survey of the Vatican Archives and of Its Medieval Holdings* (Toronto, 1972) 50f., 63f., 103-56; O. Hageneder, "Die päpstlichen Register des 13. und 14. Jahrhunderts," *Annali della scuola speciale per archivisti e bibliotecari dell'Università di Roma* 12 (1972) 45-76; E. Pásztor, "I registri camerali di lettere pontificie del secolo XIII," *AHP* 11 (1973) 7-83; P. Herde, "Die 'Registra contradictarum' des Vatikanischen Archivs (1575-1799)," in *Palaeographia, Diplomatica et Archivistica*, Festschrift for G. Battelli (Rome, 1979) 2:407-44; P. Rabikauskas, *Diplomatica pontificia* (4th ed. Rome, 1980) 66-75, 107f., 125-36; M. Giusti, *Inventario dei registri vaticani* (Vatican City, 1981); H. Hoberg, "Das Vatikanische Archivs seit 1950," *RQ* 77 (1982) 148f.; T. Frenz, *Die Kanzlei der Päpste der Hochrenaissance 1471-1527* (Tübingen, 1986); L. Schmugge et al., *Die Supplikenregister der päpstlichen Pönitentiarie aus der Zeit Pius' II. (1458-64)* (Tübingen, 1996); P. N. Zutshi, "The Registers of Common Letters of Pope Urban V (1362-70) and Gregory IX (1370-78)," *Journal of Ecclesiastical History* 51 (2000) 497-508; T. Frenz, *Papsturkunden des Mittelalters und der Neuzeit,* (2nd ed. Stuttgart, 2000).

PETER HERDE

Rome

1. History.—2. Art and Architecture.—3. Diocese.

The city of Rome (*Roma* in Latin and Italian) lies on the lower reaches of the river Tiber, in the southern foothills of Latium. In the classical period, it was the capital of the empire and the seat of the → papacy. From the mid-eighth century, it was the center of the papal → state, and it has been the capital of Italy since 1870.

1. History

Since late antiquity, Rome has enjoyed unquestioned importance, as the city of St. → Peter and of the martyrs, and as the ecclesiastical center of the West. Gregory the Great (590-604) was the first pope who succeeded in making the unity of the Western church a genuinely central factor in a supranational community of peoples. Although he himself loyally acknowledged the emperor in a period when the power of Byzantium was declining, circumstances forced him to assume civic responsibilities in central Italy, with the result that the ecclesiastical administration increasingly came to supplant the structures of the state: for example, the Roman corn supply came from lands owned by the church. The external appearance of the city changed too, not so much through magnificent church buildings as through the diaconal institutions which were often housed in former granaries. Other acts of Gregory were significant for the future of Rome: he made positive contact with the Germanic peoples, who were on the rise; he won the Langobards and West Goths for the Roman church, and he sent Augustine, prior of St. Andrew's monastery, with forty companions to the Anglo-Saxons in 596. The church that came into being in England, like the Frankish church which Boniface (Winfried) later organized, had close connections to Rome. After Jerusalem fell to the Arabs in 638, Rome became the goal of a great stream of pilgrims, and this altered the appearance of the Borgo, the quarter near → St. Peter's. Temples whose doors had been closed for more than two hundred years were now transformed into churches: thus, the Pantheon became Sancta Maria ad Martyres in 609. The church of St. Hadrian was installed in the senate building between 625 and 629, and the Forum likewise took on a distinctly Christian character.

In view of the disintegration of Byzantine power and the menace from the Langobards, the papacy allied itself with the Franks in 754. The Donation of Pippin made central Italy a papal possession, while Stephen II bestowed on Pippin the Younger the title of *patricius Romanorum*. From now on, Rome was the secular capital city of the papacy, with St. Peter its nominal sovereign,

and church, Rome, and papacy coalesced more and more in Western consciousness, so that the subsequent history of the papacy was to a large extent also the history of Rome. At this period, the forged Donation of Constantine was composed; this document was produced in support of papal claims to sovereignty until the fifteenth century. In addition, large-scale building works were undertaken between 760 and 860. These included the construction of a wall around the Borgo, which has since been known as the Leonine city, and the repair of aqueducts. At the same time, however, the aristocracy in Rome acquired more power, and it was they who controlled the papacy from the late ninth century onward. Things did not improve until Emperor Henry III succeeded in correcting these abuses at the synod of Sutri in 1046.

The reforming popes—the most important of whom, Gregory VII, affirmed the jurisdictional → primacy and the inerrancy of the Roman church in his *Dictatus Papae* (1075)—fought a hard struggle against the emperors. The outcome gave the pope the spiritual leadership in the Western church; increasing contacts between the peoples also gave Rome a new position. The Gregorian Reform sought to reestablish the structures of earliest Christianity, but it led in practice to the ascent of the papacy and to the orientation of the Western churches toward Rome.

One of the central concerns of this reform movement was to reintroduce the election of bishops, but electoral conflicts frequently resulted in appeals to the Holy See, and hence to an increase in the importance of Rome; this was also the result of the reservation of → canonization to the popes since Innocent III, of the general councils which were held under papal leadership from 1123 on, and of papal encouragement of the spiritual movements that accompanied the rise in importance of the cities: the mendicants placed themselves under the immediate authority of the pope and set up their generalates in Rome. Although Gregory VII wanted all the faithful to look directly to Rome, and the pope to be leader of the universal church, there were also critics such as Bernard of Clairvaux, who warned that the legal dimension was assuming undue importance in the life of the church. The papal claims were also resisted by the city of Rome, which on its part claimed to be the capital and mistress of the world, although it did not even succeed in attaining the status of a free commune; nevertheless, a senate was founded in 1143, and the pope and the citizens agreed in 1188 on the status of a commune under papal sovereignty. From this period on, the nobles built city fortresses that allowed them to control entire quarters. Tensions between the aristocratic families run through the whole history of the city until the fifteenth century; in the thirteenth century, these problems frequently led the popes to reside in other cities in the church state such as → Anagni and → Viterbo. After the first → Holy Year in 1300 had once again demonstrated the prestige of the papacy and of Rome, Boniface VIII unleashed a crisis with his exaggerated claims to authority. This subsequently led to the transfer of pope and curia to Avignon in France; when the city thus lost its structural center, it soon declined. Cola di Rienzo (1313-1354) attempted in vain to win autonomy for Rome and to make the pope subject to the city. Although the popes constructed a residence and an efficient administration in → Avignon, they did not forget Rome, and figures such as Bridget of Sweden and Catherine of Siena kept the memory of the city's role alive.

Gregory XI returned to Rome in 1376, but the Western Schism prevented the city from recovering from the years of decline. Nevertheless, Boniface IX did succeed in establishing papal sovereignty and in transforming Rome into the city of the popes, and none of the later aristocratic conspiracies represented a serious threat to papal rule. Naturally, Rome, with around twenty thousand inhabitants at the beginning of the fifteenth century, could not rival the flourishing cities in northern Italy. Martin V, elected as pope of a reunited Christendom in 1417, was able to enter his city only after overcoming many time-consuming difficulties. He initiated some restoration work, but this was begun on a large scale only in the mid-fifteenth century, after the schism of Basel had been resolved and the money which once again flowed in large amounts to Rome made incisive urbanistic measures possible. The fortresses of the nobles were demolished, and *palazzi* were built on the sites of their domestic towers. Streets were repaired and bridges built over the Tiber; most important of all, however, the papal residence moved definitively to the → Vatican. Members of the papal court and other ecclesiastical groups were patrons of the arts. As

the city rose in importance, its population grew; the incoming stream of persons and money not only made possible new buildings and works of art but also led under Nicholas V to a union between the papacy and humanism which made Rome a center of the Renaissance and of the arts. Under Julius II, Rome outstripped Florence. Nicholas V was the first to develop a concept embracing the Borgo as a whole, which had now become the residence of the pope; he followed the theory of the ideal state which had been elaborated by Leon Battista Alberti, a theoretician of architecture. The renovation and reconstruction of St. Peter's, of the Apostolic Palace, → Castel Sant'Angelo, and the hospital of the Holy Spirit, a work that was to take centuries, began at this period.

Literature too attested to the significance of Rome. The starting point for medieval authors was their consciousness of the historical significance of the city, which had presented the aspect of an immense field of ruins since the early Middle Ages. They did not spare their criticism of the curia when they wrote about Rome, since they measured its activity against the idea of the glorious past.

Pilgrimages to Rome were supported by the popes of the reform period through legislation designed to protect pilgrims and through the construction of hospices. From the late Middle Ages on, many pilgrims also conducted business in the curia. The contacts between Rome and the countries of Latin Christendom, as well as the financial income that accompanied these contacts, made possible the immense volume of artistic creativity which culminated in the building of new St. Peter's (begun in 1506); this met an abrupt (though temporary) end when the city was sacked by the mercenaries of Charles V in 1527.

The Reformation reduced the importance of Rome for a time, but after the popes took over the leadership of Catholic renewal, the city became the focal point for those countries that had remained faithful to the old church. Important reforming orders were founded in Rome, such as the Society of Jesus (1540), and these had a determinative influence on the formation of the post-Tridentine confessional church. It was at this period that the city also became a center of ecclesiastical studies: Ignatius of Loyola founded the Collegio Romano (the origin of the later Gregorian University) in 1551 and the German college (first foreign seminary in Rome) in 1552. Rome's importance for the post-Tridentine church was further increased by the permanent embassies which became more numerous from the time of Gregory XIII onward (Papal → Legations), by Sixtus V's reorganization of the College of → Cardinals (1586), and by his restructuring of the → curia in 1588, which made it an efficient modern institution. In terms of urban planning, Sixtus V gave visible expression to Rome's role as center of Catholic Christendom by building new streets, which gave access to the great basilicas (especially the Via Sistina), by rededicating trophies of victory and obelisks from the classical period as Christian monuments, and by founding the → Vatican Library to collect the testimonies of the Christian tradition, and the Vatican printing press to produce normative editions. The Holy Years of 1575 and 1600 showed that the papacy—and Rome with it—had retained its position in the world that was still Catholic; the difference was that the post-Tridentine orientation to Rome had a religious rather than a fiscal basis.

The impetus of reform slackened in the seventeenth century, and the Counter-Reformation came to a halt under Urban VIII, but Rome became the baroque metropolis of Europe in this period, with a fascination that reached far beyond Catholic Christendom and brought visitors on the "grand tour" to the city; pilgrimages were now less of a magnet than the interest in classical antiquity. In the eighteenth century, confessional barriers began to lose something of their importance, and the number of foreigners resident in Rome increased: not only immigrants who came to stay in the city on a permanent basis, but more and more foreigners who remained for a short period, linked by a shared ideal of education, international contacts, and cultural interests. In this period, the ancient monuments of the city were given efficient protection and were catalogued (Johann Joachim Winckelmann). This rise in cultural importance was accompanied by a decline in the ecclesiastical importance of Rome, since the popes did not succeed in imposing their authority on churches that had been increasingly subject to state authority since the fifteenth century. Although the French Revolution created the initial impression that Rome had lost its ecclesiastical significance altogether, the French concordat of 1801 showed that the papacy—and hence Rome

too—was indispensable to a reorganization of the church.

Rome as an "idea" had been secularized in the eighteenth century, but the defeat of Napoleon brought about a change of climate. The transition from the Enlightenment to the restoration generated a reaction to the universal state domination of the church. Among Catholics, this took the form of ultramontanism, an increased orientation to Rome and the papacy as the supreme ecclesiastical and moral authority. Nineteenth-century Rome drew more scholars, artists, and travelers from all confessions than ever before, with a clear shift of interest from religion to art history: the city of the martyrs became more and more the Christian metropolis of art. Fresh creativity declined, and scholarly research took the foreground. Aspects of this development were the foundation of Christian archaeology as an academic discipline and the opening of the Vatican Secret → Archive in 1881. The numerous academic institutes now made the city an important site of international scholarship in archaeology, history, and the history of art. Finally, one should not underestimate the increasing throngs of travelers and pilgrims brought to Rome by the new means of transport; in the twentieth century, this took the form of mass tourism, making an encounter with the pope an everyday occurrence. This stream of visitors reached special peaks in the Holy Years. In view of the risk posed to the church state by the movement for Italian unity, and the declining support for this state on the part of the European powers, the popes from Pius IX onward placed their hopes in the Catholic masses and sought intensive contacts with the people, e.g., in public audiences.

After the end of the church state in 1870 and the integration of Rome into the kingdom of Italy, no restriction was put on the activity of the pope, but a decisive transformation of the city took place through the expulsion of the church from many spheres of public life (e.g., through the secularization of the religious communities). In urbanistic terms, Rome was now to be presented as the capital city of the united Italy. New quarters were built for the increasing population (1870: 220,000; 1911: 500,000 inhabitants), as well as representative official buildings and monuments, some of which had an anticlerical note (e.g., the statue of Giordano Bruno on the Campo de'Fiori). Forty percent of the buildings in Rome were demolished in the course of this process. The church did not cease to be prominent in Rome, but the city did become more secular. It did not become an industrial city, but a dual capital with civil and papal central institutions and a double → diplomatic corps. The Roman Question was a burden on both sides, and was resolved only in 1929 by the signing of the → Lateran Treaties and the foundation of the → Vatican state. The fascist period saw the continuing demolition of older buildings to give access to classical buildings, to create representative official streets (Via dei Fori Imperiali, Via della Conciliazione), or to build new city quarters.

After the Second World War, the population of the city increased, above all through immigration from the southern Italian provinces (2000: 3 million inhabitants in the city, 3.8 million in the province of Rome). In the same period, the ecclesiastical presence was intensified by the construction by religious orders of new generalates and houses of study; this made the church presence more international. The new version of the Italian concordat signed in 1983 accepted the increasing pluralization and no longer emphasized "the sacred character of the eternal city" as the 1929 concordat had done. The building of the grand mosque in 1995 signaled the end of confessional homogeneity.

■ **Bibliography:** *LMA* 7:969-97; *TRE* 29:191-206; F. Gregorovius, *Geschichte der Stadt Rom im Mittelalter*, 8 vols. (Stuttgart, 1859-72); Istituto di Studi Romani, ed., *Storia di Roma*, vols. 10-31 (Bologna, 1947-87); *AHP* (bibliographical updates); R. Krautheimer, *Rome, Profile of a City 312-1308* (Princeton, N.J., 1980); J. Petersen, "Rom als Haupstadt des geeinten Italien 1870-1914," *QFIAB* 63 (1984) 261-83; R. Krautheimer, *The Rome of Alexander VII 1655-67* (Princeton, N.J., 1985); R. Schiffmann, *Roma felix: Aspekte der städtebaulichen Gestaltung Roms unter Papst Sixtus V* (Frankfurt a.M. et al., 1985); P. Vian, ed., *Speculum mundi: Roma centro internazionale di ricerche umanistiche* (Rome, 1993); S. Gensini, ed., *Roma capitale (1447-1527)* (Pisa, 1994); L. Herbers, "Rom im Frankenreich," *Mönchtum—Kirche—Herrschaft*, Festschrift for J. Semmler (Sigmaringen, 1998) 133-69; G. Spoletini, *Roma 2000: Le due anime di Roma* (Rome, 1998); G. Signorotto, ed., *La corte di Roma tra Cinque e Seicento* (Rome, 1998); J. M. H. Smith, ed., *Early Medieval Rome and the Christian West*, Festschrift for D. A. Bullough (Leiden et al., 2000).

ERWIN GATZ

2. *Art and Architecture*

Rome's surprising importance in the history of art is due to a unique constellation of particular circumstances. Artists from across Europe were drawn to Rome by the papal curia and those who worked in its vicinity, a continually changing series of patrons consisting of cardinals, prelates, families of papal "nephews" and of aristocrats, embassies, and houses of religious orders who gave both religious and secular commissions for the construction and decoration of the cardinals' titular churches, monastic and parish churches, family chapels, funeral monuments, altars, buildings of the municipal government, and private palaces and villas. Pilgrims were another significant factor: the relics that were transferred from the catacombs to the city churches had to be made accessible in an appropriate manner. The donations of the pilgrims (especially in the Holy Years, which were held from 1300 onward) permitted the repair and renovation of the station churches, and pilgrim routes are a central aspect of Roman urban development.

The artists found a rich repertoire in cults and local traditions that were often many centuries old, as well as in the surviving works of pagan and early Christian antiquity, which supplied forms, contents, and sometimes even materials, when *spolia* and valuable building materials were re-employed. This is why the roots of the art in Rome are frequently to be sought in Rome itself.

Rome set its stamp on Western art as the seat of the pope, as the place where the emperor was crowned, and as the ideological center of the empire. The Roman basilica with three naves became a common pattern in the construction of medieval churches, and the "Roman custom" was consciously followed in many places (e.g., the widespread use of the crypt in the form of a ring, and of the atrium; imitation of the transept or west apse of old → St. Peter's, e.g., in Saint-Denis, Seligenstadt, Fulda, Hersfeld, Assisi). The employment of symbols and urban planning make conscious reference to Rome and its main churches (e.g., in Aachen, Cologne, Constance, Bamberg, Fulda).

In the Renaissance, Rome became a school for artists and a center of artistic theory with the foundation of the Academy of St. Luke in 1577. The first objects of study were the classical works, which were collected and exhibited (Sixtus IV

247

founded the civic collection on the Capitoline in 1471, and the Vatican Belvedere was founded when *Laocoön* was discovered in 1506); later, the art of the high Renaissance was studied (the frescoes by Raphael and Michelangelo, the façade paintings by Polidoro da Caravaggio), and the countryside of the Roman Campagna was studied from the seventeenth century on. In the eighteenth and nineteenth centuries, it became customary for young noblemen on their educational "grand tour" and for young artists to spend a period of time in Rome (cf. the "Prix de Rome" of the French Academy).

Rome is a center of scholarly research into art history today, thanks to its important collections (→ Vatican Museums, Villa Borghese), archives, libraries, and international institutes such as the German Bibliotheca Hertziana.

The churches built in the Carolingian period tended to follow the type, building technique, liturgical layout, and furnishings of early Christian models (Santa Prassede, San Marco, Santa Maria in Domnica). Rome retained the basilica with a flat roof supported by columns throughout the Middle Ages, with only a few examples of the Byzantine method of supporting the roof (Santa Maria in Cosmedin). This retrospective architecture reached a peak in the churches of San Crisogono and Santa Maria in Trastevere, erected in the twelfth century. The twelfth and thirteenth centuries are characterized in general by a building style that plays with classical motifs and constructs bell towers, cloisters, and vestibules. The so-called Cosmati employed marble with inlaid work in colored patterns to decorate the floors, pulpits, altars, choir screens, baldachins, and paschal candlesticks in a large number of churches; this was immensely popular. The Gothic style was found only in new churches belonging to religious orders: Santa Maria in Aracoeli (Franciscans) and Santa Maria sopra Minerva (Dominicans). The transfer of the curia to Avignon (1309-1377) and the Western Schism brought building activity in Rome almost to a full stop.

The Renaissance began under Martin V (restoration of St. John → Lateran), Nicholas V (beginning of a barrel-vaulted roof for the chapter choir in → St. Peter's by Bernardo Rossellino), Paul II (Palazzo Venezia, vestibule of San Marco), and Sixtus IV (Santa Maria del Popolo, San Agostino, Palazzo della Cancelleria), but it was only with Donato Bramante that the classical vocabulary was fully assimilated (Tempietto in San Pietro in Montorio, 1504). Bramante's *chef d'oeuvre* is the new building of St. Peter's, begun in 1506, where he was inspired by the voluminous pillars and curved forms of the classical baths and crowned the crossing of the church with a dome higher than that of the Pantheon. The most important architects of the sixteenth century vied with one another to complete this gigantic construction (Raphael, Baldassare Peruzzi, Antonio da Sangallo the Younger, Michelangelo, Giacomo Vignola, Giacomo della Porta). The churches, palaces, and villas they built left their mark on the Rome of the early modern period. Separate funeral chapels were built as annexes to churches (Cappella Chigi at Santa Maria del Popolo [Raphael]; Cappella Sforza at Santa Maria Maggiore [Michelangelo]; Sistine Chapel [under Sixtus IV] and Pauline chapel [under Paul V]). Existing side chapels tended to be furnished more richly and were sometimes decorated in keeping with a systematic plan. Stronger and weightier forms are typical of the new buildings erected after the Council of Trent, e.g., the churches of the reforming orders (Il Gesù, San Andrea della Valle, Chiesa Nuova, San Carlo ai Catinari), the university known as "Sapienza," and the Jesuit Collegio Romano. The vivid visual effect of the typical Roman church façade (Santo Spirito in Sassia) was enhanced (Santa Caterina dei Funari; Il Gesù; the two churches built by Carlo Maderno, Santa Susanna and San Pietro). This development came to include the interior also in the course of the seventeenth century; this was constructed to appeal visually to the onlooker and was often enclosed in curved walls and decorated in a uniform style. Under Urban VIII, Innocent X, and Alexander VII, buildings of the high baroque were constructed (Francesco Borromini: San Carlo alle Quattro Fontane and San Ivo alla Sapienza; Pietro da Cortona: Santi Luca e Martina, façade and forecourt of Santa Maria della Pace; Giovanni Lorenzo Bernini: San Andrea al Quirinale; Carlo Rainaldi: Santa Maria in Campitello); these served as models for the whole of Europe. The eighteenth century conserved this repertoire of forms, and saw the construction of a number of internationally renowned buildings and new solutions to questions of civic architecture (Carlo Fontana: façade of San Marcello al Corso; Alessandro

Galilei: façade of St. John Lateran; Ferdinando Fuga: façade of Santa Maria Maggiore; Niccolò Salvi: Trevi fountain; Spanish steps leading up to Trinità dei Monti).

■ **Bibliography:** *Le chiese di Roma illustrate* (Rome, 1923-97); *Guide rionali di Roma* (Rome, 1967-94); R. Lanciani, *Storia degli scavi di Roma* (Rome, 1902-12); R. Krautheimer, ed., *Corpus Basilicarum Christianarum Romae,* 5 vols. (Vatican City, 1937-80); M. Armellini, *Le chiese di Roma* (2nd ed. Vatican City, 1942); L. Bruhns, *Die Kunst der Stadt Rom* (Vienna, 1951); A. A. Frutaz, *Le piante di Roma* (Rome, 1962); V. Golzio and G. Zander, *Le chiese di Roma dal XI al XVI secolo* (Rome, 1963); P. Portoghesi, *Roma barocca* (Rome, 1966); W. Buchowiecki, *Handbuch der Kirchen Roms,* 3 vols. (Vienna, 1967-97); P. Portoghesi, *Roma del Rinascimento* (Rome, 1971); F. Haskell, *Patrons and Painters* (2nd ed. London, 1980); R. Krautheimer, *Rome, Profile of a City 312-1308* (Princeton, N.J., 1980); A. Blunt, *Guide to Baroque Rome* (London, 1982); T. Magnuson, *Rome in the Age of Bernini* (Stockholm, 1982); R. Krautheimer, *The Rome of Alexander VII, 1655-1667* (Princeton, N.J., 1985); P. Bober and R. Rubinstein, *Renaissance Artists and Antique Sculpture* (London, 1986); U. Fischer-Pace, *Kunstdenkmäler in Rom* (Darmstadt, 1988); C. D'Onofrio, *Visitiamo Roma mille anni fa* (Rome, 1988); S. de Blaauw, *Cultus et Decor* (Vatican City, 1994); J. Garms, *Vedute di Roma* (Naples, 1995); L. Partridge, *Renaissance in Rom* (Cologne, 1996); S. F. Ostrow, *Art and Spirituality in Counter-Reformation Rome: The Sistine and Pauline Chapels in S. Maria Maggiore* (Cambridge, 1996).

MARTIN RASPE

3. *Diocese*

The diocese of Rome (*Urbs seu Romana*) has a special place among all the dioceses of the world, since it is the seat of the pope, who is both bishop of Rome and head of the Catholic Church. This affects not only the person of the pope in his dual function, but also the totality of ecclesiastical Rome, since the city houses both the institutions of the local church with its parishes and institutes and many priests and institutions serving the Roman → curia or the universal church. These do indeed give aid to the diocese of Rome on a subsidiary level, but their primary tasks lie in other areas. Further elements of church presence in Rome are the pontifical → universities and centers of higher education, with around one thousand professors and ten thousand students from all parts of the world, with a great variety of educational experiences, as well as a large number of religious communities, especially the generalates.

These too give at best a subsidiary service to the local church; in 1958, 58 percent of parishes were staffed by religious orders. This international variety is interesting and stimulating, but it does not make the coordination of apostolic work easier. In view of the increase in population from 1.84 million in 1984 to 2.9 million in 2000, the diocese of Rome attaches special importance to founding parishes (1900: 58; 1955: 155; 2000: 329) and building churches (74 new constructions between 1971 and 1990) with institutions and rooms that often provide important meeting places in the various parts of the city.

A papal vicar for the diocese of Rome is first attested under Innocent III in 1198, but this office took on a clear shape only with the Catholic reform. Paul IV decreed in 1558 that it should always be held by a cardinal, and there has been an unbroken line of cardinal vicars since that date. Pius X restructured the vicariate in 1912, and Paul VI undertook a far-reaching reorganization in 1977. Since then, the vicariate has had its offices in the → Lateran palace. The authority of the cardinal vicar is much greater than that of the vicar general in other dioceses.

The diocese includes most of the city of Rome, covering 881 square kilometers. In 2000, it had ca. 2.67 million Catholics (97 percent of the population) in 329 parishes. Of the 800 diocesan priests, 680 live in Rome, in addition to 835 priests from other dioceses, ca. 5,000 religious priests and 21,500 sisters.

■ **Bibliography:** Riccardi, *Roma "città sacra"?: Dalla conciliazione all'operazione Sturzo* (Milan, 1979); F. Iozzelli, *Roma religiosa all'inizio del Novecento* (Rome, 1985); *Guida alle nuove chiese di Roma* (Rome, 1990); L. Fiorani, "Un vescovo e la sua diocesi: Pio IX, 'primo pastore e parroco di Roma,'" in Ecole française de Rome, ed., *Achille Ratti—Pape Pie XI* (Rome, 1996) 423-97; *La diocesi di Roma 1996/1997* (Rome, 1996); *AnPont* (2000) 1:635, 1472-79; *Periodical: Ricerche per la storia religiosa di Roma* (1977–).

ERWIN GATZ

Rota (*Romana Rota, Sacra Romana Rota*). This is the most important court of the Apostolic See. Its name ("wheel" in Latin) probably derives from the custom in secular and ecclesiastical ceremonial of marking off an area by inlays in the floor (often of porphyry) for the performance of important rites or legal acts. Such inlays have existed in → St. Peter's in Rome since the early

Middle Ages. Important judicial cases were considered to be matters for the Rota. Other interpretations derive the name from a round table on which the legal books were laid, or from the principle of rotation in the formation of the individual collegial courts of the Rota.

1. History

The Rota's historical roots lie in the pontifical → chancellery of the high Middle Ages, whose membership included not only the (vice-)chancellor and the *Auditor contradictorum* but also the *cappellani papae*, who were probably first instituted by Lucius III (1181-1185). Their task was the examination of individual legal cases; under Innocent III, they were also given responsibility in 1212 for pronouncing verdicts. The initial limitation to the tasks of an examining judge lives on in the use of the term "auditor" to designate the judges of the Rota today. From the mid-thirteenth century onward, the *cappellani* constituted a permanent court which had no name of its own, but was merely known in general terms as *Sacrum palatium apostolicum*. Toward the end of the same century, it worked in a collegial manner (*Sacri palatii apostolici causarum auditores*), and it was divided into chambers from the beginning of the fourteenth century. The first comprehensive regulations were issued by John XXII in 1331.

Originally, the Rota was responsible only for ecclesiastical matters, but it functioned from the end of the fifteenth century at the latest as a court of appeal for secular cases in the → papal state. Its golden age was the fifteenth and sixteenth centuries. After Sixtus V had erected permanent → congregations of cardinals in 1588, these assumed much of the responsibility for ecclesiastical trials, so that the Rota's importance diminished: now it was only the highest court of appeal for secular cases from the papal states. Gregory XVI issued the legal regulations in 1834. When the papal states were extinguished, the Rota ceased to exist.

When Pius X reformed the curia in 1908, he reestablished the Rota (*AAS* 1 [1909] 15) and gave it new regulations in a "Lex propria" (ibid., 20-35), which also affected the → Apostolic Signatura, and in detailed "Regulae" (*AAS* 2 [1910] 783-850). This made the Rota the court of appeal for ecclesiastical legal disputes from the whole world. The basic function and structure of the court were not affected by the amendments promulgated in 1934 (*AAS* 26 [1934] 449-91), 1969 (X. Ochoa, *Leges Ecclesiae post Codicem Iuris Canonici editae*, 4:5550-58), and 1982 (*AAS* 74 [1982] 490-517).

2. Present-day Structure

According to the norms in force since October 1, 1994 (*AAS* 86 [1994] 508-40), the Rota continues to be a court with a collegial constitution, consisting of judges ("auditors") nominated by the pope under a dean who is appointed by the pope from among the Rota judges as "first among equals." The judges must be priests; their number is not laid down by law (in 2000, there were twenty, including the dean). The other judicial offices ("promotor," "defensor," etc.) can be held by laypersons. The Rota is a court of appeal with primary responsibility for cases that have been decided in the first or second instance by lower courts. In certain matters, it has ordinary competence in the first instance; apart from these cases, the pope can direct it to hear a case, and *avocatio* by the dean is possible (cann. 1443-1445 *CIC*; can. 1065 *CCEO*; Apostolic Constitution *Pastor Bonus* [*AAS* 80 (1988) 841-934], nos. 128f., Norms for the Rota [see above], art. 52). Decisions by the Rota (published as *Decisiones seu sententiae selectae; Decreta selecta*) and the pope's annual addresses to the Rota lay down guidelines for the judicial practice of all church courts. A three-year course of training for court personnel is held at the Rota (the "Studio rotale").

■ **Bibliography:** *DMC* 4:153ff.; *HDRG* 4:1148-54; *CATH* 13:130ff.; *Enciclopedia del diritto* (Varese, 1989) 41:137-51; *LMA* 1:1193f.; *VATL* 661ff.; D. Bernino, *Il Tribunale della Santa Rota Romana* (Rome, 1717); F. E. Schneider, *Die römische Rota* (Paderborn, 1914); N. Del Re, *La Curia Romana* (3rd ed. Rome, 1970) 243-59, 592-96; P. A. Bonnet, "La competenza del Tribunale della Rota romana e del Supremo Tribunale della Segnatura Apostolica," *Ius Ecclesiae* 7 (1995) 3-37; A. Stankiewicz, "Rilievi procedurali nel nuovo 'Ordo iudiciarius' della Rota romana," *Ius Ecclesiae* 7 (1995) 65-87; J. L. Acebal Luján, "Normas del Tribunal de la Rota Romana," *Revista Español de Derecho Canónico* 52 (1995) 231-79; S. Haering, "Die neue Ordnung der Römischen Rota aus dem Jahr 1994," *De processibus matrimonialibus* 2 (1995) 89-115; P. Bonnet and C. Gullo, eds., *Le "norme" del Tribunale della Rota Romana* (Vatican City, 1997); S. Haering, "Die Neuordnung der Römischen Rota (1994) im wissenschaftlichen Schrifttum," *De processibus matrimonialibus* 6 (1999) 181-92; *AnPont* (2000) 1298-1301, 1949f.; *Periodical: Quaderni Studio Rotale* (1987–).
STEPHAN HAERING

St. Peter's Church. The church built over the →
tomb of the apostle → Peter is the central shrine of
the Roman Catholic Church. Since the early
Middle Ages, it has been the most important pilgrim site in the West, and since the fourteenth
century it has been the center of papal activity,
serving both as a palace church and as the spiritual
center of the → Vatican. The church's unique
position suggested the principal ideas that would
shape its architecture and furnishings: virtually
everything here is related to church tradition, the
central certainties of the Catholic faith and the →
primacy of the pope.

On the site of the present building, the emperor
Constantine erected (ca. 320) the basilica of Old
St. Peter's with its five naves. A protruding
transept and a large apse finished off the west side,
while the narthex, forecourt, and a broad exterior
staircase completed the east side. Two round
buildings, the rotundas of Honorius and Andrew,
abutted the south transept arm; the latter served as
a sacristy until it was demolished in the eighteenth
century. In the fifth century, Leo the Great had the
walls of the central nave decorated with frescoes,
and the system employed—scenes from the Old
and the New Testaments that corresponded typologically to one another—became the model of
innumerable church paintings in the following
centuries. From the very beginning, the high altar
stood at the entrance to the apse above the →
tomb of Peter. Under Gregory the Great, the
direct relationship of the altar to the apostle's
tomb was more strongly emphasized, and a circular crypt was built to give the faithful access to the
grave. The final phase of decoration in Old St.
Peter's took place in the first half of the fourteenth
century: the main works, the Stefaneschi polyp-
tych and the Navicella mosaic, were executed by
Giotto and his workshop.

The building of new St. Peter's proved to be a
lengthy and complicated process. Measures taken
under Nicholas V in the mid-fifteenth century
were the prelude to the new building. The old
basilica was in need of restoration, but the decision in 1451-1452 to strengthen the nave and
rebuild the transept and choir was made primarily
because of ceremonial and liturgical considerations—indeed perhaps even as a "house-cleaning
measure" in view of the fact that the old church
was filled with tombs and altars. Work on the
choir began under the direction of Bernardo

Rossellino, probably with the participation of
Leon Battista Alberti, but this did not progress
beyond the erection of the foundation walls. The
discrepancy between the history of the church's
planning and its actual construction begins here:
from this point on, it is relatively easy to follow the
progress of the work, but scholars disagree about
the many projects that were sketched. It is, however, certain that the visionary sketches of Donato
Bramante and Michelangelo in the sixteenth century determined the "look" of the new building.
Julius II laid the foundation stone for the new
construction of the west side in 1506. He wished
to continue work on Rossellino's choir and perhaps wanted to set up a tomb for himself there.

The Latin cross was to remain the basic architectural form, as we see from the continuation of
work on the loggia of benedictions, which had
begun under Pius II in 1464, alongside the old
façade. Bramante, Julius II's master builder, seems
initially to have favored a building with a central
axis, with all the arms of the cross equal in length;
in later years, he aimed at a synthesis of a domed
building with a central axis and a basilica with a
long nave. He constructed the crossing by combin-
ing freestanding pillars with an interior diagonal
slope and a dome above pendants. The projects of
Fra Giocondo, Giuliano da Sangallo, and Raphael
(who followed Bramante as architect of St. Peter's
in 1514) remained only projects. Antonio da Sangallo the Younger (with Baldassare Peruzzi) followed Raphael in 1521. In 1538, he raised the floor
level by ca. 3.2 meters; toward the end of the sixteenth century the so-called Vatican grottoes were
constructed below this. Sangallo's model for the
new building (1538-1544) was confusingly
obsessed with small, antiquarian details and was
rejected by Michelangelo after 1546. When he was
given full authority in 1549, Michelangelo reverted
to the idea of a building with a central axis and
determined the definitive appearance of the
cupola, the west tribune, the south and north arms
of the cross. By shortening the end of the choir,
Michelangelo intended to make St. Peter's "smaller
in size, but all the greater in its effect" (Giorgio
Vasari). At his death in 1564, the drum was finished, surrounded by sixteen pairs of pillars; the
cupola with its two bowls and sloping contours
was finished only in 1588-1593, by Giacomo della
Porta with the help of Domenico Fontana (height:
132.5 meters; diameter: 42 meters).

Functional defects and the threat of profanation to the floor of old St. Peter's, which was sanctified by tradition, prompted resistance from the late sixteenth century to the project of completing the building on a central axis. In 1606, Carlo Maderno was commissioned to build the nave, which develops organically in three yokes from the crossing and is spanned by coffered barrel vaulting over huge piers. The narthex, positioned in front of the nave, provided the link to the Apostolic Palace. The façade of travertine was completed in 1612; this brought the new basilica to its present length of 211.5 meters. Where Michelangelo had probably planned a portico with columns, Maderno erected a façade punctuated by many openings. Forward-leaning half-columns and the loggia of benedictions provide the central accent. In 1612-1614, the construction of bell towers began, but these were never completed; this disturbed the proportions of the façade, although they make a powerful impression thanks to their sheer size. Although the church has only three naves, it was given five portals like old St. Peter's. The bronze doors by Filarete (1433-1445) from old St. Peter's were used for the middle portal.

The interior of the new church was originally pure white. Gregory XIII commissioned the first decoration, which was undertaken between 1574 and 1578 in the Cappella Gregoriana, erected by Della Porta in the quadrilateral between the east and the south arms of the cross. The gilded stucco, mosaics, and bright encrusted marble combine to produce a magnificent appearance. Since this chapel is not an enclosed space, its colorful pattern of decoration spread to the surrounding areas of the basilica; a similar program was employed in the "twin" chapel in the northeast part of the church, the Cappella Clementina (1583-1601). Following the plans of Giacomo Vignola, these two chapels were completed with cupolas, thus realizing at least in part Bramante's wish to have a church with many domes. Clement VIII decorated the main dome and the pendants with mosaics: Giuseppe Cesari created a deesis with apostles and saints between the ribs of the dome, angels with the instruments of the passion on a higher level, and God the Father in the lantern (1593-1612), while Giovanni de'Vecchi and Cesare Nebbia portrayed the four evangelists in the pendants (1598-1601). In 1599, Clement VIII also commissioned a cycle of paintings of Peter for

six new altars. The band of text in the lower architrave of the cupola, quoting Matt. 16:18 ("TV ES PETRVS . . ."), is also a part of Clement's program, which gave primary emphasis to the apostolic succession. The cycle of paintings of Peter had its natural center in the apostle's tomb; it was extended by Paul V at the beginning of the seventeenth century in the vestibule (mosaics with scenes from Peter's life and thirty-two seated statues of holy popes) and on the façade (a relief by Antonio Buonvicino depicting Christ handing over the keys to Peter, 1612-1614). Clement VIII, who consecrated the *mensa* of the altar in 1594, located the high altar in such a way that it honored the tomb of Peter: instead of occupying the center of the crossing, the altar was given a slightly off-center position. In keeping with early Christian tradition, this avoided separating tomb and altar. Maderno completed the open *confessio* below the high altar in 1615.

Clement VIII erected the first freestanding ciborium above this altar; a number of provisional baldachins followed, until Giovanni Lorenzo Bernini was commissioned in 1624 to give the high altar and the crossing their definitive form. The bronze baldachin which he completed in 1633 displays a continuity of ideas and form with its predecessors, but the conception and the use of materials have a completely new scale and boldness. From the niches of the pillars which support the dome, the colossal statues of Longinus (Bernini) and the apostle Andrew (François Duquesnoy) see Christ's coming in glory and are at the same time historical witnesses of the passion, which is renewed in the eucharistic mystery, and Christ's followers in their martyrdom. Statues of the empress Helena (Andrea Bolgi) and Veronica (Francesco Mochi) stand in the other two niches in the crossing. The choice of these four saints, whose biography is linked with Christ's sacrificial death, was determined when their relics were placed in the crossing in 1605; these relics are recalled in the reliefs of the upper niches in the pillars. The reference to the place of the passion is strengthened by the twisting columns of the baldachin, which evoke the legendary columns of Solomon's temple; and since these also imitate the pillars of Constantine's ciborium, they are a testimony to the unbroken continuity of the →
Petrine ministry. One-sidedly political interpretations as "tokens of papal sovereignty" fail to do

justice to the universal affirmation made by this monument, and certainly miss the primary intentions of those who created the crossing as we now see it.

Apart from the baldachin, Urban VIII, who solemnly consecrated the basilica in 1626, commissioned the leading painters in Rome (Giovanni Lanfranco, Domenichino, Guido Reni, Andrea Sacchi, Petrus da Cortona, Nicolas Poussin, etc.) to produce paintings for all the altars; more than a dozen altars were erected in St. Peter's during his pontificate. It is thanks to the harmonious collaboration between Bernini and this pope and his successors that the entire interior of the basilica was decorated successively in keeping with a single master plan from 1620 onward. After the crossing had been decorated, the tomb of Urban VIII followed (1628-1647); this was erected in the west tribune along with the tomb of Paul III. This period saw the erection of the tomb of the marchioness Matilda of Tuscany (1633-1646), the relief *Pasce oves meas* above the middle portal (1633-1646), the decoration of the piers and arcade spandrels in the nave with busts of holy popes and allegories of the Christian virtues (1645-1648), the altar of the *cathedra* (1656-1666), the equestrian statue of the emperor Constantine (1654-1668), the Scala Regia (1663-1666). Bernini gave the mighty Square before the church an oval form by enclosing it within two arms of colonnades running outward from the basilica (1656-1671). The Square and the church form a totality marked by anthropomorphic ideas—Christ (or his vicar) embracing all humanity. The obelisk from the so-called Neronian circus, in which Peter is said to have suffered martyrdom, is reinterpreted as a Christian sign of victory; it has stood on this site since 1585. Most of the ninety-six figures of saints in the inner ring of the colonnade were designed by Bernini himself, whose work achieved an overlapping of the Petrine and the christological programs. This synthesis finds its keystone in the altar of the *cathedra* in the west tribune. The throne of the Roman bishop is exalted into the mystical realm, while simultaneously descending as the empty throne of revelation (*etimasia*), above which the Holy Spirit (represented in the center of a halo of angels and clouds) imparts himself to the whole of Christianity (represented by the Latin and Greek church fathers in the lower area).

St. Peter's was not built in accord with a single master plan, but developed in many phases, often as a result of ad hoc decisions. This means that Hans Sedlmayr's interpretation of the church as a visual profession of faith is unconvincing. On the other hand, it seems that both "dogmatic" and "historical" iconology de facto collaborated here: abstract doctrinal propositions and concrete historical tradition complement one another in the decoration. Bernini united the given elements of the architecture and his own creations to form a comprehensive ecclesiology which makes visible both the contingent form and the transcendent destiny of the church. Its historicity (Scala Regia, vestibule, nave) flows into the liturgical present (high altar, crossing) against the eschatological backdrop of Christ's second coming (cupola, apse). The program of images leads from the historical, via the contemporary, to that which is to come, and affirms the unity of the church by referring to the apostle who is its guarantee.

Apart from the elements of decoration mentioned here, the most important works of art are sculptures: the bronze statue of St. Peter, probably a work of Arnolfo di Cambrio (ca. 1300); the tomb of Innocent VIII, by Antonio Pollaiuolo (1484-1498); Michelangelo's *Pietà* group (1499); the altar relief depicting the meeting of Leo the Great and Attila, by Alessandro Algardi (1646-1653); the tomb of Alexander VII, by Bernini (1671-1678); and the angels and tabernacle in the sacrament chapel, by Bernini (1673-1675).

■ **Bibliography:** *VATL* 561-71; P. Bonanni, *Numismata summorum pontificum templi Vaticani fabricam indicantia* (Rome, 1696); T. Alpharanus, *De Basilicae Vaticanae antiquissima et nova structura* (Rome, 1914); H. Sedlmayr, "Der Bilderkreis von Neu Sankt Peter in Rom," in *Epochen und Werke* (Vienna/Munich, 1960) 2:7-46; H. Siebenhüner, "Umrisse zur Geschichte der Ausstattung von Sankt Peter in Rom von Paul III. bis Paul V. (1547-1606)," in Festschrift for H. Sedlmayr (Munich, 1962) 229-320; W. Buchowiecki, *Handbuch der Kirchen Roms* (Vienna, 1967) 1:102-213; H. Thelen, *Zur Entstehungsgeschichte der Hochaltar-Architektur von Sankt Peter in Rom* (Berlin, 1967); I. Lavin, *Bernini and the Crossing of Saint Peter's* (New York, 1968); G. Grimaldi, *Descrizione della basilica antica di San Pietro in Vaticano* (Vatican City, 1972); E. Francia, *Storia della costruzione del nuovo San Pietro,* 2 vols. (Rome, 1977, 1989); A. Arbeiter, *Alt-Sankt-Peter in Geschichte und Wissenschaft* (Berlin, 1986); F. Graf Wolff Metternich and C. Thoenes, *Die frühen Sankt Peter-Entwürfe 1505-14* (Tübingen, 1987); C. Pietrangeli, ed., *La Basilica di San Pietro* (Florence,

1989); S. Schütze, "Beobachtungen zu Idee und Gestalt der Ausstattung von Neu-Sankt-Peter unter Urban VIII.," *Römisches Jahrbuch der Bibliotheca Hertziana* (1994) 213-87; C. Thoenes, "Neue Beobachtungen an Bramantes Sankt Peter-Entwürfen," *Münchener Jahrbuch der bildenden Kunst* (1994) 109-32; C. L. Frommel, "Die Baugeschichte von Sankt Peter bis zu Paul III.," in *Architekturmodelle der Renaissance* (Berlin, 1995) 74-100; C. Thoenes, "Sankt Peter 1534-46," in *Architekturmodelle der Renaissance,* 101-9; G. Rocchi Coopmans de Yoldi, ed., *San Pietro: Arte e Storia nella Basilica Vaticana* (Bergamo, 1996); W. C. Kirwin, *Powers Matchless* (New York, 1997); L. Rice, *The Altars and Altarpieces of New Saint Peter's* (New York, 1997); G. Spagnesi, ed., *L'architettura della Basilica di San Pietro: Atti del Convegno 1995* (Rome, 1997); D. Casalino, *La basilica di San Pietro in Vaticano* (Florence, 1999); H. Bredekamp, *Sankt Peter in Rom und das Prinzip der produktiven Zerstörung: Bau und Abbau von Bramante bis Bernini* (Berlin, 2000).

DAMIAN DOMBROWSKI

Secret, Pontifical (*Secretum pontificium*). An Instruction about the *Secretum pontificium* issued on February 4, 1974, by the → Secretariat of State with papal approval replaced the regulations concerning the "Secret of the Holy Office," which had been in force until that date. Various projects of the Roman → curia are subject to this especially strict obligation to maintain silence, e.g., preparations for the creation of new cardinals and the nominations of bishops, as well as the procedures followed by the Congregation for the Doctrine of the Faith to protect the faith and the sacrament of penance. Not only the pope but also the cardinals who preside over dicasteries and papal legates can place certain matters (e.g., important documents or the preparation of such texts) under the protection of the pontifical secret. Where this is broken, the penalty is determined by an ad hoc commission. The disciplinary law of the Roman curia contains a relevant penal norm.
■ **Bibliography:** H. Schwendenwein, "Secretum Pontificium," in *Ex aequo et bono,* Festschrift for W. M. Plöchl (Innsbruck, 1977) 295-306.

HUGO SCHWENDENWEIN

Secretariat of State (*Secretaria Status; Pastor Bonus,* nos. 39-47; cf. *Regolamento Generale della Curia Romana,* nos. 83-85). This is the body in the Roman → curia that works in direct association with the pope. Because of its comprehensive responsibilities, the Secretariat of State can be called the central department of the Roman curia. It is headed by the → Cardinal Secretary of State, who has a relationship of particular trust vis-à-vis the pope; this is why he has always lost his office on the death of the pope.

1. *History*

The origins of the Secretariat of State lie in the activity of the papal secretaries with regard to the political and economic-political correspondence of the pope. This was entrusted in the fifteenth century to a secret secretary (*secretarius secretus*), who was made immediately subordinate to the pope in 1487. The term "Secretary of State" is first mentioned in 1550; this term was used in Rome itself for the first time in 1605, and the Secretary of State has been a cardinal since 1644. The power struggle with the Cardinal Nephew, who was in charge of political questions, ended in 1692, when this office was abolished and the Secretary of State took over his functions, as well as responsibility for the internal affairs of the papal states. In the course of an eventful history, the Secretariat of State, as the dicastery of the Secretary of State, has developed into the most important department of the Roman curia; the most recent stages of this process can be traced to the curial reform of 1908, the *Code of Canon Law* in 1917, the curial reform of 1967, the abolition of the papal → chancellery in 1973, and finally, the abolition of the Council for the Public Affairs of the Church in 1988, when its duties were entrusted to the Secretariat of State.

2. *Canon Law*

The Secretariat of State is divided into two departments. For historical reasons, these have different organizational structures; there is no clear demarcation of their responsibilities. Section I, for general business, is headed by the Substitute, aided by an Assessor; it is, so to speak, the "presidential office" of the pope, the main instrument he employs in his ministry. It has comprehensive responsibilities and a general responsibility for coordination; it also plays the key role in the personal politics of the curia. Its duties embrace matters that go beyond the ordinary competence of other dicasteries, the oversight of the papal → legations, relationships to the embassies of secular powers (→ Diplomatic Corps), regulating the representation and activity of the Holy See in international institutions, and international Catholic institutions. Section I is also responsible for producing and sending papal documents, the publication of the → *Acta Apostolicae Sedis,* and issuing official news through the Press Office of the Holy See. It also has the oversight of the → *Osservatore Romano,* → Radio Vatican, and the Vatican television center. The Central Office for Church Statistics is attached to Section I.

Section II, for relations with states, is headed by the Secretary, aided by an undersecretary and a body of cardinals and bishops; it is, so to speak, the "foreign office" of the pope. Its duties include dealing with political questions and responsibility for diplomatic relations with states (including matters covered by concordats). The Cardinal Secretary of State is also charged by the pope with convoking meetings of the cardinals in charge of curial dicasteries to discuss important questions concerning the coordination of their work and to exchange mutual information; these are held several times a year. He must also convoke and preside over the council of cardinals for the organizational and economic affairs of the Holy See, which was set up in 1981 and usually meets twice a year (→ Finances of the Apostolic See). As occasion requires, and with the consent of the pope, he should also invite the heads of several curial bodies to joint consultations.

■ **Primary Sources:** John Paul II, Apostolic Constitution *Pastor Bonus,* June 28, 1988 (*AAS* 80 [1988] 841-934, with corrections: 87 [1995] 588); *Regolamento Generale della Curia Romana, AAS* 84 (1992) 201-43; 91 (1999) 630-99.
■ **Bibliography:** On 1: *VATL* 752ff.; A. Kraus, "Secretarius und Sekretariat: Der Ursprung der Institution des Staatssekretariats und ihr Einfluß auf die Entwicklung moderner Regierungsformen in Europa," *RQ* 55 (1960) 43-84; J. Semmler, *Das Päpstliche Staatssekretariat in den Pontifikaten Pauls V. und Gregors XV. 1605-23,* Forschungen zur Geschichte des Päpstlichen Staatssekretariats 2; *RQ Supplementheft* 33 (Rome, 1969); *AnPont* (2000) 1933f. On 2: *MKCIC* can. 360; *HKKR* 2nd ed. 370f.; W. Aymans and K. Mörsdorf, *Kanonisches Recht: Lehrbuch aufgrund des CIC* (13th ed. Paderborn et al., 1997) 2:248f.; A. Kraus, "Das Päpstliche Staatssekretariat unter Urban VIII.," *AHP* 33 (1995) 117-67; *AnPont* (2000) 1237-41.

HERIBERT SCHMITZ

Secretariats of the Holy See. After the Roman → curia was reorganized in the Apostolic Constitution *Sapienti consilio* of June 29, 1908, there were three independent "offices": the → Secretariat of State, the Secretariat for Letters to Princes, and the Secretariat for Latin Letters. These two latter offices had the duty of drawing up special papal documents in Latin (see can. 264 *CIC* 1917), and were abolished in the comprehensive curial reform carried out in the Apostolic Constitution *Regimini Ecclesiae Universae* of August 15, 1967. This reform made the Secretariat of State the central administrative body and set up three new Secretariats as a fruit of the Second Vatican Council: the Secretariats for Christian Unity, for Non-Christians, and for Non-believers. These were a new type of curial office, with a legal structure resembling the congregations, but serving pastoral tasks rather than administration. These three Secretariats were transformed into "Pontifical → Councils" in the ensuing curial reform in the Apostolic Constitution *Pastor Bonus* of June 28, 1988. This meant that they lost their original provisional character and took their place with the other nine Pontifical Councils among the dicasteries of the Roman curia, which have equal standing in law.

■ **Bibliography:** *VATL* 720ff.; W. Aymans and K. Mörsdorf, *Kanonisches Recht: Lehrbuch aufgrund des CIC* (13th ed. Paderborn et al., 1997) 2:244-61.

KONRAD HARTELT

Sede Vacante. This Latin term ("while the see is vacant") refers to the period between the end of one pontificate and the election of a new pope. The see becomes vacant either through abdication (Benedict IX, Gregory VI, Celestine V, Gregory XII) or through death (can. 332 §2 *CIC*). Present law governing the *sede vacante* is found in the Apostolic Constitution *Universi Dominici Gregis* (*AAS* 88 [1996] 305-43). On the death of the pope, all heads of Roman dicasteries lose their offices, with the exceptions of the Camerlengo of the Holy Roman church, the Grand Penitentioner, and the Vicar-General of the diocese of Rome; day-to-day business is carried on by the secretaries. The principle *sede vacante nihil innovetur* ("while the see is vacant, let no innovations be made") prohibits making any changes that would tie the hand of the next pope (can. 335 *CIC*). The *sede vacante* ends when the bishop who is elected pope accepts election; if the one elected is not yet a bishop, he must receive episcopal ordination at once (can. 332 §1).

■ **Bibliography:** *VATL* 718f.; J. H. Provost, "'De sede apostolica impedita' due to incapacity," in *Cristianesimo* *nella storia,* Festschrift for G. Alberigo (Bologna, 1996) 101-30.

BRUNO STEIMER

Sedia Gestatoria. A chair or throne borne by servants allowed crowds of people to see bearers of high office in antiquity. This was adopted by papal (and sometimes episcopal) ceremonial in the early Middle Ages. Several *sediari pontifici* bore on their shoulders the *sedia gestatoria* on which the pope sat and brought him to liturgical celebrations and other assemblies. Liturgical fans (*flabelli*) were carried on either side of the *sedia gestatoria;* these were abolished by Paul VI in 1963. The *sedia gestatoria* has fallen into desuetude today; its function is performed by a special vehicle, the "popemobile" (*papamobile*).

■ Bibliography: *LMA* 8:1665f.; *VATL* 717.

KLAUS PETER DANNECKER

Sistine Chapel. The papal domestic chapel in the Vatican was commissioned in 1473 by Sixtus IV. It was probably built by Giovannino de'Dolci and was consecrated on August 15, 1483. It is an elongated three-storey brick building in simple cubic form, lying parallel to St. Peter's church to the south, and was originally crowned with battlements for defense. The chapel on the second storey has windows with round arches and flat barreled vaulting with fan copings. The choir stalls, singers' gallery, and marble flooring were in place before 1484; the frescoes on the walls, in three ascending bands, were painted ca. 1481 by Sandro Botticelli, Domenico Ghirlandaio, Cosimo Rosselli, and Perugino. The lowest band contains painted tapestries; the middle band has scenes from the life of Moses in typological correspondence to the life of Jesus, painted on large sections of the wall framed by imitation pilasters; the clerestory has full-scale portraits of popes. Between 1508 and 1512, Michelangelo created the ceiling frescoes for Julius II, with scenes from Genesis, prophets, sibyls, and putti in a painted architectural framework; the dramatic depiction of the Last Judgment on the wall behind the altar followed between 1536 and 1541. Beginning in 1515, Raphael created tapestries for the long walls with scenes from the lives of Peter and Paul (these are in the Pinacoteca Vaticana today; the sketches are in the Victoria and Albert Museum in London). The chapel was completely restored between 1980 and 1994.

■ **Bibliography:** *VATL* 733-40; E. Steinmann, *Die Sixtinische Kapelle,* 2 vols. (Munich, 1901-5); C. de Tolnay, *Michelangelo,* II: *The Sistine Chapel* (Princeton, N.J., 1945); R. Salvini, *La Cappella Sistina* (Milan, 1965); F. Hartt and G. Colalucci, *Michelangelo: La Cappella Sistina,* 3 vols. (Milan, 1989-90); R. Richmond, *Michelangelo und die Sixtinische Kapelle* (Freiburg, 1993); H. Pfeiffer, "Gemalte Theologie in der Sixtinischen Kapelle," *AHP* 28 (1990) 99-160; 31 (1993) 69-108; 33 (1995) 91-116; 35 (1997) 49-88; 37 (1999) 85-127; L. Bestmann, *Michelangelos Sixtinische Kapelle* (Munich, 1999).

CANDIDA SYNDIKUS

Synod of Bishops. The origins of this institution in the structure of the Catholic Church lie in the discussions at the Second Vatican Council about how to realize episcopal → collegiality in responsibility for the universal church after the conclusion of the council. No. 5 of the decree *Christus Dominus* envisages that a synod be set up, and even before this document had received definitive approval, Pope Paul VI erected the synod of bishops and established its legal basis in the Motu proprio *Apostolica sollicitudo* of August 15, 1965 (*AAS* 57 [1965] 775-80). Procedural regulations were laid down by the Cardinal Secretary of State on December 8, 1966 (*AAS* 59 [1967] 91-103), in preparation for the first synod, which met on September 29, 1967. Since current law (*CIC* can. 342-48) does not regulate all the relevant questions (e.g., electoral law), the law in force until the promulgation of the *Code* in 1983 continues to be valid, in keeping with can. 6 §1 n. 4. The *CCEO* contains only one brief mention of the synod of bishops in can. 46, where it heads the list of institutions that the pope may utilize in the exercise of his office. It is not an organ of the Roman curia, but is immediately subordinate to the pope (can. 344).

In many ways, the synod of bishops has a special position among the synodal organizations of the church, especially with regard to its tasks, the kinds of sessions it holds, and its membership.

We must distinguish between its ordinary and extraordinary tasks. It is the *ordinary* advisory organ of the pope, with the task of promoting the unity of the world episcopate with the pope in faith, morals, and church discipline, through appropriate discussion of the themes on its agenda. The pope can grant it *extraordinary* authority to take decisions on particular matters, but he alone retains the authority to put such decisions into effect (can. 342, 343).

The synod of bishops is not simply summoned from time to time. Can. 342 speaks only of "specified times," but in practice a rhythm of assemblies roughly every three years has become the norm. This gives the synod something approaching a permanent organizational character. In accord with this, it has its own general secretariat and an episcopal secretariat which remains in office until the next assembly of the synod (can. 348 §1).

Nevertheless, the formation of an episcopal "leadership group" is largely avoided. The synod of bishops—unlike all other synodal organizations—is primarily a representative organ of the episcopate. One must distinguish here between elected and appointed members, as well as those who are members on the basis of their office. With certain modifications, this applies to all three forms in which the synod of bishops can be convoked. In questions concerning the universal church, we find the *ordinary general assembly,* in which the episcopal conferences are represented by between one and four elected representatives (depending on their size), and, in cases of urgency, the *extraordinary assembly,* in which the episcopal conferences are represented by their presidents. In questions of exclusively regional significance, we find the *special assembly,* where the episcopal conferences of the region concerned are represented in the same way as at the ordinary general assemblies. In all three forms, the overwhelming majority are representatives of the episcopal conferences of the Latin rite and of the most important oriental churches *sui iuris* (can. 346; Motu proprio *Apostolica sollicitudo* 3-10). The synodal office lapses with the closure of the assembly (can. 347 §1).

The discussion of the matters on the agenda usually takes place on two levels. Discussions of the topic in general, or of specific questions prompted by local initiatives, can take place in the episcopal conferences or oriental synods in advance of the synod. Nevertheless, it is not possible to bind the representatives of episcopal collegiality to follow a "mandate" in the discussions during the assembly itself.

As a legal structure, the synod of bishops is open to further development. If it proves impossible for practical reasons to hold an ecumenical council in keeping with current law, the synod of bishops might offer an acceptable alternative model. Current law (can. 337 §3 *CIC,* can. 50 §3 *CCEO*) already empowers the pope to create other structures which would allow the college of bishops to exercise its responsibility vis-à-vis the universal church.

■ **Bibliography:** W. Aymans and K. Mörsdorf, *Kanonisches Recht: Lehrbuch aufgrund des CIC* (13th ed. Paderborn et al., 1997) II, §62 (with further bibliography); *New Commentary on the Code of Canon Law,* ed. J. P. Beal, J. A. Coriden, T. Green (New York, 2000) 454f..

WINFRIED AYMANS

Throne, Assistants to. These are first recorded in the third century and were given the structure of a college of priests and laymen from the mid-seventeenth century. They stood around the throne of the pope during papal ceremonies. This title is no longer bestowed on clergy, but lay assistants—most of whom belong to the Roman aristocracy—continue to perform their honorary service under the direction of the Prefect of the Pontifical → Household in solemn Masses and on other occasions, in keeping with the Motu proprio *Pontificalis Domus* (*AAS* 60 [1968] 305-15).

■ **Bibliography:** *VATL* 779f.; *AnPont* (2000) 1969.

MARTIN HÜLSKAMP

Tiara. This external head covering for the pope is first attested in the fourth century. Like the miter, its origins are to be sought in the Phrygian pointed cap, which stood upright on the wearer's head. In the course of time, this crown, which was understood to have both a priestly and a triumphant royal significance, acquired its three-storied decoration (hence the name *triregnum*), intended to display the threefold authority of the pope as "father of princes and kings, ruler of the world, and vicar of Christ on earth" (*Pontificale Romanum,* 1596). Paul VI abandoned the use of this expression of universal authority after his own coronation in 1963, and replaced the tiara in liturgical celebrations with the miter. From 1978, the → pallium has been laid on the shoulders of the newly elected pope as a sign of his universal episcopal authority.

■ **Bibliography:** *VATL* 780f.; B. Sirch, *Der Ursprung der bischöflichen Mitra und päpstlichen Tiara* (St. Ottilien, 1975).

MARTIN HÜLSKAMP

Titles, Papal. The Papal Year-Book (*AnPont* [2000] 27*) lists the following titles for the pope, some of which are also employed in ecclesiastical law.

1. *Bishop of Rome.* The pope is first of all bishop of a local church, the "bishop of the church of Rome" (can. 331 *CIC*; can. 43 *CCEO*). As a bishop, the pope belongs to the college of bishops; as bishop of Rome, he is the "head of the college of bishops," a term first used at the Second Vatican Council (cf. *Lumen Gentium* 22, 25.2).

2. *Vicar of Jesus Christ.* This title goes back to the fifth century and was originally used both of bishops and of priests. The pope is *vicarius Iesu Christi* for the universal church (see *Lumen Gentium* 18.2); individual bishops are "vicars of Jesus Christ" in the local churches entrusted to each of them (27.1). The *CIC* narrows this conciliar usage by applying the title exclusively to the pope; *CCEO* takes a different line (see can. 178).

3. *Successor of the Prince of the Apostles.* Put more simply, the pope is "Peter's successor" (can. 330 *CIC*; can. 42 *CCEO*). The title *successor Petri* is closely linked to the episcopal title, since it refers to Peter's dual function as head of the college of the apostles and bishop of Rome.

4. *Supreme Pontiff of the Universal Church.* The term *pontifex,* which comes from the pre-Christian Roman period, was used as a synonym for "bishop" toward the end of the fourth century; *summus pontifex* was used especially of metropolitans, and later exclusively of the pope. The title expresses the fact that the pope has the highest authority in the church (see, e.g., can. 336 *CIC*), although according to *Lumen Gentium* 21.1, this title is in fact reserved to Christ. This is why it is more customary to speak of *Romanus Pontifex* (see cann. 332-34 *CIC*; cann. 44-46 *CCEO*), a title that indicates also that the papal office is linked to a specific local church. The role of the pope in the universal church is expressed in a way that gives greater emphasis to his pastoral ministry when he is called "shepherd of the universal church" (*universae Ecclesiae his in sacris Pastor*): can. 331 *CIC*; can. 43 *CCEO*; *Lumen Gentium* 22.2.

5. *Patriarch of the West.* This is a purely honorific title, entailing no authority to govern in the Latin church (can. 438 *CIC*). In the uniate Eastern churches, however, the dignity of patriarch is linked with the authority to govern (cf. can. 78 *CCEO*).

6. *Primate of Italy,* a purely honorific title, like no. 5 (see can. 438 *CIC*).

7. *Archbishop and Metropolitan of the Roman Province.* The pope is the head of the Roman church province, a role that entails particular rights and obligations in keeping with cann. 435-37 *CIC*.

8. *Sovereign of the State of the Vatican City.* This title expresses the independence of the pope vis-à-vis secular powers, guaranteed by the territory of a state of his own.

9. *Servant of the Servants of God.* The formula *servus servorum Dei,* first used as a papal title by Gregory I (590-604), indicates that the papal office is one of service. Even today, it is employed at the beginning of important papal documents.

The title "pope" (from Greek *pappas* and Latin *papa*; → Papacy) was originally used for abbots, bishops, and patriarchs. From the end of Christian antiquity, it has been increasingly reserved in the Western church for the bishop of Rome. Today, it is the common title used by others and by himself to refer to him. Frequently, titles are used (even in addressing the pope) which are the fruit of questionable exaggerations. The → International Theological Commission has suggested that the following titles should be preferred: *Papa, Sanctus Pater, Episcopus Romanus, Successor Petri, Supremus Ecclesiae Pastor* (see Congar 543).

■ **Bibliography:** *HKKR* 254-57; *MKCIC* can. 331; Y. Congar, "Titel, welche für den Papst verwendet werden," *Concilium* 11 (1975) 538-44.

PETER KRÄMER

Titular Churches. This term applies today to the Roman churches bestowed on cardinals. According to the → *Liber Pontificalis,* Clement I (88-97) divided the churches of Rome into seven regions, which in turn were subdivided into titular churches; the same source says that Popes Evaristus (101?-107?) and Dionysius (259?-268?) bestowed titular churches on Roman presbyters, as did Marcellus I (307?-309?), who allegedly raised the number of such churches to twenty-five. Only eighteen titular churches can be shown to have existed at the beginning of the fourth century, however; seven others were erected in the same century, so that the number twenty-five would not have been reached before ca. 400. All the other churches in Rome were in a certain sense subordinate to the titular churches, since these provided priests for them. The titular churches, taken as a whole, formed the church of Rome.

The origin of the term *titulus ecclesiae* has not yet been explained satisfactorily. It has been suggested that the church gave its title to the cardinal; or that it derives from the name of the owner, which was indicated by an inscription on the Roman dwelling; or that it was bestowed as a "title" on those Roman presbyters who were appointed to the service of the church of Rome. This third hypothesis agrees best with the information given by classical and legal authors. The titular churches were forerunners of today's parish churches. It is uncertain whether the presbyters and other clergy were ordained for service in their titular church, or whether their "title of ordination" was the Roman church itself. As members of the bishop's presbyterate, the titular presbyters enjoyed not only the rights common to all priests but also the right to baptize (shown by the presence of a baptistery in Sant'Anastasia from 402/3; later baptisteries are found in San Vitale, Santa Sabina, San Lorenzo in Lucina, etc.), to administer the sacrament of penance, and to celebrate the Eucharist. The titular priests celebrated services in the cemetery basilicas from the fourth century onward; this was later reserved exclusively to the three great burial churches, viz., St. Peter's, St. Paul's Outside the Walls, and St. Laurence Outside the Walls. The titular churches were "branches" of the church of Rome, headed by the pope, with its administrative center in the → Lateran from the fourth century.

The priests entrusted with the direction of the titular churches (*presbyteri titulorum*) later became the *presbyteri cardinales* (the reference is to the *cardo,* or "hinge," of the bishop's church), as distinct from the *presbyteri parochiales* of the suburbicarian churches. They took part in the papal liturgy, but they were permitted to celebrate only after receiving the *fermentum,* which they placed in the chalice as a sign of their fellowship with the pope. These Roman *presbyteri titulorum* were the persons most affected by the changes in the constitution of the city church in Rome from the sixth century on, and especially in the first decades of the eighth century. Only the *presbyter prior* of each titular church remained a member of the presbyterate of the bishop of Rome. This meant that the term *cardinalis* in Rome had become applicable to priests; indeed, this became their generic name to such an extent that, until the twelfth century, *cardinalis* on its own usually

meant only a cardinal priest. In the twelfth century, under Alexander III, the cardinal priests also enjoyed quasi-episcopal rights in their titular churches.

The oldest known titular church buildings (basilicas) from the second half of the fourth century include Santa Pudenziana, San Pietro in Vincoli, Santa Cecilia, Santa Sabina and the Titulus Pammachii (Santi Giovanni e Paolo). Most of the titular churches seem to have been built under Constantine. Further sources of information about them are the Roman synods of 499 (with the earliest historically reliable list) and 595, the catalogue of Salzburg from the Carolingian period, the anonymous list from Einsiedeln (ninth century) and the catalogue of Leo III (795-816) in the *Liber Pontificalis*. A list by Pietro Mallio from the pontificate of Alexander III (1159-1181) mentions twenty-eight titular churches, seven for each of the four patriarchal churches. St. Peter's has the following churches: Santa Maria in Trastevere, San Crisogono, Santa Cecilia, Sant'Anastasia, San Lorenzo in Damaso, San Marco, Santi Martino e Silvestro. St. Paul's has Santa Sabina, Santi Nereo e Achilleo, Santa Prisca, San Sisto, Santa Balbina, San Marcello, Santa Susanna. St. Mary Major has Santi XII Apostoli, San Ciriaco in Thermis, San Eusebio, Santa Pudenziana, San Vitale, Santi Marcellino e Pietro, San Clemente. St. Laurence has Santa Prassede, San Pietro in Vincoli, San Lorenzo in Lucina, Santa Croce in Gerusalemme, San Stefano in Celio Monte (San Stefano Rotondo), Santi Quattro Coronati. Other titular churches were added to the list at a later date, as the number of cardinal priests grew.

■ **Bibliography:** *DACL* 14:2883-95; *EC* 12:152-58; *LMA* 8:814f.; P. Hinschius, *Das Kirchenrecht der Katholiken und Protestanten in Deutschland* (Nuremberg, 1869) 1:309ff.; J. P. Kirsch, *Die römischen Titelkirchen im Altertum* (Paderborn, 1918; repr. New York, 1967); A. Kalsbach, "Die Umwandlung des heidnischen in das christliche römische Stadtbild," in *Scientia Sacra,* Festschrift for K. J. Schulte (Cologne, 1935) 71-83; V. Monachino, *La cura pastorale a Milano, Cartagine e Roma nel secolo IV* (Rome, 1947); R. Vielliard, *Recherches sur les origines de la Rome chrétienne* (2nd ed. Rome, 1959); G. Matthiae, *Le chiese di Roma dal IV. al X. secolo* (Bologna, 1962) 54-77; C. G. Fürst, *Cardinalis* (Munich, 1967) passim; F. Guidobaldi, "L'inserimento delle Chiese Titolari nel tessuto urbano preesistente," in *Quaeritur inventus colitur,* Festschrift for U. M. Fasola (Vatican City, 1989) 1:381-96; L. Reekmans, "L'implantation monumentale chrétienne dans le paysage urbaine de Rome de 300 à 850," in *Actes du XIe Congrès international d'archéologie chrétienne* (Rome, 1989) 861-915, at 867-72; C. Pietri, "Régions ecclésiastiques et paroisses romaines," in *Actes du XIe Congrès international d'archéologie chrétienne,* 1035-67; R. Weigand, "Unbekannte Dekretalen zum Kardinalskollegium," in Festschrift for A. M. Stickler (Rome, 1992) 612-17.

RICHARD PUZA

Tomb of Peter.

1. Site.—2. Monument.—3. Interpretation.

1. *Site*

At the foot of the hilly area called *Vaticanum* (→ Vatican), lying beyond the northwest bank of the Tiber (outside the city of Rome in the classical period), lay gardens belonging to the emperors Caligula and Nero. Here there was probably also a villa with a circus attached to it. Two cross-country roads, the Via Cornelia and the Via Triumphalis, led from Rome over the Neronian Bridge and went through this area in the direction of southern Etruria. As was often the case, cemeteries were built beside these roads outside the city; some of these, from the first to the fourth centuries, have been excavated on the territory of the modern → Vatican state.

The inscription on a funeral monument of the early second century, found in the necropolis which was partly brought to light under → St. Peter's between 1940 and 1949, states that this tomb was built *iuxta circum Neronis,* "alongside the circus of Nero." The location of this circus is known both from excavations carried out in recent decades and from the original site of the obelisk, immediately to the south of today's basilica, from which it was moved to St. Peter's Square in 1587: it lay at the foot of the Vatican Hill, about 600 meters in length from west to east, roughly parallel to today's basilica, which is constructed above the northern part of the circus.

According to the Roman historian Tacitus (*Annals* 15.44.6-9), it appears that many Christians were executed on this site in an imperial persecution ca. 64-67. The fact that → Peter is mentioned as a Roman martyr in *1 Clement* 1:5-6 (cf. Ignatius of Antioch, *Rom.* 4.3; Dionysius of Corinth *apud* Eusebius of Caesarea, *Historia Ecclesiastica* 2.25.8) and in other sources (*Apocalypse of Peter* 14.4) attests that the tradition of his martyrdom existed in Rome from the end of the first cen-

tury onward. This gives the tradition a high degree of historical probability, although the sources do not permit us to affirm with certainty that his martyrdom was connected to the Neronian persecution and execution in the circus of which Tacitus speaks. Nevertheless, according to Eusebius, the Roman presbyter Gaius attests the existence of Peter's tomb (called *tropaion,* "monument of victory") on the Vatican around the year 200, and the → *Liber Pontificalis* bears witness to the tradition that the tomb, above which Constantine built the basilica on the Vatican Hill (*LP* XX-XIII, 17ff.), lay beside the place of martyrdom and the palace of Nero (I, 1-16). This makes it likely that the circus on the Vatican, attested by the Roman funeral inscription from the necropolis under St. Peter's and by the excavations, was the place of Peter's martyrdom. According to tradition, his tomb lay close to this site.

2. *Monument*

When the tomb of Pius XI was under construction in the grottoes under St. Peter's in 1939, ancient walls were discovered. The excavations undertaken from 1940 to 1949 and 1953 to 1957 have revealed, between the foundation walls of the Constantinian basilica of St. Peter's and below the dome of today's church, a Roman necropolis on the slope of the hill from west to east, ca. 65 meters in length. This was in use from the early second century to the beginning of the fourth. Between the monumental tombs constructed along a street of graves—all of which are pagan, with a few Christian exceptions from the third and early fourth centuries—lies a small area on which nothing was built, called "campo P" by the excavating teams, measuring ca. 3.4 x 7.5 meters. This may originally have been a path up the hill. Numerous simple earth burials were discovered here. Some lie underneath the red wall (and therefore are older), while others probably date from the late second or third centuries. To the east and the south, this area is bounded by monumental tombs constructed in the second century, and to the west by the supporting wall of a staircase leading to other tombs (R, R^1) and a cistern lying somewhat higher up, which was soon converted to use as a tomb. This supporting wall, with red plasterwork, has been dated between 147 and 161 on the basis of coins found on the site and of stamps on the tiles.

A small monument, ca. 2.3 meters in height, which may have been built at the same time as the red wall, adjoins it, standing before a niche in the wall. A projecting marble console or entablature in the upper section of the niche is supported by two small columns, 1.4 meters in height. A broken section above this construction may have been a second niche, but the reconstruction of the upper structure of the monument in the manner of an edicule, and the height of the red wall above it, must remain hypothetical. A roughly hewn recess—a niche, according to the excavators—below the floor level of the edicule in the area of the foundations of the red wall lies above an irregular, ill-defined cavity in the earth measuring only 100 x 80 cm. The excavators and other scholars believe that the original tomb of Peter stood on this site, which is bounded to the south only by three small walls. The measurements of the cavity and the discoveries do not in fact match those of even a simple grave; but although no material traces of a grave have survived, it is certain that the niche in the red wall, and perhaps the edicule too, were erected in the mid-second century as Peter's memorial, since further constructions in the third century strengthened them (walls g and s in the publications of the excavations), and pilgrims left their graffiti here, along with invocations of the saint by visitors. Although many other burials were undertaken near the memorial, its existence on this site is the probable reason why nothing was built on campo P.

Finally, the unbroken tradition of the memorial site to Peter led Constantine to make the edicule the cultic center of the basilica he built to honor the prince of the apostles soon after 320. He broke down the red wall on both sides of the edicule and filled up the surrounding area with soil, leveling the graves to such an extent that the memorial was higher than the floor of the basilica which he constructed over the necropolis. At the same time, the edicule was covered with slabs of precious Pavonazetto marble, framed by strips of porphyry; this can still be seen today, in the chapel of Clement VIII in the grottoes. This elaborate decoration was in keeping with the dominant position of the monument before the apse, in a specially erected room, viz., the transept flooded with light, which stood to the west, before the Constantinian basilica with its five naves, which was reserved for the solemn celebration of the Eucharist. The costly

decoration of the edicule was completed by a baldachin with columns of Roman marble bearing reliefs. The basilica was oriented to the memorial and was the first basilica to be constructed with a special transept, in order that the architecture might give special emphasis to the memorial. This shows clearly that the monument was regarded as the memorial to Peter's tomb in the tradition of the Christian community in Rome from the mid-second century to the time of Constantine. As the graffiti indicate, it was continuously cared for and revered.

3. *Interpretation*

Archaeological evidence leaves it doubtful whether the original tomb of the apostle lay at this precise spot below the memorial. In the first place, the edicule lies in the line of tombs which (as the inscription mentioned above shows) were built immediately beside the northernmost rows of seats in the abandoned circus from the early second century onward, i.e., at the very edge of the site, and it is scarcely likely that the apostle was buried there immediately after his execution. Second, it is only in the third century that the veneration of the martyrs at their tombs begins in Rome.

Clarification of these questions can be supplied only by the archaeological evidence, but this is not reproduced correctly in the publications, since the excavations were not carried out on methodological principles following the stratification, and the drawings and plans which accompany the publications (*Esplorazioni*) are interpretative sketches rather than documentations drawn to scale which would permit an objective analysis of the excavations and the constructions that were found. On the basis of what has been published, one must conclude that Peter's tomb was at an unidentified place in the area north of the circus, at the incline of the hill. When the circus was abandoned early in the second century, and monumental tombs were erected on the site, the Christian community in Rome erected the edicule as a memorial beside the supporting wall, on a site that remained free, in order that they might preserve the memory of Peter close to the place where the apostle had suffered martyrdom and been buried.

About 600, Gregory the Great built a podium around the edicule, in keeping with the contemporary understanding of the cult of the martyrs, so that he could set up the altar immediately above the memorial, which was viewed as Peter's funeral monument. The circular crypt constructed by Gregory in this podium in the apse of the Constantinian basilica gives pilgrims to this day access to the monument from the rear (western) side. Callistus II (1119-1124) restored the altar over the edicule. When the new basilica of St. Peter's was built (1506-1626), the memorial was included in the lower storey of St. Peter's, the so-called grottoes, on the floor level of the Constantinian basilica. It can be seen and venerated there in its medieval decoration in the *Confessio,* with its front niche in which the → pallium is kept. Clement VIII (1592-1605) had the high altar of the new church built on an elevated podium above the memorial and the older altar. Giovanni Lorenzo Bernini's bronze baldachin (1633) with its twisting columns is the direct formal continuation of Constantine's baldachin over the memorial.

Thus, the edicule as Peter's memorial has been venerated in an unbroken tradition that goes back to the second century, and it has lost none of its force even today. After the grave of Christ in the church of the Holy Sepulcher in Jerusalem, it is the most significant memorial in Christendom; historically speaking, it is the most significant archaeological memorial of all.

■ **Bibliography:** *VATL* 577-80; B. M. Apolloni-Ghetti et al., *Esplorazioni sotto la confessione di San Pietro in Vaticano, eseguite negli anni 1940-49,* 2 vols. (Vatican City, 1951); A. von Gerkan, "Kritische Studie zu den Ausgrabungen unter der Peterskirche in Rom," *Zeitschrift für Geschichte und Kunst des Trierer Landes* 22 (1954) 26-55; T. Klauser, *Die römische Petrus-Tradition im Lichte der neuen Ausgrabungen unter der Peterskirche* (Cologne, 1956); J. M. C. Toynbee and J. B. Ward Perkins, *The Shrine of Saint Peter and the Vatican Excavations* (London, 1957); A. Prandi, *La zona archeologica della Confessio Vaticana: I monumenti del II secolo* (Vatican City, 1957); M. Guarducci, *I graffiti sotto la Confessione di San Pietro in Vaticano,* 3 vols. (Vatican City, 1958); A. von Gerkan, "Zu den Problemen des Petrusgrabes," *Jahrbuch für Antike und Christentum* 1 (1958) 79-93; idem, "Petrus in Vaticano et in Catacumbas," *Jahrbuch für Antike und Christentum* 5 (1962) 23-32; A. A. de Marco, *The Tomb of Saint Peter* (Vatican City, 1964); M. Guarducci, *Le reliquie di Pietro sotto la Confessione della basilica vaticana* (Vatican City, 1965); E. Kirschbaum, *Die Gräber der Apostelfürsten,* with appendix by E. Dassmann (3rd ed. Frankfurt a.M., 1974); E. Dinkler, "Petrus und Paulus in Rom: Die literarische und archäologische Frage nach den Tropaia ton

apostolon," *Gymnasium* 87 (1980) 1-37; M. Guarducci, "Pietro in Vaticano," *Archeologia Classica* 36 (1984) 266-69; K. Gaertner, H. Mielsch, H. von Hesberg, *Die heidnische Nekropole unter St. Peter in Rom,* 2 vols. (Vatican City, 1986-96); F. J. Fink, *Das Petrusgrab in Rom* (Innsbruck, 1988); P. Liverani, "Preesistenze archeologiche: La necropoli vaticana e la tomba dell'apostolo, Il circolo di Caligola, L'obelisco," in C. Pietrangeli, ed., *La basilica di San Pietro* (Vatican City, 1989) 18-38; M. Cecchelli, "Il complesso culturale vaticano dalla fondazione costantiniana ai lavori eseguiti fino al pontificato di Gregorio Magno (anno 604)," in C. Pietrangeli, ed., *La basilica di San Pietro* (Vatican City, 1989) 39-56, 325f.; M. Guarducci, *La tomba di San Pietro: Una straordinaria vicenda* (Milan, 1989); A. Ferrua, "La tomba di San Pietro," *La civiltà cattolica* 141 (1990) 460-67; idem, *La tomba di San Pietro* (Bari, 1991) 325-29; H. Temporini and W. Haase, *Aufstieg und Niedergang der römischen Welt,* II, vol. 26/1 (Berlin/New York, 1991) 539-95; H. G. Thümmel, "Die Archäologie der Petrusmemorie in Rom," *Boreas* 16 (1993) 97-113; P. Silvan, "From the Tomb to the Dome: The Architectural Evolution of the 'Memorial' to the Apostle Peter," in *Vatican Treasures: 2000 Years of Art and Culture in the Vatican and Italy,* exhibition catalogue (Milan, 1993) 27ff.; L. Reekmans, "De opgraving onder de St. Pietersbasiliek op de Vatikaan," *Medelingen van de Koninklijk Academie van België Klasse der Letteren* 56 (1994) 1-20; S. De Blaauw, *Cultus et Decor: Liturgia e architettura nella Roma tardoantica e medievale* (Vatican City, 1994) 2:470-79; A. Sperandio, ed., *La tomba di San Pietro: Restauro e illuminazione della necropoli Vaticana. Restoration and Enlighting [sic] of Vatican Necropolis* (Milan, 1999); L. Bianchi, *Ad limina Petri: Spazio e memoria della Roma cristiana* (Rome, 1999).

HUGO BRANDENBURG

Universities and Faculties, Pontifical. The right of an ecclesiastical center of higher studies (university, faculty, institute) to call itself "pontifical" (*pontificius*) depends, apart from long-standing customary right, on a specific act of the Holy See bestowing this right, either when it is erected or else later, to signify that it is the pope who founds and maintains the center of studies. The honorific designation "pontifical" is given in order to emphasize the importance of the center or in acknowledgment of its merits; or else because this title appears desirable and is therefore requested by the center itself.

Despite this, ecclesiastical centers of higher studies are often automatically referred to as "pontifical." However, while canonical foundation or approval by the Holy See, the bestowal of the right to award doctorates, a link to the (papal) canon law of the universal church, or the fact of supervision by the Holy See do entitle the center of higher studies to be called "of pontifical right," these factors do not bestow the title "pontifical." The designation "Catholic" may be employed only with the consent of the responsible ecclesiastical authority (can. 808 *CIC*; cf. can. 216 *CIC*; can. 19 *CCEO*).

The draft of the Apostolic Constitution *Ex corde Ecclesiae* of August 15, 1990, on Catholic universities envisaged a section on the title "pontifical," but this was not included in the final version.

According to *AnPont* (2000) there are six universities in Rome with the title "pontifical": the Gregorian (Jesuits), the Lateran, Urbaniana, Angelicum (Dominicans), Salesiana (Salesians), Holy Cross (Opus Dei), and eleven other centers of higher learning with this title, including the Anselmianum (Benedictines) and the Antonianum (Franciscans). Of fifty-one Catholic universities, eighteen bear this title; of sixty-eight ecclesiastical faculties, eighteen are "pontifical."

The prefixing of "pontifical" to the names of Pontifical Academies and other ecclesiastical educational institutions is to be understood in the same manner.

■ **Bibliography:** H. Schmitz, "Kirchliche Hochschulen—Päpstliche Hochschulen?" *Trierer theologische Zeitschrift* 81 (1972) 310-15, reprinted in idem, *Studien zum kirchlichen Hochschulrecht*, Forschungen zur Kirchenrechtswissenschaft 8 (Würzburg, 1990) 201-6; J. Ammer, *Zum Recht der "katholischen Universität,"* Forschungen zur Kirchenrechtswissenschaft 17 (Würzburg, 1994) 81, 170, 182, 251, 273, 297; *AnPont* (2000) 1833-94, 1904-20.

HERIBERT SCHMITZ

Urbi et Orbi. This formula is employed by the Roman → curia to indicate that a particular document concerns both the city of Rome (Latin *urbs*) and the whole Catholic world (*orbis*). The promulgation of some decrees by congregations of the Roman curia, especially that for the Causes of the Saints, and the proclamation of certain indulgences, are addressed *urbi et orbi*. This formula is best known from the papal → blessing imparted on special occasions, e.g., the presentation of a newly elected pope or the blessings from the loggia of → St. Peter's at Easter and Christmas.

■ **Bibliography:** *VATL* 800.

JOSEF AMMER

Vatican. In ordinary usage, this term designates both the residence of the pope and of the Roman → curia, and the → Vatican state.

1. History

The name derives from the Vatican Hill (*mons vaticanus*) on the right bank of the Tiber in Rome. The → tomb of Peter has been venerated on the lower slope of this hill since the second century, and Constantine the Great erected the basilica of old → St. Peter's above it. The papal residence and central administrative offices of the Roman curia have been located to the north of St. Peter's since the fifteenth century.

In classical antiquity, this area was crossed by the Via Aurelia Nova, the Via Cornelia, and the Via Triumphalis, where there were extensive cemeteries. It was also the site of the circus of Caligula and Nero, where (according to Tacitus's account) Roman Christians were put to death on charges of arson; these are venerated as the protomartyrs of the church of Rome. The popes took up residence not next to old St. Peter's but rather beside St. John → Lateran. St. Peter's, which lay outside the city (like all cemeteries and cemetery basilicas), developed into a site of pilgrimage, and its significance increased after the fall of Jerusalem in 614 and 638 made pilgrimages to the Holy City more difficult.

In the early Middle Ages, a large number of churches, chapels, and national hospices (*scholae*) were built in the area surrounding St. Peter's, which was now known as the "Borgo." A secondary papal residence beside St. Peter's is first attested in 498. When Charlemagne visited Rome, Leo III erected a palace beside St. Peter's which could still be seen in the twelfth century. Under Leo IV, the threat from the Saracens led to the construction of a wall around the Borgo between 847 and 853; parts of it survive. Since then, the Borgo has also been called the "Leonine city." It had its own legal status, but was a part of the city of Rome, with which it was linked by the Ponte Sant'Angelo, controlled from the → Castel Sant' Angelo. In the twelfth century, when the safety of the residence in the Lateran could no longer be guaranteed, the popes resided for some periods beside St. Peter's. In the thirteenth century, they often resided in → Anagni, → Viterbo, Orvieto, and Perugia. The oldest parts of today's Apostolic Palace date to Innocent III.

A new development began after the Council of Constance, with the overcoming of the Western Schism and the new papal ascendancy. In the mid-fifteenth century, the popes transferred their residence from the Lateran to St. Peter's. This meant that their court and a large part of the curia also moved to the Vatican, which took on a new appearance with the extension of the Apostolic Palace (the largest palace site in the world until the seventeenth century) and the construction of new St. Peter's, as well as the development of Castel Sant'Angelo as a papal fortress, linked to the Vatican palace by an escape route, and the building of the Hospital of the Holy Spirit, which was exemplary in its period. Until the end of the → papal states, the Borgo remained the papal district in Rome, but the majority of its inhabitants voted to join the kingdom of Italy after Rome was occupied by the Italian troops in 1871. When Rome became the capital of Italy, extensive building activity began in the area around the Vatican, which was eventually encircled by new city districts.

■ **Bibliography:** *LMA* 8:1429f.; *TRE* 29:357-379; F. Castagnoli, *Il Vaticano nell'antichità classica* (Vatican City, 1992).

ERWIN GATZ

2. *Architectural History*
The basilica of St. Peter's forms the spiritual and material point of departure for the architectual complex of buildings in the Vatican. In the aftermath of the Saracen attack in 846, Leo IV built a fortified suburb (the Leonine city) to the north of St. Peter's, and building works in the following centuries concentrated on this area. The interior of the papal fortification was divided into the *curia inferior* and the *curia superior*. The "lower" palace, seat of the administration, stood on the level of the old forecourt; it was razed in the seventeenth century when the new church and forecourt were built. The "upper" palace was the residence; the basic outlines of this medieval site can still be seen. In the late thirteenth century, Nicholas III began the construction of a citadel-like building here; this should be understood as a precautionary measure, in view of the party struggles which lacerated Rome in the Middle Ages. The southern wing and a part of the eastern wing, constructed under Nicholas, are the oldest parts of the architectural complex around the "Parrot court," and hence the nucleus of all subsequent palace buildings in the Vatican. The façade of the three-storey

eastern wing was decorated with loggias overlooking the city of Rome.

After the exile in Avignon, when the Vatican became the new principal seat of the Apostolic See, the older rooms proved too small for the representative and ceremonial demands and for the volume of administrative work; however, it was only after the end of the Western Schism that the architectural reorganization of the residence was carried out in a systematic manner. The architect commissioned by Nicholas V, one of the humanist popes, to extend the north wing of the palace was probably Bernardo Rossellino; the Cappella Nicolina, his private chapel, was installed in a tower from the period of Innocent III and decorated with frescoes by Fra Angelico. Pius II began the construction of the loggia of benedictions alongside St. Peter's; although this had religious functions, it also formed the façade of the lower palace, facing the forecourt. It initiated a new architectural style inspired by classical antiquity, a remarkable departure from the fortress character of earlier Vatican buildings. Under Sixtus IV, the Parrot court was completed by the construction of the west wing, and the → Vatican Library was given new quarters in the ground floor of the north wing. The name of this pope is linked above all with the → Sistine Chapel, called after him.

Under Innocent VIII, the palace site began to take in further territory to the north. The Vatican Belvedere, planned by Antonio Pollaiuolo or Baccio Pontelli, was constructed on Monte San Egidio. At the beginning of the sixteenth century, the courtyard of the Belvedere—with architecture appropriate to a villa, hovering in a strangely indecisive way between medieval elements and the new forms of the Renaissance—was the site of the first Vatican collection of antiquities. Generations of artists and sculptors learned their profession by studying the works of art displayed here (including the Belvedere *Apollo* and *Laocoön*). From ca. 1500 onward, the Renaissance popes enriched the palace with the finest masterpieces in Europe. Alexander VI took up residence in the "Borgia apartment," named after him, on the first floor of the north wing, and commissioned Bernardo Pinturicchio to decorate it with stucco and frescoes. His successors Julius II and Leo X wished to transform the Vatican into a residence modeled on imperial Roman antiquity. The papal chambers (*stanze*) were moved to the second floor and were

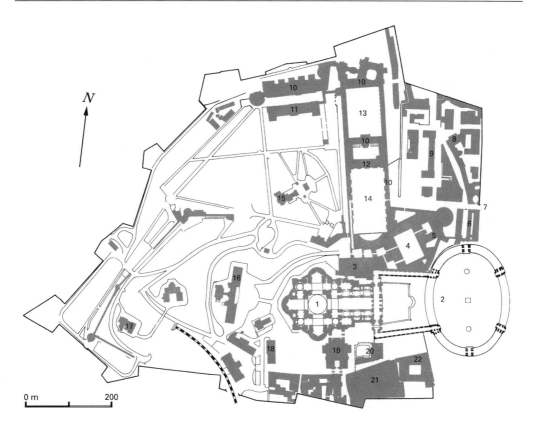

Vatican City

1. St. Peter's
2. St. Peter's Square
3. Sistine Chapel
4. Courtyard of Damasus
5. Apostolic Palace
6. Swiss Guard
7. St. Anne's Gate
8. Osservatore Romano
9. Belvedere Palace
10. Vatican Museums
11. Vatican Art Gallery
12. Vatican Library
13. Cortile della Pigna
14. Cortile del Belvedere
15. Casina of Pius IV (Papal Academy of Sciences)
16. Governatorate
17. Radio transmitter
18. Rota
19. Sacristy
20. Campo Santo Teutonico
21. Audience hall
22. Palace of the Holy Office

decorated from 1508 on by Raphael, whose frescoes became very famous (e.g., the School of Athens, the Disputation, Parnassus, the fire in the Borgo). After his death in 1520, his pupils executed his sketches for the decoration of the Sala di Costantino, the easternmost of the *stanze*. A new façade in the form of three stories of loggias was added to the adjacent side of the palace, which looked toward Rome. This was begun by Bramante in 1509 and continued by Raphael, whose pupils decorated the middle loggia with stucco work, grotesque figures, and biblical frescoes. Raphael created two other Renaissance incunabula in the little loggia and the bathroom of Cardinal Bernardo Dovizi da Bibbiena on the third floor of the palace, where techniques and ornamental motifs from Nero's Domus Aurea are given new life. The largest project of this period was the Belvedere court, planned by Bramante: 300 meters in length and surrounded by porticoes and threefold terraces, it was intended to be a match for the imperial buildings on the Palatine Hill. Bramante himself erected only a part of the eastern corridor; his work was continued by Raphael and Antonio da Sangallo the Younger. Piro Ligorio constructed the vestibule which finishes off the northern side as a colossal niche (*nicchione*), and began work on the western corridor, which was completed by Ottavio Mascarino in 1585. The upper storey was occupied by the gallery of maps, 120 meters in length; Gregory XIII built the Tower of Winds (the first Vatican observatory) at the north end of this corridor. In order to extend the Library, Sixtus V divided the Belvedere court by a transverse wing; from that time, the upper part has been called the Cortile della Pigna, after a bronze pinecone from old St. Peter's. In the meantime, Sangallo had been commissioned by Paul III to restructure the southwest zone of the palace. He built the Sala Regia as a representative reception room with frescoes by Giorgio Vasari and other artists, and the Cappella Paolina, in which Michelangelo executed his last important fresco commission from 1542 to 1550 (the crucifixion of Peter, the conversion of Paul). Ligorio built the Casina of Paul IV between 1558 and 1563, in the Vatican Gardens to the west of St. Peter's; this small villa is decorated in sumptuous mannerist style (classicist stucco works on the exterior, and frescoes by Federigo Zuccari, Santi di Tito, and Federigo Barocci in the interior). The façade of loggias built by Bramante and Raphael was continued eastward on the palace by Ligorio, Martino Longhi the Elder, and Mascarino, covering the medieval area of the façade and laid the foundations of the courtyard of Damasus.

In 1589-1590, Domenico Fontana erected new residential quarters in the northeast, the palace of Sixtus. When the western façade of this palace was completed, the courtyard of Damasus was now enclosed by loggias on three sides; the side that remained open was closed in the mid-nineteenth century by a one-storey portico. Under Clement VIII, the Sala Clementina was built in the new palace; this forms the majestic vestibule of the apartments in which the popes have lived until the present day. This more or less completed the complex of buildings to the north of the basilica, but there was no connection between palace and basilica until 1663-1666, when Giovanni Lorenzo Bernini linked the narthex of St. Peter's and the Sala Regia in the upper storey of the palace by means of a monumental staircase (the Scala Regia), which gives an impression of great size in a small space. In the eighteenth century, the Museo Pio-Clementino formed the nucleus of the → Vatican Museums; in the following period, these museums accounted for most of the building work in the northern part of the Vatican site.

To the south of the basilica, half hidden between the palace of the Holy Office and the → Campo Santo Teutonico, lies the modern audience hall erected by Luigi Nervi under Paul VI and dedicated in 1971. The concave floor and the vault, which admits light, form a lens-shaped room that can take up to twelve thousand visitors.

■ **Bibliography:** *VATL* 812-20; D. Redig de Campos, *I Palazzi Vaticani* (Bologna, 1967); idem, *Der Apostolische Palast: Der Vatikan und das christliche Rom* (Vatican City, 1975); C. Pietrangeli, ed., *Il Palazzo Apostolico Vaticano* (Florence, 1992); P. N. Pagliara, in *Der Vatikanische Palast: Ausstellungskatalog "Hochrenaissance im Vatikan"* (Ostfildern, 1999) 207-26.

DAMIAN DOMBROWSKI

Vatican Library (*Bibliotheca Apostolica Vaticana*). The Vatican Library was founded by Nicholas V, who acquired ca. 1,250 manuscripts. Its first independent head was Platina, appointed by Sixtus IV in 1475. After 1550, the Librarian of the Holy Roman Church has always been a cardinal. In the course of time, he was given assistants: a first and second custodian, writers, a prefect, and a vice-prefect. In 1588, Sixtus V commissioned Domenico Fontana to build the library room (the Sala Sistina).

The library was enriched by the gift of the Palatine Library from Heidelberg by Maximilian of Bavaria in 1623; by the library of the dukes of Urbino (Bibliotheca Urbinates) in 1657; and by the library of Queen Christina of Sweden (Bibliotheca Reginae Christinae) in 1690. Clement XI formed the department "Bibliotheca Orientalis Clementina" on the basis *inter alia* of the collections of Abraham Ecchellensis and the manuscripts purchased in Syria and Egypt by Elias Assemani. Benedict XIV acquired the private libraries of the marquis Alessandro Gregorio Capponi (1746) and Cardinal Pietro Ottoboni (1748: Bibliotheca Capponiana and Ottoboniana). The Vatican Library suffered considerable losses as a result of the Treaty of Colentino (1797), but most of the works were returned by Paris in 1815. Pius IX, who acquired the library of Giuseppe Mezzofanti, had the library rooms renovated. Under Leo XIII, Cardinal Librarian Franz Ehrle, as prefect of the Vatican Library, was able to acquire the family libraries of the Borghese (1891) and Barberini (1902), as well as the library of Cardinal Stefano Borgia (1902). Under Benedict XV, the Bibliotheca Rossiana was acquired (1921). Under Pius XI, the collections of the houses of Chigi (1923) and Ferrajoli (1926) were acquired, and the catalogues were reorganized. Under Pius XII and John XXIII, the holdings of the Vatican Library were extended (chapter archive of St. Peter's, 1940; Federico Patetta, 1945) and the cataloguing of manuscripts was continued.

The library's rooms were extended under Paul VI (a new depot for periodicals) and John Paul II (an underground depot for manuscripts, a new catalogue of printed books). In the mid-1990s, the four sections (manuscripts, printed books, museum, collection of coins) were automated. The Library has maintained a school for librarianship studies since 1934. The Vatican Library has a photographic laboratory and a workshop for restoration of books. Approximately four hundred volumes have been published by the Vatican Library since 1900 in the scholarly series *Studi e Testi*. Today the Vatican Library has ca. 150,000 manuscripts, 8,300 incunabula, and 1.6 million books.

■ **Bibliography:** *VATL* 802ff.; J. Bignami Odier, *La Bibliothèque Vaticana de Sixte IV à Pie XI* (Vatican City, 1973); P. De Nicolò, *Biblioteca Apostolica Vaticana* (Florence, 1985); W. Berschin, *Die Palatina in der Vaticana* (Stuttgart, 1992); C. Grafinger, *Die Ausleihe vatikanischer Handschriften und Druckwerke (1563-1700)* (Vatican City, 1992); A. Manfredi, *I codici di Nicolò IV* (Vatican City, 1994); C. Grafinger, *Beiträge zur Geschichte der Bibliotheca Vaticana* (Vatican City, 1997); M. Ceresa, *Bibliografia dei fondi manoscritti della Biblioteca Vaticana 1986-1990* (Vatican City, 1998); *AnPont* (2000) 1376-79, 1984f.

RAFFAELE FARINA

Vatican Museums.
1. Vatican Museums.—2. Vatican Art Gallery.

1. *Vatican Museums*
The Vatican collections of art began with the placing of classical works of art (e.g., *Apollo, Laocoön*)

in the courtyard of the Villa Belvedere by the popes of the high Renaissance, but as an institution, the Vatican Museums were founded only in the eighteenth century. Clement XI and Clement XII made space available by transforming the porticoes of the courtyard between the Belvedere and the Apostolic Palace into closed galleries; Benedict XIV installed a museum for classical inscriptions and the museum of the → Vatican Library here. Clement XIII founded the Museo Profano, headed (from 1763) by Johann Joachim Winckelmann. Its collection included *Aldobrandini Wedding,* a masterpiece of classical painting. Alessandro Dori and Michelangelo Simonetti were commissioned by Clement XIV to restructure the Belvedere complex between 1771 and 1773, and this led to the construction of several galleries for sculpture. The old courtyard of statues was transformed into an octagonal atrium. Pius VI extended the museum by erecting buildings in neoclassical style, linked with the Museo Profano by a monumental flight of stairs (the Scala Simonetti). This new site was opened in 1787 as the Museo Pio-Clementino. Giulio Camporese built the entrance in 1792-1793 as a domed quadratic construction, the Atrio dei Quattro Cancelli, with the circular Sala della Biga on the upper floor.

During Napoleon's rule, the most important pieces from the Vatican Museums were carried off to Paris. Pius VI attempted to make good the losses by new acquisitions, a task he entrusted to Antonio Canova in 1802. This was so successful that the Museo Chiaramonti could be installed in the east wing of the Cortile della Pigna as early as 1807. The works of art returned by France in 1816 created new problems of space, and Raffaele Stern built a transverse wing (the Braccio Nuovo) in this courtyard in 1822. Gregory XVI extended the collections to include Etruscology and Egyptology; beside the great vestibule of the Cortile della Pigna, the Museo Gregoriano Etrusco opened its doors in 1837, and the Museo Gregoriano Egizio in 1839. Because space was short, the same pope founded a second museum of antiquities in the → Lateran (Museo Profano Gregoriano); Pius IX founded the Museo Pio Cristiano for early Christian art in the Lateran in 1854, and Pius XI the Museum of Missionary Ethnology in 1926. John XXIII erected a modern museum building to house these three collections alongside the Vatican art gallery.

The new entrance area to the Vatican museums, with its elegant staircase in the form of a double spiral, was created in 1932. The newest development is the collection of modern religious art, consisting entirely of donations, which Paul VI, following an initiative of Pius XII, installed in the Vatican art gallery.

■ Bibliography: *VATL* 229-36, 497-508; "Die Vatikanischen Museen," in *Der Vatikan und das christliche Rom* (Vatican City, 1975) 166-305; C. Pietrangeli, *I Musei Vaticani* (Rome, 1985; Eng. tr., Rome, 1993); B. Andreae, ed., *Bildkatalog der Skulpturen des Vatikanischen Museums* (Berlin et al., 1995ff.) Iff.; M. Winner, B. Andreae, and C. Pietrangeli, eds., *Il Cortile delle Statue* (Mainz, 1998).

2. *Vatican Art Gallery (Pinacoteca Vaticana)*

Today's collection of paintings, tapestries, and icons was formed in the course of a general reorganization of the Vatican museums (see [1] above) after the church property plundered by Napoleon was returned. The paintings, most of which came from churches and monasteries in the papal states, were moved many times within the Apostolic Palace, before being placed in the west wing of the Belvedere courtyard in 1909. Pius XI had a building specially constructed for them.

The → Lateran Treaties had acknowledged the sovereignty of the → Vatican over its artistic treasures, but had also obliged the Vatican to make them available to the public. Between 1929 and 1932, Luca Beltrami erected a three-story building in an elegant eclectic style in the Vatican Gardens, to the west of the museums. This became the home of the art collection and of research institutes and restorers' workshops. The eighteen rooms of the Vatican gallery contain in chronological order works of all the important Italian schools since the Middle Ages, especially from the Renaissance. Among the great masters represented by outstanding works are Giotto di Bondone (the Stefaneschi altar), Melozzo da Forlì, Perugino, and Leonardo da Vinci. Raphael's altarpieces form the high point (the coronation of Mary, the Madonna of Foligno, the transfiguration). Other artists represented are Titian, Federigo Barocci, Guido Reni, Domenichino, Michelangelo da Caravaggio (the burial of Christ), and Nicolas Poussin.

■ Bibliography: *VATL* 807ff.; C. Pietrangeli, *Die Gemälde des Vatikans* (Munich, 1996).

DAMIAN DOMBROWSKI

Vatican State. After what remained of the → papal states had been occupied by the kingdom of Italy in 1870, Rome became the capital of a united Italy and the pope declared himself a "prisoner" in the Vatican. The Roman Question was resolved in 1929 by the conclusion of the → Lateran Treaties, and the state of the Vatican City (SCV, *Stato della Città del Vaticano*) was erected as the smallest state in the world (0.44 square kilometers). It is not the continuation of the papal states, but a new foundation.

Surrounded by Italian state territory, it comprises → St. Peter's with St. Peter's Square, the Vatican palaces (→ Vatican) and Gardens. Besides this, the privilege of extraterritoriality is enjoyed by the patriarchal basilicas in the city of → Rome and its environs, the official buildings of the Roman → curia and the papal summer residence in → Castelgandolfo. The Vatican state serves the tasks of the pope or of the → Holy See in terms of international law and provides support to the spiritual sovereignty of the pope. Its constitutional form is that of an elective monarchy, in which the pope possesses legislative, judicial, and executive authority, which he exercises either in person or by means of delegated organs such as the Papal Commission for the Vatican state (founded 1939), which is subordinate to the Governatorate. As a sovereign state, the Vatican state possesses its own judicial organs and its own ecclesiastical administration (the parishes of St. Peter's and St. Anne's). The population numbers fewer than one thousand, drawn from various nationalities. It has its own flag (gold and white, with crossed keys and tiara), its own coat of arms, national anthem, and postal service. It issues coins (not banknotes) and followed Italy in adopting the euro. The territory of the Vatican state is neutral and inviolable. Since 1958, the state and its cultural goods have been protected by the Hague Convention; in a case of armed conflict, it is protected by the Director General of the United Nations. The Vatican state as a whole was included in the list of World Cultural Patrimony in 1982.

■ Bibliography: *VATL* 747-51; *TRE* 29:357-79; H. F. Köck, *Die völkerrechtliche Stellung des Heiligen Stuhles* (Berlin, 1975); E. Gallina, *Il Vaticano è di tutti: straordinari riconoscimenti internazionali della Città del Vaticano e dei Beni extraterritoriali* (Vatican City, 1991); K. Sonne et al., eds., *Der Vatikan als Staatsorganisation* (Munich, 1995); W. Schultz, "Der Staat der Vatikanstadt, der Heilige Stuhl und die Römische Kurie in den

Schriften von W. Schulz," in Festschrift for F. X. Walter (Frankfurt a.M., 1999); *AnPont* (2000) 1458-71; *Bibliography:* M. J. Walsh, ed., *Vatican City State* (Oxford, 1983).

ERWIN GATZ

Vatican–U.S. Relations. From the time of American independence, the American Republic and its church were frequently mysteries to the Holy See. In 1783, the Holy See asked the new American government for its opinion on appointing a vicar apostolic, but the U.S. rejected this overture since it pertained to a religious matter. This Roman initiative without any consultation of the American clergy, moreover, antagonized John Carroll, the leader of the American priests, all of whom had been Jesuits before their order's suppression in 1773. The clergy gained the right to elect one of their own as the first bishop. They chose Carroll as the first bishop of Baltimore.

In the nineteenth century, as the church expanded across the continent, the bishops developed a strong sense of collegiality. In a series of seven provincial councils between 1829 and 1849 and three plenary ones in 1852, 1866, and 1884, they not only acted corporately for the whole American church but also spoke of the infallibility of the college of the bishops under the presidency of the pope. In 1849, other metropolitan sees were established, and the bishops requested that Baltimore be named the primatial see—a title rejected, since Roman officials feared the American church was too independent. In 1853, Archbishop Bedini, nuncio to Brazil, conducted an official visitation of the American church and recommended a nuncio to the government as preferable to a primate for preserving episcopal unity—a recommendation the Holy See did not follow. After Vatican I, American bishops gradually lost their theology of collegiality. They held a final plenary council in 1884, but this was called at Roman initiative. They did, however, retain the practice, but not the theory, of collegiality. Between 1890 and 1919, the archbishops met annually. In 1919, the entire hierarchy formed the National Catholic Welfare Council (NCWC), which held annual meetings and had a standing secretariat in Washington. In 1922, the Consistorial Congregation ordered this body disbanded, but the overwhelming majority of the American bishops prevailed on Rome to allow it to continue with its name changed to NCW Conference to avoid any implication that it was a legislative body.

Diplomatic relations between the United States and the Holy See were complicated by anti-Catholicism and the American separation of church and state. The U.S. established consular relations with the papal states in 1797 and official diplomatic relations from 1848 to 1867, when Congress cut off funding for the Roman mission—this legislation was repealed only in 1983 in preparation for the establishment of full diplomatic relations. In 1893, the Holy See appointed a permanent apostolic delegate to the American hierarchy, but had no representative to the government; communication between the Vatican and the White House took place through one of the American bishops. In 1939, as World War II drew near, President Franklin D. Roosevelt, under the influence of Archbishop Francis Spellman of New York, wanted closer ties with the Vatican as a neutral listening post. He therefore appointed Myron C. Taylor as his personal representative to Pius XII, a position that did not need Senate approval. Taylor held this position until he resigned in 1950. In 1951, President Harry S. Truman nominated General Mark Clark as "ambassador to the Vatican," but Clark withdrew in the face of increased anti-Catholic opposition. In 1970, President Richard M. Nixon reinstituted the office of "personal representative," a position retained by Presidents Gerald Ford, Jimmy Carter, and Ronald Reagan. In January 1984, the U.S. and the Holy See announced the establishment of full diplomatic relations, with Archbishop Pio Laghi, the delegate, named the first pro-nuncio, and William Wilson, the former personal representative, named the first ambassador. One of President Reagan's motivations for establishing diplomatic relations was to curtail the activism of the American bishops, who had issued a pastoral letter in 1983 challenging the first use of nuclear arms and tolerating deterrence only if accompanied by negotiations for nuclear disarmament. Although Reagan's efforts on this level were unsuccessful, the closer ties between John Paul II and the U.S. probably contributed to the collapse of Communism and the Soviet Union.

After Vatican II, the NCWC was disbanded and two new entities were formed, the National Conference of Catholic Bishops (NCCB) and the United States Catholic Conference (USCC). The

USCC has a standing secretariat in Washington coordinating Catholic efforts between the annual meetings of the NCCB. In 2001, the two bodies were merged into the United States Conference of Catholic Bishops (USCCB).

■ **Bibliography:** *The Vatican and the American Hierarchy from 1870 to 1965* (Stuttgart, 1982).

GERALD FOGARTY

Vexillum Sancti Petri. This flag was blessed by the pope and given to princes in order to declare a war as a "holy war" or a crusade, thereby justifying claims in feudal law. It is first attested in the mid-eleventh century (Benedict IX, Leo IX, Alexander II). The history of the *vexillum* leads to the honorific office of *Vexillifer Ecclesiae* (Italian: *gonfaloniere*, "standard-bearer"), conferred on high-ranking laymen by popes from Boniface VIII to the nineteenth century.

■ **Bibliography:** *LMA* 8:1607; *VATL* 754f.

BRUNO STEIMER

Viterbo. The Franks gave the territory of this city in Latium to the pope in 787, and it formed the kernel of the later Patrimony of Peter (→ Papal States). Popes often resided in Viterbo in the thirteenth century; the construction of a papal palace began in 1266. Five conclaves (Papal → Election) were held here in the second half of the thirteenth century, including the longest in history (1268-1271).

■ **Bibliography:** *LMA* 8:1121f., 1771f.

MARIA LUPI

Works, Pontifical. These organizations disburse aid on behalf of the Holy See.

1. Pontifical Work for Priestly Vocations (Pontificia Opera delle Vocazioni Sacerdotali)
This was founded in Freiburg, Germany in 1926 by Maria Immaculata, duchess of Saxony, as the Women's Aid Organization for Priestly Vocations, a lay organization to encourage and support candidates for the priesthood; it was prohibited by the German government in 1939. It took its place alongside other, older diocesan works which aided priests. Taking up this initiative, Pius XII set up the Pontifical Work for Priestly Vocations for the universal church in 1941. After 1945, the Women's Aid Organization and other works in aid of priests were aggregated to this Pontifical

Work; in 1955, the Pontifical Work for Vocations to the Religious Life was erected.

The basis of the Pontifical Work, which is attached to the Congregation for Catholic Education, is formed by the diocesan Works where groups meet to pray for vocations. It wishes to make concern for vocations an integral dimension of pastoral work as a whole today, promoting vocations to the priesthood and the religious life and encouraging the apostolate prayer in parishes, by means of monthly days of prayer and the yearly World Day of Prayer for Vocations.

■ **Primary Sources:** *AAS* 33 (1941) 479; 47 (1955) 266.

■ **Bibliography:** *VATL* 840f.; E. von Schönau, *Eine königliche Frau und ihr Werk* (Freiburg, 1951); A. Schuldis, *Werk alle Werke* (2nd ed. Freiburg, 1955); R. Schmucker, *Das Gebet hat große Kraft: Zur Gründungsgeschichte des Frauenhilfswerkes* (Freiburg, 1996); *AnPont* (2000) 1291.

ROBERT SCHMUCKER

2. Pontifical Missionary Works
(a) Three originally private church associations for the promotion of Catholic world missions (1, 2, and 3) were given the status of official "pontifical" missionary works in 1922; a fourth (4) received this status in 1956. The most recent reorganization of these Works was carried out in the statutes of June 26, 1980.

(1) Pontifical Work for the Propagation of the Faith (Pontificium Opus Missionale a Propagatione Fidei), founded in Lyons in 1822 by a group of laypersons led by Marie-Pauline Jaricot and introduced to Germany as the Francis Xavier Missionary Association (in Aachen) or the Louis Missionary Association (in Munich). Its goal is to enhance general awareness of the missions, to provide spiritual and material missionary aid, and to promote contacts between the loal churches. It is called "Missio" in Germany, Austria, and Switzerland. According to its statutes, its period of special activity is the month of October, with the celebration of World Missionary Sunday.

(2) Pontifical Work of St. Peter the Apostle (Pontificium Opus Missionale a Sancto Petro Apostolo), founded in 1889 in Caen by Stephanie and Jeanne Bigard, helps promote indigenous vocations to the priesthood and the religious life by means of information, prayer, and financial help for seminaries and novitiates.

(3) Pontifical Work of the Holy Childhood (Pon-

tificium Opus Missionale a Sancta Infantia), founded in 1843 by Charles de Forbin-Janson, bishop of Nancy; it spread to Germany in 1846 as the Association of the Childhood of Jesus. Its task is "to make children conscious of the universal mission and to lead them to share their faith and their material goods too, with the children of regions and churches who are less well off" (statutes, no. 17).

(4) Pontifical Missionary Association of Priests and Religious (Pontificia Unio Missionalis). Formerly the Missionary Association of Priests, founded in 1916 by Paolo Manna of the Pontifical Institute for Foreign Missions in Milan. Its aim is to encourage "missionary formation and information of priests, religious, seminarians, and novices, as well as of other persons active in the church's pastoral work" (statutes, no. 23).

According to the 1980 statutes, these four Works form *"one* institution . . . which is subject to the Congregation for the Evangelization of the Peoples" (no. 31). They are headed by national directors in the individual countries, assisted by a national council of diocesan directors. The central direction is entrusted to a committee of directors and a higher council drawn from all four Works. Apart from donations strictly earmarked for a specific purpose, all the income from donations, members' dues, and collections is transmitted to a central fund in Rome, where national directors from the Third World share in the process of distribution of funds to the poorer churches. The 1980 statutes emphasize both the papal and the diocesan character of these Works: "They are institutions both of the universal church and of each local church," and hence "the official organization of a worldwide missionary cooperation," which must "always take priority among all the aid organizations within the church" (see also can. 791, §2 *CIC*).

(b) The Missionary Association of Catholic Women and Girls (to use the name given in 1902), which had been founded in Germany in 1893 by Katharina Schynse, was accorded the honorific title "pontifical" by Pius XII in 1942. Its statutes were approved by the Congregation for the Evangelization of the Peoples in 1970, and the association was given the name Pontifical Missionary Work of Women in Germany. It supports the celebration of the liturgy in Africa, Asia, Latin America, and Eastern Europe, especially by making available liturgical vessels and vestments appropriate to the local cultures. It also helps women in these countries whose rights are severely disregarded. It has a diocesan structure; its direction is in Koblenz-Pfaffenhofen.

■ **Bibliography:** On (a): *VATL* 489f.; A. Olichon, *Les origines françaises de l'oeuvre Pontificale de Saint Pierre Apôtre* (Paris, 1929); F. Baeumker, *Dr. Heinrich Hahn* (Aachen, 1930); W. Mathäser, *Der Ludwig-Missionsverein* (Munich, 1939); La Pontificia Unione Missionaria del Clero, *Vade-Mecum* (Rome, 1963); Oeuvres Pontificales Missionaires de la Propagation de la Foi et de Saint Pierre Apôtre, *Vademecum* (Rome, 1964); W. Jansen, *Das Päpstliche Missionwerk der Kinder in Deutschland* (Mönchengladbach, 1970); *Statuten der Päpstlichen Missionswerke 26.6.1980,* Verlautbarungen des Apostolischen Stuhls 26 (Bonn, 1980); J. López Gay, "The New Statutes of the Pontifical Mission-Aid Societies," *Bibliographia Missionaria 1980* (Vatican City, 1981); *AnPont* (2000) 1277ff.

On (b): B. Arens, *Die katholischen Missionsvereine* (Freiburg, 1922); G. Kummer, *Die Leopoldinenstiftung (1829-1914)* (Vienna, 1966); E. Gatz, ed., *Katholiken in der Minderheit,* Geschichte des kirchlichen Lebens in den deutschsprachigen Ländern seit dem Ende des 18. Jahrhunderts 3 (Freiburg, 1993) 215-313.

LUDWIG WIEDENMANN

Zelanti (from Greek *zēlos,* "zeal"). This term is employed in papal historiography to designate highly conservative groups among the hierarchy, at the opposite end of the scale from those "moderates" and "liberals" who were open to new developments. These terms play an especially important role in the description of conclaves.

KLAUS GANZER

INDEX OF SUBJECTS